Houghton
Mifflin
Harcourt

collections

A&E
HISTORY
bio.

Cover, Title Page Photo Credits: Image Ideas/jupiterimages/Getty Images

Printed in the U.S.A.

ISBN 978-0-544-56955-3

5 6 7 8 9 10 0868 24 23 22 21 20 19 18 17 16

4500598717 B C D E F

Houghton
Mifflin
Harcourt

collections

GRADE 12

Program Consultants:
Kylene Beers
Martha Hougen
Carol Jago
William L. McBride
Erik Palmer
Lydia Stack

bio.

About Our Program Consultants

Kylene Beers Nationally known lecturer and author on reading and literacy; 2011 recipient of the Conference on English Leadership Exemplary Leader Award; coauthor of *Notice and Note: Strategies for Close Reading*; former president of the National Council of Teachers of English. Dr. Beers is the nationally known author of *When Kids Can't Read: What Teachers Can Do* and coeditor of *Adolescent Literacy: Turning Promise into Practice*, as well as articles in the *Journal of Adolescent and Adult Literacy*. Former editor of *Voices from the Middle*, she is the 2001 recipient of NCTE's Richard W. Halley Award, given for outstanding contributions to middle-school literacy. She recently served as Senior Reading Researcher at the Comer School Development Program at Yale University as well as Senior Reading Advisor to Secondary Schools for the Reading and Writing Project at Teachers College.

Martha Hougen National consultant, presenter, researcher, and author. Areas of expertise include differentiating instruction for students with learning difficulties, including those with learning disabilities and dyslexia; and teacher and leader preparation improvement. Dr. Hougen has taught at the middle school through graduate levels. Recently her focus has been on working with teacher educators to enhance teacher and leader preparation to better meet the needs of all students. Currently she is working with the University of Florida at the Collaboration for Effective Educator Development, Accountability, and Reform Center (CEEDAR Center) to improve the achievement of students with disabilities by reforming teacher and leader licensure, evaluation, and preparation. She has led similar efforts in Texas with the Higher Education Collaborative and the College & Career Readiness Initiative Faculty Collaboratives. In addition to peer-reviewed articles, curricular documents, and presentations, Dr. Hougen has published two college textbooks: *The Fundamentals of Literacy Assessment and Instruction Pre-K–6* (2012) and *The Fundamentals of Literacy Assessment and Instruction 6–12* (2014).

Carol Jago Teacher of English with 32 years of experience at Santa Monica High School in California; author and nationally known lecturer; and former president of the National Council of Teachers of English. Currently serves as Associate Director of the California Reading and Literature Project at UCLA. With expertise in standards assessment and secondary education, Ms. Jago is the author of numerous books on education, including *With Rigor for All* and *Papers, Papers, Papers*, and is active with the California Association of Teachers of English, editing its scholarly journal *California English* since 1996. Ms. Jago also served on the planning committee for the 2009 NAEP Framework and the 2011 NAEP Writing Framework.

William L. McBride Curriculum specialist. Dr. McBride is a nationally known speaker, educator, and author who now trains teachers in instructional methodologies. He is coauthor of *What's Happening?*, an innovative, high-interest text for middle-grade readers, and author of *If They Can Argue Well, They Can Write Well.* A former reading specialist, English teacher, and social studies teacher, he holds a master's degree in reading and a doctorate in curriculum and instruction from the University of North Carolina at Chapel Hill. Dr. McBride has contributed to the development of textbook series in language arts, social studies, science, and vocabulary. He is also known for his novel *Entertaining an Elephant*, which tells the story of a veteran teacher who becomes reinspired with both his profession and his life.

Erik Palmer Veteran teacher and education consultant based in Denver, Colorado. Author of *Well Spoken: Teaching Speaking to All Students* and *Digitally Speaking: How to Improve Student Presentations*. His areas of focus include improving oral communication, promoting technology in classroom presentations, and updating instruction through the use of digital tools. He holds a bachelor's degree from Oberlin College and a master's degree in curriculum and instruction from the University of Colorado.

Lydia Stack Internationally known teacher educator and author. She is involved in a Stanford University project to support English Language Learners, *Understanding Language*. The goal of this project is to enrich academic content and language instruction for English Language Learners (ELLs) in grades K-12 by making explicit the language and literacy skills necessary to meet the Common Core State Standards (CCSS) and Next Generation Science Standards. Her teaching experience includes twenty-five years as an elementary and high school ESL teacher, and she is a past president of Teachers of English to Speakers of Other Languages (TESOL). Her awards include the TESOL James E. Alatis Award and the San Francisco STAR Teacher Award. Her publications include *On Our Way to English, Visions: Language, Literature, Content,* and *American Themes*, a literature anthology for high school students in the ACCESS program of the U.S. State Department's Office of English Language Programs.

Additional thanks to the following Program Reviewers

Rosemary Asquino
Sylvia B. Bennett
Yvonne Bradley
Leslie Brown
Haley Carroll
Caitlin Chalmers
Emily Colley-King
Stacy Collins
Denise DeBonis
Courtney Dickerson
Sarah Easley
Phyllis J. Everette
Peter J. Foy Sr.
Carol M. Gibby
Angie Gill
Mary K. Goff
Saira Haas
Lisa M. Janeway
Robert V. Kidd Jr.
Kim Lilley
John C. Lowe
Taryn Curtis MacGee
Meredith S. Maddox
Cynthia Martin
Kelli M. McDonough
Megan Pankiewicz
Linda Beck Pieplow
Molly Pieplow
Mary-Sarah Proctor
Jessica A. Stith
Peter Swartley
Pamela Thomas
Linda A. Tobias
Rachel Ukleja
Lauren Vint
Heather Lynn York
Leigh Ann Zerr

COLLECTION 1

Chasing Success

KEY LEARNING OBJECTIVES

- Cite text evidence to support inferences.
- Determine central ideas.
- Analyze conflict in drama.
- Analyze symbols in drama.
- Analyze word choice.
- Analyze structure of an argument.
- Analyze drama interpretations.
- Integrate and evaluate information.

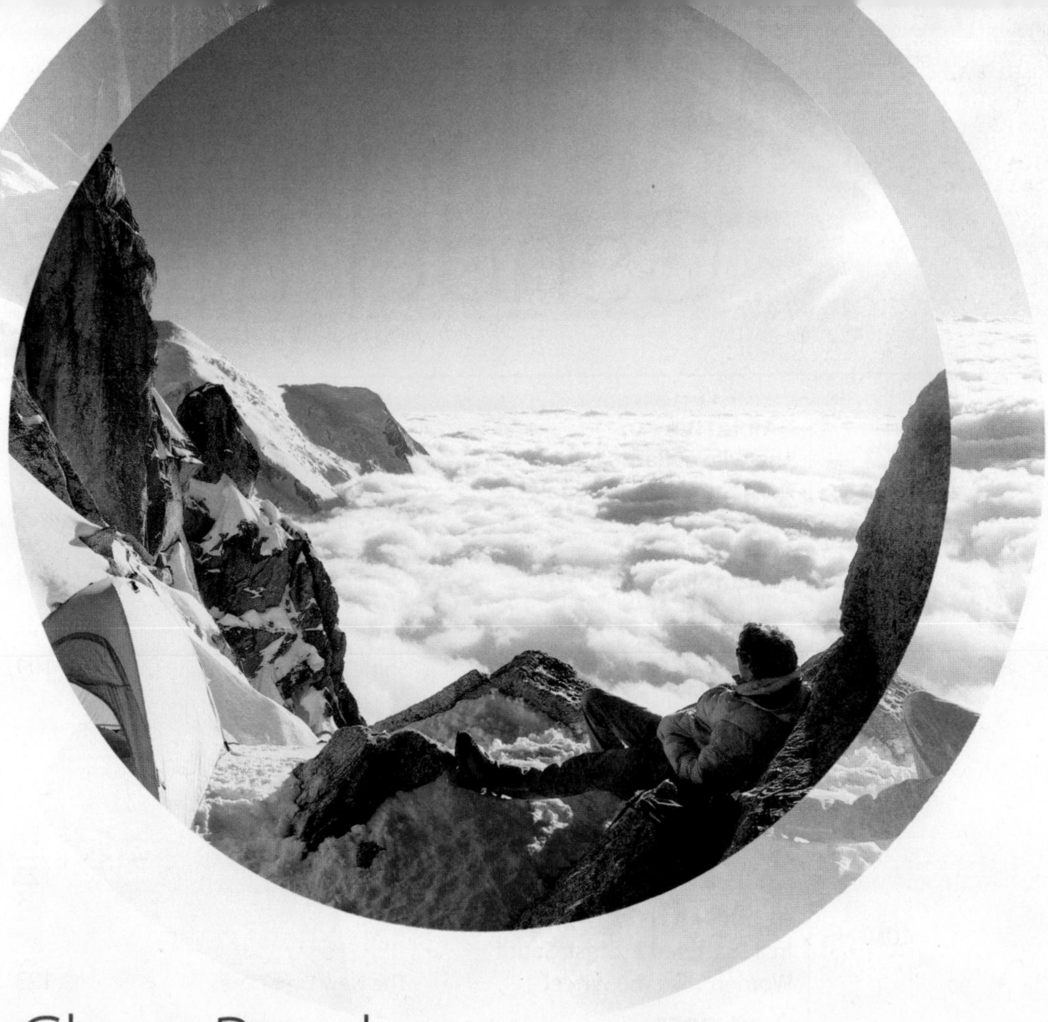

Close Reader

eBook *Explore It!*

Visit hmhfyi.com for current articles and informational texts.

COLLECTION **2**

Gender Roles

KEY LEARNING OBJECTIVES

Support inferences and draw conclusions.
Determine central ideas.
Summarize text.
Analyze ideas and events.
Analyze narrator of a poem.
Analyze setting of a story.
Determine figurative meanings.
Analyze frame story.
Analyze counterarguments.
Analyze rhetorical devices.
Determine author's point of view.
Integrate and evaluate information.

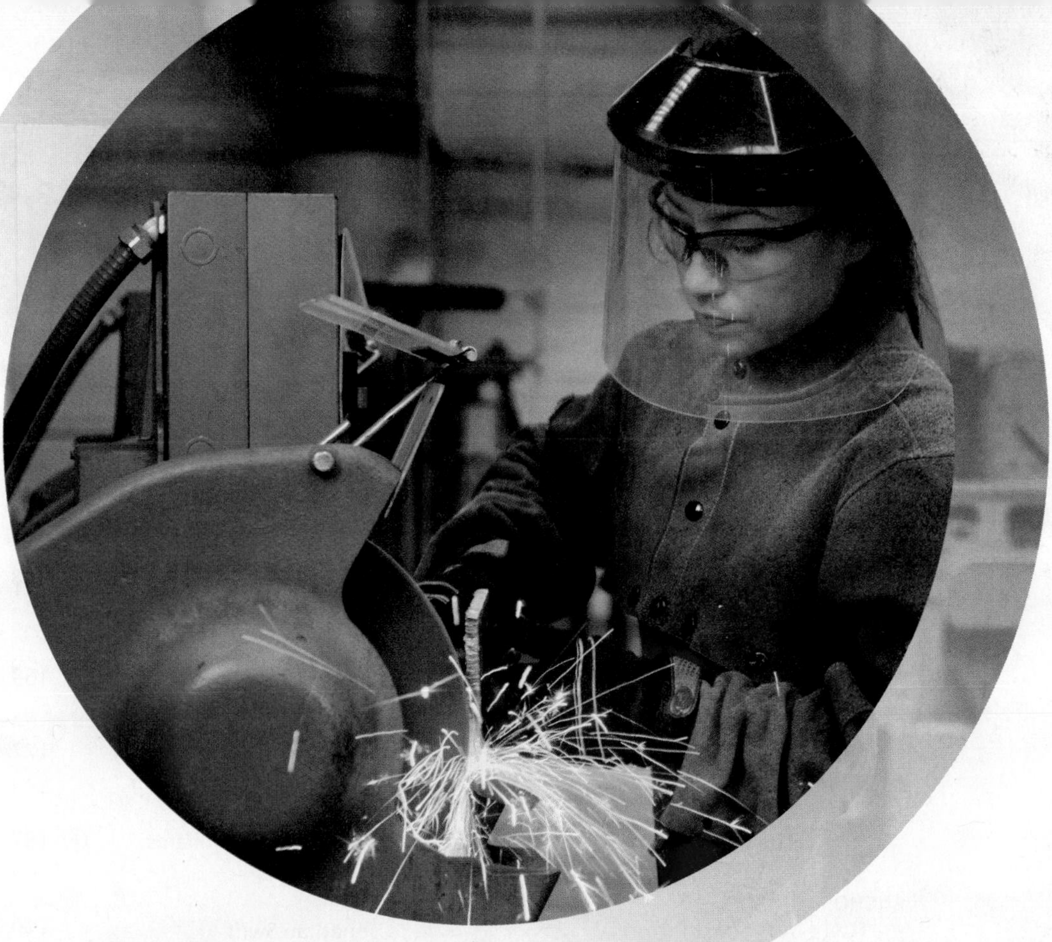

Close Reader

eBook *Explore It!*

Video Links

Visit hmhfyi.com for current articles and informational texts.

COLLECTION **3**

Voices of Protest

KEY LEARNING OBJECTIVES

Cite text evidence to support inferences.
Analyze cause and effect.
Analyze word choice and tone.
Determine connotative meanings.
Analyze satire.
Integrate and evaluate information.
Delineate and evaluate an argument.
Analyze foundational documents.
Comprehend historical context.

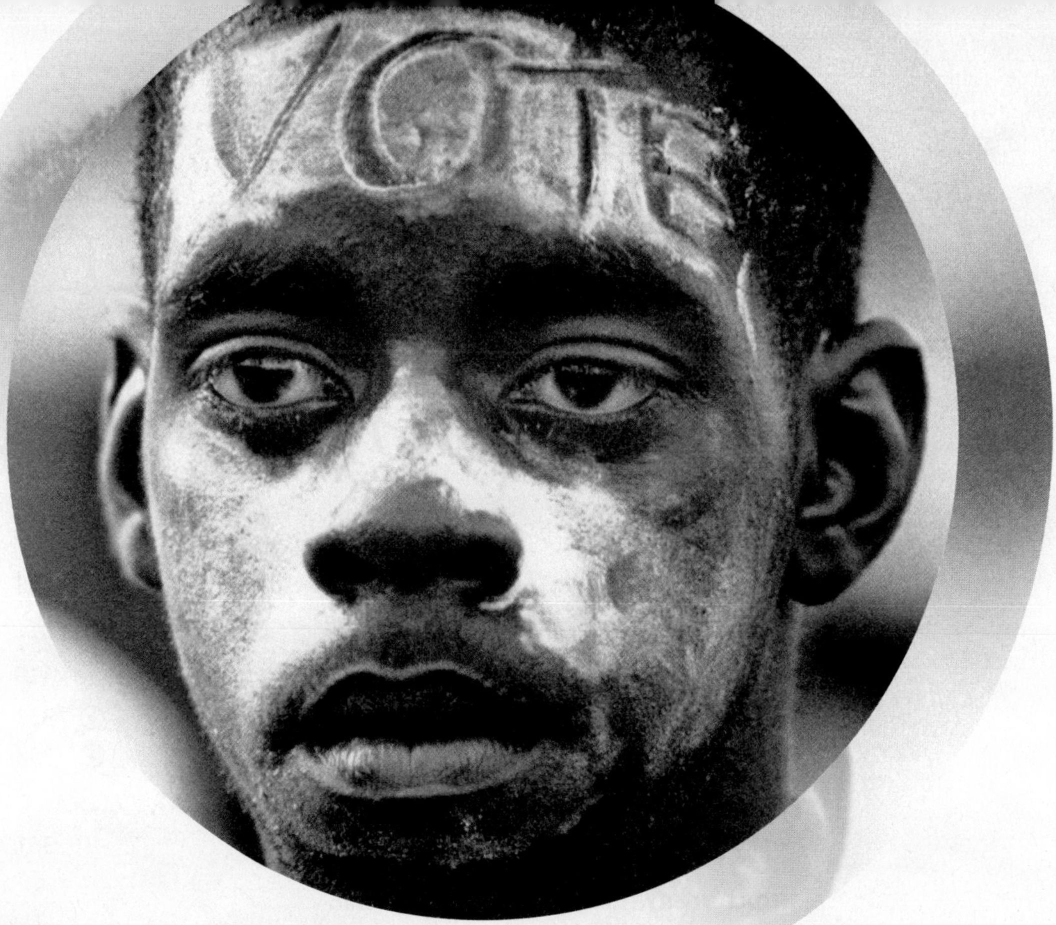

Close Reader

Image Credits: ©Steve Schapiro/Corbis

eBook *Explore It!*

Visit hmhfyi.com for current articles and informational texts.

COLLECTION **4**

Seeking Justice, Seeking Peace

KEY LEARNING OBJECTIVES

Support inferences and draw conclusions.
Determine central ideas.
Analyze ideas and events.
Analyze conflict in drama.
Determine figurative meanings.
Analyze language in soliloquies.
Analyze story structure.
Analyze structure of an argument.
Analyze irony.
Analyze drama interpretations.

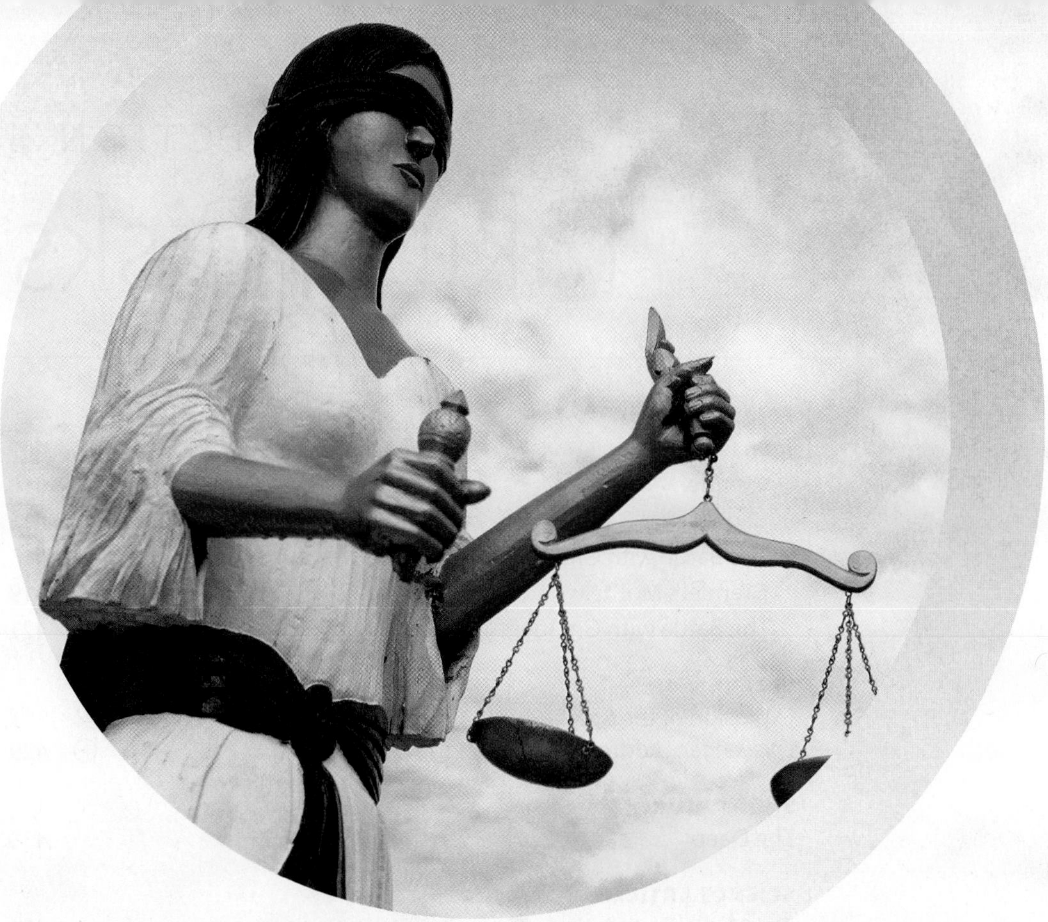

Close Reader

eBook *Explore It!*

Video Links

Visit hmhfyi.com for current articles and informational texts.

COLLECTION **5**

Taking Risks

KEY LEARNING OBJECTIVES

Support inferences and draw conclusions.
Determine themes.
Summarize text.
Analyze setting of a story.
Analyze characteristics of an epic.
Analyze Old English poetry.
Determine author's purpose.
Delineate and evaluate an argument.

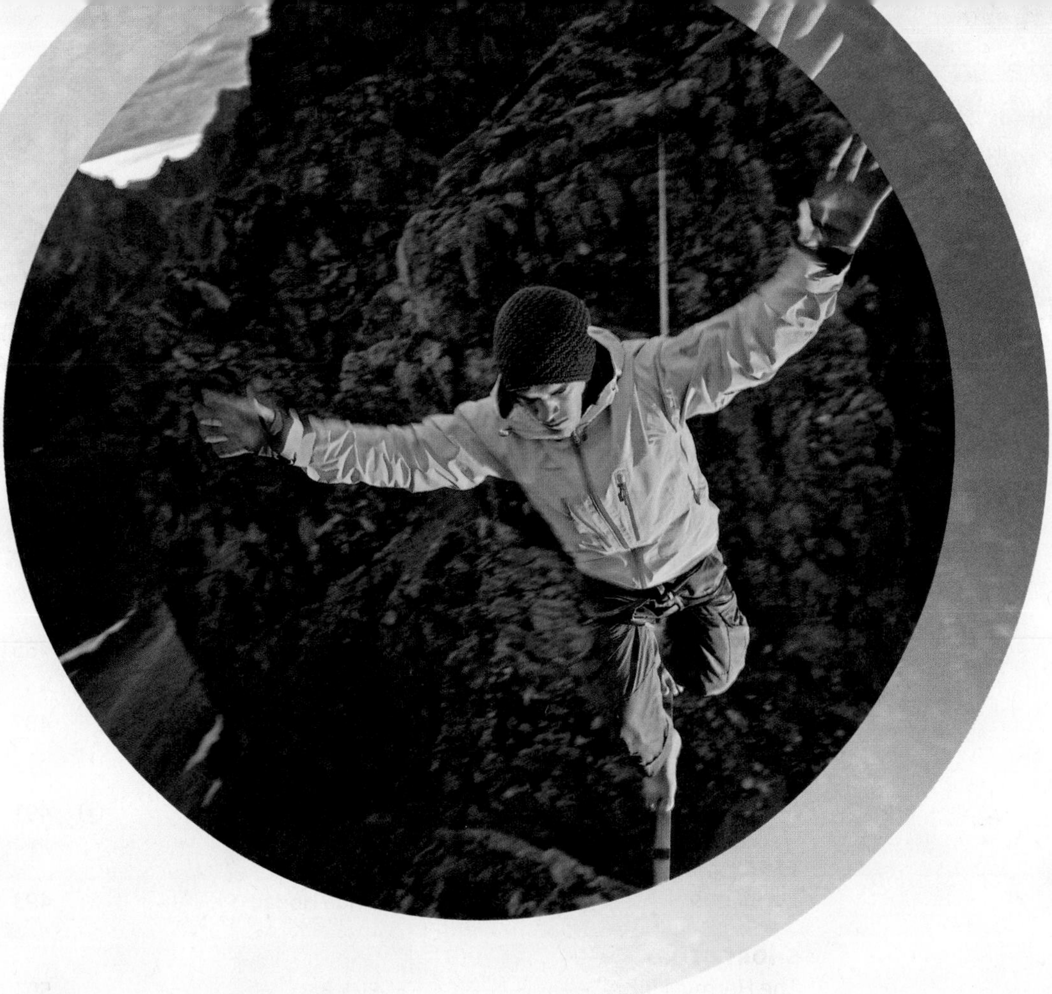

Close Reader

eBook *Explore It!*

Visit hmhfyi.com for current articles and informational texts.

COLLECTION **6**

Finding Ourselves in Nature

KEY LEARNING OBJECTIVES

Cite text evidence to support inferences.
Determine theme.
Determine figurative meanings.
Analyze structure.
Analyze frame story.
Analyze style.
Integrate and evaluate information.
Demonstrate knowledge of foundational works.
Comprehend cultural context in nonfiction.

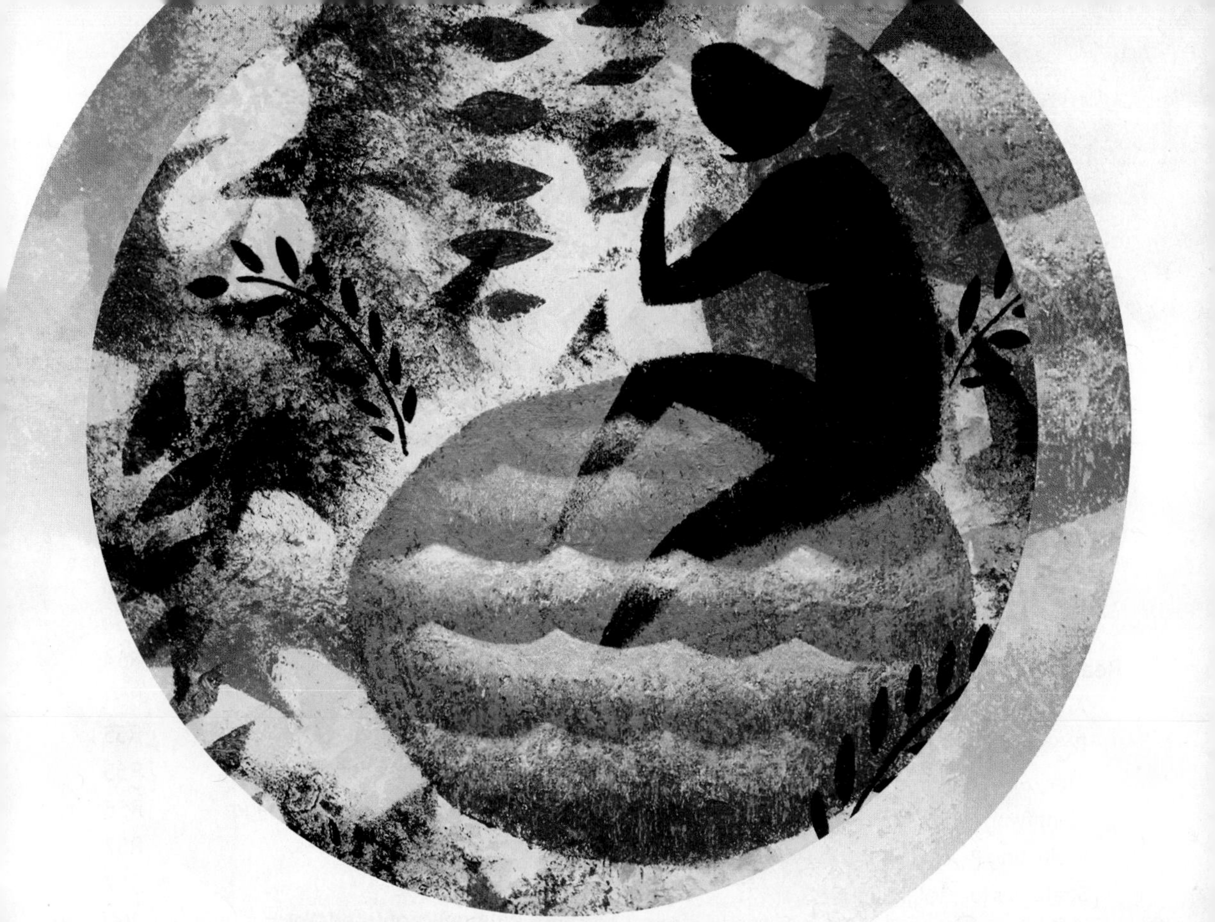

Close Reader

Video Links

Visit hmhfyi.com for current articles and informational texts.

Student Resources

DIGITAL OVERVIEW

Connecting to Your World

Every time you read something, view something, write to someone, or react to what you've read or seen, you're participating in a world of ideas. You do this every day, inside the classroom and out. These skills will serve you not only at home and at school, but eventually in your career.

The digital tools in this program will tap into the skills you already use and help you sharpen those skills for the future.

Start your exploration at my.hrw.com

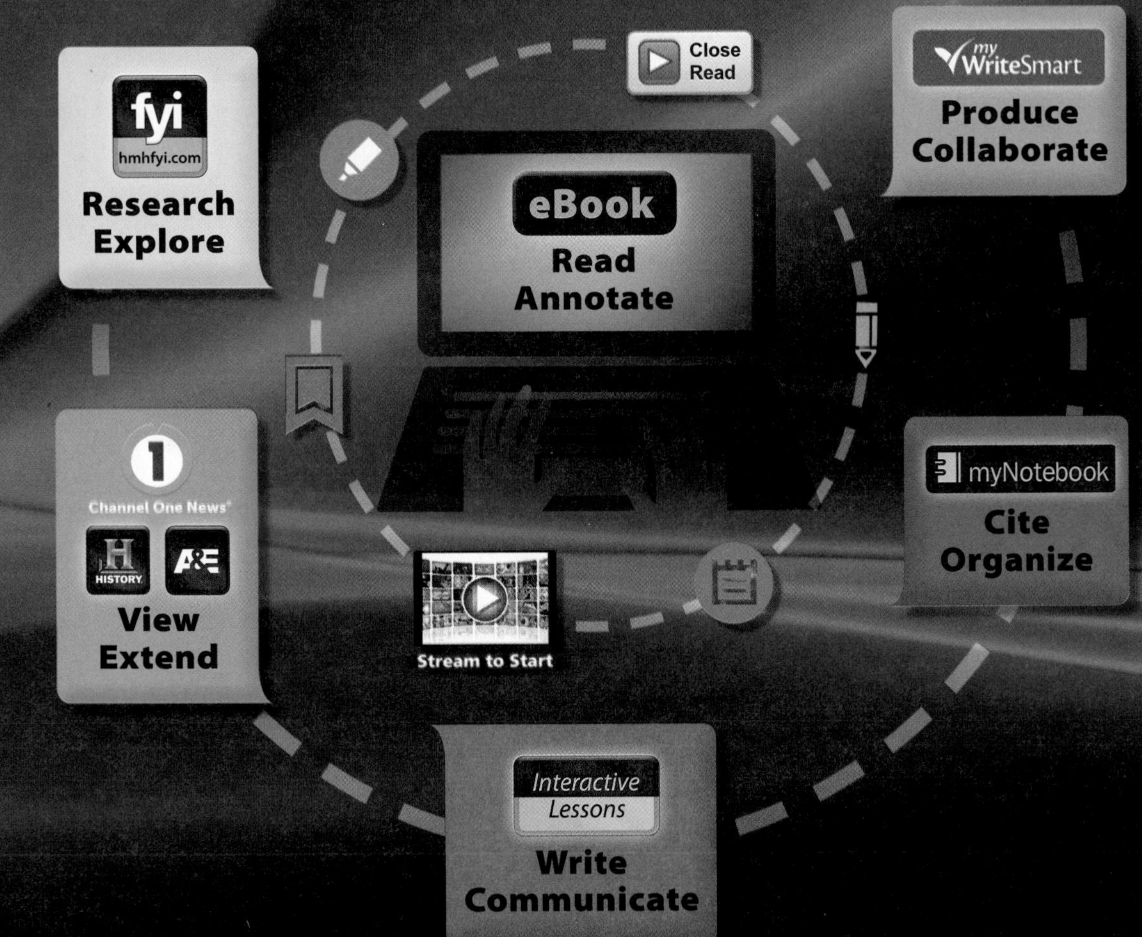

››INTERACTIVE LESSONS

Writing and Speaking & Listening

Communication in today's world requires quite a variety of skills. To express yourself and win people over, you have to be able to write for print, for online media, and for spoken presentations. To collaborate, you have to work with people who might be sitting right next to you or at the other end of an Internet connection.

Available Only in Your eBook

Interactive Lessons

These interactive lessons will help you master the skills needed to become an expert communicator.

What Does a Strong Argument Look Like?

Read this argument and answer the questions about how the writer states and supports his position.

Tip

Pitching Perfect Pitch
by José Alvarez

Did you know that when you are listening to your favorite vocalist, you might be hearing a computer-generated pitch? Many record companies use pitch-correction software to ensure that their performers are pitch-perfect. **While perfectionism is an admirable goal, there is a fine line between using technology to enhance music and using it to make performers into something they're not. Whether recording in the studio or playing a live performance, musicians should not use pitch-correction software.**

Music production has become a digital experience. Producers use software to cut and paste pieces of music together, just like you cut and paste words together in your word-processing software. When editing these different things together digitally, slight imperfections can occur where the pieces are joined. Enter the correction software. What began as a method to streamline the digital editing process has turned into an almost industry-wide standard of altering a musician"s work. "Think of it like plastic surgery," says a Grammy-winning recording engineer.

What is the writer's position, or **claim**, on the use of pitch-correction software?

- [ ] Musicians should learn to live with their imperfections.
- [x] Musicians should never use the software.
- [ ] Musicians should use the software to enhance live performances only.

Writing Arguments

Master the art of proving your point.

W 1, W 10

Interactive Lessons

1. Introduction
2. What Is a Claim?
3. Support: Reasons and Evidence
4. Building Effective Support
5. Creating a Coherent Argument
6. Persuasive Techniques
7. Formal Style
8. Concluding Your Argument

Writing Informative Texts

W 2, W 10

Shed light on complex ideas and topics.

Interactive Lessons

1. Introduction
2. Developing a Topic
3. Organizing Ideas
4. Introductions and Conclusions
5. Elaboration
6. Using Graphics and Multimedia
7. Precise Language and Vocabulary
8. Formal Style

Writing Narratives

W 3, W 10

A good storyteller can always capture an audience.

Interactive Lessons

1. Introduction
2. Narrative Context
3. Point of View and Characters
4. Narrative Structure
5. Narrative Techniques
6. The Language of Narrative

W 4, W 5, W 10

Writing as a Process

Get from the first twinkle of an idea to a sparkling final draft.

Interactive Lessons

1. Introduction
2. Task, Purpose, and Audience
3. Planning and Drafting
4. Revising and Editing
5. Trying a New Approach

W 6

Producing and Publishing with Technology

Learn how to write for an online audience.

Interactive Lessons

1. Introduction
2. Writing for the Internet
3. Interacting with Your Online Audience
4. Using Technology to Collaborate

W 6, W 7, W 8, W 9, W 10

Conducting Research

There's a world of information out there. How do you find it?

Interactive Lessons

1. Introduction
2. Starting Your Research
3. Types of Sources
4. Using the Library for Research
5. Conducting Field Research
6. Using the Internet for Research
7. Taking Notes
8. Refocusing Your Inquiry

Evaluating Sources

W 8

Approach all sources with a critical eye.

Interactive Lessons

1. Introduction
2. Evaluating Sources for Usefulness
3. Evaluating Sources for Reliability

Using Textual Evidence

W 7, W 8, W 9

Put your research into writing.

Interactive Lessons

1. Introduction
2. Synthesizing Information
3. Writing an Outline
4. Summarizing, Paraphrasing, and Quoting
5. Attribution

Participating in Collaborative Discussions

SL 1

There's power in putting your heads together.

Interactive Lessons

1. Introduction
2. Preparing for Discussion
3. Establishing and Following Procedure
4. Speaking Constructively
5. Listening and Responding
6. Wrapping Up Your Discussion

Analyzing and Evaluating Presentations

SL 2, SL 3

Is there substance behind the style?

Interactive Lessons

1. Introduction
2. Analyzing a Presentation
3. Evaluating a Speaker's Reliability
4. Tracing a Speaker's Argument
5. Rhetoric and Delivery
6. Synthesizing Media Sources

Giving a Presentation

SL 4, SL 6

Learn how to talk to a roomful of people.

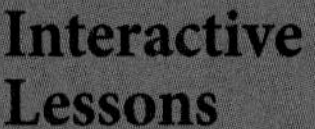

Interactive Lessons

1. Introduction
2. Knowing Your Audience
3. The Content of Your Presentation: Argument

3a. The Content of Your Presentation: Narrative

4. Style in Presentation
5. Delivering Your Presentation

Using Media in a Presentation

SL 5

If a picture is worth a thousand words, just think what you can do with a video.

Interactive Lessons

1. Introduction
2. Types of Media: Audio, Video, and Images
3. Using Presentation Software
4. Practicing Your Presentation

DIGITAL SPOTLIGHT

eBook | myNotebook | fyi | myWriteSmart

Supporting 21st-Century Skills

The amount of information people encounter each day keeps increasing. Whether you're working alone or collaborating with others, it takes effort to analyze the complex texts and competing ideas that bombard us in this fast-paced world. What can allow you to succeed? Staying engaged and organized. The digital tools in this program will help you to think critically and take charge of your learning.

Stream to Start

Ignite your Investigation

You learn best when you're engaged. The **Stream to Start** video at the beginning of each collection is designed to inspire interest in the topics being explored. Watch it and then let your curiosity lead your investigations.

Learn How to Do a Close Read

An effective close read is all about the details; you have to examine the language and ideas a writer includes. See how it's done by accessing the **Close Read Screencasts** in your eBook. Hear modeled conversations about anchor texts.

Contents
Resources
Bookmarks
Notes
Page View

Who, almost dead for breath, had scarcely more
Than would make up his message.

Lady Macbeth. Give him tending.
He brings great news.

[Messenger *exits.*]

The raven himself is hoarse
That croaks the fatal entrance of Duncan
Under my battlements. Come, you spirits
That tend on mortal thoughts, unsex me here,

Close Read

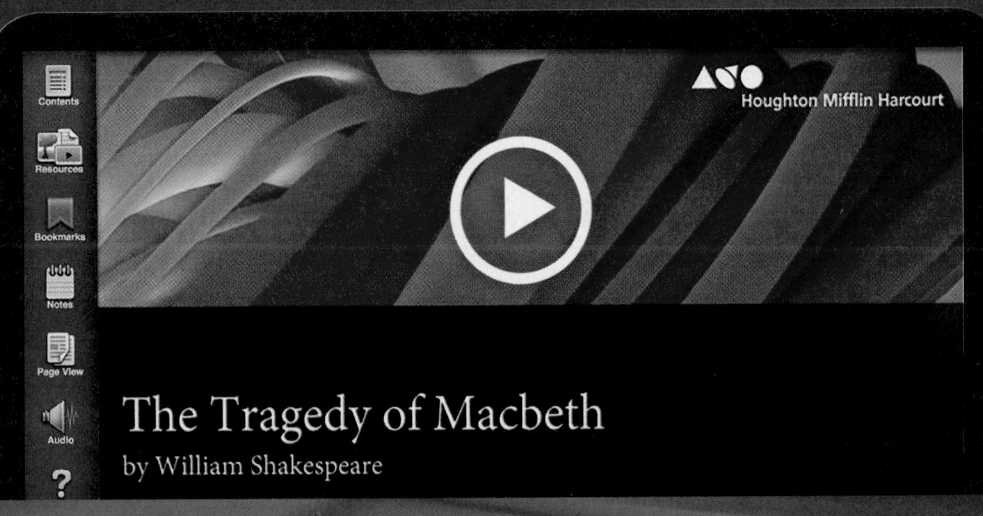

Contents
Resources
Bookmarks
Notes
Page View

The raven himself is hoarse
That croaksthe fatal entrance of Duncan
Under my battlements. Come, you spirits
Thattend on mortalthoughts, unsex me here,
And fill me from the crown to the toe top-full
Of direst cruelty. Make thick my blood.
Stop up th' access and passage to remorse,
That no compunctious visitings of nature

The raven is a symbol of death and evil.

Annotate the Texts

Practice close reading by utilizing the powerful annotation tools in your eBook. Mark up key ideas and observations using highlighters and sticky notes. Tag unfamiliar words to create a personal word list in *my*Notebook.

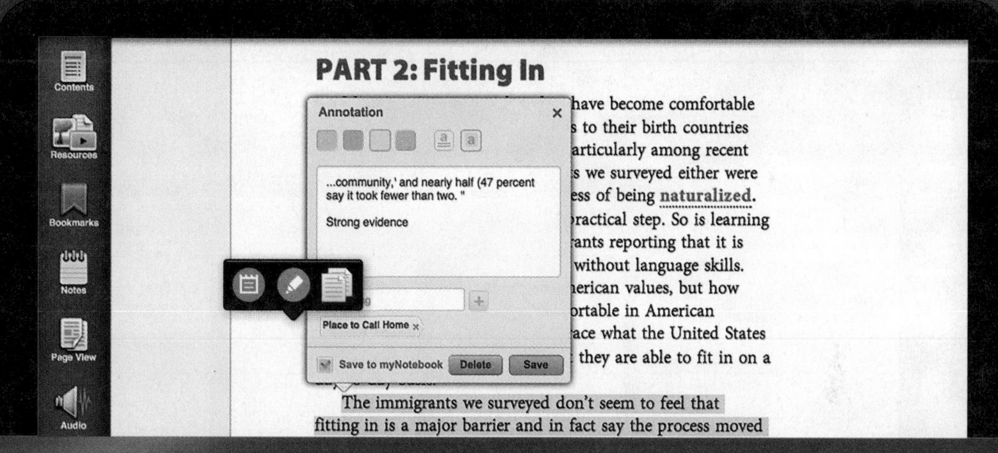

Find More Text Evidence on the Web

Tap into the *FYI* website for links to high-interest informational texts about collection topics. Synthesize information and connect notes and text evidence from any Web source by including it in *my*Notebook.

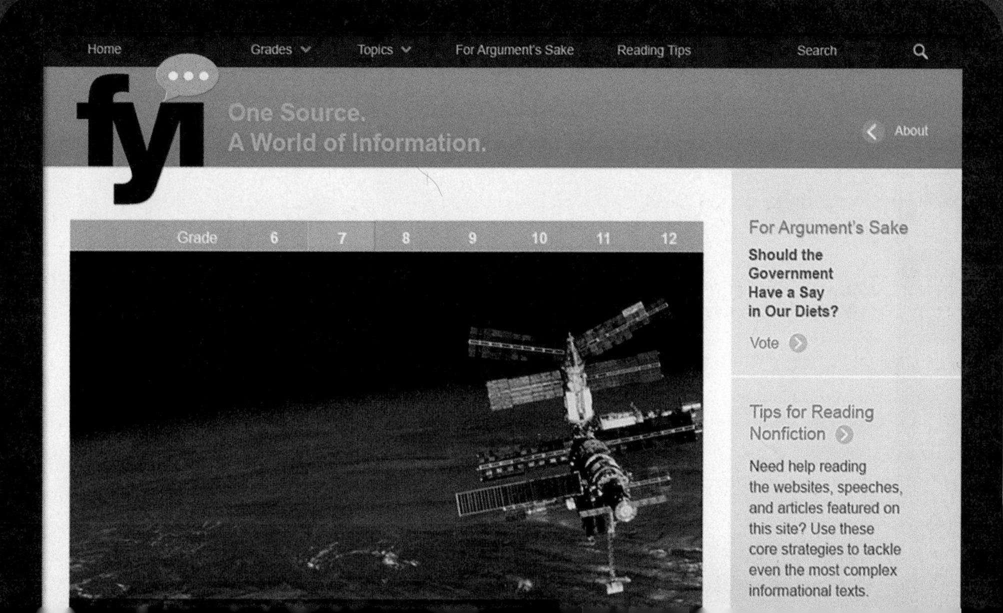

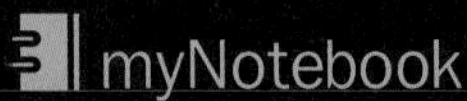

Save and Organize Your Notes

Save your annotations to *my*Notebook, where you can organize them to use as text evidence in performance tasks and other writing assignments. You can also organize the unfamiliar words you tagged by creating word lists, which will help you grow your vocabulary.

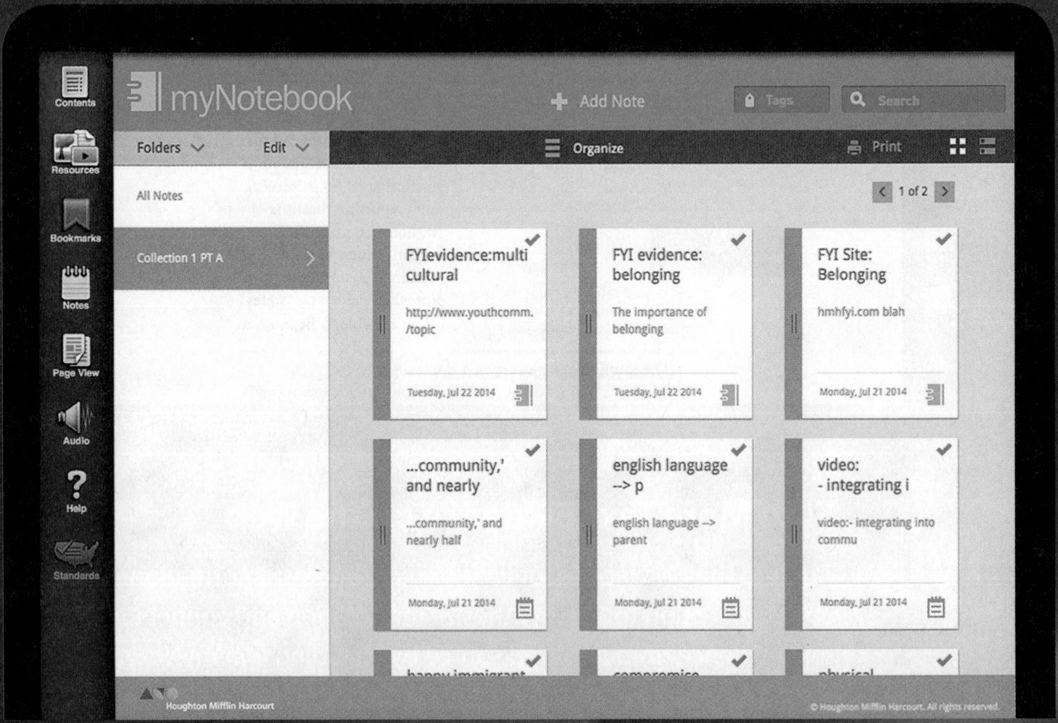

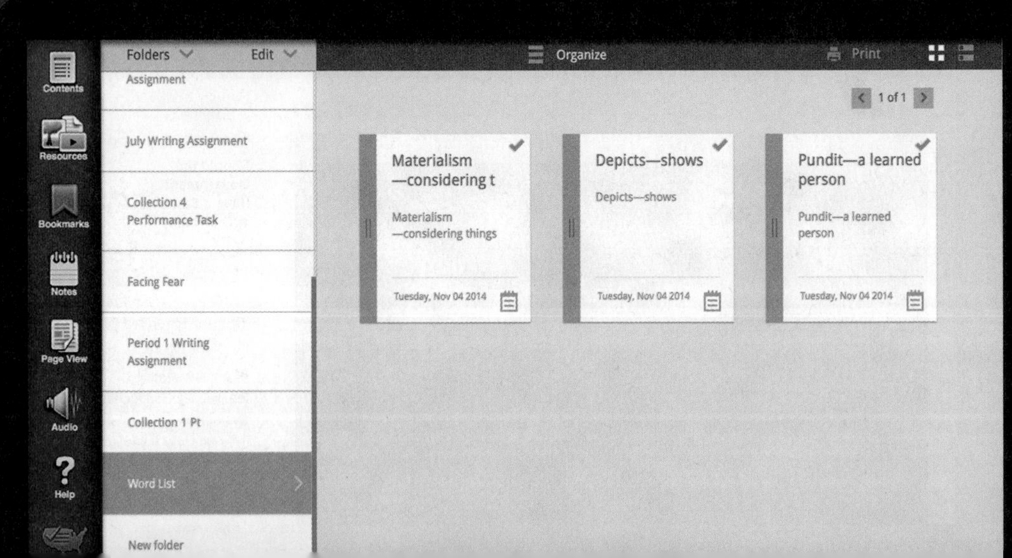

Create, Communicate, and Collaborate

Use the technology provided by the ***my*WriteSmart** tool to keep track of your writing assignments, create drafts, and collaborate and communicate with peers and your teacher. Use the evidence you've gathered in ***my*Notebook** to support your ideas.

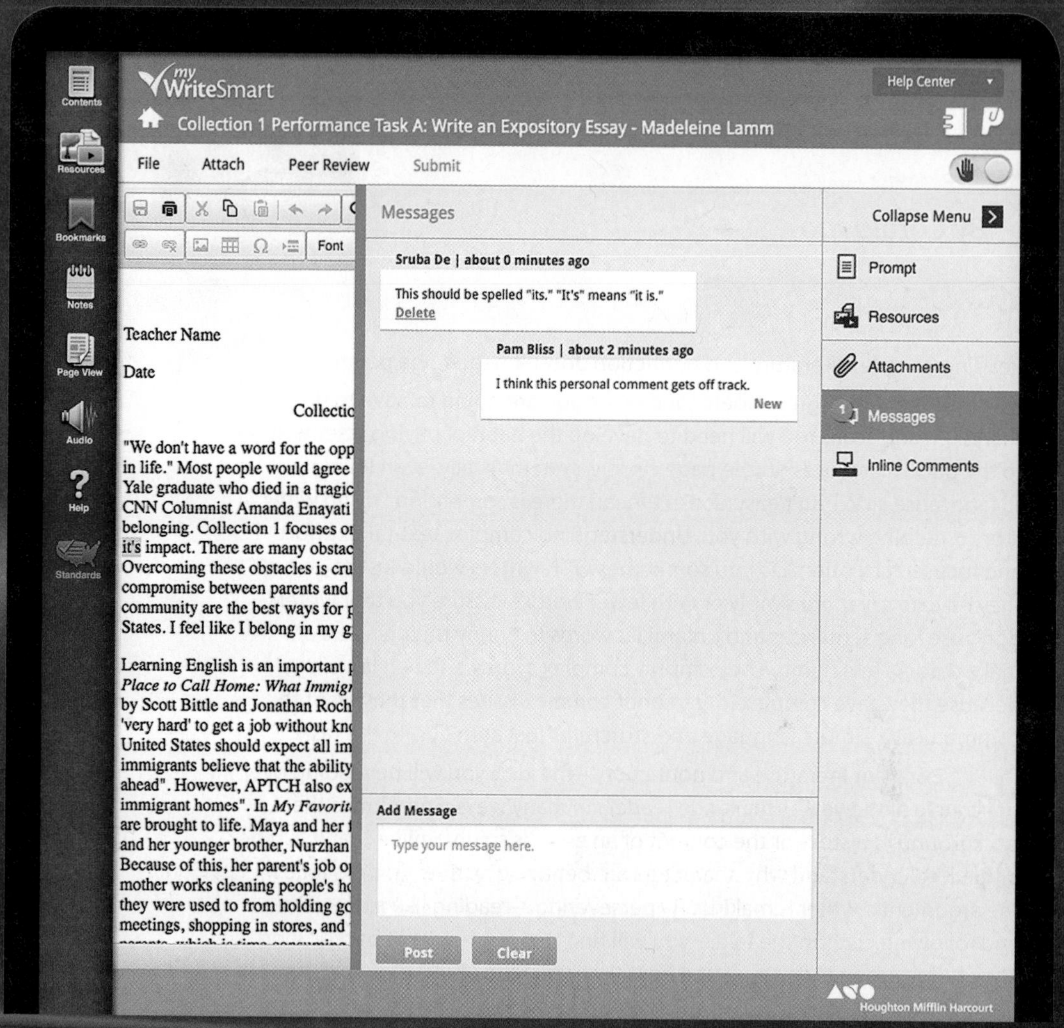

Navigating Complex Texts in the 21st Century

By Carol Jago

Reading complex literature and nonfiction doesn't need to be painful.

But to enjoy great poetry and prose you are going to have to do more than skim and scan. You will need to develop the habit of paying attention to the particular words on the page closely, systematically, even lovingly. Just because a text isn't easy doesn't mean there is something wrong with it or something wrong with you. Understanding complex text takes effort and focused attention. Do you sometimes wish writers would just say what they have to say more simply or with fewer words? I assure you that writers don't use long sentences and unfamiliar words to annoy their readers or make readers feel dumb. They employ complex syntax and rich language because they have complex ideas about complex issues that they want to communicate. Simple language and structures just aren't up to the task.

Excellent literature and nonfiction—the kind you will be reading over the course of the year—challenge readers in many ways. Sometimes the background of a story or the content of an essay is so unfamiliar that it can be difficult to understand why characters are behaving as they do or to follow the argument a writer is making. By persevering—reading like a detective and following clues in the text—you will find that your store of background knowledge grows. As a result, the next time you read about global issues, financial matters, political events, environmental news (like the California drought), or health research, the text won't seem nearly as hard. Navigating a terrain you have been over once before never seems quite as rugged the second time through. The more you read, the better reader you become.

Good readers aren't scared off by challenging text. When the going gets rough, they know what to do. Let's take vocabulary, a common measure of text complexity, as an example. Learning new words is the business of a lifetime. Rather than shutting down when you meet a word you don't know, take a moment to think about the word. Is any part of the word familiar to you? Is there something in the context of the sentence or paragraph that can help you figure out its meaning? Is there someone or something that can provide you with a definition? When we read literature or nonfiction from a time period other than our own, the text is often full of words we don't know. Each time you meet those words in succeeding readings you will be adding to your understanding of the word and its use. Your brain is a natural word-learning machine. The more you feed it complex text, the larger vocabulary you'll have and as a result, the easier navigating the next book will be.

Have you ever been reading a long, complicated sentence and discovered that by the time you reached the end you had forgotten the beginning? Unlike the sentences we speak or dash off in a note to a friend, complex text is often full of sentences that are not only lengthy but also constructed in intricate ways. Such sentences require readers to slow down and figure out how phrases relate to one another as well as who is doing what to whom. Remember, rereading isn't cheating. It is exactly what experienced readers know to do when they meet dense text on the page. On the pages that follow you will find stories and articles that challenge you at a sentence level. Don't be intimidated. By paying careful attention to how those sentences are constructed, you will see their meanings unfold before your eyes.

"Your brain is a natural word-learning machine. The more you feed it complex text, the larger vocabulary you'll have."

That same kind of attention is required for reading the media. Every day you are bombarded with messages—online, offline, everywhere you look. These, too, are complex texts that you want to be able to see through; that is, to be able to recognize the message's source, purpose, context, intended audience, and appeals. This is what it takes to be a 21st century reader.

Another way text can be complex is in terms of the density of ideas. Sometimes a writer piles on so much information that you find even if your eyes continue to move down the page, your brain has stopped taking in anything. At times like this, turning to a peer and discussing particular lines or concepts can help you pay closer attention and begin to unpack the text. Sharing questions and ideas, exploring a difficult passage together, makes it possible to tease out the meaning of even the most difficult text.

Poetry is by its nature particularly dense and for that reason poses particular challenges for casual readers. Don't ever assume that once through a poem is enough. Often, seemingly simple poems in terms of word choice and length—for example an Emily Dickinson, Mary Oliver, or W.H. Auden poem—express extremely complex feelings and insights. Poets also often make reference to mythological and Biblical allusions which contemporary readers are not always familiar with. Skipping over such references robs your reading of the richness the poet intended. Look up that bird. Check out the note on the page. Ask your teacher.

You will notice a range of complexity within each collection of readings. This spectrum reflects the range of texts that surround us: some easy, some hard, some seemingly easy but hard, some seemingly hard but easy. Navigating this sea of texts should stretch you as a reader and a thinker. How could it be otherwise when your journey is in the realms of gold? Please accept this invitation to an intellectual voyage I think you will enjoy.

Understanding the Common Core State Standards

What are the English Language Arts Common Core State Standards?

The Common Core State Standards for English Language Arts indicate what you should know and be able to do by the end of your grade level. These understandings and skills will help you be better prepared for future classes, college courses, and a career. For this reason, the standards for each strand in English Language Arts (such as Reading Informational Text or Writing) directly relate to the College and Career Readiness Anchor Standards for each strand. The Anchor Standards broadly outline the understandings and skills you should master by the end of high school so that you are well prepared for college or for a career.

How do I learn the English Language Arts Common Core State Standards?

Your textbook is closely aligned to the English Language Arts Common Core State Standards. Every time you learn a concept or practice a skill, you are working on mastery of one of the standards. Each collection, each selection, and each performance task in your textbook connects to one or more of the standards for English Language Arts listed on the following pages.

The English Language Arts Common Core State Standards are divided into five strands: Reading Literature, Reading Informational Text, Writing, Speaking and Listening, and Language.

©svetikd/The Agency Collection/Getty Images

Strand	What It Means to You
Reading Literature (RL)	This strand concerns the literary texts you will read at this grade level: stories, drama, and poetry. The Common Core State Standards stress that you should read a range of texts of increasing complexity as you progress through high school.
Reading Informational Text (RI)	Informational text includes a broad range of literary nonfiction, including exposition, argument, and functional text, in such genres as personal essays, speeches, opinion pieces, memoirs, and historical and technical accounts. The Common Core State Standards stress that you will read a range of informational texts of increasing complexity as you progress from grade to grade.
Writing (W)	The Writing strand focuses on your generating three types of texts—arguments, informative or explanatory texts, and narratives—while using the writing process and technology to develop and share your writing. The Common Core State Standards also emphasize research and specify that you should write routinely for both short and extended time frames.
Speaking and Listening (SL)	The Common Core State Standards focus on comprehending information presented in a variety of media and formats, on participating in collaborative discussions, and on presenting knowledge and ideas clearly.
Language (L)	The standards in the Language strand address the conventions of standard English grammar, usage, and mechanics; knowledge of language; and vocabulary acquisition and use.

Common Core Code Decoder

The codes you find on the pages of your textbook identify the specific knowledge or skill for the standard addressed in the text.

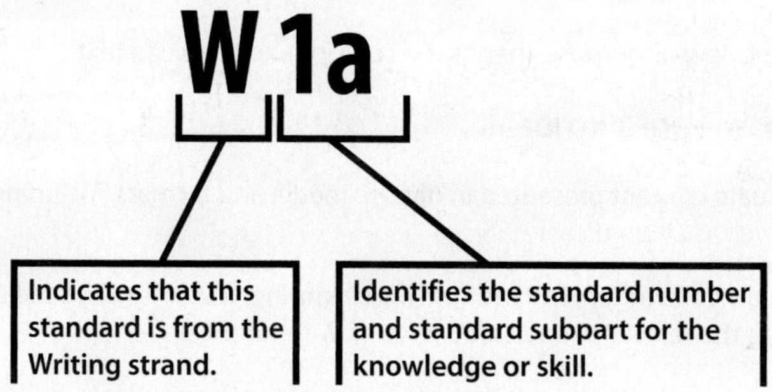

English Language Arts Common Core State Standards

Listed below are the English Language Arts Common Core State Standards that you are required to master by the end of grade 12. We have provided a summary of the concepts you will learn on your way to mastering each standard. The CCR anchor standards and high school grade-specific standards for each strand work together to define college and career readiness expectations—the former providing broad standards, the latter providing additional specificity.

College and Career Readiness Anchor Standards for Reading

Common Core State Standards
KEY IDEAS AND DETAILS
1. Read closely to determine what the text says explicitly and to make logical inferences from it; cite specific textual evidence when writing or speaking to support conclusions drawn from the text.
2. Determine central ideas or themes of a text and analyze their development; summarize the key supporting details and ideas.
3. Analyze how and why individuals, events, and ideas develop and interact over the course of a text.
CRAFT AND STRUCTURE
4. Interpret words and phrases as they are used in a text, including determining technical, connotative, and figurative meanings, and analyze how specific word choices shape meaning or tone.
5. Analyze the structure of texts, including how specific sentences, paragraphs, and larger portions of the text (e.g., a section, chapter, scene, or stanza) relate to each other and the whole.
6. Assess how point of view or purpose shapes the content and style of a text.
INTEGRATION OF KNOWLEDGE AND IDEAS
7. Integrate and evaluate content presented in diverse media and formats, including visually and quantitatively, as well as in words.
8. Delineate and evaluate the argument and specific claims in a text, including the validity of the reasoning as well as the relevance and sufficiency of the evidence.
9. Analyze how two or more texts address similar themes or topics in order to build knowledge or to compare the approaches the authors take.
RANGE OF READING AND LEVEL OF TEXT COMPLEXITY
10. Read and comprehend complex literary and informational texts independently and proficiently.

Reading Standards for Literature, Grades 11–12 Students

The College and Career Readiness Anchor Standards for Reading apply to both literature and informational text.

Common Core State Standards	What It Means to You
KEY IDEAS AND DETAILS	
1. Cite strong and thorough textual evidence to support analysis of what the text says explicitly as well as inferences drawn from the text, including determining where the text leaves matters uncertain.	You will use strong evidence from a text to support your analysis of its central ideas—both those that are stated directly and those that are suggested—and to show where the text leaves matters uncertain.
2. Determine two or more themes or central ideas of a text and analyze their development over the course of the text, including how they interact and build on one another to produce a complex account; provide an objective summary of the text.	You will analyze the development of at least two of a text's key ideas and themes by showing how they progress and interact throughout the text. You will also summarize the text as a whole without adding your own ideas or opinions.
3. Analyze the impact of the author's choices regarding how to develop and relate elements of a story or drama (e.g., where a story is set, how the action is ordered, how the characters are introduced and developed).	You will analyze the author's choices related to setting, plot structure, and characterization in a story or drama.
CRAFT AND STRUCTURE	
4. Determine the meaning of words and phrases as they are used in the text, including figurative and connotative meanings; analyze the impact of specific word choices on meaning and tone, including words with multiple meanings or language that is particularly fresh, engaging, or beautiful. (Include Shakespeare as well as other authors.)	You will analyze specific words and phrases in the text to determine both their figurative and connotative meanings, as well as how they contribute to the text's tone and meaning as a whole. You will also consider multiple-meaning words and vivid language.
5. Analyze how an author's choices concerning how to structure specific parts of a text (e.g., the choice of where to begin or end a story, the choice to provide a comedic or tragic resolution) contribute to its overall structure and meaning as well as its aesthetic impact.	You will analyze the ways in which the author has chosen to structure and order the text and determine how those choices shape the text's meaning and affect the reader.
6. Analyze a case in which grasping point of view requires distinguishing what is directly stated in a text from what is really meant (e.g., satire, sarcasm, irony, or understatement).	You will understand a point of view in which what is really meant is different from what is said or stated.

Reading Standards for Literature, Grades 11–12 Students, continued

Common Core State Standards	What It Means to You
INTEGRATION OF KNOWLEDGE AND IDEAS	
7. Analyze multiple interpretations of a story, drama, or poem (e.g., recorded or live production of a play or recorded novel or poetry), evaluating how each version interprets the source text. (Include at least one play by Shakespeare and one play by an American dramatist.)	You will compare and contrast multiple interpretations of a story, drama, or poem, and analyze how each draws from and uses the source text.
8. (Not applicable to literature)	
9. Demonstrate knowledge of eighteenth-, nineteenth- and early-twentieth-century foundational works of American literature, including how two or more texts from the same period treat similar themes or topics.	You will analyze, compare, and contrast important eighteenth-, nineteenth-, and early-twentieth-century works of American literature.
RANGE OF READING AND LEVEL OF TEXT COMPLEXITY	
10. By the end of grade 12, read and comprehend literature, including stories, dramas, and poems, at the high end of the grades 11–CCR text complexity band independently and proficiently.	You will read and understand grade-level appropriate literary texts by the end of grade 12.

Reading Standards for Informational Text, Grades 11–12 Students

Common Core State Standards	What It Means to You
KEY IDEAS AND DETAILS	
1. Cite strong and thorough textual evidence to support analysis of what the text says explicitly as well as inferences drawn from the text, including determining where the text leaves matters uncertain.	You will use details and information from the text to support your analysis of its central ideas—both those that are stated directly and those that are suggested—and to show where the text leaves matters uncertain.
2. Determine two or more central ideas of a text and analyze their development over the course of the text, including how they interact and build on one another to provide a complex analysis; provide an objective summary of the text.	You will analyze the development of at least two of a text's key ideas by showing how they progress and interact throughout the text. You will also summarize the text as a whole without adding your own ideas or opinions.

Common Core State Standards	What It Means to You
3. Analyze a complex set of ideas or sequence of events and explain how specific individuals, ideas, or events interact and develop over the course of the text.	You will analyze the specific interactions among a set of ideas, individuals, or a sequence of events in a text.
CRAFT AND STRUCTURE	
4. Determine the meaning of words and phrases as they are used in a text, including figurative, connotative, and technical meanings; analyze how an author uses and refines the meaning of a key term or terms over the course of a text (e.g., how Madison defines *faction* in *Federalist* No. 10).	You will analyze specific words and phrases in the text to determine their figurative, connotative, and technical meanings, as well as to uncover how an author uses them throughout a text.
5. Analyze and evaluate the effectiveness of the structure an author uses in his or her exposition or argument, including whether the structure makes points clear, convincing, and engaging.	You will examine a text's structure and evaluate whether it makes the author's claims clear, convincing, and interesting.
6. Determine an author's point of view or purpose in a text in which the rhetoric is particularly effective, analyzing how style and content contribute to the power, persuasiveness, or beauty of the text.	You will understand the author's purpose and perspective on a topic and analyze how the author uses language to affect the reader.
INTEGRATION OF KNOWLEDGE AND IDEAS	
7. Integrate and evaluate multiple sources of information presented in different media or formats (e.g., visually, quantitatively) as well as in words in order to address a question or solve a problem.	You will integrate multiple and varied sources of information to address a question or solve a problem.
8. Delineate and evaluate the reasoning in seminal U.S. texts, including the application of constitutional principles and use of legal reasoning (e.g., in U.S. Supreme Court majority opinions and dissents) and the premises, purposes, and arguments in works of public advocacy (e.g., *The Federalist*, presidential addresses).	You will analyze the reasoning and underlying principles of important historical U.S. texts for their support of the principles of democracy.

Reading Standards for Informational Text, Grades 11–12 Students, continued

Common Core State Standards	What It Means to You
9. Analyze seventeenth-, eighteenth-, and nineteenth-century foundational U.S. documents of historical and literary significance (including The Declaration of Independence, the Preamble to the Constitution, the Bill of Rights, and Lincoln's Second Inaugural Address) for their themes, purposes, and rhetorical features.	You will read and analyze important eighteenth-, nineteenth-, and early-twentieth-century documents pertaining to American history to determine their themes, purposes, and use of language.
RANGE OF READING AND LEVEL OF TEXT COMPLEXITY	
10. By the end of grade 12, read and comprehend literary nonfiction in the grades 11–CCR text complexity band independently and proficiently.	You will demonstrate the ability to read and understand grade-level appropriate literary nonfiction texts by the end of grade 12.

College and Career Readiness Anchor Standards for Writing

Common Core State Standards
TEXT TYPES AND PURPOSES
1. Write arguments to support claims in an analysis of substantive topics or texts, using valid reasoning and relevant and sufficient evidence.
2. Write informative/explanatory texts to examine and convey complex ideas and information clearly and accurately through the effective selection, organization, and analysis of content.
3. Write narratives to develop real or imagined experiences or events using effective technique, well-chosen details, and well-structured event sequences.
PRODUCTION AND DISTRIBUTION OF WRITING
4. Produce clear and coherent writing in which the development, organization, and style are appropriate to task, purpose, and audience.
5. Develop and strengthen writing as needed by planning, revising, editing, rewriting, or trying a new approach.
6. Use technology, including the Internet, to produce and publish writing and to interact and collaborate with others.
RESEARCH TO BUILD AND PRESENT KNOWLEDGE
7. Conduct short as well as more sustained research projects based on focused questions, demonstrating understanding of the subject under investigation.
8. Gather relevant information from multiple print and digital sources, assess the credibility and accuracy of each source, and integrate the information while avoiding plagiarism.

Common Core State Standards
9. Draw evidence from literary and/or informational texts to support analysis, reflection, and research.
RANGE OF WRITING
10. Write routinely over extended time frames (time for research, reflection, and revision) and shorter time frames (a single sitting or a day or two) for a range of tasks, purposes, and audiences.

Writing Standards, Grades 11–12 Students

Common Core State Standards	What It Means to You
TEXT TYPES AND PURPOSES	
1. Write arguments to support claims in an analysis of substantive topics or texts, using valid reasoning and relevant and sufficient evidence.	You will write and develop arguments with strong evidence and valid reasoning that include
a. Introduce precise, knowledgeable claim(s), establish the significance of the claim(s), distinguish the claim(s) from alternate or opposing claims, and create an organization that logically sequences claim(s), counterclaims, reasons, and evidence.	**a.** a clear organization of precise claims and counterclaims
b. Develop claim(s) and counterclaims fairly and thoroughly, supplying the most relevant evidence for each while pointing out the strengths and limitations of both in a manner that anticipates the audience's knowledge level, concerns, values, and possible biases.	**b.** relevant and unbiased support for claims that incorporates audience considerations
c. Use words, phrases, and clauses as well as varied syntax to link the major sections of the text, create cohesion, and clarify the relationships between claim(s) and reasons, between reasons and evidence, and between claim(s) and counterclaims.	**c.** use of transitional words, phrases, and clauses and varied sentence structures to link information and clarify relationships
d. Establish and maintain a formal style and objective tone while attending to the norms and conventions of the discipline in which they are writing.	**d.** a tone and style that is appropriate and that adheres to the conventions, or expectations, of the discipline

Writing Standards, Grades 11–12 Students, continued

Common Core State Standards	What It Means to You
e. Provide a concluding statement or section that follows from and supports the argument presented.	**e.** a strong concluding statement or section that summarizes the evidence presented
TEXT TYPES AND PURPOSES	
2. Write informative/explanatory texts to examine and convey complex ideas, concepts, and information clearly and accurately through the effective selection, organization, and analysis of content.	You will write clear, well-organized, and thoughtful informative and explanatory texts with
a. Introduce a topic; organize complex ideas, concepts, and information so that each new element builds on that which precedes it to create a unified whole; include formatting (e.g., headings), graphics (e.g., figures, tables), and multimedia when useful to aiding comprehension.	**a.** a clear introduction and an organization that builds on each successive idea, including formats, headings, graphic organizers (when appropriate), and multimedia
b. Develop the topic thoroughly by selecting the most significant and relevant facts, extended definitions, concrete details, quotations, or other information and examples appropriate to the audience's knowledge of the topic.	**b.** a sufficient variety of support and background information
c. Use appropriate and varied transitions and syntax to link the major sections of the text, create cohesion, and clarify the relationships among complex ideas and concepts.	**c.** appropriate and varied transitions and sentence structures
d. Use precise language, domain-specific vocabulary, and techniques such as metaphor, simile, and analogy to manage the complexity of the topic.	**d.** precise language, relevant vocabulary, and the use of comparisons to express complex ideas
e. Establish and maintain a formal style and objective tone while attending to the norms and conventions of the discipline in which they are writing.	**e.** an appropriate tone and style that adheres to the conventions, or expectations, of the discipline

Common Core State Standards	What It Means to You
f. Provide a concluding statement or section that follows from and supports the information or explanation presented (e.g., articulating implications or the significance of the topic).	**f.** a strong concluding statement or section that logically relates to the information presented in the text and that restates the importance or relevance of the topic
TEXT TYPES AND PURPOSES	
3. Write narratives to develop real or imagined experiences or events using effective technique, well-chosen details, and well-structured event sequences.	You will write clear, well-structured, detailed narrative texts that
a. Engage and orient the reader by setting out a problem, situation, or observation and its significance, establishing one or multiple point(s) of view, and introducing a narrator and/or characters; create a smooth progression of experiences or events.	**a.** draw your readers in with a clear topic, well-developed point(s) of view, a well-developed narrator and characters, and an interesting progression of events or ideas
b. Use narrative techniques, such as dialogue, pacing, description, reflection, and multiple plot lines, to develop experiences, events, and/or characters.	**b.** use a range of literary techniques to develop and expand on events and/or characters
c. Use a variety of techniques to sequence events so that they build on one another to create a coherent whole and build toward a particular tone and outcome (e.g., a sense of mystery, suspense, growth, or resolution).	**c.** have a coherent sequence and structure that create the appropriate tone and ending for readers
d. Use precise words and phrases, telling details, and sensory language to convey a vivid picture of the experiences, events, setting, and/or characters.	**d.** use precise words, sensory details, and language in order to keep readers interested
e. Provide a conclusion that follows from and reflects on what is experienced, observed, or resolved over the course of the narrative.	**e.** have a strong and logical conclusion that reflects on the topic

Writing Standards, Grades 11–12 Students, continued

Common Core State Standards	What It Means to You
PRODUCTION AND DISTRIBUTION OF WRITING	
4. Produce clear and coherent writing in which the development, organization, and style are appropriate to task, purpose, and audience.	You will produce writing that is appropriate to the task, purpose, and audience for whom you are writing.
5. Develop and strengthen writing as needed by planning, revising, editing, rewriting, or trying a new approach, focusing on addressing what is most significant for a specific purpose and audience.	You will revise and refine your writing, using a variety of strategies, to address what is most important for your purpose and audience.
6. Use technology, including the Internet, to produce, publish, and update individual or shared writing products in response to ongoing feedback, including new arguments or information.	You will use technology to share your writing, provide links to other relevant information, and to update your information as needed.
RESEARCH TO BUILD AND PRESENT KNOWLEDGE	
7. Conduct short as well as more sustained research projects to answer a question (including a self-generated question) or solve a problem; narrow or broaden the inquiry when appropriate; synthesize multiple sources on the subject, demonstrating understanding of the subject under investigation.	You will engage in short and more complex research tasks that include answering a question or solving a problem by using multiple sources. Your understanding of the subject will be evident in the product you develop.
8. Gather relevant information from multiple authoritative print and digital sources, using advanced searches effectively; assess the strengths and limitations of each source in terms of the task, purpose, and audience; integrate information into the text selectively to maintain the flow of ideas, avoiding plagiarism and overreliance on any one source and following a standard format for citation.	You will effectively conduct searches to gather information from a variety of print and digital sources and will evaluate each source in terms of the goal of your research. You will appropriately cite your sources of information and will follow a standard format for citation, such as the MLA or APA guidelines.

Common Core State Standards	What It Means to You
RESEARCH TO BUILD AND PRESENT KNOWLEDGE	
9. Draw evidence from literary or informational texts to support analysis, reflection, and research.	You will paraphrase, summarize, quote, and cite primary and secondary sources, using both literary and informational texts, to support your analysis, reflection, and research, for purposes including
a. Apply *grades 11–12 Reading standards* to literature (e.g., "Demonstrate knowledge of eighteenth-, nineteenth- and early-twentieth-century foundational works of American literature, including how two or more texts from the same period treat similar themes or topics").	**a.** written analysis of themes, author's choices, or point of view in American literature
b. Apply *grades 11–12 Reading standards* to literary nonfiction (e.g., "Delineate and evaluate the reasoning in seminal U.S. texts, including the application of constitutional principles and use of legal reasoning [e.g., in U.S. Supreme Court Case majority opinions and dissents] and the premises, purposes, and arguments in works of public advocacy [e.g., *The Federalist*, presidential addresses]").	**b.** written analysis of central ideas, text structure, word choice, point of view, or reasoning in American literary nonfiction
RANGE OF WRITING	
10. Write routinely over extended time frames (time for research, reflection, and revision) and shorter time frames (a single sitting or a day or two) for a range of tasks, purposes, and audiences.	You will write a variety of texts for different purposes and audiences over both short and extended periods of time.

College and Career Readiness Anchor Standards for Speaking and Listening

Common Core State Standards
COMPREHENSION AND COLLABORATION
1. Prepare for and participate effectively in a range of conversations and collaborations with diverse partners, building on others' ideas and expressing their own clearly and persuasively.
2. Integrate and evaluate information presented in diverse media and formats, including visually, quantitatively, and orally.

Common Core State Standards
3. Evaluate a speaker's point of view, reasoning, and use of evidence and rhetoric.
PRESENTATION OF KNOWLEDGE AND IDEAS
4. Present information, findings, and supporting evidence such that listeners can follow the line of reasoning and the organization, development, and style are appropriate to task, purpose, and audience.
5. Make strategic use of digital media and visual displays of data to express information and enhance understanding of presentations.
6. Adapt speech to a variety of contexts and communicative tasks, demonstrating command of formal English when indicated or appropriate.

Speaking and Listening Standards, Grades 11–12 Students

Common Core State Standards	What It Means to You
COMPREHENSION AND COLLABORATION	
1. Initiate and participate effectively in a range of collaborative discussions (one-on-one, in groups, and teacher-led) with diverse partners on grades 11–12 topics, texts, and issues, building on others' ideas and expressing their own clearly and persuasively.	You will actively participate in a variety of discussions in which you
a. Come to discussions prepared, having read and researched material under study; explicitly draw on that preparation by referring to evidence from texts and other research on the topic or issue to stimulate a thoughtful, well-reasoned exchange of ideas.	**a.** have read any relevant material beforehand and have come to the discussion prepared with background research
b. Work with peers to promote civil, democratic discussions and decision-making, set clear goals and deadlines, and establish individual roles as needed.	**b.** work with others to establish goals, processes, and roles within the group in order to have reasonable discussions
c. Propel conversations by posing and responding to questions that probe reasoning and evidence; ensure a hearing for a full range of positions on a topic or issue; clarify, verify, or challenge ideas and conclusions; and promote divergent and creative perspectives.	**c.** ask and respond to questions, encourage a range of positions, and relate the current topic to other relevant information and perspectives

Common Core State Standards	What It Means to You
d. Respond thoughtfully to diverse perspectives; synthesize comments, claims, and evidence made on all sides of an issue; resolve contradictions when possible; and determine what additional information or research is required to deepen the investigation or complete the task.	**d.** respond to different perspectives, summarize points of agreement or disagreement when needed, help to resolve unclear points, and set out a plan for additional research as needed
2. Integrate multiple sources of information presented in diverse formats and media (e.g., visually, quantitatively, orally) in order to make informed decisions and solve problems, evaluating the credibility and accuracy of each source and noting any discrepancies among the data.	You will integrate multiple and varied sources of information, assessing the credibility and accuracy of each source to aid the group-discussion process.
3. Evaluate a speaker's point of view, reasoning, and use of evidence and rhetoric, assessing the stance, premises, links among ideas, word choice, points of emphasis, and tone used.	You will evaluate a speaker's argument and analyze the nature of the speaker's reasoning or evidence.
PRESENTATION OF KNOWLEDGE AND IDEAS	
4. Present information, findings, and supporting evidence, conveying a clear and distinct perspective, such that listeners can follow the line of reasoning, alternative or opposing perspectives are addressed, and the organization, development, substance, and style are appropriate to purpose, audience, and a range of formal and informal tasks.	You will organize and present information, evidence, and your perspective to your listeners in a logical sequence and style that are appropriate to your task, purpose, and audience.
5. Make strategic use of digital media (e.g., textual, graphical, audio, visual, and interactive elements) in presentations to enhance understanding of findings, reasoning, and evidence and to add interest.	You will use digital media to enhance understanding and to add interest to your presentations.
6. Adapt speech to a variety of contexts and tasks, demonstrating a command of formal English when indicated or appropriate.	You will adapt the formality of your speech appropriately, depending on its context and purpose.

College and Career Readiness Anchor Standards for Language

Common Core State Standards
CONVENTIONS OF STANDARD ENGLISH
1. Demonstrate command of the conventions of standard English grammar and usage when writing or speaking.
2. Demonstrate command of the conventions of standard English capitalization, punctuation, and spelling when writing.
KNOWLEDGE OF LANGUAGE
3. Apply knowledge of language to understand how language functions in different contexts, to make effective choices for meaning or style, and to comprehend more fully when reading or listening.
VOCABULARY ACQUISITION AND USE
4. Determine or clarify the meaning of unknown and multiple-meaning words and phrases by using context clues, analyzing meaningful word parts, and consulting general and specialized reference materials, as appropriate.
5. Demonstrate understanding of figurative language, word relationships, and nuances in word meanings.
6. Acquire and use accurately a range of general academic and domain-specific words and phrases sufficient for reading, writing, speaking, and listening at the college- and career-readiness level; demonstrate independence in gathering vocabulary knowledge when encountering an unknown term important to comprehension or expression.

Language Standards, Grades 11–12 Students

Common Core State Standards	What It Means to You
CONVENTIONS OF STANDARD ENGLISH	
1. Demonstrate command of the conventions of standard English grammar and usage when writing or speaking.	You will correctly use the conventions of English grammar and usage, including
a. Apply the understanding that usage is a matter of convention, can change over time, and is sometimes contested.	**a.** demonstrating that usage follows accepted standards and can change or be contested
b. Resolve issues of complex or contested usage, consulting references (e.g., *Merriam-Webster's Dictionary of English Usage, Garner's Modern American Usage*) as needed.	**b.** using references to resolve disagreements or uncertainty about usage

Common Core State Standards	What It Means to You
2. Demonstrate command of the conventions of standard English capitalization, punctuation, and spelling when writing. **a.** Observe hyphenation conventions.	You will correctly use the conventions of standard English capitalization, punctuation, and spelling, including **a.** hyphens
b. Spell correctly.	**b.** spelling
KNOWLEDGE OF LANGUAGE	
3. Apply knowledge of language to understand how language functions in different contexts, to make effective choices for meaning or style, and to comprehend more fully when reading or listening.	You will apply your knowledge of language in different contexts to guide choices in your own writing and speaking by
a. Vary syntax for effect, consulting references (e.g., Tufte's *Artful Sentences*) for guidance as needed; apply an understanding of syntax to the study of complex texts when reading.	**a.** using appropriate references for guidance to vary your syntax and to understand syntax in complex texts
VOCABULARY ACQUISITION AND USE	
4. Determine or clarify the meaning of unknown and multiple-meaning words and phrases based on grades 11–12 reading and content, choosing flexibly from a range of strategies.	You will understand the meaning of grade-level appropriate words and phrases by
a. Use context (e.g., the overall meaning of a sentence, paragraph, or text; a word's position or function in a sentence) as a clue to the meaning of a word or phrase.	**a.** using context clues
b. Identify and correctly use patterns of word changes that indicate different meanings or parts of speech (e.g., *conceive, conception, conceivable*).	**b.** applying various forms of words according to meaning or part of speech

Language Standards, Grades 11–12 Students, continued

Common Core State Standards	What It Means to You
c. Consult general and specialized reference materials (e.g., dictionaries, glossaries, thesauruses), both print and digital, to find the pronunciation of a word or determine or clarify its precise meaning, its part of speech, its etymology, or its standard usage.	**c.** using reference materials to determine and clarify word meaning, part of speech, etymology, and standard usage
d. Verify the preliminary determination of the meaning of a word or phrase (e.g., by checking the inferred meaning in context or in a dictionary).	**d.** inferring and verifying the meanings of words in context
VOCABULARY ACQUISITION AND USE	
5. Demonstrate understanding of figurative language, word relationships, and nuances in word meanings.	You will understand figurative language, word relationships, and slight differences in word meanings by
a. Interpret figures of speech (e.g., hyperbole, paradox) in context and analyze their role in the text.	**a.** interpreting figures of speech in context
b. Analyze nuances in the meaning of words with similar denotations.	**b.** analyzing slight differences in the meanings of similar words
6. Acquire and use accurately general academic and domain-specific words and phrases, sufficient for reading, writing, speaking, and listening at the college and career readiness level; demonstrate independence in gathering vocabulary knowledge when considering a word or phrase important to comprehension or expression.	You will develop and use a range of vocabulary at the college and career readiness level and will demonstrate that you can successfully acquire new vocabulary independently.

Image Credits: ©Jonathan Griffith/Aurora Photos/Corbis

Chasing Success

Success may be sweet, but as this collection shows, it sometimes requires great sacrifice.

COLLECTION

PERFORMANCE TASK Preview

At the end of this collection, you will have the opportunity to complete two tasks:

- Debate with classmates the merits of extending the school year to provide more time for learning, citing evidence from texts in the collection.
- Write an essay in which you compare and contrast the experiences of two characters or people from the texts, focusing on the sacrifices they make to succeed.

ACADEMIC VOCABULARY

Study the words and their definitions in the chart below. You will use these words as you discuss and write about the texts in this collection.

Word	Definition	Related Forms
accumulate (ə-kyoom´yə-lāt´) *v.*	to gather or pile up	accumulation, accumulative
appreciation (ə-prē´shē-ā´shən) *n.*	recognition of the quality, significance, or value of someone or something	appreciable, appreciate, appreciative
conform (kən-fôrm´) *v.*	to be similar to or match something or someone; to act or be in accord or agreement	conformable, conformance, conformation, conformist, conformity
persistence (pər-sĭs´təns) *n.*	the act or quality of holding firmly to a purpose or task in spite of obstacles	persist, persistency, persistent

Malcolm Gladwell *(b. 1963) was born to an English father and a Jamaican mother. He grew up in rural Ontario, Canada. The author of several bestselling books, he is a staff writer for* The New Yorker. *Gladwell typically analyzes aspects of daily life, offering intriguing ideas about social phenomena and human behavior. "Marita's Bargain" is excerpted from Gladwell's third book,* Outliers: The Story of Success, *in which he explores the reasons why some people achieve success and others do not.*

Marita's Bargain

Essay by Malcolm Gladwell

AS YOU READ Pay attention to details that describe KIPP students. Write down any questions you generate during reading.

As you read, save new words to ***myWordList***.

In the mid-1990s, an experimental public school called the KIPP Academy opened on the fourth floor of Lou Gehrig Junior High School in New York City.[1] Lou Gehrig is in the seventh school district, otherwise known as the South Bronx, one of the poorest neighborhoods in New York City. It is a squat, gray 1960s-era building across the street from a bleak-looking group of high-rises. A few blocks over is Grand Concourse, the borough's main thoroughfare. These are not streets that you'd happily walk down, alone, after dark.

KIPP is a middle school. Classes are large: the fifth grade has two sections of thirty-five students each. There are no entrance exams or admissions requirements. Students are chosen by lottery, with any fourth grader living in the Bronx eligible to apply. Roughly half of the students are African American; the rest are Hispanic. Three-quarters of the children come from single-parent homes. Ninety percent qualify for "free or reduced lunch," which is to say that their families earn

[1] **KIPP:** "Knowledge Is Power Program," a national organization of charter schools.

so little that the federal government chips in so the children can eat properly at lunchtime.

KIPP Academy seems like the kind of school in the kind of neighborhood with the kind of student that would make educators despair—except that the minute you enter the building, it's clear that something is different. The students walk quietly down the hallways in single file. In the classroom, they are taught to turn and address anyone talking to them in a protocol known as "SSLANT": smile, sit up, listen, ask questions, nod when being spoken to, and track with your eyes. On the walls of the school's corridors are hundreds of pennants from the colleges that KIPP graduates have gone on to attend. Last year, hundreds of families from across the Bronx entered the lottery for KIPP's two fifth-grade classes. It is no exaggeration to say that just over ten years into its existence, KIPP has become one of the most desirable public schools in New York City.

What KIPP is most famous for is mathematics. In the South Bronx, only about 16 percent of all middle school students are performing at or above their grade level in math. But at KIPP, by the end of fifth grade, many of the students call math their favorite subject. In seventh grade, KIPP students start *high school* algebra. By the end of eighth grade, 84 percent of the students are performing at or above their grade level, which is to say that this **motley** group of randomly chosen lower-income kids from dingy apartments in one of the country's worst neighborhoods—whose parents, in an overwhelming number of cases, never set foot in a college—do as well in mathematics as the privileged eighth graders of America's wealthy suburbs. "Our kids' reading is on point," said David Levin, who founded KIPP with a fellow teacher, Michael Feinberg, in 1994. "They struggle a little bit with writing skills. But when they leave here, they rock in math."

motley
(mŏt´lē) *adj.* unusually varied or mixed.

There are now more than fifty KIPP schools across the United States, with more on the way. The KIPP program represents one of the most promising new educational philosophies in the United States. But its success is best understood not in terms of its curriculum, its teachers, its resources, or some kind of institutional innovation. KIPP is, rather, an organization that has succeeded by taking the idea of cultural legacies seriously.

In the early nineteenth century, a group of reformers set out to establish a system of public education in the United States. What passed for public school at the time was a haphazard assortment of locally run one-room schoolhouses and overcrowded urban classrooms scattered around the country. In rural areas, schools closed in the spring and fall and ran all summer long, so that children could help out in the busy planting and harvesting seasons. In the city, many schools mirrored the long and chaotic schedules of the children's working-class parents. The reformers wanted to make sure that all

> Just over ten years into its existence, KIPP has become one of the most desirable public schools in New York City.

children went to school and that public school was comprehensive, meaning that all children got enough schooling to learn how to read and write and do basic arithmetic and function as productive citizens.

But as the historian Kenneth Gold has pointed out, the early educational reformers were also tremendously concerned that children not get *too much* schooling. In 1871, for example, the US commissioner of education published a report by Edward Jarvis on the "Relation of Education to Insanity." Jarvis had studied 1,741 cases of insanity and concluded that "over-study" was responsible for 205 of them. "Education lays the foundation of a large portion of the causes of mental disorder," Jarvis wrote. Similarly, the pioneer of public education in Massachusetts, Horace Mann, believed that working students too hard would create a "most pernicious influence upon character and habits. . . . Not infrequently is health itself destroyed by overstimulating the mind." In the education journals of the day, there were constant worries about overtaxing students or blunting their natural abilities through too much schoolwork.

The reformers, Gold writes:

> strove for ways to reduce time spent studying, because long periods of respite could save the mind from injury. Hence the elimination of Saturday classes, the shortening of the school day, and the lengthening of vacation—all of which occurred over the course of the nineteenth century. Teachers were cautioned that "when [students] are required to study, their bodies should not be exhausted by long confinement, nor their minds bewildered by prolonged application." Rest also presented particular opportunities for strengthening **cognitive** and analytical skills. As one contributor to the *Massachusetts Teacher* suggested, "it is when thus relieved from the state of tension belonging to actual study that boys and girls, as well as men and women, acquire the habit of thought and reflection, and of forming their own conclusions, independently of what they are taught and the authority of others."

cognitive
(kŏg′nĭ-tĭv) *adj.* related to knowledge or understanding.

This idea—that effort must be balanced by rest—could not be more different from Asian notions about study and work, of course. But then again, the Asian worldview was shaped by the rice paddy. In the Pearl River Delta, the rice farmer planted two and sometimes three crops a year.[2] The land was fallow only briefly. In fact, one of the singular features of rice cultivation is that because of the nutrients carried by the water used in irrigation, the more a plot of land is cultivated, the more fertile it gets.

But in Western agriculture, the opposite is true. Unless a wheat- or cornfield is left fallow every few years, the soil becomes exhausted. Every winter, fields are empty. The hard labor of spring planting and fall harvesting is followed, like clockwork, by the slower pace of summer and winter. This is the logic the reformers applied to the cultivation of young minds. We formulate new ideas by analogy, working from what we know toward what we don't know, and what the reformers knew were the rhythms of the agricultural seasons. A mind must be cultivated. But not too much, lest it be exhausted. And what was the remedy for the dangers of exhaustion? The long summer vacation—a peculiar and distinctive American legacy that has had profound consequences for the learning patterns of the students of the present day.

Summer vacation is a topic seldom mentioned in American educational debates. It is considered a permanent and **inviolate** feature of school life, like high school football or the senior prom. But take a look at the following sets of elementary school test-score results, and see if your faith in the value of long summer holidays isn't profoundly shaken.

inviolate (ĭn-vī´ə-lĭt) *adj.* secure against change or violation.

These numbers come from research led by the Johns Hopkins University sociologist Karl Alexander. Alexander tracked the progress of 650 first graders from the Baltimore public school system, looking at how they scored on a widely used math- and reading-skills exam called the California Achievement Test. These are reading scores for the first five years of elementary school, broken down by socioeconomic class—low, middle, and high.

Class	1st Grade	2nd Grade	3rd Grade	4th Grade	5th Grade
Low	329	375	397	433	461
Middle	348	388	425	467	497
High	361	418	460	506	534

Look at the first column. The students start in first grade with meaningful, but not overwhelming, differences in their knowledge and

[2] **rice paddy . . . three crops a year:** The Pearl River Delta is an area in southeastern China where the Pearl River enters the South China Sea. It contains many rice paddies, flooded land used to grow rice.

ability. The first graders from the wealthiest homes have a 32-point advantage over the first graders from the poorest homes—and by the way, first graders from poor homes in Baltimore are *really* poor. Now look at the fifth-grade column. By that point, four years later, the initially modest gap between rich and poor has more than doubled.

This "achievement gap" is a phenomenon that has been observed over and over again, and it typically provokes one of two responses. The first response is that disadvantaged kids simply don't have the same inherent ability to learn as children from more privileged backgrounds. They're not as smart. The second, slightly more optimistic conclusion is that, in some way, our schools are failing poor children: we simply aren't doing a good enough job of teaching them the skills they need. But here's where Alexander's study gets interesting, because it turns out that neither of those explanations rings true.

The city of Baltimore didn't give its kids the California Achievement Test just at the end of every school year, in June. It gave them the test in September too, just after summer vacation ended. What Alexander realized is that the second set of test results allowed him to do a slightly different analysis. If he looked at the difference between the score a student got at the beginning of the school year, in September, and the score he or she got the following June, he could measure—precisely—how much that student learned over the school year. And if he looked at the difference between a student's score in June and then in the following September, he could see how much that student learned over the course of the summer. In other words, he could figure out—at least in part—how much of the achievement gap is the result of things that happen during the school year, and how much it has to do with what happens during summer vacation.

Let's start with the school-year gains. This table shows how many points students' test scores rose from the time they started classes in September to the time they stopped in June. The "Total" column represents their cumulative classroom learning from all five years of elementary school.

Class	1st Grade	2nd Grade	3rd Grade	4th Grade	5th Grade	Total
Low	55	46	30	33	25	189
Middle	69	43	34	41	27	214
High	60	39	34	28	23	184

Here is a completely different story from the one suggested by the first table. The first set of test results made it look like lower-income kids were somehow failing in the classroom. But here we see plainly that isn't true. Look at the "Total" column. Over the course of five years of elementary school, poor kids "out-learn" the wealthiest kids

189 points to 184 points. They lag behind the middle-class kids by only a modest amount, and, in fact, in one year, second grade, they learn more than the middle- or upper-class kids.

Next, let's see what happens if we look just at how reading scores change during summer vacation.

Class	After 1st	After 2nd	After 3rd	After 4th	Total
Low	−3.67	−1.70	2.74	2.89	0.26
Middle	−3.11	4.18	3.68	2.34	7.09
High	15.38	9.22	14.51	13.38	52.49

Do you see the difference? Look at the first column, which measures what happens over the summer after first grade. The wealthiest kids come back in September and their reading scores have jumped more than 15 points. The poorest kids come back from the holidays and their reading scores have *dropped* almost 4 points. Poor kids may out-learn rich kids during the school year. But during the summer, they fall far behind.

Now take a look at the last column, which totals up all the summer gains from first grade to fifth grade. The reading scores of the poor kids go up by .26 points. *When it comes to reading skills, poor kids learn nothing when school is not in session.* The reading scores of the rich kids, by contrast, go up by a whopping 52.49 points. Virtually all of the advantage that wealthy students have over poor students is the result of differences in the way privileged kids learn while they are *not* in school. . . .

What Alexander's work suggests is that the way in which education has been discussed in the United States is backwards. An enormous amount of time is spent talking about reducing class size, rewriting curricula, buying every student a shiny new laptop, and increasing school funding—all of which assumes that there is something fundamentally wrong with the job schools are doing. But look back at the second table, which shows what happens between September and June. Schools *work*. The only problem with school, for the kids who aren't achieving, is that there isn't enough of it.

Alexander, in fact, has done a very simple calculation to demonstrate what would happen if the children of Baltimore went to school year-round. The answer is that poor kids and wealthy kids would, by the end of elementary school, be doing math and reading at almost the same level.

Suddenly the causes of Asian math superiority become even more obvious. Students in Asian schools don't have long summer vacations. Why would they? Cultures that believe that the route to success lies in rising before dawn 360 days a year are scarcely going to give their children three straight months off in the summer. The school year in the United States is, on average, 180 days long. The South Korean school year is 220 days long. The Japanese school year is 243 days long.

One of the questions asked of test takers on a recent math test given to students around the world was how many of the algebra, calculus, and geometry questions covered subject matter that they had previously learned in class. For Japanese twelfth graders, the answer was 92 percent. That's the value of going to school 243 days a year. You have the time to learn everything that needs to be learned—and you have less time to unlearn it. For American twelfth graders, the comparable figure was 54 percent. For its poorest students, America doesn't have a school problem. It has a summer vacation problem, and that's the problem the KIPP schools set out to solve. They decided to bring the lessons of the rice paddy to the American inner city.

"They start school at seven twenty-five," says David Levin of the students at the Bronx KIPP Academy. "They all do a course called thinking skills until seven fifty-five. They do ninety minutes of English, ninety minutes of math every day, except in fifth grade, where they do two hours of math a day. An hour of science, an hour of social science, an hour of music at least twice a week, and then you have an hour and fifteen minutes of orchestra on top of that. Everyone does orchestra. The day goes from seven twenty-five until five p.m. After five, there are homework clubs, detention, sports teams. There are kids here from seven twenty-five until seven p.m. If you take an average day, and you take out lunch and recess, our kids are spending fifty to sixty percent more time learning than the traditional public school student."

Levin was standing in the school's main hallway. It was lunchtime and the students were trooping by quietly in orderly lines, all of them in their KIPP Academy shirts. Levin stopped a girl whose shirttail was out. "Do me a favor, when you get a chance," he called out, miming a tucking-in movement. He continued: "Saturdays they come in nine to one. In the summer, it's eight to two." By summer, Levin was referring to the fact that KIPP students do three extra weeks of school, in July. These are, after all, precisely the kind of lower-income kids who Alexander identified as losing ground over the long summer vacation, so KIPP's response is simply to not have a long summer vacation.

"The beginning is hard," he went on. "By the end of the day they're restless. Part of it is endurance, part of it is motivation. Part of it is incentives and rewards and fun stuff. Part of it is good old-fashioned discipline. You throw all of that into the stew. We talk a lot here about grit and self-control. The kids know what those words mean."

Levin walked down the hall to an eighth-grade math class and stood quietly in the back. A student named Aaron was at the front of the class, working his way through a problem from the page of thinking-skills exercises that all KIPP students are required to do each morning. The teacher, a ponytailed man in his thirties named Frank Corcoran, sat in a chair to the side, only occasionally jumping in to guide the discussion. It was the kind of scene repeated every day in American classrooms—with one difference. Aaron was up at the front, working on that single problem, for *twenty* minutes—methodically, carefully, with the participation of the class, working his way through not just the answer but also the question of whether there was more than one way to get the answer. . . .

"What that extra time does is allow for a more relaxed atmosphere," Corcoran said, after the class was over. "I find that the problem with math education is the sink-or-swim approach. Everything is rapid fire, and the kids who get it first are the ones who are rewarded. So there comes to be a feeling that there are people who can do math and there are people who aren't math people. I think that extended amount of time gives you the chance as a teacher to explain things, and more time for the kids to sit and digest everything that's going on—to review, to do things at a much slower pace. It seems **counterintuitive** but we do things at a slower pace and as a result we get through a lot more. There's a lot more retention, better understanding of the material. It lets me be a little bit more relaxed. We have time to have games. Kids can ask any questions they want, and if I'm explaining something, I don't feel pressed for time. I can go back over material and not feel time pressure." The extra time gave Corcoran the chance to make mathematics *meaningful:* to let his students see the clear relationship between effort and reward.

counterintuitive (koun′tər-ĭn-to͞o′ĭ-tĭv) *adj.* contrary to what one expects.

On the walls of the classroom were dozens of certificates from the New York State Regents exam, testifying to first-class honors for Corcoran's students. "We had a girl in this class," Corcoran said. "She was a horrible math student in fifth grade. She cried every Saturday when we did remedial stuff. Huge tears and tears." At the memory, Corcoran got a little emotional himself. He looked down. "She just e-mailed us a couple weeks ago. She's in college now. She's an accounting major."

The story of the miracle school that transforms losers into winners is, of course, all too familiar. It's the stuff of inspirational books and sentimental Hollywood movies. But the reality of places like KIPP is a good deal less glamorous than that. To get a sense of what 50 to 60 percent more learning time means, listen to the typical day in the life of a KIPP student.

The student's name is Marita. She's an only child who lives in a single-parent home. Her mother never went to college. The two of them share a one-bedroom apartment in the Bronx. Marita used to go to a parochial school down the street from her home, until her mother heard of KIPP. "When I was in fourth grade, me and one of my other friends, Tanya, we both applied to KIPP," Marita said. "I remember Miss Owens. She interviewed me, and the way she was saying made it sound so hard I thought I was going to prison. I almost started crying.

> Our kids are spending fifty to sixty percent more time learning than the traditional public school student.

And she was like, If you don't want to sign this, you don't have to sign this. But then my mom was right there, so I signed it."

With that, her life changed. (Keep in mind, while reading what follows, that Marita is twelve years old.)

"I wake up at five-forty-five a.m. to get a head start," she says. "I brush my teeth, shower. I get some breakfast at school, if I am running late. Usually get yelled at because I am taking too long. I meet my friends Diana and Steven at the bus stop, and we get the number one bus."

A 5:45 wakeup is fairly typical of KIPP students, especially given the long bus and subway commutes that many have to get to school. Levin, at one point, went into a seventh-grade music class with seventy kids in it and asked for a show of hands on when the students woke up. A handful said they woke up after six. Three quarters said they woke up before six. And almost half said they woke up before 5:30. One classmate of Marita's, a boy named José, said he sometimes wakes up at three or four a.m., finishes his homework from the night before, and then "goes back to sleep for a bit."

Marita went on:

> I leave school at five p.m., and if I don't lollygag around, then I will get home around five-thirty. Then I say hi to my mom really quickly and start my homework. And if it's not a lot of homework that day, it will take me two to three hours, and I'll be done around nine p.m. Or if we have essays, then I will be done like ten p.m., or ten-thirty p.m.
>
> Sometimes my mom makes me break for dinner. I tell her I want to go straight through, but she says I have to eat. So around eight, she makes me break for dinner for, like, a half hour, and then I get back to work. Then, usually after that, my mom wants to hear about school, but I have to make it quick because I have to get in bed by eleven p.m. So I get all my stuff ready, and then I get into bed. I tell her all about the day and what happened, and by

> the time we are finished, she is on the brink of sleeping, so that's probably around eleven-fifteen. Then I go to sleep, and the next morning we do it all over again. We are in the same room. But it's a huge bedroom and you can split it into two, and we have beds on other sides. Me and my mom are very close.

She spoke in the matter-of-fact way of children who have no way of knowing how unusual their situation is. She had the hours of a lawyer trying to make partner, or of a medical resident. All that was missing were the dark circles under her eyes and a steaming cup of coffee, except that she was too young for either.

"Sometimes I don't go to sleep when I'm supposed to," Marita continued. "I go to sleep at, like, twelve o'clock, and the next afternoon, it will hit me. And I will doze off in class. But then I have to wake up because I have to get the information. I remember I was in one class, and I was dozing off and the teacher saw me and said, 'Can I talk to you after class?' And he asked me, 'Why were you dozing off?' And I told him I went to sleep late. And he was, like, 'You need to go to sleep earlier.'"

Marita's life is not the life of a typical twelve-year-old. Nor is it what we would necessarily wish for a twelve-year-old. Children, we like to believe, should have time to play and dream, and sleep. Marita has responsibilities. . . . Her community does not give her what she needs. So what does she have to do? Give up her evenings and weekends and friends—all the elements of her old world—and replace them with KIPP.

Here is Marita again, in a passage that is little short of heartbreaking:

> Well, when we first started fifth grade, I used to have contact with one of the girls from my old school, and whenever I left school on Friday, I would go to her house and stay there until my mom would get home from work. So I would be at her house and I would be doing my homework. She would never have any homework. And she would say, "Oh, my God, you stay there late." Then she said she wanted to go to KIPP, but then she would say that KIPP is too hard and she didn't want to do it. And I would say, "Everyone says that KIPP is hard, but once you get the hang of it, it's not really that hard." She told me, "It's because you are smart." And I said, "No, every one of us is smart." And she was so discouraged because we stayed until five and we had a lot of homework, and I told her that us having a lot of homework helps us do better in class. And she told me she didn't want to hear the whole speech. All my friends now are from KIPP.

Is this a lot to ask of a child? It is. But think of things from Marita's perspective. She has made a bargain with her school. She will get up at five-forty-five in the morning, go in on Saturdays, and do homework until eleven at night. In return, KIPP promises that it will take kids like her who are stuck in poverty and give them a chance to get out. It will get 84 percent of them up to or above their grade level in mathematics. On the strength of that performance, 90 percent of KIPP students get scholarships to private or parochial high schools instead of having to attend their own **desultory** high schools in the Bronx. And on the strength of that high school experience, more than 80 percent of KIPP graduates will go on to college, in many cases being the first in their family to do so. . . .

desultory (dĕs′əl-tôr′ē) *adj.* lacking a fixed plan.

Marita doesn't need a brand-new school with acres of playing fields and gleaming facilities. She doesn't need a laptop, a smaller class, a teacher with a PhD, or a bigger apartment. She doesn't need a higher IQ or a mind as quick as Chris Langan's. All those things would be nice, of course. But they miss the point. Marita just needed a *chance.* And look at the chance she was given! Someone brought a little bit of the rice paddy to the South Bronx and explained to her the miracle of meaningful work.

COLLABORATIVE DISCUSSION Are KIPP students different from other public school students? With a partner, discuss the qualities that KIPP students possess and how their circumstances distinguish them from other students. Cite evidence from the text to support your views.

Determine Central Ideas

RI 2

A **central idea** is an important idea or message that an author wants to convey. Although a central idea may be stated, more often readers must infer it from details in the text. Use these steps to identify the central ideas in "Marita's Bargain":

- Identify the **topic** of the work. The central ideas present insights or perspectives on this subject. Gladwell's broad topic is education; more specifically, he explores the impact of an experimental kind of public school on students.
- Analyze the **details** used to develop the discussion. Consider the kind of information these details present and how they reveal the author's view of the subject. For example, the facts, examples, and quotations about the rigorous schedule of KIPP Academy support Gladwell's opinion about this educational approach.
- Use subheadings, the title, and other **text features** as clues to help identify central ideas.
- Evaluate how the organization, or **structure,** of the work helps develop important ideas. For example, Gladwell devotes the last two sections of his essay to Marita's story, suggesting that he wants to convey a specific idea about the hard work that goes into achieving success.

Integrate and Evaluate Information

RI 7

Information can be presented in a variety of formats and media, including maps, photographs, diagrams, charts, and video. **Quantitative formats,** which present numerical or statistical data, include tables and graphs, such as line graphs, bar graphs, and circle graphs. In "Marita's Bargain," Gladwell uses several **tables** to support his ideas. To analyze the information in a table, follow these steps:

- If the table has a title, read it to see what the table is about. Gladwell's tables do not have titles, but he introduces each one in the text immediately before it.
- Read the labels on the columns and rows, and make sure you understand what they mean. For example, the label "Class" in Gladwell's tables refers to the socioeconomic class of each group of students. The row labels divide the students into three groups: low, middle, and high.
- Scan the numbers to identify any obvious trends. Look across each row from left to right, and read each column from top to bottom. Do the numbers grow consistently larger or smaller? What might this mean?
- Read what the text says about the table. Gladwell follows each table with an explanation of the conclusions he draws from it. Then review the numbers in the table again to see if you agree with the author's interpretation.

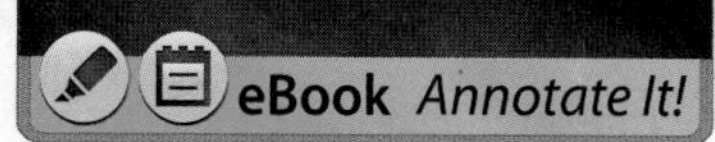

Analyzing the Text

RI 1, RI 2, RI 4, RI 5, RI 7, W 3a, W 3d

Cite Text Evidence Support your responses with evidence from the selection.

1. **Connect** This essay originally appeared in a book that explores whether success comes more from talent or opportunity. Based on the details in section 1 (lines 1–52), what does Gladwell believe about the success of students enrolled in the KIPP Academy?
2. **Analyze** Gladwell examines the history of the U.S. public school system in section 2 (lines 53–115) before he discusses summer vacation in section 3 (lines 116–221). How do the ideas and information in section 2 support his discussion in section 3?
3. **Evaluate** What is the function of the tables in section 3 (lines 116–221)? Are they effective in conveying Gladwell's central idea in this part of the essay? Explain why or why not.
4. **Cite Evidence** Is the success of the KIPP Academy based solely on the extended school day and year? Cite evidence from the essay to support your conclusion.
5. **Analyze** What is Gladwell's purpose in the last part of the essay? How does he achieve this purpose? Support your explanation with specific details from the text.
6. **Summarize** What are the central ideas of Gladwell's essay? Summarize these ideas in two or three sentences.
7. **Draw Conclusions** Why does Gladwell use the word "bargain" instead of "agreement" or "deal"? Explain how the connotation of this word helps to reinforce readers' understanding of Gladwell's perspective on the KIPP Academy.
8. **Synthesize** One critic suggested that "Marita's Bargain" and other essays in *Outliers* made it a more "political" book than his others. Does "Marita's Bargain" have a political message? Why or why not?

PERFORMANCE TASK

Writing Activity: Diary Gladwell describes how attending the KIPP Academy has affected Marita's relationships with her old friends who do not go to the school. Write a diary entry in which she reflects on the change in these friendships. Consider the following:

- Marita's feelings about the importance of succeeding in school
- the reaction of her old friends to the demands of the Kipp Academy
- the amount of free time Marita has outside of school
- Marita's relationship with her mother

Critical Vocabulary

motley **inviolate** **desultory**

cognitive **counterintuitive**

Practice and Apply Complete each of the following sentence stems in a way that reflects the meaning of the Critical Vocabulary word.

1. Going to bed at a later hour to cure insomnia seems *counterintuitive* because . . .
2. The costumes worn by a harlequin or clown are described as *motley* because . . .
3. The town hall meeting was *desultory* because . . .
4. The trainer tested the player's *cognitive* skills after the concussion because . . .
5. The bank deposits were *inviolate* because . . .

Vocabulary Strategy: Context Clues

The context of an unfamiliar word—other words, sentences, and paragraphs around the word—often gives clues to its meaning. For example, the Critical Vocabulary word *motley* occurs in this context in the essay: "this motley group of randomly chosen lower-income kids from dingy apartments." The chart shows the kinds of context clues you could use to figure out the meaning of *motley* and other challenging words.

Synonym	A word or phrase before or after the unknown term has the same meaning. For example, the phrase "randomly chosen" suggests that *motley* means "varied" or "different from each other."
Example	The context may include examples that help illustrate a word's meaning. For example, Gladwell writes that summer vacation is an "inviolate feature of school life, like high school football or the senior prom." The examples that follow the signal word *like* suggest that *inviolate* means "secure against change."
Antonym	Sometimes a word that is the opposite of the unknown term appears in the context. This relationship is signaled by *but* or *unlike*. For example in this sentence, the word *organized* is the opposite of *desultory*: "Unlike her organized speech, his was desultory."
Restatement	Look for a restatement of a word's meaning before or after it. For example, "The house painter's efforts were desultory—rather hit or miss—making us wonder if the job would ever be completed."

Practice and Apply Find each of these words in the selection. Define it and explain the context clues that help you identify its meaning as it is used in the essay.

1. protocol
2. pernicious
3. respite
4. singular

Language and Style: Subject-Verb Agreement

L1

Agreement in number means that if the subject of a clause is singular, the verb must also be singular. A plural subject requires a plural verb. Ensuring that each subject and verb pair is in agreement enables writers to communicate their ideas precisely and clearly to their audience.

Read this sentence from "Marita's Bargain":

Virtually all of the advantage that wealthy students have over poor students is the result of differences in the way privileged kids learn while they are *not* in school.

Note that the verb of each subordinate clause agrees with its subject (students have; kids learn; they are). The subject of the main clause is the indefinite pronoun *all* followed by the prepositional phrase *of the advantage,* making *all* singular in this instance and requiring the use of the singular verb *is.*

Here are some examples of different circumstances affecting subject-verb agreement:

Examples	Situation
Most of the sugar is gone. Most of the cookies were eaten.	**Phrases and clauses between the subject and verb:** Generally, phrases or clauses between the subject and verb do not influence number. **Exception:** The indefinite pronouns *all, any, most, more, none,* and *some* can be either singular or plural, depending whether they refer to a quantity (sugar) or a number of things (cookies). The prepositional phrase or context of the sentence must be used to determine the pronoun's number.
Why has only one student responded so far? On the counter are numerous blank applications.	**Sentences beginning with *Here* or *There,* questions, inverted sentences:** Look for the subject after the verb to make sure that the verb agrees with it.
The rain and wind have decreased. Fish and chips is my favorite dinner. Each book and DVD is available to borrowers.	**Subjects joined by *and:*** Most compound subjects joined by *and* require a plural verb. **Exceptions:** If the compound subject refers to one thing, use a singular verb. Compound subjects preceded by *every, each,* or *many a* require a singular verb.
Neither my reluctance nor your threats are enough to keep me from carrying out the mission.	**Subjects joined by *or, nor, either/or, neither/nor:*** The verb should agree with the part of the subject closest to it.

Practice and Apply Create a two-column chart. List the types of situations governing subject-verb agreement in one column. Copy examples of sentences from Gladwell's essay or write original sentences that illustrate each situation in the second column. Be sure to identify the subject-verb pairs. Explain your examples to a partner.

Michael Lewis *(b. 1960) is the author of several bestselling books, including* The Blind Side *and* Moneyball, *both of which were made into successful movies. In his first book,* Liar's Poker, *he examines Wall Street practices based on his personal experiences as an investment banker. Lewis is a contributing editor for* Vanity Fair *and writes for the* New York Times *as well as other publications. A graduate of Princeton University, he returned to the school in 2012 during graduation weekend to deliver the baccalaureate address recorded in this video.*

MEDIA ANALYSIS

Don't Eat Fortune's Cookie

Graduation Speech by Michael Lewis

AS YOU VIEW Pay attention to Lewis's ideas about success and rewards.

COLLABORATIVE DISCUSSION What ideas does Lewis express about success and how people are rewarded? With a partner, discuss how these ideas relate to students preparing to graduate from college.

Support Inferences

RI 1

Ideas are usually stated explicitly in nonfiction writing. However, there may be some unstated thoughts and feelings that require readers to make **inferences**, or logical assumptions based on evidence in the text. When viewing a recorded speech such as "Don't Eat Fortune's Cookie," you can support your inferences with observations about the speaker's tone and gestures as well as with specific words.

In the following quotation, Michael Lewis describes how he once experienced a speech such as the one he is delivering:

> **Thirty years ago I sat where you sat. I must have listened to some older person share his life experiences. I don't remember a word of it. I couldn't even tell you who spoke. And you won't be able to either.**

You might infer from the author's words, humorous tone, and smile that although he is speaking at a prestigious event, he doesn't want the audience to think he has an inflated opinion of himself.

Analyzing the Media

RI 1, RI 2, RI 6, W 4

Cite Text Evidence Support your responses with evidence from the selection.

1. **Identify** What is the central idea of Lewis's speech? Why might he have chosen to express this idea at a Princeton graduation ceremony?
2. **Analyze** Why does Lewis share his personal experiences at the beginning of the speech? How does this part of the speech affect his credibility?
3. **Analyze** Explain how the discussion of ***Moneyball*** relates to Lewis's central idea.
4. **Infer** What can you infer from Lewis's vivid description of the way the team leaders ate the extra cookies?
5. **Draw Conclusions** What is Lewis's overall purpose in this speech? How does the specific content of the speech contribute to that purpose?

PERFORMANCE TASK

Writing Activity: Review Write a review of Michael Lewis's address for the alumni newsletter from the viewpoint of a graduate in the audience. Comment on these areas:

- the relevance of his central idea
- the development of his central idea
- the focus and organization of his speech
- the style of his delivery

The Secret to Raising Smart Kids

Science Article by Carol S. Dweck

AS YOU READ Pay attention to the details that explain two different mind-sets about intelligence and learning.

A brilliant student, Jonathan sailed through grade school. He completed his assignments easily and routinely earned A's. Jonathan puzzled over why some of his classmates struggled, and his parents told him he had a special gift. In the seventh grade, however, Jonathan suddenly lost interest in school, refusing to do homework or study for tests. As a consequence, his grades plummeted. His parents tried to boost their son's confidence by assuring him that he was very smart. But their attempts failed to motivate Jonathan (who is a composite drawn from several children). Schoolwork, their son maintained, was boring and pointless.

Our society worships talent, and many people assume that possessing superior intelligence or ability—along with confidence in that ability—is a recipe for success. In fact, however, more than 30 years of scientific investigation suggests that an overemphasis on intellect or talent leaves people vulnerable to failure, fearful of challenges and unwilling to remedy their shortcomings.

The result plays out in children like Jonathan, who coast through the early grades under the dangerous notion that no-effort academic achievement defines them as smart or gifted. Such children hold an **implicit** belief that intelligence is **innate** and fixed, making striving to learn seem far less important than being (or looking) smart. This belief also makes them see challenges, mistakes and even the need to exert effort as threats to their ego rather than as opportunities to improve. And it causes them to lose confidence and motivation when the work is no longer easy for them.

implicit
(ĭm-plĭs´ĭt) *adj.* understood but not directly stated.

innate
(ĭ-nāt´) *adj.* possessed at birth.

Praising children's innate abilities, as Jonathan's parents did, reinforces this mind-set, which can also prevent young athletes or people in the workforce and even marriages from living up to their potential. On the other hand, our studies show that teaching people to have a "growth mind-set," which encourages a focus on effort rather than on intelligence or talent, helps make them into high achievers in school and in life.

The Opportunity of Defeat

I first began to investigate the underpinnings of human motivation—and how people persevere after setbacks—as a psychology graduate student at Yale University in the 1960s. Animal experiments by psychologists Martin Seligman, Steven Maier and Richard Solomon of the University of Pennsylvania had shown that after repeated failures, most animals conclude that a situation is hopeless and beyond their control. After such an experience, the researchers found, an animal often remains passive even when it can effect change—a state they called learned helplessness.

People can learn to be helpless, too, but not everyone reacts to setbacks this way. I wondered:

Why do some students give up when they encounter difficulty, whereas others who are no more skilled continue to strive and learn? One answer, I soon discovered, lay in people's beliefs about why they had failed.

In particular, attributing poor performance to a lack of ability depresses motivation more than does the belief that lack of effort is to blame. In 1972, when I taught a group of elementary and middle school children who displayed helpless behavior in school that a lack of effort (rather than lack of ability) led to their mistakes on math problems, the kids learned to keep trying when the problems got tough. They also solved many of the problems even in the face of difficulty. Another group of helpless children who were simply rewarded for their success on easy problems did not improve their ability to solve hard math problems. These experiments were an early indication that a focus on effort can help resolve helplessness and **engender** success.

engender
(ĕn-jĕn´dər) *v.* to bring into existence.

Subsequent studies revealed that the most persistent students do not ruminate about their own failure much at all but instead think of mistakes as problems to be solved. At the University of Illinois in the 1970s I, along with my then graduate student Carol Diener, asked 60 fifth graders to think out loud while they solved very difficult pattern-recognition problems. Some students reacted defensively to mistakes, denigrating their skills with comments such as "I never did have a good rememory," and their problem-solving strategies deteriorated.

Others, meanwhile, focused on fixing errors and honing their skills. One advised himself: "I should slow down and try to figure this out." Two schoolchildren were particularly inspiring. One, in the wake of difficulty, pulled up his chair, rubbed his hands together, smacked his lips and said, "I love a challenge!" The other, also confronting the hard problems, looked up at the experimenter and approvingly declared, "I was hoping this would be informative!" Predictably, the students with this attitude outperformed their **cohorts** in these studies.

cohort (kō′hôrt′) *n.* a companion or associate.

Two Views of Intelligence

Several years later I developed a broader theory of what separates the two general classes of learners—helpless versus mastery-oriented. I realized that these different types of students not only explain their failures differently, but they also hold different "theories" of intelligence. The helpless ones believe that intelligence is a fixed trait: you have only a certain amount, and that's that. I call this a "fixed mind-set." Mistakes crack their self-confidence because they attribute errors to a lack of ability, which they feel powerless to change. They avoid challenges because challenges make mistakes more likely and looking smart less so. Like Jonathan, such children shun effort in the belief that having to work hard means they are dumb.

The mastery-oriented children, on the other hand, think intelligence is **malleable** and can be developed through education and hard work. They want to learn above all else. After all, if you believe that you can expand your intellectual skills, you want to do just that. Because slipups stem from a lack of effort, not ability, they can be remedied by more effort. Challenges are energizing rather than intimidating; they offer opportunities to learn. Students with such a growth mind-set, we predicted, were destined for greater academic success and were quite likely to outperform their counterparts.

malleable (măl′ē-ə-bəl) *adj.* able to be shaped or molded.

We validated these expectations in a study published in early 2007. Psychologists Lisa Blackwell of Columbia University and Kali H. Trzesniewski of Stanford University and I monitored 373 students for two years during the transition to junior high school, when the work gets more difficult and the grading more stringent, to determine how their mind-sets might affect their math grades. At the beginning of seventh grade, we assessed the students' mind-sets by asking them to agree or disagree with statements such as "Your intelligence is something very basic about you that you can't really change." We then assessed their beliefs about other aspects of learning and looked to see what happened to their grades.

As we had predicted, the students with a growth mind-set felt that learning was a more important goal in school than getting good grades. In addition, they held hard work in high regard, believing that the more you labored at something, the better you would become at it. They understood that even geniuses have to work hard for their great accomplishments. Confronted by a setback such as a disappointing test grade, students with a growth mind-set said they would study harder or try a different strategy for mastering the material.

The students who held a fixed mind-set, however, were concerned about looking smart with little regard for learning. They had negative views of effort, believing that having to work hard at something was a sign of low ability. They thought that a person with talent or intelligence did not need to work hard to do well. Attributing a bad grade to their own lack of ability, those with a fixed mind-set said that they would study less in the future, try never to take that subject again and consider cheating on future tests.

Such divergent outlooks had a dramatic impact on performance. At the start of junior high, the math achievement test scores of the students with a growth mind-set were comparable to those of students who displayed a fixed mind-set. But as the work became more difficult, the students with a growth mind-set showed greater persistence. As a result, their math grades overtook those of the other students by the end of the first semester—and the gap between the two groups continued to widen during the two years we followed them.

Along with Columbia psychologist Heidi Grant, I found a similar relation between mind-set and achievement in a 2003 study of 128 Columbia freshman premed students who were enrolled in a challenging general chemistry course. Although all the students cared about grades, the ones who earned the best grades were those who placed a high premium on learning rather than on showing that they were smart in chemistry. The focus on learning strategies, effort and persistence paid off for these students.

Confronting Deficiencies

A belief in fixed intelligence also makes people less willing to admit to errors or to confront and remedy their deficiencies in school, at work and in their social relationships. In a study published in 1999 of 168 freshmen entering the University of Hong Kong, where all instruction and coursework are in English, three Hong Kong colleagues and I found that students with a growth mind-set who scored poorly on their English proficiency exam were far more inclined to take a remedial English course than were low-scoring students with a fixed mind-set. The students with a stagnant view of intelligence were presumably unwilling to admit to their deficit and thus passed up the opportunity to correct it.

A fixed mind-set can similarly hamper communication and progress in the workplace by leading managers and employees to discourage or ignore constructive criticism and advice. Research by psychologists Peter Heslin and Don VandeWalle of Southern Methodist University and Gary Latham of the University of Toronto shows that managers who have a fixed mind-set are less likely to seek or welcome feedback from their employees than are managers with a growth mind-set. Presumably, managers with a growth mind-set see themselves as works-in-progress and understand that they need feedback to improve, whereas bosses with a fixed mind-set are more likely to see criticism as reflecting their underlying level of competence. Assuming that other people are not capable of changing either, executives with a fixed mind-set are also less likely to mentor their underlings. But after Heslin, VandeWalle and Latham gave managers a tutorial on the value and principles of the growth mind-set, supervisors became more willing to coach their employees and gave more useful advice.

Mind-set can affect the quality and longevity of personal relationships as well, through people's willingness—or unwillingness—to deal with difficulties. Those with a fixed mind-set are less likely than those with a growth mind-set to broach problems in their relationships and to try to solve them, according to a 2006 study I conducted with psychologist Lara Kammrath of Wilfrid Laurier University in Ontario. After all, if you think that human personality traits are more or less fixed, relationship repair seems largely futile. Individuals who believe people can change and grow, however, are more confident that confronting concerns in their relationships will lead to resolutions.

Proper Praise

How do we transmit a growth mind-set to our children? One way is by telling stories about achievements that result from hard work. For instance, talking about math geniuses who were more or less born that way puts students in a fixed mind-set, but descriptions of great mathematicians who fell in love with math and developed amazing skills engenders a growth mindset, our studies have shown. People also communicate mind-sets through praise. Although many, if not most, parents believe that they should build up a child by telling him or her how brilliant and talented he or she is, our research suggests that this is misguided.

In studies involving several hundred fifth graders published in 1998, for example, Columbia psychologist Claudia M. Mueller and I gave children questions from a nonverbal IQ test. After the first 10 problems, on which most children did fairly well, we praised them. We praised some of them for their intelligence: "Wow…that's a really good score. You must be smart at this." We commended others for their effort: "Wow…that's a really good score. You must have worked really hard."

We found that intelligence praise encouraged a fixed mind-set more often than did pats on the back for effort. Those congratulated for their intelligence, for example, shied away from a challenging assignment—they wanted an easy one instead—far more often than the kids applauded for their effort. (Most of those lauded for their hard work wanted the difficult problem set from which they would learn.) When we gave everyone hard problems anyway, those praised for being smart became discouraged, doubting their ability. And their scores, even on an easier problem set we gave them afterward, declined as compared with their previous results on equivalent problems. In contrast, students praised for their effort did not lose confidence when faced with the harder questions, and their performance improved markedly on the easier problems that followed.

Making Up Your Mind-Set

In addition to encouraging a growth mind-set through praise for effort, parents and teachers can help children by providing explicit instruction regarding the mind as a learning machine. Blackwell, Trzesniewski and I recently designed an eight-session workshop for 91 students whose math grades were declining in their first year of junior high. Forty-eight of the students received instruction in study skills only, whereas the others attended a combination of study skills sessions and classes in which they learned about the growth mind-set and how to apply it to schoolwork.

In the growth mind-set classes, students read and discussed an article entitled "You Can Grow Your Brain." They were taught that the brain is like a muscle that gets stronger with use and that learning prompts neurons in the brain to grow new connections. From such instruction, many students began to see themselves as agents of their own brain development. Students who had been disruptive or bored sat still and took note. One particularly unruly boy looked up during the discussion and said, "You mean I don't have to be dumb?" . . .

Teaching children such information is not just a ploy to get them to study. People do differ in intelligence, talent and ability. And yet research is converging on the conclusion that great accomplishment, and even what we call genius, is typically the result of years of passion and dedication and not something that flows naturally from a gift. Mozart, Edison, Curie, Darwin and Cézanne were not simply born with talent; they cultivated it through tremendous and sustained effort. Similarly, hard work and discipline contribute much more to school achievement than IQ does.

Such lessons apply to almost every human endeavor. For instance, many young athletes value talent more than hard work and have consequently become unteachable. Similarly, many people accomplish little in their jobs without constant praise and encouragement to maintain their motivation. If we foster a growth mind-set in our homes and schools, however, we will give our children the tools to succeed in their pursuits and to become responsible employees and citizens.

COLLABORATIVE DISCUSSION With a partner, discuss the most important differences between the two mind-sets Dweck writes about. Cite specific evidence from the text to support your comparison.

Analyze Structure: Argument

RI 5, RI 10

An **argument** expresses the writer's opinion on an issue or problem and supports it with reasons and evidence. A sound argument includes these elements:

- The **claim** is the statement of the writer's position on an issue or problem. It should be clear and specific. Often the claim is presented near the beginning of an argument, which enables readers to evaluate the strength of the supporting evidence that follows. **Example:** Walking for thirty minutes or more several times a week will significantly improve the quality of a person's life.
- **Reasons** are statements that justify or explain the claim. Valid reasons are accurate and relevant. They support the writer's position and rely on logic rather than emotion. **Example:** Walking has been proven to result in measurable health benefits.
- **Evidence** includes details that support the reasons, such as facts, quotations, examples, statistics, and expert views. To be convincing, the evidence must be sound, relevant, and substantial. **Example:** As a result of walking for thirty minutes a day, enzymes are produced that destroy bad cholesterol.
- Good arguments may also include **counterarguments.** These are arguments that anticipate possible opposing views and answer them. Counterarguments show that the writer has thorough knowledge of the issue and has clearly thought about both sides.

Strong support is the foundation of a good argument. The questions in the chart can help you assess the reasons and evidence in "The Secret to Raising Smart Kids."

Evaluating Support	
Can the information be verified?	Check the accuracy of facts by confirming them in another source, such as a reference work or a trustworthy website. In "The Secret to Raising Smart Kids," Dweck provides dates, locations, and names of professionals involved in the studies she cites.
Is there sufficient evidence?	Insufficient evidence leaves readers with unanswered questions and doubt. The organization of "The Secret to Raising Smart Kids" into separate sections helps readers determine whether each reason is amply supported.
Is the evidence authoritative?	In "The Secret to Raising Smart Kids," much of the evidence comes from studies carried out by psychologists whose credentials establish them as experts in their fields. Reference works, reliable websites, or accredited organizations are also credible sources of information on a topic.
Are the reasons logical?	Watch for errors in logic, such as oversimplifying a complex problem, making a generalization that is too broad or is drawn from too little information, or cause-and-effect fallacies (assuming that because one event followed another, the first event caused the second one to occur).

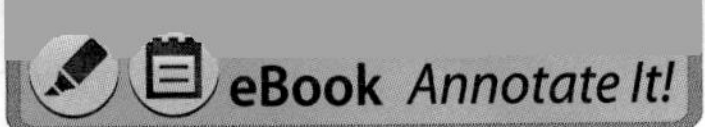

eBook *Annotate It!*

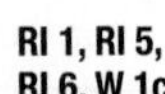

RI 1, RI 5, RI 6, W 1c

Analyzing the Text

Cite Text Evidence Support your responses with evidence from the selection.

1. **Summarize** What is Dweck's claim in this article?
2. **Analyze** In the section entitled "The Opportunity of Defeat," Dweck presents her first reason, which is that students with a growth mind-set show more persistence when faced with obstacles. What evidence does she use to support her view that "attributing poor performance to a lack of ability depresses motivation more than does the belief that lack of effort is to blame"?
3. **Analyze** What idea is supported by the evidence presented in "Two Views of Intelligence"? Why does Dweck include the information about premed students in the last paragraph?
4. **Analyze** What reason does Dweck provide to support her claim in the section entitled "Confronting Deficiencies"? How does this section strengthen her argument?
5. **Analyze** What specific advice does Dweck provide on how parents and educators can influence the mind-sets of children? Explain how this advice could help persuade readers to accept her claim.
6. **Evaluate** Dweck opens her article with the story of a brilliant student named Jonathan who experiences difficulties at school. How effective is this introduction? Give reasons for your opinion.
7. **Evaluate** Does Dweck provide a thorough and balanced argument in her article? Consider the following structural elements in your response: claim, reasons, evidence, counterarguments.
8. **Critique** Is the style of this article appropriate for a persuasive text? Why or why not? Be sure to consider Dweck's word choices and **syntax,** or arrangement of words.

PERFORMANCE TASK

Writing Activity With a partner, write an additional paragraph to be included in one of these sections of the article: "The Opportunity of Defeat," "Two Views of Intelligence," or "Confronting Deficiencies."

- In your paragraph, develop two examples in the context of a high-school setting that support the point the author is making in that part of the article. Your hypothetical examples should be drawn from your own experience and observations and illustrate the characteristics of each mind-set described in that section of the text.
- Use transitional words and phrases to link your paragraph to the main idea.

Critical Vocabulary

L 4b

implicit **innate** **engender**

cohort **malleable**

Practice and Apply Answer each question, explaining your choice.

1. Which is *innate,* a dog's ability to bark or a dog's ability to obey commands?
2. Which is an *implicit* form of communication, a wink or the statement "I'm joking"?
3. Which *engenders* football enthusiasm, a stadium band or the officials?
4. Who is your *cohort,* your aunt in another country or your study partner?
5. What would make taffy *malleable,* freezing it or keeping it out on a warm day?

Vocabulary Strategy: Prefixes with Multiple Meanings

The Critical Vocabulary words *engender* and *innate* are formed with prefixes. Knowing the meaning of a prefix can help you define unfamiliar words. For example, putting together the meaning of the prefix *in-* ("in") with the meaning of the root *nate* ("born") enables you to figure out that *innate* means "inborn," or "possessed at birth." If a prefix has more than one meaning, such as those shown in the chart, use the context of the unfamiliar word to help you confirm its precise definition.

Prefix	Meanings
a-	**1.** without, not: *amoral* **2.** on, in: *aboard*
en-	**1.** to put into or onto: *encapsulate* **2.** to cause to be: *engender*
im-, in-	**1.** not: *inhumane* **2.** in, into, within: *immigrate*
pro-	**1.** supporting or in favor of: *pronuclear* **2.** forward, in front of: *propel* **3.** earlier, before: *proactive*

Practice and Apply Write a definition for each underlined word. Explain how context clues help you identify which meaning of the prefix is used.

1. The young boy remained afloat in the rough water.
2. The technician installed the new software on the computer for the nervous customer.
3. A play may begin with a prologue introducing the characters and plot.
4. The charismatic speaker enkindled passion in his audience with his fiery words.
5. After seeing her asymmetrical bangs, she vowed never to cut her own hair again.

Language and Style: Participles and Participial Phrases

Participial phrases act as adjectives, modifying nouns or pronouns. A participial phrase includes a **participle** (verb form ending in *-ed* or *-ing*), modifiers, and complements. Writers use participial phrases to add detail that will make their meaning more precise. They also use participial phrases to vary their sentence structure and keep the attention of their readers.

In "The Secret to Raising Smart Kids," the author places participial phrases next to the nouns or pronouns that they modify to make her meaning clear. As a result, the phrases appear in different positions in sentences throughout her article.

A participial phrase that begins a sentence is set off with a comma.

Attributing a bad grade to their own lack of ability, those with a fixed mind-set said that they would study less in the future. . . .

A participial phrase in the middle of a sentence is set off by commas if it contains nonessential information.

The other, also confronting the hard problems, looked up at the experimenter. . . .

Most participial phrases that occur at the end of a sentence are not set off by commas if they follow the noun or pronoun they are modifying.

We validated these expectations in a study published in early 2007.

A careless writer might have written the last two sentences like this:

The other looked up at the experimenter, also confronting the hard problems. . . .
Published in early 2007 we validated these expectations in a study.

These sentences create confusion because it is not clear which pronoun or noun the participial phrases modify.

Practice and Apply Look back at the paragraph you wrote with a partner in response to this selection's Performance Task. With your partner, rewrite two sentences to include participial phrases. Then compare the before and after versions. Discuss how the use of participial phrases helped you to add detail, improve the clarity of your writing, or vary your sentence structure.

Jamaica Kincaid *(b. 1949) was born Elaine Potter Richardson on the Caribbean island of Antigua in 1949. She left at seventeen to work in New York City. After a series of jobs, she became a writer for the* New Yorker. *In 1985, she published her first novel,* Annie John, *the last chapter of which is "A Walk to the Jetty." Like Kincaid herself, the protagonist is emotionally estranged from her mother at a young age. Kincaid revisits this theme often in her works. She also expresses her abhorrence of British colonial rule in Antigua, most notably in the nonfiction work* A Small Place, *which excited controversy for its deeply angry tone.*

A Walk to the Jetty

from Annie John

Novel by Jamaica Kincaid

AS YOU READ Look for details that tell you how the narrator feels about the people and places in her life.

"My name is Annie John." These were the first words that came into my mind as I woke up on the morning of the last day I spent in Antigua, and they stayed there, lined up one behind the other, marching up and down, for I don't know how long. At noon on that day, a ship on which I was to be a passenger would sail to Barbados, and there I would board another ship, which would sail to England, where I would study to become a nurse. My name was the last thing I saw the night before, just as I was falling asleep; it was written in big, black letters all over my trunk, sometimes followed by my address in Antigua, sometimes followed by my address as it would be in England. I did not want to go to England, I did not want to be a nurse, but I would have chosen going off to live in a cavern and keeping house for seven unruly men rather than go on with my life as it stood. I never wanted to lie in this bed again, my legs hanging out way past the foot of it, tossing and turning on my mattress, with its cotton stuffing all lumped just where it wasn't a good place to be lumped. I never wanted to lie in my bed again and hear Mr. Ephraim driving his sheep to pasture—a signal to my mother that she should get up to prepare my father's and my bath and breakfast. I never wanted to lie in my bed and hear her get dressed, washing her face, brushing her teeth, and gargling. I especially never wanted to lie in my bed and hear my mother gargling again.

Lying there in the half-dark of my room, I could see my shelf, with my books—some of them prizes I had won in school, some of them gifts from my mother—and with photographs of people I was supposed to love forever no matter what, and with my old thermos, which was given to me for my eighth birthday, and some shells I had gathered at different times I spent at the sea. In one corner stood my washstand and its beautiful basin of white enamel with blooming red hibiscus painted at the bottom and an urn that matched. In another corner were my old school shoes and my Sunday shoes. In still another corner, a bureau held my old clothes. I knew everything in this room, inside out and outside in. I had lived in this room for thirteen of my seventeen years. I could see in my mind's eye even the day my father was adding it onto the rest of the house. Everywhere I looked stood something that had meant a lot to me, that had given me pleasure at some point, or could remind me of a time that was a happy time. But as I was lying there my heart could have burst open with joy at the thought of never having to see any of it again.

If someone had asked me for a little summing up of my life at that moment as I lay in bed, I would have said, "My name is Annie John. I was born on the fifteenth of September, seventeen years ago, at

Holberton Hospital, at five o'clock in the morning. At the time I was born, the moon was going down at one end of the sky and the sun was coming up at the other. My mother's name is Annie also. My father's name is Alexander, and he is thirty-five years older than my mother. Two of his children are four and six years older than she is. Looking at how sickly he has become and looking at the way my mother now has to run up and down for him, gathering the herbs and barks that he boils in water, which he drinks instead of the medicine the doctor has ordered for him, I plan not only never to marry an old man but certainly never to marry at all. The house we live in my father built with his own hands. The bed I am lying in my father built with his own hands. If I get up and sit on a chair, it is a chair my father built with his own hands. When my mother uses a large wooden spoon to stir the porridge we sometimes eat as part of our breakfast, it will be a spoon that my father has carved with his own hands. The sheets on my bed my mother made with her own hands. The curtains hanging at my window my mother made with her own hands. The nightie I am wearing, with **scalloped** neck and hem and sleeves, my mother made with her own hands. When I look at things in a certain way, I suppose I should say that the two of them made me with their own hands. For most of my life, when the three of us went anywhere together I stood between the two of them or sat between the two of them. But then I got too big, and there I was, shoulder to shoulder with them more or less, and it became not very comfortable to walk down the street together. And so now there they are together and here I am apart. I don't see them now the way I used to, and I don't love them now the way I used to. The bitter thing about it is that they are just the same and it is I who have changed, so all the things I used to be and all the things I used to feel are as false as the teeth in my father's head. Why, I wonder, didn't I see the **hypocrite** in my mother when, over the years, she said that she loved me and could hardly live without me, while at the same time proposing and arranging separation after separation, including this one, which, unbeknownst to her, *I* have arranged to be permanent? So now I, too, have hypocrisy, and breasts (small ones), and hair growing in the appropriate places, and sharp eyes, and I have made a vow never to be fooled again."

scalloped (skŏl´əpt) *adj.* having a wavy edge, border, or design.

hypocrite (hĭp´ə-krĭt´) *n.* one who professes good qualities but does not demonstrate or possess them.

Lying in my bed for the last time, I thought, This is what I add up to. At that, I felt as if someone had placed me in a hole and was forcing me first down and then up against the pressure of gravity. I shook myself and prepared to get up. I said to myself, "I am getting up out of this bed for the last time." Everything I would do that morning until I got on the ship that would take me to England I would be doing for the last time, for I had made up my mind that, come what may, the road for me now went only in one direction: away from my home, away from my mother, away from my father, away from the everlasting blue sky, away from the everlasting hot sun, away from people who said to me, "This happened during the time your mother was carrying you."

If I had been asked to put into words why I felt this way, if I had been given years to reflect and come up with the words of why I felt this way, I would not have been able to come up with so much as the letter "A." I only knew that I felt the way I did, and that this feeling was the strongest thing in my life.

The Anglican church bell struck seven. My father had already bathed and dressed and was in his workshop puttering around. As if the day of my leaving were something to celebrate, they were treating it as a holiday, and nothing in the usual way would take place. My father would not go to work at all. When I got up, my mother greeted me with a big, bright "Good morning"—so big and bright that I shrank before it. I bathed quickly in some warm bark water that my mother had prepared for me. I put on my underclothes—all of them white and all of them smelling funny. Along with my earrings, my neck chain, and my bracelets, all made of gold from British Guiana, my underclothes had been sent to my mother's obeah[1] woman, and whatever she had done to my jewelry and underclothes would help protect me from evil spirits and every kind of misfortune. The things I never wanted to see or hear or do again now made up at least three weeks' worth of grocery lists. I placed a mark against obeah women, jewelry, and white underclothes. Over my underclothes, I put on an around-the-yard dress of my mother's. The clothes I would wear for my voyage were a dark-blue pleated skirt and a blue-and-white checked blouse (the blue in the blouse matched exactly the blue of my skirt) with a large sailor collar and with a tie made from the same material as the skirt—a blouse that came down a long way past my waist, over my skirt. They were lying on a chair, freshly ironed by my mother. Putting on my clothes was the last thing I would do just before leaving the house. Miss Cornelia came and pressed my hair and then shaped it into what felt like a hundred corkscrews, all lying flat against my head so that my hat would fit properly.

At breakfast, I was seated in my usual spot, with my mother at one end of the table, my father at the other, and me in the middle, so that as they talked to me or to each other I would shift my head to the left or to the right and get a good look at them. We were having a Sunday breakfast, a breakfast as if we had just come back from Sunday-morning services: salt fish and antroba[2] and souse[3] and hard-boiled eggs, and even special Sunday bread from Mr. Daniel, our baker. On Sundays, we ate this big breakfast at eleven o'clock and then we didn't eat again until four o'clock, when we had our big Sunday dinner. It was the best breakfast we ate, and the only breakfast better than that was the one we ate on Christmas morning. My parents were in a festive mood, saying what a wonderful time I would have in my new life, what

[1] **obeah** (o′bē-ə): an African-based religion practiced in the Caribbean.

[2] **antroba:** a blend of crushed eggplant and spices.

[3] **souse:** pickled meat.

a wonderful opportunity this was for me, and what a lucky person I was. They were eating away as they talked, my father's false teeth making that clop-clop sound like a horse on a walk as he talked, my mother's mouth going up and down like a donkey's as she chewed each mouthful thirty-two times. (I had long ago counted, because it was something she made me do also, and I was trying to see if this was just one of her rules that applied only to me.) I was looking at them with a smile on my face but disgust in my heart when my mother said, "Of course, you are a young lady now, and we won't be surprised if in due time you write to say that one day soon you are to be married."

Without thinking, I said, with bad feeling that I didn't hide very well, "How absurd!"

My parents immediately stopped eating and looked at me as if they had not seen me before. My father was the first to go back to his food. My mother continued to look. I don't know what went through her mind, but I could see her using her tongue to dislodge food stuck in the far corners of her mouth.

Many of my mother's friends now came to say goodbye to me, and to wish me God's blessings. I thanked them and showed the proper amount of joy at the glorious things they pointed out to me that my future held and showed the proper amount of sorrow at how much my parents and everyone else who loved me would miss me. My body ached a little at all this false going back and forth, at all this taking in of people gazing at me with heads tilted, love and pity on their smiling faces. I could have left without saying any goodbyes to them and I wouldn't have missed it. There was only one person I felt I should say goodbye to, and that was my former friend Gwen. We had long ago drifted apart, and when I saw her now my heart nearly split in two with embarrassment at the feelings I used to have for her and things I had shared with her. She had now **degenerated** into complete silliness, hardly able to complete a sentence without putting in a few giggles. Along with the giggles, she had developed some other schoolgirl traits that she did not have when she was actually a schoolgirl, so beneath her were such things then. When we were saying our goodbyes, it was all I could do not to say cruelly, "Why are you behaving like such a monkey?" Instead, I put everything on a friendly plain, wishing her well and the best in the future. It was then that she told me that she was more or less engaged to a boy she had known while growing up early on in Nevis, and that soon, in a year or so, they would be married. My reply to her was "Good luck," and she thought I meant her well, so she grabbed me and said, "Thank you. I knew you would be happy about it." But to me it was as if she had shown me a high point from which she was going to jump and hoped to land in one piece on her feet. We parted, and when I turned away I didn't look back.

degenerate (dĭ-jĕn′ə-rāt′) *v.* to decline in quality.

My mother had arranged with a stevedore[4] to take my trunk to the jetty ahead of me. At ten o'clock on the dot, I was dressed, and we set off for the jetty. An hour after that, I would board a launch that would take me out to sea, where I then would board the ship. Starting out, as if for old time's sake and without giving it a thought, we lined up in the old way: I walking between my mother and my father. I loomed way above my father and could see the top of his head. We must have made a strange sight: a grown girl all dressed up in the middle of a morning, in the middle of the week, walking in step in the middle between her two parents, for people we didn't know stared at us. It was all of half an hour's walk from our house to the jetty, but I was passing through most of the years of my life. We passed by the house where Miss Dulcie, the seamstress that I had been apprenticed to for a time, lived, and just as I was passing by, a wave of bad feeling for her came over me, because I suddenly remembered that the months I spent with her all she had me do was sweep the floor, which was always full of threads and pins and needles, and I never seemed to sweep it clean enough to please her. Then she would send me to the store to buy buttons or thread, though I was only allowed to do this if I was given a sample of the button or thread, and then she would find fault even though they were an exact match of the samples she had given me. And all the while she said to me, "A girl like you will never learn to sew properly, you know." At the time, I don't suppose I minded it, because it was customary to treat the first-year apprentice with such scorn, but now I placed on the dustheap of my life Miss Dulcie and everything that I had had to do with her.

We were soon on the road that I had taken to school, to church, to Sunday school, to choir practice, to Brownie meetings, to Girl Guide meetings, to meet a friend. I was five years old when I first walked on this road unaccompanied by someone to hold my hand. My mother had placed three pennies in my little basket, which was a duplicate of her bigger basket, and sent me to the chemist's shop[5] to buy a pennyworth of senna leaves, a pennyworth of eucalyptus leaves, and a pennyworth of camphor. She then instructed me on what side of the road to walk, where to make a turn, where to cross, how to look carefully before I crossed, and if I met anyone that I knew to politely pass greetings and keep on my way. I was wearing a freshly ironed yellow dress that had printed on it scenes of acrobats flying through the air and swinging on a trapeze. I had just had a bath, and after it, instead of powdering me with my baby-smelling talcum powder, my mother had, as a special favor, let me use her own talcum powder, which smelled quite perfumy and came in a can that had painted on it people going out to dinner in nineteenth-century London and was called Mazie. How it pleased me to walk out the door and bend

[4] **stevedore:** dock worker who loads and unloads ships.

[5] **chemist's shop:** pharmacy.

my head down to sniff at myself and see that I smelled just like my mother. I went to the chemist's shop, and he had to come from behind the counter and bend down to hear what it was that I wanted to buy, my voice was so little and timid then. I went back just the way I had come, and when I walked into the yard and presented my basket with its three packages to my mother, her eyes filled with tears and she swooped me up and held me high in the air and said that I was wonderful and good and that there would never be anybody better. If I had just conquered Persia, she couldn't have been more proud of me.

We passed by our church—the church in which I had been christened and received and had sung in the junior choir. We passed by a house in which a girl I used to like and was sure I couldn't live without had lived. Once, when she had mumps, I went to visit her against my mother's wishes, and we sat on her bed and ate the cure of roasted, buttered sweet potatoes that had been placed on her swollen jaws, held there by a piece of white cloth. I don't know how, but my mother found out about it, and I don't know how, but she put an end to our friendship. Shortly after, the girl moved with her family across the sea to somewhere else. We passed the doll store, where I would go with my mother when I was little and point out the doll I wanted that year for Christmas. We passed the store where I bought the much-fought-over shoes I wore to church to be received in. We passed the bank. On my sixth birthday, I was given, among other things, the present of a sixpence.[6] My mother and I then went to this bank, and with the

[6] **sixpence:** a coin worth six pennies in the old British system, with four farthings in a penny, twelve pennies in a shilling, and 20 shillings in a pound.

> "We must have made a strange sight: a grown girl all dressed up in the middle of a morning, in the middle of the week, walking in step in the middle between her two parents."

sixpence I opened my own savings account. I was given a little gray book with my name in big letters on it, and in the balance column it said "6d." Every Saturday morning after that, I was given a sixpence—later a shilling, and later a two-and-sixpence piece—and I would take it to the bank for deposit. I had never been allowed to withdraw even a farthing from my bank account until just a few weeks before I was to leave; then the whole account was closed out, and I received from the bank the sum of six pounds ten shillings and two and a half pence.

We passed the office of the doctor who told my mother three times that I did not need glasses, that if my eyes were feeling weak a glass of carrot juice a day would make them strong again. This happened when I was eight. And so every day at recess I would run to my school gate and meet my mother, who was waiting for me with a glass of juice from carrots she had just grated and then squeezed, and I would drink it and then run back to meet my chums. I knew there was nothing at all wrong with my eyes, but I had recently read a story in *The Schoolgirl's Own Annual* in which the heroine, a girl a few years older than I was then, cut such a figure to my mind with the way she was always adjusting her small, round, hornrimmed glasses that I felt I must have a pair exactly like them. When it became clear that I didn't need glasses, I began to complain about the glare of the sun being too much for my eyes, and I walked around with my hands shielding them—especially in my mother's presence. My mother then bought for me a pair of sunglasses with the exact horn-rimmed frames I wanted, and how I enjoyed the gestures of blowing on the lenses, wiping them with the hem of my uniform, adjusting the glasses when they slipped down my nose, and just removing them from their case and putting them on. In three weeks, I grew tired of them and they found a nice resting place in a drawer, along with some other things that at one time or another I couldn't live without.

We passed the store that sold only grooming aids, all imported from England. This store had in it a large porcelain dog—white, with black spots all over and a red ribbon of satin tied around its neck.

The dog sat in front of a white porcelain bowl that was always filled with fresh water, and it sat in such a way that it looked as if it had just taken a long drink. When I was a small child, I would ask my mother, if ever we were near this store, to please take me to see the dog, and I would stand in front of it, bent over slightly, my hands resting on my knees, and stare at it and stare at it. I thought this dog more beautiful and more real than any actual dog I had ever seen or any actual dog I would ever see. I must have outgrown my interest in the dog, for when it disappeared I never asked what became of it. We passed the library, and if there was anything on this walk that I might have wept over leaving, this most surely would have been the thing. My mother had been a member of the library long before I was born. And since she took me everywhere with her when I was quite little, when she went to the library she took me along there, too. I would sit in her lap very quietly as she read books that she did not want to take home with her. I could not read the words yet, but just the way they looked on the page was interesting to me. Once, a book she was reading had a large picture of a man in it, and when I asked her who he was she told me that he was Louis Pasteur and that the book was about his life. It stuck in my mind, because she said it was because of him that she boiled my milk to purify it before I was allowed to drink it, that it was his idea, and that that was why the process was called pasteurization. One of the things I had put away in my mother's old trunk in which she kept all my childhood things was my library card. At that moment, I owed sevenpence in overdue fees.

As I passed by all these places, it was as if I were in a dream, for I didn't notice the people coming and going in and out of them, I didn't feel my feet touch ground, I didn't even feel my own body—I just saw these places as if they were hanging in the air, not having top or bottom, and as if I had gone in and out of them all in the same moment. The sun was bright; the sky was blue and just above my head. We then arrived at the jetty.

My heart now beat fast, and no matter how hard I tried, I couldn't keep my mouth from falling open and my nostrils from spreading to the ends of my face. My old fear of slipping between the boards of the jetty and falling into the dark-green water where the dark-green eels lived came over me. When my father's stomach started to go bad, the doctor had recommended a walk every evening right after he ate his dinner. Sometimes he would take me with him. When he took me with him, we usually went to the jetty, and there he would sit and talk to the night watchman about cricket or some other thing that didn't interest me, because it was not personal; they didn't talk about their wives, or their children, or their parents, or about any of their likes and dislikes. They talked about things in such a strange way, and I didn't see what they found funny, but sometimes they made each other laugh so much that their guffaws would bound out to sea and send back an echo. I was always sorry when we got to the jetty and saw that the night watchman on duty was the one he enjoyed speaking to; it was like being locked up in a book filled with numbers and diagrams and what-ifs. For the thing about not being able to understand and enjoy what they were saying was I had nothing to take my mind off my fear of slipping in between the boards of the jetty.

Now, too, I had nothing to take my mind off what was happening to me. My mother and my father—I was leaving them forever. My home on an island—I was leaving it forever. What to make of everything? I felt a familiar hollow space inside. I felt I was being held down against my will. I felt I was burning up from head to toe. I felt that someone was tearing me up into little pieces and soon I would be able to see all the little pieces as they floated out into nothing in the deep blue sea. I didn't know whether to laugh or cry. I could see that it would be better not to think too clearly about any one thing. The launch was being made ready to take me, along with some other passengers, out to the ship that was anchored in the sea. My father paid our fares, and we joined a line of people waiting to board. My mother checked my bag to make sure that I had my passport, the money she had given me, and a sheet of paper placed between some pages in my Bible on which were written the names of the relatives—people I had not known existed—with whom I would live in England. Across from the jetty was a wharf, and some stevedores were loading and unloading barges. I don't know why seeing that struck me so, but suddenly a wave of strong feeling came over me, and my heart swelled with a great gladness as the words "I shall never see this again" spilled out inside me. But then, just as quickly, my heart shriveled up and the words "I shall never see this again" stabbed at me. I don't know what stopped me from falling in a heap at my parents' feet.

When we were all on board, the launch headed out to sea. Away from the jetty, the water became the customary blue, and the launch left a wide path in it that looked like a road. I passed by sounds and smells that were so familiar that I had long ago stopped paying any attention to them. But now here they were, and the ever-present "I shall never see this again" bobbed up and down inside me. There was the sound of the seagull diving down into the water and coming up with something silverish in its mouth. There was the smell of the sea and the sight of small pieces of rubbish floating around in it. There were boats filled with fishermen coming in early. There was the sound of their voices as they shouted greetings to each other. There was the hot sun, there was the blue sea, there was the blue sky. Not very far away, there was the white sand of the shore, with the run-down houses all crowded in next to each other, for in some places only poor people lived near the shore. I was seated in the launch between my parents, and when I realized that I was gripping their hands tightly I glanced quickly to see if they were looking at me with scorn, for I felt sure that they must have known of my never-see-this-again feelings. But instead my father kissed me on the forehead and my mother kissed me on the mouth, and they both gave over their hands to me, so that I could grip them as much as I wanted. I was on the verge of feeling that it had all been a mistake, but I remembered that I wasn't a child anymore, and that now when I made up my mind about something I had to see it through. At that moment, we came to the ship, and that was that.

> "My mother and my father—I was leaving them forever. My home on an island—I was leaving it forever."

The goodbyes had to be quick, the captain said. My mother introduced herself to him and then introduced me. She told him to keep an eye on me, for I had never gone this far away from home on my own. She gave him a letter to pass on to the captain of the next ship that I would board in Barbados. They walked me to my cabin, a small space that I would share with someone else—a woman I did not know. I had never before slept in a room with someone I did not know. My father kissed me goodbye and told me to be good and to write home often. After he said this, he looked at me, then looked at the floor and swung his left foot, then looked at me again. I could see that he wanted to say something else, something that he had never said to me before, but then he just turned and walked away. My mother said, "Well," and then she threw her arms around me. Big tears streamed down her face, and it must have been that—for I could not bear to see my mother cry—which started me crying, too. She then tightened her arms around me and held me to her close, so that I felt that I couldn't breathe. With that, my tears dried up and I was suddenly on my guard. "What does she want now?" I said to myself. Still holding me close to her, she said, in a voice that raked across my skin, "It doesn't matter what you do or where you go, I'll always be your mother and this will always be your home."

I dragged myself away from her and backed off a little, and then I shook myself, as if to wake myself out of a stupor. We looked at each other for a long time with smiles on our faces, but I know the opposite of that was in my heart. As if responding to some invisible cue, we both said, at the very same moment, "Well." Then my mother turned around and walked out the cabin door. I stood there for I don't know how long, and then I remembered that it was customary to stand on deck and wave to your relatives who were returning to shore. From the deck, I could not see my father, but I could see my mother facing the ship, her eyes searching to pick me out. I removed from my bag a red cotton handkerchief that she had earlier given me for this purpose, and I waved it wildly in the air. Recognizing me immediately, she waved back just as wildly, and we continued to do this until she became just a dot in the matchbox-size launch swallowed up in the big blue sea.

I went back to my cabin and lay down on my berth. Everything trembled as if it had a spring at its very center. I could hear the small waves lap-lapping around the ship. They made an unexpected sound, as if a vessel filled with liquid had been placed on its side and now was slowly emptying out.

COLLABORATIVE DISCUSSION With a partner, discuss Annie John's view of her life on the island. Cite details from the text that reveal her perspective.

Support Inferences

RL 1, RL 10

Inferences are logical assumptions that readers make based on evidence in the text to figure out what is not directly stated. Making inferences enables readers to understand characters' motives, traits, feelings, and relationships. For example, in "A Walk to the Jetty," Annie John's mother goes to the school every day at recess time with fresh-squeezed carrot juice to improve her daughter's eyesight. From the mother's action, readers can infer that she is completely devoted to her daughter. In turn, the fact that Annie is fabricating her eye problems, despite the worry she is causing her mother, enables readers to infer that she doesn't appreciate her mother's devotion and is careless of others' feelings.

When you make inferences about a story, be sure that you can support them with strong textual evidence. Also be aware that authors deliberately leave some matters uncertain. Sometimes this creates tension as readers wonder what might happen later in the story. In other cases, the story is simply open to interpretation. Several different inferences may be equally plausible, but none of them can be proven correct.

Analyze Word Choice

RL 4

Diction refers to an author's choice of words, including both vocabulary (individual words) and syntax (the order or arrangement of words). In "A Walk to the Jetty," Kincaid creates a distinctive **tone,** or attitude toward a subject, through the diction of her narrator, Annie John. Use the following questions to help you analyze an author's diction:

- **Does the writer choose simple or sophisticated words?** Kincaid makes her seventeen-year-old narrator sound realistic by choosing a suitable level of vocabulary.
- **Does the writer use mostly concrete words, which name specific things, or abstract words that identify concepts?** Kincaid uses concrete words to create fresh, vivid descriptions. For example, as Annie looks around her bedroom, she lists the items that she sees. "In one corner stood my washstand and its beautiful basin of white enamel with blooming red hibiscus painted at the bottom. . . ." These words not only create clear images but also reflect the way Annie John views her surroundings.
- **Does the writer select words with strong connotations, or associated feelings?** When Annie says, "I loomed way above my father," the word *loomed* suggests her emotional distance from him. A more neutral word, such as *stood,* would not have the same effect.
- **Is the writer's syntax formal or informal?** Kincaid varies the length of her sentences, but in general Annie's narration has an informal syntax, following the rhythm of everyday speech. In the third paragraph, Annie offers a summary of her life that mimics the more formal syntax of a school essay.

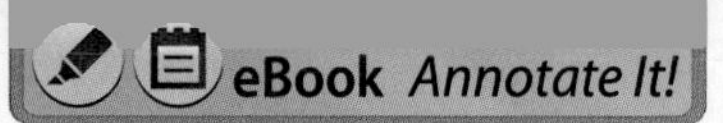

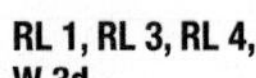

Analyzing the Text

RL 1, RL 3, RL 4, W 3d

Cite Text Evidence Support your responses with evidence from the selection.

1. **Infer** Reread lines 69–78. What do Annie's statements about hypocrisy reveal about her conflict with her mother?

2. **Infer** Referring to her height, Annie says that in bed her legs were "hanging out way past the foot of it" and that she "loomed way above my father and could see the top of his head." What do these details suggest about Annie John's perspective on the island and her life there?

3. **Analyze** Annie describes her parents as the family eats breakfast for the last time together (lines 121–149). What is her tone in this passage? What words convey that attitude?

4. **Analyze** A **symbol** is a person, place, or object that represents something beyond itself. Think about the island setting and Annie John's voyage to England. What might each represent?

5. **Analyze** Much of this selection describes Annie's walk with her parents to the jetty. How does Kincaid use this description to provide insight into Annie's character?

6. **Analyze** In lines 349–352, Annie says that "suddenly a wave of strong feeling came over me, and my heart swelled with a great gladness as the words 'I shall never see this again' spilled out inside me. But then, just as quickly, my heart shriveled up and the words 'I shall never see this again' stabbed at me." Explain how the author's word choices in this passage affect readers' understanding of Annie's emotions.

7. **Draw Conclusions** In the last sentence of the story, Annie compares the "lap-lapping" of the waves to the sound of liquid "slowly emptying out" from a vessel. What does this simile suggest about how leaving home has affected her?

8. **Evaluate** Kincaid uses the first-person point of view to tell Annie's story. Is this an effective technique for developing her narrative? Explain why or why not.

PERFORMANCE TASK

Writing Activity: Letter At the end of the selection, Annie realizes that leaving home is harder than she expected. Write a letter from Annie to her parents after she arrives in England. In the letter, have her reflect on what she has given up and whether she feels the sacrifice was worthwhile.

- Maintain a consistent first-person point of view.
- Include details that develop readers' understanding of Annie's feelings and the circumstances causing those feelings.
- Incorporate elements of Kincaid's style to capture Annie's voice.

L 4c

Critical Vocabulary

scalloped **hypocrite** **degenerate**

Practice and Apply For each Critical Vocabulary word, identify which example below it best illustrates the word's meaning. Be sure to explain why the example you chose is more accurate.

scalloped	hypocrite	degenerate
A skirt is edged with a series of curves.	A person talks about healthy habits but eats only fast food.	Two friends have a big fight but later apologize to each other.
A skirt dips in the back and is shorter in the front.	A person doesn't understand why fast food is not healthy.	Two friends who disagree end up shouting at each other.

Vocabulary Strategy: Etymology

Etymology is the history of a word. Most dictionary entries include etymologies that identify which language the word came from and what the original word meant. The etymology also traces the route by which a word passed into the English language.

The entry below gives the history of the Critical Vocabulary word *hypocrite*. It shows that *hypocrite* comes from an ancient Greek word that meant "to play a part or pretend." From Greek, the word passed into Latin, then French, and finally Middle English. You can see that the meaning of the Greek root is closely related to what *hypocrite* means today.

hyp•o•crite (hĭp´ə-krĭt´) *n.* a person given to saying beliefs or feelings that are not genuine. [Middle English *ipocrite,* from Old French, from Late Latin *hypocrite,* from Greek *hupokritēs,* actor, from *hupokrīnesthai,* to play a part, pretend]

Practice and Apply Look up the remaining Critical Vocabulary words in a college-level dictionary and trace their etymology. Discuss with a partner how closely the original meaning resembles the usage of the word today.

Language and Style: Dashes

L 2

In "A Walk to the Jetty," Kincaid uses dashes in many of her sentences. This chart explains some grammatical functions of the dash.

Purpose	Example
to amplify or extend an idea	She would not visit the library again—even though she still owed sevenpence for overdue books.
to show an abrupt break in thought or speech	When it was time to leave—and this annoyed Annie so much—her parents lingered over their breakfast.
in place of parentheses	Her outfit for the trip—a dark-blue skirt and checked blouse—had been carefully ironed.

Kincaid also uses dashes as a style element. With them she helps readers "hear" the narrator's tone and focus on important ideas.

Read this sentence from the story:

Big tears streamed down her face, and it must have been that—for I could not bear to see my mother cry—which started me crying, too.

The dashes in this sentence interrupt the description of an emotional scene and make the narrator's excuse the focus of the sentence. She wants to justify her tears and make sure that there is no confusion about why she is crying. At the same time, the dashes suggest that the narrator is impatient or annoyed with her mother for leading her to display this weakness.

Now consider the effect of replacing the dashes with parentheses or commas.

Big tears streamed down her face, and it must have been that (for I could not bear to see my mother cry) which started me crying, too.

Big tears streamed down her face, and it must have been that, for I could not bear to see my mother cry, which started me crying, too.

The use of parentheses or commas changes the tone, making the narrator seem almost apologetic rather than defiant. Her excuse for crying is no longer the most important idea in the sentence. Rather, readers are left with the impression of the mother's grief and the narrator's response.

Practice and Apply Look back at the letter that you wrote from the point of view of Annie John in response to this selection's Performance Task. Insert dashes into existing sentences or add sentences with dashes that amplify or extend an idea, show an interruption, or take the place of parentheses. Share your sentences with a partner and discuss how the insertion of dashes affects their tone or meaning.

ILE

Drama by Eugene O'Neill

Eugene O'Neill (1888–1953) *won the Nobel Prize for Literature as well as four Pulitzer Prizes. Brooks Atkinson, theater critic for the* New York Times, *credited him with transforming American drama into a serious art form. Until his late twenties, however, he seemed destined for obscurity.*

O'Neill was born in New York City. His father was a popular touring actor, whose profession resulted in an insecure life for the family. As a young man, O'Neill lacked direction. He was expelled from Princeton University; tried a series of occupations, including that of a sailor; and then finally began to write. In 1916, his play Bound East for Cardiff *was produced in New York by the Provincetown Players, launching his literary career.*

The play Ile, *written in 1917, is one of several one-act plays about the sea that O'Neill wrote during this early period. He based the characters and plot on actual residents of Provincetown, Massachusetts: Captain Cook and his wife, Viola, who went to sea with her husband for two years. After Viola returned home, she was never the same.*

O'Neill's literary output between 1920 and 1943 included 20 full-length plays as well as shorter works. Most of his plays explore tragic themes and troubled relationships. Mourning Becomes Electra *(1931) sets the Greek tragedy* Oresteia *in Civil War–era New England.* The Iceman Cometh *(1939) suggests that without illusions, people cannot escape despair. His autobiographical play* Long Day's Journey into Night *(1941) reveals the searing pain of O'Neill's family life, including his mother's drug addiction. He did not want the play performed until 25 years after his death. However, its first production in 1956 earned O'Neill his fourth Pulitzer Prize.*

AS YOU READ Pay attention to the clues that reveal Captain Keeney's character.

CHARACTERS

BEN, *the cabin boy*
THE STEWARD
CAPTAIN KEENEY
SLOCUM, *second mate*
MRS. KEENEY
JOE, *a harpooner*

Members of the crew of the steam whaler Atlantic Queen.

[SCENE—CAPTAIN KEENEY*'s cabin on board the steam whaling ship* Atlantic Queen*—a small, square compartment about eight feet high with a skylight in the center looking out on the poop deck. On the left (the stern of the ship) a long bench with rough cushions is built in against the wall. In front of the bench, a table. Over the bench, several curtained portholes.*

In the rear, left, a door leading to the captain's sleeping quarters. To the right of the door a small organ, looking as if it were brand new, is placed against the wall.

On the right, to the rear, a marble-topped sideboard. On the sideboard, a woman's sewing basket. Farther forward, a doorway leading to the companion way, and past the officer's quarters to the main deck.

In the center of the room, a stove. From the middle of the ceiling a hanging lamp is suspended. The walls of the cabin are painted white.

There is no rolling of the ship, and the light which comes through the skylight is sickly and faint, indicating one of those gray days of calm when ocean and sky are alike dead. The silence is unbroken except for the measured tread of some one walking up and down on the poop deck overhead.

It is nearing two bells—one o'clock—in the afternoon of a day in the year 1895.

At the rise of the curtain there is a moment of intense silence. Then the STEWARD *enters and commences to clear the table of the few dishes which still remain on it after the* CAPTAIN*'s dinner. He is an old, grizzled man dressed in dungaree pants, a sweater, and a woolen cap with ear flaps. His manner is sullen and angry. He stops stacking up the plates and casts a quick glance upward at the skylight; then tiptoes over to the closed door in rear and listens with his ear pressed to the crack. What he hears makes his face darken and he mutters a furious curse. There is a noise from the doorway on the right and he darts back to the table.*

BEN *enters. He is an over-grown, gawky boy with a long, pinched face. He is dressed in sweater, fur cap, etc. His teeth are chattering with the cold and he hurries to the stove, where he stands for a moment shivering, blowing on his hands, slapping them against his sides, on the verge of crying.*]

THE STEWARD (*In relieved tones—seeing who it is*). Oh, 'tis you, is it? What're ye shiverin' 'bout? Stay by the stove where ye belong and ye'll find no need of chatterin'.

BEN. It's c-c-cold. (*Trying to control his chattering teeth—derisively.*) Who d'ye think it were—the Old Man?

THE STEWARD (*Makes a threatening move—*BEN *shrinks away*). None o' your lip, young un, or I'll learn ye. (*More kindly.*) Where was it ye've been all o' the time—the fo'c's'tle?[1]

BEN. Yes.

THE STEWARD. Let the Old Man see ye up for'ard monkeyshinin' with the hands and ye'll get a hidin' ye'll not forget in a hurry.

BEN. Aw, he don't see nothin'. (*A trace of awe in his tones—he glances upward.*) He just walks up and down like he didn't notice nobody—and stares at the ice to the no'the'ard.

THE STEWARD (*The same tone of awe creeping into his voice*). He's always starin' at the ice. (*In a sudden rage, shaking his fist at the skylight.*) Ice, ice, ice! Damn him and damn the ice! Holdin' us in for nigh on a year—nothin' to see but ice—stuck in it like a fly in molasses!

BEN (*Apprehensively*). Ssshh! He'll hear ye.

THE STEWARD (*Raging*). Aye, damn him, and damn the Arctic seas, and damn this stinkin' whalin' ship of his, and damn me for a fool to ever ship on it! (*Subsiding as if realizing the uselessness of this outburst—shaking his head—slowly, with deep conviction.*) He's a hard man—as hard a man as ever sailed the seas.

BEN (*Solemnly*). Aye.

THE STEWARD. The two years we all signed up for are done this day. Blessed Christ! Two years o' this dog's life, and no luck in the fishin', and the hands half starved with the food runnin' low, rotten as it is; and not a sign of him turnin' back for home! (*Bitterly.*) Home! I begin to doubt if ever I'll set foot on land again. (*Excitedly.*) What is it he thinks he' goin' to do? Keep us all up here after our time is worked out till the last man of us is starved to death or frozen? We've grub enough hardly to last out the voyage back if we started now. What are the men goin' to do 'bout it? Did ye hear any talk in the fo'c's'tle?

BEN (*Going over to him—in a half whisper*). They said if he don't put back south for home today they're goin' to mutiny.

THE STEWARD (*With grim satisfaction*). Mutiny? Aye, 'tis the only thing they can do; and serve him right after the manner he's treated them—'s if they weren't no better nor dogs.

BEN. The ice is all broke up to s'uth'ard. They's clear water 's far 's you can see. He ain't got no excuse for not turnin' back for home, the men says.

THE STEWARD (*Bitterly*). He won't look nowheres but no'the'ard where they's only the ice to see. He don't want to see no clear water. All he thinks on is gittin' the ile[2]—'s if it was our fault he ain't had good luck with the whales. (*Shaking his head.*) I think the man's mighty nigh losin' his senses.

BEN (*Awed*). D'you really think he's crazy?

THE STEWARD. Aye, it's the punishment o' God on him. Did ye ever hear of a man who wasn't crazy do the things he does? (*Pointing to the door in rear.*) Who but a man that's mad would take his woman—and as sweet a woman

[1] **forecastle** (fōk′səl): the top deck near the bow (front) of a ship.

[2] **ile** (īl): a regional pronunciation of "oil."

as ever was—on a stinkin' whalin' ship to the Arctic seas to be locked in by the rotten ice for nigh on a year, and maybe lose her senses forever—for it's sure she'll never be the same again.

BEN (*Sadly*). She useter be awful nice to me before—(*His eyes grow wide and frightened.*) she got—like she is.

THE STEWARD. Aye, she was good to all of us. 'Twould have been hell on board without her; for he's a hard man—a hard, hard man—a driver if there ever was one. (*With a grim laugh.*) I hope he's satisfied now—drivin' her on till she's near lost her mind. And who could blame her? 'Tis a God's wonder we're not a ship full of crazed people—with the damned ice all the time, and the quiet so thick you're afraid to hear your own voice.

BEN (*With a frightened glance toward the door on right*). She don't never speak to me no more—jest looks at me 's if she didn't know me.

THE STEWARD. She don't know no one—but him. She talks to him—when she does talk—right enough.

BEN. She does nothin' all day long now but sit and sew—and then she cries to herself without makin' no noise. I've seen her.

THE STEWARD. Aye, I could hear her through the door a while back.

BEN (*Tiptoes over to the door and listens*). She's cryin' now.

THE STEWARD (*Furiously—shaking his fist*). God send his soul to hell for the devil he is! (*There is the noise of some one coming slowly down the companionway stairs.* THE STEWARD *hurries to his stacked up dishes. He is so nervous from fright that he knocks off the top one, which falls and breaks on the floor. He stands aghast, trembling with dread.* BEN *is violently rubbing off the organ with a piece of cloth which he has snatched from his pocket.* CAPTAIN KEENEY *appears in the doorway on right and comes into the cabin,*

removing his fur cap as he does so. He is a man of about forty, around five-ten in height but looking much shorter on account of the enormous proportions of his shoulders and chest. His face is massive and deeply lined, with gray-blue eyes of a bleak hardness, and a tightly clenched, thin-lipped mouth. His thick hair is long and gray. He is dressed in a heavy blue jacket and blue pants stuffed into his seaboots.

(*He is followed into the cabin by the* SECOND MATE, *a rangy six-footer with a lean weather-beaten face. The* MATE *is dressed about the same as the captain. He is a man of thirty or so.*)

KEENEY (*Comes toward the STEWARD—with a stern look on his face. The STEWARD is visibly frightened and the stack of dishes rattles in his trembling hands.* KEENEY *draws back his fist and the* STEWARD *shrinks away. The fist is gradually lowered and* KEENEY *speaks slowly*). 'Twould be like hitting a worm. It is nigh on two bells, Mr. Steward, and this truck not cleared yet.

THE STEWARD (*Stammering*). Y-y-yes, sir.

KEENEY. Instead of doin' your rightful work ye've been below here gossipin' old woman's talk with that boy. (*To* BEN, *fiercely.*) Get out o' this, you! Clean up the chart room. (BEN *darts past the* MATE *to the open doorway.*) Pick up that dish, Mr. Steward!

THE STEWARD (*Doing so with difficulty*). Yes, sir.

KEENEY. The next dish you break, Mr. Steward, you take a bath in the Bering Sea at the end of a rope.

THE STEWARD (*Tremblingly*). Yes, sir. (*He hurries out. The* SECOND MATE *walks slowly over to the* CAPTAIN.)

MATE. I warn't 'specially anxious the man at the wheel should catch what I wanted to say to you, sir. That's why I asked you to come below.

KEENEY (*Impatiently*). Speak your say, Mr. Slocum.

MATE (*Unconsciously lowering his voice*). I'm afeard there'll be trouble with the hands by the look o' things. They'll likely turn ugly, every blessed one o' them, if you don't put back. The two years they signed up for is up to-day.

KEENEY. And d'you think you're tellin' me somethin' new, Mr. Slocum? I've felt it in the air this long time past. D'you think I've not seen their ugly looks and the grudgin' way they worked? (*The door in rear is opened and* MRS. KEENEY *stands in the doorway. She is a slight, sweet-faced little woman primly dressed in black. Her eyes are red from weeping and her face drawn and pale. She takes in the cabin with a frightened glance and stands as if fixed to the spot by some nameless dread, clasping and unclasping her hands nervously. The two men turn and look at her.*)

KEENEY (*With rough tenderness*). Well, Annie?

MRS. KEENEY (*As if awakening from a dream*). David, I—(*She is silent. The* MATE *starts for the doorway.*)

KEENEY (*Turning to him—sharply*). Wait!

MATE. Yes, sir.

KEENEY. D'you want anything, Annie?

MRS. KEENEY (*After a pause, during which she seems to be endeavoring to collect her thoughts*). I thought maybe—I'd go up on deck, David, to get a breath of fresh air. (*She stands humbly awaiting his permission. He and the* MATE *exchange a significant glance.*)

KEENEY. It's too cold, Annie. You'd best stay below to-day. There's nothing to look at on deck—but ice.

MRS. KEENEY (*Monotonously*). I know—ice, ice, ice! But there's nothing to see down here but these walls. (*She makes a gesture of loathing.*)

KEENEY. You can play the organ, Annie.

MRS. KEENEY (*Dully*). I hate the organ. It puts me in mind of home.

KEENEY (*A touch of resentment in his voice*). I got it jest for you.

MRS. KEENEY (*Dully*). I know. (*She turns away from them and walks slowly to the bench on left. She lifts up one of the curtains and looks through a porthole; then utters an exclamation of joy.*) Ah, water! Clear water! As far as I can see! How good it looks after all these months of ice! (*She turns round to them, her face transfigured with joy.*) Ah, now I must go upon deck and look at it, David.

KEENEY (*Frowning*). Best not to-day, Annie. Best wait for a day when the sun shines.

MRS. KEENEY (*Desperately*). But the sun never shines in this terrible place.

KEENEY (*A tone of command in his voice*). Best not to-day, Annie.

MRS. KEENEY (*Crumbling before this command—abjectly*). Very well, David. (*She stands there staring straight before her as if in a daze. The two men look at her uneasily.*)

KEENEY (*Sharply*). Annie!

MRS. KEENEY (*Dully*). Yes, David.

KEENEY. Me and Mr. Slocum has business to talk about—ship's business.

MRS. KEENEY. Very well, David. (*She goes slowly out, rear, and leaves the door three-quarters shut behind her.*)

KEENEY. Best not have her on deck if they's goin' to be any trouble.

MATE. Yes, sir.

KEENEY. And trouble they's goin' to be. I feel it in my bones. (*Takes a revolver from the pocket of his coat and examines it.*) Got your'n?

MATE. Yes, sir.

KEENEY. Not that we'll have to use 'em—not if I know their breed of dog—jest to frighten' em up a bit. (*Grimly.*) I ain't never been forced to use one yit; and trouble I've had by land and by sea 's long as I kin remember, and will have till my dyin' day, I reckon.

MATE (*Hesitatingly*). Then you ain't goin'—to turn back?

KEENEY. Turn back! Mr. Slocum, did you ever hear o' me pointin' s'uth for home with only a measly four hundred barrel of ile in the hold?

MATE (*Hastily*). No, sir—but the grub's gittin' low.

KEENEY. They's enough to last a long time yit, if they're careful with it; and they's plenty o' water.

MATE. They say it's not fit to eat—what's left; and the two years they signed on fur is up to-day. They might make trouble for you in the courts when we git home.

KEENEY. To hell with' em! Let them make what law trouble they kin. I don't give a damn 'bout the money. I've got to git the ile! (*Glancing sharply at the* MATE.) You ain't turnin' no damned sea lawyer, be you, Mr. Slocum?

MATE (*Flushing*). Not by a hell of a sight, sir.

KEENEY. What do the fools want to go home fur now? Their share o' the four hundred barrel wouldn't keep 'em in chewin' terbacco.

MATE (*Slowly*). They wants to git back to their folks an' things, I s'pose.

KEENEY (*Looking at him searchingly*). 'N you want to turn back, too. (*The* MATE *looks down confusedly before his sharp gaze.*) Don't lie, Mr. Slocum. It's writ down plain in your eyes. (*With grim sarcasm.*) I hope, Mr. Slocum, you ain't agoin' to jine the men agin me.

MATE (*Indignantly*). That ain't fair, sir, to say sich things.

KEENEY (*With satisfaction*). I warn't much afeard o' that, Tom. You been with me nigh on ten year and I've learned ye whalin'. No man kin say I ain't a good master, if I be a hard one.

MATE. I warn't thinkin' of myself, sir—'bout turnin' home, I mean. (*Desperately.*) But Mrs. Keeney, sir—seems like she ain't jest satisfied up here, ailin' like—what with the cold an' bad luck an' the ice an' all.

KEENEY (*His face clouding—rebukingly but not severely*). That's my business, Mr. Slocum. I'll thank you to steer a clear course o' that. (*A pause.*) The ice'll break up soon to no'th'ard. I could see it startin' to-day. And when it goes and we git some sun Annie'll perk up. (*Another pause—then he bursts forth:*) It ain't the damned money what's keepin' me up in the Northern seas, Tom. But I can't go back to Homeport with a measly four hundred barrel of ile. I'd die fust. I ain't never come back home in all my days without a full ship. Ain't that truth?

MATE. Yes, sir; but this voyage you been icebound, an'—

KEENEY (*Scornfully*). And d'you s'pose any of 'em would believe that—any o' them skippers I've beaten voyage after voyage? Can't you hear 'em laughin' and sneerin'—Tibbots 'n' Harris 'n' Simms and the rest—and all o' Homeport makin' fun o' me? "Dave Keeney what boasts he's the best whalin' skipper out o' Homeport comin' back with a measly four hundred barrel of ile?" (*The thought of this drives him into a frenzy, and he smashes his fist down on the marble top of the sideboard.*) Hell! I got to git the ile, I tell you. How could I figger on this ice? It's never been so bad before in the thirty year I been acomin' here. And now it's breakin' up. In a couple o' days it'll be all gone. And they's whale here, plenty of 'em. I know they is and I ain't never gone wrong yit. I got to git the ile! I got to git it in spite of all hell, and by God, I ain't agoin' home till I do git it! (*There is the sound of subdued sobbing from the door in rear. The two men stand silent for a moment, listening. Then* KEENEY *goes over to the door and looks in. He hesitates for a moment as if he were going to enter—then closes the door softly.* JOE, *the harpooner, an enormous six-footer with a battered, ugly face, enters from right and stands waiting for the captain to notice him.*)

KEENEY (*Turning and seeing him*). Don't be standin' there like a gawk, Harpooner. Speak up!

JOE (*Confusedly*). We want—the men, sir—they wants to send a depitation aft to have a word with you.

KEENEY (*Furiously*). Tell 'em to go to—(*Checks himself and continues grimly.*) Tell 'em to come. I'll see 'em.

JOE. Aye, aye, sir. (*He goes out.*)

KEENEY (*With a grim smile*). Here it comes, the trouble you spoke of, Mr. Slocum, and we'll make short shift of it. It's better to crush such things at the start than let them make headway.

MATE (*Worriedly*). Shall I wake up the First and Fourth, sir? We might need their help.

KEENEY. No, let them sleep. I'm well able to handle this alone, Mr. Slocum. (*There is the shuffling of footsteps from outside and five of the crew crowd into the cabin, led by* JOE. *All are dressed alike—sweaters, seaboots, etc. They glance uneasily at the* CAPTAIN, *twirling their fur caps in their hands.*)

KEENEY (*After a pause*). Well? Who's to speak fur ye?

JOE (*Stepping forward with an air of bravado*). I be.

KEENEY (*Eyeing him up and down coldly*). So you be. Then speak your say and be quick about it.

JOE (*Trying not to wilt before the* CAPTAIN'S *glance and avoiding his eyes*). The time we signed up for is done to-day.

KEENEY (*Icily*). You're tellin' me nothin' I don't know.

JOE. You ain't pintin' fur home yit, far's we kin see.

KEENEY. No, and I ain't agoin' to till this ship is full of ile.

JOE. You can't go no further no'the with the ice afore ye.

KEENEY. The ice is breaking up.

JOE (*After a slight pause during which the others mumble angrily to one another*). The grub we're gittin' now is rotten.

KEENEY. It's good enough fur ye. Better men than ye are have eaten worse. (*There is a chorus of angry exclamations from the crowd.*)

JOE (*Encouraged by this support*). We ain't agoin' to work no more less you puts back for home.

KEENEY (*Fiercely*). You ain't, ain't you?

JOE. No; and the law courts'll say we was right.

KEENEY. To hell with your law courts! We're at sea now and I'm the law on this ship. (*Edging up toward the harpooner.*) And every mother's son of you what don't obey orders goes in irons. (*There are more angry exclamations from the crew.* MRS. KEENEY *appears in the doorway in rear and looks on with startled eyes. None of the men notice her.*)

JOE (*With bravado*). Then we're agoin' to mutiny and take the old hooker home ourselves. Ain't we, boys? (*As he turns his head to look at the others,* KEENEY'*s fist shoots out to the side of his jaw.* JOE *goes down in a heap and lies there.* MRS. KEENEY *gives a shriek and hides her face in her hands. The men pull out their sheath knives and start a rush, but stop when they find themselves confronted by the revolvers of* KEENEY *and the* MATE.)

KEENEY (*His eyes and voice snapping*). Hold still! (*The men stand huddled together in a sullen silence.* KEENEY'*s voice is full of mockery.*) You've found out it ain't safe to mutiny on this ship, ain't you? And now git for'ard where ye belong, and—(*He gives* JOE'*s body a contemptuous kick.*) Drag him with you. And remember the first man of ye I see shirkin' I'll shoot dead as sure as there's a sea under us, and you can tell the rest the same. Git for'ard now! Quick! (*The men leave in cowed silence, carrying* JOE *with them.* KEENEY *turns to the* MATE *with a short laugh and puts his revolver back in his pocket.*) Best get up on deck, Mr. Slocum, and see to it they don't try none of their skulkin' tricks. We'll have to keep an eye peeled from now on. I know 'em.

MATE. Yes, sir. (*He goes out, right.* KEENEY *hears his wife's hysterical weeping and turns around in surprise—then walks slowly to her side.*)

KEENEY (*Putting an arm around her shoulder—with gruff tenderness*). There, there, Annie. Don't be afeard. It's all past and gone.

MRS. KEENEY (*Shrinking away from him*). Oh, I can't bear it! I can't bear it any longer!

KEENEY (*Gently*). Can't bear what, Annie?

MRS. KEENEY (*Hysterically*). All this horrible brutality, and these brutes of men, and this terrible ship, and this prison cell of a room, and the ice all around, and the silence. (*After this outburst she calms down and wipes her eyes with her handkerchief.*)

KEENEY (*After a pause during which he looks down at her with a puzzled frown*). Remember, I warn't hankerin' to have you come on this voyage, Annie.

MRS. KEENEY. I wanted to be with you, David, don't you see? I didn't want to wait back there in the house all alone as I've been doing these last six years since we were married—waiting, and watching, and fearing—with nothing to keep my mind occupied—not able to go back teaching school on account of being Dave Keeney's wife. I used to dream of sailing on the great, wide, glorious ocean. I wanted to be by your side in the danger and vigorous life of it all. I wanted to see you the hero they make you out to be in Homeport. And instead—(*Her voice grows tremulous.*) All I find is ice and cold—and brutality! (*Her voice breaks.*)

KEENEY. I warned you what it'd be, Annie. "Whalin' ain't no ladies' tea party," I says to you, and "you better stay to home where you've got all your woman's comforts." (*Shaking his head.*) But you was so set on it.

MRS. KEENEY (*Wearily*). Oh, I know it isn't your fault, David. You see, I didn't believe you. I guess I was dreaming about the old Vikings in the story books and I thought you were one of them.

KEENEY (*Protestingly*). I done my best to make it as cozy and comfortable as could be. (MRS. KEENEY *looks around her in wild scorn.*) I even sent to the city for that organ for ye, thinkin' it might be soothin' to ye to be playin' it times when they was calms and things was dull like.

MRS. KEENEY (*Wearily*). Yes, you were very kind, David. I know that. (*She goes to left and lifts the curtains from the porthole and looks out—then suddenly bursts forth:*) I won't stand it—I can't stand it—pent up by these walls like a prisoner. (*She runs over to him and throws her arms around him, weeping. He puts his arm protectingly over her shoulders.*) Take me away from here, David! If I don't get away from here, out of this terrible ship, I'll go mad! Take me home, David! I can't think any more. I feel as if the cold and the silence were crushing down on my brain. I'm afraid. Take me home!

KEENEY (*Holds her at arm's length and looks at her face anxiously*). Best go to bed, Annie. You ain't yourself. You got fever. Your eyes look so strange like. I ain't never seen you look this way before.

MRS. KEENEY (*Laughing hysterically*). It's the ice and the cold and the silence—they'd make any one look strange.

KEENEY (*Soothingly*). In a month or two, with good luck, three at the most, I'll have her filled with ile and then we'll give her everything she'll stand and pint for home.

MRS. KEENEY. But we can't wait for that—I can't wait. I want to get home. And the men won't wait. They want to get home. It's cruel, it's brutal for you to keep them. You must sail back. You've got no excuse. There's clear water to the south now. If you've a heart at all you've got to turn back.

KEENEY (*Harshly*). I can't, Annie.

MRS. KEENEY. Why can't you?

KEENEY. A woman couldn't rightly understand my reason.

MRS. KEENEY (*Wildly*). Because it's a stupid, stubborn reason. Oh, I heard you talking with the second mate. You're afraid the other captains will sneer at you because you didn't come back with a full ship. You want to live up to your silly reputation even if you do have to beat and starve men and drive me mad to do it.

KEENEY (*His jaw set stubbornly*). It ain't that, Annie. Them skippers would never dare sneer to my face. It ain't so much what any one'd say—but—(*He hesitates, struggling to express his meaning.*) You see—I've always done it—since my first voyage as skipper. I always come back—with a full ship—and—it don't seem right not to—somehow. I been always first whalin' skipper out o' Homeport, and—Don't you see my meanin', Annie? (*He glances at her. She is not looking at him but staring dully in front of her, not hearing a word he is saying.*) Annie! (*She comes to herself with a start.*) Best turn in, Annie, there's a good woman. You ain't well.

MRS. KEENEY (*Resisting his attempts to guide her to the door in rear*). David! Won't you please turn back?

KEENEY (*Gently*). I can't, Annie—not yet awhile. You don't see my meanin'. I got to git the ile.

MRS. KEENEY. It'd be different if you needed the money, but you don't. You've got more than plenty.

KEENEY (*Impatiently*). It ain't the money I'm thinkin' of. D'you think I'm as mean as that?

MRS. KEENEY (*Dully*). No—I don't know—I can't understand—(*Intensely*). Oh, I want to be home in the old house once more and see my own kitchen again, and hear a woman's voice talking to me and be able to talk to her. Two years! It seems so long ago—as if I'd been dead and could never go back.

KEENEY (*Worried by her strange tone and the far-away look in her eyes*). Best go to bed, Annie. You ain't well.

MRS. KEENEY (*Not appearing to hear him*). I used to be lonely when you were away. I used to think Homeport was a stupid, monotonous place. Then I used to go down on the beach, especially when it was windy and the breakers were rolling in, and I'd dream of the fine free life you must be leading. (*She gives a laugh which is half a sob.*) I used to love the sea then. (*She pauses; then continues with slow intensity:*) But now—I don't ever want to see the sea again.

KEENEY (*Thinking to humor her*). 'Tis no fit place for a woman, that's sure. I was a fool to bring ye.

MRS. KEENEY (*After a pause—passing her hand over her eyes with a gesture of pathetic weariness*). How long would it take us to reach home—if we started now?

KEENEY (*Frowning*). 'Bout two months, I reckon, Annie, with fair luck.

MRS. KEENEY (*Counts on her fingers—then murmurs with a rapt smile*). That would be August, the latter part of August, wouldn't it? It was on the twenty-fifth of August we were married, David, wasn't it?

KEENEY (*Trying to conceal the fact that her memories have moved him—gruffly*). Don't you remember?

MRS. KEENEY (*Vaguely—again passes her hand over her eyes.*) My memory is leaving me—up here in the ice. It was so long ago. (*A pause—then she smiles dreamily.*) It's June now. The lilacs will be all in bloom in the front yard—and the climbing roses on the trellis to the side of the house—they're budding. (*She suddenly covers her face with her hands and commences to sob.*)

KEENEY (*Disturbed*). Go in and rest, Annie. You're all wore out cryin' over what can't be helped.

MRS. KEENEY (*Suddenly throwing her arms around his neck and clinging to him*). You love me, don't you, David?

KEENEY (*In amazed embarrassment at this outburst*). Love you? Why d'you ask me such a question, Annie?

MRS. KEENEY (*Shaking him—fiercely*). But you do, don't you, David? Tell me!

KEENEY. I'm your husband, Annie, and you're my wife. Could there be aught but love between us after all these years?

MRS. KEENEY (*Shaking him again—still more fiercely*). Then you do love me. Say it!

KEENEY (*Simply*). I do, Annie.

MRS. KEENEY (*Gives a sigh of relief—her hands drop to her sides. Keeney regards her anxiously. She passes her hand across her eyes and murmurs half to herself:*) I sometimes think if we could only have had a child. (KEENEY *turns away from her, deeply moved. She grabs his arm and turns him around to face her—intensely.*) And I've always been a good wife to you, haven't I, David?

KEENEY (*His voice betraying his emotion*). No man has ever had a better, Annie.

MRS. KEENEY. And I've never asked for much from you, have I, David? Have I?

KEENEY. You know you could have all I got the power to give ye, Annie.

MRS. KEENEY (*Wildly*). Then do this this once for my sake, for God's sake—take me home! It's killing me, this life—the brutality and cold and horror of it. I'm going mad. I can feel the threat in the air. I can hear the silence threatening me—day after gray day and every day the same. I can't bear it. (*Sobbing*). I'll go mad, I know I will. Take me home, David, if you love me as you say. I'm afraid. For the love of God, take me home! (*She throws her arms around him, weeping against his shoulder. His face betrays the tremendous struggle going on within him. He holds her out at arm's length, his expression softening. For a moment his shoulders sag, he becomes old, his iron spirit weakens as he looks at her tear-stained face.*)

KEENEY (*Dragging out the words with an effort*). I'll do it, Annie—for your sake—if you say it's needful for ye.

MRS. KEENEY (*With wild joy—kissing him*). God bless you for that, David! (*He turns away from her silently and walks toward the companionway. Just at that moment there is a clatter of footsteps on the stairs and the* SECOND MATE *enters the cabin.*)

MATE (*Excitedly*). The ice is breakin' up to no'the'ard, sir. There's a clear passage through the floe, and clear water beyond, the lookout says. (KEENEY *straightens himself like a man coming out of a trance.* MRS. KEENEY *looks at the* MATE *with terrified eyes.*)

KEENEY (*Dazedly—trying to collect his thoughts*). A clear passage? To no'the'ard?

MATE. Yes, sir.

KEENEY (*His voice suddenly grim with determination*). Then get her ready and we'll drive her through.

MATE. Aye, aye, sir.

MRS. KEENEY (*Appealingly*). David!

KEENEY (*Not heeding her*). Will the men turn to willin' or must we drag 'em out?

MATE. They'll turn to willin' enough. You put the fear o' God into 'em, sir. They're meek as lambs.

KEENEY. Then drive 'em—both watches. (*With grim determination.*) They's whale t'other side o' this floe and we're going to git 'em.

MATE. Aye, aye, sir. (*He goes out hurriedly. A moment later there is the sound of scuffling feet from the deck outside and the* MATE*'s voice shouting orders.*)

KEENEY (*Speaking aloud to himself—derisively*). And I was agoin' home like a yaller dog!

MRS. KEENEY (*Imploringly*). David!

KEENEY (*Sternly*). Woman, you ain't adoin' right when you meddle in men's business and weaken 'em. You can't know my feelin's. I got to prove a man to be a good husband for ye to take pride in. I got to git the ile, I tell ye.

MRS. KEENEY (*Supplicatingly*). David! Aren't you going home?

KEENEY (*Ignoring this question—commandingly*). You ain't well. Go and lay down a mite. (*He starts for the door.*) I got to git on deck. (*He goes out. She cries after him in anguish:*) David! (*A pause. She passes her hand across her eyes—then commences to laugh hysterically and goes to the organ. She sits down and starts to play wildly an old hymn.* KEENEY *reenters from the doorway to the deck and stands looking at* *her angrily. He comes over and grabs her roughly by the shoulder.*)

KEENEY. Woman, what foolish mockin' is this? (*She laughs wildly and he starts back from her in alarm.*) Annie! What is it? (*She doesn't answer him.* KEENEY*'s voice trembles.*) Don't you know me, Annie? (*He puts both hands on her shoulders and turns her around so that he can look into her eyes. She stares up at him with a stupid expression, a vague smile on her lips. He stumbles away from her, and she commences softly to play the organ again.*)

KEENEY (*Swallowing hard—in a hoarse whisper, as if he had difficulty in speaking*). You said—you was a-goin' mad—God! (*A long wail is heard from the deck above.*) Ah bl-o-o-o-ow! (*A moment later the* MATE*'s face appears through the skylight. He cannot see* MRS. KEENEY.)

MATE (*In great excitement*). Whales, sir—a whole school of 'em—off the star'b'd quarter 'bout five mile away—big ones!

KEENEY (*Galvanized into action*). Are you lowerin' the boats?

MATE. Yes, sir.

KEENEY (*With grim decision*). I'm a-comin' with ye.

MATE. Aye, aye, sir. (*Jubilantly.*) You'll git the ile now right enough, sir. (*His head is withdrawn and he can be heard shouting orders.*)

KEENEY (*Turning to his wife*). Annie! Did you hear him? I'll git the ile. (*She doesn't answer or seem to know he is there. He gives a hard laugh, which is almost a groan.*) I know you're foolin' me, Annie. You ain't out of your mind—(*Anxiously.*) be you? I'll git the ile now right enough—jest a little while longer, Annie—then we'll turn hom'ard. I can't turn back now, you see that, don't ye? I've got to git the ile. (*In sudden terror.*) Answer me! You ain't mad, be you? (*She keeps on playing the organ, but makes no reply. The* MATE*'s face appears again through the skylight.*)

MATE. All ready, sir. (KEENEY *turns his back on his wife and strides to the doorway, where he stands for a moment and looks back at her in anguish, fighting to control his feelings.*)

MATE. Comin', sir?

KEENEY (*His face suddenly grown hard with determination*). Aye. (*He turns abruptly and goes out.* MRS. KEENEY *does not appear to notice his departure. Her whole attention seems centered in the organ. She sits with half-closed eyes, her body swaying a little from side to side to the rhythm of the hymn. Her fingers move faster and faster and she is playing wildly and discordantly as*

(*The Curtain Falls*)

COLLABORATIVE DISCUSSION What are Captain Keeney's predominant character traits? With a partner, discuss whether these qualities are necessary for a ship's captain to have. Cite specific textual evidence to support your ideas.

Analyze Drama Elements: Conflict

RL 3

The action of any play is driven by **conflict,** or a struggle between opposing forces. The plot unfolds as the play's characters try to solve problems that stem from the conflict. **Internal conflict** occurs within a character's own mind. **External conflict** exists between a character and an outside force. The following list provides details about the specific kinds of conflict you may find in the play *Ile.*

- **Character Versus Self** A character with an internal conflict struggles to reconcile opposing values, desires, needs, or emotions in order to act or make a decision. The character's words and actions reveal this conflict to the audience.
- **Character Versus Character** A conflict between two characters is external. Although a fight is the most obvious sign of external conflict, often there is more subtle tension between characters that is revealed through dialogue and the characters' actions and reactions. For example, Annie exerts pressure on her husband when she reminds him of their anniversary and asks him if he loves her.
- **Character Versus Nature** Another type of external conflict occurs when a character is pitted against nature. The sailors are in conflict with the ice that traps them. This conflict with nature leads to other issues, including the confrontation between the crew and the captain.
- **Character Versus Society** Sometimes what a character wants puts him or her in direct opposition to what society considers acceptable. This kind of external conflict may result in the character's being ostracized by his or her community.

Analyze Drama Elements: Symbol

RL 3

A **symbol** is a person, place, or object that represents something beyond itself. Some commonplace symbols are easy to interpret. For example, the Garden of Eden symbolizes innocence. Other symbols are invented by authors to have meaning within the context of a specific literary work. To understand them, readers must analyze how they relate to characters, plot, and theme.

Eugene O'Neill incorporates several symbols into his play. One is the organ Captain Keeney bought for his wife, "thinkin' it might be soothin' to ye to be playin' it." The organ might symbolize the domestic life in which Annie feels comfortable, in contrast to the captain's harsher world aboard the ship. Annie's wild playing at the end shows that these worlds are incompatible.

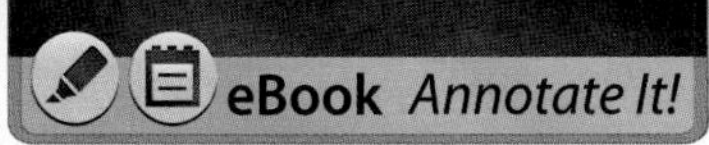

Analyzing the Text

RL 1, RL 3, W 4, SL 1a

Cite Text Evidence Support your responses with evidence from the selection.

1. **Analyze** What information does O'Neill reveal in the exchange between the Steward and Ben? How does this first scene set the **mood,** or atmosphere, of the play?
2. **Infer** Review the stage directions that describe the confrontation between the crew members and Captain Keeney (lines 461–537). What is the men's attitude toward the captain? What insight into the captain's character do the stage directions provide?
3. **Interpret** When Mrs. Keeney questions why Captain Keeney won't turn back, he replies, "It ain't so much what any one'd say—but. . . . You see—I've always done it—since my first voyage as a skipper. I always come back—with a full ship—and it don't seem right not to—somehow." What does the full ship of oil symbolize for him?
4. **Analyze** Mrs. Keeney convinces the captain to turn the ship around, but he abruptly changes his mind when he learns that the ice is breaking up. What internal conflict of the captain's is revealed in this section of the play?
5. **Analyze** Why is Mrs. Keeney on the ship? How does this information influence your opinion about the conflict between the captain and his wife?
6. **Analyze** Ice is an important symbol in the play. Does it have the same meaning for all of the characters, or does it symbolize different things? Explain your response.

PERFORMANCE TASK

Speaking Activity: Response to Literature The captain and Mrs. Keeney have different perspectives on life. In a small group, examine the following lines of dialogue. Discuss how they reveal the conflict between the two characters' viewpoints. Together, write a summary of your discussion and present it to the class.

- "I used to dream of sailing on the great, wide, glorious ocean. I wanted to be by your side in the danger and vigorous life of it all. I wanted to see you the hero. . . ." [Mrs. Keeney]
- "I warned you what it'd be, Annie. 'Whalin' ain't no ladies' tea party,' I says to you." [Captain Keeney]
- "You see I didn't believe you. I guess I was dreaming about the old Vikings in the story books and I thought you were one of them." [Mrs. Keeney]

Language and Style: Dialect

L 1a, L 3

Dialect is a type of language spoken in a particular place by a certain group of people. Writers use dialect to evoke a specific setting or to develop characters. In *Ile,* the title itself, which means "oil," is part of the dialect spoken by the characters in the play. The dialect helps establish the setting as the late 1800s. It also creates realism. The language fits the rough-and-ready men who battle the elements of nature. In contrast, O'Neill chooses to have Mrs. Keeney speak in more standard English.

Read the following dialogue from the play:

Let the Old Man see ye up for'ard monkeyshinin' with the hands and ye'll get a hidin' ye'll not forget in a hurry.

Then compare the effect of the dialect with this statement written in standard English:

Don't let the Captain see you wasting time with the crew members; you will get in trouble.

This second version lacks the authenticity of the first. It could have been spoken anywhere by anyone, whereas the original version establishes a sense of place, time, and character.

This chart identifies some of the characteristics of the dialect found in this play:

Characteristic	Example
The dialect includes specialized vocabulary words and colloquial expressions. Readers can use context to help them define these words and phrases.	"It is nigh on two bells, Mr. Steward, and this truck not cleared yet."
The grammatical constructions do not follow the standard conventions of written and spoken English.	"She don't never speak to me no more . . ."
Some terms, such as "ile," and the lack of a final *g* on progressive verb forms reflect a regional pronunciation.	"She's cryin' now."

Practice and Apply With a partner, write four lines of dialogue between Captain Keeney and Mrs. Keeney. This dialogue should occur directly after she witnesses his confrontation with the crew members; it may include specific details about what upset her as well as the captain's explanation for his actions. Be sure to incorporate characteristics of the captain's dialect and Mrs. Keeney's pattern of speech, and have the dialogue reflect what you know about their characters and the plot. Share your dialogue with a partner.

MEDIA ANALYSIS

Media Versions of *ILE*

Opera by Ezra Donner

Production Image

AS YOU VIEW Consider how the music of the opera helps convey the story. Write down any questions you generate during viewing.

COLLABORATIVE DISCUSSION How would you describe the overall mood, or feeling, of the opera? With a partner, discuss which elements of the performance contribute to this atmosphere. Cite examples from the video to support your ideas.

COMPARE TEXT AND MEDIA

Analyze Interpretations of Drama: Operatic Interpretation

RL 7

Music is the key element in any opera. It helps communicate the story by influencing the audience's interpretation of the characters' words and actions:

- Music sets the **mood**, or emotional atmosphere, of a scene, affecting how the audience feels. Fast music may create a feeling of urgency; slow music may set a somber or sad mood. For example, in *Ile*, a series of quick, emphatic notes intensifies the mood of excitement when the mate announces that the ice is breaking up.
- Music influences the way the audience feels about a **character**. If uplifting music is played when a character enters, the audience may perceive that character in a more positive way.
- Music can be used to draw attention to **dialogue** as well as to a character's gestures or movements. For example, when Captain Keeney goes back on deck after his decision to keep sailing, the music fades, focusing the audience's attention on Annie's actions.

Analyzing the Text and Media

RL 7, W 4, SL 6

Cite Text Evidence Support your responses with evidence from the selection.

1. **Analyze** What emotion is conveyed by the music that accompanies much of Annie Keeney's dialogue? How might this music influence the way the audience perceives her character?
2. **Analyze** How do the music and performers' singing contribute to your understanding of the characters? Cite specific examples from the video.
3. **Compare** The opera version of the discussion between Captain Keeney and his wife omits several passages of dialogue, including his explanation of why he has to get the oil and his reminder that he asked her not to come on the voyage. How do these omissions affect the way the audience understands the central conflict?

PERFORMANCE TASK

Writing Activity: Critique Is the opera version of *Ile* a faithful interpretation of O'Neill's play?

- Prepare a written response to the question, citing specific examples to support your view.
- Identify classmates with opposing viewpoints. Take turns presenting your responses to the class.
- As a class, decide which viewpoint is most compelling.

MEDIA

AS YOU VIEW This image shows a scene from a 2009 production of ***Ile*** that was staged during the summer on a 19th-century schooner docked at the Mystic Seaport Museum in Connecticut. Compare the actors, costumes, and set in the photograph with the images you had in your mind after reading O'Neill's play. Write down any questions you generate as you view the image.

COLLABORATIVE DISCUSSION With a partner, discuss your reaction to the production shown in the photograph. Which scene from O'Neill's play is most likely represented in the image? What specific choices did the director make in staging it? Cite evidence from both the play and the photograph to support your points.

COMPARE TEXT AND MEDIA

Analyze Interpretations of Drama: Casting and Staging

RL 7

Before staging a play, directors must decide how they want to interpret the original work. They might choose to stay true to the writer's vision of the characters and setting. Or they might decide on a more radical interpretation of these elements. Their interpretation determines the casting and staging.

- **Casting** involves choosing actors to play the specific roles. The director's criteria for a particular character may include age, gender, personality, and physical appearance. The photograph of the production of *Ile* in Mystic, Connecticut, shows how one director chose to "see" the characters of Captain and Mrs. Keeney.
- **Staging** depends on where and when the director envisions the action taking place. The setting of a play might be created by elaborate sets within a theater. The photograph from the Mystic production shows the choice of an outdoor location that is meaningful to the play and produces the effect the director wants.

Even if audience members do not consciously think about a play's casting and staging, both elements contribute to their reactions to the play and their interpretation of its meaning.

Analyzing the Text and Media

RL 7, SL 4

Cite Text Evidence Support your responses with evidence from the selection.

1. **Analyze** In what ways is the casting consistent with O'Neill's text? In what ways does the casting depart from the text?
2. **Analyze** What is the director's purpose in staging the play on an actual schooner anchored off the Connecticut coast? How might this staging, compared to a more traditional theater staging, change the play's impact on the audience?

PERFORMANCE TASK

Media Activity: Set Design How would you stage O'Neill's play?

- With a partner, decide on your vision of the setting of O'Neill's play. Write a brief explanation of the reasons you would choose this setting.
- Draw or find images of the set design that would be used in your staging of the play.
- Present your set design to the class, explaining the reasons behind your decisions.

Debate an Issue

This collection focuses on the sacrifices people make to achieve success. In the anchor text "Marita's Bargain," the author describes a school in which the days are longer, summer vacation is shorter, and students are very successful. With a group of classmates, conduct a debate on whether *all* students should have longer school days and shorter vacations.

SL 1a–d Initiate and participate in a range of collaborative discussions, building on others' ideas and expressing their own.

SL 3 Evaluate a speaker's point of view, reasoning, and use of evidence and rhetoric.

SL 4 Present information, findings, and supporting evidence, conveying a clear and distinct perspective, such that listeners can follow the line of reasoning, alternative or opposing perspectives are addressed, and the organization, development, substance, and style are appropriate to purpose, audience, and a range of formal and informal tasks.

Each team in an effective debate

- takes a clear position, either for or against the idea of students spending more time in school
- selects relevant evidence from "Marita's Bargain" and one or more other texts in the collection to support the claims
- follows an orderly format in which speakers from each team take turns presenting their claims, counterclaims, reasons, and evidence
- communicates ideas formally and objectively, using precise language
- engages in an exchange of ideas in which participants respond to diverse perspectives, build on ideas, and evaluate others' reasoning

PLAN

Get Organized Work with your classmates to prepare for the debate.

- Divide the class into teams. An equal number of students should be on each team. One will argue for more time in school, and one will argue against.
- Select one student to be the moderator for the debate. The moderator will play a neutral role, promoting civil discussion.

Gather Evidence Use the annotation tools in your eBook to find evidence in the texts. Save each piece of evidence to ***myNotebook*** in a folder titled *Collection 1 Performance Task A.*

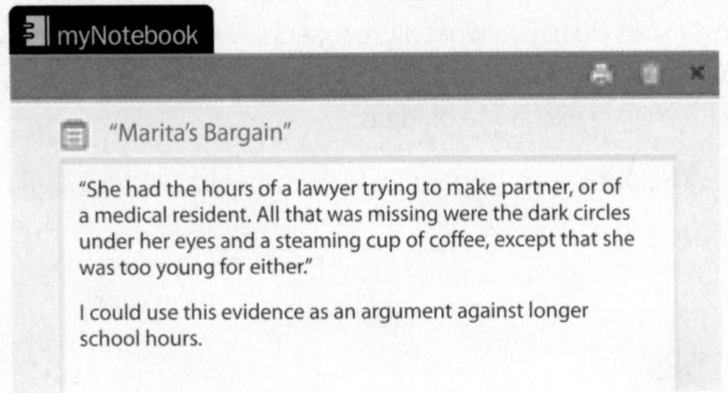

ACADEMIC VOCABULARY

As you build your argument, be sure to use these words.

accumulate
appreciation
conform
persistence
reinforce

PRODUCE

Build Your Argument

Build Your Argument Organize the reasons and evidence you have accumulated into an effective argument.

- Write a clear statement of your claim or position.
- Outline the main reasons that support your claim.
- Sort through the evidence you have collected from "Marita's Bargain," the other texts, and your own experience. Match each piece of evidence with the reason it most clearly supports.
- Think about the opposing claims the other team will likely make to refute your ideas. Plan the counterclaims you will make to challenge their opposing claims.
- Assign a debate role for each member of the team. One member will introduce the team's claim with supporting reasons and evidence. Other team members will exchange questions with a member of the opposing team to clarify and challenge reasoning. The last member will present a strong closing argument.
- Each debate team member should write out or make notes on the part of the argument he or she will present.
- Draft a closing statement that your last speaker will use to reinforce the strongest reasons for your position.

Working with your peers, develop a debate plan in *my*WriteSmart. Your group should focus on getting ideas down, rather than on perfecting the language.

Interactive Lessons

To help you write your argument, complete the following lesson:

- Writing Arguments: Building Effective Support

Language and Style: Offer and Justify Opinions

In a formal debate, the goal of each team is to negotiate with others and persuade members of the other team to change their position. In addition, a team member offers counterpoints to their opponent. Following are some ways students can negotiate with others to make sure their points are getting across:

To ask for clarification: Could you repeat that please?

To present a counterpoint: You make a valid point but my view is …

Have each team review their notes and use these phrases during the debate as applicable.

REVISE

Practice for the Debate A debate is more than a series of prepared statements read aloud. Participants listen closely to what all speakers say so that they can respond appropriately and build on others' ideas. Divide your team into two groups to practice for a lively exchange of ideas.

- Assign one group to argue for your team's position and the other to argue against it.
- The first speaker in each group should clearly state a position and provide reasons and evidence to support it. Subsequent speakers should provide additional support.

Interactive Lessons

To help you practice your debate, use:

- Participating in Collaborative Discussions: Listening and Responding

- The last speakers should summarize their groups' positions.
- When your practice debate is over, evaluate each other's reasoning and use of evidence. Discuss how you can improve your performance in the actual debate.
- Use appropriate eye contact, adequate volume, and clear pronunciations when you speak.

When your practice debate is over, review your argument as a team and make any revisions necessary to strengthen it. Use the chart below to help your revision.

Questions	Tips	Revision Techniques
Does my claim reflect my opinion on the issue?	**Underline** your claim.	If needed, **clarify** your position.
Do I have evidence to support my opinion?	**Circle** your evidence.	**Add** evidence from one or more texts if needed.
Have I anticipated opposing claims and refuted them with counterclaims?	**Highlight** text that refutes possible opposing claims.	**Add** counterclaims if needed to refute opposing claims.
Does the last speaker effectively sum up the argument?	**Underline** the conclusion.	**Clarify** your team's conclusion, adding a summary statement.

PRESENT

Hold the Debate With guidance from your teacher, stage your debate.

- The moderator should begin by introducing the topic of the debate and then recognizing speakers, alternating between the two teams.
- Take notes during the debate, noting any errors in reasoning or insufficient evidence from the other team. Be prepared to address these flaws when it is your turn to speak.
- When the debate is over, express appreciation for your opponents' work. Then vote on whether extending the amount of time students spend in school is a good idea.
- Discuss the reasons and evidence that you found most compelling.

PERFORMANCE TASK A RUBRIC
DEBATE

	Ideas and Evidence	Organization	Language
4	• The claim clearly states a position on a substantive topic or issue. • The debater's background research is noticeably thorough and accurate. • Valid reasons and relevant evidence from the texts convincingly support the claim. • Opposing claims are anticipated and effectively rebutted with counterclaims. • The concluding section effectively summarizes the claim.	• The reasons and textual evidence are organized consistently and logically throughout the argument. • Varied exchanges support opinions, offer counterpoints, and defend opinions.	• The speaker uses an appropriately formal style and an objective, or controlled, tone. • The debater speaks with confidence, clarity, and precision and completely keeps the audience's attention. • Grammar and usage are correct.
3	• The claim adequately states a position on an issue or topic. • The debater's research on the issue or topic is mostly thorough, but could be more extensive. • Most reasons and evidence from the texts support the speaker's claim, but they could be more convincing. • Opposing claims are anticipated, but the counterclaims need to be developed more. • The concluding section restates the claim.	• The organization of reasons and textual evidence is confusing in a few places. • One or more exchanges offer a counterpoint and defend opinions.	• The style is informal in a few places, and the tone is defensive at times. • The debater speaks with some confidence and clarity and mostly keeps the audience's attention. • Some grammatical and usage errors are repeated in the argument.
2	• The claim identifies an issue, but the speaker's position is not clearly stated. • The debater's research on the topic or issue is obviously limited. • The reasons and evidence from the texts are not always logical or relevant. • Opposing claims are anticipated but not addressed logically. • The concluding section includes an incomplete summary of the claim.	• The organization of reasons and textual evidence is logical in some places, but it often doesn't follow a pattern. • A counterpoint is not offered. Opinions are defended.	• The style becomes informal in many places, and the tone is often dismissive of the opposing team's viewpoints. • The debater speaks with uncertainty and minimally holds the audience's attention. • Grammar and usage are incorrect in many places, but the debater's ideas are still clear.
1	• The introduction and the statement of the claim are missing. • The debater shows little or no evidence of researching the issue or topic. • Significant supporting reasons and evidence from the texts are missing. • Opposing claims are neither anticipated nor rebutted. • The concluding section is missing.	• An organizational strategy is not used; reasons and textual evidence are presented randomly. • Counterpoints are not offered and opinions are not defended.	• The style is inappropriate, and the tone is disrespectful and combative. • The speaker sounds monotonous and does not capture the audience's attention. • Many grammatical and usage errors change the meaning of the debater's ideas.

Write a Compare-Contrast Essay

W 2a–f Write informative/explanatory texts.
W 4 Produce clear and coherent writing.
W 5 Develop writing by planning, revising, editing, rewriting.
W 9 Draw evidence from literary or informational texts.

The texts in this collection show the price some people are willing to pay to fulfill their ambitions. In the anchor text, "A Walk to the Jetty," the narrator goes abroad so she can get ahead in life, despite her painfully conflicted feelings about leaving behind her family and home. Write an essay in which you compare and contrast Annie John's experience with that of another character or person profiled in the collection. Discuss the sacrifices these individuals make and whether they are worth it.

An effective compare-contrast essay

- includes a controlling idea, or thesis statement, that contrasts Annie John's experience with that of another character or person in a collection text
- engages readers by introducing the topic with an interesting observation, quotation, or detail from one of the texts
- has an effective organization, such as subject-by-subject or point-by-point comparison
- develops the comparison with thorough evidence
- has a concluding section that synthesizes information from both texts and leaves the reader with an interesting insight

PLAN

Gather Evidence Use the annotation tools in your eBook to find evidence from "A Walk to the Jetty" and one other text. Save each piece of evidence to *my*Notebook, in a folder titled *Collection 1 Performance Task B.*

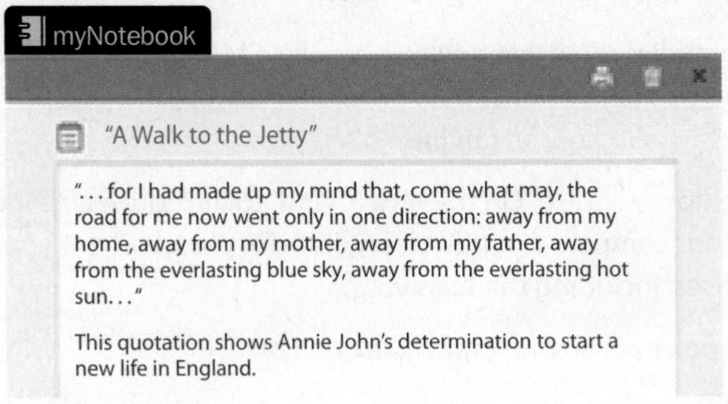

ACADEMIC VOCABULARY

As you write your essay, be sure to use these words.

accumulate
appreciation
conform
persistence
reinforce

Get Organized

Organize your details and evidence in an outline.

- Develop a thesis statement that will establish the focus of your comparison.
- Decide what organizational pattern you will use for your essay. Will you write everything you have to say about Annie John first, and then write about the other person or character (subject by subject)? Or, will you discuss one point as it relates to both Annie John and the other subject, and then move on to the next point (point by point)?
- Select an interesting quotation or detail to introduce your essay.
- Jot down some ideas for your concluding section.

Interactive Lessons

To help you create an outline, complete the following lesson:

- Using Textual Evidence: Writing an Outline

PRODUCE

*my*WriteSmart

Write your rough draft in *my*WriteSmart. Focus on getting your ideas down, rather than on perfecting your choice of language.

Draft Your Essay

Write a draft of your essay, following your outline.

- Introduce the subjects of your essay and the points you will compare. Be sure to give readers enough information to appreciate your thesis statement even if they are not familiar with the texts.
- Present your details, quotations, and examples from the texts in logically ordered paragraphs.
- Establish and maintain a formal style by avoiding contractions and slang. Adopt a neutral attitude to convey an objective tone.
- Write a final paragraph that synthesizes the ideas you have presented in the body of your essay. Explain why you think the sacrifices made were or were not worth the pain they involved, and draw your own conclusion about personal ambition.

Language and Style: Use Transitions

To make texts cohesive, writers use **transitions,** or connecting words, to link ideas, events, or reasons. Read this excerpt from "The Secret to Raising Smart Kids":

> "On the other hand, our studies show that teaching people to have a 'growth mind set,' which encourages a focus on effort rather than on intelligence or talent, helps make them into high achievers in school and in life."

Note how Dweck uses the transitional phrase "On the other hand" to introduce a new point to her argument. As you write your compare-contrast essay, look for places where you can add transitional words and phrases, including the following:

first, finally, meanwhile, however, on the contrary, in addition

REVISE

Improve Your Draft Use the following chart to improve your draft.

Questions	Tips	Revision Techniques
Does my introduction clearly state my thesis statement?	**Underline** your thesis statement.	If needed, **clarify** your thesis statement.
Have I used relevant evidence from each text to support my thesis?	**Highlight** your evidence.	**Add** or **change** evidence from one or more texts if needed.
Have I shown both similarities and differences between Annie John and the other individual?	**Underline** the similarities and differences.	**Add** more comparisons if necessary.
Have I used transitions to link the sections of my essay?	**Highlight** each transitional word or phrase.	**Add** transitions to clarify relationships between sections.
Does my conclusion synthesize information from the body of my essay?	**Underline** the conclusion.	**Clarify** your conclusion by adding a summary statement, if necessary.

Have your partner or a group of peers review your draft in *my*WriteSmart. Ask your reviewers to note any evidence that does not support your thesis.

Interactive Lessons

To help you revise your essay, complete the following lesson:

- Writing as a Process: Revising and Editing

PRESENT

Exchange Essays When your final draft is completed, exchange essays with a partner. Read your partner's essay and provide written feedback. Reread the criteria for an effective compare-contrast essay and ask the following questions:

- Which aspects of the essay are particularly strong?
- Which areas could be improved?

PERFORMANCE TASK B RUBRIC

COMPARE-CONTRAST ESSAY

	Ideas and Evidence	Organization	Language
4	• The introduction is appealing; the thesis statement clearly identifies the subjects and sets up points for comparison and contrast. • Concrete, relevant details and examples from the texts skillfully support each key point. • The concluding section effectively synthesizes the ideas, summarizes the points of comparison and contrast, and leaves the reader with a thought-provoking idea.	• Key points and supporting textual evidence are organized logically, effectively, and consistently throughout the essay. • Varied transitions successfully show the relationships between ideas.	• The essay has an appropriately formal style and a knowledgeable, objective tone. • Language is precise and effectively emphasizes similarities and differences. • Spelling, capitalization, and punctuation are correct. If handwritten, the essay is legible. • Grammar and usage are correct.
3	• The introduction could be more engaging; the thesis statement identifies the subjects and sets up one or two points for comparison and contrast. • One or two key points need more textual support. • The concluding section synthesizes most of the ideas and summarizes most points of comparison and contrast but offers no new insight.	• The organization of key points and supporting textual evidence is confusing in a few places. • A few more transitions are needed to connect ideas.	• The style becomes informal in a few places, and the tone does not always communicate confidence. • Most language is precise. • Several spelling, capitalization, and punctuation mistakes occur. If handwritten, the essay is mostly legible. • Some grammatical and usage errors are repeated in the essay.
2	• The introduction is commonplace; the thesis statement identifies the subjects and only hints at the points of comparison and contrast. • Evidence from the texts supports some key points but is often too general. • The concluding section gives an incomplete summary of the points of comparison and contrast and restates the thesis.	• Most key points are organized logically, but many supporting details from the texts are out of place. • More transitions are needed throughout the comparison to connect ideas.	• The style is informal in many places, and the tone communicates a superficial understanding of the subjects. • Language is repetitive or vague at times. • Spelling, capitalization, and punctuation are often incorrect but do not make reading the essay difficult. If handwritten, the essay may be partially illegible. • Grammar and usage are incorrect in many places, but the writer's ideas are still clear.
1	• The appropriate elements of an introduction are missing. • Evidence from the texts is irrelevant or missing. • An identifiable concluding section is missing.	• A logical organization is not apparent; ideas are presented randomly. • Transitions are not used, making the comparison-contrast essay difficult to understand.	• The style is informal, and the tone is inappropriate. • Language is inaccurate, repetitive, and vague. • Spelling, capitalization, and punctuation are incorrect throughout. If handwritten, the essay may be partially or mostly illegible. • Many grammatical and usage errors change the meaning of the writer's ideas.

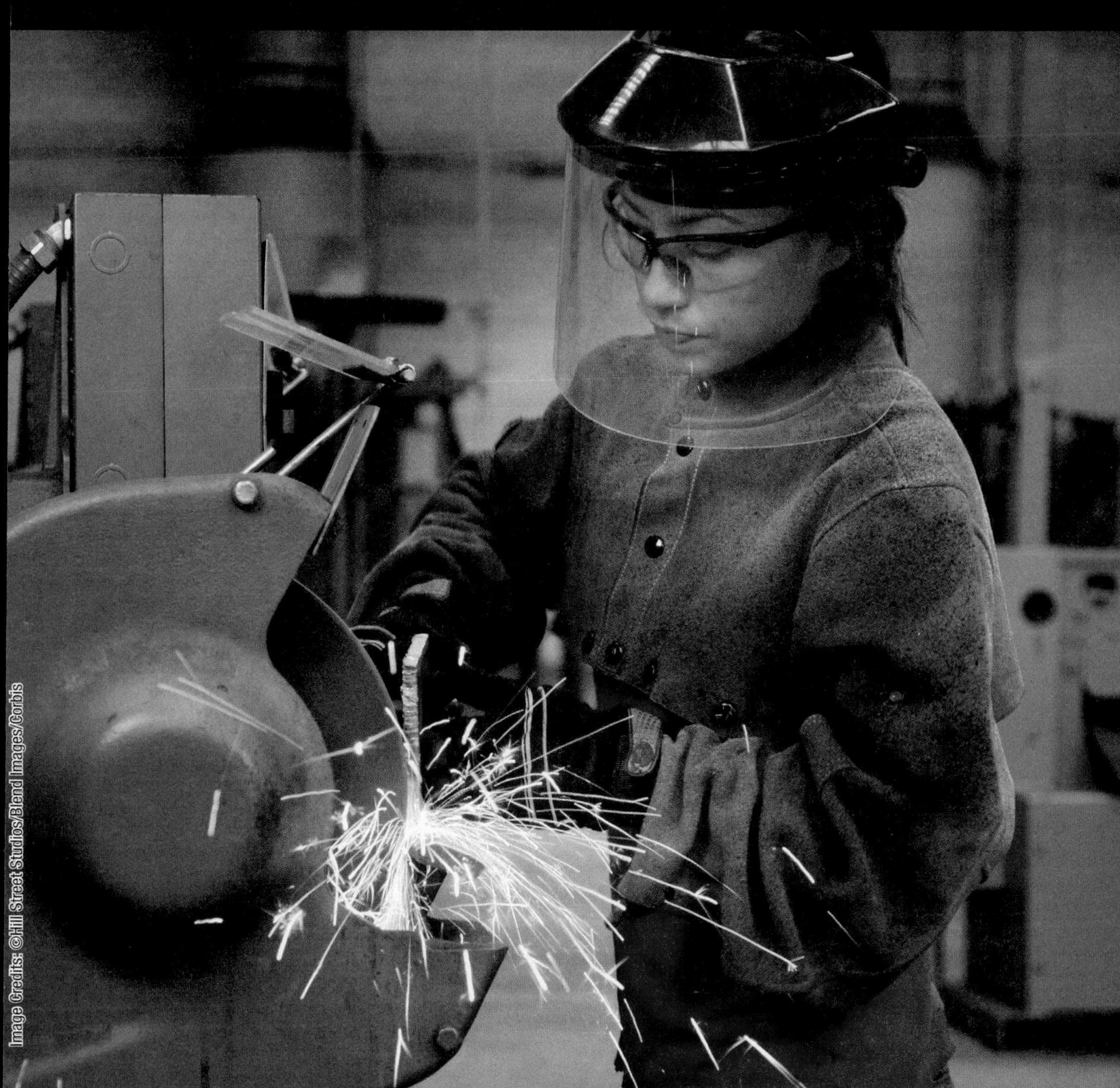

Image Credits: ©Hill Street Studios/Blend Images/Corbis

Gender Roles

"Like it or not, today we are all pioneers. . . . The old rules are no longer reliable guides to work out modern gender roles."

—Stephanie Coontz

This collection explores the traditional roles of men and women as well as changes in gender roles that have occurred in recent decades.

COLLECTION

PERFORMANCE TASK Preview

At the end of this collection, you will have the opportunity to complete two tasks:

- Write an essay about understanding between men and women.
- Present a reflective narrative about a significant experience in your life that has challenged or strengthened your beliefs in the differences between men and women.

ACADEMIC VOCABULARY

Study the words and their definitions in the chart below. You will use these words as you discuss and write about the texts in this collection.

Word	Definition	Related Forms
bias (bī´əs) *n.*	predisposition toward; preference for one thing over another	biased
complementary (kŏm´plə-mĕn´tə-rē) *adj.*	completing; forming a whole	complement, complementarity
exploit (ĭk-sploit´) *v.*	to take advantage of; to use for selfish or unethical purposes	exploitation, exploitative
inclinations (ĭn´klə-nā´shənz) *n.*	leanings toward; propensities for	incline, inclinable
predominance (prĭ-dŏm´ə-nəns) *v.*	superiority in control, force, or influence	predominate, predominant

HISTORY VIDEO

The Wife of Bath's Tale

from The Canterbury Tales

Narrative Poem by Geoffrey Chaucer translated by Nevill Coghill

Background *In 14th-century England, literacy was becoming more widespread and books more easily available. During this period, a number of narrative works were written in Middle English, which was starting to replace French and Latin as the main literary language. They included romances based on the King Arthur legends, short narrative poems known as ballads, and moral tales. The most important one, written in the late 1300s by Geoffrey Chaucer, was a long narrative work called* The Canterbury Tales.

Written mostly in verse, The Canterbury Tales *depicts a group of pilgrims traveling to the shrine of St. Thomas à Becket in Canterbury, England. At the beginning of their journey, the host of a tavern where they stop to rest proposes a story-telling contest, with the winner to receive a free dinner at the tavern.*

The Canterbury Tales *is distinguished by its realism, earthy humor, and shrewd insights into human nature. Chaucer's pilgrims represent a cross-section of medieval society, which allowed him to satirize institutions and practices of his time. The tales are preceded by prologues in which the characters often exchange comments and argue with one another. The selection you will read contains one of Chaucer's best-known tales and an excerpt from its prologue.*

Geoffrey Chaucer *(1342?–1400) held political positions for most of his adult life. In addition to* The Canterbury Tales, *he wrote the tragic verse romance* Troilus and Criseyde. *Upon his death, as a mark of respect, he was buried in Westminster Abbey, an honor rarely given to a commoner.*

AS YOU READ Pay attention to details that reveal the personality of the Wife of Bath. Write down any questions you generate during reading.

As you read, mark up the text. Save your work to ***myNotebook***.

- Highlight details
- Add notes and questions
- Add new words to ***myWordList***

The Wife of Bath's Prologue

The Friar laughed when he had heard all this.
"Well, Ma'am," he said, "as God may send me bliss,
This is a long **preamble** to a tale!"
But when the Summoner heard the Friar rail,
"Just look!" he cried, "by the two arms of God!
These meddling friars are always on the prod!
Don't we all know a friar and a fly
Go prod and buzz in every dish and pie!
What do you mean with your 'preambulation'?
Amble yourself, trot, do a meditation!
You're spoiling all our fun with your commotion."
The Friar smiled and said, "Is that your motion?
I promise on my word before I go
To find occasion for a tale or so
About a summoner that will make us laugh."
"Well, damn your eyes, and on my own behalf,"
The Summoner answered, "mine be damned as well
If I can't think of several tales to tell
About the friars that will make you mourn
Before we get as far as Sittingbourne.
Have you no patience? Look, he's in a huff!"
Our Host called out, "Be quiet, that's enough!
Shut up, and let the woman tell her tale.
You must be drunk, you've taken too much ale.
Now, Ma'am, you go ahead and no demur."
"All right," she said, "it's just as you prefer,
If I have licence from this worthy friar."
"Nothing," said he, "that I should more desire."

preamble (prē´ăm´bəl) *n.* an introductory statement.

The Wife of Bath's Tale

When good King Arthur ruled in ancient days
(A king that every Briton loves to praise)
This was a land brim-full of fairy folk.
The Elf-Queen and her courtiers joined and broke
Their elfin dance on many a green mead,
Or so was the opinion once, I read,
Hundreds of years ago, in days of yore.
But no one now sees fairies any more.
For now the saintly charity and prayer
Of holy friars seem to have purged the air;
They search the countryside through field and stream
As thick as motes that speckle a sun-beam,
Blessing the halls, the chambers, kitchens, bowers,
Cities and boroughs, castles, courts and towers,

33 mead: meadow.

40 motes: specks of dust.

41 bowers: bedrooms.

Thorpes, barns and stables, outhouses and dairies,
And that's the reason why there are no fairies.
Wherever there was wont to walk an elf
Today there walks the holy friar himself
As evening falls or when the daylight springs,
Saying his matins and his holy things,
Walking his limit round from town to town.
Women can now go safely up and down
By every bush or under every tree;
There is no other incubus but he,
So there is really no one else to hurt you
And he will do no more than take your **virtue**.

Now it so happened, I began to say,
Long, long ago in good King Arthur's day,
There was a knight who was a lusty liver.
One day as he came riding from the river
He saw a maiden walking all forlorn
Ahead of him, alone as she was born.
And of that maiden, spite of all she said,
By very force he took her maidenhead.
This act of violence made such a stir,
So much petitioning to the king for her,
That he condemned the knight to lose his head
By course of law. He was as good as dead
(It seems that then the statutes took that view)
But that the queen, and other ladies too,
Implored the king to exercise his grace
So ceaselessly, he gave the queen the case
And granted her his life, and she could choose
Whether to show him mercy or refuse.

The queen returned him thanks with all her might,
And then she sent a summons to the knight
At her convenience, and expressed her will:
"You stand, for such is the position still,
In no way certain of your life," said she,
"Yet you shall live if you can answer me:
What is the thing that women most desire?
Beware the axe and say as I require.

"If you can't answer on the moment, though,
I will concede you this: you are to go
A twelvemonth and a day to seek and learn
Sufficient answer, then you shall return.
I shall take gages from you to extort
Surrender of your body to the court."

43 thorpes: villages; **outhouses:** sheds.

45 wherever . . . elf: wherever an elf was accustomed to walk.

49 limit: the area to which a friar was restricted in his begging for donations.

52 incubus (ĭn´kyə-bəs): an evil spirt beliveed to descend on women.

virtue
(vûr´cho͞o) *n.* purity or virginity.

61–62 of that maiden . . . maidenhead: in spite of the maiden's protests, he robbed her of her virginity.

85 gages: pledges.

Sad was the knight and sorrowfully sighed,
But there! All other choices were denied,
And in the end he chose to go away
And to return after a year and day
Armed with such answer as there might be sent
To him by God. He took his leave and went.

He knocked at every house, searched every place,
Yes, anywhere that offered hope of grace.
What could it be that women wanted most?
But all the same he never touched a coast,
Country or town in which there seemed to be
Any two people willing to agree.

Some said that women wanted wealth and treasure,
"Honor," said some, some "Jollity and pleasure,"
Some "Gorgeous clothes" and others "Fun in bed,"
"To be oft widowed and remarried," said
Others again, and some that what most mattered
Was that we should be cosseted and flattered.
That's very near the truth, it seems to me;
A man can win us best with flattery.
To dance attendance on us, make a fuss,
Ensnares us all, the best and worst of us.

Some say the things we most desire are these:
Freedom to do exactly as we please,
With no one to reprove our faults and lies,
Rather to have one call us good and wise.
Truly there's not a woman in ten score
Who has a fault, and someone rubs the sore,
But she will kick if what he says is true;
You try it out and you will find so too.
However vicious we may be within
We like to be thought wise and void of sin.
Others assert we women find it sweet
When we are thought dependable, discreet
And secret, firm of purpose and controlled,
Never betraying things that we are told.
But that's not worth the handle of a rake;
Women conceal a thing? For Heaven's sake!
Remember Midas? Will you hear the tale?

Among some other little things, now stale,
Ovid relates that under his long hair
The unhappy Midas grew a splendid pair
Of ass's ears; as subtly as he might,
He kept his foul deformity from sight;

104 cosseted (kŏs´ĭ-tĭd): pampered.

113 ten score: 200.

115 but she will: who will not.

118 void of sin: sinless.

125 Midas: a legendary king of Phrygia, in Asia Minor.

127 Ovid (ŏv´ĭd): an ancient Roman poet whose *Metamorphoses* is a storehouse of Greek and Roman legends.

Save for his wife, there was not one that knew.
He loved her best, and trusted in her too.
He begged her not to tell a living creature
That he possessed so horrible a feature.
And she—she swore, were all the world to win,
She would not do such villainy and sin
As saddle her husband with so foul a name;
Besides to speak would be to share the shame.
Nevertheless she thought she would have died
Keeping this secret bottled up inside;
It seemed to swell her heart and she, no doubt,
Thought it was on the point of bursting out.

131 save: except.

Fearing to speak of it to woman or man,
Down to a reedy marsh she quickly ran
And reached the sedge. Her heart was all on fire
And, as a bittern bumbles in the mire,
She whispered to the water, near the ground,
"Betray me not, O water, with thy sound!
To thee alone I tell it: it appears
My husband has a pair of ass's ears!
Ah! My heart's well again, the secret's out!
I could no longer keep it, not a doubt."
And so you see, although we may hold fast
A little while, it must come out at last,
We can't keep secrets; as for Midas, well,
Read Ovid for his story; he will tell.

145 sedge: marsh grasses.

146 bumbles in the mire: booms in the swamp. (The bittern, a wading bird, is famous for its loud call.)

This knight that I am telling you about
Perceived at last he never would find out
What it could be that women loved the best.
Faint was the soul within his sorrowful breast,
As home he went, he dared no longer stay;
His year was up and now it was the day.

As he rode home in a dejected mood
Suddenly, at the margin of a wood,
He saw a dance upon the leafy floor
Of four and twenty ladies, nay, and more.
Eagerly he approached, in hope to learn
Some words of wisdom ere he should return;
But lo! Before he came to where they were,
Dancers and dance all vanished into air!
There wasn't a living creature to be seen
Save one old woman crouched upon the green.
A fouler-looking creature I suppose
Could scarcely be imagined. She arose
And said, "Sir knight, there's no way on from here.

Tell me what you are looking for, my dear,
For peradventure that were best for you;
We old, old women know a thing or two."

177 peradventure: maybe, possibly.

"Dear Mother," said the knight, "alack the day!
I am as good as dead if I can't say
What thing it is that women most desire;
If you could tell me I would pay your hire."
"Give me your hand," she said, "and swear to do
Whatever I shall next require of you
—If so to do should lie within your might—
And you shall know the answer before night."
"Upon my honor," he answered, "I agree."
"Then," said the crone, "I dare to guarantee
Your life is safe; I shall make good my claim.
Upon my life the queen will say the same.
Show me the very proudest of them all
In costly coverchief or jewelled caul
That dare say no to what I have to teach.
Let us go forward without further speech."
And then she crooned her gospel in his ear
And told him to be glad and not to fear.

179 alack the day: an exclamation of sorrow, roughly equivalent to "Woe is me!"

192 coverchief: kerchief; **caul** (kaul): an ornamental hairnet.

195 gospel: message.

They came to court. This knight, in full array,
Stood forth and said, "O Queen, I've kept my day
And kept my word and have my answer ready."

197 in full array: in all his finery.

There sat the noble matrons and the heady
Young girls, and widows too, that have the grace
Of wisdom, all assembled in that place,
And there the queen herself was throned to hear
And judge his answer. Then the knight drew near
And silence was commanded through the hall.

200 heady: giddy; impetuous.

201 grace: gift.

The queen gave order he should tell them all
What thing it was that women wanted most.
He stood not silent like a beast or post,
But gave his answer with the ringing word
Of a man's voice and the assembly heard:

"My liege and lady, in general," said he,
"A woman wants the self-same **sovereignty**
Over her husband as over her lover,
And master him; he must not be above her.
That is your greatest wish, whether you kill
Or spare me; please yourself. I wait your will."

211 liege (lēj): lord.

sovereignty (sŏv′ər-ĭn-tē) *n.* independent rule or authority.

In all the court not one that shook her head
Or contradicted what the knight had said;
Maid, wife and widow cried, "He's saved his life!"

And on the word up started the old wife,
The one the knight saw sitting on the green,
And cried, "Your mercy, sovereign lady queen!
Before the court disperses, do me right!
'Twas I who taught this answer to the knight,
For which he swore, and pledged his honor to it,
That the first thing I asked of him he'd do it,
So far as it should lie within his might.
Before this court I ask you then, sir knight,
To keep your word and take me for your wife;
For well you know that I have saved your life.
If this be false, deny it on your sword!"

"Alas!" he said, "Old lady, by the Lord
I know indeed that such was my behest,
But for God's love think of a new request,
Take all my goods, but leave my body free."
"A curse on us," she said, "if I agree!
I may be foul, I may be poor and old,
Yet will not choose to be, for all the gold
That's bedded in the earth or lies above,
Less than your wife, nay, than your very love!"

"My love?" said he. "By heaven, my damnation!
Alas that any of my race and station
Should ever make so foul a misalliance!"
Yet in the end his pleading and defiance
All went for nothing, he was forced to wed.

233 behest (bĭ-hĕst´): promise.

242 race and station: family and rank.

243 misalliance (mĭs´ə-lī´əns): an unsuitable marriage.

He takes his ancient wife and goes to bed.

Now peradventure some may well suspect
A lack of care in me since I neglect
To tell of the rejoicing and display
Made at the feast upon their wedding-day.
I have but a short answer to let fall;
I say there was no joy or feast at all,

Nothing but heaviness of heart and sorrow.
He married her in private on the morrow
And all day long stayed hidden like an owl,
It was such torture that his wife looked foul.

Great was the anguish churning in his head
When he and she were piloted to bed;
He wallowed back and forth in desperate style.
His ancient wife lay smiling all the while;
At last she said, "Bless us! Is this, my dear,
How knights and wives get on together here?
Are these the laws of good King Arthur's house?
Are knights of his all so contemptuous?
I am your own beloved and your wife,
And I am she, indeed, that saved your life;
And certainly I never did you wrong.
Then why, this first of nights, so sad a song?
You're carrying on as if you were half-witted.
Say, for God's love, what sin have I committed?
I'll put things right if you will tell me how."

"Put right?" he cried. "That never can be now!
Nothing can ever be put right again!
You're old, and so abominably plain,
So poor to start with, so low-bred to follow;
It's little wonder if I twist and wallow!
God, that my heart would burst within my breast!"

"Is that," said she, "the cause of your unrest?"

"Yes, certainly," he said, "and can you wonder?"

"I could set right what you suppose a blunder,
That's if I cared to, in a day or two,
If I were shown more courtesy by you.
Just now," she said, "you spoke of gentle birth,
Such as descends from ancient wealth and worth.
If that's the claim you make for gentlemen
Such arrogance is hardly worth a hen.

258 piloted: led. (In the Middle Ages, the wedding party typically escorted the bride and groom to their bedchamber.).

259 wallowed: (wŏl´ōd) rolled around; thrashed about.

Whoever loves to work for virtuous ends,
Public and private, and who most intends
To do what deeds of gentleness he can,
Take him to be the greatest gentleman.
Christ wills we take our gentleness from Him,
Not from a wealth of ancestry long dim,
Though they **bequeath** their whole establishment
By which we claim to be of high descent.
Our fathers cannot make us a bequest
Of all those virtues that became them best
And earned for them the name of gentlemen,
But bade us follow them as best we can.

"Thus the wise poet of the Florentines,
Dante by name, has written in these lines,
For such is the opinion Dante launches:
'Seldom arises by these slender branches
Prowess of men, for it is God, no less,
Wills us to claim of Him our gentleness.'
For of our parents nothing can we claim
Save temporal things, and these may hurt and maim.

"But everyone knows this as well as I;
For if gentility were implanted by
The natural course of lineage down the line,
Public or private, could it cease to shine
In doing the fair work of gentle deed?
No vice or villainy could then bear seed.

"Take fire and carry it to the darkest house
Between this kingdom and the Caucasus,
And shut the doors on it and leave it there,
It will burn on, and it will burn as fair
As if ten thousand men were there to see,
For fire will keep its nature and degree,
I can assure you, sir, until it dies.

"But gentleness, as you will recognize,
Is not annexed in nature to possessions.
Men fail in living up to their professions;
But fire never ceases to be fire.
God knows you'll often find, if you enquire,
Some lording full of villainy and shame.
If you would be esteemed for the mere name
Of having been by birth a gentleman
And stemming from some virtuous, noble clan,
And do not live yourself by gentle deed
Or take your father's noble code and creed,

bequeath (bĭ-kwēth´) *v.* to pass on to heirs.

299 Florentines: the people of Florence, Italy.

300 Dante (dän´tā): a famous medieval Italian poet. Lines 302–304 refer to a passage in Dante's most famous work, *The Divine Comedy*.

306 temporal: worldly, rather than spiritual.

308 gentility (jĕn-tĭl´ĭ-tē): the quality possessed by a gentle, or noble, person.

314 Caucasus (kô´kə-səs): a region of western Asia, between the Black and Caspian seas.

322 professions: beliefs; ideals.

325 lording: lord; nobleman.

“Gentility must come from God alone.”

You are no gentleman, though duke or earl.
Vice and bad manners are what make a churl.

“Gentility is only the renown
For bounty that your fathers handed down,
Quite foreign to your person, not your own;
Gentility must come from God alone.
That we are gentle comes to us by grace
And by no means is it bequeathed with place.

“Reflect how noble (says Valerius)
Was Tullius surnamed Hostilius,
Who rose from poverty to nobleness.
And read Boethius, Seneca no less,
Thus they express themselves and are agreed:
‘Gentle is he that does a gentle deed.’
And therefore, my dear husband, I conclude
That even if my ancestors were rude,
Yet God on high—and so I hope He will—
Can grant me grace to live in virtue still,
A gentlewoman only when beginning
To live in virtue and to shrink from sinning.

“As for my poverty which you reprove,
Almighty God Himself in whom we move,
Believe and have our being, chose a life
Of poverty, and every man or wife,
Nay, every child can see our Heavenly King
Would never stoop to choose a shameful thing.
No shame in poverty if the heart is gay,
As Seneca and all the learned say.
He who accepts his poverty unhurt
I’d say is rich although he lacked a shirt.
But truly poor are they who whine and fret
And covet what they cannot hope to get.
And he that, having nothing, covets not,
Is rich, though you may think he is a sot.

332 churl (chûrl): low-class person; boor.

339 Valerius (və-lîr´ē-əs): Valerius Maximus, a Roman writer who compiled a collection of historical anecdotes.

340 Tullius (tŭl´ē-əs) surnamed Hostilius (hŏ-stĭl´ē-əs): the third king of the Romans.

342 Boethius (bō-ē´thē-əs): a Christian philosopher of the Dark Ages; **Seneca** (sĕn´ĭ-kə): an ancient Roman philosopher, writer, teacher, and politician.

364 sot: fool.

"True poverty can find a song to sing.
Juvenal says a pleasant little thing:
'The poor can dance and sing in the relief
Of having nothing that will tempt a thief.'
Though it be hateful, poverty is good,
A great incentive to a livelihood,
And a great help to our capacity
For wisdom, if accepted patiently.
Poverty is, though wanting in estate,
A kind of wealth that none calumniate.
Poverty often, when the heart is lowly,
Brings one to God and teaches what is holy,
Gives knowledge of oneself and even lends
A glass by which to see one's truest friends.
And since it's no offense, let me be plain;
Do not **rebuke** my poverty again.

"Lastly you taxed me, sir, with being old.
Yet even if you never had been told
By ancient books, you gentlemen engage,
Yourselves in honor to respect old age.
To call an old man 'father' shows good breeding,
And this could be supported from my reading.

"You say I'm old and fouler than a fen.
You need not fear to be a cuckold, then.
Filth and old age, I'm sure you will agree,
Are powerful wardens over chastity.
Nevertheless, well knowing your delights,
I shall fulfil your worldly appetites.

"You have two choices; which one will you try?
To have me old and ugly till I die,
But still a loyal, true, and humble wife
That never will displease you all her life,
Or would you rather I were young and pretty
And chance your arm what happens in a city
Where friends will visit you because of me,
Yes, and in other places too, maybe.
Which would you have? The choice is all your own."

The knight thought long, and with a piteous groan
At last he said, with all the care in life,
"My lady and my love, my dearest wife,
I leave the matter to your wise decision.
You make the choice yourself, for the provision
Of what may be agreeable and rich

366 Juvenal (jo͞o′və-nəl): an ancient Roman satirist.

373 wanting in estate: lacking in grandeur.

374 calumniate (kə-lŭm′nē-āt′): criticize with false statements; slander.

rebuke (rĭ-byo͞ok′) *v.* to reprimand or scold.

387 fen: marsh.

388 cuckold (kŭk′əld): a husband whose wife is unfaithful.

398 chance your arm: take your chance on.

In honor to us both, I don't care which;
Whatever pleases you suffices me."

"And have I won the mastery?" said she,
"Since I'm to choose and rule as I think fit?"
"Certainly, wife," he answered her, "that's it."
"Kiss me," she cried. "No quarrels! On my oath
And word of honor, you shall find me both,
That is, both fair and faithful as a wife;
May I go howling mad and take my life
Unless I prove to be as good and true
As ever wife was since the world was new!
And if tomorrow when the sun's above
I seem less fair than any lady-love,
Than any queen or empress east or west,
Do with my life and death as you think best.
Cast up the curtain, husband. Look at me!"

And when indeed the knight had looked to see,
Lo, she was young and lovely, rich in charms.
In ecstasy he caught her in his arms,
His heart went bathing in a bath of blisses
And melted in a hundred thousand kisses,
And she responded in the fullest measure
With all that could delight or give him pleasure.

So they lived ever after to the end
In perfect bliss; and may Christ Jesus send
Us husbands meek and young and fresh in bed,
And grace to overbid them when we wed.
And—Jesu hear my prayer!—cut short the lives
Of those who won't be governed by their wives;
And all old, angry niggards of their pence,
God send them soon a very pestilence!

COLLABORATIVE DISCUSSION With a partner, discuss your impression of the Wife of Bath. Explain whether you think her tale is well-suited to her personality.

Analyze Structure: Frame Story

RL 5

The Canterbury Tales has a complex structure that features a **frame story**—a story that surrounds and binds together one or more different narratives in a single work. The frame story in *The Canterbury Tales* is made up of the General Prologue, in which the characters, setting, and storytelling premise are introduced, as well as the main narrator's account of what the pilgrims say and do between each of their tales.

In addition to unifying the tales told by the pilgrims, the frame story provides a vivid portrait of each pilgrim. Through the initial descriptions as well as the later interactions among the pilgrims, readers learn about the places they occupy in medieval society. These interactions enable Chaucer to present insights about practices and institutions in this time period; for example, his portrayals of the clergy and church officials reveal the corruption of the church.

Chaucer also uses the frame story to explore relationships between pilgrims. In "The Wife of Bath's Prologue," the Friar interrupts the Wife of Bath's long account of her five husbands, which prefaces her actual story: "Well, Ma'am, . . . as God may send me bliss,/ This is a long preamble to a tale!" His comment reveals the antagonism between the two of them, which is further developed in the Wife's tale.

Analyze Story Elements: Narrator

RL 3

The **narrator** of a story is the character or voice that relates the story's events to the reader. Chaucer created multiple narrators for *The Canterbury Tales*. The narrator of the frame story describes the pilgrims and records their exchanges with one another. The pilgrims, in turn, narrate their own tales. You can gain insight into the Wife of Bath by examining the following elements in her narration:

Subject and Theme	Direct Statements	Tone
Narrators who are characters in a story usually choose subjects and themes relevant to their own experiences. For example, the Wife of Bath, who has been married five times, tells a tale about relationships between men and women.	Narrators sometimes comment directly on characters and events. The Wife of Bath makes statements on a variety of topics, such as the type of husband she values and the ability of women to keep secrets.	A narrator's tone, or attitude toward a subject, provides clues about the narrator's personality. Usually tone is communicated through word choice and details. Notice the words that the Wife of Bath uses to describe the knight's predicament. What kind of person comes across through this tone?

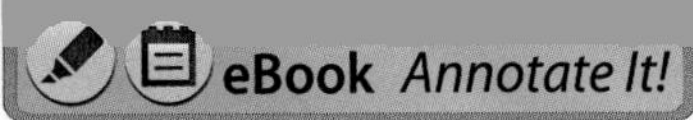

Analyzing the Text

RL 1, RL 2, RL 3, RL 5, W 4

Cite Text Evidence Support your responses with evidence from the selection.

1. **Identify** The interaction between the Wife of Bath and the Friar in "The Wife of Bath's Prologue" is part of Chaucer's frame story. What connections can be made between this section of the prologue and the tale itself?
2. **Infer** As a narrator, the Wife of Bath comments extensively about the various answers to the knight's question. What do her comments reveal about her own values and ideas? Use evidence from the poem to support your analysis.
3. **Draw Conclusions** The story of Midas appears to be unrelated to the tale of the knight. What narrative purpose or purposes does this digression serve?
4. **Analyze** What is the Wife's tone as she narrates the account of the knight's wedding night? How does her tone influence readers' view of this scene?
5. **Analyze** Chaucer explores the idea that "appearances can be deceiving" through the character of the old woman. How does this theme relate to the earlier events in the tale?
6. **Evaluate** Review the last two stanzas of the poem. Does this happy ending provide a satisfying conclusion, or is it disturbing? Explain your response.
7. **Critique** In "The Wife of Bath's Prologue," the Friar complains about the Wife of Bath's long, rambling preamble. How effective is she at narrating her tale about the knight? Explain your response.

PERFORMANCE TASK

Writing Activity: Character Analysis When the queen demands that the knight find out "What is the thing that women most desire?" he searches for a whole year to find an answer. Does the knight gain understanding of women over the course of the story, or is he still essentially the same as he was at the beginning? Respond to this question by writing a character analysis. Consider the following:

- the knight's initial crime
- his reaction to the old woman after she insists that he marry her
- his response to the choice she offers him on their wedding night

Critical Vocabulary

L 1a, L 1b

preamble **virtue** **sovereignty**

bequeath **rebuke**

Practice and Apply Use your knowledge of the Critical Vocabulary words to respond to each question.

1. The Wife of Bath chose some of her husbands based on what they could *bequeath* to her. What characteristic did these husbands share?
2. The nuns on the pilgrimage wear clothes that protect their *virtue*. What do their outfits probably look like?
3. After the Friar tells his tale, the Wife of Bath *rebukes* him. What does the Wife think of the tale?
4. As a widow, the Wife of Bath has *sovereignty* over her financial affairs. What can she spend her money on? Explain.
5. Because of the long *preamble*, listeners were prepared for the surprising nature of the tale. Explain why.

Vocabulary Strategy: Usage

The English language is dynamic. New words become part of it; other words are dropped; still others are used in a way that is different from their original or earlier meanings. In line 54 of the poem, Chaucer uses the Critical Vocabulary word *virtue*. "And he will do no more than take your virtue." In this line, *virtue* means "chastity" or "purity." Readers today, however, more commonly interpret *virtue* to mean "a good quality." The chart shows examples of other words found in the poem that are used differently today than they were in Chaucer's time:

Word in the Poem	Meaning in the 14th Century
gentle: "Gentle is he that does a gentle deed."	noble
rude: "even if my ancestors were rude"	of low birth
fair: "And if tomorrow when the sun's above I seem less fair than any lady-love"	beautiful

Practice and Apply Complete the following steps:

1. Define the word in the chart as it is commonly used today.
2. Write a sentence that illustrates a current usage of each word.
3. Work in a small group to identify other words in the poem that have changed their meanings over the years. Share the words and their old and new usages with the class.

Language and Style: Inverted Sentences

L 3a

An **inverted sentence** is one in which the normal order of a subject followed by a verb is reversed. Notice how Chaucer uses inversion in these lines from the poem:

This knight that I am telling you about
Perceived at last he never would find out
What it could be that women loved the best.
Faint was the soul within his sorrowful breast,
As home he went, he dared no longer stay;
His year was up and now it was the day.

If Chaucer had chosen not to use inversion, his lines might have appeared this way:

This knight that I am telling you about
Perceived at last he never would find out
What it could be that women loved the best.
His soul within his sorrowful breast was faint,
As home he went, he dared no longer stay;
His year was up and now it was the day.

By inverting the sentence in the fourth line, Chaucer preserves his rhyming couplet. Just as importantly he maintains the effective rhythm of his poem. In the second version of the lines with the subject placed before the verb, the rhyme is lost. In addition, the rhythm of the line is stilted and awkward and takes away from the effectiveness of the whole stanza.

Writers of prose also use inversion. Varying sentence structure by reversing the subject-verb order enables writers to refocus the attention of their readers. In addition, inverted sentences add emphasis by building up suspense with words and phrases before arriving at the verb and subject. When inverting sentences in your own writing, it is important to remember to check that the subject and verb agree in number.

Regular Order	Inverted Order
The old woman lurks behind the knights.	Behind the knights lurks the old woman.
The knights travel over the fields and through every village.	Over the fields and through every village travel the knights.

Practice and Apply Write three inverted sentences about events in "The Wife of Bath's Tale."

Mohammed Naseehu Ali (b. 1971) *was born in Ghana, a country in western Africa. He came to the United States in 1988 at the age of 16 to pursue his education, graduating from Bennington College in Vermont. Although he lives in New York City, the roots of his writing are in Ghana. He wants "to document the history of the Ghanaian people, so that civilization doesn't only see Africa and African people as an exotic people—but as normal people." "Mallam Sile" is from* The Prophet of Zongo Street, *his first published collection. It is set in a fictional Muslim neighborhood in Ghana.*

Mallam Sile

Short Story by Mohammed Naseehu Ali

AS YOU READ Take note of the details that help you understand the character of Mallam Sile. Write down any questions you generate during reading.

He was popularly known as *mai tea*, or the tea seller. His shop was situated right in the navel of Zongo Street—a stone's throw from the chief's assembly shed and adjacent to the kiosk where Mansa BBC, the town gossip, sold her provisions. Along with fried eggs and white butter bread, Mallam Sile carried all kinds of beverages: regular black tea, Japanese green tea, Milo, Bournvita, cocoa drink, instant coffee. But on Zongo Street all hot beverages were referred to just as tea, and it was common, therefore, to hear people say, "Mallam Sile, may I have a mug of cocoa tea?" or "Sile, may I have a cup of coffee tea?"

The tea shop had no windows. It was built of *wawa*, a cheap wood easily infested by termites. The floor was uncemented, and heaps of dust rose in the air whenever a customer walked in. Sile protected his merchandise from the dust by keeping everything in plastic bags. An enormous wooden "chop box," the top of which he used as a serving table, covered most of the space in the shop. There was a tall chair behind the chop box for Sile, but he never used it, preferring instead to stand on his feet even when the shop was empty. There were also three benches that were meant to be used only by those who bought tea, though the idle gossips who crowded the shop and never spent any money occupied the seats most of the time.

Old Sile had an irrational fear of being electrocuted and so he'd never tapped electricity into his shack, as was usually done on Zongo Street. Instead, he used kerosene lanterns, three of which hung from the low wooden ceiling. Sile kept a small radio in the shop, and whenever he had no customers he listened, in meditative silence, to the English programs on GBC 2, as though he understood what was being said. Mallam Sile was fluent only in his northern Sisaala tongue, though he understood Hausa—the language of the street's inhabitants—and spoke just enough pidgin to be able to conduct his business.

The mornings were usually slow for the tea seller, as a majority of the street folks preferred the traditional breakfast of *kókó da mása*, or corn porridge with rice cake. But, come evening, the shop was crowded with the street's young men and women, who gossiped and talked about the "laytes' neus" in town. Some came to the shop just to meet their loved ones. During the shop's peak hours—from eight in the evening until around midnight—one could hardly hear oneself talk because of the boisterous chattering that went on. But anytime Mallam Sile opened his mouth to add to a conversation people would say, "Shut up, Sile, what do you know about this?" or "Close your beak, Sile, who told you that?" The tea seller learned to swallow his words, and eventually spoke only when he was engaged in a transaction with a customer. But nothing said or even whispered in the shop escaped his sharp ears.

Mallam Sile was a loner, without kin on the street or anywhere else in the city. He was born in Nanpugu, a small border town in the north. He left home at age sixteen, and, all by himself, journeyed more than nine hundred miles in a cow truck to find work down south in Kumasi—the capital city of Ghana's gold-rich Ashanti region.

Within a week of his arrival in the city, Sile landed a job as a house servant. Although his monthly wages were meagre, he sent a portion of them home to his ailing parents, who lived like paupers in their drought-stricken village. Even so, Sile's efforts were not enough to save his parents from the claws of Death, who took them away in their sleep one night. They were found clinging tightly to each other, as if one of them had seen what was coming and had grabbed onto the other so that they could go together.

The young Sile received the news of his parents' death with mixed emotions. He was sad to lose them, of course, but he saw it as a well-deserved rest for them, as they both had been ill and bedridden for many months. Though Sile didn't travel up north to attend their funeral, he sent money for a decent burial. With his parents deceased, Sile suddenly found himself with more money in his hands. He quit his house-servant job and found another, selling iced *kenkey* in

Kumasi's central market. Sile kept every pesewa[1] he earned, and two years later he was able to use his savings to open a tea business. It was the first of such establishments on Zongo Street, and would remain the only one for many years to come.

Mallam Sile was short—so short, in fact, that many claimed he was a Pygmy. He stood exactly five feet one inch tall. Although he didn't have the broad, flat nose, poorly developed chin, and round head of the Pygmies, he was stout and hairy all over, as they were. A childhood illness that had caused Sile's vision to deteriorate had continued to plague him throughout his adult life. Yet he refused to go to the hospital and condemned any form of medication, traditional or Western. "God is the one who brings illness, and he is the only true healer"—this was Sile's simple, if rather mystical, explanation.

Sile's small face was covered with a thick, long beard. The wrinkles on his dark forehead and the moistness of his soft, squinted eyes gave him the appearance of a sage, one who had lived through and conquered many adversities in his life. His smile, which stretched from one wrinkled cheek to the other, baring his kola-stained teeth, radiated strength, wisdom, and self-confidence.

Sile wore the same outfit every day: a white polyester djellabah[2] and its matching *wando*, a loose pair of slacks that tied with strings at the waist. He had eight of these suits, and wore a different one each day of the week. Also, his head was perpetually shaved, and he was never without his white embroidered Mecca hat—worn by highly devout Muslims as a reflection of their submission to Allah. Like most of the street's dwellers, Sile owned just one pair of slippers at a time, and replaced them only when they were worn out beyond repair. An unusual birth defect that caused the tea seller to grow an additional toe on each foot had made it impossible for him to find footwear that fit him properly; special slippers were made for him by Anaba the cobbler, who used discarded car tires for the soles of the shoes he made. The rascals of Zongo Street, led by Samadu, the street's most notorious bully, poked at Sile's feet and his slippers, which they called *kalabilwala*, a nonsensical term that no one could understand, let alone translate.

At forty-six, Mallam Sile was still a virgin. He routinely made passes at the divorcées and widows who came to his shop, but none showed any interest in him whatsoever. "What would I do with a dwarf?" the women would ask, feeling ashamed of having had passes made at them by Sile. A couple of them seemed receptive to tea seller Sile's advances, but everyone knew that they were flirting with him only in order to get free tea.

Eventually, Sile resigned himself to his lack of success with women. He was convinced that he would die a virgin. Yet late at night,

[1] **pesewa** (pə-sā´wə): a small Ghanaian coin.

[2] **djellabah** (je-lä´bə): a long, hooded robe.

Eventually, Sile resigned himself to his lack of success with women. He was convinced that he would die a virgin.

after all the customers, idlers, and rumormongers had left the shop to seek refuge in their shanties and on their bug-ridden grass mattresses, Sile could be heard singing love songs, hoping that a woman somewhere would respond to his passionate cries:

A beautiful woman, they say,
Is like an elephant's meat.
And only the man with the sharpest knife
Can cut through.
That's what they say.

Young girl, I have no knife,
I am not a hunter of meat,
And I am not savage.
I am only looking for love.
This is what I say.

Up north where I am from,
Young girls are not what they are here.
Up north where I am from,
People don't judge you by your knife.
They look at the size of your heart.

Young girl, I don't know what you look like.
I don't know where to look for you.
I don't even know who you are, young girl.
All I know is: my heart is aching.
Oh, oh, oh! My heart is aching for you.

Sile's voice rang with melancholy when he sang his songs. But still the rascals derided him. "When are you going to give up, Sile?" they would say. "Can't you see that no woman would marry you?"

"I have given up on them long, long ago," he would reply. "But I am never going to give up on myself!"

"You keep fooling yourself," they told him, laughing.

The rascals' mocking didn't end there. Knowing that Mallam Sile couldn't see properly, they often used fake or banned cedi[3] notes to purchase tea from him at night. The tea seller pinned the useless bills to the walls of his shop as if they were good-luck charms. He believed that it was hunger—and not mischief—that had led the rascals to cheat him. And, since he considered it inhuman to refuse a hungry person food, Mallam Sile allowed them to get away with their frauds.

To cool off the hot tea for his customers, Sile poured the contents of one mug into another, raising one over the other. The rascals would push Sile in the middle of this process, causing the hot liquid to spill all over his arms. The tea seller was never angered by such pranks. He merely grinned and, without saying a word, wiped off the spilled tea and continued to serve his customers. And when the rascals blew out the lanterns in the shop, so as to steal bread and Milo while he was trying to rekindle the light, Sile accepted that, too. He managed to rid his heart of any ill feelings. He would wave his short arms to anyone who walked past his shop, and shout, by way of greeting, "How are the heavens with you, boy?" Sile called everyone "boy," including women and older people, and he hardly ever uttered a sentence without referring to the heavens.

He prided himself on his hard work, and smiled whenever he looked in the mirror and saw his dwarfish body and ailing eyes, two abnormalities that he had learned to love. A few months before the death of his parents, he had come to the conclusion that if Allah had made him any differently he would not have been Mallam Sile—and Mallam Sile was an individual whom Sile's heart, mind, and spirit had come to accept and respect. This created within him a peace that made it possible for him not only to tolerate the rascals' ill treatment but also to forgive them. Though in their eyes Sile was only a buffoon.

One sunny afternoon during the dry season, Mallam Sile was seen atop the roof of his shack with hammers, saws, pliers, and all kinds of building tools. He lingered there all day long like a stray monkey, and by dusk he had dismantled all the aluminum roofing sheets that had once sheltered him and his business. He resumed work early the following morning, and by about one-thirty, before *azafar*, the first of the two afternoon prayers, Sile had no place to call either home or tea shop—he had demolished the shack down to its dusty floor.

At three-thirty, after *la-asar*, the second afternoon worship, Mallam Sile moved his personal belongings and all his tea

[3] **cedi** (sā´dē): basic unit of currency in Ghana.

paraphernalia to a room in the servants' quarters of the chief's palace. The room had been arranged for him by the chief's wazir, or right-hand man, who was sympathetic to the tea seller.

paraphernalia (păr´ə-fər-nāl´yə) *n.* necessary equipment or utensils.

During the next two days, Mallam Sile ordered plywood and planks of *odum*, a wood superior to the *wawa* used for the old shop. He also ordered a few bags of cement and truckloads of sand and stones, and immediately began building a new shack, much bigger than the first.

The street folks were shocked by Sile's new building—they wondered where he had got the money to embark on such an enterprise. Sile was rumored to be constructing a mini-market store to compete with Alhaji Saifa, the owner of the street's provision store. (And though the tea seller denied the rumor, it rapidly spread up and down the street, eventually creating bad blood between Sile and Alhaji Saifa.)

It took three days for Mallam Sile to complete work on the new shop's foundation, and an additional three weeks for him to erect the wooden walls and the aluminum roofing sheets. While Sile was busy at work, passersby would call out, "How is the provision store coming?" or "*Mai tea*, how is the mansion coming?" Sile would reply simply, "It is coming well, boy. It will be completed soon, *Inshallah*."[4] He would grin his usual wide grin and wave his short hairy arms, and then return to his work.

Meanwhile, as the days and weeks passed, the street folks grew impatient and somewhat angry at the closing of Sile's shop. The nearest tea shack was three hundred metres away, on Zerikyi Road—and not only that but the owner of the shack, Abongo, was generally abhorred. And for good reason. Abongo, also a northerner, was quite unfriendly even to his loyal customers. He maintained a rigid no-credit policy, and made customers pay him even before they were served. No one was an exception to this policy—even if he or she was dying of hunger. And, unlike Sile, Abongo didn't tolerate idlers or loud conversation in his shop. If a customer persisted in chatting, Abongo reached for the customer's mug, poured the contents in a plastic basin, and refunded his money. He then chased the customer out of the shop, brandishing his bullwhip and cursing after him, "If your mama and papa never teach you manners, I'll teach you some! I'll sew those careless lips of yours together, you bastard son of a bastard woman!"

As soon as work on the shop was completed, Sile left for his home town. Soon afterward, yet another rumor surfaced: it was said that the tea seller had travelled up north in search of "black medicine" for his bad eyesight.

Sile finally returned one Friday evening, some six weeks after he'd begun work on the shop, flanked by a stern woman who looked to be in her late thirties and was three times larger than the tea seller. The

[4] **Inshallah** (ĭn-shä´lə): Arabic for "God willing."

woman, whose name was Abeeba, turned out to be Mallam Sile's wife. She was tall and massive, with a face as gloomy as that of someone mourning a dead relative. Like her husband, Abeeba said very little to people in or out of the shop. She, too, grinned and waved her huge arms whenever she greeted people, though, unlike the tea seller, she seemed to have something harder lurking behind her cheerful smile. Abeeba carried herself with the grace and confidence of a lioness, and covered her head and part of her face with an Islamic veil, a practice that had been dropped by most of the married women on Zongo Street.

The rascals asked Sile, when they ran into him at the market, "From where did you get this elephant? Better not get on her bad side; she'll sit on you till you sink into the ground." To this, the tea seller did not say a word.

Exactly one week after Sile's return from his village, he and his wife opened the doors of the new shop to their customers. Among the most talked-about features were the smooth concrete floor and the bright gas lantern that illuminated every corner. In a small wooden box behind the counter, Sile and his wife burned *tularen mayu*, or witches' lavender, a strong yet sweet-smelling incense that doubled as a jinx repellent—to drive bad spirits away from the establishment.

On the first night, the tea shop was so crowded that some customers couldn't find a seat, even with the twelve new metal folding chairs that Sile had bought. The patrons sang songs of praise to the variety of food on the new menu, which included meat pies, brown bread, custard, and Tom Brown, an imported grain porridge. Some of the patrons even went so far as to thank Sile and his wife for relieving them of "Abongo's nastiness." But wise old Sile, who was as familiar with the street folks' cynicism as he was with the palms of his hands, merely nodded and grinned his sheepish grin. He knew that, despite their praise, and despite the smiles they flashed his way, some customers were at that very moment thinking of ways to cheat him.

While Sile prepared the tea and food, Abeeba served and collected the money. Prior to the shop's reopening, Abeeba had tried to convince her husband that they, too, should adopt Abongo's no-credit policy. Sile had quickly frowned upon the idea, claiming that it was inhumane to do such a thing.

The tea seller and his wife debated the matter for three days before they came to a compromise. They agreed to extend credit, but only in special cases and also on condition that the debtor swear by the Koran to pay on time; if a debtor didn't make a payment, he or she would not be given any credit in the future. But, even with the new policy in place, it wasn't long before some of the customers reverted to their old habits and began skipping payments. Then an encounter between Abeeba and one of the defaulters changed everything.

What took place was this: Samadu, the **pugnacious** sixteen-year-old whose fame had reached every corner of the city, was the tough guy of Zongo Street. He was of medium height, muscular, and a natural-born athlete. For nine months running, no one in the neighborhood had managed to put Samadu's back to the ground in the haphazard wrestling contests held beside the central market's latrine. Samadu's "power" was such that parents paid him to protect their children from other bullies at school. He was also known for having tortured and even killed the livestock of the adults who denounced him. If they didn't have pets or domestic animals, he harassed their children for several days until he was appeased with cash or goods. Some parents won Samadu's friendship for their children by bribing him with gifts of money, food, or clothing.

pugnacious (pŭg-nā´shəs) *adj.* belligerent, inclined to quarrel.

Samadu, of course, was deeply in debt to Mallam Sile—he owed him eighty cedis, about four dollars. Early one Tuesday morning, Mallam Sile's wife showed up at Samadu's house to collect the money. Abeeba had tried to collect the debt amicably, but after her third futile attempt she had suggested to Sile that they use force to persuade the boy to pay. Sile had responded by telling his wife, "Stay out of that boy's way—he is dangerous. If he has decided not to pay, let him keep it. He will be the loser in the end."

"But, Mallam, it is an insult what he is doing," Abeeba argued. "I think people to whom we have been generous should only be generous in return. I am getting fed up with their ways, and the sooner the folks

here know that even the toad gets sick of filling his belly with the same dirty pond water every day, the better!" Though Sile wasn't sure what his wife meant, he let the matter drop.

When Abeeba arrived at Samadu's house, a number of housewives and young women were busily doing their morning chores in and around the compound—some sweeping and stirring up dust, others fetching water from the tap in the compound's center or lighting up charcoal pots to warm the food left over from the previous night. Abeeba greeted them politely and asked to be shown to the tough guy's door. The women tried to turn Abeeba away, as they feared that Samadu would humiliate her in some way. But Abeeba insisted that she had important business with him, and so the housewives reluctantly directed her to Samadu's room, which, like all the young men's rooms, was situated just outside the main compound.

The usual tactic that the street's teen-age boys used when fighting girls or women was to strip them of the wrapper around their waist, knowing that they would be reluctant to continue fighting half-naked. But Abeeba had heard young boys in the shop discussing Samadu's bullying ways and had come prepared for anything. She wore a sleeveless shirt and a pair of tight-fitting khaki shorts, and, for the first time ever, she had left her veil at home.

"You rogue! If you call yourself a man, come out and pay your debt!" Abeeba shouted, as she pounded on Samadu's door.

"Who do you think you are, ruining my sleep because of some useless eighty cedis?" Samadu screamed from inside.

"The money may be useless, but it is certainly worthier than you, and that's why you haven't been able to pay, you rubbish heap of a man!" Abeeba's voice was coarse and full of menace. The veins on her neck stood out, like those of the *juju* fighters at the annual wrestling contest. Her eyes moved rapidly inside her head, as though she were having a fit of some sort.

One of the onlookers, a famished-looking housewife, pleaded with the tea seller's wife, "Go back to your house, woman. Don't fight him, he will disgrace you in public." Another woman in the background added, "What kind of a woman thinks she can fight a man? Be careful, oh!"

Abeeba didn't pay any attention to the women's **admonitions**. Just then, a loud bang was heard inside the room. The door swung open, and Samadu stormed out, his face red with anger. "No one gets away with insulting me. No one!" he shouted. There was a line of dried drool on his right cheek, and whitish mucus had gathered in the corners of his eyes. "You ugly elephant-woman. After I am done with you today, you'll learn a lesson or two about why women don't grow beards!"

admonition (ăd′mə-nĭsh′ən) *n.* critical advice.

"Ha, you teach me a lesson? You?" Abeeba said. "I, too, will educate you about the need to have money in your pocket before you flag the candy man!" With this, she lunged at Samadu.

The women placed their palms on their breasts, and their bodies shook with dread. "Where are the men on the street? Come and separate the fight, oh! Men, come out, oh!" they shouted. The children in the compound, though freshly aroused from sleep, hopped about excitedly, as if they were watching a ritual. Half of them called out, "*Piri pirin-pi!,*" while the other half responded, "*Wein son!,*" as they chanted and cheered for Samadu.

Samadu knew immediately that if he engaged Abeeba in a wrestling match she would use her bulky mass to force him to the ground. His strategy, therefore, was to throw punches and kicks from a safe distance, thereby avoiding close contact. But Abeeba was a lot quicker than he imagined, and she managed to dodge the first five punches he threw. He threw a sixth punch, and missed. He stumbled over his own foot when he tried to connect the seventh, and landed inches from Abeeba. With blinding quickness, she seized him by the sleeping wrapper tied around his neck and began to punch him. The exuberant crowd was hushed by this unexpected turn of events.

But Samadu wasn't heralded as the street's tough guy for nothing. He threw a sharp jab at Abeeba's stomach and succeeded in releasing himself from her grip by deftly undoing the knot of his sleeping cloth. He was topless now, clad only in a pair of corduroy knickers. He danced on his feet, swung his arms, and moved his torso from side to side, the way true boxers do. The crowd got excited again and picked up the fight song, "*Piri pirin-pi, Wein son! Piri pirin-pi, Wein son!*" Some among them shouted "Ali! Ali! Ali!" as Samadu danced and pranced, carefully avoiding Abeeba, who watched his movements with the keenness of a hungry lioness.

The women in the crowd went from holding their breasts to slapping their massive thighs. They jumped about nervously, moving their bodies in rhythm to the chants. The boys booed Abeeba, calling her all sorts of names for the beasts of the jungle. "Destroy that elephant!" they shouted.

The harder the crowd cheered for Samadu, the fancier his footwork became. He finally threw a punch that landed on Abeeba's left shoulder, though she seemed completely unfazed and continued to chase him around the small circle created by the spectators. When Samadu next threw his fist, Abeeba anticipated it. She dodged, then grabbed his wrist and twisted his arm with such force that he let out a high-pitched cry: "*Wayyo* Allah!" The crowd gasped as the tough guy attempted to **extricate** himself from Abeeba's grip. He tightened all the muscles in his body and craned his neck. But her strength was just too much for him.

extricate (ĕk´strĭ-kāt´) *v.* to free from difficulty.

The crowd booed, "Wooh, ugly rhinoceros." Then, in a sudden, swift motion, Abeeba lifted the tough guy off the ground, raised him above her head (the crowd booed louder), and dumped him back down like a sack of rice. She then jumped on top of him and began to whack him violently.

The women, now frantic, shouted, "Where are the men in this house? Men, come out, oh! There is a fight!"

A handful of men came running to the scene, followed by many more a few minutes later.

Meanwhile, with each punch Abeeba asked, "Where is our money?"

"I don't have it, and wouldn't pay even if I did!" Samadu responded. The men drew nearer and tried to pull Abeeba off, but her grip on Samadu's waistband was too firm. The men pleaded with Abeeba to let go. "I will not release him until he pays us back our money!" she shouted. "And if he doesn't I'll drag his ass all the way to the Zongo police station."

On hearing this, an elderly man who lived in Samadu's compound ran inside the house; he returned a few minutes later with eighty cedis, which he placed in the palm of Abeeba's free hand. With one hand gripping Samadu's waistband, she used the fingers of the other to flip and count the money. Once she was sure the amount was right, she released the boy, giving him a mean, hard look as she left. The crowd watched silently, mouths agape, as though they had just witnessed something from a cinema reel.

Mallam Sile was still engaged in his morning *zikhr*, or meditation, when Abeeba returned to the shack. He, of course, had no inkling of what had taken place. Later, when Abeeba told him that Samadu had paid the money he owed, the tea seller, though surprised, didn't think to ask how this had happened. In his **naïveté**, he concluded that Samadu had finally been entered by the love and fear of God. Abeeba's news therefore confirmed Mallam Sile's long-standing belief that every man was capable of goodness, just as he was capable of evil.

naïveté (nī′ēv-tā′) *n.* lack of knowledge or experience.

The tea seller's belief was further solidified when he ran into Samadu a fortnight later. The tough guy greeted him politely, something he had never done before. When Mallam Sile related this

> "In a sudden, swift motion, Abeeba lifted the tough guy off the ground, raised him above her head (the crowd booed louder), and dumped him back down like a sack of rice."

to his wife, she restrained herself from telling him the truth. Abeeba knew that Sile would be quite displeased with her methods. Just a week ago, he had spoken to her about the pointlessness of using fire to put out fire, of how it "worsens rather than extinguishes the original flame." Abeeba prayed that no one else would tell her husband about her duel with Samadu, although the entire city seemed to know about it by now. Tough guys from other neighborhoods came to the tea shop just to steal a glance at the woman who had conquered the tough guy of Zongo Street.

Then one night during the fasting month of Ramadan,[5] some two months after the fight, a voice in Mallam Sile's head asked, "Why is everyone calling my wife 'the man checker'? How come people I give credit to suddenly pay me on time? Why am I being treated with such respect, even by the worst and most stubborn rascals on the street?" Sile was lying in bed with his wife when these questions came to him. But, in his usual fashion, he didn't try to answer them. Instead, he drew in a deep breath and began to pray. He smiled and thanked Allahu-Raheemu, the Merciful One, for curing the street folks of the prejudice they had nursed against him for so long. Mallam Sile also thanked Allah for giving his neighbors the will and the courage to finally accept him just as he was created. He flashed a grin in the darkness and moved closer to his slumbering wife. He buried his small body in her massive, protective frame and soon fell into a deep, dreamless sleep.

---

[5] **Ramadan:** a month-long religious event that features fasting during daylight hours.

COLLABORATIVE DISCUSSION With a partner, describe Mallam Sile. Discuss his major character traits and how those traits compare and contrast with his wife's traits. Cite specific textual evidence from the story to support your ideas.

Analyze Story Elements: Setting

RL 3

In "Mallam Sile," the **setting** involves not only the specific location of Zongo Street in Kumasi, Ghana, but also the culture of the Ghanaian Muslims who live and work there. Their beliefs, social structure, religious practices, and customs infuse the story. This **cultural setting** is important for understanding the conflicts experienced by the main characters, Mallam Sile and his wife, who depart from the social norms of their neighbors. The setting is also related to the story's theme.

The author, Mohammed Naseehu Ali, conveys a vivid sense of Mallam Sile's world at the beginning of the story: "He was popularly known as *mai tea,* or the tea seller. His shop was situated right in the navel of Zongo Street—a stone's throw from the chief's assembly shed and adjacent to the kiosk where Mansa BBC, the town gossip, sold her provisions." These first sentences draw readers into the intimacy of this neighborhood in which everyone knows everyone else's business and talks about it. In addition, details such as the term *mai tea*, the reference to the chief's assembly shed, and even Mansa's nickname "BBC" after the British Broadcasting Corporation, establish the cultural context and help readers to understand its predominance in the story.

Support Inferences: Draw Conclusions

RL 1

Readers use evidence from a text and their own knowledge to make **inferences,** logical assumptions about something that is not directly stated in the text. For example, the phrase "situated right in the navel of Zongo Street" might lead readers to infer that Mallam's tea shop is central to the life of the residents of Zongo Street. Sometimes the evidence in a text leaves matters uncertain, and readers must understand that their inferences are only guesses.

Conclusions are more general statements about a text. They often are based on inferences that the reader has already made. For example, after reading "Mallam Sile," readers can use details from the story and inferences they have made to draw a conclusion about the author's purpose for choosing the setting of Kumasi, Ghana.

Details	Inferences	Conclusion
The story is set in Kumasi, Ghana, where the author is from. The description of the setting is vivid and realistic.	Ghana is important to the author. The author wants readers to be able to visualize what life in Ghana is like.	The author wants others to know about the Ghanaian way of life and what makes it special.

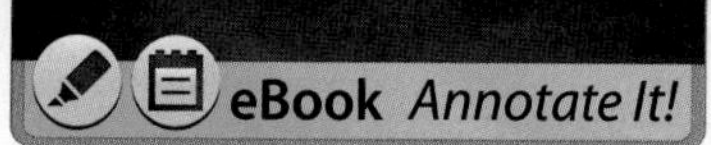

RL 1, RL 2, RL 3, W 3d, W 4, SL 1

Analyzing the Text

Cite Text Evidence Support your responses with evidence from the selection.

1. **Analyze** What words and phrases evoke a sense of the liveliness of Mallam's tea shop? What is revealed about the importance of speech in the Ghanaian culture from this description of the setting?
2. **Infer** Mallam is told to "shut up" whenever he tries to speak, so that eventually "the tea seller learned to swallow his words." Why is Mallam treated in this way? What does this behavior towards Mallam add to readers' understanding of both his character and Ghanaian society?
3. **Cause and Effect** How does Mallam's religion shape his character? How do these aspects of his character lead to conflict? Include details from the text to support your explanation.
4. **Infer** Why does Mallam Sile build a new tea shop? In what way might this be seen as a turning point in the story?
5. **Draw Conclusions** The fight between Abeeba and Samadu is developed in great detail. Why does the author include this scene in the story? Cite details from the story to support your conclusion.
6. **Analyze** What is the **theme,** or underlying message, of the story? How is it related to the setting?
7. **Draw Conclusions** At the end of the story, Mallam Sile questions the changes in his neighbors' attitude toward him as he lies in bed next to his wife. How much does he understand about her role in forcing these changes? Explain your response.

PERFORMANCE TASK

Writing Activity: Description Using Ali's style as a model, write two or three paragraphs describing a familiar setting that is a gathering place in your school or community.

- Include specific sensory details that convey a vivid picture of your setting as well as its atmosphere.
- Organize your details in a way that allows readers to perceive the relationship of setting elements to each other.
- Share and discuss your description in a small group.

Critical Vocabulary

L 4c, L 4d

paraphernalia **pugnacious** **admonition** **extricate** **naïveté**

Practice and Apply Complete each sentence in a way that reflects the meaning of the Critical Vocabulary word.

1. Abeeba stopped pestering customers to pay their bills after Mallam Sile's *admonition* to her because . . .
2. Mallam worried about confronting the *pugnacious* Samadu because . . .
3. Mallam needed new cupboards to hold his tea-making *paraphernalia* because . . .
4. The women warned Abeeba that she might not be able to *extricate* herself from Samadu's grasp because . . .
5. Mallam's *naïveté* enabled bullies to exploit him because . . .

Vocabulary Strategy: Consult a Dictionary

Although readers often use the context clues in a text that point to the meaning of an unfamiliar word to help them define it, they need to consult dictionaries to find other information about words or to verify meanings. Both print and digital college-level **dictionaries** include the pronunciation, part of speech, etymology, and precise meanings of a word. Sometimes the entry will also identify synonyms or antonyms for the word. Look at the entry for the Vocabulary word *paraphernalia.*

par•a•pher•na•lia (păr´ə-fər-nāl´yə, -fə-nāl´yə) *pl.n. (used with a sing. or pl. verb)* 1. The articles used in a particular activity; equipment: *a photographer's paraphernalia.* See Synonyms at **equipment.** 2. *Law* Personal property used by a married woman that, although actually owned by her husband and subject to claims by his creditors, becomes her personal property after his death. [Medieval *Latin paraphernālia,* neuter pl. of *paraphernālis*, pertaining to the *parapherna*, a married woman's property exclusive of her dowry, from Late Latin, from Greek : *para-*, beyond; see PARA-[1] + *phernē*, dowry; see **bher-**[1] in Indo-European roots.]

Practice and Apply Use a dictionary to answer these questions about the Critical Vocabulary words.

1. Which meaning of *paraphernalia* is most closely related to the word's origin?
2. What is the meaning of the Latin root from which *extricate* is formed?
3. Where is the long *a* sound in *naïveté*?
4. Based on its dictionary definition, is the connotation of *admonition* "harsh" or "gentle"?
5. What is a synonym for *pugnacious?*

Language and Style: Adjectives and Adverbs

L1

Adjectives are words used to modify nouns or pronouns. They are located close to the word they modify or come after a linking verb. **Adverbs** are words used to modify verbs, other adverbs, or adjectives. Some may end in *-ly*; others do not.

Adjectives tell . . .	Adverbs tell . . .
which one: *That* cat is mine.	**when:** Call me *later.*
what kind: We ordered *pink* cupcakes.	**where:** We stayed *inside* during the storm.
how many: The bride invited *two hundred* guests.	**how:** He spoke *angrily.*
how much: We needed *less* dirt than we anticipated.	**to what extent:** The acrobat was *very* agile.

Adjectives and adverbs can be valuable tools for a writer. Ali's skillful use of them brings his setting and characters to life in "Mallam Sile."

Read this sentence from the story.

Although he didn't have the broad, flat nose, poorly developed chin, and round head of the Pygmies, he was stout and hairy all over, as they were.

The author could instead have written the sentence this way:

He didn't have the nose, chin, and head of the Pygmies, but he looked like them in other ways.

In contrast to the original sentence, which creates a vivid image in readers' minds of both Pygmies and Mallam Sile, the second version is dull and unhelpful to readers. The lack of descriptive adjectives and adverbs gives them nothing to visualize.

In addition to choosing modifiers for the specific meaning they impart, Ali also chooses adverbs and adjectives for their connotation and level of intensity. For example, he describes the noise in the tea shop as "boisterous chattering," using the more intense *boisterous* instead of the less powerful synonym *loud*.

Practice and Apply Return to the descriptive paragraphs about a familiar setting that you wrote in response to this selection's Performance Task. Revise your paragraphs to include more specific adjectives and adverbs. Compare the "before" and "after" versions of your sentences with a partner and discuss the effect of your revisions.

Shirley Geok-lin Lim (b. 1944) *was born in Malacca, Malaysia. She came to the United States to pursue her education and now teaches at the University of California at Santa Barbara. Lim is a prolific writer, publishing poems, novels, short stories, memoirs, criticism, and other nonfiction works. But she considers herself first and foremost a poet. In 1980, she was the first woman and the first Asian to win the Commonwealth Poetry Prize. In her writing, she explores themes such as identity, transitions, race, gender, and relationships, referring to and drawing from her difficult childhood.*

My Father's Sadness

Poem by Shirley Geok-lin Lim

AS YOU READ Examine the poem for clues that reveal how the speaker views the father's life. Write down any questions you generate during reading.

My father's sadness appears in my dreams.
His young body is dying of responsibility.
So many men and women march out of his mouth
each time he opens his heart for fullness,
he is shot down; so many men and women
like dragons' teeth[1] rising in the instance
of his lifetime. He is an oriental. He claims
paternity. But in his dreams he is a young body
with only his life before him.

[1] **dragons' teeth:** an allusion to a Greek myth in which a dragon's teeth, when planted, grow into fierce warriors.

My father's sadness masks my face. It is hard
to see through his tears, his desires drum in my chest.
I tense like a young man with a full moon
and no woman in sight. My father broke
with each child, finer and finer, the clay
of his body crumbling to a drizzle of silicone
in the hour-glass. How hard it is
to be a father, a bull under the axle,
the mangrove[2] netted by lianas,[3] the host
perishing of its lavishness.

---

[2] **mangrove:** a tree that grows along the shore in tropical areas.

[3] **lianas** (lē-ä´nəz): long vines that grow in tropical forests and often climb around trees.

COLLABORATIVE DISCUSSION What is the image of the father that the speaker sees in dreams? With a partner, discuss how this image conveys the speaker's perspective on the father's life. Cite specific textual evidence from the poem to support your ideas.

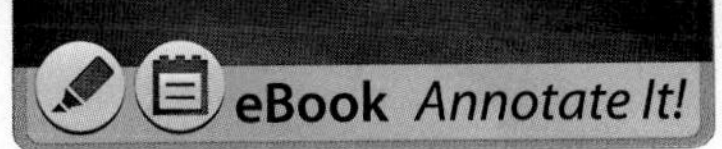

Determine Figurative Meanings

RL 4, L 5a

Figurative language is language that communicates ideas beyond the literal meaning of the words. Shirley Geok-lin Lim uses figurative language in the form of **similes** and **metaphors** to evoke images of the father and the speaker's perceptions of him in "My Father's Sadness."

A **simile** compares two dissimilar things using the word *like* or *as*.	"I tense like a young man with a full moon / and no woman in sight." (lines 12–13)
A **metaphor** compares two things directly, without using *like* or *as*.	"How hard it is to be a father, / a bull under the axle" (lines 16–17)

To understand the figurative language in the chart, identify what the things that are compared have in common. In the simile, the speaker and the young man both feel the tension of being frustrated. In the metaphor, the father and the bull are both burdened by heavy labor.

Analyzing the Text

RL 1, RL 2, RL 4, L 5a, SL 6

Cite Text Evidence Support your responses with evidence from the selection.

1. **Interpret** What theme about fatherhood is developed in the first stanza? Explain how the poet uses figurative language to convey this meaning.
2. **Cite Evidence** What is the **tone**, or attitude, of the speaker toward the father? How do the details in lines 10–13 communicate this tone?
3. **Analyze** Explain how the metaphor in lines 13–16 contributes to the theme of the poem.
4. **Evaluate** Are lines 18–19, "the mangrove netted by lianas, the host perishing of its lavishness," an effective ending for the poem? Support your view by explaining both the literal image created by the lines as well as their figurative meaning.

PERFORMANCE TASK

Speaking Activity: Oral Interpretation Prepare an oral reading of the poem:

- On a copy of the poem, highlight important words and phrases that you want to emphasize in your reading to bring out your interpretation.
- Present your reading in a small group. Discuss similarities and differences in the oral interpretations presented by you and your classmates.

Language and Style: Alliteration and Consonance

In a poem, the sound and language are complementary. A poem's meaning relies on both. In her poem, Lim uses the sound devices **alliteration** and **consonance** to create a particular mood, or feeling, and to emphasize ideas.

Sound Devices in Poetry	
Alliteration is the repetition of consonant sounds at the beginning of words.	"So many men and women march out of his mouth" (line 3)
Consonance is the repetition of consonant sounds within and at the end of words.	"My father's sadness appears in my dreams." (line 1)

In the first example in the chart, the *m* is repeated. This alliteration adds emphasis to the words. It also draws readers' attention to the startling image presented. In the second example, the *s* sound is repeated at the end of several words. This consonance slows the line, helping to create a mood of sadness, which reinforces the poem's meaning.

Lim weaves both devices into several of her lines. Read lines 4–5 from the poem:

each time he opens his heart for fullness,
he is shot down; so many men and women

Together the alliteration and the consonance create a link between the sounds of the two lines. The repetition of the initial consonant *h* in the words *he*, *his*, *heart*, and *he* again in the second line helps connect the ideas, while the slower pace established by the *s* at the end of several words is brought to an abrupt halt by the use of the word *down*, which repeats none of the sounds. The word ends the pattern, helping to convey the harsh ending of the father's hopes as well.

Practice and Apply In the style of Lim, write four lines of a poem about a particular person. Incorporate alliteration and consonance. Share your lines with a partner and discuss the effectiveness of your devices in creating mood and meaning.

Background *In the eighteenth century, the daughters of English gentlemen were mostly taught reading, languages, playing the piano, singing, drawing, and needlework. This was thought to be adequate preparation for their lives as wives, mothers, governesses, or companions to wealthy ladies.*

Mary Wollstonecraft *(1759–1797) is considered by many to be the mother of feminism. Inspired by the ideas of liberal reformers, she wrote about the rights of women and others. Her 1790 book,* A Vindication of the Rights of Man, *attacked class and privilege; she followed that with* A Vindication of the Rights of Woman *in 1792.*

from A Vindication of the Rights of Woman

Political Argument by Mary Wollstonecraft

AS YOU READ Look for details that tell you about the nature of women's education in the eighteenth century.

From the Introduction

After considering the historic page, and viewing the living world with anxious solicitude, the most melancholy emotions of sorrowful indignation have depressed my spirits, and I have sighed when obliged to confess, that either nature has made a great difference between man and man, or that the civilization which has hitherto taken place in the world has been very partial. I have turned over various books written on the subject of education, and patiently observed the conduct of parents and the management of schools; but what has been the result?—a profound conviction that the neglected education of my fellow-creatures is the grand source of the misery I deplore; and that women, in particular, are rendered weak and wretched by a variety of concurring causes, originating from one hasty conclusion. The conduct and manners of women, in fact, evidently prove that their minds are not in a healthy state; for, like the flowers which are planted in too rich a soil, strength and usefulness are sacrificed to beauty; and the flaunting leaves, after having pleased a fastidious eye, fade, disregarded on the stalk, long before the season when they ought to have arrived at maturity. One cause of this barren

vindication (vĭn′dĭ-kā′shən) *n.* justification.

blooming I attribute to a false system of education, gathered from the books written on this subject by men who, considering females rather as women than human creatures, have been more anxious to make them alluring mistresses than affectionate wives and rational mothers; and the understanding of the sex has been so bubbled by this specious homage,[1] that the civilized women of the present century, with a few exceptions, are only anxious to inspire love, when they ought to cherish a nobler ambition, and by their abilities and virtues exact respect.

In a treatise,[2] therefore, on female rights and manners, the works which have been particularly written for their improvement must not be overlooked; especially when it is asserted, in direct terms, that the minds of women are enfeebled by false refinement; that the books of instruction, written by men of genius, have had the same tendency as more frivolous productions; and that . . . they are treated as a kind of subordinate beings, and not as a part of the human species, when improvable reason is allowed to be the dignified distinction which raises men above the brute creation, and puts a natural scepter in a feeble hand.

Yet, because I am a woman, I would not lead my readers to suppose that I mean violently to agitate the contested question respecting the quality or inferiority of the sex; but as the subject lies in my way, and I cannot pass it over without subjecting the main tendency of my reasoning to misconstruction, I shall stop a moment to deliver, in a few words, my opinion. In the government of the physical world it is observable that the female in point of strength is, in general, inferior to the male. This is the law of nature; and it does not appear to be suspended or **abrogated** in favor of woman. A degree of physical superiority cannot, therefore, be denied—and it is a noble prerogative! But not content with this natural preeminence, men endeavor to sink us still lower merely to render us alluring objects for a moment; and women, intoxicated by the adoration which men, under the influence of their senses, pay them, do not seek to obtain a durable interest in their hearts, or to become the friends of the fellow creatures who find amusement in their society.

abrogate (ăb´rə-gāt´) *v.* to revoke or nullify.

I am aware of an obvious inference: from every quarter have I heard exclamations against masculine women; but where are they to be found? If by this appellation men mean to inveigh against their ardor[3] in hunting, shooting, and gaming, I shall most cordially join in the cry; but if it be against the imitation of manly virtues, or, more properly speaking, the attainment of those talents and virtues, the exercise of which ennobles the human character, and which raise

---

[1] **bubbled by this specious homage** (spē´shəs hŏm´ĭj): deceived by this false honor.

[2] **treatise:** a formal, detailed article or book on a particular subject.

[3] **If by . . . inveigh** (ĭn-vā´) **against their ardor:** if by this term ("masculine women") men mean to condemn some women's enthusiasm.

females in the scale of animal being, when they are comprehensively termed mankind; all those who view them with a philosophic eye must, I should think, wish with me, that they may every day grow more and more masculine. . . .

My own sex, I hope, will excuse me, if I treat them like rational creatures, instead of flattering their *fascinating* graces, and viewing them as if they were in a state of perpetual childhood, unable to stand alone. I earnestly wish to point out in what true dignity and human happiness consists—I wish to persuade women to endeavor to acquire strength, both of mind and body, and to convince them that the soft phrases, **susceptibility** of heart, delicacy of sentiment, and refinement of taste, are almost synonymous with epithets[4] of weakness, and that those beings who are only the objects of pity and that kind of love, which has been termed its sister, will soon become objects of contempt. . . .

susceptibility (sə-sĕp´tə-bĭl´ĭ-tē) *n.* vulnerability, or the likeliness to be affected.

The education of women has, of late, been more attended to than formerly; yet they are still reckoned a frivolous sex, and ridiculed or pitied by the writers who endeavor by satire or instruction to improve them. It is acknowledged that they spend many of the first years of their lives in acquiring a smattering of accomplishments;[5] meanwhile strength of body and mind are sacrificed to libertine[6] notions of beauty, to the desire of establishing themselves—the only way women can rise in the world—by marriage. And this desire making mere animals of them, when they marry they act as such children may be expected to act: they dress; they paint, and nickname God's creatures. Surely these weak beings are only fit for a seraglio![7] Can they be expected to govern a family with judgment, or take care of the poor babes whom they bring into the world?

If then it can be fairly deduced from the present conduct of the sex, from the prevalent fondness for pleasure which takes place of ambition and those nobler passions that open and enlarge the soul; that the instruction which women have hitherto received has only tended, with the constitution of civil society, to render them insignificant objects of desire—mere propagators of fools!—if it can be proved that in aiming to accomplish them, without cultivating their understandings, they are taken out of their sphere of duties, and made ridiculous and useless when the short-lived bloom of beauty is over, I presume that *rational* men will excuse me for endeavoring to persuade them to become more masculine and respectable.

[4] **epithets** (ĕp´ə-thĕts´): descriptive terms.

[5] **accomplishments:** This term, when applied to women, designated only those achievements then considered suitable for middle- and upper-class women, such as painting, singing, playing a musical instrument, and embroidery.

[6] **libertine** (lĭb´ər-tēn´): indecent or unseemly.

[7] **seraglio** (sə-răl´yō): harem.

Indeed the word masculine is only a bugbear:[8] there is little reason to fear that women will acquire too much courage or fortitude; for their apparent inferiority with respect to bodily strength, must render them, in some degree, dependent on men in the various relations of life; but why should it be increased by prejudices that give a sex to virtue, and confound simple truths with sensual reveries?[9]

From Chapter 2

Youth is the season for love in both sexes; but in those days of thoughtless enjoyment provision should be made for the more important years of life, when reflection takes place of sensation. But Rousseau,[10] and most of the male writers who have followed his steps, have warmly inculcated that the whole tendency of female education ought to be directed to one point: to render them[11] pleasing.

Let me reason with the supporters of this opinion who have any knowledge of human nature, do they imagine that marriage can eradicate the habitude of life? The woman who has only been taught to please will soon find that her charms are oblique sunbeams, and that they cannot have much effect on her husband's heart when they are seen every day, when the summer is passed and gone. Will she then have sufficient native energy to look into herself for comfort, and cultivate her dormant faculties? or, is it not more rational to expect that she will try to please other men; and, in the emotions raised by the expectation of new conquests, endeavor to forget the mortification her love or pride has received? When the husband ceases to be a lover—and the time will inevitably come, her desire of pleasing will then grow languid, or become a spring of bitterness; and love, perhaps, the most evanescent of all passions, gives place to jealousy or vanity.

I now speak of women who are restrained by principle or prejudice; such women, though they would shrink from an intrigue with real abhorrence, yet, nevertheless, wish to be convinced by the homage of gallantry that they are cruelly neglected by their husbands; or, days and weeks are spent in dreaming of the happiness enjoyed by **congenial** souls till their health is undermined and their spirits broken by discontent. How then can the great art of pleasing be such a necessary study? it is only useful to a mistress; the chaste wife, and serious mother, should only consider her power to please as the polish of her virtues, and the affection of her husband as one of the comforts that render her talk less difficult and her life happier. But, whether she be loved or neglected, her first wish should be to make herself

congenial (kən-jēn´yəl) *adj.* agreeable, sympathetic.

[8] **bugbear:** an object of exaggerated fear.

[9] **confound . . . reveries** (rĕv´ə-rēz): confuse simple truths with men's sexual daydreams.

[10] **Rousseau** (ro͞o-sō´): The Swiss-born French philosopher Jean-Jacques Rousseau (1712–1778) presented a plan for female education in his famous 1762 novel *Émile.*

[11] **them:** that is, females.

respectable, and not to rely for all her happiness on a being subject to like infirmities with herself.

The worthy Dr. Gregory fell into a similar error. I respect his heart; but entirely disapprove of his celebrated Legacy to his Daughters.[12] . . .

He actually recommends **dissimulation**, and advises an innocent girl to give the lie to her feelings, and not dance with spirit, when gaiety of heart would make her feet eloquent without making her gestures immodest. In the name of truth and common sense, why should not one woman acknowledge that she can take more exercise than another? or, in other words, that she has a sound constitution; and why, to damp innocent vivacity, is she darkly to be told that men will draw conclusions which she little thinks of? Let the libertine draw what inference he pleases; but, I hope, that no sensible mother will restrain the natural frankness of youth by instilling such indecent cautions. Out of the abundance of the heart the mouth speaketh; and a wiser than Solomon[13] hath said, that the heart should be made clean, and not trivial ceremonies observed, which it is not very difficult to fulfil with scrupulous exactness when vice reigns in the heart.

dissimulation (dĭ-sĭm′yə-lā′shən) *n.* deceit or pretense.

Women ought to endeavor to purify their heart; but can they do so when their uncultivated understandings make them entirely dependent on their senses for employment and amusement, when no noble pursuit sets them above the little vanities of the day, or enables them to curb the wild emotions that agitate a reed over which every passing breeze has power? To gain the affections of a virtuous man, is affectation necessary? Nature has given woman a weaker frame than man; but, to ensure her husband's affections, must a wife, who by the exercise of her mind and body whilst she was discharging the duties of a daughter, wife, and mother, has allowed her constitution to retain its natural strength, and her nerves a healthy tone, is she, I say, to condescend to use art and feign a sickly delicacy in order to secure her husband's affection? Weakness may excite tenderness, and gratify the arrogant pride of man; but the lordly caresses of a protector will not gratify a noble mind that pants for, and deserves to be respected. Fondness is a poor substitute for friendship! . . .

Besides, the woman who strengthens her body and exercises her mind will, by managing her family and practicing various virtues, become the friend, and not the humble dependent of her husband; and if she, by possessing such substantial qualities, merit his regard, she

[12] **Dr. Gregory . . . Daughters:** In his 1774 work *A Father's Legacy for His Daughters*, John Gregory (1724–1773) offered a plan for female education that remained popular for decades.

[13] **a wiser than Solomon:** King David, reputed author of many psalms in the Bible and the father of King Solomon, who was known for his wisdom. The words that follow draw on ideas in Psalm 24, which states that only those with "clean hands, and a pure heart" shall ascend into Heaven.

will not find it necessary to conceal her affection, nor to pretend to an unnatural coldness of constitution to excite her husband's passions. . . .

If all the faculties of woman's mind are only to be cultivated as they respect her dependence on man; if, when a husband be obtained, she have arrived at her goal, and meanly proud rests satisfied with such a paltry crown, let her grovel contentedly, scarcely raised by her employments above the animal kingdom; but, if, struggling for the prize of her high calling, she look beyond the present scene, let her cultivate her understanding without stopping to consider what character the husband may have whom she is destined to marry. Let her only determine, without being too anxious about present happiness, to acquire the qualities that ennoble a rational being, and a rough inelegant husband may shock her taste without destroying her peace of mind. She will not model her soul to suit the frailties of her companion, but to bear with them: his character may be a trial, but not an impediment to virtue. . . .

These may be termed Utopian dreams. Thanks to that Being who impressed them on my soul, and gave me sufficient strength of mind to dare to exert my own reason, till, becoming dependent only on him for the support of my virtue, I view, with indignation, the mistaken notions that enslave my sex.

I love man as my fellow; but his scepter, real, or usurped, extends not to me, unless the reason of an individual demands my homage; and even then the submission is to reason, and not to man. In fact, the conduct of an accountable being must be regulated by the operations of its own reason; or on what foundation rests the throne of God?

It appears to me necessary to dwell on these obvious truths, because females have been insulated, as it were; and, while they have been stripped of the virtues that should clothe humanity, they have been decked with artificial graces that enable them to exercise a short-lived tyranny. Love, in their bosoms, taking place of every nobler passion, their sole ambition is to be fair, to raise emotion instead of inspiring respect; and this ignoble desire, like the servility in absolute monarchies, destroys all strength of character. Liberty is the mother of virtue, and if women be, by their very constitution, slaves, and not allowed to breathe the sharp invigorating air of freedom, they must ever languish like exotics,[14] and be reckoned beautiful flaws in nature.

[14] **languish** (lăng´gwĭsh) **like exotics:** wilt like plants grown away from their natural environment.

COLLABORATIVE DISCUSSION What does Wollstonecraft see as the rationale guiding the education of women in her society? With a partner, discuss the harm that she thinks results from this view of education. Cite specific textual evidence from the essay to support your ideas.

Analyze Structure: Counterarguments

RI 5, RI 10

In an argument, writers support their **claims,** or positions on an issue, by presenting logical reasons and valid evidence. Writers may also include **counterarguments** in which they anticipate opposing views and refute them. Mary Wollstonecraft provides several counterarguments in her argument, which show that she has thought about the issue from all sides. Her counterarguments acknowledge her opponents' perspective, making readers who might disagree with her more open to her ideas.

Examine Wollstonecraft's counterargument in lines 43–49: "In the government of the physical world it is observable that the female in point of strength is, in general, inferior to the male . . . But not content with this natural preeminence, men endeavor to sink us still lower merely to render us alluring objects for a moment. . . ." Wollstonecraft starts by agreeing that men do have a physical advantage over women. Then she points out that this advantage is limited to their strength, so it does not justify keeping women in an inferior status in which they merely serve as attractive and charming ornaments for the pleasure of men.

Analyze Style: Rhetorical Devices

RI 6

In her argument, Mary Wollstonecraft uses a variety of **rhetorical devices.** The devices shown in the chart make her points clearer and more persuasive.

Rhetorical Device	Example
Analogies are detailed comparisons made between dissimilar things to explain an unfamiliar idea in terms of a familiar one.	Wollstonecraft develops an analogy in her introduction that helps to explain her view of how inadequate or "false" education affects the lives of women.
Antithesis juxtaposes sharply contrasting words, phrases, clauses, or sentences to emphasize a point, often using a parallel grammatical structure.	In speaking of Dr. Gregory, Wollstonecraft says, "I respect his heart; but entirely disapprove of his celebrated Legacy to his Daughters."
Rhetorical questions are questions inserted into a text to which no answer is expected. They emphasize meaning and evoke an emotional response.	Wollstonecraft asks, "Can they [women] be expected to govern a family with judgment, or take care of the poor babes whom they bring into the world?"

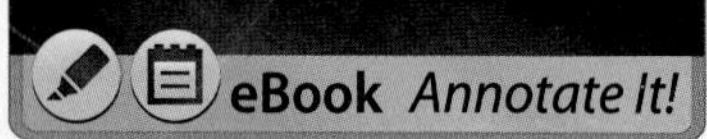

Analyzing Text

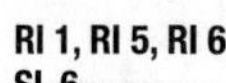

Cite Text Evidence Support your responses with evidence from the selection.

1. **Identify** What is Mary Wollstonecraft's claim in her argument? Identify three reasons that she provides to support this claim.
2. **Analyze** What analogy does Wollstonecraft present in the first paragraph of her argument? How does this analogy clarify the point she is making?
3. **Analyze** Wollstonecraft includes a series of rhetorical questions in lines 157–169. How does her use of this device contribute to her purpose?
4. **Analyze** What rhetorical device does Wollstonecraft use in lines 190–192? What idea is emphasized by the use of this device?
5. **Analyze** What reasons does Wollstonecraft offer to refute the following opposing views in her counterarguments?
   - the concern that improved education will make women too masculine (lines 76–105)
   - Rousseau's contention that the purpose of education for females is to make them more pleasing to men (106–139)
   - Dr. Gregory's belief that women should dissemble, or hide their true feelings and energies (lines 140–172).
6. **Connect** In the eighteenth century, intellectuals in Europe and the American colonies promoted the expansion of liberty and equality. Reread lines 193–213 of Wollstonecraft's argument. In what ways does she appeal to these ideals in support of her argument for reforming women's education?

PERFORMANCE TASK

Speaking Activity: Oral Presentation Present an oral response to the views and ideas expressed in Wollstonecraft's argument.

To prepare your response, jot down answers to these and other questions:

- Which of Wollstonecraft's views are still relevant?
- What evidence can you present in a counterargument to ideas of Wollstonecraft's with which you disagree?
- What ideas might Wollstonecraft have added if she had written the argument today?
- Develop speaking notes that present your ideas using a logical organization.
- Support your major points with details and evidence.
- Rehearse your speech with a partner, giving each other feedback.

L 4a, L 4d

Critical Vocabulary

vindication **abrogate** **susceptibility**

congenial **dissimulation**

Practice and Apply Answer each question, referring to the Critical Vocabulary words in your response.

1. If someone writes an editorial in favor of a new tax on junk food, is the editorial a *vindication* or *dissimulation* of the tax proposal?
2. Did women in the eighteenth century show *susceptibility* or *dissimulation* when they accepted men's view of themselves as helpless and frail?
3. If someone's rights were *abrogated*, would that person's response be *congenial?* Explain.

Vocabulary Strategy: Multiple Meanings

Many words in English have more than one meaning. For example, the dictionary entry for the Vocabulary word *vindication* lists several definitions. To determine which meaning matches the way the word is used in the title of the argument, readers must use context clues. The remaining words in the title, as well as what readers know about the content of the text, can help them figure out that *vindication* means "justification." The chart presents two meanings of the Vocabulary word *congenial*. Notice how the context clues in the sentences help to reveal the intended meaning.

Definition	Example
"having the same tastes, habits, or temperament"	When sharing a room at college, it helps if you and your roommate have congenial living habits.
"friendly and sociable"	Although our host was outwardly congenial, I sensed he was ready for us to leave.

Practice and Apply The following words from the argument have multiple meanings: *conduct, render, exact, sound.* Complete these steps for each word:

1. Identify two of its meanings.
2. Write a sentence illustrating each meaning, including context clues.
3. Exchange sentences with a partner and use the context clues to define the word as it is used in each sentence.

L 1

Language and Style: Sentence Structure

Wollstonecraft expresses her ideas in long, detailed sentences that rely heavily on **coordinating** and **subordinating conjunctions** to connect words, phrases, and clauses smoothly in a way that shows the relationships between ideas.

Coordinating Conjunctions	Purpose	Sample Sentences
and, but, for, nor, or, so, yet	connect words or groups of words that have the same function in a sentence	We were so close yet so far. They lost the debate, but they still believed in themselves.
Subordinating Conjunctions	**Purpose**	**Sample Sentences**
after, although, as, as if, because, before, if, since, so that, than, though, unless, until, when, whenever, where, wherever, while	introduce subordinate clauses—clauses that cannot stand by themselves as complete sentences	Although they read her essay, they were not convinced. She was sorry that she had not published it sooner.

Read this sentence from the argument:

I love man as my fellow; but his scepter, real, or usurped, extends not to me, unless the reason of an individual demands my homage; and even then the submission is to reason, and not to man.

The author could have chosen to write the same ideas in this way:

I love man as my fellow. His scepter, real, or usurped, extends not to me. The reason of an individual may demand my homage. The submission is to reason. The submission is not to man.

The elimination of the conjunctions *but, unless,* and *and* makes it harder for readers to understand the relationships between the ideas.

Practice and Apply Look back at the notes you created for your oral response to the argument when you completed this selection's Performance Task. Insert conjunctions that help to clarify the relationship between ideas. Present your changes to a partner and discuss how they improve the flow and clarity of your speech.

MEDIA ANALYSIS

News Coverage of a Women's Rights Campaign

In a Scattered Protest, Saudi Women Take the Wheel

from the **New York Times,** June 17, 2011
Online Article by Neil MacFarquhar and Dina Salah Amer, Cairo

AS YOU READ Pay attention to details about the reasons for the protest. Write down any questions you generate during reading.

Several dozen women drove in defiance of the law in major cities of Saudi Arabia on Friday, according to reports on social media and by an informal network of activists in the country. There appeared to be few confrontations reported with either the traffic or morals police, and at least half a dozen women who were stopped were escorted home and admonished not to drive again, said activists reached by telephone.

From its inception in April, the protest against the longstanding ban was far smaller than initially anticipated, but it was not meant to be a mass driving effort. Rather, women with legal driver's licenses from other countries were urged to run mundane errands—going to the grocery store, perhaps—in order to underscore the fact that it should be normal for women to drive.

Maha al-Qahtani, an information technology specialist for the government, drove around the capital, Riyadh, for 45 minutes with her husband, Mohamed, a human rights activist, in the car. She braced for a siren after passing each of about five police cars, she said, but they ignored her.

"I woke up today believing with every part of me that this is my right, I woke up believing this is my duty, and I was no longer afraid," said Mrs. Qahtani, adding that she had brought a change of clothes and a prayer rug with her in case she was detained.

“I woke up believing this is my duty, and I was no longer afraid.”

Manal al-Sharif, a 32-year-old single mother, started the call for the June 17 protest in April with a Facebook page. But after posting videos of herself driving around Al Khobar in the Eastern Province, she was arrested in late May and jailed for nine days—a punishment that was stricter than expected. Many supporters were disappointed, feeling that she had jumped the gun and jeopardized them all by taking a confrontational approach.

Women driving remains a sensitive issue in Saudi Arabia. For religious conservatives, it is a kind of Alamo, with the ban a sign that the kingdom still holds to its traditions and has not caved to Western pressure.

The ruling family has been especially dependent on this base of supporters in recent months as protests erupted across the region and has been mute as the mufti, the highest religious figure in the kingdom, rolled out a fatwa[1] banning protests.

Many Saudi activists considered the treatment meted out to Ms. Sharif a warning from the monarchy against trying to organize any kind of movement via social media. The initiative for women to drive was the strongest effort so far in the kingdom inspired by the regional climate.

“Women in Saudi Arabia see other women in the Middle East making revolutions, women in Yemen and Egypt at the forefront of revolutions, being so bold, toppling entire governments,” said Waleed Abu Alkhair, whose wife drove around Jidda. “The women of Saudi Arabia looked at themselves and they realized, ‘Wow! We can’t even drive!’ ”

Mr. Abu Alkhair said he knew about many women who drove, and aside from one being questioned by the police for two hours, none were bothered. Once the campaign had been announced there were frequent threats by opponents to punish female drivers either by beating them or by smashing their cars.

[1] **fatwa:** a ruling or opinion on Islamic law.

"We want women to keep fighting this fight and to be free," he said. "It will help to liberate the entire society."

In the weeks after Ms. Sharif's arrest, a debate erupted between conservative clerics and their followers and the kingdom's increasingly outspoken women. Opponents largely argued that Saudi society was not ready, that a woman should not be thrown into the wilds of Saudi driving habits or be held responsible for any accidents.

Worse, opponents argued, it would lead to the public mingling of the sexes. Supporters mocked the clerics for putting everything in a sexual context and asked why it was O.K. for Saudi women to be driven around by an army of some 800,000 male drivers imported from Southeast Asia.

Although the arrest of Ms. Sharif discouraged women from driving, the fact that it enlivened the debate was in contrast to the first (and last) such protest in November 1990. Clerics branded the 47 women amoral and the royal family confiscated their passports, firing those working for the government. Many went into isolation for their own safety.

In addition to religious opposition there is widespread suspicion in the country that those who control the visa process—and in Saudi

Image Credits: ©Hassan Ammar/AP/Corbis

Arabia that means the princes of the ruling family—have made a business out of controlling the black market in visas for drivers, which can cost more than $3,000 apiece.

Many young married women decry the fact that they cannot afford that, not to mention the driver's salary, about $600 a month.

The more liberal princes support allowing women to drive. Prince Talal bin Abdul-Aziz al-Saud, 79 years old and long among the most outspoken members of the royal family, argues that such reforms lag because the leading members of the family have failed to yield any power or influence to younger generations.

"Bravo to the women!" the prince said in an interview. "Why should women drive in the countryside and not in the cities?" (Women have long driven in rural areas.)

King Abdullah and other royals have said in interviews with foreign reporters that they expected Saudi women to drive one day soon but have done little lately.

"Saudi Arabian women are going to have to fight for our rights, men are not going to just hand them over to us," said Amira Kashgary, a professor who drove through Jidda on Friday for 45 minutes with her 21-year-old daughter. Women are tired of being stranded or missing appointments because their drivers disappear for the day, Professor Kashgary said. "We want to drive today, tomorrow, and every day—it's not a one-day show. We want to make it a norm."

COLLABORATIVE DISCUSSION With a partner, discuss how and why the participants organized the protest. Was the protest effective? Cite specific textual evidence from the article to support your ideas.

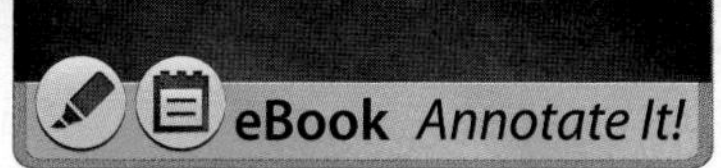

Summarize the Text

RI 2

When readers summarize a text, they use their own words to tell what it is about. A **summary** includes only the central ideas and most important details of a text. It follows the order of the original text and is written in a way that is objective and accurate. Readers may summarize paragraphs, passages, or entire selections to help them clarify meaning or remember essential information.

Compare these two summaries of the first paragraph of the article. Note the differences that make the second summary more accurate than the first.

Summary	Analysis
Dozens of women drove in Saudi Arabia according to reports. Some were stopped, but there were not a lot of confrontations, or so activists said. The women who participated were brave.	This summary copies much of the original text, merely leaving out some words to shorten the length. Too many unimportant details are included as well as a statement of the writer's opinion.
A planned protest against the ban on female drivers in Saudi Arabia drew dozens of women but passed without serious incident for participants.	This summary retells the major ideas of the first paragraph in the writer's own words and eliminates unimportant details. The writer maintains an objective tone.

Analyzing the Media

RI 1, RI 2, RI 4,RI 5, RI 6

Cite Text Evidence Support your responses with evidence from the selection.

1. **Analyze** What does driving represent to Saudi women? Why is it "a kind of Alamo" to supporters of the ban?
2. **Analyze** What is the purpose of this article? How do the authors accomplish their purpose? Explain.
3. **Evaluate** Think about how the authors structure their article. Why is this structure effective?
4. **Summarize** What are the central ideas in this article? Write a brief summary that includes those ideas and the most important details.

Saudi Women Defy Driving Ban

News Video
June 23, 2011

AS YOU VIEW Consider how the depiction of the protest in the news video is similar to and different from the article. Write down any questions you generate during viewing.

COLLABORATIVE DISCUSSION With a partner, think about whether the video explains all aspects of the issue behind the protest. Discuss why multiple sources of information are helpful in understanding an issue. Cite specific elements of the video to support your ideas.

Analyze Ideas and Events

RI 3

The way events or ideas are presented in a video, even one not produced by professional filmmakers, influences how the audience perceives them. Examining some of the elements of the video clip "Saudi Women Defy Driving Ban" will help viewers understand the filmmakers' purpose and message more clearly.

Element	Analysis
Opening/Closing Shots	The camera in the opening sequence is placed to reflect the driver's view of the road. The closing shot is of the note left on the car with the broken side mirror, requesting that Azza Al-Shamasi not drive. What do these choices by the filmmakers suggest about the perspective from which they want viewers to understand the events?
Types of Images	The women in the video are each wearing a *niqab*, a veil covering the face and hair that is worn by some Muslim women. The filmmakers also include images of the road, the note, the smashed mirror, and Azza's hands. Think about the message sent by these images and how they build upon the central idea of the film.
Interviews	The women are the only ones who speak in the video. Compare their comments and tones. What ideas do the filmmakers want viewers to learn from these interviews?

Analyzing the Media

RI 1, RI 3

Cite Text Evidence Support your responses with evidence from the selection.

1. **Analyze** Do the opening and closing shots suggest a bias, or an inclination to one side of the story, on the part of the filmmakers? Explain.
2. **Compare** What views do both women who are interviewed share? How do their comments affect the audience's sense of where their efforts might lead?
3. **Infer** At one point, the camera zooms in on Azza's hands. What idea is conveyed by this image?

News Coverage of a Women's Rights Campaign

Integrate and Evaluate Information

RI 7, SL 2

Both the news article and the video clip present information on the Saudi women's protest. As a reader/viewer, you must integrate the ideas that are communicated and evaluate their accuracy and credibility in order to form your own understanding. To do this, examine these aspects of each source of information:

- Purpose: The choice of medium is often dictated by the intended purpose of the piece. For example, the authors chose to write a news article because they wanted to inform readers of what took place in Saudi Arabia. Readers would expect to find facts in the article.
- Perspective: The perspective, or viewpoint, of the piece determines the content. For example, to convey a certain perspective in the video, specific images were used. Being aware of the perspective can help viewers or readers recognize bias.
- Meaning: If sources of information convey similar ideas, then readers/viewers can be more confident that the ideas are valid. If there are major differences, readers or viewers have to decide what the discrepancies mean about the validity of the information.

Analyzing the Media

RI 1, RI 2, RI 7, SL 1, SL 2, SL 5

Cite Text Evidence Support your responses with evidence from the selections.

1. **Compare** What central ideas are conveyed by both the article and the video clip? What do the differences reveal about the purpose of each?
2. **Analyze** Are the article and the video clip complementary or conflicting? Explain, citing specific examples.
3. **Compare** What are the advantages of each medium? Why is it important to have a choice of methods for conveying information?

PERFORMANCE TASK

Media Activity: News Video With a partner, produce your own news video on a local or school event.

- Decide on your purpose. Then organize your ideas for written, visual, and sound elements.
- Using available video equipment, shoot footage of relevant sites, events, or people; include interviews with participants or those affected by the event.
- Create your script and decide on sound effects.
- Put all of your elements together, editing to create a unified story.
- Present to the class. Have class members comment on how well you achieved your purpose.

Scott Russell Sanders (b. 1945) *was born in Tennessee. He won a scholarship to attend Cambridge University, where he acquired his Ph.D. in English. His professional life was spent teaching at Indiana University. Much of his writing focuses on the relationship between humans and nature and on the importance of conservation. Sanders is particularly known for his essays. He says that an essay usually begins "in a state of strong emotion and equally strong puzzlement. Some event, recollection . . . provokes me, and sets me asking questions that drive the writing forward."*

The Men We Carry in Our Minds

Essay by Scott Russell Sanders

AS YOU READ Note the experiences that have influenced Sanders's views about men and women.

"This must be a hard time for women," I say to my friend Anneke. "They have so many paths to choose from, and so many voices calling them."

"I think it's a lot harder for men," she replies.

"How do you figure that?"

"The women I know feel excited, innocent, like crusaders in a just cause. The men I know are eaten up with guilt."

We are sitting at the kitchen table drinking sassafras tea, our hands wrapped around the mugs because this April morning is cool and drizzly. "Like a Dutch morning," Anneke told me earlier. She is Dutch herself, a writer and midwife and peacemaker, with the round face and sad eyes of a woman in a Vermeer[1] painting who might be waiting for the rain to stop, for a door to open. She leans over to sniff a sprig of lilac, pale lavender, that rises from a vase of cobalt blue.

"Women feel such pressure to be everything, do everything," I say. "Career, kids, art, politics. Have their babies and get back to the office

[1] **Vermeer:** Johannes Vermeer (1632–1675), a Dutch painter known for his interior household scenes.

a week later. It's as if they're trying to overcome a million years' worth of evolution in one lifetime."

"But we help one another. We don't try to lumber on alone, like so many wounded grizzly bears, the way men do." Anneke sips her tea. I gave her the mug with owls on it, for wisdom. "And we have this deep-down sense that we're in the *right*—we've been held back, passed over, used—while men feel they're in the wrong. Men are the ones who've been **discredited**, who have to search their souls."

discredit
(dĭs-krĕd´ĭt) *v.* to damage the reputation of.

I search my soul. I discover guilty feelings aplenty—toward the poor, the Vietnamese, Native Americans, the whales, an endless list of debts—a guilt in each case that is as bright and unambiguous as a neon sign. But toward women I feel something more confused, a snarl of shame, envy, wary tenderness, and amazement. This muddle troubles me. To hide my unease I say, "You're right, it's tough being a man these days."

"Don't laugh." Anneke frowns at me, mournful-eyed, through the sassafras steam. "I wouldn't be a man for anything. It's much easier being the victim. All the victim has to do is break free. The persecutor has to live with his past."

How deep is that past? I find myself wondering after Anneke has left. How much of an inheritance do I have to throw off? Is it just the beliefs I breathed in as a child? Do I have to scour memory back through father and grandfather? Through St. Paul?[2] Beyond Stonehenge and into the twilit caves? I'm convinced the past we must contend with is deeper even than speech. When I think back on my childhood, on how I learned to see men and women, I have a sense of ancient, dizzying depths. The back roads of Tennessee and Ohio where I grew up were probably closer, in their sexual patterns, to the campsites of Stone Age hunters than to the genderless cities of the future into which we are rushing.

The first men, besides my father, I remember seeing were black convicts and white guards, in the cottonfield across the road from our farm on the outskirts of Memphis. I must have been three or four. The prisoners wore dingy gray-and-black zebra suits, heavy as canvas, sodden with sweat. Hatless, stooped, they chopped weeds in the fierce heat, row after row, breathing the **acrid** dust of boll-weevil poison. The overseers wore dazzling white shirts and broad shadowy hats. The oiled barrels of their shotguns flashed in the sunlight. Their faces in memory are utterly blank. Of course those men, white and black, have become for me an emblem of racial hatred. But they have also come to stand for the twin poles of my early vision of manhood—the brute toiling animal and the boss.

acrid
(ăk´rĭd) *adj.* strongly unpleasant in smell or taste.

When I was a boy, the men I knew labored with their bodies. They were **marginal** farmers, just scraping by, or welders, steelworkers,

marginal
(mär´jə-nəl) *adj.* just meeting a very low standard of success.

---

[2] **St. Paul:** an influential first-century Christian teacher and writer who, in the view of some theologians, reinforced the secondary status of women in the early church.

carpenters; they swept floors, dug ditches, mined coal, or drove trucks, their forearms ropy with muscle; they trained horses, stoked furnaces, built tires, stood on assembly lines wrestling parts onto cars and refrigerators. They got up before light, worked all day long whatever the weather, and when they came home at night they looked as though somebody had been whipping them. In the evenings and on weekends they worked on their own places, tilling gardens that were lumpy with clay, fixing broken-down cars, hammering on houses that were always too drafty, too leaky, too small.

The bodies of the men I knew were twisted and maimed in ways visible and invisible. The nails of their hands were black and split, the hands tattooed with scars. Some had lost fingers. Heavy lifting had given many of them finicky backs and guts weak from hernias. Racing against conveyor belts had given them ulcers. Their ankles and knees ached from years of standing on concrete. Anyone who had worked for long around machines was hard of hearing. They squinted, and the skin of their faces was creased like the leather of old work gloves. There were times, studying them, when I dreaded growing up. Most of them coughed, from dust or cigarettes, and most of them drank cheap wine or whiskey, so their eyes looked bloodshot and bruised. The fathers of my friends always seemed older than the mothers. Men wore out sooner. Only women lived into old age.

As a boy I also knew another sort of men, who did not sweat and break down like mules. They were soldiers, and so far as I could tell

they scarcely worked at all. During my early school years we lived on a military base, an arsenal in Ohio, and every day I saw GIs in the guardshacks, on the stoops of barracks, at the wheels of olive drab Chevrolets. The chief fact of their lives was boredom. Long after I left the Arsenal I came to recognize the sour smell the soldiers gave off as that of souls in limbo. They were all waiting—for wars, for transfers, for leaves, for promotions, for the end of their hitch—like so many braves waiting for the hunt to begin. Unlike the warriors of older tribes, however, they would have no say about when the battle would start or how it would be waged. Their waiting was broken only when they practiced for war. They fired guns at targets, drove tanks across the churned-up fields of the military reservation, set off bombs in the wrecks of old fighter planes. I knew this was all play. But I also felt certain that when the hour for killing arrived, they would kill. When the real shooting started, many of them would die. This was what soldiers were *for*, just as a hammer was for driving nails.

Warriors and toilers: those seemed, in my boyhood vision, to be the chief destinies for men. They weren't the only destinies, as I learned from having a few male teachers, from reading books, and from watching television. But the men on television—the politicians, the astronauts, the generals, the **savvy** lawyers, the philosophical doctors, the bosses who gave orders to both soldiers and laborers—seemed as remote and unreal to me as the figures in tapestries. I could no more imagine growing up to become one of these cool, potent creatures than I could imagine becoming a prince.

savvy
(săv´ē) *adj.* shrewd, confidently clever.

A nearer and more hopeful example was that of my father, who had escaped from a red-dirt farm to a tire factory, and from the assembly line to the front office. Eventually he dressed in a white shirt and tie. He carried himself as if he had been born to work with his mind. But his body, remembering the earlier years of slogging work, began to give out on him in his fifties, and it quit on him entirely before he turned sixty-five. Even such a partial escape from man's fate as he had accomplished did not seem possible for most of the boys I knew. They joined the Army, stood in line for jobs in the smoky plants, helped build highways. They were bound to work as their fathers had worked, killing themselves or preparing to kill others.

A scholarship enabled me not only to attend college, a rare enough feat in my circle, but even to study in a university meant for the children of the rich. Here I met for the first time young men who had assumed from birth that they would lead lives of comfort and power. And for the first time I met women who told me that men were guilty of having kept all the joys and privileges of the earth for themselves. I was baffled. What privileges? What joys? I thought about the maimed, dismal lives of most of the men back home. What had they stolen from their wives and daughters? The right to go five days a week, twelve months a year, for thirty or forty years to a steel mill or a coal mine? The right to drop bombs and die in war? The right to feel every leak in

“Warriors and toilers: those seemed, in my boyhood vision, to be the chief destinies for men.”

the roof, every gap in the fence, every cough in the engine, as a wound they must mend? The right to feel, when the lay-off comes or the plant shuts down, not only afraid but ashamed?

I was slow to understand the deep grievances of women. This was because, as a boy, I had envied them. Before college, the only people I had ever known who were interested in art or music or literature, the only ones who read books, the only ones who ever seemed to enjoy a sense of ease and grace were the mothers and daughters. Like the menfolk, they fretted about money, they scrimped and made-do. But, when the pay stopped coming in, they were not the ones who had failed. Nor did they have to go to war, and that seemed to me a blessed fact. By comparison with the narrow, ironclad days of fathers, there was an expansiveness, I thought, in the days of mothers. They went to see neighbors, to shop in town, to run errands at school, at the library, at church. No doubt, had I looked harder at their lives, I would have envied them less. It was not my fate to become a woman, so it was easier for me to see the graces. Few of them held jobs outside the home, and those who did filled thankless roles as clerks and waitresses. I didn't see, then, what a prison a house could be, since houses seemed to me brighter, handsomer places than any factory. I did not realize—because such things were never spoken of—how often women suffered from men's bullying. I did learn about the wretchedness of abandoned wives, single mothers, widows; but I also learned about the wretchedness of lone men. Even then I could see how exhausting it was for a mother to cater all day to the needs of young children. But if I had been asked, as a boy, to choose between tending a baby and tending a machine, I think I would have chosen the baby. (Having now tended both, I know I would choose the baby.)

So I was baffled when the women at college accused me and my sex of having cornered the world's pleasures. I think something like my bafflement has been felt by other boys (and by girls as well) who grew up in dirt-poor farm country, in mining country, in black ghettos, in Hispanic barrios, in the shadows of factories, in Third World nations—any place where the fate of men is as grim and bleak as the fate of women. Toilers and warriors. I realize now how ancient these identities are, how deep the tug they exert on men, the undertow of a thousand generations. The miseries I saw, as a boy, in the lives of nearly all men I continue to see in the lives of many—the body-breaking toil, the tedium, the call to be tough, the humiliating powerlessness, the battle for a living and for territory.

When the women I met at college thought about the joys and privileges of men, they did not carry in their minds the sort of men I had known in my childhood. They thought of their fathers, who were bankers, physicians, architects, stockbrokers, the big wheels of the big cities. These fathers rode the train to work or drove cars that cost more than any of my childhood houses. They were attended from morning to night by female helpers, wives and nurses and secretaries. They were never laid off, never short of cash at month's end, never lined up for welfare. These fathers made decisions that mattered. They ran the world.

The daughters of such men wanted to share in this power, this glory. So did I. They yearned for a say over their future, for jobs worthy of their abilities, for the right to live at peace, unmolested, whole. Yes, I thought, yes yes. The difference between me and these daughters was that they saw me, because of my sex, as destined from birth to become like their fathers, and therefore as an enemy to their desires. But I knew better. I wasn't an enemy, in fact or in feeling. I was an ally. If I had known, then, how to tell them so, would they have believed me? Would they now?

COLLABORATIVE DISCUSSION With a partner, discuss how Sanders's views have developed over time.

Determine Author's Point of View

RI 6

"The Men We Carry in Our Minds" is a **personal essay**, a particular type of writing in which writers express their points of view on subjects by reflecting on events or incidents in their own lives. Sanders's essay is informal; it starts with a casual conversation between the writer and a female friend. This discussion in which Anneke calls men "persecutors" prompts the writer to think about how his perception of male roles and responsibilities has been shaped by his past experiences. In this passage he describes the men of his childhood:

> **The bodies of the men I knew were twisted and maimed in ways visible and invisible. The nails of their hands were black and split, the hands tattooed with scars. Some had lost fingers.**

Through these details and the words he chooses—*twisted, maimed, split*, and *scars*—Sanders's perspective on the lives of the men he knew is clearly conveyed to readers.

Determine Central Ideas

RI 2

A **central idea** is an important point about a topic that the writer wants to convey. In this essay, Sanders presents more than one central idea as he reflects on the role of men in society from his own perspective as well as the perspectives of his female friends. By the end of his essay, he has reconciled the ideas conveyed by both viewpoints. He comes to a new understanding of gender roles, as well as the way in which people's past lives shape their present outlooks.

To identify a central idea implied in a paragraph, passage, or selection, examine the details that the writer includes. Consider what point about the topic these details communicate. Then express that idea in a statement.

In this example notice how the details from one of the paragraphs in the essay develop the main idea:

Details	Central Idea
The men of his youth barely earned a living. They did hard physical labor that required them to get up before light and work all day long. In their free time, they repaired their cars and houses and tilled gardens that were lumpy with clay.	Men led dreary lives filled with hard work and little pleasure.

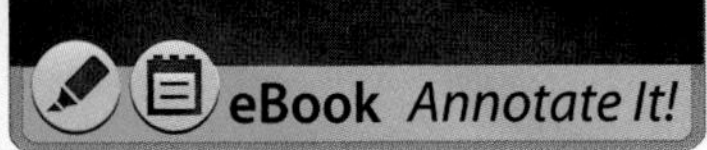

RI 1, RI 2, RI 3, RI 4, RI 6, W 1, SL 3, SL 4

Analyzing the Text

Cite Text Evidence Support your responses with evidence from the selection.

1. **Identify** The term **irony** describes a contrast between expectation and reality. What is ironic about Anneke's statement that life is a lot harder for men?
2. **Interpret** Explain what Sanders means by the phrases "Stone Age hunters" and "genderless cities" in this quotation: "The back roads of Tennessee and Ohio where I grew up were probably closer, in their sexual patterns, to the campsites of Stone Age hunters than to the genderless cities of the future into which we are rushing" (lines 43–46).
3. **Analyze** What central idea about how women view gender roles is conveyed through Anneke's comments and the author's descriptions of his female friends in college?
4. **Analyze** What does the phrase "I dreaded growing up" reveal about the author's perspective on the men he observed in his youth?
5. **Draw Conclusions** Why does Sanders include the paragraph about the women in his childhood (lines 135–159)? How does the contrast between men's and women's lives in this paragraph help support his central idea about men?
6. **Analyze** How does Sanders reconcile his understanding of what men's lives are like with the perspective of his female friends?
7. **Evaluate** Reread lines 59–82. Identify elements of Sanders's style in this passage. **Style** is the distinctive way in which a writer uses language. How effective is Sanders's style in conveying his point of view?
8. **Critique** Is the title "The Men We Carry in Our Minds" appropriate for the essay? Explain why or why not.

PERFORMANCE TASK

Speaking Activity: Debate Sanders presents varying views on gender roles in his essay. As a class, debate which view has more validity and relevance today.

1. Form a team with classmates to support one of the positions.
2. Create an outline stating your claim and identifying the evidence that supports this claim.
3. Take turns presenting each argument and answering questions from the listeners.
4. Students in the audience should write an evaluation of the persuasiveness of each side's argument and decide the "winner" of the debate.

L 4a

Critical Vocabulary

discredit **acrid** **marginal** **savvy**

Practice and Apply Explain which choice accurately fits the meaning of the Critical Vocabulary word.

1. Is a *savvy* professional easily exploited or hard to deceive? Explain.
2. Would peppermint tea or burning rubber have an *acrid* odor?
3. If investigators *discredit* a politician, is the politician likely to get reelected or voted out of office?
4. Does a *marginal* worker enjoy a rich lifestyle or live on a small amount of money?

Vocabulary Strategy: Context Clues

When readers encounter an unfamiliar word, they can use context clues to determine its meaning. **Context clues** are the words, phrases, or sentences that surround an unfamiliar word. Sometimes a clue will be in the same sentence. Other times readers must look before or after the sentence to find the familiar words that help them decide on the meaning of the unknown word. The chart shows the context clues in the essay that could be used to define vocabulary words:

Context Clues	
Quotation	**Clue**
". . . while men feel they're in the wrong. Men are the ones who've been *discredited,* who have to search their souls."	"in the wrong"
"They were *marginal* farmers, just scraping by, or welders . . ."	"just scraping by"

Practice and Apply Return to the essay to find context clues that define each of these words: *lumber* (line 19), *maimed* (line 70), *potent* (line 108), *expansiveness* (line 144).

1. Write the definition based on the clues.
2. Use each word in an original sentence.

Language and Style: Syntax

L 3a

Syntax refers to the way words are arranged in a sentence. Writers use syntax to establish the tone of their writing—for example, the use of complex sentence structures can help create a formal tone. Varying syntax can also make writing more engaging or emphasize certain ideas. The chart shows examples of how Sanders varies his syntax.

Syntax	Purpose	Example
Alternating between short and long sentences	to make writing more engaging	"I search my soul. I discover guilty feelings aplenty—toward the poor, the Vietnamese, Native Americans, the whales, an endless list of debts—a guilt in each case that is as bright and unambiguous as a neon sign."
Sentence fragments	to create an informal tone	"What privileges? What joys?"
Parallel structure	to emphasizes ideas	"Before college, the only people I had ever known who were interested in art or music or literature, the only ones who read books, the only ones who ever seemed to enjoy a sense of ease and grace were the mothers and daughters."

Practice and Apply Write a paragraph in which you express your reaction to the essay, using all three of the types of syntax identified in the chart. Compare your use of varied syntax with a partner.

Write an Informative Essay

W 2a–f Write informative/explanatory texts.
W 4 Produce clear and coherent writing.
W 9 Draw evidence from literary or informational texts.

This collection focuses on gender roles through a variety of viewpoints and genres as well as from a range of cultures and time periods. In the anchor text "The Wife of Bath's Tale," a knight goes on a year-long quest to find out what women most desire in life. What does Chaucer suggest about the ability of people to understand someone of the opposite sex? Write an informative essay about understanding between men and women, drawing on "The Wife of Bath's Tale" and two other selections in this collection.

An effective informative essay includes

- an introduction with a clearly stated thesis statement about understanding between men and women
- a logically structured body that thoroughly develops the topic with relevant examples, concrete details, quotations, and other evidence
- transitions to clarify the relationships between ideas
- a conclusion that follows from the ideas conveyed in the essay
- precise use of language with appropriate tone and style for an informative essay

PLAN

Analyze the Texts Reread "The Wife of Bath's Tale" and take notes on what Chaucer is trying to convey about our ability to understand someone of the opposite sex. Does our inclination to make generalizations about the opposite sex prevent us from understanding each other?

Gather Evidence Use the annotation tools in your eBook to find evidence from two other collection texts. Save your notes in a folder titled *Collection 2 Performance Task A*.

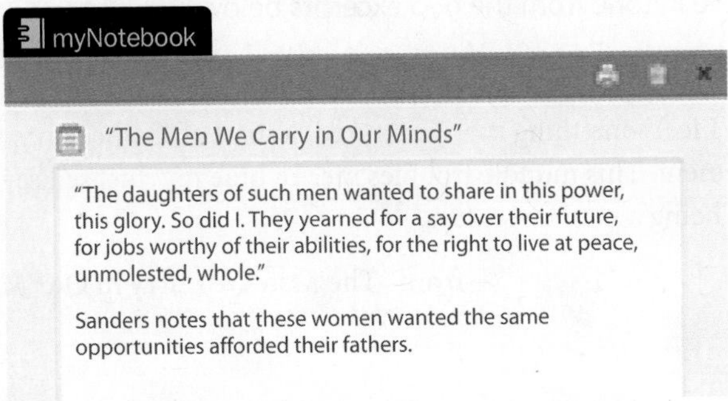

ACADEMIC VOCABULARY

As you write your informative essay, be sure to use these words.

bias
complementary
exploit
inclinations
predominance

Get Organized

Organize your details and evidence in an outline.

- Choose the textual evidence that is the most relevant to your thesis statement.
- Decide what organizational pattern you will use for your essay. For example, will you present your first idea about the ability of men and women to understand each other, citing evidence from all three texts, and then move on to the next idea? Or, will you discuss the texts one at a time, presenting all your ideas and evidence for one selection before turning to the next selection?
- Use your organizational pattern to sort evidence into a logical order.
- Select an interesting quotation or detail from one of the texts to use in the introduction.
- List some ideas for your concluding section. Think about how you can relate your topic to a broader concept regarding gender biases or the roles of men and women.

Interactive Lessons

For help organizing your draft, use

- Writing Informative Texts: Organizing Ideas

PRODUCE

Draft Your Essay

Write a draft of your essay, following your outline.

- Introduce your thesis statement about understanding the opposite sex. Present your topic in an interesting way that will make readers want to continue reading.
- Present your details, facts, quotations, and examples from the texts in logically ordered paragraphs.
- Use appropriate transitions to create cohesion between sections of your essay and to clarify relationships between your topic and the provided evidence.
- Write a concluding section that summarizes the main points of your topic.

myWriteSmart

Write your rough draft in *my*WriteSmart. Focus on getting your ideas down, rather than on perfecting your choice of language.

Interactive Lessons

For more on formal language, use

- Writing Informative Texts: Formal Style

Language and Style: Formal and Informal Language

In an informative essay, your goal as a writer is to remain objective and unbiased—you are not making an argument or stating your opinion. You should also make sure you use formal language. Note the difference in tone from the two excerpts below.

Informal Language

> "But toward women I feel something more confused, a snarl of shame, envy, wary tenderness, and amazement. This muddle troubles me. To hide my unease I say, 'You're right, it's tough being a man these days.'"
>
> —from "The Men We Carry in Our Minds"

Formal Language

> “There appeared to be few confrontations reported with either the traffic or morals police, and at least half a dozen women who were stopped were escorted home and admonished not to drive again, said activists reached by telephone.”
>
> —from “In a Scattered Protest, Saudi Women Take the Wheel”

In the first excerpt, the author uses fragments and contractions to create an informal conversational tone. The second excerpt uses formal language and complex sentences. Review your essay to make sure you have used formal language.

REVISE

myWriteSmart

Have your partner or a group of peers review your draft in *my*WriteSmart. Ask your reviewers to note any evidence that does not support the central ideas.

Improve Your Draft Use the following chart to revise your draft:

Questions	Tips	Revision Techniques
Does the introduction clearly state my thesis statement?	**Underline** your thesis statement.	If needed, **clarify** your thesis statement.
Have I used relevant evidence from each text to support my thesis?	**Highlight** your evidence.	**Add** evidence from one or more texts if needed.
Have I used formal English language?	**Note** any sentence fragments or use of contractions.	**Revise** sentence fragments or contractions to create more formal language.
Does my conclusion follow logically from the body of my essay?	**Underline** the conclusion.	**Clarify** your conclusion by adding a summary statement, if necessary.

PRESENT

Present Your Essay When your final draft is completed, present your essay to a small group. Your classmates will listen attentively, take notes, and ask questions. Group members should pay attention to whether or not the presenter maintained an objective tone throughout the essay and point out aspects of the presenter’s essay that are particularly strong, as well as areas that could be improved.

PERFORMANCE TASK A RUBRIC

INFORMATIVE ESSAY

	Ideas and Evidence	Organization	Language
4	• The introduction is intriguing and informative; the thesis statement clearly identifies a compelling topic. • The topic is strongly developed with relevant facts, concrete details, interesting quotations, and examples from the texts. • The concluding section capably follows from and supports the ideas presented.	• The organization is effective and logical throughout the essay. • Transitions are well crafted and successfully connect related ideas.	• The writing reflects a formal style and an objective, knowledgeable tone. • Language is vivid and precise. • Sentence beginnings, lengths, and structures vary and have a rhythmic flow. • Spelling, capitalization, and punctuation are correct. If handwritten, the essay is legible. • Grammar and usage are correct.
3	• The introduction could do more to attract the reader's curiosity; the thesis statement identifies a topic. • One or two key points could use additional support in the form of relevant facts, concrete details, quotations, and examples from the texts. • The concluding section mostly follows from and supports the ideas presented.	• The organization is confusing in a few places. • A few more transitions are needed to connect related ideas.	• The style is inconsistent in a few places, and the tone is subjective at times. • Vague language is used in a few places. • Sentence beginnings, lengths, and structures vary somewhat. • Some spelling, capitalization, and punctuation mistakes occur. If handwritten, the essay is mostly legible. • Some grammatical and usage errors are repeated in the essay.
2	• The introduction provides some information about a topic but does not include a thesis statement. • Most key points need additional support in the form of relevant facts, concrete details, quotations, and examples from the texts. • The concluding section is confusing and does not follow from the ideas presented.	• The organization is confusing in some places and often doesn't follow a pattern. • More transitions are needed throughout to connect related ideas.	• The style is too informal; the tone conveys subjectivity and a lack of understanding of the topic. • Vague, general language is used in many places. • Sentence structures barely vary, and some fragments or run-on sentences are present. • Spelling, capitalization, and punctuation are often incorrect but do not make reading the essay difficult. If handwritten, the essay may be partially illegible. • Grammar and usage are incorrect in many places, but the writer's ideas are still clear.
1	• The appropriate elements of an introduction are missing. • Facts, details, quotations, and examples from the texts are missing. • The essay lacks an identifiable concluding section.	• A logical organization is not used; information is presented randomly. • Transitions are not used, making the essay difficult to understand.	• The style and tone are inappropriate for the essay. • Language is too vague or general to convey the information. • Repetitive sentence structure, fragments, and run-on sentences make the writing monotonous and difficult to follow. • Spelling, capitalization, and punctuation are incorrect throughout. If handwritten, the essay may be partially or mostly illegible. • Many grammatical and usage errors change the meaning of the writer's ideas.

COLLECTION 2
PERFORMANCE TASK B

Interactive Lessons

To help you complete this task, use
- *Writing as a Process*
- *Giving a Presentation*

W 3a–e Write narratives.
SL 4 Present information.

Deliver a Reflective Narrative

This collection explores traditional roles of men and women as well as changes in gender roles that have occurred in recent decades. Look back at the texts and think about how gender roles have evolved over time. In the anchor text "The Men We Carry in Our Minds," Scott Russell Sanders offers a nuanced view of feminism, arguing that the jobs that were once monopolized by men were not always so enviable. How have the texts in this collection changed the way that you think about gender roles? Think about an experience in your own life that has challenged or strengthened your beliefs in the differences between men and women. Write a reflective narrative about your experience and then present it to the class.

An effective reflective narrative

- explores the significance of a personal experience, event, or concern
- uses sensory language to convey a vivid picture
- includes appropriate narrative techniques such as dialogue, pacing, and description
- draws comparisons between the specific incident and broader themes about gender roles

Mentor Text Note how Sanders reflects on his changing opinions of women as he ages in "The Men We Carry in Our Minds."

> "I didn't see, then, what a prison a house could be, since houses seemed to me brighter, handsomer places than any factory. I did not realize—because such things were never spoken of—how often women suffered from men's bullying. I did learn about the wretchedness of abandoned wives, single mothers, widows; but I also learned about the wretchedness of lone men."

PLAN

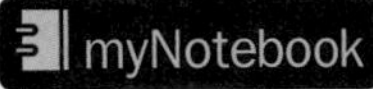

Use the annotation tools in your eBook to find evidence about changing gender roles. Save each piece of evidence to your notebook.

Analyze the Texts Think about the author's experiences and ask yourself if they remind you of an experience in your own life. When did you become aware of the differences between genders? How have your views about gender changed as you've grown? Which texts in this collection challenged your thinking about gender roles, and why? Pick a specific incident from your life that has influenced your views on gender and write about it.

Create an Outline Pick a specific incident from your life that has influenced your views on gender and write about it.

- What texts from this collection reminded you of that incident, and why? Use quotations or examples from one of the collection texts to create the introduction to your narrative.
- What happened during the incident? Make sure to explain the experience in a logical, sequential order.
- What did the experience mean to you? How did the experience change your thinking about gender roles? Use your conclusion to summarize and reflect on your thoughts.

Write your outline in *my*WriteSmart. Follow a logical outline format so your notes are easy to refer to later.

Reread "The Men We Carry in Our Minds," and take notes about how Sanders conveys his view on gender roles. Gather evidence from the text, and note any specific details, quotations, or examples. Then review and take notes on your other chosen text(s). Pay attention to ways in which the texts may make suggestions about the continued evolution of gender roles in the next ten years. Will we see a change in the predominance of men in positions of power? Will existing gender biases change or disappear? Will women continue to break barriers to equality?

PRODUCE

Draft Your Reflective Narrative Using your notes and outline, write a draft of your narrative.

- Begin with an interesting quotation from one of the collection texts to catch readers' interest. Provide an explanation for why this piece resonated with you.
- Transition into describing your personal experience. Make sure you use narrative techniques such as dialogue, pacing, description, and sensory language.
- Provide a conclusion that reflects on your experience and summarizes your beliefs about gender roles.

ACADEMIC VOCABULARY

As you draft your narrative, use these words.

bias
complementary
exploit
inclinations
predominance

Interactive Lessons

For help planning and drafting your essay, use

- Writing as a Process: Planning and Drafting

Language and Style: Sensory Language

To capture your audience's interest, you will want to bring your experience to life for them. Use vivid details and sensory language in your narrative to convey a vivid picture. Note how Sanders uses details in the passage below to describe "the first men" he remembers seeing—

> "The prisoners wore dingy gray-and-black zebra suits, heavy as canvas, sodden with sweat. Hatless, stooped, they chopped weeds in the fierce heat, row after row, breathing the acrid dust of boll-weevil poison. The overseers wore dazzling white shirts and broad shadowy hats. The oiled barrels of their shotguns flashed in the sunlight. Their faces in memory are utterly blank."

Look for places in your essay where you can create a more vivid memory by using sensory language.

REVISE

Practice Your Presentation

Practice Your Presentation Present your narrative aloud. Try speaking in front of a mirror or make a recording of yourself and listen to it. Remember to use appropriate eye contact, adequate volume, and clear pronunciation. Use the chart below to help you evaluate your presentation.

Questions	Tips	Revision Techniques
Does the introduction grab the audience's attention?	**Underline** sentences that provide interest to your audience.	If needed, **add** an attention-grabber to your introduction.
Do you use narrative techniques and descriptive details to relate the events in your narrative?	**Highlight** where you include narrative techniques and descriptive details.	**Add** variety to your presentation by using dialogue and vivid description.
Does the presentation explore the significance of a personal experience or concern?	**Note** sentences that explore the significance of your experience.	**Clarify** for your listener the personal impact of your experience.
Does the conclusion sum up your ideas and draw comparisons to broader ideas about gender roles?	**Underline** your conclusion.	If needed, **add** a sentence or two relating your personal experience to broader ideas.

PRESENT

Deliver Your Presentation Present your narrative to the whole class. The audience should listen and take notes. You should be prepared to answer questions about your experience. Remember to use both verbal and nonverbal techniques when delivering your presentation.

- Use formal language to present your ideas, but if using dialogue in your narrative, use informal expressions.
- Speak clearly and at an appropriate volume and pace.
- Invite students to ask you questions about your experience.

Interactive Lessons
For help with your presentation, use
- Giving a Presentation: Delivering Your Presentation

PERFORMANCE TASK B RUBRIC

REFLECTIVE NARRATIVE

	Ideas and Evidence	Organization	Language
4	• The speaker effectively narrates an event and its importance. • The speaker concludes by reflecting on the importance of the experience.	• The speaker makes an insightful link between a collection text and the experience described. • Ideas and events progress in a logical order and are linked with effective transitions.	• Vivid sensory descriptions and precise language bring the experience to life. • The speaker is easy to understand and adapts volume and pacing to audience needs.
3	• The event and its significance are clear to listeners. • The conclusion summarizes most of the speaker's feelings.	• A link or comparison is made between a collection text and the speaker's experience. • The order of ideas and events is logical, and transitions are generally used.	• The speaker describes events and ideas using some sensory language and some precise word choices. • The speaker is generally easy to understand and uses appropriate volume and pacing.
2	• The narrative is hard to follow or its significance to the speaker is vague at times. • The conclusion lacks reflection on the importance of the experience.	• A collection text is mentioned, but the connection between it and the speaker's experience may be weak. • Ideas and events may seem disorganized, and the narrative may lack some needed transitions.	• The speaker uses one or two precise word choices or details that appeal to the senses. • The speaker is occasionally difficult to understand.
1	• The speaker fails to communicate the event clearly or identify its significance. • The narrative lacks a conclusion.	• The speaker makes no link to a text from the collection. • Ideas and events are presented in a disorganized way with no transitions.	• Descriptions of events and ideas are vague and fail to create an impression of what the experience was like. • The speaker is often difficult to understand.

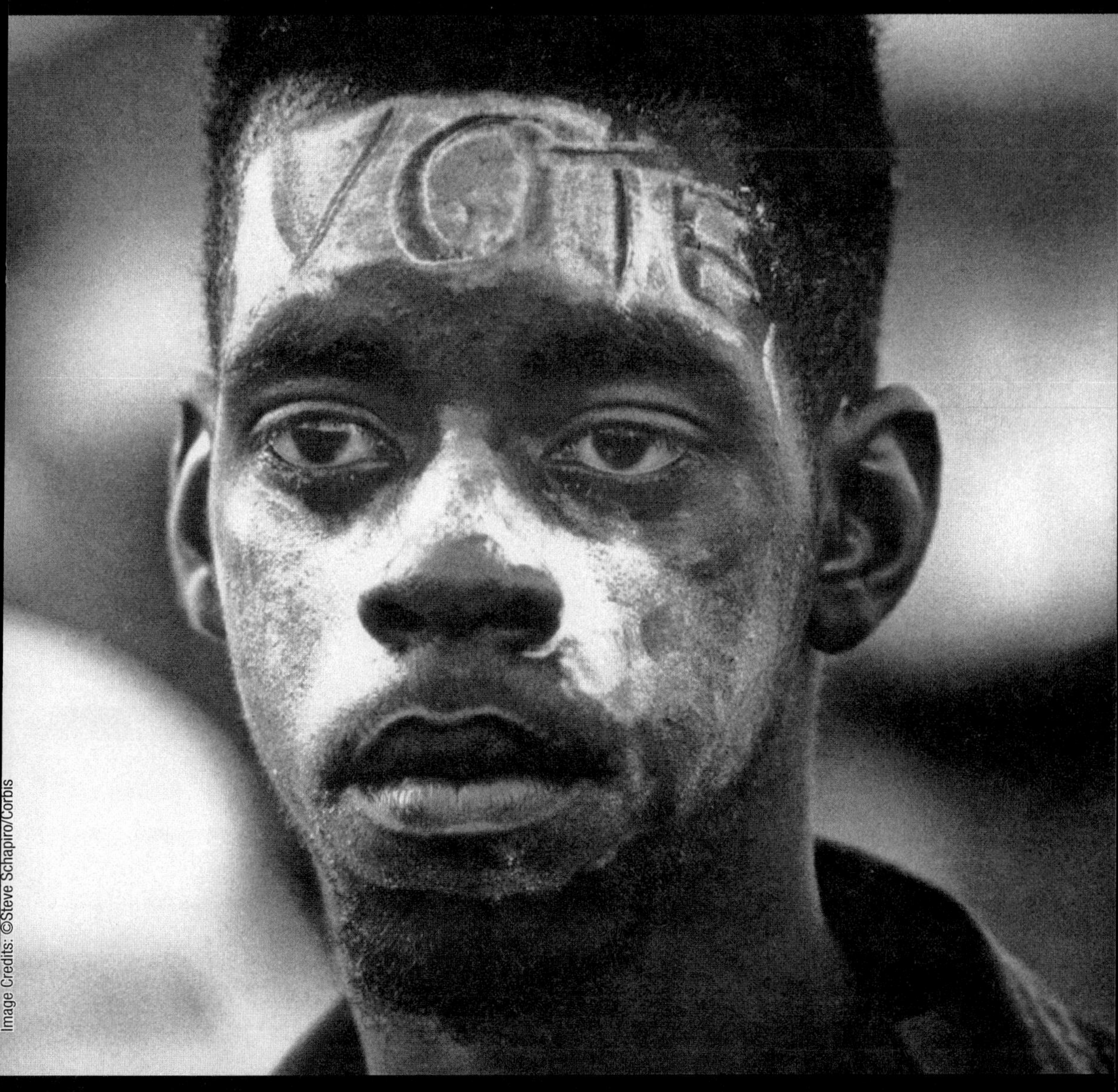

Image Credits: ©Steve Schapiro/Corbis

Voices of Protest

COLLECTION **3**

Voices of Protest

This collection represents nearly three centuries of opposition to injustice, addressing problems such as tyranny, hunger, and pollution.

Stream to Start

Channel One News®

COLLECTION

PERFORMANCE TASK Preview

At the end of this collection, you will have the opportunity to complete two tasks:

- Participate in a group discussion about the nature of injustice and ways to end it.
- Using "A Modest Proposal" as a model, write a satire on a topic discussed in one of the selections.

ACADEMIC VOCABULARY

Study the words and their definitions in the chart below. You will use these words as you discuss and write about the texts in this collection.

Word	Definition	Related Forms
controversy (kŏn´trə-vûr´sē) *n.*	public disagreement, argument	controversial, controvert
convince (kən-vĭns´) *n.*	persuade or lead to agreement by means of argument	convict, conviction
ethics (ĕth´ĭks) *n.*	rules of conduct or set of principles	ethical, ethicist
radical (răd´ĭ-kəl) *adj.*	extreme; desirous of change in established institutions or practices	radicalism, radicalize
tension (tĕn´shən) *n.*	mental strain or excitement	tense, tensive

HISTORY VIDEO

Martin Luther King Jr. (1929–1968), a Baptist minister and social activist, was the most prominent leader of the civil rights movement from the mid-1950s until his assassination in 1968. He was committed to using nonviolent protest to end legal discrimination and segregation in the United States. His efforts aided in the passage of the Civil Rights Act of 1964 and the Voting Rights Act of 1965. In the mid-1960s, he grew concerned about the involvement of the United States in the Vietnam War. He gradually became more vocal in his opposition to the war, giving this speech on April 4, 1967, at the Riverside Church in New York City.

Speech on the Vietnam War, 1967

Speech by Martin Luther King Jr.

AS YOU READ Look for connections between King's opposition to the war and his civil rights work. Note any questions you have as you read.

As you read, mark up the text. Save your work to ***myNotebook***.

- Highlight details
- Add notes and questions
- Add new words to ***myWordList***

I come to this platform tonight to make a passionate plea to my beloved nation. This speech is not addressed to Hanoi or to the National Liberation Front.[1] It is not addressed to China or to Russia. Nor is it an attempt to overlook the ambiguity of the total situation and the need for a collective solution to the tragedy of Vietnam. Neither is it an attempt to make North Vietnam or the National Liberation Front paragons of virtue, nor to overlook the role they must play in the successful resolution of the problem. While they both may have justifiable reasons to be suspicious of the good faith of the United States, life and history give eloquent testimony to the fact that conflicts are never resolved without trustful give and take on both sides. Tonight, however, I wish not to speak with Hanoi and the National Liberation Front, but rather to my fellow Americans.

Since I am a preacher by calling, I suppose it is not surprising that I have seven major reasons for bringing Vietnam into the field of my moral vision. There is at the outset a very obvious and almost **facile**

facile (făs′əl) *adj.* easy to make or understand.

[1] **National Liberation Front:** also known as the Vietcong, revolutionary fighters in South Vietnam.

connection between the war in Vietnam and the struggle I and others have been waging in America. A few years ago there was a shining moment in that struggle. It seemed as if there was a real promise of hope for the poor, both black and white, through the poverty program.[2] There were experiments, hopes, new beginnings. Then came the buildup in Vietnam, and I watched this program broken and **eviscerated** as if it were some idle political plaything of a society gone mad on war. And I knew that America would never invest the necessary funds or energies in rehabilitation of its poor so long as adventures like Vietnam continued to draw men and skills and money like some demonic, destructive suction tube. So I was increasingly compelled to see the war as an enemy of the poor and to attack it as such.

eviscerate (ĭ-vĭs´ə-rāt´) *v.* to remove the necessary or important parts of.

Perhaps a more tragic recognition of reality took place when it became clear to me that the war was doing far more than devastating the hopes of the poor at home. It was sending their sons and their brothers and their husbands to fight and to die in extraordinarily high proportions relative to the rest of the population. We were taking the black young men who had been crippled by our society and sending them eight thousand miles away to guarantee liberties in Southeast Asia which they had not found in southwest Georgia and East Harlem. So we have been repeatedly faced with the cruel irony of watching Negro and white boys on TV screens as they kill and die together for a nation that has been unable to seat them together in the same schools. So we watch them in brutal solidarity burning the huts of a poor village, but we realize that they would hardly live on the same block in Chicago. I could not be silent in the face of such cruel manipulation of the poor.

My third reason moves to an even deeper level of awareness, for it grows out of my experience in the ghettos of the North over the last three years, especially the last three summers. As I have walked among the desperate, rejected, and angry young men, I have told them that Molotov cocktails[3] and rifles would not solve their problems. I have tried to offer them my deepest compassion while maintaining my conviction that social change comes most meaningfully through nonviolent action. But they asked, and rightly so, "What about Vietnam?" They asked if our own nation wasn't using massive doses of violence to solve its problems, to bring about the changes it wanted. Their questions hit home, and I knew that I could never again raise my voice against the violence of the oppressed in the ghettos without having first spoken clearly to the greatest purveyor of violence in the world today: my own government. For the sake of those boys, for the

[2] **poverty program:** legislation, often called the "War on Poverty," enacted in 1964 during Lyndon Johnson's administration.

[3] **Molotov cocktails:** home-made incendiary weapons made by filling breakable bottles with a flammable liquid, attaching and lighting wicks, and throwing them at a target.

sake of this government, for the sake of the hundreds of thousands trembling under our violence, I cannot be silent.

For those who ask the question, "Aren't you a civil rights leader?" and thereby mean to exclude me from the movement for peace, I have this further answer. In 1957, when a group of us formed the Southern Christian Leadership Conference, we chose as our motto: "To save the soul of America." We were convinced that we could not limit our vision to certain rights for black people, but instead affirmed the conviction that America would never be free or saved from itself until the descendants of its slaves were loosed completely from the shackles they still wear. In a way we were agreeing with Langston Hughes, that black bard of Harlem, who had written earlier:

O, yes, I say it plain,
America never was America to me,
And yet I swear this oath—
America will be!

Now it should be incandescently clear that no one who has any concern for the integrity and life of America today can ignore the present war. If America's soul becomes totally poisoned, part of the autopsy must read "Vietnam." It can never be saved so long as it destroys the deepest hopes of men the world over. So it is that those of us who are yet determined that "America will be" are led down the path of protest and dissent, working for the health of our land.

As if the weight of such a commitment to the life and health of America were not enough, another burden of responsibility was placed upon me in 1964. And I cannot forget that the Nobel Peace Prize[4] was also a commission, a commission to work harder than I had ever worked before for the brotherhood of man. This is a calling that takes me beyond national allegiances.

But even if it were not present, I would yet have to live with the meaning of my commitment to the ministry of Jesus Christ. To me, the relationship of this ministry to the making of peace is so obvious that I sometimes marvel at those who ask me why I am speaking against the war. Could it be that they do not know that the Good News[5] was meant for all men—for communist and capitalist, for their children and ours, for black and for white, for revolutionary and conservative? Have they forgotten that my ministry is in obedience to the one who loved his enemies so fully that he died for them? What then can I say to the Vietcong[6] or to Castro or to Mao as a faithful minister of this one? Can I threaten them with death or must I not share with them my life?

[4] **Nobel Peace Prize:** an annual award given to an individual who best promotes international friendship, reduces military forces, and fosters peaceful relations. King won the prize in 1964.

[5] **Good News:** the Gospels, or the written accounts of Jesus and his teachings.

[6] **Vietcong:** the National Liberation Front, South Vietnamese revolutionaries.

Finally, as I try to explain for you and for myself the road that leads from Montgomery[7] to this place, I would have offered all that was most valid if I simply said that I must be true to my conviction that I share with all men the calling to be a son of the living God. Beyond the calling of race or nation or creed is this vocation of sonship and brotherhood. Because I believe that the Father is deeply concerned, especially for His suffering and helpless and outcast children, I come tonight to speak for them. This I believe to be the privilege and the burden of all of us who deem ourselves bound by allegiances and loyalties which are broader and deeper than nationalism and which go beyond our nation's self-defined goals and positions. We are called to speak for the weak, for the voiceless, for the victims of our nation, for those it calls "enemy," for no document from human hands can make these humans any less our brothers.

And as I ponder the madness of Vietnam and search within myself for ways to understand and respond in compassion, my mind goes constantly to the people of that peninsula. I speak now not of the soldiers of each side, not of the ideologies of the Liberation Front, not of the junta in Saigon, but simply of the people who have been living under the curse of war for almost three continuous decades now. I think of them, too, because it is clear to me that there will be no meaningful solution there until some attempt is made to know them and hear their broken cries.

They must see Americans as strange liberators. The Vietnamese people proclaimed their own independence in 1954—in 1945 rather—after a combined French and Japanese occupation and before the communist revolution in China. They were led by Ho Chi Minh. Even though they quoted the American Declaration of Independence in their own document of freedom, we refused to recognize them. Instead, we decided to support France in its reconquest of her former colony. Our government felt then that the Vietnamese people were not ready for independence, and we again fell victim to the deadly Western arrogance that has poisoned the international atmosphere for so long. With that tragic decision we rejected a revolutionary government seeking self-determination and a government that had been established not by China—for whom the Vietnamese have no great love—but by clearly **indigenous** forces that included some communists. For the peasants this new government meant real land reform, one of the most important needs in their lives.

indigenous (ĭn-dĭj´ə-nəs) *adj.* native to a land.

For nine years following 1945 we denied the people of Vietnam the right of independence. For nine years we vigorously supported the French in their abortive effort to recolonize Vietnam. Before the end of the war we were meeting 80 percent of the French war costs. Even before the French were defeated at Dien Bien Phu, they began to

[7] **Montgomery:** Alabama city and site of the 1955 bus boycott, a civil rights protest that brought King to national prominence.

despair of their reckless action, but we did not. We encouraged them with our huge financial and military supplies to continue the war even after they had lost the will. Soon we would be paying almost the full costs of this tragic attempt at recolonization.

After the French were defeated, it looked as if independence and land reform would come again through the Geneva Agreement. But instead there came the United States, determined that Ho should not unify the temporarily divided nation, and the peasants watched again as we supported one of the most vicious modern dictators, our chosen man, Premier Diem.[8] The peasants watched and cringed as Diem ruthlessly rooted out all opposition, supported their **extortionist** landlords, and refused even to discuss reunification with the North. The peasants watched as all of this was presided over by United States influence and then by increasing numbers of United States troops who came to help quell the **insurgency** that Diem's methods had aroused. When Diem was overthrown they may have been happy, but the long line of military dictators seemed to offer no real change, especially in terms of their need for land and peace.

extortionist (ĭk-stôr′shən-ĭst) *n.* one who obtains something by force or threat.

insurgency (ĭn-sûr′jən-sē) *n.* rebellion or revolt.

The only change came from America as we increased our troop commitments in support of governments which were singularly corrupt, inept, and without popular support. All the while the people read our leaflets and received the regular promises of peace and democracy and land reform. Now they languish under our bombs and consider us, not their fellow Vietnamese, the real enemy. They move sadly and apathetically as we herd them off the land of their fathers into concentration camps where minimal social needs are rarely met. They know they must move on or be destroyed by our bombs.

So they go, primarily women and children and the aged. They watch as we poison their water, as we kill a million acres of their crops. They must weep as the bulldozers roar through their areas preparing to destroy the precious trees. They wander into the hospitals with at least twenty casualties from American firepower for one Vietcong-inflicted injury. So far we may have killed a million of them, mostly children. They wander into the towns and see thousands of the children, homeless, without clothes, running in packs on the streets like animals. They see the children degraded by our soldiers as they beg for food. They see the children selling their sisters to our soldiers, soliciting for their mothers.

What do the peasants think as we ally ourselves with the landlords and as we refuse to put any action into our many words concerning land reform? What do they think as we test out our latest weapons on them, just as the Germans tested out new medicine and new tortures in the concentration camps of Europe? Where are the

[8] **Premier Diem** (dē-ĕm′): Ngo Dinh Diem (1901–1963), the first president of South Vietnam in 1955, who was later killed in a military coup.

roots of the independent Vietnam we claim to be building? Is it among these voiceless ones?

We have destroyed their two most cherished institutions: the family and the village. We have destroyed their land and their crops. We have cooperated in the crushing of the nation's only noncommunist revolutionary political force, the unified Buddhist Church. We have supported the enemies of the peasants of Saigon. We have corrupted their women and children and killed their men.

Now there is little left to build on, save bitterness. Soon the only solid physical foundations remaining will be found at our military bases and in the concrete of the concentration camps we call "fortified hamlets." The peasants may well wonder if we plan to build our new Vietnam on such grounds as these. Could we blame them for such thoughts? We must speak for them and raise the questions they cannot raise. These, too, are our brothers.

Perhaps a more difficult but no less necessary task is to speak for those who have been designated as our enemies. What of the National Liberation Front, that strangely anonymous group we call "VC" or "communists"? What must they think of the United States of America when they realize that we permitted the repression and cruelty of Diem, which helped to bring them into being as a resistance group in the South? What do they think of our condoning the violence which led to their own taking up of arms? How can they believe in our integrity when now we speak of "aggression from the North" as if there were nothing more essential to the war? How can they trust us when now we charge them with violence after the murderous reign of

Diem and charge them with violence while we pour every new weapon of death into their land? Surely we must understand their feelings, even if we do not condone their actions. Surely we must see that the men we supported pressed them to their violence. Surely we must see that our own computerized plans of destruction simply dwarf their greatest acts.

How do they judge us when our officials know that their membership is less than 25 percent communist, and yet insist on giving them the blanket name? What must they be thinking when they know that we are aware of their control of major sections of Vietnam, and yet we appear ready to allow national elections in which this highly organized political parallel government will not have a part? They ask how we can speak of free elections when the Saigon press is censored and controlled by the military junta. And they are surely right to wonder what kind of new government we plan to help form without them, the only party in real touch with the peasants. They question our political goals and they deny the reality of a peace settlement from which they will be excluded. Their questions are frighteningly relevant. Is our nation planning to build on political myth again, and then shore it up upon the power of a new violence?

Here is the true meaning and value of compassion and nonviolence, when it helps us to see the enemy's point of view, to hear his questions, to know his assessment of ourselves. For from his view we may indeed see the basic weaknesses of our own condition, and if we are mature, we may learn and grow and profit from the wisdom of the brothers who are called the opposition.

So, too, with Hanoi. In the North, where our bombs now pummel the land, and our mines endanger the waterways, we are met by a deep but understandable mistrust. To speak for them is to explain this lack of confidence in Western words, and especially their distrust of American intentions now. In Hanoi are the men who led the nation to independence against the Japanese and the French, the men who sought membership in the French Commonwealth and were betrayed by the weakness of Paris and the willfulness of the colonial armies. It was they who led a second struggle against French domination at tremendous costs, and then were persuaded to give up the land they controlled between the thirteenth and seventeenth parallel as a temporary measure at Geneva. After 1954 they watched us conspire with Diem to prevent elections which could have surely brought Ho Chi Minh to power over a united Vietnam, and they realized they had been betrayed again. When we ask why they do not leap to negotiate, these things must be remembered.

Also, it must be clear that the leaders of Hanoi considered the presence of American troops in support of the Diem regime to have been the initial military breach of the Geneva Agreement concerning foreign troops. They remind us that they did not begin to send troops in large numbers and even supplies into the South until American forces had moved into the tens of thousands.

Hanoi remembers how our leaders refused to tell us the truth about the earlier North Vietnamese overtures for peace, how the president claimed that none existed when they had clearly been made. Ho Chi Minh has watched as America has spoken of peace and built up its forces, and now he has surely heard the increasing international rumors of American plans for an invasion of the North. He knows the bombing and shelling and mining we are doing are part of traditional pre-invasion strategy. Perhaps only his sense of humor and of irony can save him when he hears the most powerful nation of the world speaking of aggression as it drops thousands of bombs on a poor, weak nation more than eight hundred, or rather, eight thousand miles away from its shores.

At this point I should make it clear that while I have tried in these last few minutes to give a voice to the voiceless in Vietnam and to understand the arguments of those who are called "enemy," I am as deeply concerned about our own troops there as anything else. For it occurs to me that what we are submitting them to in Vietnam is not simply the brutalizing process that goes on in any war where armies face each other and seek to destroy. We are adding cynicism to the process of death, for they must know after a short period there that none of the things we claim to be fighting for are really involved. Before long they must know that their government has sent them into a struggle among Vietnamese, and the more sophisticated surely realize that we are on the side of the wealthy, and the secure, while we create a hell for the poor.

Somehow this madness must cease. We must stop now. I speak as a child of God and brother to the suffering poor of Vietnam. I speak for those whose land is being laid waste, whose homes are being destroyed, whose culture is being subverted. I speak for the poor of America who are paying the double price of smashed hopes at home, and dealt death and corruption in Vietnam. I speak as a citizen of the world, for the world as it stands aghast at the path we have taken. I speak as one who loves America, to the leaders of our own nation: The great initiative in this war is ours; the initiative to stop it must be ours.

This is the message of the great Buddhist leaders of Vietnam. Recently one of them wrote these words, and I quote:

> Each day the war goes on the hatred increases in the heart of the Vietnamese and in the hearts of those of humanitarian instinct. The Americans are forcing even their friends into becoming their enemies. It is curious that the Americans, who calculate so carefully on the possibilities of military victory, do not realize that in the process they are incurring deep psychological and political defeat. The image of America will never again be the image of

revolution, freedom, and democracy, but the image of violence and militarism.

Unquote.

If we continue, there will be no doubt in my mind and in the mind of the world that we have no honorable intentions in Vietnam. If we do not stop our war against the people of Vietnam immediately, the world will be left with no other alternative than to see this as some horrible, clumsy, and deadly game we have decided to play. The world now demands a maturity of America that we may not be able to achieve. It demands that we admit that we have been wrong from the beginning of our adventure in Vietnam, that we have been detrimental to the life of the Vietnamese people. The situation is one in which we must be ready to turn sharply from our present ways. In order to atone for our sins and errors in Vietnam, we should take the initiative in bringing a halt to this tragic war.

I would like to suggest five concrete things that our government should do immediately to begin the long and difficult process of extricating ourselves from this nightmarish conflict:

Number one: End all bombing in North and South Vietnam.

Number two: Declare a unilateral cease-fire in the hope that such action will create the atmosphere for negotiation.

Three: Take immediate steps to prevent other battlegrounds in Southeast Asia by curtailing our military buildup in Thailand and our interference in Laos.

Four: Realistically accept the fact that the National Liberation Front has substantial support in South Vietnam and must thereby play a role in any meaningful negotiations and any future Vietnam government.

Five: Set a date that we will remove all foreign troops from Vietnam in accordance with the 1954 Geneva Agreement. [*Sustained applause*]

Part of our ongoing [*Applause continues*], part of our ongoing commitment might well express itself in an offer to grant asylum to any Vietnamese who fears for his life under a new regime which included the Liberation Front. Then we must make what **reparations** we can for the damage we have done. We must provide the medical aid that is badly needed, making it available in this country if necessary. Meanwhile [*Applause*], meanwhile, we in the churches and synagogues have a continuing task while we urge our government to disengage itself from a disgraceful commitment. We must continue to raise our voices and our lives if our nation persists in its perverse ways in Vietnam. We must be prepared to match actions with words by seeking out every creative method of protest possible.

reparations (rĕp′ə-rā′shəns) *n.* compensation or payment from a nation for damage or injury during a war.

As we counsel young men concerning military service, we must clarify for them our nation's role in Vietnam and challenge them with the alternative of conscientious objection.[9] [*Sustained applause*] I am pleased to say that this is a path now chosen by more than seventy students at my own alma mater, Morehouse College, and I recommend it to all who find the American course in Vietnam a dishonorable and unjust one. [*Applause*] Moreover, I would encourage all ministers of draft age to give up their ministerial exemptions and seek status as conscientious objectors. [*Applause*] These are the times for real choices and not false ones. We are at the moment when our lives must be placed on the line if our nation is to survive its own folly. Every man of humane convictions must decide on the protest that best suits his convictions, but we must all protest.

Now there is something seductively tempting about stopping there and sending us all off on what in some circles has become a popular crusade against the war in Vietnam. I say we must enter that struggle, but I wish to go on now to say something even more disturbing.

The war in Vietnam is but a symptom of a far deeper malady within the American spirit, and if we ignore this sobering reality [*Applause*], and if we ignore this sobering reality, we will find ourselves organizing "clergy and laymen concerned" committees for the next generation. They will be concerned about Guatemala and Peru. They will be concerned about Thailand and Cambodia. They will be concerned about Mozambique and South Africa. We will be marching for these and a dozen other names and attending rallies without end unless there is a significant and profound change in American life and policy. [*Sustained applause*] So such thoughts take us beyond Vietnam, but not beyond our calling as sons of the living God.

In 1957 a sensitive American official overseas said that it seemed to him that our nation was on the wrong side of a world revolution. During the past ten years we have seen emerge a pattern of suppression which has now justified the presence of U.S. military advisors in Venezuela. This need to maintain social stability for our investments accounts for the counter-revolutionary action of American forces in Guatemala. It tells why American helicopters are being used against guerrillas in Cambodia and why American napalm and Green Beret forces have already been active against rebels in Peru.

It is with such activity in mind that the words of the late John F. Kennedy come back to haunt us. Five years ago he said, "Those who make peaceful revolution impossible will make violent revolution inevitable." [*Applause*] Increasingly, by choice or by accident, this is the role our nation has taken, the role of those who make peaceful revolution impossible by refusing to give up the privileges and the pleasures that come from the immense profits of overseas investments. I am convinced that if we are to get on the right side of the world

[9] **conscientious objection:** the refusal to participate in military actions because of moral or religious beliefs.

“The war in Vietnam is but a symptom of a far deeper malady within the American spirit.”

revolution, we as a nation must undergo a radical revolution of values. We must rapidly begin [*Applause*], we must rapidly begin the shift from a thing-oriented society to a person-oriented society. When machines and computers, profit motives and property rights, are considered more important than people, the giant triplets of racism, extreme materialism, and militarism are incapable of being conquered.

A true revolution of values will soon cause us to question the fairness and justice of many of our past and present policies. On the one hand we are called to play the Good Samaritan on life’s roadside, but that will be only an initial act. One day we must come to see that the whole Jericho Road[10] must be transformed so that men and women will not be constantly beaten and robbed as they make their journey on life’s highway. True compassion is more than flinging a coin to a beggar. It comes to see that an edifice which produces beggars needs restructuring. [*Applause*]

A true revolution of values will soon look uneasily on the glaring contrast of poverty and wealth. With righteous indignation, it will look across the seas and see individual capitalists of the West investing huge sums of money in Asia, Africa, and South America, only to take the profits out with no concern for the social betterment of the countries, and say, “This is not just.” It will look at our alliance with the landed gentry of South America and say, “This is not just.” The Western arrogance of feeling that it has everything to teach others and nothing to learn from them is not just.

A true revolution of values will lay hand on the world order and say of war, “This way of settling differences is not just.” This business of burning human beings with napalm,[11] of filling our nation’s homes with orphans and widows, of injecting poisonous drugs of hate into the veins of peoples normally humane, of sending men home from dark and bloody battlefields physically handicapped and

[10] **Jericho Road:** an ancient route between Jerusalem and Jericho. In the New Testament, the Good Samaritan stops on this road to help an injured robbery victim.

[11] **napalm:** an incendiary fuel used in U.S. bombs to burn Vietnamese opponents.

psychologically deranged, cannot be reconciled with wisdom, justice, and love. A nation that continues year after year to spend more money on military defense than on programs of social uplift is approaching spiritual death. [*Sustained applause*]

America, the richest and most powerful nation in the world, can well lead the way in this revolution of values. There is nothing except a tragic death wish to prevent us from reordering our priorities so that the pursuit of peace will take precedence over the pursuit of war. There is nothing to keep us from molding a **recalcitrant** status quo with bruised hands until we have fashioned it into a brotherhood.

recalcitrant
(rĭ-kăl´sĭ-trənt) *adj.* uncooperative and resistant of authority.

This kind of positive revolution of values is our best defense against communism. [*Applause*] War is not the answer. Communism will never be defeated by the use of atomic bombs or nuclear weapons. Let us not join those who shout war and, through their misguided passions, urge the United States to relinquish its participation in the United Nations. These are days which demand wise restraint and calm reasonableness. We must not engage in a negative anticommunism, but rather in a positive thrust for democracy [*Applause*], realizing that our greatest defense against communism is to take offensive action in behalf of justice. We must with positive action seek to remove those conditions of poverty, insecurity, and injustice, which are the fertile soil in which the seed of communism grows and develops.

These are revolutionary times. All over the globe men are revolting against old systems of exploitation and oppression, and out of the wounds of a frail world, new systems of justice and equality are being born. The shirtless and barefoot people of the land are rising up as never before. The people who sat in darkness have seen a great light. We in the West must support these revolutions.

It is a sad fact that because of comfort, complacency, a morbid fear of communism, and our proneness to adjust to injustice, the Western nations that initiated so much of the revolutionary spirit of the modern world have now become the arch antirevolutionaries. This has driven many to feel that only Marxism has a revolutionary spirit. Therefore, communism is a judgment against our failure to make democracy real and follow through on the revolutions that we initiated. Our only hope today lies in our ability to recapture the revolutionary spirit and go out into a sometimes hostile world declaring eternal hostility to poverty, racism, and militarism. With this powerful commitment we shall boldly challenge the status quo and unjust mores, and thereby speed the day when every valley shall be exalted, and every mountain and hill shall be made low [*Audience:*] (*Yes*); the crooked shall be made straight, and the rough places plain.[12]

A genuine revolution of values means in the final analysis that our loyalties must become ecumenical rather than sectional. Every nation

[12] **every valley shall be . . . plain:** biblical quote from the Old Testament book of Isaiah describing the arrival of the Messiah.

must now develop an overriding loyalty to mankind as a whole in order to preserve the best in their individual societies.

This call for a worldwide fellowship that lifts neighborly concern beyond one's tribe, race, class, and nation is in reality a call for an all-embracing and unconditional love for all mankind. This oft misunderstood, this oft misinterpreted concept, so readily dismissed by the Nietzsches[13] of the world as a weak and cowardly force, has now become an absolute necessity for the survival of man. When I speak of love I am not speaking of some sentimental and weak response. I'm not speaking of that force which is just emotional bosh. I am speaking of that force which all of the great religions have seen as the supreme unifying principle of life. Love is somehow the key that unlocks the door which leads to ultimate reality. This Hindu-Muslim-Christian-Jewish-Buddhist belief about ultimate reality is beautifully summed up in the first epistle of Saint John: "Let us love one another (*Yes*), for love is God. (*Yes*) And every one that loveth is born of God and knoweth God. He that loveth not knoweth not God, for God is love. . . . If we love one another, God dwelleth in us and his love is perfected in us." Let us hope that this spirit will become the order of the day.

We can no longer afford to worship the god of hate or bow before the altar of retaliation. The oceans of history are made turbulent by the ever-rising tides of hate. History is cluttered with the wreckage of nations and individuals that pursued this self-defeating path of hate. As Arnold Toynbee says: "Love is the ultimate force that makes for the saving choice of life and good against the damning choice of death and evil. Therefore the first hope in our inventory must be the hope that love is going to have the last word." Unquote.

We are now faced with the fact, my friends, that tomorrow is today. We are confronted with the fierce urgency of now. In this unfolding conundrum of life and history, there is such a thing as being too late. Procrastination is still the thief of time. Life often leaves us standing bare, naked, and dejected with a lost opportunity. The tide in the affairs of men does not remain at flood—it ebbs. We may cry out desperately for time to pause in her passage, but time is **adamant** to every plea and rushes on. Over the bleached bones and jumbled residues of numerous civilizations are written the pathetic words, "Too late." There is an invisible book of life that faithfully records our vigilance or our neglect. Omar Khayyam[14] is right: "The moving finger writes, and having writ moves on."

We still have a choice today: nonviolent coexistence or violent coannihilation. We must move past indecision to action. We must find new ways to speak for peace in Vietnam and justice throughout the developing world, a world that borders on our doors. If we do not

adamant (ăd´ə-mənt) *adj.* inflexible and insistent, unchanging.

[13] **Nietzsches** (nē´chəz): a reference to the German philosopher Friedrich Nietzsche (1844–1900), who rejected Christianity and its associated morality.

[14] **Omar Khayyam:** (1048–c. 1132) influential Persian poet and scholar.

act, we shall surely be dragged down the long, dark, and shameful corridors of time reserved for those who possess power without compassion, might without morality, and strength without sight.

Now let us begin. Now let us rededicate ourselves to the long and bitter, but beautiful, struggle for a new world. This is the calling of the sons of God, and our brothers wait eagerly for our response. Shall we say the odds are too great? Shall we tell them the struggle is too hard? Will our message be that the forces of American life militate against their arrival as full men, and we send our deepest regrets? Or will there be another message—of longing, of hope, of solidarity with their yearnings, of commitment to their cause, whatever the cost? The choice is ours, and though we might prefer it otherwise, we must choose in this crucial moment of human history.

As that noble bard of yesterday James Russell Lowell eloquently stated:

Once to every man and nation comes a moment to decide,
In the strife of Truth and Falsehood, for the good or evil side;
Some great cause, God's new Messiah offering each the bloom or
blight,
And the choice goes by forever 'twixt that darkness and that light.
Though the cause of evil prosper, yet 'tis truth alone is strong
Though her portions be the scaffold, and upon the throne be
wrong
Yet that scaffold sways the future, and behind the dim unknown
Standeth God within the shadow, keeping watch above his own.

And if we will only make the right choice, we will be able to transform this pending cosmic elegy into a creative psalm of peace. If we will make the right choice, we will be able to transform the jangling discords of our world into a beautiful symphony of brotherhood. If we will but make the right choice, we will be able to speed up the day, all over America and all over the world, when justice will roll down like waters, and righteousness like a mighty stream. [*Sustained applause*]

COLLABORATIVE DISCUSSION How does King relate the war and the civil rights issues in America? With a partner, discuss how he brings the two movements together. Cite specific textual evidence from the speech to support your ideas.

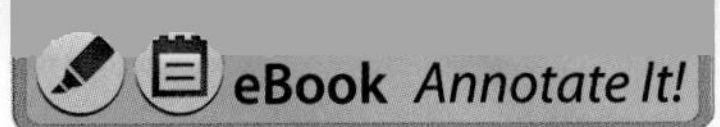

Delineate and Evaluate an Argument: Inductive Reasoning

In his complex speech, Martin Luther King Jr. wants to persuade listeners to agree with his views about the Vietnam War. To do this, he uses **inductive reasoning**, a method of argument in which the writer first presents evidence about an issue or problem and then draws a conclusion from it. The conclusion presents the writer's belief about what should be done or how the issue or problem should be resolved.

In evaluating an inductive argument, consider the following:

Is the evidence valid?	The facts presented by the writer must be accurate and verifiable. A fact can be verified in an eyewitness account, a newspaper article, an encyclopedia, a history book, or another reputable source.
Is the evidence thorough?	Make sure that the writer has examined enough evidence to support his or her conclusions. Question any generalizations drawn from a small sample of evidence.
Does the conclusion follow logically from the evidence?	Look for errors in logic that would undermine the argument. For example, the writer may oversimplify a complex issue or mistakenly assume that because one event followed another, the first event caused the second one to occur.

Determine Connotative Meanings

RI 4

The term **connotation** refers to the shades of meaning associated with a word beyond its basic dictionary definition. Good writers carefully select words with connotations that will help convey their ideas or persuade people. Such choices may include **loaded language**, words with strongly positive or negative connotations. In his speech, Martin Luther King Jr. selects words that will resonate with his listeners—he relies on the words' connotative meanings to convince the audience to feel the way he does about certain issues and ideas.

Read this passage from his speech.

And I knew that America would never invest the necessary funds or energies in rehabilitation of its poor so long as adventures like Vietnam continued to draw men and skills and money like some demonic, destructive suction tube.

The phrase "demonic, destructive suction tube" expresses King's view of the war as a colossal waste of resources. His loaded language suggests that the war is "demonic," or associated with the devil, and that it acts like a destructive machine. In other words, the war represents something evil and inhuman, gobbling up all that is good.

Analyzing the Text

RI 1, RI 4, RI 5, RI 6, RI 8, RI 10, W 9b

Cite Text Evidence Support your responses with evidence from the selection.

1. **Interpret** At the beginning of the speech, why does King explain his reasons for speaking out against the Vietnam War?
2. **Cite Evidence** What evidence does King offer to support his suggestion in line 123 that the United States is not really acting to liberate the Vietnamese people?
3. **Analyze** Questions that are posed for effect, without any expectation of a reply, are called **rhetorical questions.** Explain the effect of this rhetorical device in lines 182–188 and lines 203–214.
4. **Draw Conclusions** Why does King try to help his audience understand the enemy's point of view in lines 202–272?
5. **Analyze** In lines 319–334, King presents five specific steps that the U.S. should take. How do these proposals relate to the preceding part of his argument?
6. **Compare** In the civil rights movement, King and his followers refused to obey racial laws that they considered unjust. How does this strategy compare with his recommendation that young men in the United States become conscientious objectors?
7. **Evaluate** What conclusion does King reach through inductive reasoning? Does this conclusion logically follow from the evidence he has presented? Why or why not?
8. **Evaluate** What words with strongly positive connotations does King use in lines 513–539? Is his use of this loaded language an effective way to end the speech? Expain your response.

PERFORMANCE TASK

Writing Activity: Review What would have been newsworthy about Dr. King's speech in 1967? Write an article about the speech from the viewpoint of a journalist.

- Identify the purpose of the argument and its major points. Then evaluate the evidence presented and the logic of the conclusion reached.
- Include discussion of King's style and the devices that he uses to command attention.
- Use conventions of standard written English.

Critical Vocabulary

facile **eviscerate** **indigenous** **extortionist**

insurgency **reparations** **recalcitrant** **adamant**

Practice and Apply Create a semantic map for each Critical Vocabulary word. Use a dictionary or thesaurus as needed. This example is for a word in line 43 of the speech.

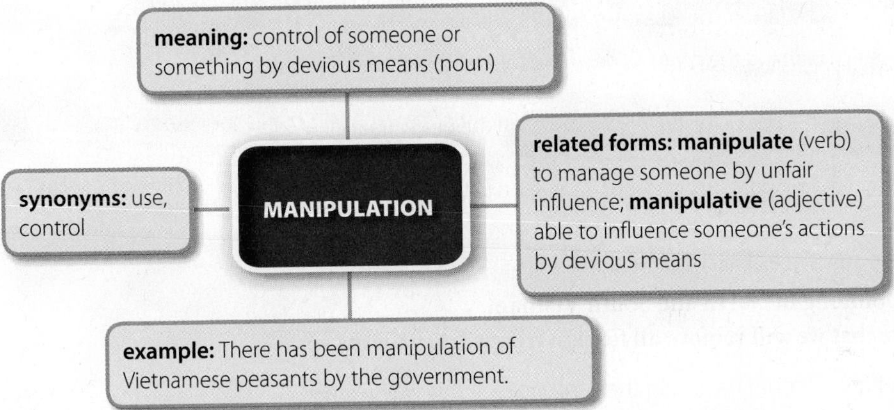

Vocabulary Strategy: Suffixes

Several Critical Vocabulary words have suffixes that indicate their part of speech and meaning. For example, the suffix *-ous* means "relating to or having the quality of." This suffix forms an adjective, as in *indigenous*. Knowing some common suffixes and the part of speech they form will help you define unfamiliar terms.

	Noun suffixes	Adjective suffixes
Suffix **Meaning** **Example**	*-ation, -tion* action, resulting state ***desperation***	*-ate* having, characterized by ***desperate***
Suffix **Meaning** **Example**	*-ism* belief or doctrine ***nationalism***	*-al* of or relating to ***national***
Suffix **Meaning** **Example**	*-ence* action or process, quality or state ***incandescence***	*-ent* being in a specified state or condition ***incandescent***

Practice and Apply Identify a new word that uses a suffix shown in each row of the chart.

- Identify the base, or main word part without the suffix.
- Note the word's part of speech.
- Write a definition for the base word's meaning and the suffix's meaning.
- Write a sentence for each word.

Language and Style: Imperative Mood

L 3

The **mood** of a verb shows the way in which a thought or idea is expressed. The **indicative mood** is the one most commonly used in writing to state ideas, opinions, or facts, or to ask questions. The **imperative mood** is used to give orders, make requests, or issue advice. In the imperative mood, the subject is not typically stated but is understood. The chart shows how the same idea is stated in both moods.

Indicative Mood	Imperative Mood
We must stop bombing the countryside.	Stop bombing the countryside.
Would you sign the peace treaty?	Sign the peace treaty.
Returning soldiers should be given jobs.	Give jobs to returning soldiers.

Read these sentences from the speech.

End all bombing in North and South Vietnam.
Set a date that we will remove all foreign troops from Vietnam.

Martin Luther King Jr. could have said the sentences in this way instead:

The government should end all bombing in North and South Vietnam.
The government should set a date that we will remove all foreign troops from Vietnam.

Notice that the mood is changed to indicative in the second set of sentences by adding a subject and helping verb. In these sentences, the emphasis on the verb, or the action, is diluted. As a result, the intensity of the original version is lost, making the sentences less effective in conveying emotion and meaning.

Practice and Apply Rewrite this paragraph, changing some of the sentences to the imperative mood.

These are tips that I have found helpful for successful speech-giving. First, it is important to make sure that you have prepared a set of speaking notes. Your main ideas and most important details should be written on large index cards. You should be able to see your notes at a glance. Second, you should practice in front of a mirror by yourself, incorporating gestures and working on eye contact. Third, it is a good idea to ask a friend or family member to listen to your speech. Finally, you should get a good night's sleep before the big day. If you are well rested, you will be able to do your best.

COMPARE TEXTS

from The Crisis

Essay by Thomas Paine

from Civil Disobedience

Essay by Henry David Thoreau

Thomas Paine (1737–1809) *came to America from London in 1774 and rapidly made a name for himself as a revolutionary writer. Embracing the colonists' cause, in 1776 he wrote* Common Sense, *a 50-page pamphlet that attacked the injustices of hereditary rule and advocated independence. His pamphlet sold 120,000 copies in three months. Later that year, he began to publish his "Crisis" papers, the first of which is included here. Paine wrote this essay while he was camped with troops from the Colonial Army following a retreat. General Washington ordered his officers to read the essay aloud to the troops to boost their morale. Once the war was over, Paine left for Europe, where similar movements were underway. There, however, he offended many with his brashness and alienated others with his last published work,* The Age of Reason, *which attacked organized religion. Upon returning to America in 1802, he had few friends left. He lived the rest of his life in poverty and obscurity.*

Henry David Thoreau (1817–1862) *published only two books before his death at the age of 44. Neither book sold well, but in the years following his death, his renown grew. Today he is highly regarded for both his nature writing and his political ideas. The nonviolent principles he espouses in* Civil Disobedience *have influenced activists throughout the world, including Mohandas Gandhi and Martin Luther King Jr. Thoreau lived a life of nonconformity, refusing to do anything that conflicted with the dictates of his own conscience. For example, he refused to pay his poll tax to protest the war in Mexico and slavery. As a result, he spent a night in jail, which he refers to in this essay.*

AS YOU READ Think about how Paine catches and keeps your attention with his writing. Write down any questions you generate during reading.

from The Crisis

by Thomas Paine

These are the times that try men's souls: The summer soldier and the sunshine patriot will, in this crisis, shrink from the service of his country; but he that stands it NOW, deserves the love and thanks of man and woman. **Tyranny**, like hell, is not easily conquered; yet we have this consolation with us, that the harder the conflict, the more glorious the triumph. What we obtain too cheap, we esteem too lightly:— 'Tis dearness only that gives every thing its value. Heaven knows how to set a proper price upon its goods; and it would be strange indeed, if so celestial an article as FREEDOM should not be highly rated. Britain, with an army to enforce her tyranny, has declared, that she has a right (*not only to* TAX) but "TO BIND us in ALL CASES WHATSOEVER,"[1] and if *being bound in that manner* is not slavery, then there is not such a thing as slavery upon earth. Even the expression is impious, for so unlimited a power can only belong to God.

tyranny
(tĭr´ə-nē) *n.*
oppressive rule by an absolute power.

Whether the Independence of the Continent was declared too soon, or delayed too long, I will not now enter into as an argument; my own simple opinion is, that had it been eight months earlier, it would have been much better. We did not make a proper use of last winter, neither could we, while we were in a dependant state. However, the fault, if it were one, was all our own; we have none to blame but ourselves. But no great deal is lost yet; all that Howe has been doing for this month past is rather a ravage than a conquest which the spirit of the Jersies a year ago would have quickly repulsed, and which time and a little **resolution** will soon recover.

resolution
(rĕz´ə-lo͞o´shən) *n.*
determination.

I have as little superstition in me as any man living, but my secret opinion has ever been, and still is, that God almighty will not give up a people to military destruction, or leave them unsupportedly to perish, who had so earnestly and so repeatedly sought to avoid the **calamities** of war, by every decent method which wisdom could invent. Neither have I so much of the infidel in me, as to suppose, that he has relinquished the government of the world, and given us up to the care of devils; and as I do not, I cannot see on what grounds the king of Britain can look up to heaven for help against us: A common murderer, a highwayman, or a housebreaker, has as good a pretense as he. . . .

calamity
(kə-lăm´ĭ-tē) *n.*
a disaster or catastrophe.

[1] **"TO BIND us in ALL CASES WHATSOEVER":** a reference to wording in the Declaratory Act of 1766, in which the British parliament asserted its "power and authority" to make and enforce laws over the American colonies.

"The harder the conflict, the more glorious the triumph."

I once felt all that kind of anger, which a man ought to feel, against the mean principles that are held by the Tories:[2] A noted one, who kept a tavern at Amboy,[3] was standing at his door, with as pretty a child in his hand, about eight or nine years old, as most I ever saw, and after speaking his mind as freely as he thought was prudent, finished with this unfatherly expression, "*Well! give me peace in my day.*" Not a man lives on the Continent but fully believes that a separation must some time or other finally take place, and a generous parent would have said, "*If there must be trouble, let it be in my day, that my child may have peace;*" and this single reflection, well applied, is sufficient to awaken every man to duty. Not a place upon earth might be so happy as America. Her situation is remote from all the wrangling world, and she has nothing to do but trade with them. A man may easily distinguish in himself between temper and principle, and I am as confident, as I am that God governs the world, that America will never be happy until she gets clear of foreign dominion. Wars, without ceasing, will break out until that period arrives, and the Continent must in the end be conqueror; for, though the flame of liberty may sometimes cease to shine, the coal never can expire. . . .

I turn with the warm ardor of a friend to those who have nobly stood, and are yet determined to stand the matter out: I call not upon a few, but upon all; not on this State or that State, but on every State; up and help us; lay your shoulders to the wheel; better have too much force than too little, when so great an object is at stake. Let it be told to the future world, that in the depth of winter, when nothing but hope and virtue could survive, that the city and the country, alarmed at one common danger, came forth to meet and to repulse it. Say not, that thousands are gone, turn out your tens of thousands; throw not the burden of the day upon Providence, but "*shew your faith by your works,*" that God may bless you. It matters not where you live, or what rank of life you hold, the evil or the blessing will reach you all. The far

[2] **the mean principles . . . Tories:** the small-minded beliefs of those colonists who remain loyal to Great Britain.

[3] **Amboy:** probably Perth Amboy, a town in New Jersey.

and the near, the home counties and the back, the rich and the poor, shall suffer or rejoice alike. The heart that feels not now, is dead: The blood of his children shall curse his cowardice, who shrinks back at a time when a little might have saved the whole, and made *them* happy. I love the man that can smile in trouble, that can gather strength from distress, and grow brave by reflection. 'Tis the business of little minds to shrink; but he whose heart is firm, and whose conscience approves his conduct, will pursue his principles unto death. My own line of reasoning is to myself as strait and clear as a ray of light. Not all the treasures of the world, so far as I believe, could have induced me to support an offensive war, for I think it murder; but if a thief break into my house, burn and destroy my property, and kill or threaten to kill me, or those that are in it, and to "*bind me in all cases whatsoever,*" to his absolute will, am I to suffer it? What **signifies** it to me, whether he who does it, is a king or a common man; my countryman or not my countryman? whether it is done by an individual villain, or an army of them? If we reason to the root of things we shall find no difference; neither can any just cause be assigned why we should punish in the one case, and pardon in the other. Let them call me rebel, and welcome, I feel no concern from it; but I should suffer the misery of devils, were I to make a whore of my soul by swearing allegiance to one, whose character is that of a sottish, stupid, stubborn, worthless, brutish man. I conceive likewise a horrid idea in receiving mercy from a being, who at the last day shall be shrieking to the rocks and mountains to cover him, and fleeing with terror from the orphan, the widow and the slain of America.

signify
(sĭg′nə-fī′) *v.* to have meaning or importance.

There are cases which cannot be overdone by language, and this is one. There are persons too who see not the full extent of the evil that threatens them; they **solace** themselves with hopes that the enemy, if they succeed, will be merciful. It is the madness of folly to expect mercy from those who have refused to do justice; and even mercy, where conquest is the object, is only a trick of war: The cunning of the fox is as murderous as the violence of the wolfe; and we ought to guard equally against both. Howe's first object is partly by threats and partly by promises, to terrify or seduce the people to deliver up their arms, and receive mercy. The ministry recommended the same plan to Gage, and this is what the Tories call making their peace; "*a peace which passeth all understanding*" *indeed!* A peace which would be the immediate forerunner of a worse ruin than any we have yet thought of. Ye men of Pennsylvania, do reason upon those things! Were the back counties to give up their arms, they would fall easy prey to the Indians, who are all armed: This perhaps is what some Tories would not be sorry for. Were the home counties to deliver up their arms, they would be exposed to the resentment of the back counties, who would then have it at their power to chastise their defection at pleasure. And were any one State to give up its arms, that State must be garrisoned by all Howe's army of Britons and Hessians to preserve it from the anger of

solace
(sŏl′ĭs) *v.* give comfort or relief to.

the rest. Mutual fear is a principal link in the chain of mutual love, and woe be the State that breaks the compact. Howe is mercifully inviting you to barbarous destruction, and men must be either rogues or fools that will not see it. I dwell not upon the vapours of imagination; I bring reason to your ears; and in language, as plain as A, B, C, hold up truth to your eyes.

I thank God that I fear not. I see no real cause for fear. I know our situation well, and can see the way out of it. While our army was collected, Howe dared not risk a battle, and it is no credit to him that he decamped from the White Plains, and waited a mean opportunity to ravage the defenceless Jersies; but it is great credit to us, that, with an handful of men, we sustained an orderly retreat for near an hundred miles, brought off our ammunition, all our field-pieces, the greatest part of our stores, and had four rivers to pass. None can say that our retreat was precipitate, for we were near three weeks in performing it, and the country might have time to come in. Twice we marched back to meet the enemy and remained out till dark. The sign of fear was not seen in our camp, and had not some of the cowardly and disaffected inhabitants spread false alarms through the country, the Jersies had never been ravaged. Once more we are again collected and collecting; our new army at both ends of the Continent is recruiting fast, and we shall be able to open the next campaign with sixty thousand men, well armed and clothed. This is our situation, and who will may know it. By perseverance and fortitude we have the prospect of a glorious issue; by cowardice and submission, the sad choice of a variety of evils—a ravaged country—a depopulated city—habitations without safety, and slavery without hope—our homes turned into barracks and bawdy-houses for Hessians, and a future race to provide for whose fathers we shall doubt of. Look on this picture, and weep over it!—and if there yet remains one thoughtless wretch who believes it not, let him suffer it unlamented.

COLLABORATIVE DISCUSSION To whom is Paine addressing his essay? With a partner, discuss those characteristics of Paine's writing that make his essay effective for his audience. Cite specific textual evidence from the essay to support your ideas.

Analyze Foundational Documents

RI 9

Through his essay, Thomas Paine hopes to persuade those colonists who have not yet done so to take up arms against the British and for the rest to keep faith with the cause. To achieve his patriotic purpose, he incorporates a number of persuasive techniques.

Technique	Example
Emotional appeals are attempts to persuade by eliciting strong feelings, such as pity or fear. These appeals rely on **loaded language,** words with strong positive or negative connotations.	Paine's use of phrases such as "flame of liberty" in line 54 helps to stir feelings of patriotism in his readers.
Ethical appeals call upon readers' sense of right and wrong.	Paine's story of a father in Amboy in lines 37–47 appeals to readers' ethics.
Appeals to association imply that one will gain acceptance or prestige by taking the writer's position.	"I turn with the warm ardor of a friend to those who have nobly stood . . ."
Appeals to authority call upon experts or others who warrant respect.	"My secret opinion is that God almighty will not give up a people to military destruction . . ."

In addition to these persuasive techniques, Paine's literary style includes these rhetorical devices that strengthen his meaning:

Parallel structure	Analogy	Repetition
Paine uses similar grammatical constructions to express ideas of equal importance. Notice in this quotation that the parallel structure emphasizes the reward of persevering through hard conflict: "yet we have this consolation with us, that the harder the conflict, the more glorious the triumph."	In lines 75–86, Paine makes a point-by-point comparison between two situations to present the war from another perspective.	To emphasize meaning and add intensity to the rhythm of his prose, Paine repeats words and phrases, as in this quotation: "I thank God that I fear not. I see no real cause for fear."

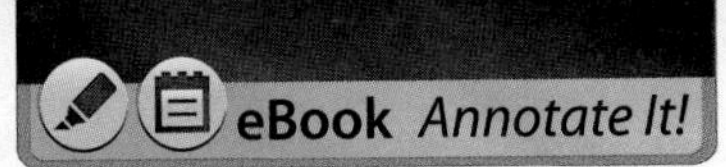

RI 2, RI 3, RI 4, RI 9, W 4

Analyzing the Text

Cite Text Evidence Support your responses with evidence from the selection.

1. **Interpret** The opening sentence of this essay is one of the most famous in American literature. Explain the point that Paine is making here. Which word choices help make the sentence memorable?
2. **Identify** Find examples of loaded language in lines 1–15. To which emotions do these words appeal?
3. **Infer** What is Paine calculating will be the result of the ethical appeal he uses in lines 37–47? Explain.
4. **Analyze** A writer's **tone** is his or her attitude toward a subject. What is Paine's tone in lines 56–71? What persuasive and rhetorical techniques help convey this tone?
5. **Analyze** What analogy does Paine make in lines 75–86? What conclusion does he want readers to draw from this analogy?
6. **Analyze** According to Paine in lines 101–120, what would happen if colonists acceded to Howe's demand to relinquish their arms? What does he want to persuade readers about in this passage?
7. **Evaluate** Reread lines 121–138. What is Paine's purpose in including these details about the war? Is this an effective way to conclude his essay? Explain.

PERFORMANCE TASK

Writing Activity: Letter Paine read this essay to General Washington's troops to boost their morale. Imagine that you are one of the soldiers. Write a letter to a family member back home, explaining how you felt upon hearing it.

- Analyze the impact of the speech on you as a listener. Refer to the parts of the speech that you found memorable and why.
- Use conventions of standard written English.

Critical Vocabulary

L 4c

tyranny **resolution** **calamity**

signify **solace**

Practice and Apply Explain whether the words in each pair are synonyms or antonyms. Use a college-level dictionary to check your work if necessary.

1. resolution/weakness
2. solace/comfort
3. tyranny/oppression
4. calamity/good fortune
5. signify/matter

Vocabulary Strategy: Clarify Precise Meaning

Some words have several meanings that may be closely related. To find out the precise meaning of a word as it is used in a sentence, readers need to look at the context of the word, or the words and phrases surrounding it, and consult a college-level dictionary.

The Critical Vocabulary word *resolution* has a number of definitions. In this phrase from the essay, "and which time and a little resolution will soon recover," the adjective "little" tells readers that it is something that can be measured. Looking in the dictionary confirms that *resolution* means "the condition or quality of being firmly determined."

Use of the dictionary can help readers to extend their understanding of words and be more exact in the way that they define them.

Practice and Apply Use a college-level dictionary as well as context clues to define each of the italicized words in these sentences from the essay.

1. "All that Howe has been doing for this month past is rather a *ravage* than a conquest."
2. "I turn with the warm *ardor* of a friend to those who have nobly stood, and are yet determined to stand the matter out. . . ."
3. "Howe's first object is partly by threats and partly by promises, to terrify or *seduce* the people to deliver up their arms."
4. "I bring *reason* to your ears; and in language, as plain as A, B, C, hold up truth to your eyes."

AS YOU READ Pay attention to details that tell you how Thoreau feels about government. Write down any questions you generate during reading.

from Civil Disobedience

by Henry David Thoreau

I heartily accept the motto, "That government is best which governs least;" and I should like to see it acted up to more rapidly and systematically. Carried out, it finally amounts to this, which also I believe,—"That government is best which governs not at all;" and when men are prepared for it, that will be the kind of government which they will have. Government is at best but an expedient; but most governments are usually, and all governments are sometimes, inexpedient. The objections which have been brought against a standing army, and they are many and weighty, and deserve to prevail, may also at last be brought against a standing government. The standing army is only an arm of the standing government. The government itself, which is only the mode which the people have chosen to execute their will, is equally liable to be abused and perverted before the people can act through it. Witness the present Mexican war,[1] the work of comparatively a few individuals using the standing government as their tool; for, in the outset, the people would not have consented to this measure. . . .

But, to speak practically and as a citizen, unlike those who call themselves no-government men, I ask for, not at once no government, but *at once* a better government. Let every man make known what kind of government would command his respect, and that will be one step toward obtaining it.

After all, the practical reason why, when the power is once in the hands of the people, a majority are permitted, and for a long period continue, to rule is not because they are most likely to be in the right, nor because this seems fairest to the minority, but because they are physically the strongest. But a government in which the majority rule in all cases cannot be based on justice, even as far as men understand it. Can there not be a government in which majorities do not virtually decide right and wrong, but conscience?—in which majorities decide only those questions to which the rule of expediency is applicable? Must the citizen ever for a moment, or in the least degree, resign his conscience to the legislator? Why has every man a conscience, then? I think that we should be men first, and subjects afterward. It is not desirable to cultivate a respect for the law, so much as for the right. The only obligation which I have a right to assume is to do at any time

[1] **the present Mexican war:** the 1846–1848 war between Mexico and the United States.

“The only obligation which I have a right to assume is to do at any time what I think right.”

what I think right. It is truly enough said, that a corporation has no conscience; but a corporation of conscientious men is a corporation *with* a conscience. Law never made men a whit more just; and, by means of their respect for it, even the well-disposed are daily made the agents of injustice. A common and natural result of an undue respect for law is, that you may see a file of soldiers, colonel, captain, corporal, privates, powder-monkeys,[2] and all, marching in admirable order over hill and dale to the wars, against their wills, ay, against their common sense and consciences, which makes it very steep marching indeed, and produces a palpitation of the heart. They have no doubt that it is a damnable business in which they are concerned; they are all peaceably inclined. Now, what are they? Men at all? or small movable forts and magazines,[3] at the service of some unscrupulous man in power? Visit the Navy-Yard, and behold a marine, such a man as an American government can make, or such as it can make a man with its black arts[4]—a mere shadow and reminiscence of humanity, a man laid out alive and standing, and already, as one may say, buried under arms with funeral accompaniments, though it may be,—

“Not a drum was heard, not a funeral note,
As his corse to the rampart we hurried;
Not a soldier discharged his farewell shot
O'er the grave where our hero we buried.”[5]

The mass of men serve the state thus, not as men mainly, but as machines, with their bodies. They are the standing army, and the militia, jailers, constables, *posse comitatus*,[6] etc. In most cases there is no free exercise whatever of the judgment or of the moral sense; but they put themselves on a level with wood and earth and stones;

---

[2] **powder-monkeys:** boys with the job of carrying gunpowder to artillery crews.

[3] **magazines:** places where ammunition is stored.

[4] **black arts:** witchcraft.

[5] **“Not a drum . . . we buried”:** opening lines of “The Burial of Sir John Moore After Corunna” by the Irish poet Charles Wolfe (1791–1823).

[6] ***posse comitatus*** (pŏs´ē kŏm-ə-tā´təs): group of people that can be called on by the sheriff to help enforce the law [*Latin*, literally, the power of the county].

and wooden men can perhaps be manufactured that will serve the purpose as well. Such command no more respect than men of straw or a lump of dirt. They have the same sort of worth only as horses and dogs. Yet such as these even are commonly esteemed good citizens. Others—as most legislators, politicians, lawyers, ministers, and office-holders—serve the state chiefly with their heads; and, as they rarely make any moral distinctions, they are as likely to serve the Devil, without *intending* it, as God. A very few—as heroes, patriots, martyrs, reformers in the great sense, and *men*—serve the state with their consciences also, and so necessarily resist it for the most part; and they are commonly treated as enemies by it. . . .

Unjust laws exist: shall we be content to obey them, or shall we endeavor to amend them, and obey them until we have succeeded or shall we transgress them at once? Men generally, under such a government as this, think that they ought to wait until they have persuaded the majority to alter them. They think that, if they should resist, the remedy would be worse than the evil. But it is the fault of the government itself that the remedy *is* worse than the evil. *It* makes it worse. Why is it not more apt to anticipate and provide for reform? Why does it not cherish its wise minority? Why does it cry and resist before it is hurt? Why does it not encourage its citizens to be on the alert to point out its faults, and *do* better than it would have them? Why does it always crucify Christ, and excommunicate Copernicus and Luther,[7] and pronounce Washington and Franklin rebels? . . .

If the injustice is part of the necessary friction of the machine of government, let it go, let it go: perchance it will wear smooth, certainly the machine will wear out. If the injustice has a spring, or a pulley, or a rope, or a crank, exclusively for itself, then perhaps you may consider whether the remedy will not be worse than the evil; but if it is of such a nature that it requires you to be the agent of injustice to another, then, I say, break the law. Let your life be a counter-friction to stop the machine. What I have to do is to see, at any rate, that I do not lend myself to the wrong which I condemn. . . .

I meet this American government, or its representative, the state government, directly, and face to face, once a year—no more—in the person of its tax-gatherer; this is the only mode in which a man situated as I am necessarily meets it; and it then says distinctly, Recognize me; and the simplest, most effectual, and, in the present posture of affairs,[8] the indispensablest mode of treating with it on this head, of expressing your little satisfaction with and love for it, is to deny it then. My civil neighbor, the tax-gatherer, is the very man I have to deal with,—for it is, after all, with men and not with parchment

[7] **Copernicus** (kō-pûr´nə-kəs) **and Luther:** Radicals in their time, Polish astronomer Nicolaus Copernicus theorized that the sun rather than the Earth was the center of our planetary system; German theologian Martin Luther was a leader in the Protestant Reformation.

[8] **posture of affairs:** situation.

that I quarrel,—and he has voluntarily chosen to be an agent of the government. How shall he ever know well what he is and does as an officer of the government, or as a man, until he is obliged to consider whether he shall treat me, his neighbor, for whom he has respect, as a neighbor and well-disposed man, or as a maniac and disturber of the peace, and see if he can get over this obstruction to his neighborliness without a ruder and more impetuous thought or speech corresponding with his action. I know this well, that if one thousand, if one hundred, if ten men whom I could name,—if ten *honest* men only,—ay, if *one* honest man, in this State of Massachusetts, *ceasing to hold slaves*, were actually to withdraw from this copartnership, and be locked up in the county jail therefor, it would be the abolition of slavery in America. For it matters not how small the beginning may seem to be: what is once well done is done forever. But we love better to talk about it: that we say is our mission. Reform keeps many scores of newspapers in its service, but not one man. . . .

Under a government which imprisons any unjustly, the true place for a just man is also a prison. The proper place today, the only place which Massachusetts has provided for her freer and less desponding spirits, is in her prisons, to be put out and locked out of the State by her own act, as they have already put themselves out by their principles. It is there that the fugitive slave, and the Mexican prisoner on parole, and the Indian come to plead the wrongs of his race should find them; on that separate, but more free and honorable ground, where the State places those who are not *with* her, but *against* her,—the only house in a slave State in which a free man can abide with honor. If any think that their influence would be lost there, and their voices no longer afflict the ear of the State, that they would not be as an enemy within its walls, they do not know by how much truth is stronger than error, nor how much more eloquently and effectively he can combat injustice who has experienced a little in his own person. Cast your whole vote, not a strip of paper merely, but your whole influence. A minority is powerless while it conforms to the majority; it is not even a minority then; but it is irresistible when it clogs by its whole weight. If the alternative is to keep all just men in prison, or give up war and slavery, the State will not hesitate which to choose. If a thousand men were not to pay their tax bills this year, that would not be a violent and bloody measure, as it would be to pay them, and enable the State to commit violence and shed innocent blood. This is, in fact, the definition of a peaceable revolution, if any such is possible. If the tax-gatherer, or any other public officer, asks me, as one has done, "But what shall I do?" my answer is, "If you really wish to do anything, resign your office." When the subject has refused allegiance, and the officer has resigned his office, then the revolution is accomplished. But even suppose blood should flow. Is there not a sort of blood shed when the conscience is wounded? Through this wound a man's real manhood and immortality flow out, and he bleeds to an everlasting death. I see this blood flowing now. . . .

I have paid no poll-tax for six years. I was put into a jail once on this account, for one night; and, as I stood considering the walls of solid stone, two or three feet thick, the door of wood and iron, a foot thick, and the iron grating which strained the light, I could not help being struck with the foolishness of that institution which treated me as if I were mere flesh and blood and bones, to be locked up. I wondered that it should have concluded at length that this was the best use it could put me to, and had never thought to avail itself of my services in some way. I saw that, if there was a wall of stone between me and my townsmen, there was a still more difficult one to climb or break through before they could get to be as free as I was. I did not for a moment feel confined, and the walls seemed a great waste of stone and mortar. I felt as if I alone of all my townsmen had paid my tax. They plainly did not know how to treat me, but behaved like persons who are underbred.[9] In every threat and in every compliment there was a blunder; for they thought that my chief desire was to stand the other side of that stone wall. I could not but smile to see how industriously they locked the door on my meditations, which followed them out again without let or hindrance,[10] and *they* were really all that was dangerous. As they could not reach me, they had resolved

[9] **underbred:** ill-mannered.

[10] **without let or hindrance:** without encountering obstacles.

to punish my body; just as boys, if they cannot come at some person against whom they have a spite, will abuse his dog. I saw that the State was half-witted, that it was timid as a lone woman with her silver spoons, and that it did not know its friends from its foes, and I lost all my remaining respect for it, and pitied it.

Thus the State never intentionally confronts a man's sense, intellectual or moral, but only his body, his senses. It is not armed with superior wit or honesty, but with superior physical strength. I was not born to be forced. I will breathe after my own fashion. Let us see who is the strongest. What force has a multitude? They only can force me who obey a higher law than I. They force me to become like themselves. I do not hear of *men* being *forced* to live this way or that by masses of men. What sort of life were that to live? When I meet a government which says to me, "Your money or your life," why should I be in haste to give it my money? It may be in a great strait, and not know what to do: I cannot help that. It must help itself; do as I do. It is not worth the while to snivel about it. I am not responsible for the successful working of the machinery of society. I am not the son of the engineer. I perceive that, when an acorn and a chestnut fall side by side, the one does not remain inert to make way for the other, but both obey their own laws, and spring and grow and flourish as best they can, till one, perchance, overshadows and destroys the other. If a plant cannot live according to its nature, it dies; and so a man.

COLLABORATIVE DISCUSSION With a partner, discuss Thoreau's beliefs about government. Cite specific textual evidence from the essay to support your ideas.

RI 8

Delineate and Evaluate an Argument

"Civil Disobedience" is a work of public advocacy—that is, it seeks to influence the opinions or attitudes of the general public to bring about change. To evaluate Thoreau's argument, it is necessary to examine each of the elements shown in the chart.

Claim	After identifying the claim, readers need to look at whether it is convincingly supported by reasons and evidence. Illogical reasoning or insufficient evidence can undermine the credibility of the claim.
Reasoning	**Premises:** Premises are statements from which a conclusion is drawn or upon which the argument is based. To evaluate the soundness of Thoreau's reasoning, it is helpful to question the legitimacy of his premises. For example: • Is the general principle that "government is best which governs least" sound? • Can a government function if it lets all people obey their own conscience? • Is civil disobedience—breaking laws and refusing to pay taxes—always preferable to legal efforts to reform government, such as voting and petitioning? **Logical errors:** A writer may sound convincing but base his or her conclusions on errors in logic, such as these: • non sequitur: a conclusion that does not follow logically from the proof offered in support of it • false analogy: a comparison that doesn't hold up because of major differences between the subjects • overgeneralization: a generalization that is too broad
Evidence	The facts, examples, and other details have to be valid, authoritative, relevant, sufficient, and up to date.

For example, to analyze the first five lines of "Civil Disobedience," readers must first consider the validity of the premise "That government is best which governs least." If this premise is not sound—in other words, if there are exceptions to this statement—then any reasoning based on it is flawed also. Thoreau draws a conclusion based on that statement, which is that "government is best which governs not at all." In evaluating this conclusion, readers must decide whether Thoreau offers proof that supports it, or whether it is a non sequitur.

By questioning the validity of Thoreau's premises and examining the relationships between evidence and conclusions, readers will be able to ascertain the soundness of his argument.

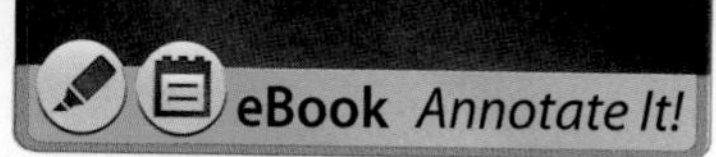

Analyzing the Text

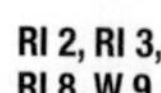

Cite Text Evidence Support your responses with evidence from the selection.

1. **Interpret** Why does Thoreau believe that "a government in which the majority rule in all cases cannot be based on justice, even as far as men understand it"?
2. **Analyze** What claim does Thoreau make about his obligation as a citizen? How does this claim relate to the premise, "That government is best which governs least"?
3. **Cite Evidence** What reasons and evidence does Thoreau offer to justify his view that the people who truly serve the state are those who often resist it?
4. **Analyze** How do the ideas expressed in lines 88–96 help to qualify or clarify some of Thoreau's earlier points?
5. **Evaluate** In lines 122–153, Thoreau argues that civil disobedience is an effective way of bringing about change. How convincing is this argument? Explain.
6. **Analyze** A statement that seems to contradict itself but nevertheless suggests an important truth is called a **paradox**. What is paradoxical about Thoreau's observations of the night he spent in prison?
7. **Critique** At the end of the excerpt, Thoreau uses an analogy of an acorn and a chestnut to convey his point about human nature. Is this an effective way to communicate his message? Why or why not?

PERFORMANCE TASK

Research Activity: Report How did later activists, such as Martin Luther King Jr., or Mohandas Gandhi, interpret the principles set forth by Thoreau in "Civil Disobedience"?

- Find sources that explain the connection between the activist you have chosen and Thoreau. Identify key similarities and differences in their approaches to nonviolent resistance.
- Organize your ideas into a report. Include charts or other text features to convey your important ideas.
- Document your sources, including endnotes or footnotes as appropriate.
- Use the conventions of standard written English.

L 3a

Language and Style: Combining Sentences

A series of short sentences can result in a terse style that fails to clearly show the relationship between ideas. One way writers can combine their sentences is by connecting two or more complete sentences with one of these coordinating conjunctions:

Coordinating Conjunction	Sample Sentence
and: builds upon or adds to an idea	"Walden" is an account of his years spent in nature, and "Civil Disobedience" presents his political philosophy.
but: shows opposition or contrast	Paine's rhetoric is fiery and intense, but Thoreau chose a more measured style.
or: identifies a choice	Would you like to write a report on the historical controversy surrounding Paine, or would you prefer to create a poster about the radical theories of Thoreau?

In his essay "Civil Disobedience," Thoreau uses coordinating conjunctions to build compound sentences that show how the ideas in each sentence relate to each other. By combining ideas, he creates a smooth, rhythmical prose.

Read this sentence from the essay.

Government is at best but an expedient; but most governments are usually, and all governments are sometimes, inexpedient.

This compound sentence could have been written as a series of simple sentences:

Government is at best but an expedient. Most governments are usually inexpedient. All governments are sometimes inexpedient.

Breaking the sentence into three separate statements takes away the elegance of Thoreau's style. The three sentences are functional but bland. They have a choppy rhythm, and to convey the correct meaning they must repeat the adjective "inexpedient." Thoreau's meaning is weakened as well with the loss of the conjunction "but," which helps emphasize the point that most governments are inexpedient rather than expedient.

Practice and Apply Return to the report about Thoreau's influence on later activists that you wrote in response to this selection's Performance Task, or return to another essay you have recently written. Find places where you could create a smoother flow and clarify your meaning by combining sentences with a coordinating conjunction. Remember to include a comma before the conjunction. Share the changes you make with a partner.

from The Crisis
from Civil Disobedience

eBook *Annotate It!*

Analyze Foundational Documents

RI 9

By comparing foundational documents from different periods in American history, readers can gain insight into how important ideas evolved over time and how they were influenced by historical events.

Thomas Paine and Henry David Thoreau both argue for resistance to injustice in their essays, but in different ways. Paine argues that the colonists must be united in opposition to the British. Thoreau argues that individuals must follow their own consciences, even if it means opposing the majority. Paine argues in favor of war; Thoreau advocates nonviolent resistance through refusing to cooperate. Both works, however, have had a major impact on political thought and movements in America and around the world.

Analyzing the Text

RI 1, RI 6, RI 9, W 2b, SL 1a

Cite Text Evidence Support your responses with evidence from the selections.

1. **Analyze** Compare the **tone**, or attitude of the author toward his subject, in each work, citing details to show how it is conveyed. Explain how the tone relates to each author's purpose.
2. **Compare** Examine lines 1–15 of "The Crisis" and lines 75–96 of "Civil Disobedience." Compare elements of each author's style, including the use of **rhetorical devices**, such as repetition and parallel structure.
3. **Analyze** Discuss the influence of the historical context on each author's philosophy of resistance, and explain whether their ideas transcend this historical context.

PERFORMANCE TASK

Speaking Activity: Role Play What would Paine and Thoreau have to say about some of today's political issues?

- Working in a group, decide on two or three current events. Develop questions pertaining to these issues and work together to prepare answers from both writers' perspectives, citing specific evidence.
- Choose two members to represent Paine and Thoreau. In a whole-class setting, ask the prepared questions of the two students, who should respond in their roles.
- Invite other class members to ask questions. As a class, summarize the relevance of each writer's approach to current issues.

A&E BIO

Terry Tempest Williams *(b. 1955) was raised by a large Mormon family in Utah. Both Utah and Mormonism have influenced her writing. Her book* Refuge: An Unnatural History of Family and Place, *from which the selection is taken, tells about her mother's cancer diagnosis, and the unprecedented rise of the Great Salt Lake that flooded a wildlife refuge. This link between people and nature is one that Williams often explores in her writing. Her concern for the environment has led her to testify before Congress.*

The Clan of One-Breasted Women

Essay by Terry Tempest Williams

AS YOU READ Look for the details that the author includes to show how her family and nature are engaged in the same struggle.

I belong to a Clan of One-Breasted Women. My mother, my grandmothers, and six aunts have all had mastectomies. Seven are dead. The two who survive have just completed rounds of chemotherapy and radiation.

I've had my own problems: two biopsies for breast cancer and a small tumor between my ribs diagnosed as a "borderline malignancy."

This is my family history.

Most statistics tell us breast cancer is genetic, hereditary, with rising percentages attached to fatty diets, childlessness, or becoming pregnant after thirty. What they don't say is living in Utah may be the greatest hazard of all.

We are a Mormon family with roots in Utah since 1847. The "word of wisdom" in my family aligned us with good foods—no coffee, no tea, tobacco, or alcohol.[1] For the most part, our women were finished having their babies by the time they were thirty. And only one faced

[1] **The "word of wisdom" . . . alcohol:** law of the Mormon religion concerning health, as revealed by the Prophet Joseph Smith in 1833.

breast cancer prior to 1960. Traditionally, as a group of people, Mormons have a low rate of cancer.

Is our family a cultural **anomaly**? The truth is, we didn't think about it. Those who did, usually the men, simply said, "bad genes." The women's attitude was **stoic**. Cancer was part of life. On February 16, 1971, the eve of my mother's surgery, I accidently picked up the telephone and overheard her ask my grandmother what she could expect.

anomaly (ə-nŏm′ə-lē) *n.* peculiarity; an unusual example.

stoic (stō′ĭk) *adj.* enduring difficulty without expressing emotion or complaint.

"Diane, it is one of the most spiritual experiences you will ever encounter."

I quietly put down the receiver.

Two days later, my father took my brothers and me to the hospital to visit her. She met us in the lobby in a wheelchair. No bandages were visible. I'll never forget her radiance, the way she held herself in a purple velvet robe, and how she gathered us around her.

"Children, I am fine. I want you to know I felt the arms of God around me."

We believed her. My father cried. Our mother, his wife, was thirty-eight years old.

A little over a year after Mother's death, Dad and I were having dinner together. He had just returned from St. George, where the Tempest Company was completing the gas lines that would service southern Utah. He spoke of his love for the country, the sandstoned landscape, bare-boned and beautiful. He had just finished hiking the Kolob trail in Zion National Park. We got caught up in reminiscing, recalling with fondness our walk up Angel's Landing on his fiftieth birthday and the years our family had vacationed there.

Over dessert, I shared a recurring dream of mine. I told my father that for years, as long as I could remember, I saw this flash of light in the night in the desert—that this image had so permeated my being that I could not venture south without seeing it again, on the horizon, illuminating buttes and mesas.

"You did see it," he said.

"Saw what?"

"The bomb. The cloud. We were driving home from Riverside, California. You were sitting on Diane's lap. She was pregnant. In fact, I remember the day, September 7, 1957. We had just gotten out of the Service.[2] We were driving north, past Las Vegas. It was an hour or so before dawn, when this explosion went off. We not only heard it, but felt it. I thought the oil tanker in front of us had blown up. We pulled over and suddenly, rising from the desert floor, we saw it, clearly, this golden-stemmed cloud, the mushroom. The sky seemed to vibrate with an eerie pink glow. Within a few minutes, a light ash was raining on the car."

---

[2] **the Service:** many Mormons volunteer to serve as missionaries for a two-year period, during which they attempt to convert others to their faith.

I stared at my father.

"I thought you knew that," he said. "It was a common occurrence in the fifties."

It was at this moment that I realized the deceit I had been living under. Children growing up in the American Southwest, drinking contaminated milk from contaminated cows, even from the contaminated breasts of their mothers, my mother—members, years later, of the Clan of One-Breasted Women.

It is a well-known story in the Desert West, "The Day We Bombed Utah," or more accurately, the years we bombed Utah: above ground atomic testing in Nevada took place from January 27, 1951, through July 11, 1962. Not only were the winds blowing north covering "low-use segments of the population" with fallout and leaving sheep dead in their tracks, but the climate was right. The United States of the 1950s was red, white, and blue. The Korean War was raging. McCarthyism[3] was **rampant**. Ike[4] was it, and the cold war was hot. If you were against nuclear testing, you were for a communist regime.

rampant (răm′pənt) *adj.* growing wildly without restraint or limit.

Much has been written about this "American nuclear tragedy." Public health was secondary to national security. The Atomic Energy

[3] **McCarthyism:** criticizing and denouncing people for their belief or sympathy for Communism, often without evidence, as practiced by Senate committees led by Joseph McCarthy of Wisconsin.

[4] **Ike:** Dwight David Eisenhower (1890–1969), World War II military leader and President of the U.S. between 1953 and 1961.

> **"Children . . . . drinking contaminated milk from contaminated cows, even from the contaminated breasts of their mothers."**

Commissioner, Thomas Murray, said, "Gentlemen, we must not let anything interfere with this series of tests, nothing."

Again and again, the American public was told by its government, in spite of burns, blisters, and nausea, "It has been found that the tests may be conducted with adequate assurance of safety under conditions prevailing at the bombing reservations." Assuaging public fears was simply a matter of public relations. "Your best action," an Atomic Energy Commission booklet read, "is not to be worried about fallout." A news release typical of the times stated, "We find no basis for concluding that harm to any individual has resulted from radioactive fallout."

On August 30, 1979, during Jimmy Carter's presidency, a suit was filed, *Irene Allen* v. *The United States of America*. Mrs. Allen's case was the first on an alphabetical list of twenty-four test cases, representative of nearly twelve hundred plaintiffs seeking compensation from the United States government for cancers caused by nuclear testing in Nevada.

Irene Allen lived in Hurricane, Utah. She was the mother of five children and had been widowed twice. Her first husband, with their two oldest boys, had watched the tests from the roof of the local high school. He died of leukemia in 1956. Her second husband died of pancreatic cancer in 1978.

In a town meeting conducted by Utah Senator Orrin Hatch, shortly before the suit was filed, Mrs. Allen said, "I am not blaming the government, I want you to know that, Senator Hatch. But I thought if my testimony could help in any way so this wouldn't happen again to any of the generations coming up after us . . . I am happy to be here this day to bear testimony of this."

God-fearing people. This is just one story in an anthology of thousands.

On May 10, 1984, Judge Bruce S. Jenkins handed down his opinion. Ten of the plaintiffs were awarded damages. It was the first time a federal court had determined that nuclear tests had been the cause of cancers. For the remaining fourteen test cases, the proof of causation was not sufficient. In spite of the split decision, it was considered a landmark ruling. It was not to remain so for long.

In April 1987, the Tenth Circuit Court of Appeals overturned Judge Jenkins's ruling on the ground that the United States was protected from suit by the legal doctrine of sovereign immunity, a centuries-old idea from England in the days of absolute monarchs.

In January 1988, the Supreme Court refused to review the Appeals Court decision. To our court system it does not matter whether the United States government was irresponsible, whether it lied to its citizens, or even that citizens died from the fallout of nuclear testing. What matters is that our government is immune: "The King can do no wrong."

In Mormon culture, authority is respected, obedience is revered, and independent thinking is not. I was taught as a young girl not to "make waves" or "rock the boat."

"Just let it go," Mother would say. "You know how you feel, that's what counts."

For many years, I have done just that—listened, observed, and quietly formed my own opinions, in a culture that rarely asks questions because it has all the answers. But one by one, I have watched the women in my family die common, heroic deaths. We sat in waiting rooms hoping for good news, but always receiving the bad. I cared for them, bathed their scarred bodies, and kept their secrets. I watched beautiful women become bald as Cytoxan, cisplatin, and Adriamycin[5] were injected into their veins. I held their foreheads as they vomited green-black bile, and I shot them with morphine when the pain became inhuman. In the end, I witnessed their last peaceful breaths, becoming a midwife to the rebirth of their souls.

The price of obedience has become too high.

The fear and inability to question authority that ultimately killed rural communities in Utah during atmospheric testing of atomic weapons is the same fear I saw in my mother's body. Sheep. Dead sheep. The evidence is buried.

I cannot prove that my mother, Diane Dixon Tempest, or my grandmothers, Lettie Romney Dixon and Kathryn Blackett Tempest, along with my aunts developed cancer from nuclear fallout in Utah. But I can't prove they didn't.

My father's memory was correct. The September blast we drove through in 1957 was part of Operation Plumbbob, one of the most intensive series of bomb tests to be initiated. The flash of light in the night in the desert, which I had always thought was a dream, developed into a family nightmare. It took fourteen years, from 1957 to 1971, for cancer to manifest in my mother—the same time, Howard L. Andrews, an authority in radioactive fallout at the National

[5] **Cytoxan, cisplatin, and Adriamycin** (sī-tŏk´sän, sĭs-plā´tn, and ă-drē´ă-mī´sĭn): drugs used in chemotherapy to treat cancer.

Institutes of Health, says radiation cancer requires to become evident. The more I learn about what it means to be a "downwinder," the more questions I drown in.

What I do know, however, is that as a Mormon woman of the fifth generation of Latter-day Saints, I must question everything, even if it means losing my faith, even if it means becoming a member of a border tribe among my own people. Tolerating blind obedience in the name of patriotism or religion ultimately takes our lives.

When the Atomic Energy Commission described the country north of the Nevada Test Site as "virtually uninhabited desert terrain," my family and the birds at Great Salt Lake were some of the "virtual uninhabitants."

One night, I dreamed women from all over the world circled a blazing fire in the desert. They spoke of change, how they hold the moon in their bellies and wax and wane with its phases. They mocked the presumption of even-tempered beings and made promises that they would never fear the witch inside themselves. The women danced wildly as sparks broke away from the flames and entered the night sky as stars.

And they sang a song given to them by Shoshone grandmothers:

Ah ne nah, nah	Consider the rabbits
nin nah nah—	How gently they walk on the earth—
ah ne nah, nah	Consider the rabbits
nin nah nah—	How gently they walk on the earth—
Nyaga mutzi	We remember them
oh ne nay—	We can walk gently also—
Nyaga mutzi	We remember them
oh ne nay—	We can walk gently also—

The women danced and drummed and sang for weeks, preparing themselves for what was to come. They would reclaim the desert for the sake of their children, for the sake of the land.

A few miles downwind from the fire circle, bombs were being tested. Rabbits felt the tremors. Their soft leather pads on paws and feet recognized the shaking sands, while the roots of mesquite and sage were smoldering. Rocks were hot from the inside out and dust devils hummed unnaturally. And each time there was another nuclear test, ravens watched the desert heave. Stretch marks appeared. The land was losing its muscle.

The women couldn't bear it any longer. They were mothers. They had suffered labor pains but always under the promise of birth. The red hot pains beneath the desert promised death only, as each bomb became a stillborn. A contract had been made and broken between human beings and the land. A new contract was being drawn by the women, who understood the fate of the earth as their own.

Under the cover of darkness, ten women slipped under a barbed-wire fence and entered the contaminated country. They were trespassing. They walked toward the town of Mercury, in moonlight, taking their cues from coyote, kit fox, antelope squirrel, and quail. They moved quietly and deliberately through the maze of Joshua trees. When a hint of daylight appeared they rested, drinking tea and sharing their rations of food. The women closed their eyes. The time had come to protest with the heart, that to deny one's genealogy[6] with the earth was to commit treason against one's soul.

At dawn, the women draped themselves in mylar, wrapping long streamers of silver plastic around their arms to blow in the breeze. They wore clear masks, that became the faces of humanity. And when they arrived at the edge of Mercury, they carried all the butterflies of a summer day in their wombs. They paused to allow their courage to settle.

The town that forbids pregnant women and children to enter because of radiation risks was asleep. The women moved through the streets as winged messengers, twirling around each other in slow motion, peeking inside homes and watching the easy sleep of men and women. They were astonished by such stillness and periodically would utter a shrill note or low cry just to verify life.

The residents finally awoke to these strange **apparitions**. Some simply stared. Others called authorities, and in time, the women were apprehended by wary soldiers dressed in desert fatigues. They were taken to a white, square building on the other edge of Mercury. When asked who they were and why they were there, the women replied, "We are mothers and we have come to reclaim the desert for our children."

apparition (ăp′ə-rĭsh′ən) *n.* an unexpected, unexplained vision; a ghostly image of a person.

The soldiers arrested them. As the ten women were blindfolded and handcuffed, they began singing:

You can't forbid us everything
You can't forbid us to think—
You can't forbid our tears to flow
And you can't stop the songs that we sing.

The women continued to sing louder and louder, until they heard the voices of their sisters moving across the mesa:

Ah ne nah, nah
nin nah nah—
Ah ne nah, nah
nin nah nah—
Nyaga mutzi
oh ne nay—
Nyaga mutzi
oh ne nay—

[6] **genealogy:** Mormons believe that their connections with ancestors are eternal, and that those who have died can still become members of the church.

"Call for reinforcements," one soldier said.

"We have," interrupted one woman, "we have—and you have no idea of our numbers."

I crossed the line at the Nevada Test Site and was arrested with nine other Utahns for trespassing on military lands. They are still conducting nuclear tests in the desert. Ours was an act of civil disobedience. But as I walked toward the town of Mercury, it was more than a gesture of peace. It was a gesture on behalf of the Clan of One-Breasted Women.

As one officer cinched the handcuffs around my wrists, another frisked my body. She found a pen and a pad of paper tucked inside my left boot.

"And these?" she asked sternly.

"Weapons," I replied.

Our eyes met. I smiled. She pulled the leg of my trousers back over my boot.

"Step forward, please," she said as she took my arm.

We were booked under an afternoon sun and bused to Tonopah, Nevada. It was a two-hour ride. This was familiar country. The Joshua trees standing their ground had been named by my ancestors, who believed they looked like prophets pointing west to the Promised Land. These were the same trees that bloomed each spring, flowers appearing like white flames in the Mojave. And I recalled a full moon in May, when Mother and I had walked among them, flushing out mourning doves and owls.

The bus stopped short of town. We were released.

The officials thought it was a cruel joke to leave us stranded in the desert with no way to get home. What they didn't realize was that we were home, soul-centered and strong, women who recognized the sweet smell of sage as fuel for our spirits.

COLLABORATIVE DISCUSSION In Williams's view, what has caused her family's health problems? What is this same cause doing to the landscape? With a partner, discuss what point the author is making by linking the two consequences to the same cause. Cite specific textual evidence from the essay to support your ideas.

Support Inferences

RI 1

Inferences are logical assumptions that readers make based on details in the text as well as what they know from their own experiences. Making inferences enables readers to understand thoughts and feelings that are not directly stated in the text. Sometimes these unstated thoughts and feelings are fairly easy to infer; in other cases, the author deliberately leaves matters uncertain.

In the following quotation, Williams describes seeing her mother after her cancer surgery:

> **She met us in the lobby . . . I'll never forget her radiance, the way she held herself in a purple velvet robe, and how she gathered us around her.**

Williams's use of the word *radiance* and the details she includes might lead readers to infer that her mother was a very strong woman with a deep faith; that it was important to her mother to reassure the family that she was all right; and that Williams actually believed her mother might survive.

Analyze Ideas and Events: Cause and Effect

RI 3

To understand how the author moves from "blind obedience" to "civil disobedience," readers must examine the **cause-and-effect** relationship between the events. In a cause-and-effect relationship, one or more actions or events cause another action or event to occur. As this organizer shows, the major events in the essay all contribute to the author's changed attitude and her deliberate act of protest.

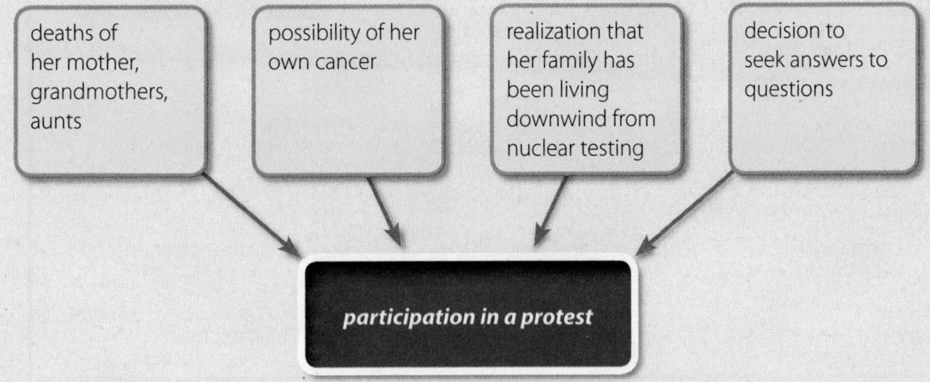

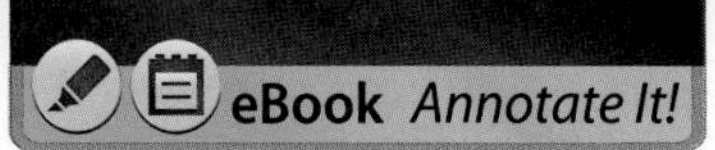

Analyzing the Text

RI 1, RI 3, RI 4, RI 6, RI 7, W 7, W 8, SL 5

Cite Text Evidence Support your responses with evidence from the selection.

1. **Infer** What can readers infer about the ethics and attitudes of the Mormon faith from what the author shares about her mother and grandmother? Why does the author want readers to understand the Mormon culture?
2. **Analyze** Explain how the author's perspective on her Mormon faith changes. Why must this shift occur before she can participate in the protest?
3. **Cause/Effect** Which event or moment has the greatest effect on the author's decision to protest? Cite details from the essay that support your response.
4. **Analyze** What is the author's **tone**, or attitude, toward the government? What words and phrases convey her tone?
5. **Analyze** What is the author's purpose in including her dream in the essay? How does this dream affect readers' understanding of the author's feelings and the protest itself?
6. **Cite Evidence** In this essay, the author presents facts, but she also uses **imagery**, words and phrases that create vivid sensory perceptions for readers. Explain how imagery heightens readers' understanding of important parts of the essay. Cite specific examples to support this analysis.
7. **Synthesize** Terry Tempest Williams has described her writing by saying, "I write through my biases of gender, geography, and culture." How does this point of view influence both her writing and her social activism? Explain what the essay and her protest at the Nevada Test Site have in common.

PERFORMANCE TASK

Media Activity: Report With a small group, present a multimedia report on the nuclear testing in Utah.

- Research the topic, using reliable web sites, reference books, and other resources. Remember to document your sources and write notes in your own words.
- Decide on the major point you want to convey through your presentation. Create a storyboard to help organize the visual, audio, and verbal elements of your report.
- Present your report to the class.

L 5b

Critical Vocabulary

anomaly **stoic** **rampant** **apparition**

Practice and Apply Answer each question, referring to the meaning of the Critical Vocabulary word in the statement.

1. The woman was *stoic* during her controversial testimony. How did she behave?
2. The girl thought she saw an *apparition* in her bedroom. How did she react? Why?
3. The disease was *rampant* in the area. Were public health officials worried or not? Explain.
4. The pickpocketing incident in the neighborhood was an *anomaly*. Should more police be assigned to the neighborhood in response? Explain why or why not.

Vocabulary Strategy: Denotation and Connotation

In her essay, Williams states, "McCarthyism was rampant." The Critical Vocabulary word *rampant* means "uncontrolled or out of hand." *Rampant* has many synonyms, including "wild," "excessive," "riotous," and "unchecked." The author chose *rampant*, however, because it is associated with something harmful or malicious. While the **denotation**, or dictionary definition of a word, is important, a word's **connotation**—ideas and feelings associated with it—helps convey the author's tone or attitude. The chart includes other words from the essay that were chosen for their connotations.

Word	Example	Denotation	Connotation
revered	"Obedience is revered."	held in deep respect	sacred
inhuman	"The pain became inhuman."	not ordinary; cruel	beyond a person's ability to survive
heave	"Ravens watched the desert heave."	shift or raise with great effort; throw	violent; painful

Practice and Apply For each word in the chart, identify a synonym—a word with the same denotation. Follow these steps:

1. Write the synonym and define it.
2. Use the synonym in a sentence.
3. Explain how the connotation of the new word differs from the connotation of the original.

Language and Style: Gerunds and Gerund Phrases

Gerunds are verb forms that end in *-ing* and are used as nouns. **Gerund phrases** include the gerund plus its modifiers and complements. As this chart shows, gerunds and gerund phrases can appear in any part of a sentence where a noun could be used.

Part of the sentence	Example
subject	**Bombing in Utah** was at its height in the 1950s.
direct object	The women finished **chanting**.
indirect object	The women gave **petitioning** a try.
subject complement	Her cure for tension was **writing in her journal**.
object of the preposition	She thought for a long time before **protesting at the site**.

Williams uses gerunds and gerund phrases in her essay. Read these sentences from the essay.

We got caught up in reminiscing . . .

Tolerating blind obedience in the name of patriotism or religion ultimately takes our lives.

The author could instead have replaced the gerunds with nouns:

We got caught up in our memories . . .

The toleration of blind obedience in the name of patriotism or religion ultimately takes our lives.

Although both versions of each sentence say the same thing, notice that the use of a gerund makes the sentences livelier. The *-ing* form of the verb creates a sense of motion and energy that helps to keep the readers' attention.

Practice and Apply Return to the multimedia report that you created in response to this selection's Performance Task. Identify places where you could replace a noun with a gerund or gerund phrase to make your speaking more lively. Discuss your changes with a partner.

Background *In the 1720s, the Catholics in Ireland suffered from the repressive rule of England, which stripped them of their rights and forced them into poverty. Their misery increased with a series of crop failures; many had to beg or face starvation. Swift wrote "A Modest Proposal" to protest England's policies in Ireland.*

Jonathan Swift (1667–1745) *was born of English parents in Dublin, Ireland. He became an Anglican priest and a writer, whose satires took aim at injustice and vice. He is probably best known for* Gulliver's Travels. *This satire is now enjoyed as a story, although Swift wrote it as a criticism of political corruption.*

A Modest Proposal

for preventing the children of poor people in Ireland from being a burden to their parents or country, and for making them beneficial to the public

Satire by Jonathan Swift

AS YOU READ Pay attention to details that Swift includes to make his proposal sound convincing. Note questions you have during reading.

It is a melancholy object to those who walk through this great town[1] or travel in the country, when they see the streets, the roads, and cabin doors, crowded with beggars of the female sex, followed by three, four, or six children, all in rags and importuning every passenger for an alms.[2] These mothers, instead of being able to work for their honest livelihood, are forced to employ all their time in strolling to beg sustenance for their helpless infants, who, as they grow up, either turn thieves for want[3] of work, or leave their dear native country to fight for the Pretender[4] in Spain, or sell themselves to the Barbadoes.[5]

---

[1] **this great town:** Dublin, Ireland.

[2] **importuning** (ĭm′pôr-to͞on′ĭng) **. . . alms** (ämz): begging from every passerby for a charitable handout.

[3] **want:** lack; need.

[4] **Pretender:** James Edward Stuart, who claimed the English throne, from which his now deceased father, James II, had been removed in 1688. Because James II and his son were Catholic, the common people of Ireland were loyal to them.

[5] **sell . . . Barbadoes:** To escape poverty, some Irish migrated to the West Indies, obtaining money for their passage by agreeing to work as slaves on plantations there for a set period.

I think it is agreed by all parties that this **prodigious** number of children in the arms, or on the backs, or at the heels of their mothers, and frequently of their fathers, is in the present deplorable state of the kingdom a very great additional grievance; and therefore whoever could find out a fair, cheap, and easy method of making these children sound, useful members of the commonwealth would deserve so well of the public as to have his statue set up for a preserver of the nation.

prodigious (prə-dĭj´əs) *adj.* remarkably great; huge.

But my intention is very far from being confined to provide only for the children of professed beggars; it is of a much greater extent, and shall take in the whole number of infants at a certain age who are born of parents in effect as little able to support them as those who demand our charity in the streets.

As to my own part, having turned my thoughts for many years upon this important subject, and maturely weighed the several schemes of other projectors,[6] I have always found them grossly mistaken in their computation. It is true, a child just dropped from its dam[7] may be supported by her milk for a solar year, with little other nourishment; at most not above the value of two shillings, which the mother may certainly get, or the value in scraps, by her lawful occupation of begging; and it is exactly at one year old that I propose to provide for them in such a manner as instead of being a charge upon their parents or the parish, or wanting food and raiment for the rest of their lives, they shall on the contrary contribute to the feeding, and partly to the clothing, of many thousands.

There is likewise another great advantage in my scheme, that it will prevent those voluntary abortions, and that horrid practice of women murdering their bastard children, alas, too frequent among us, sacrificing the poor innocent babes, I doubt,[8] more to avoid the expense than the shame, which would move tears and pity in the most savage and inhuman breast.

The number of souls in this kingdom being usually reckoned one million and a half, of these I calculate there may be about two hundred thousand couples whose wives are breeders; from which number I subtract thirty thousand couples who are able to maintain their own children, although I apprehend there cannot be so many under the present distresses of the kingdom; but this being granted, there will remain an hundred and seventy thousand breeders. I again subtract fifty thousand for those women who miscarry, or whose children die by accident or disease within the year. There only remain an hundred and twenty thousand children of poor parents annually born. The question therefore is, how this number shall be reared and provided for, which, as I have already said, under the present situation of affairs, is utterly impossible by all the methods hitherto proposed. For we can

[6] **projectors:** persons who propose public projects or plans.

[7] **dam** (dăm): female parent. The term is used mostly for farm animals.

[8] **doubt:** suspect.

> Whoever could find out a fair, cheap, and easy method of making these children sound, useful members of the commonwealth would deserve so well of the public.

neither employ them in handicraft or agriculture; we neither build houses (I mean in the country) nor cultivate land. They can very seldom pick up a livelihood by stealing till they arrive at six years old, except where they are of towardly parts;[9] although I confess they learn the **rudiments** much earlier, during which time they can however be looked upon only as probationers, as I have been informed by a principal gentleman in the county of Cavan, who protested to me that he never knew above one or two instances under the age of six, even in a part of the kingdom so renowned for the quickest proficiency in that art.

rudiment: (roo͞′də-mənt) *n.* basic principle or aspect.

I am assured by our merchants that a boy or girl before twelve years old is no salable commodity; and even when they come to this age they will not yield above three pounds, or three pounds and half a crown at most on the Exchange; which cannot turn to account[10] either to the parents or the kingdom, the charge of nutriment and rags having been at least four times that value.

I shall now therefore humbly propose my own thoughts, which I hope will not be liable to the least objection.

I have been assured by a very knowing American of my acquaintance in London, that a young healthy child well nursed is at a year old a most delicious, nourishing, and wholesome food, whether stewed, roasted, baked, or boiled; and I make no doubt that it will equally serve in a fricassee or a ragout.[11]

I do therefore humbly offer it to public consideration that of the hundred and twenty thousand children, already computed, twenty thousand may be reserved for breed,[12] whereof only one fourth part to be males, which is more than we allow to sheep, black cattle, or swine; and my reason is that these children are seldom the fruits of marriage, a circumstance not much regarded by our savages, therefore one male will be sufficient to serve four females. That the remaining

---

[9] **are of towardly** (tôrd′lē) **parts:** have a promising talent.

[10] **turn to account:** earn a profit; benefit; prove useful.

[11] **fricassee** (frĭk′ə-sē′) . . . **ragout** (ră-goo͞′): types of meat stews.

[12] **reserved for breed:** kept for breeding (instead of being slaughtered).

hundred thousand may at a year old be offered in sale to the persons of quality and fortune through the kingdom, always advising the mother to let them suck plentifully in the last month, so as to render them plump and fat for a good table. A child will make two dishes at an entertainment for friends; and when the family dines alone, the fore or hind quarter will make a reasonable dish, and seasoned with a little pepper or salt will be very good boiled on the fourth day, especially in winter.

I have reckoned upon a medium that a child just born will weigh twelve pounds, and in a solar year if tolerably nursed increaseth to twenty-eight pounds.

I grant this food will be somewhat dear, and therefore very proper for landlords, who, as they have already devoured most of the parents, seem to have the best title to the children.

Infant's flesh will be in season throughout the year, but more plentiful in March, and a little before and after. For we are told by a grave author, an eminent French physician,[13] that fish being a prolific[14] diet, there are more children born in Roman Catholic countries about nine months after Lent[15] than at any other season; therefore, reckoning a year after Lent, the markets will be more glutted than usual, because the number of popish infants is at least three to one in this kingdom; and therefore it will have one other **collateral** advantage, by lessening the number of Papists[16] among us.

collateral (kə-lăt´ər-əl) *adj.* additional, accompanying.

I have already computed the charge of nursing a beggar's child (in which list I reckon all cottagers, laborers, and four fifths of the farmers), to be about two shillings per annum, rags included; and I believe no gentleman would repine to give ten shillings for the carcass of a good fat child, which, as I have said, will make four dishes of excellent nutritive meat, when he hath only some particular friend or his own family to dine with him. Thus the squire will learn to be a good landlord, and grow popular among the tenants; the mother will have eight shillings net profit, and be fit for work till she produces another child.

Those who are more thrifty (as I must confess the times require) may flay the carcass; the skin of which artificially dressed will make admirable gloves for ladies, and summer boots for fine gentlemen.

As to our city of Dublin, shambles[17] may be appointed for this purpose in the most convenient parts of it, and butchers we may be assured will not be wanting; although I rather recommend buying the

---

[13] **grave . . . physician:** François Rabelais (răb´ə-lā´), a 16th-century French satirist.

[14] **prolific:** promoting fertility.

[15] **Lent:** Catholics traditionally do not eat meat during Lent, the 40 days leading up to Easter, and instead eat a lot of fish.

[16] **popish** (pō´pĭsh) . . . **Papists:** hostile or contemptuous terms referring to Roman Catholics.

[17] **shambles:** slaughterhouses.

children alive, and dressing them hot from the knife as we do roasting pigs.

A very worthy person, a true lover of his country, and whose virtues I highly esteem, was lately pleased in discoursing on this matter to offer a refinement upon my scheme. He said that many gentlemen of this kingdom, having of late destroyed their deer, he conceived that the want of venison might be well supplied by the bodies of young lads and maidens, not exceeding fourteen years of age nor under twelve, so great a number of both sexes in every county being now ready to starve for want of work and service; and these to be disposed of by their parents, if alive, or otherwise by their nearest relations. But with due deference to so excellent a friend and so deserving a patriot, I cannot be altogether in his sentiments; for as to the males, my American acquaintance assured me from frequent experience that their flesh was generally tough and lean, like that of our schoolboys, by continual exercise, and their taste disagreeable; and to fatten them would not answer the charge. Then as to the females, it would, I think with humble submission, be a loss to the public, because they soon would become breeders themselves; and besides, it is not improbable that some **scrupulous** people might be apt to censure such a practice (although indeed very unjustly) as a little bordering upon cruelty; which, I confess, hath always been with me the strongest objection against any project, how well soever intended.

scrupulous: (skro͞o′pyə-ləs) *adj.* honorable; moral.

But in order to justify my friend, he confessed that this expedient was put into his head by the famous Psalmanazar, a native of the island Formosa,[18] who came from thence to London above twenty years ago, and in conversation told my friend that in his country when any young person happened to be put to death, the executioner sold the carcass to persons of quality as a prime dainty; and that in his time the body of a plump girl of fifteen, who was crucified for an attempt to poison the emperor, was sold to his Imperial Majesty's prime minister of state, and other great mandarins of the court, in joints from the gibbet,[19] at four hundred crowns. Neither indeed can I deny that if the same use were made of several plump young girls in this town, who without one single groat[20] to their fortunes cannot stir abroad without a chair,[21] and appear at the playhouse and assemblies in foreign fineries which they never will pay for, the kingdom would not be the worse.

Some persons of a desponding spirit are in great concern about that vast number of poor people who are aged, diseased, or maimed, and I have been desired to employ my thoughts what course may be

---

[18] **Psalmanazar** (săl′mə-năz′ər) . . . **Formosa** (fôr-mō′sə): a French imposter in London who called himself George Psalmanazar and pretended to be from Formosa (now Taiwan), where, he said, cannibalism was practiced.

[19] **gibbet** (jĭb′ĭt): gallows.

[20] **groat:** an old British coin worth four pennies.

[21] **cannot stir . . . chair:** cannot go outside without using an enclosed chair carried on poles by two men.

taken to ease the nation of so grievous an encumbrance. But I am not in the least pain upon that matter, because it is very well known that they are every day dying and rotting by cold and famine, and filth and vermin, as fast as can be reasonably expected. And as to the younger laborers, they are now in almost as hopeful a condition. They cannot get work, and consequently pine away for want of nourishment to a degree that if at any time they are accidentally hired to common labor, they have not strength to perform it; and thus the country and themselves are happily delivered from the evils to come.

I have too long digressed, and therefore shall return to my subject. I think the advantages by the proposal which I have made are obvious and many, as well as of the highest importance.

For first, as I have already observed, it would greatly lessen the number of Papists, with whom we are yearly overrun, being the principal breeders of the nation as well as our most dangerous enemies; and who stay at home on purpose to deliver the kingdom to the Pretender, hoping to take their advantage by the absence of so many good Protestants, who have chosen rather to leave their country than stay at home and pay tithes against their conscience to an Episcopal curate.[22]

Secondly, the poorer tenants will have something valuable of their own, which by law may be made liable to distress,[23] and help to pay their landlord's rent, their corn and cattle being already seized and money a thing unknown.

Thirdly, whereas the maintenance of an hundred thousand children, from two years old and upwards, cannot be computed at less than ten shillings a piece per annum, the nation's stock will be thereby increased fifty thousand pounds per annum, besides the profit of a new dish introduced to the tables of all gentlemen of fortune in the kingdom who have any refinement in taste. And the money will circulate among ourselves, the goods being entirely of our own growth and manufacture.

Fourthly, the constant breeders, besides the gain of eight shillings sterling per annum by the sale of their children, will be rid of the charge of maintaining them after the first year.

Fifthly, this food would likewise bring great custom to taverns, where the vintners will certainly be so prudent as to procure the best receipts[24] for dressing it to perfection, and consequently have their houses frequented by all the fine gentlemen, who justly value themselves upon their knowledge in good eating; and a skillful cook, who understands how to oblige his guests, will contrive to make it as expensive as they please.

[22] **Protestants . . . curate** (kyŏŏr´ĭt): Swift is criticizing absentee Anglo-Irish landowners who lived—and spent their income from their property—in England.

[23] **distress:** seizure of a person's property for the payment of debts.

[24] **receipts:** recipes.

> **"No gentleman would repine to give ten shillings for the carcass of a good fat child."**

Sixthly, this would be a great **inducement** to marriage, which all wise nations have either encouraged by rewards or enforced by laws and penalties. It would increase the care and tenderness of mothers toward their children, when they were sure of a settlement for life to the poor babes, provided in some sort by the public, to their annual profit instead of expense. We should see an honest emulation among the married women, which of them could bring the fattest child to the market. Men would become as fond of their wives during the time of their pregnancy as they are now of their mares in foal, their cows in calf, or sows when they are ready to farrow; nor offer to beat or kick them (as is too frequent a practice) for fear of a miscarriage.

inducement: (ĭn-do͞os′mənt) *n.* an incentive or stimulus.

Many other advantages might be enumerated. For instance, the addition of some thousand carcasses in our exportation of barreled beef, the propagation of swine's flesh, and improvement in the art of making good bacon, so much wanted among us by the great destruction of pigs, too frequent at our tables, which are no way comparable in taste or magnificence to a well-grown, fat, yearling child, which roasted whole will make a considerable figure at a lord mayor's feast or any other public entertainment. But this and many others I omit, being studious of brevity.

Supposing that one thousand families in this city would be constant customers for infants' flesh, besides others who might have it at merry meetings, particularly weddings and christenings, I compute that Dublin would take off annually about twenty thousand carcasses, and the rest of the kingdom (where probably they will be sold somewhat cheaper) the remaining eighty thousand.

I can think of no one objection that will possibly be raised against this proposal, unless it should be urged that the number of people will be thereby much lessened in the kingdom. This I freely own, and it was indeed one principal design in offering it to the world. I desire the reader will observe, that I calculate my remedy for this one individual kingdom of Ireland and for no other that ever was, is, or I think ever can be upon earth. Therefore let no man talk to me of other expedients: of taxing our absentees at five shillings a pound: of using neither clothes nor household furniture except what is of our own growth and manufacture: of utterly rejecting the materials and instruments that promote foreign luxury: of curing the expensiveness of pride, vanity, idleness, and gaming in our women: of introducing a vein of parsimony,[25] prudence, and temperance: of learning to love our country, in the want of which we differ even from Laplanders and the inhabitants of Topinamboo:[26] of quitting our animosities and factions, nor acting any longer like the Jews, who were murdering one another at the very moment their city was taken:[27] of being a little cautious not to sell our country and conscience for nothing: of teaching landlords to have at least one degree of mercy toward their tenants: lastly, of putting a spirit of honesty, industry, and skill into our shopkeepers; who, if a resolution could now be taken to buy only our native goods, would immediately unite to cheat and exact upon us in the price, the measure, and the goodness, nor could ever yet be brought to make one fair proposal of just dealing, though often and earnestly invited to it.

Therefore I repeat, let no man talk to me of these and the like expedients,[28] till he hath at least some glimpse of hope that there will ever be some hearty and sincere attempt to put them in practice.

But as to myself, having been wearied out for many years with offering vain, idle, visionary thoughts, and at length utterly despairing of success, I fortunately fell upon this proposal, which, as it is wholly new, so it hath something solid and real, of no expense and little trouble, full in our own power, and whereby we can incur no danger in disobliging England. For this kind of commodity will not bear exportation, the flesh being of too tender a consistence to admit a long continuance in salt, although perhaps I could name a country which would be glad to eat up our whole nation without it.

After all, I am not so violently bent upon my own opinion as to reject any offer proposed by wise men, which shall be found equally innocent, cheap, easy, and effectual. But before something of that kind shall be advanced in contradiction to my scheme, and offering a better, I desire the author or authors will be pleased maturely to consider two points. First, as things now stand, how they will be able to find food and raiment for an hundred thousand useless mouths and backs. And secondly, there being a round million of creatures in human figure throughout this kingdom, whose sole subsistence put into a common stock[29] would leave them in debt two millions of pounds sterling, adding those who are beggars by profession to the bulk of farmers,

---

[25]**parsimony** (pär′sə-mō′nē): frugality; thrift.

[26]**Topinamboo** (tŏp′ĭ-năm′bo͞o): an area in Brazil supposedly inhabited by wild savages.

[27]**Jews . . . taken:** In AD 70, during a Jewish revolt against Roman rule, the inhabitants of Jerusalem, by fighting among themselves, made it easier for the Romans to capture the city.

[28]**let no man . . . expedients:** In his writings, Swift had suggested "other expedients" without success.

[29]**common stock:** ordinary stock in a company or business venture.

cottagers, and laborers, with their wives and children who are beggars in effect; I desire those politicians who dislike my overture, and may perhaps be so bold to attempt an answer, that they will first ask the parents of these mortals whether they would not at this day think it a great happiness to have been sold for food at a year old in the manner I prescribe, and thereby have avoided such a perpetual scene of misfortunes as they have since gone through by the oppression of landlords, the impossibility of paying rent without money or trade, the want of common sustenance, with neither house nor clothes to cover them from the inclemencies of the weather, and the most inevitable prospect of entailing the like or greater miseries upon their breed forever.

I profess, in the sincerity of my heart, that I have not the least personal interest in endeavoring to promote this necessary work, having no other motive than the public good of my country, by advancing our trade, providing for infants, relieving the poor, and giving some pleasure to the rich. I have no children by which I can propose to get a single penny; the youngest being nine years old, and my wife past childbearing.

COLLABORATIVE DISCUSSION With a partner, discuss how Swift increases the impact of his satire by making his proposal appear legitimate. Cite specific textual evidence from the essay in support.

Analyze Author's Point of View: Satire

RL 6, RI 6

Satire is a literary technique in which institutions, practices, or behaviors are ridiculed for the purpose of bringing about reform. The effectiveness of satire depends on the ability of readers to distinguish between what is directly stated and what is really meant.

Although some satirical works are lighthearted and humorous, in "A Modest Proposal," Swift's satire is dark and scathing. He shows his contempt for England's policies in Ireland through the outrageousness of his proposal. To develop his satire, he relies on several literary devices, including the two described in the chart.

Device	Example
Verbal irony occurs when a writer says the opposite of what is meant.	The title of Swift's essay, "A Modest Proposal," is an example of verbal irony because the actual proposal is outrageous rather than reasonable.
Understatement occurs when the writer says less than is expected or appropriate.	Swift says that a plan to hunt boys and girls 12 to 14 years old might be criticized as "a little bordering upon cruelty."

Comprehend Literary Nonfiction: Historical Context

RI 10

Some literary works, particularly satires, can be more fully appreciated if readers understand the **historical context**—the conditions or events that inspired them. "A Modest Proposal" conveys a universal message about injustice, but its true purpose is to serve as an indictment of English policies in Ireland.

To comprehend Swift's satire, you should examine the footnotes that explain eighteenth-century references. In addition, keep in mind that at the time Swift was writing, Irish Catholics could not vote, hold public office, buy land, or receive an education. Land was mostly owned by English or Anglo-Irish Protestants, many of whom were absentee landlords. Tenants were forced to pay rent to these landlords, even during the years when the crops failed. Little money paid to the English found its way back into the Irish economy. Swift had protested these injustices before the publication of "A Modest Proposal." In fact, he actually presented the solutions that he ironically dismisses in lines 236–241 of the satire, but his ideas were not accepted. "A Modest Proposal" was his last great published satire that attempted to right the wrongs he saw.

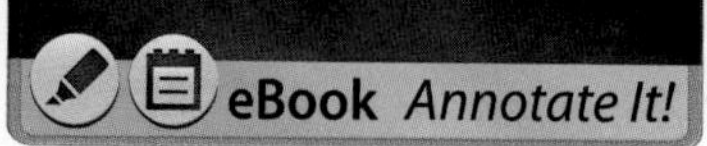

Analyzing the Text

RL 6, RI 3, RI 4, RI 5, RI 6, RI 10, W 4, L 5a

Cite Text Evidence Support your responses with evidence from the selection.

1. **Analyze** Swift uses a fictional narrator to present the proposal in his essay. Describe the tone of this narrator toward the ideas he is proposing, citing words and phrases that reveal his attitude. How does this tone contribute to the effectiveness of the satire?
2. **Infer** What idea about the English view of the Irish does Swift convey through his use of words such as *breeder, carcasses,* and *flesh*? How does his inclusion of statistical data develop this idea?
3. **Analyze** Discuss examples of verbal irony in the following passages:
   - lines 69–70 ("I shall now . . . least objection.")
   - lines 124–144 ("A very worthy . . . soever intended.")
   - lines 159–170 ("Some persons . . . evils to come.")
4. **Analyze** Another device that Swift uses to develop his satire is **hyperbole**, a figure of speech in which the truth is exaggerated for emphasis or to create humor. Identify an example of hyperbole in Swift's essay and describe its effect.
5. **Analyze** Swift says that he has "digressed" in lines 159–170. Explain how this digression actually serves his purpose of exposing English injustice.
6. **Draw Conclusions** Reread lines 236–256, in which Swift dismisses alternate "expedients" as impractical. What point does he make by referring to his own proposals in this way?
7. **Connect** The period from the late 1600s through the 1700s is known as the Enlightenment, a time when many writers promoted scientific reasoning as a means of solving social problems. Swift was often critical of such writers. How is this historical context reflected in "A Modest Proposal"?

PERFORMANCE TASK

Writing Activity: Context Guide Working with a partner, reread the essay to identify a section where you need more historical context to understand Swift's references.

- With your partner, research the history behind a certain reference or passage in the text.
- Record the line numbers of your reference or passage and your sources on a sheet of paper.
- Take notes about your findings and write a short summary statement.
- Review your work for accuracy and standard English grammar and usage. Then share it with the class.
- Gather all notes and summaries into a "Context Guide" folder to help other students who read "A Modest Proposal."

L 4a, L 4d

Critical Vocabulary

prodigious **rudiment** **collateral**
scrupulous **inducement**

Practice and Apply Choose the situation that fits the meaning of the Critical Vocabulary word. Explain your decision.

1. If you have a *prodigious* talent for satire, would people reject your work or want to read it?
2. What would be an *inducement* to the English to settle in Ireland, the offer of land or the inability to understand the language?
3. What is a *rudiment* of farming, grinding the wheat or preparing the soil?
4. If a landlord is *scrupulous*, would he live on site or visit his tenants every few years?
5. What is *collateral* damage from a famine, higher food prices or diseased crops?

Vocabulary Strategy: Context Clues

Context clues are often found in the words and sentences around an unknown term. A context clue may consist of definition or restatement of the meaning of the unfamiliar word, an example following the word, a comparison or contrast, or a nearby synonym. The unknown word's position or function in a sentence can also be a clue.

For example, the placement and suffix of the Critical Vocabulary word *prodigious* in line 10 tell you that it is an adjective. Knowing this makes the word easier to define. The Vocabulary word *inducement* appears in this sentence with the context clue "encouraged": "Sixthly, this would be a great inducement to marriage, which all wise nations have either encouraged by rewards or enforced by laws and penalties." After using context clues to get a preliminary understanding of a word, you can verify the word's meaning by looking it up in a dictionary.

Practice and Apply Use the context clues in each sentence to define the italicized words from the essay. Check your meanings in a dictionary.

1. Their *sustenance*, a bland potato soup, kept them alive through the winter.
2. He *reckoned* the cost of raising a child, computing it to the penny.
3. The *inclemency* of the country's weather, the bitter wind and constant rain, added to the misery of those who lacked shelter.
4. Those who crave such a delicacy would not *repine* for an instant at the thought of spending the money.

Language and Style: Active and Passive Voice

L 3a

Swift uses both active and passive voice in his essay. When a verb is in the **active voice**, the subject performs the action. When the verb is in the **passive voice**, the subject is the receiver of the action. The passive voice is formed with the verb *to be* and the past participle of a verb. Typically, the active voice is preferred because it conveys more energy and is more direct. To develop a more formal tone fitting for his proposal, however, Swift turns to the passive voice.

Read these sentences from the essay.

It is agreed by all parties that this prodigious number of children . . . is . . . a very great additional grievance.

I am assured by our merchants that a boy or girl before twelve years old is no salable commodity.

Swift could have chosen to use the active voice in both sentences:

All parties agree that this prodigious number of children . . . is . . . a very great additional grievance.

Our merchants assure me that a boy or girl before twelve years old is no salable commodity.

Altering the verb from passive to active makes the writing more vigorous and less like the bureacratic language that might be used in a real proposal. Sometimes, the passive voice is preferred for other reasons as explained in the chart.

Uses of Passive Voice	
Purpose	**Example**
to emphasize the receiver of the action	The truce was shattered by the accidental firing.
when the doer of the action is not known or not important	The votes were counted.

Practice and Apply Write four sentences about "A Modest Proposal" in passive voice. Exchange sentences with a partner and rewrite each other's sentences in active voice. Compare the differences between the two versions.

Alison Wright *is a photojournalist whose work has taken her around the world. Her photographs capture people struggling for survival and coping with human-rights issues. She also records traditions of changing cultures to preserve them. Her pictures have appeared in many publications including* National Geographic *magazine. In addition, her photos and writing have been published in several books. One of her books recounts her recovery after surviving a life-threatening bus accident in Laos.*

MEDIA ANALYSIS

Third World America

Photojournalism by Alison Wright

AS YOU VIEW Notice details in the photographs that provide insight into the living conditions of the people shown in them.

This project covers an array of social and ethnic borders; the black families of the Mississippi Delta who live in the first town started after slavery was abolished; the struggles of a single woman raising three children on the minimum wage while working at Wendy's in Ohio; the food bank in Appalachia where 800 cars a day line up for groceries; migrant workers who live in Texas and raise children in this country so they can have a better life as American citizens; Indians on a Navaho reservation who instill a cultural sense of pride to their children in the native powwows, yet have no running water or electricity in their basic hogans.

The face of poverty in this country is not the rail thin visage as in developing countries, but due to such a poor innutritious diet, obesity is a ubiquitous problem. Children's health is so affected that diabetes is prevalent, and many are overweight with severe psychological problems. With the cost of living outweighing the average income, many families across America are just one pay check away from being on the edge, especially when it comes to healthcare issues.

MEDIA

Texas: The bedroom for seven children, Rio Grande Valley.

Ohio, Appalachia: This food bank feeds over 1,000 people per day.

Arizona: This family lives in a bus with no electricity or water on a Navaho Indian reservation.

Mississippi Delta: Woman raising her children alone.

COLLABORATIVE DISCUSSION With a partner, share your impressions of the people in the photographs. Cite specific details from the photos to support your discussion.

Integrate and Evaluate Information

RI 7

In her photo essay, Alison Wright uses text and images to communicate her message about poverty in America. In order to appreciate the meaning conveyed by each photo as well as their cumulative effect, viewers need to analyze the following elements:

- **Camera angle:** Does Wright take close-up shots or use a wider angle? How does this choice affect what viewers see in the photographs?
- **Subject:** Does Wright show people in isolation or photograph them in groups? What do their poses suggest about them? How does the surrounding text enhance the information in the photos?
- **Lighting:** A photographer might create an effect through lighting. What choices does Wright make in these photos?
- **Mood:** Through lighting, choice of setting, and props, a photographer can create a particular mood, or atmosphere, that helps convey a message.

Analyzing the Media

RI 7, SL 4, SL 5

Cite Text Evidence Support your responses with evidence from the selection.

1. **Analyze** Explain why Wright chooses a wider angle from which to view her subjects. How does this view enhance readers' understanding of the context of each photograph?
2. **Analyze** How do the captions add to the effectiveness of the photo essay? What is the relationship between the captions and the introductory text?
3. **Cite Evidence** Choose one photograph, and explain how it communicates Wright's message. Identify details that help convey the meaning.
4. **Critique** Describe the photographer's style as revealed through this series of photographs, commenting on her choice of subjects, the use of lighting, and the mood conveyed by each. How is Wright's style related to her purpose?

PERFORMANCE TASK

Media Activity: Photo Essay With a partner, create your own photo essay to convince an audience of your perspective on an aspect of poverty in the United States.

- Conduct research and find or take photographs to illustrate your point. Be sure to consider copyright restrictions.
- Write a brief preface, assemble the photographs, and write captions.
- Display your photo essay in a gallery in the classroom.

Martín Espada (b. 1957) *was born in Brooklyn, New York. Growing up in a rough neighborhood, he experienced many of the conditions that he writes about in his poetry. Espada says that when he worked as a tenant lawyer, he used law as a political tool, and he uses poetry for the same purpose. A professor at the University of Massachusetts at Amherst, Espada has written several volumes of poetry, including* Imagine the Angels of Bread, *which won an American Book Award. He believes that "poetry humanizes. It makes the abstract concrete. It makes the general specific and particular."*

Imagine the Angels of Bread

Poem by Martín Espada

AS YOU READ Pay attention to images of suffering and injustice in the poem. Write down any questions that you generate during reading.

This is the year that squatters evict landlords,
gazing like admirals from the rail
of the roofdeck
or levitating hands in praise
of steam in the shower;
this is the year
that shawled refugees deport judges
who stare at the floor
and their swollen feet
as files are stamped
with their destination;
this is the year that police revolvers,
stove-hot, blister the fingers
of raging cops,
and nightsticks splinter
in their palms;
this is the year
that darkskinned men
lynched a century ago

return to sip coffee quietly
with the apologizing descendants
of their executioners.

This is the year that those
who swim the border's undertow
and shiver in boxcars
are greeted with trumpets and drums
at the first railroad crossing
on the other side;
this is the year that the hands
pulling tomatoes from the vine
uproot the deed to the earth that sprouts the vine,
the hands canning tomatoes
are named in the will
that owns the bedlam of the cannery;
this is the year that the eyes
stinging from the poison that purifies toilets
awaken at last to the sight
of a rooster-loud hillside,
pilgrimage of immigrant birth;
this is the year that cockroaches
become extinct, that no doctor
finds a roach embedded
in the ear of an infant;

this is the year that the food stamps
of adolescent mothers
are auctioned like gold doubloons,
and no coin is given to buy machetes
for the next bouquet of severed heads
in coffee plantation country.

If the abolition of slave-manacles
began as a vision of hands without manacles,
then this is the year;
if the shutdown of extermination camps
began as imagination of a land
without barbed wire or the crematorium,
then this is the year;
if every rebellion begins with the idea
that conquerors on horseback
are not many-legged gods, that they too drown
if plunged in the river,
then this is the year.

So may every humiliated mouth,
teeth like desecrated headstones,
fill with the angels of bread.

COLLABORATIVE DISCUSSION With a partner, discuss how Espada uses imagery to reverse common forms of suffering and injustice in the world. Cite specific examples in the text.

eBook *Annotate It!*

Analyze Word Choice: Tone

RL 4

The **tone** of a poem is the speaker's attitude toward the subject. Often tone can be described with a single word, such as *sarcastic, bitter*, or *affectionate*. In some works, such as "Imagine the Angels of Bread," the tone is more complicated because the speaker mixes together hopeful statements with disturbing imagery. As you analyze this poem's tone, consider how the following elements contribute to it:

Word choices and their **connotations** (the thoughts and feelings associated with the words)	For example, *blister* in line 13 has a harsh connotation, while *sip* in line 20 evokes a calm and soothing mood.
Imagery used to depict the subject or action	The poem contains many images associated with oppression, but also more hopeful images such as "levitating hands in praise."

Analyzing the Text

RL 1, RL 4, W 10

Cite Text Evidence Support your responses with evidence from the selection.

1. **Identify Patterns** Lines 1–3 of the poem include a **simile**, a comparison between two unlike things that uses the word *like* or *as*. What idea does the simile convey? Explain how this simile helps establish a pattern in the poem.

2. **Analyze** Identify the tone in each of the following passages. Cite specific words and images that help create this tone.
   - lines 12–16
   - lines 26–28
   - lines 36–38

3. **Analyze** What words and phrases are repeated in the poem? Explain how this repetition is used to emphasize ideas and emotions.

4. **Draw Conclusions** Reread the poem's last stanza. What is the significance of the phrase "angels of bread" used here and in the title?

PERFORMANCE TASK

Writing Activity: Poem Write a short poem inspired by one of the images or statements in "Imagine the Angels of Bread."

- Decide on a theme, or message, that you want to convey in the poem.
- Choose words and images that create an appropriate tone.
- Read the completed poem to a small group.

Interactive Lessons

To help you complete this task, use
- *Participating in Collaborative Discussions*
- *Using Textual Evidence*

Participate in a Group Discussion

Look back at the anchor text "Speech on the Vietnam War, 1967" and at the other texts in the collection. What connections do you see between the examples of injustice explored in each text? Have a group discussion on the topic, and then write a summary of the discussion.

SL 1a–d Initiate and participate in collaborative discussions.
SL 4 Present information, findings, and supporting evidence.

Participants in a successful group discussion

- present quotations or examples from "Speech on the Vietnam War, 1967" and other collection texts to illustrate ideas about injustice
- make clear, logical, and well-developed connections among the texts' views of injustice
- pose and respond to questions to keep the conversation going
- respond to the ideas of others in the group, adapting or expanding upon their own ideas or politely challenging others' assertions
- use appropriate eye contact, adequate volume, and clear pronunciation
- write an accurate and objective summary of the discussion

Mentor Text See how this example from "The Crisis" illustrates an idea about injustice.

> "Britain, with an army to enforce her tyranny, has declared, that she has a right (*not only to* TAX) but "to BIND US in ALL CASES WHATSOEVER," and if *being bound in that manner* is not slavery, then there is not such a thing as slavery upon earth."

myNotebook

Use the annotation tools in your eBook to find examples of injustice from the selections that you will discuss. Save each example to your notebook.

PLAN

Get Organized Work with your classmates to prepare for the discussion.

- In the anchor text "Speech on the Vietnam War, 1967," Martin Luther King Jr. outlines many intersecting areas of injustice that relate to the war. Get together with your group and choose two other texts from this collection, in addition to King's speech, that you will use to discuss relationships between various examples of injustice.
- Choose a moderator and a note-taker. The moderator will keep track of the time and make sure all members participate equally. The note-taker will write down important ideas from the discussion.
- Set deadlines to make sure all tasks related to the discussion can be completed on time. Tasks include analyzing the texts, holding the discussion, and writing summaries.

ACADEMIC VOCABULARY

As you plan your discussion on the issue of injustice, try to use these words.

controversy
convince
ethics
radical
tension

Analyze the Texts Work independently to review your group's chosen texts.

- Reread "Speech on the Vietnam War, 1967" and identify examples of injustice cited by Martin Luther King Jr. Take note of any details or quotations you might want to mention in a discussion about the speech.
- Then review the other chosen texts, also taking notes on examples of injustice.
- Consider how the examples you have identified are related. Do the injustices stem from the same root cause, for example, or do they interact in ways that make the problems grow?

Interactive Lessons

To help you plan your discussion, complete the following lessons:

- Participating in Collaborative Discussions: Preparing for Discussion
- Using Textual Evidence: Writing an Outline

Outline Your Ideas Put your ideas in order so that you can refer to them quickly during the discussion. You might create an outline or use a graphic organizer.

- Write down your central ideas about how the examples of injustice in the three texts are related to each other. State your ideas clearly and concisely so that others will easily understand them.
- Sort through the evidence you have collected from the texts. Match each piece of evidence with the central idea it most clearly supports. Make sure your reasoning is sound enough to convince other group members of your ideas.
- Think of questions that the moderator or other group members may ask you. Be prepared to answer them.
- Develop some suggestions to end the injustices that your group is going to discuss. Recall the steps that Martin Luther King Jr. outlines in lines 322–333 of his speech. You may need to do some additional research on the specific problems before you can suggest reasonable solutions to them.

PRODUCE

Write your outline in *my*WriteSmart. Focus on putting your ideas in a logical order.

Have the Discussion Join your group members to exchange ideas in a discussion.

- The moderator may start the discussion by calling on a student to speak first. After that, everyone in the group should take responsibility for building on others' ideas and posing questions to keep the conversation going.
- Be sure that listeners understand your ideas. When you speak, be sure to maintain eye contact, use adequate volume, and pronounce your words clearly.
- Maintain a respectful tone toward your fellow group members, even when you disagree with each other's ideas. It is the moderator's job

Interactive Lessons

To help you plan your discussion, complete the following lessons in *Participating in Collaborative Discussions*:

- Speaking Constructively
- Listening and Responding

to ease any tension among group members and keep the discussion focused on the topic.

- Listen closely to what all speakers say so that you can respond appropriately and ask relevant questions.
- If the discussion gets off track, the moderator may ask the note-taker to read back his or her notes on the last relevant part of the conversation.
- Take your own notes throughout the discussion. You will use these notes to write your summary.

REVISE

Write your summary in *my*WriteSmart. Make sure that you include all of your group's key points.

Evaluate the Discussion Conclude your discussion by evaluating the ideas that have been brought up. Use the chart on the following page to review the characteristics of an effective discussion.

- Discuss the reasons and evidence that you found most compelling.
- Synthesize the ideas expressed by the group and resolve any controversial ideas, if possible.
- Decide on the most important points from the discussion that the note-taker will report back to the class.
- Work independently to write a summary of the conclusions that your group reached and your suggestions for addressing the problems.

PRESENT

Present to the Class The note-taker should summarize the main points from the group discussion for the rest of the class. Then give your classmates a chance to ask questions about your analysis and your suggested solutions. All group members can respond to the questions.

PERFORMANCE TASK A RUBRIC

GROUP DISCUSSION

	Ideas and Evidence	Organization	Language
4	• Group members identify clear and relevant examples of injustice from three collection texts, including the King speech. • Students propel discussion by posing thoughtful questions and offering new ideas. • Students offer well-reasoned analysis of the connections between examples. • Students propose reasonable, real-world solutions to the problems discussed.	• The group completes all tasks on schedule. • Group members' remarks are based on well-organized notes that clearly identify their central ideas. • The conversation stays focused on the topic and makes logical connections between ideas and examples. • Group members accurately summarize their discussion in writing and in a class presentation.	• Group members adapt speech to the context of the discussion, using appropriately formal English to discuss texts and ideas. • Students quote accurately from the texts to support ideas. • Students use appropriate eye contact, adequate volume, and clear pronunciation throughout the discussion. • Students maintain a polite and thoughtful tone throughout the discussion.
3	• Group members identify examples of injustice from three collection texts, including the King speech. • Students pose questions and offer new ideas, but the discussion lapses occasionally. • Students analyze some connections between examples. • Students propose solutions to the problems discussed.	• The group completes most tasks on schedule. • Group members' remarks are based on notes that identify their central ideas. • The conversation mostly stays focused on the topic and makes connections between ideas and examples. • Group members adequately summarize their discussion in writing and in a class presentation.	• Group members mostly use formal English to discuss texts and ideas. • Students quote accurately from the texts to support ideas. • Students use appropriate eye contact, adequate volume, and clear pronunciation throughout most of the discussion. • Students maintain a polite and thoughtful tone throughout most of the discussion.
2	• Group members identify a few examples of injustice from collection texts. • The discussion is not fluid, and students depend on the moderator to ask questions. • Students make few connections between the text examples. • Students propose solutions to some of the problems, but the solutions are not practical or appropriate.	• The group completes many tasks late. • Group members' notes do not clearly identify their central ideas. • The conversation wanders off the topic and makes few connections between ideas and examples. • Students' summaries are incomplete or unfocused.	• Group members use some formal and some informal English to discuss texts and ideas. • Students' quotations and examples sometimes do not accurately reflect the texts. • Students sometimes forget to use appropriate eye contact, adequate volume, and clear pronunciation. • Students sometimes forget to maintain a polite tone when responding to others' comments and questions.
1	• Group members do not identify clear examples of injustice. • There is no real discussion of ideas; the moderator fails to keep group members engaged. • Students make no connections between the text examples. • Students propose no solutions to the problems, or the solutions are illogical.	• The group seems unaware of deadlines. • Group members do not prepare notes that can help them express their central ideas about the texts. • The conversation is unfocused and makes no connections between ideas and examples. • Students' summaries of the discussion are inaccurate.	• Group members use informal English and/or slang, resulting in ideas that are not clearly expressed. • Students' quotations and examples do not accurately reflect the texts. • Students do not use appropriate eye contact, adequate volume, and clear pronunciation. • Students do not maintain a polite tone when responding to others' comments and questions.

Write a Satire

In "A Modest Proposal," Jonathan Swift proposes a satirical solution to one particular injustice as a way of exposing its horrors. Using Swift's essay as a model, write a satire on a topic covered in one of the other texts in the collection.

W 1 Write arguments.
W 4 Produce clear and coherent writing.
W 5 Develop and strengthen writing.
W 6 Use technology to produce, publish, and update writing projects.
W 9 Draw evidence from literary or informational texts.

An effective satire

- introduces a particular idea, custom, behavior, or institution to be the target of satire with the goal of convincing readers to change their view of the target or of bringing about social reform
- includes irony, humor, exaggeration, and understatement to show the target in a critical light
- identifies the object of the satire, but makes the reader infer the writer's true perspective on the issue
- uses the form of a problem-solution essay, as in "A Modest Proposal"
- concludes with a summary or global statement about the issue
- uses precise language with appropriate tone and style for a satire

Mentor Text See how Swift uses irony in this excerpt from "A Modest Proposal" by suggesting that the solution to Irish poverty is to raise children to the age of two and then sell them as a culinary delicacy.

> "Thirdly, whereas the maintenance of an hundred thousand children, from two years old and upwards, cannot be computed at less than ten shillings a piece per annum, the nation's stock will be thereby increased fifty thousand pounds per annum, besides the profit of a new dish introduced to the tables of all gentlemen of fortune in the kingdom who have any refinement in taste."

PLAN

Analyze "A Modest Proposal" Reread Swift's essay and take note of the problem-solution format. Model the structure of your own satire after "A Modest Proposal." Your satire should

- clearly identify a problem and its causes
- propose a solution to the problem and explain how to implement it
- provide support for the solution in the form of reasons and evidence
- note other possible solutions and argue against them

myNotebook

Use the annotation tools in your eBook to identify features of the format of Swift's essay. Save each note to your notebook.

Brainstorm Review the other texts in the collection, paying attention to the types of injustices presented in each text.

- Choose one topic covered in the collection and use a graphic organizer to help you generate ideas for a satire on that topic.
- Think of the target of your satire as a specific problem, and come up with a satirical solution for it. Gather supporting reasons and evidence. Identify other solutions and offer opposing arguments.
- The overall tone of a satire is ironic. That is, the ideas you state should be the opposite of what you really mean. Readers will infer your meaning once they recognize the ironic tone of your writing.

Get Organized Organize your ideas and evidence in an outline.

- Using the organizational pattern of "A Modest Proposal," create an outline of your ideas for the satire.
- Sort your textual evidence into a logical order.
- Select a controversial detail or example to introduce the target of your satire in a humorous way.
- List some ideas for your concluding section.

Interactive Lessons

To help you plan your satire, complete the following lesson:

- Writing Arguments: Create a Coherent Argument

ACADEMIC VOCABULARY

As you draft your satire, try to use these words.

controversy
convince
ethics
radical
tension

PRODUCE

Draft Your Satire Write a draft of your satire, following your outline.

- Introduce the type of injustice that is the target of your satire. Use humor or exaggeration to draw your reader in.
- Present your problem, solution, alternative solutions, and counterarguments in logically ordered paragraphs.
- Use appropriate transitions to create overall cohesion of the text.
- Write a concluding section that summarizes your central ideas and follows logically from the body of the essay.

myWriteSmart

Write your rough draft in *my*WriteSmart. Focus on getting your ideas down, rather than on perfecting your choice of language.

Interactive Lessons

To help you draft your satire, complete these lessons:

- Writing as a Process: Planning and Drafting
- Writing Arguments: Form and Style

Language and Style: Connect Ideas

An effective argument shows a clear connection between ideas. Read this passage from Martin Luther King Jr.'s "Speech on the Vietnam War, 1967."

> "Every nation must now develop an overriding loyalty to mankind as a whole in order to preserve the best in their individual societies."

Note how King uses the words "in order to" to express a reason—linking the "what" to the "why." By linking abstract and concrete ideas, you can show how they are related. Look for places in your satire where you can combine ideas.

REVISE

Have your partner review your draft in *my*WriteSmart. Ask your reviewer to evaluate whether the tone of your essay clearly indicates your satirical intent, and also whether you have organized your ideas effectively.

Interactive Lessons

To help you revise your satire, complete the following lesson:

- Writing as a Process: Revising and Editing

Improve Your Draft Revise your draft to make sure it is clear, coherent, and engaging. Use the following questions to revise your draft.

Questions	Tips	Revision Techniques
Does the introduction grab the reader's attention and clearly state the topic?	**Underline** sentences that grab the reader's attention. **Highlight** the statement of the topic.	**Add** words that will grab the reader's attention. **Add** or **reword** a statement of the topic.
Does the satire present a problem and propose a solution?	**Highlight** the words that explain the problem. **Underline** the words that propose a solution.	**Add** an explanation of the problem to be solved. **Add** a clear proposal of the solution.
Are ideas, reasons, and evidence presented in a logical order?	**Underline** transition words that connect the sections of the satire.	**Reorder** the sections of the satire to be more logical.
Is the tone appropriate for satire?	**Highlight** examples of humor, exaggeration, and understatement.	**Add** humor, exaggeration, and understatement to create an ironic tone.
Does the satire maintain a formal style of English?	**Underline** slang and informal language.	**Rewrite** text to replace informal language with formal language.
Does the conclusion summarize the issue and make a global statement about the topic?	**Highlight** the summary of the issue. **Underline** the global statement about the topic.	**Add** a summary of the issue. **Add** a global statement about the injustice that serves as the target of the satire.

PRESENT

Exchange Satires When your final draft is completed, publish it as a blog on a classroom or school website. Then have a partner review your satire, using the rubric on the following page. Read your partner's satire and provide feedback. Be sure to point out aspects of the satire that are strong, as well as areas that could be improved.

Update Your Satire Consider your partner's feedback. Did your satire have the intended effect? Use your partner's suggestions to update your published satire.

PERFORMANCE TASK B RUBRIC

SATIRE

	Ideas and Evidence	Organization	Language
4	• The introduction is compelling; it introduces an injustice and promises a bold but satirical solution. • Relevant reasons and evidence logically support the solution. • Opposing solutions are anticipated and addressed effectively. • Humor, exaggeration, and understatement enhance the satire. • The concluding section effectively summarizes the ideas and clearly emphasizes the advantages of the proposed solution.	• The reasons and evidence are organized consistently and logically throughout the essay. • Varied transitions successfully connect reasons and evidence to the problem and the proposed solution.	• The writing reflects a formal style and an ironic tone. • Sentence beginnings, lengths, and structures vary and have a rhythmic flow. • Spelling, capitalization, and punctuation are correct. If handwritten, the essay is legible. • Grammar and usage are correct.
3	• The introduction introduces an injustice and promises a solution. • Reasons and evidence support the solution. • Opposing solutions are anticipated and addressed adequately. • The writer uses humor, exaggeration, and/or understatement to create a satirical effect. • The concluding section summarizes ideas and emphasizes the advantages of the proposed solution.	• The organization of reasons and evidence is confusing in a few places. • A few more transitions are needed to connect reasons and evidence to the problem and the proposed solution.	• The style is inconsistent in a few places, and the ironic tone disappears in some passages. • Sentence beginnings, lengths, and structures vary somewhat. • Several spelling, capitalization, and punctuation mistakes occur. If handwritten, the essay is mostly legible. • Some grammatical and usage errors are repeated in the description.
2	• The introduction suggests an injustice and a solution, but the formulation is vague. • Reasons and evidence support the solution but are not sufficient or consistently logical. • Opposing solutions may be acknowledged but are not addressed adequately. • There are a few examples of humor, exaggeration, and/or understatement. • The concluding section summarizes some of the writer's ideas and repeats the proposed solution.	• The organization of reasons and evidence is logical in some places, but it often doesn't follow a pattern. • Many more transitions are needed throughout to connect reasons and evidence to the problem and the proposed solution.	• The style becomes informal in many places, and the ironic tone is very inconsistent. • Sentence structures barely vary, and some fragments or run-on sentences are present. • Spelling, capitalization, and punctuation are often incorrect but do not make reading the essay difficult. If handwritten, the essay may be partially illegible. • Grammar and usage are incorrect in many places, but the writer's ideas are still clear.
1	• The introduction hints at an injustice but does not allow readers to see that the essay is a satire. • Reasons and evidence in support of the solution are missing or insufficient. • Opposing solutions are neither acknowledged nor addressed. • Any examples of humor, exaggeration, and/or understatement do not support the purpose of a satire. • The concluding section does not summarize the writer's ideas or reinforce the proposed solution.	• A logical organization is not apparent; ideas are presented randomly. • Transitions are not used, making the essay difficult to understand.	• The style and tone are inappropriate for the essay. • Repetitive sentence structure, fragments, and run-on sentences make the writing monotonous. • Spelling, capitalization, and punctuation are incorrect throughout. If handwritten, the essay may be partially or mostly illegible. • Many grammatical and usage errors change the meaning of the writer's ideas.

Seeking Justice, Seeking Peace

"Forgiving means abandoning your right to pay back the perpetrator in his own coin, but it is a loss which liberates the victim."

—Desmond Tutu

COLLECTION **4**

Seeking Justice, Seeking Peace

This collection raises the issue of whether it is better to avenge evil acts or end conflict through reconciliation.

COLLECTION

PERFORMANCE TASK Preview

At the end of this collection, you will have the opportunity to complete two tasks:

- Write an analytical essay that considers how violence intrudes upon and affects the course of people's lives.
- Develop an argumentative essay that addresses the question of whether revenge is ever justifiable.

ACADEMIC VOCABULARY

Study the words and their definitions in the chart below. You will use these words as you discuss and write about the texts in this collection.

Word	Definition	Related Forms
drama (drä´mə) *n.*	a prose or verse composition that is intended to be acted out	dramatic, dramatist, dramatization
integrity (ĭn-tĕg´rĭ-tē) *n.*	quality of being ethically or morally upright	integrate, integration
mediate (mē´dē-āt´) *v.*	to settle differences between two individuals or groups	mediation, mediator
restrain (rĭ-strān´) *v.*	to hold back or control	restraint, restrainedly, restrainer
trigger (trĭg´ər) *v.*	to set off a chain of events	trigger (*n.*)

Shakespearean Drama

Shakespeare wrote *Hamlet* sometime around 1600. The story originated in an old folktale that became part of Denmark's legendary history. Shakespeare may have read a French retelling of the story, but he seems to have based his tragedy mainly on an English play about Hamlet from the 1580s. This earlier play had fallen out of fashion among Elizabethan audiences, but Shakespeare's version was an immediate success. Shakespeare transformed the genre of revenge tragedy by introducing a hero whose insights, doubts, and moral dilemmas often overshadow the play's action. *Hamlet's* psychological complexity helps explain the play's lasting popularity and influence.

The Globe Theater In Shakespeare's time, most plays were performed in outdoor public theaters. These theaters resembled courtyards, with the stage surrounded on three sides by galleries. The most famous theater in London was the Globe, where Shakespeare and his acting company performed. The Globe was a three-story wooden structure that could hold as many as 3,000 people. Plays were performed in the afternoon on a platform stage in the theater's center. The poorer patrons, or "groundlings," stood around the stage to watch the performance. Wealthier patrons sat in the covered galleries. The stage was mostly bare, which allowed for quick changes of scene. A trapdoor gave the stage added flexibility; in *Hamlet* it was used for the Ghost's entrances and exits and also in a scene set around a grave.

The Players Actors worked in close proximity to the groundlings, who stood around the stage, often eating and drinking. If they disapproved of certain characters or lines, they would let the actors know by jeering or even throwing food. The large crowds also attracted pickpockets and other rough elements. The rowdiness of the audiences and the location of theaters near taverns and other unsavory establishments gave theaters, and actors, an immoral reputation. Because the theater was viewed as disreputable, women were not allowed to perform; boys normally played the female roles.

Shakespearean Tragedy

Renaissance Drama During the Middle Ages, English drama focused mainly on religious themes, teaching moral lessons or retelling Bible stories to a populace that by and large could not read. In the Renaissance, however, a revival of interest in ancient Greek and Roman literature led playwrights to model their plays on classical drama. These plays fell into two main categories: comedies and tragedies. In Renaissance England, **comedy** was broadly defined as a dramatic work with a happy ending; many comedies contained humor, but humor was not required. A **tragedy**, in contrast, was a work in which the main character, or **tragic hero**, came to an unhappy end. In addition to comedies and tragedies, Shakespeare wrote plays classified as **histories**, which present stories about England's monarchs.

A modern reconstruction of Shakespeare's theater was built near the site of the original Globe. Since opening in 1997, the new Globe has become one of London's most popular tourist attractions. As in the original Globe, performances only take place during the warmer months of the year because the theater is not enclosed.

The Greek Origins of Tragedy Both tragedy and comedy originated in ancient Greece, where plays were performed as part of elaborate outdoor festivals. According to the ancient Greek philosopher Aristotle, tragedy arouses pity and fear in the audience—pity for the hero and fear for all human beings, who are subject to character flaws and an unknown destiny. Seeing a tragedy unfold produces a **catharsis**, or cleansing, of these emotions in the audience. In ancient Greek tragedies, the hero's tragic flaw is often **hubris**—excessive pride that leads the tragic hero to challenge the gods. Angered by such hubris, the gods unleash their retribution, or nemesis, on the hero.

Characteristics of Tragedy The intention of tragedy is to exemplify the idea that human beings are doomed to suffer, fail, or die because of their own flaws, destiny, or fate. As part of this tradition, Shakespeare's tragedies share the following characteristics with the classical Greek tragedies.

Characteristics of Tragedy	
The Tragic Hero	• is the main character who comes to an unhappy or miserable end. • is generally a person of importance in society, such as a king or queen. • exhibits extraordinary abilities but also a **tragic flaw**, a fatal error in judgment or weakness of character that leads directly to his or her downfall.
The Plot	• involves a **conflict** between the hero and a person or force, called the **antagonist**, which the hero must battle. Inevitably the conflict contributes to the hero's downfall. • is built upon a series of causally related events that lead to the **catastrophe**, or tragic resolution. This final stage of the plot usually involves the death of the hero. • is resolved when the tragic hero meets his or her doom with courage and dignity, reaffirming the grandeur of the human spirit.
The Theme	• is the central idea conveyed by the work and usually focuses on an aspect of fate, ambition, loss, defeat, death, loyalty, impulse, or desire. Tragedies may contain several themes.

One way in which Shakespearean tragedy differs from classical tragedy is that Shakespeare's tragic works are not uniformly serious. He often eased the intensity of the action by using the device of **comic relief**—a light, mildly humorous scene preceding or following a serious one.

Shakespeare's Conventions of Drama

The printed text of a Shakespeare play is like that of most traditional dramas. The play is divided into **acts** and **scenes.** The **dialogue** is labeled to show who is speaking, and **stage directions**, written in italics and in parentheses, specify the setting (time and place) and how the characters should behave and speak. In addition, Shakespeare typically used the following literary devices in his dramas.

Blank Verse Like many plays written before the 19th century, *Hamlet* is a **verse drama**, a play in which the dialogue consists almost entirely of poetry with a fixed pattern of rhythm, or **meter**. Many English verse dramas are written in **blank verse**, or unrhymed **iambic pentameter**, a meter in which the normal line contains five stressed syllables, each preceded by an unstressed syllable.

> A little more than kin and less than kind.

Soliloquy and Aside Shakespeare often used two conventions, the soliloquy and the aside, to give audiences access to characters' private thoughts and feelings.

- A **soliloquy** is a speech that a character makes while alone on stage to reveal his or her thoughts to the audience.

- An **aside** is a remark that a character makes in an undertone to the audience or another character but that others on stage are not supposed to hear. A stage direction clarifies that a remark is an aside; unless otherwise specified, the aside is to the audience. Here is an example from *Hamlet*.

> **Polonius.** Fare you well, my lord.
> **Hamlet** [*aside*]. These tedious old fools.

Dramatic Irony **Irony** is based on a contrast between appearance or expectation and reality. In **dramatic irony**, the audience knows something that one or more characters do not know. For example, the audience knows why Hamlet behaves strangely in much of the play, but most characters are confused by this behavior.

Foreshadowing **Foreshadowing** is a writer's use of hints or clues to suggest what events will occur later in a work. In Act One, Scene 3, Hamlet's friends are worried after he decides to follow a ghost that appears to be his father. Their reactions provide clues about what the ghost will reveal and also hint at Hamlet's behavior later in the play:

> **Horatio.** He waxes desperate with imagination.
> **Marcellus.** Let's follow. 'Tis not fit thus to obey him.
> **Horatio.** Have after. To what issue will this come?
> **Marcellus.** Something is rotten in the state of Denmark.

Shakespearean Language

The English language in which Shakespeare wrote was quite different from today's. As you read a Shakespearean play, pay attention to the following.

Shakespearean Language	
Grammatical Forms	In Shakespeare's day, people still commonly used the pronouns ***thou, thee, thy, thine,*** and ***thyself*** in place of forms of ***you***. Verb forms that are now outdated were also in use—***art*** for ***are*** and ***cometh*** for ***comes***, for example.
Unusual Word Order	Shakespeare often put verbs before subjects, objects before verbs, and other sentence parts in positions that now seem unusual. For instance, Polonius advises his son, "Neither a borrower nor a lender be," instead of saying, "Be neither a borrower nor a lender."
Unfamiliar Vocabulary	Shakespeare's vocabulary included many words no longer in use (like ***seeling***, meaning "blinding") or words with meanings different from their meanings today (like ***choppy***, meaning "chapped"). Shakespeare also coined new words, some of which (like ***assassination***) have become a permanent part of the language.

A&E BIO

The Tragedy of Hamlet

Drama by William Shakespeare

William Shakespeare (1564–1616) *was born in Stratford-upon-Avon, a market town in central England. His father was a prosperous tradesman. Shakespeare probably attended Stratford's grammar school, where he would have studied Latin and read classical authors. In 1582 he married Anne Hathaway. The next year she gave birth to a daughter, Susanna. Their twins Hamnet and Judith followed in 1585.*

Sometime during the next seven years, Shakespeare found work in London as an actor; he also began to write plays. In 1594 he joined the Lord Chamberlain's Men, which became the most prestigious theater company in London. Shakespeare soon grew affluent from his share in the company's profits. He bought a large house in Stratford, where his wife and children remained.

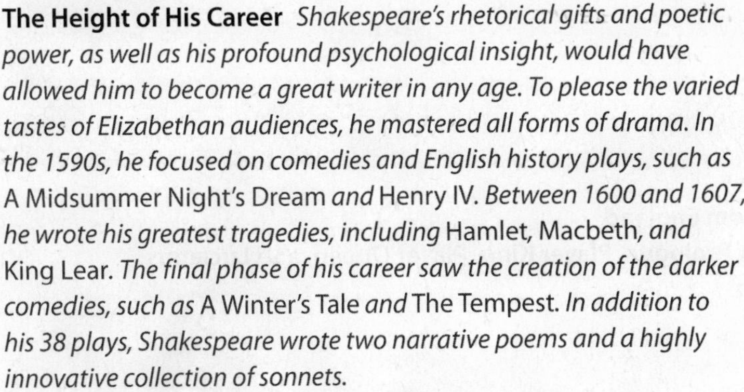

The Height of His Career *Shakespeare's rhetorical gifts and poetic power, as well as his profound psychological insight, would have allowed him to become a great writer in any age. To please the varied tastes of Elizabethan audiences, he mastered all forms of drama. In the 1590s, he focused on comedies and English history plays, such as* A Midsummer Night's Dream *and* Henry IV. *Between 1600 and 1607, he wrote his greatest tragedies, including* Hamlet, Macbeth, *and* King Lear. *The final phase of his career saw the creation of the darker comedies, such as* A Winter's Tale *and* The Tempest. *In addition to his 38 plays, Shakespeare wrote two narrative poems and a highly innovative collection of sonnets.*

His Legacy *Shakespeare died in Stratford when he was 52 years old. At the time, some of his plays existed in cheap, often badly flawed editions; others had never appeared in print. In 1623, two theater colleagues published a collected edition of his plays known as the* First Folio, *which ensured the survival of his work. Ben Jonson, a rival playwright, wrote an introduction for the volume in which he declared that Shakespeare "was not of an age, but for all time." Four centuries after Shakespeare's death, his plays, which have been translated into many languages, continue to be performed around the world.*

AS YOU READ More has been written about Hamlet than about any other Shakespearean character. Pay attention to details that show his complexity or that help explain why audiences find him so intriguing. Write down any questions you generate during reading.

CHARACTERS

The Ghost

Hamlet, Prince of Denmark, son of the late King Hamlet and Queen Gertrude

Queen Gertrude, widow of King Hamlet, now married to Claudius

King Claudius, brother to the late King Hamlet

Polonius, councillor to King Claudius

Ophelia, daughter of Polonius

Laertes, son of Polonius

Reynaldo, servant to Polonius

Horatio, Hamlet's friend and confidant

COURTIERS AT THE DANISH COURT

Voltemand
Cornelius
Rosencrantz
Guildenstern
Osric
Gentlemen
A Lord

DANISH SOLDIERS

Francisco
Barnardo
Marcellus

Fortinbras, Prince of Norway

A Captain in Fortinbras's army

Ambassadors to Denmark from England

Players who take the roles of Prologue, Player King, Player Queen, and Lucianus in *The Murder of Gonzago*

Two Messengers

Sailors

Gravedigger

Gravedigger's companion

Doctor of Divinity

Attendants, Lords, Guards, Musicians, Laertes's Followers, Soldiers, Officers

***Place*: Denmark**

ACT I

Scene 1 *A guard platform at Elsinore Castle.*

[*Enter* Barnardo *and* Francisco, *two sentinels.*]

Barnardo. Who's there?

Francisco. Nay, answer me. Stand and unfold yourself.

2 unfold yourself: show who you are.

Barnardo. Long live the King!

Francisco. Barnardo.

Barnardo. He.

Francisco. You come most carefully upon your hour.

Barnardo. 'Tis now struck twelve. Get thee to bed,
Francisco.

Francisco. For this relief much thanks. 'Tis bitter cold,
And I am sick at heart.

Barnardo. Have you had quiet guard?

Francisco. Not a mouse stirring.

Barnardo. Well, good night.
If you do meet Horatio and Marcellus,
The rivals of my watch, bid them make haste.

14 rivals of my watch: the other soldiers on guard duty with me.

[*Enter* Horatio *and* Marcellus.]

Francisco. I think I hear them.—Stand ho! Who is there?

Horatio. Friends to this ground.

Marcellus. And liegemen to the Dane.

Francisco. Give you good night.

Marcellus. O farewell, honest soldier. Who hath relieved you?

16–17 Horatio and Marcellus identify themselves as friendly to Denmark (**this ground**) and loyal subjects of the Danish king (**the Dane**).

Francisco. Barnardo hath my place. Give you good night.

[Francisco *exits.*]

Marcellus. Holla, Barnardo.

Barnardo. Say, what, is Horatio there?

Horatio. A piece of him.

Barnardo. Welcome, Horatio.—Welcome, good Marcellus.

Horatio. What, has this thing appeared again tonight?

Barnardo. I have seen nothing.

Marcellus. Horatio says 'tis but our fantasy
And will not let belief take hold of him
Touching this dreaded sight twice seen of us.
Therefore I have entreated him along

27–33 Marcellus explains that Horatio doubts their story about having twice seen a ghost (**apparition**), so he has brought Horatio to confirm what they saw (**approve our eyes**).

With us to watch the minutes of this night,
That, if again this apparition come,
He may approve our eyes and speak to it.

Horatio. Tush, tush, 'twill not appear.

Barnardo. Sit down a while,
And let us once again assail your ears,
That are so fortified against our story,
What we have two nights seen.

Horatio. Well, sit we down,
And let us hear Barnardo speak of this.

Barnardo. Last night of all,
When yond same star that's westward from the pole
Had made his course t' illume that part of heaven
Where now it burns, Marcellus and myself,
The bell then beating one—

[*Enter* Ghost.]

Marcellus. Peace, break thee off! Look where it comes again.

Barnardo. In the same figure like the King that's dead.

Marcellus [*to* Horatio]. Thou art a scholar. Speak to it, Horatio.

Barnardo. Looks he not like the King? Mark it, Horatio.

Horatio. Most like. It harrows me with fear and wonder.

Barnardo. It would be spoke to.

Marcellus. Speak to it, Horatio.

Horatio. What art thou that usurp'st this time of night,
Together with that fair and warlike form
In which the majesty of buried Denmark
Did sometimes march? By heaven, I charge thee, speak.

Marcellus. It is offended.

Barnardo. See, it stalks away.

Horatio. Stay! speak! speak! I charge thee, speak!

[Ghost *exits.*]

Marcellus. 'Tis gone and will not answer.

Barnardo. How now, Horatio, you tremble and look pale.
Is not this something more than fantasy?
What think you on 't?

Horatio. Before my God, I might not this believe
Without the sensible and true avouch
Of mine own eyes.

Marcellus. Is it not like the King?

40 star . . . pole: the North Star.

41 his: its.

46–50 It was commonly believed that a ghost could only speak after it was spoken to, preferably by someone learned enough (**a scholar**) to ask the proper questions.

48 harrows: torments.

50 usurp'st: unlawfully takes over.

52 majesty of buried Denmark: the buried King of Denmark.

53 sometimes: formerly.

61–62 Without . . . eyes: without seeing the proof (**avouch**) with my own eyes.

Horatio. As thou art to thyself.
Such was the very armor he had on
When he the ambitious Norway combated.
So frowned he once when, in an angry parle,
He smote the sledded Polacks on the ice.
'Tis strange.

Marcellus. Thus twice before, and jump at this dead hour,
With martial stalk hath he gone by our watch.

Horatio. In what particular thought to work I know not,
But in the gross and scope of mine opinion
This bodes some strange eruption to our state.

Marcellus. Good now, sit down, and tell me, he that knows,
Why this same strict and most observant watch
So nightly toils the subject of the land,
And why such daily cast of brazen cannon
And foreign mart for implements of war,
Why such impress of shipwrights, whose sore task
Does not divide the Sunday from the week.
What might be toward that this sweaty haste
Doth make the night joint laborer with the day?
Who is 't that can inform me?

Horatio. That can I.
At least the whisper goes so: our last king,
Whose image even but now appeared to us,
Was, as you know, by Fortinbras of Norway,
Thereto pricked on by a most emulate pride,
Dared to the combat; in which our valiant Hamlet
(For so this side of our known world esteemed him)
Did slay this Fortinbras, who by a sealed compact,
Well ratified by law and heraldry,
Did forfeit, with his life, all those his lands
Which he stood seized of, to the conqueror.
Against the which a moiety competent
Was gagèd by our king, which had returned
To the inheritance of Fortinbras
Had he been vanquisher, as, by the same comart
And carriage of the article designed,
His fell to Hamlet. Now, sir, young Fortinbras,
Of unimprovèd mettle hot and full,
Hath in the skirts of Norway here and there
Sharked up a list of lawless resolutes
For food and diet to some enterprise
That hath a stomach in 't; which is no other
(As it doth well appear unto our state)
But to recover of us, by strong hand

65 Norway: the King of Norway.

66 parle: parley, meeting with an enemy.

67 smote: defeated; **sledded Polacks:** Polish soldiers riding in sleds.

69 jump: exactly.

72–73 This is a bad omen (**bodes some strange eruption**) for Denmark.

74–78 Can anyone explain why the Danes weary themselves each night with sentry duty and why there is so much casting of armaments (**brazen cannon**) and foreign trade (**mart**) for weapons?

81 toward: approaching, in preparation.

90–104 By prior agreement and according to laws governing combat, Hamlet gained all the land that Fortinbras had possessed (**stood seized of**). Hamlet had pledged an equivalent portion (**moiety competent**) of his land, which would have gone to Fortinbras if he won the battle, as was specified in the same agreement. Young Fortinbras, who has an undisciplined character (**unimproved mettle**), has gathered hastily (**Sharked up**) in outlying districts (**skirts**) of Norway a troop of lawless desperadoes to serve in some undertaking that requires courage (**hath a stomach in 't**).

And terms compulsatory, those foresaid lands
So by his father lost. And this, I take it,
Is the main motive of our preparations,
The source of this our watch, and the chief head
Of this posthaste and rummage in the land.

Barnardo. I think it be no other but e'en so.
Well may it sort that this portentous figure
Comes armèd through our watch so like the king
That was and is the question of these wars.

Horatio. A mote it is to trouble the mind's eye.
In the most high and palmy state of Rome,
A little ere the mightiest Julius fell,
The graves stood tenantless, and the sheeted dead
Did squeak and gibber in the Roman streets;
As stars with trains of fire and dews of blood,
Disasters in the sun; and the moist star,
Upon whose influence Neptune's empire stands,
Was sick almost to doomsday with eclipse.
And even the like precurse of feared events,
As harbingers preceding still the fates
And prologue to the omen coming on,
Have heaven and earth together demonstrated
Unto our climatures and countrymen.

[*Enter* Ghost.]

But soft, behold! Lo, where it comes again!
I'll cross it though it blast me.—Stay, illusion!

[*It spreads his arms.*]

If thou hast any sound or use of voice,
Speak to me.
If there be any good thing to be done
That may to thee do ease and grace to me,
Speak to me.
If thou art privy to thy country's fate,
Which happily foreknowing may avoid,
O, speak!
Or if thou hast uphoarded in thy life
Extorted treasure in the womb of earth,
For which, they say, you spirits oft walk in death,
Speak of it.

[*The cock crows.*]

Stay and speak!—Stop it, Marcellus.

Marcellus. Shall I strike it with my partisan?

Horatio. Do, if it will not stand.

110 head: source.

111 rummage: bustle.

113 Well . . . sort: it may be fitting.

116 mote: dust speck.

117 palmy: thriving.

119 sheeted: wrapped in shrouds.

120 gibber: chatter.

122 disasters: menacing signs; **moist star:** the moon, which controls the Earth's tides.

123 Neptune: Roman god of the sea.

125–129 A similar foreshadowing (**precurse**) has occurred in Denmark, where a terrible event (**omen**) was preceded by signs that were like forerunners (**harbingers**) announcing the approach of someone.

130 soft: be quiet, hold off.

131 cross: confront.

138 happily . . . avoid: perhaps (**happily**) may be avoided if known in advance.

141 extorted: ill-gotten.

144 partisan: a long-handled weapon.

Barnardo. 'Tis here.

Horatio. 'Tis here.

[Ghost *exits.*]

Marcellus. 'Tis gone.
We do it wrong, being so majestical,
To offer it the show of violence,
For it is as the air, invulnerable,
And our vain blows malicious mockery.

Barnardo. It was about to speak when the cock crew.

Horatio. And then it started like a guilty thing
Upon a fearful summons. I have heard
The cock, that is the trumpet to the morn,
Doth with his lofty and shrill-sounding throat
Awake the god of day, and at his warning,
Whether in sea or fire, in earth or air,
Th' extravagant and erring spirit hies
To his confine, and of the truth herein
This present object made probation.

Marcellus. It faded on the crowing of the cock.
Some say that ever 'gainst that season comes
Wherein our Savior's birth is celebrated,
This bird of dawning singeth all night long;
And then, they say, no spirit dare stir abroad,
The nights are wholesome; then no planets strike,
No fairy takes, nor witch hath power to charm,
So hallowed and so gracious is that time.

Horatio. So have I heard and do in part believe it.
But look, the morn in russet mantle clad
Walks o'er the dew of yon high eastward hill.
Break we our watch up, and by my advice
Let us impart what we have seen tonight
Unto young Hamlet; for, upon my life,
This spirit, dumb to us, will speak to him.
Do you consent we shall acquaint him with it
As needful in our loves, fitting our duty?

Marcellus. Let's do 't, I pray, and I this morning know
Where we shall find him most convenient.

[*They exit.*]

154 started: made a sudden movement.

160 extravagant and erring: wandering out of bounds.

162 made probation: demonstrated.

164–165 ever . . . celebrated: just before Christmas.

168 strike: put forth an evil influence.

169 takes: bewitches.

Scene 2 *A state room at the castle.*

[*Flourish. Enter* Claudius, *King of Denmark,* Gertrude the Queen, *the* Council, *as* Polonius, *and his son* Laertes, Hamlet, *with others, among them* Voltemand *and* Cornelius.]

King. Though yet of Hamlet our dear brother's death
The memory be green, and that it us befitted
To bear our hearts in grief, and our whole kingdom
To be contracted in one brow of woe,
Yet so far hath discretion fought with nature
That we with wisest sorrow think on him
Together with remembrance of ourselves.
Therefore our sometime sister, now our queen,
Th' imperial jointress to this warlike state,
Have we (as 'twere with a defeated joy,
With an auspicious and a dropping eye,
With mirth in funeral and with dirge in marriage,
In equal scale weighing delight and dole)
Taken to wife. Nor have we herein barred
Your better wisdoms, which have freely gone
With this affair along. For all, our thanks.
Now follows that you know. Young Fortinbras,
Holding a weak supposal of our worth
Or thinking by our late dear brother's death
Our state to be disjoint and out of frame,
Colleaguèd with this dream of his advantage,
He hath not failed to pester us with message
Importing the surrender of those lands
Lost by his father, with all bonds of law,
To our most valiant brother—so much for him.
Now for ourself and for this time of meeting.
Thus much the business is: we have here writ
To Norway, uncle of young Fortinbras,
Who, impotent and bedrid, scarcely hears
Of this his nephew's purpose, to suppress
His further gait herein, in that the levies,
The lists, and full proportions are all made
Out of his subject; and we here dispatch
You, good Cornelius, and you, Voltemand,
For bearers of this greeting to old Norway,
Giving to you no further personal power
To business with the King more than the scope
Of these dilated articles allow.

[*Giving them a paper.*]

Farewell, and let your haste commend your duty.

8 our sometime sister: my former sister-in-law. (Claudius uses the royal "we.")

9 jointress: a woman who owns property with her husband.

11–12 With . . . eye: with one eye reflecting good fortune and the other eye, sorrow; **dirge:** a song of mourning.

21 Colleaguèd . . . advantage: connected with this false hope of his superior position.

23 Importing: relating to.

29 impotent: helpless.

30–33 Since Fortinbras has obtained all of his troops and supplies from Norway, Claudius has asked the King of Norway to stop him from proceeding further.

37 To business: to negotiate.

38 dilated articles: detailed instructions.

Laurence Olivier's 1948 film *Hamlet*. Background: Hamlet (Laurence Olivier). Foreground, left to right: Claudius (Basil Sidney), Gertrude (Eileen Herlie), Polonius (Felix Aylmer).

Cornelius/Voltemand. In that and all things will we show our duty.

King. We doubt it nothing. Heartily farewell.

[Voltemand *and* Cornelius *exit.*]

And now, Laertes, what's the news with you?
You told us of some suit. What is 't, Laertes?
You cannot speak of reason to the Dane
And lose your voice. What wouldst thou beg, Laertes,
That shall not be my offer, not thy asking?
The head is not more native to the heart,
The hand more instrumental to the mouth,
Than is the throne of Denmark to thy father.
What wouldst thou have, Laertes?

Laertes. My dread lord,
Your leave and favor to return to France,
From whence though willingly I came to Denmark
To show my duty in your coronation,

45 lose your voice: waste your breath.

47 native: closely connected.

Yet now I must confess, that duty done,
My thoughts and wishes bend again toward France
And bow them to your gracious leave and pardon.

King. Have you your father's leave? What says Polonius?

Polonius. Hath, my lord, wrung from me my slow leave
By laborsome petition, and at last
Upon his will I sealed my hard consent.
I do beseech you give him leave to go.

King. Take thy fair hour, Laertes. Time be thine,
And thy best graces spend it at thy will.—
But now, my cousin Hamlet and my son—

Hamlet [*aside*]. A little more than kin and less than kind.

King. How is it that the clouds still hang on you?

Hamlet. Not so, my lord; I am too much in the sun.

Queen. Good Hamlet, cast thy nighted color off,
And let thine eye look like a friend on Denmark.
Do not forever with thy vailèd lids
Seek for thy noble father in the dust.
Thou know'st 'tis common; all that lives must die,
Passing through nature to eternity.

Hamlet. Ay, madam, it is common.

Queen. If it be,
Why seems it so particular with thee?

Hamlet. "Seems," madam? Nay, it is. I know not "seems."
'Tis not alone my inky cloak, good mother,
Nor customary suits of solemn black,
Nor windy suspiration of forced breath,
No, nor the fruitful river in the eye,
Nor the dejected havior of the visage,
Together with all forms, moods, shapes of grief,
That can denote me truly. These indeed "seem,"
For they are actions that a man might play;
But I have that within which passes show,
These but the trappings and the suits of woe.

King. 'Tis sweet and commendable in your nature, Hamlet,
To give these mourning duties to your father.
But you must know your father lost a father,
That father lost, lost his, and the survivor bound
In filial obligation for some term
To do obsequious sorrow. But to persever
In obstinate condolement is a course
Of impious stubbornness. 'Tis unmanly grief.
It shows a will most incorrect to heaven,

60 Upon . . . consent: I reluctantly agreed to his wishes.

64 cousin: kinsman.

65 Hamlet plays off two meanings of **kind:** "loving" and "natural." He does not resemble Claudius in nature or feel a son's affection for him.

67 sun: the sunlight of royal favor (also a pun on **son**, suggesting annoyance at Claudius's use of the word).

68 nighted color: dark mood.

70 vailèd lids: lowered eyes.

74 Hamlet plays off two meanings of **common:** "universal" and "vulgar."

75 particular: special, personal.

77–83 'Tis not . . . truly: My feelings are not limited to my black mourning clothes, heavy sighs, tears, downcast expression, and other outward signs of grief.

89–94 Claudius says that a surviving son must dutifully mourn (**do obsequious sorrow**) for a while, but to remain stubbornly in grief (**obstinate condolement**) beyond that appropriate period is perverse.

A heart unfortified, a mind impatient,
An understanding simple and unschooled.
For what we know must be and is as common
As any the most vulgar thing to sense,
Why should we in our peevish opposition
Take it to heart? Fie, 'tis a fault to heaven,
A fault against the dead, a fault to nature,
To reason most absurd, whose common theme
Is death of fathers, and who still hath cried,
From the first corse till he that died today,
"This must be so." We pray you, throw to earth
This unprevailing woe and think of us
As of a father; for let the world take note,
You are the most immediate to our throne,
And with no less nobility of love
Than that which dearest father bears his son
Do I impart toward you. For your intent
In going back to school in Wittenberg,
It is most retrograde to our desire,
And we beseech you, bend you to remain
Here in the cheer and comfort of our eye,
Our chiefest courtier, cousin, and our son.

Queen. Let not thy mother lose her prayers, Hamlet.
I pray thee, stay with us. Go not to Wittenberg.

Hamlet. I shall in all my best obey you, madam.

King. Why, 'tis a loving and a fair reply.
Be as ourself in Denmark.—Madam, come.
This gentle and unforced accord of Hamlet
Sits smiling to my heart, in grace where of
No jocund health that Denmark drinks today
But the great cannon to the clouds shall tell,
And the King's rouse the heaven shall bruit again,
Respeaking earthly thunder. Come away.

[*Flourish. All but* Hamlet *exit.*]

Hamlet. O, that this too, too sullied flesh would melt,
Thaw, and resolve itself into a dew,
Or that the Everlasting had not fixed
His canon 'gainst self-slaughter! O God, God,
How weary, stale, flat, and unprofitable
Seem to me all the uses of this world!
Fie on 't, ah fie! 'Tis an unweeded garden
That grows to seed. Things rank and gross in nature
Possess it merely. That it should come to this:
But two months dead—nay, not so much, not two.
So excellent a king, that was to this

96 unfortified: unstrengthened against adversity.

99 As . . . sense: as the most common experience.

104 still: always.

105 corse: corpse.

107 unprevailing: not yielding to persuasion.

108–112 Claudius claims that he offers (**impart toward**) Hamlet, who is next in line (**most immediate**) to succeed to the throne, all the love that the most affectionate father feels for his son.

113 Wittenberg University (founded in 1502) was famous for being the school of German theologian Martin Luther, whose challenge to Roman Catholic doctrine started the Reformation.

114 retrograde: contrary.

125–128 Claudius boasts that he will not merely drink a happy toast (**jocund health**) that day, but a deep drink (**rouse**) accompanied by fanfare, which heaven will echo with thunder.

129 sullied: stained, defiled.

132 canon: law.

139–140 Hamlet says that comparing his father to Claudius would be like comparing the sun god **Hyperion** to a **satyr** (a mythical creature, half man and half goat, associated with lechery).

Hyperion to a satyr; so loving to my mother
That he might not beteem the winds of heaven
Visit her face too roughly. Heaven and earth,
Must I remember? Why, she would hang on him
As if increase of appetite had grown
By what it fed on. And yet, within a month
(Let me not think on 't; frailty, thy name is woman!),
A little month, or ere those shoes were old
With which she followed my poor father's body,
Like Niobe, all tears—why she, even she
(O God, a beast that wants discourse of reason
Would have mourned longer!), married with my uncle,
My father's brother, but no more like my father
Than I to Hercules. Within a month,
Ere yet the salt of most unrighteous tears
Had left the flushing in her gallèd eyes,
She married. O, most wicked speed, to post
With such dexterity to incestuous sheets!
It is not, nor it cannot come to good.
But break, my heart, for I must hold my tongue.

[*Enter* Horatio, Marcellus, *and* Barnardo.]

Horatio. Hail to your lordship.

Hamlet. I am glad to see you well.
Horatio—or I do forget myself!

Horatio. The same, my lord, and your poor servant ever.

Hamlet. Sir, my good friend. I'll change that name with you.
And what make you from Wittenberg, Horatio?—Marcellus?

Marcellus. My good lord.

Hamlet. I am very glad to see you. [*To* Barnardo.] Good even, sir.—
But what, in faith, make you from Wittenberg?

Horatio. A truant disposition, good my lord.

Hamlet. I would not hear your enemy say so,
Nor shall you do my ear that violence
To make it truster of your own report
Against yourself. I know you are no truant.
But what is your affair in Elsinore?
We'll teach you to drink deep ere you depart.

Horatio. My lord, I came to see your father's funeral.

Hamlet. I prithee, do not mock me, fellow student.
I think it was to see my mother's wedding.

Horatio. Indeed, my lord, it followed hard upon.

141 beteem: allow.

147 or ere: before.

149 Niobe: a Greek mythological figure who continued weeping for her slaughtered children even after she was turned to stone.

155 Had . . . eyes: had stopped reddening her inflamed (**gallèd**) eyes.

157 incestuous: Marriage between a widow and her late husband's brother was often considered incestuous in Shakespeare's time and was prohibited by church law.

163 Horatio refers to himself as a "servant" out of respect for Hamlet.

169 what . . . from: what are you doing away from.

173 truster: believer.

180 hard upon: soon after.

Hamlet. Thrift, thrift, Horatio. The funeral baked meats
Did coldly furnish forth the marriage tables.
Would I had met my dearest foe in heaven
Or ever I had seen that day, Horatio!
My father—methinks I see my father.

Horatio. Where, my lord?

Hamlet. In my mind's eye, Horatio.

Horatio. I saw him once. He was a goodly king.

Hamlet. He was a man. Take him for all in all,
I shall not look upon his like again.

Horatio. My lord, I think I saw him yesternight.

Hamlet. Saw who?

Horatio. My lord, the King your father.

Hamlet. The King my father?

Horatio. Season your admiration for a while
With an attent ear, till I may deliver
Upon the witness of these gentlemen
This marvel to you.

Hamlet. For God's love, let me hear!

Horatio. Two nights together had these gentlemen,
Marcellus and Barnardo, on their watch,
In the dead waste and middle of the night,
Been thus encountered: a figure like your father,
Armèd at point exactly, cap-à-pie,
Appears before them and with solemn march
Goes slow and stately by them. Thrice he walked
By their oppressed and fear-surprisèd eyes
Within his truncheon's length, whilst they, distilled
Almost to jelly with the act of fear,
Stand dumb and speak not to him. This to me
In dreadful secrecy impart they did,
And I with them the third night kept the watch,
Where, as they had delivered, both in time,
Form of the thing (each word made true and good),
The apparition comes. I knew your father;
These hands are not more like.

Hamlet. But where was this?

Marcellus. My lord, upon the platform where we watch.

Hamlet. Did you not speak to it?

Horatio. My lord, I did,
But answer made it none. Yet once methought

181–182 The funeral . . . tables: Leftovers from the funeral were served cold at the marriage feast.

183 dearest: most hated.

184 Or ever: before.

187 goodly: fine, admirable.

193–194 Season . . . ear: Control your astonishment for a moment and listen carefully.

201 Armèd . . . cap-à-pie: armed properly in every detail, from head to foot.

205 Within his truncheon's length: no farther away than the length of his short staff.

205–206 distilled . . . fear: reduced almost to jelly by fear.

207–208 This . . . did: They told me this in terrified (**dreadful**) secrecy.

210 delivered: asserted.

It lifted up its head and did address
Itself to motion, like as it would speak;
But even then the morning cock crew loud,
And at the sound it shrunk in haste away
And vanished from our sight.

Hamlet. 'Tis very strange.

Horatio. As I do live, my honored lord, 'tis true.
And we did think it writ down in our duty
To let you know of it.

Hamlet. Indeed, sirs, but this troubles me.
Hold you the watch tonight?

All. We do, my lord.

Hamlet. Armed, say you?

All. Armed, my lord.

Hamlet. From top to toe?
All My lord, from head to foot.

Hamlet. Then saw you not his face?

Horatio. O, yes, my lord, he wore his beaver up.

Hamlet. What, looked he frowningly?

Horatio. A countenance more in sorrow than in anger.

Hamlet. Pale or red?

Horatio. Nay, very pale.

Hamlet. And fixed his eyes upon you?

Horatio. Most constantly.

Hamlet. I would I had been there.

Horatio. It would have much amazed you.

Hamlet. Very like. Stayed it long?

Horatio. While one with moderate haste might tell a hundred.

Barnardo/Marcellus. Longer, longer.

Horatio. Not when I saw 't.

Hamlet. His beard was grizzled, no?

Horatio. It was as I have seen it in his life,
A sable silvered.

Hamlet. I will watch tonight.
Perchance 'twill walk again.

Horatio. I warrant it will.

217–218 did . . . speak: began to move as if it were going to speak.

219 even then: just then.

230 beaver: movable front piece of a helmet.

238–239 While . . . hundred: for as long as one could count (**tell**) to one hundred at a moderate pace.

240 grizzled: gray.

242 A sable silvered: black hair with white hair mixed through it.

Hamlet. If it assume my noble father's person,
I'll speak to it, though hell itself should gape
And bid me hold my peace. I pray you all,
If you have hitherto concealed this sight,
Let it be tenable in your silence still;
And whatsomever else shall hap tonight,
Give it an understanding but no tongue.
I will requite your loves. So fare you well.
Upon the platform, 'twixt eleven and twelve,
I'll visit you.

All. Our duty to your Honor.

Hamlet. Your loves, as mine to you. Farewell.

[*All but* Hamlet *exit.*]

My father's spirit—in arms! All is not well.
I doubt some foul play. Would the night were come!
Till then, sit still, my soul. Foul deeds will rise,
Though all the earth o'erwhelm them, to men's eyes.

[*He exits.*]

Scene 3 *Polonius's chambers.*

[*Enter* Laertes *and* Ophelia, *his sister.*]

Laertes. My necessaries are embarked. Farewell.
And, sister, as the winds give benefit
And convey is assistant, do not sleep,
But let me hear from you.

Ophelia. Do you doubt that?

Laertes. For Hamlet, and the trifling of his favor,
Hold it a fashion and a toy in blood,
A violet in the youth of primy nature,
Forward, not permanent, sweet, not lasting,
The perfume and suppliance of a minute,
No more.

Ophelia. No more but so?

Laertes. Think it no more.
For nature, crescent, does not grow alone
In thews and bulk, but, as this temple waxes,
The inward service of the mind and soul
Grows wide withal. Perhaps he loves you now,
And now no soil nor cautel doth besmirch
The virtue of his will; but you must fear,
His greatness weighed, his will is not his own,
For he himself is subject to his birth.
He may not, as unvalued persons do,

248 tenable: held.

249 whatsomever: whatever; **hap:** happen.

251 I . . . loves: I will reward your devotion.

256 doubt: suspect.

6 fashion . . . blood: a temporary enthusiasm and an amorous whim.

7 in . . . nature: at the beginning of its prime.

8 Forward: early blooming.

9–10 The . . . more a sweet but temporary diversion.

11–14 A growing person does not only increase in strength (**thews**) and size, but as the body grows (**this temple waxes**), the inner life (**inward service**) of mind and soul grows along with it.

15 cautel: deceit.

17 His . . . weighed: if you consider his high position.

Carve for himself, for on his choice depends
The safety and the health of this whole state.
And therefore must his choice be circumscribed
Unto the voice and yielding of that body
Whereof he is the head. Then, if he says he loves you,
It fits your wisdom so far to believe it
As he in his particular act and place
May give his saying deed, which is no further
Than the main voice of Denmark goes withal.
Then weigh what loss your honor may sustain
If with too credent ear you list his songs
Or lose your heart or your chaste treasure open
To his unmastered importunity.
Fear it, Ophelia; fear it, my dear sister,
And keep you in the rear of your affection,
Out of the shot and danger of desire.
The chariest maid is prodigal enough
If she unmask her beauty to the moon.
Virtue itself 'scapes not calumnious strokes.
The canker galls the infants of the spring
Too oft before their buttons be disclosed,
And, in the morn and liquid dew of youth,
Contagious blastments are most imminent.
Be wary, then; best safety lies in fear.
Youth to itself rebels, though none else near.

Ophelia. I shall the effect of this good lesson keep
As watchman to my heart. But, good my brother,
Do not, as some ungracious pastors do,
Show me the steep and thorny way to heaven,
Whiles, like a puffed and reckless libertine,
Himself the primrose path of dalliance treads
And recks not his own rede.

Laertes. O, fear me not.

[*Enter* Polonius.]

I stay too long. But here my father comes.
A double blessing is a double grace.
Occasion smiles upon a second leave.

Polonius. Yet here, Laertes? Aboard, aboard, for shame!
The wind sits in the shoulder of your sail,
And you are stayed for. There, my blessing with thee.
And these few precepts in thy memory
Look thou character. Give thy thoughts no tongue,
Nor any unproportioned thought his act.
Be thou familiar, but by no means vulgar.
Those friends thou hast, and their adoption tried,

20 Carve: choose.

22–24 And . . . head: His choice must be limited (**circumscribed**) by the opinion and consent (**voice and yielding**) of Denmark.

30 credent: trustful, **list:** listen to.

31–32 your chaste . . . importunity: lose your virginity to his uncontrolled pleading.

34 keep . . . affection: Don't go as far as your emotions would lead.

39 canker galls: cankerworm destroys; **infants:** early flowers.

40 buttons: buds; **disclosed:** opened.

42 contagious blastments: withering blights, harm or injury, catastrophes.

44 Youth . . . near: Youth by nature is prone to rebel.

46–51 Ophelia warns him not to act like a hypocritical pastor, preaching virtue and abstinence while leading a life of promiscuity and ignoring his own advice.

58–65 Polonius tells Laertes to write down (**character**) these few rules of conduct (**precepts**) in his memory. He should keep his thoughts to himself and not act on any unfit (**unproportioned**) thoughts, be friendly but not vulgar, remain loyal to friends proven (**tried**) worthy of being accepted but not shake hands with every swaggering youth (**unfledged courage**) who comes along.

Ophelia (Jean Simmons)

Grapple them unto thy soul with hoops of steel,
But do not dull thy palm with entertainment
Of each new-hatched, unfledged courage. Beware
Of entrance to a quarrel, but, being in,
Bear 't that th' opposèd may beware of thee.
Give every man thy ear, but few thy voice.
Take each man's censure, but reserve thy judgment.
Costly thy habit as thy purse can buy,
But not expressed in fancy (rich, not gaudy),
For the apparel oft proclaims the man,
And they in France of the best rank and station
Are of a most select and generous chief in that.
Neither a borrower nor a lender be,
For loan oft loses both itself and friend,
And borrowing dulls the edge of husbandry.
This above all: to thine own self be true,
And it must follow, as the night the day,
Thou canst not then be false to any man.
Farewell. My blessing season this in thee.

Laertes. Most humbly do I take my leave, my lord.

Polonius. The time invests you. Go, your servants tend.

Laertes. Farewell, Ophelia, and remember well
What I have said to you.

73–74 And they . . . that: Upper-class French people especially show their refinement and nobility in their choice of apparel.

77 husbandry: thrift, proper handling of money.

81 Polonius hopes that his advice will ripen (**season**) in Laertes.

83 invests: is pressing.

Ophelia. 'Tis in my memory locked,
And you yourself shall keep the key of it.

Laertes. Farewell.

[Laertes *exits.*]

Polonius. What is 't, Ophelia, he hath said to you?

Ophelia. So please you, something touching the Lord Hamlet.

Polonius. Marry, well bethought.
'Tis told me he hath very oft of late
Given private time to you, and you yourself
Have of your audience been most free and bounteous.
If it be so (as so 'tis put on me,
And that in way of caution), I must tell you
You do not understand yourself so clearly
As it behooves my daughter and your honor.
What is between you? Give me up the truth.

Ophelia. He hath, my lord, of late made many tenders
Of his affection to me.

Polonius. Affection, puh! You speak like a green girl
Unsifted in such perilous circumstance.
Do you believe his "tenders," as you call them?

Ophelia. I do not know, my lord, what I should think.

Polonius. Marry, I will teach you. Think yourself a baby
That you have ta'en these tenders for true pay,
Which are not sterling. Tender yourself more dearly,
Or (not to crack the wind of the poor phrase,
Running it thus) you'll tender me a fool.

Ophelia. My lord, he hath importuned me with love
In honorable fashion—

Polonius. Ay, "fashion" you may call it. Go to, go to!

Ophelia. And hath given countenance to his speech, my lord,
With almost all the holy vows of heaven.

Polonius. Ay, springes to catch woodcocks. I do know,
When the blood burns, how prodigal the soul
Lends the tongue vows. These blazes, daughter,
Giving more light than heat, extinct in both
Even in their promise as it is a-making,
You must not take for fire. From this time
Be something scanter of your maiden presence.
Set your entreatments at a higher rate
Than a command to parle. For Lord Hamlet,
Believe so much in him that he is young,
And with a larger tether may he walk

91 Marry: a mild oath, shortened from "by the Virgin Mary."

95 put on: told to.

100–110 Tenders: offers (lines 100 and 107). Polonius uses the word in line 107 to refer to coins that are not legal currency (**sterling**). He then warns Ophelia to offer (**tender**) herself at a higher rate (**more dearly**), or she will tender Polonius a fool—meaning either that she will present herself as a fool, that she will make him look like a fool, or that she will give him a grandchild.

116 springes . . . woodcocks: snares to catch birds that are easily caught.

117 prodigal: lavishly.

118–121 These blazes . . . fire: These blazes, which lose their light and heat almost immediately, should not be mistaken for fire.

123–135 Polonius, metaphorically referring to Ophelia as a besieged castle, tells her not to enter into negotiations (**entreatments**) for surrender merely because the enemy wants to meet (**parle**) with her. Hamlet's vows are go-betweens (**brokers**) that are not like their outward appearance; these solicitors (**implorators**) of sinful petitions (**unholy suits**) speak in pious terms in order to deceive. Polonius orders her never to disgrace (**slander**) a moment of her time by speaking to Hamlet.

Than may be given you. In few, Ophelia,
Do not believe his vows, for they are brokers,
Not of that dye which their investments show,
But mere implorators of unholy suits,
Breathing like sanctified and pious bawds
The better to beguile. This is for all:
I would not, in plain terms, from this time forth
Have you so slander any moment leisure
As to give words or talk with the Lord Hamlet.
Look to 't, I charge you. Come your ways.

Ophelia. I shall obey, my lord.

[*They exit.*]

Scene 4 *A guard platform at the castle.* ✕

[*Enter* Hamlet, Horatio, *and* Marcellus.]

Hamlet. The air bites shrewdly; it is very cold.

Horatio. It is a nipping and an eager air.

Hamlet. What hour now?

Horatio. I think it lacks of twelve.

Marcellus. No, it is struck.

Horatio. Indeed, I heard it not. It then draws near the season
Wherein the spirit held his wont to walk.

[*A flourish of trumpets and two pieces goes off.*]

What does this mean, my lord?

Hamlet. The King doth wake tonight and takes his rouse,
Keeps wassail, and the swagg'ring upspring reels;
And, as he drains his draughts of Rhenish down,
The kettledrum and trumpet thus bray out
The triumph of his pledge.

Horatio. Is it a custom?

Hamlet. Ay, marry, is 't,
But, to my mind, though I am native here
And to the manner born, it is a custom
More honored in the breach than the observance.
This heavy-headed revel east and west
Makes us traduced and taxed of other nations.
They clepe us drunkards and with swinish phrase
Soil our addition. And, indeed, it takes
From our achievements, though performed at height,
The pith and marrow of our attribute.
So oft it chances in particular men
That for some vicious mole of nature in them,

1 shrewdly: keenly.

2 eager: cutting.

9–13 The King stays up tonight drinking and dancing wildly; as he drinks down a glass of wine, kettledrums and trumpets play.

17 to the manner born: familiar since birth with this custom.

19–24 This drunken festivity makes us slandered and blamed by other nations. They call us drunkards and pigs, soiling our good name. Even when we do something outstanding, the essence of our reputation (**pith and marrow of our attribute**) is lost through drunkenness.

26 mole: defect.

As in their birth (wherein they are not guilty,
Since nature cannot choose his origin),
By the o'ergrowth of some complexion
(Oft breaking down the pales and forts of reason),
Or by some habit that too much o'erleavens
The form of plausive manners—that these men,
Carrying, I say, the stamp of one defect,
Being nature's livery or fortune's star,
His virtues else, be they as pure as grace,
As infinite as man may undergo,
Shall in the general censure take corruption
From that particular fault. The dram of evil
Doth all the noble substance of a doubt
To his own scandal.

[*Enter* Ghost.]

Horatio. Look, my lord, it comes.

Hamlet. Angels and ministers of grace, defend us!
Be thou a spirit of health or goblin damned,
Bring with thee airs from heaven or blasts from hell,
Be thy intents wicked or charitable,
Thou com'st in such a questionable shape
That I will speak to thee. I'll call thee "Hamlet,"
"King," "Father," "Royal Dane." O, answer me!
Let me not burst in ignorance, but tell
Why thy canonized bones, hearsèd in death,
Have burst their cerements; why the sepulcher,
Wherein we saw thee quietly interred,
Hath oped his ponderous and marble jaws
To cast thee up again. What may this mean
That thou, dead corse, again in complete steel,
Revisits thus the glimpses of the moon,
Making night hideous, and we fools of nature
So horridly to shake our disposition
With thoughts beyond the reaches of our souls?
Say, why is this? Wherefore? What should we do?

[Ghost *beckons.*]

Horatio. It beckons you to go away with it
As if it some impartment did desire
To you alone.

Marcellus. Look with what courteous action
It waves you to a more removèd ground.
But do not go with it.

Horatio. No, by no means.

Hamlet. It will not speak. Then I will follow it.

29–32 Hamlet describes reason as a castle whose fortified walls are broken by the excessive growth of a natural trait or by a corrupting habit.

34 nature's . . . star: which they are born with or acquire.

35 His virtues else: their other virtues.

38–40 The dram . . . scandal: A small amount of evil blots out all of a person's good qualities.

45 questionable: capable of responding to questions.

48–50 tell . . . cerements: Tell me why your bones, which were placed in a coffin and received a proper church burial, have escaped from their burial clothes.

57 horridly... disposition: disturb us terribly.

61–62 As if...alone: as if it has something to tell you on your own.

Horatio. Do not, my lord.

Hamlet. Why, what should be the fear?
I do not set my life at a pin's fee.
And for my soul, what can it do to that,
Being a thing immortal as itself?
It waves me forth again. I'll follow it.

67 pin's fee: the value of a pin.

Horatio. What if it tempt you toward the flood, my lord?
Or to the dreadful summit of the cliff
That beetles o'er his base into the sea,
And there assume some other horrible form
Which might deprive your sovereignty of reason
And draw you into madness? Think of it.
The very place puts toys of desperation,
Without more motive, into every brain
That looks so many fathoms to the sea
And hears it roar beneath.

71–76 Horatio is worried that the Ghost might lead Hamlet toward the sea (**flood**) or to the top of the cliff that hangs (**beetles**) over the sea, and then take on some horrible appearance that would drive Hamlet insane.

77 toys of desperation: irrational impulses.

Hamlet. It waves me still.—Go on, I'll follow thee.

Marcellus. You shall not go, my lord.

[*They hold back* Hamlet.]

Hamlet. Hold off your hands.

Horatio. Be ruled. You shall not go.

Hamlet. My fate cries out
And makes each petty arture in this body
As hardy as the Nemean lion's nerve.
Still am I called. Unhand me, gentlemen.
By heaven, I'll make a ghost of him that lets me!
I say, away!—Go on. I'll follow thee.

84 arture: artery.

85 Nemean lion's nerve: the sinews of a mythical lion strangled by Hercules.

87 lets: hinders.

[Ghost *and* Hamlet *exit.*]

Horatio. He waxes desperate with imagination.

Marcellus. Let's follow. 'Tis not fit thus to obey him.

Horatio. Have after. To what issue will this come?

91 Have after: Let's go after him.

Marcellus. Something is rotten in the state of Denmark.

Horatio. Heaven will direct it.

Marcellus. Nay, let's follow him.

[*They exit.*]

Scene 5 *Another part of the fortifications.*

[*Enter* Ghost *and* Hamlet.]

Hamlet. Whither wilt thou lead me? Speak. I'll go no further.

Ghost. Mark me.

Hamlet. I will.

Ghost. My hour is almost come
When I to sulf'rous and tormenting flames
Must render up myself.

Hamlet. Alas, poor ghost!

Ghost. Pity me not, but lend thy serious hearing
To what I shall unfold.

Hamlet. Speak. I am bound to hear.

Ghost. So art thou to revenge, when thou shalt hear.

Hamlet. What?

Ghost. I am thy father's spirit.
Doomed for a certain term to walk the night
And for the day confined to fast in fires
Till the foul crimes done in my days of nature
Are burnt and purged away. But that I am forbid
To tell the secrets of my prison house,
I could a tale unfold whose lightest word
Would harrow up thy soul, freeze thy young blood,
Make thy two eyes, like stars, start from their spheres,
Thy knotted and combinèd locks to part,
And each particular hair to stand an end,
Like quills upon the fearful porpentine.
But this eternal blazon must not be
To ears of flesh and blood. List, list, O list!
If thou didst ever thy dear father love—

Hamlet. O God!

Ghost. Revenge his foul and most unnatural murder.

Hamlet. Murder?

Ghost. Murder most foul, as in the best it is,
But this most foul, strange, and unnatural.

Hamlet. Haste me to know 't, that I, with wings as swift
As meditation or the thoughts of love,
May sweep to my revenge.

Ghost. I find thee apt;
And duller shouldst thou be than the fat weed
That roots itself in ease on Lethe wharf,

7 bound: obligated.

13 crimes: sins.

17 harrow up: tear up, disturb.

18 Make . . . spheres: make your two eyes like stars jump from their assigned places in the universe.

19 knotted . . . locks: carefully arranged hair.

20 an end: on end.

21 fearful porpentine: frightened porcupine.

22–23 The Ghost says he must not describe life beyond death to a living person.

28 as . . . is: which murder in general (**it**) is at the very least.

32–35 I find . . . this: I think you are willing, and you would have to be duller than the thick weed that grows on the banks of Lethe (the river of forgetfulness in the underworld) to not be roused by this.

Wouldst thou not stir in this. Now, Hamlet, hear.
'Tis given out that, sleeping in my orchard,
A serpent stung me. So the whole ear of Denmark
Is by a forgèd process of my death
Rankly abused. But know, thou noble youth,
The serpent that did sting thy father's life
Now wears his crown.

Hamlet. O, my prophetic soul! My uncle!

Ghost. Ay, that incestuous, that adulterate beast,
With witchcraft of his wit, with traitorous gifts—
O wicked wit and gifts, that have the power
So to seduce!—won to his shameful lust
The will of my most seeming-virtuous queen.
O Hamlet, what a falling off was there!
From me, whose love was of that dignity
That it went hand in hand even with the vow
I made to her in marriage, and to decline
Upon a wretch whose natural gifts were poor
To those of mine.
But virtue, as it never will be moved,
Though lewdness court it in a shape of heaven,
So, lust, though to a radiant angel linked,
Will sate itself in a celestial bed
And prey on garbage.
But soft, methinks I scent the morning air.
Brief let me be. Sleeping within my orchard,
My custom always of the afternoon,
Upon my secure hour thy uncle stole,
With juice of cursèd hebona in a vial,
And in the porches of my ears did pour
The leprous distilment, whose effect
Holds such an enmity with blood of man
That swift as quicksilver it courses through
The natural gates and alleys of the body,
And with a sudden vigor it doth posset
And curd, like eager droppings into milk,
The thin and wholesome blood. So did it mine,
And a most instant tetter barked about,
Most lazar-like, with vile and loathsome crust
All my smooth body.
Thus was I, sleeping, by a brother's hand
Of life, of crown, of queen at once dispatched,
Cut off, even in the blossoms of my sin,
Unhouseled, disappointed, unaneled,
No reck'ning made, but sent to my account
With all my imperfections on my head.

36 orchard: garden.

37–39 So...abused: Thus all of Denmark is deceived by a false account of my death.

43 adulterate: adulterous.

54–58 The Ghost compares virtue, which remains pure even if indecency courts it in a heavenly form, with lust, which grows weary of a virtuous marriage and seeks depravity.

63 hebona: a poisonous plant.

64 porches: entrances.

65 leprous distilment: a distilled liquid that causes disfigurement similar to that caused by leprosy.

69–71 doth . . . blood: The poison curdles the blood like something sour dropped into milk.

72–74 most instant . . . body: An eruption of sores (**tetter**) instantly covered my smooth body, leper-like (**lazar-like**), with a vile crust like the bark on a tree.

76 dispatched: deprived.

77–80 The Ghost regrets that he had no chance to receive the last rites of the church; he died with all his sins unabsolved.

O horrible, O horrible, most horrible!
If thou hast nature in thee, bear it not.
Let not the royal bed of Denmark be
A couch for luxury and damnèd incest.
But, howsomever thou pursues this act,
Taint not thy mind, nor let thy soul contrive
Against thy mother aught. Leave her to heaven
And to those thorns that in her bosom lodge
To prick and sting her. Fare thee well at once.
The glowworm shows the matin to be near
And 'gins to pale his uneffectual fire.
Adieu, adieu, adieu. Remember me.

[*He exits.*]

Hamlet. O all you host of heaven! O earth! What else?
And shall I couple hell? O fie! Hold, hold, my heart,
And you, my sinews, grow not instant old,

84 luxury: lust.

86–89 The Ghost tells Hamlet not to think of revenge against his mother.

90 matin: morning.

94 couple: add.

But bear me stiffly up. Remember thee?
Ay, thou poor ghost, whiles memory holds a seat
In this distracted globe. Remember thee?
Yea, from the table of my memory
I'll wipe away all trivial, fond records,
All saws of books, all forms, all pressures past,
That youth and observation copied there,
And thy commandment all alone shall live
Within the book and volume of my brain,
Unmixed with baser matter. Yes, by heaven!
O most pernicious woman!
O villain, villain, smiling, damnèd villain!
My tables—meet it is I set it down
That one may smile and smile and be a villain.
At least I am sure it may be so in Denmark.

[*He writes.*]

So, uncle, there you are. Now to my word.
It is "adieu, adieu, remember me."
I have sworn 't.

[*Enter* Horatio *and* Marcellus.]

Horatio. My lord, my lord!

Marcellus. Lord Hamlet.

Horatio. Heavens secure him!

Hamlet. So be it.

Marcellus. Illo, ho, ho, my lord!

Hamlet. Hillo, ho, ho, boy! Come, bird, come!

Marcellus. How is 't, my noble lord?

Horatio. What news, my lord?

Hamlet. O, wonderful!

Horatio. Good my lord, tell it.

Hamlet. No, you will reveal it.

Horatio. Not I, my lord, by heaven.

Marcellus. Nor I, my lord.

Hamlet. How say you, then? Would heart of man once think it?
But you'll be secret?

Horatio/Marcellus. Ay, by heaven, my lord.

Hamlet. There's never a villain dwelling in all Denmark
But he's an arrant knave.

98 globe: head.

99–105 Hamlet vows to erase from the slate (**table**) of his memory all foolish notes (**fond records**), wise sayings (**saws**) he copied from books, and past impressions (**pressures past**) so that the Ghost's command will live in his mind unmixed with ordinary, insignificant thoughts.

119 Hamlet responds to Marcellus's greeting (**illo, ho, ho**) with the call of a falconer to his hawk.

128 arrant knave: thoroughly dishonest person.

Horatio. There needs no ghost, my lord, come from the grave.
To tell us this.

Hamlet. Why, right, you are in the right.
And so, without more circumstance at all,
I hold it fit that we shake hands and part,
You, as your business and desire shall point you
(For every man hath business and desire,
Such as it is), and for my own poor part,
I will go pray.

131 circumstance: elaboration.

Horatio. These are but wild and whirling words, my lord.

Hamlet. I am sorry they offend you, heartily;
Yes, faith, heartily.

Horatio. There's no offense, my lord.

Hamlet. Yes, by Saint Patrick, but there is, Horatio,
And much offense, too. Touching this vision here,
It is an honest ghost—that let me tell you.
For your desire to know what is between us,
O'ermaster 't as you may. And now, good friends,
As you are friends, scholars, and soldiers,
Give me one poor request.

142 honest: genuine.

Horatio. What is 't, my lord? We will.

Hamlet. Never make known what you have seen tonight.

Horatio/Marcellus. My lord, we will not.

Hamlet. Nay, but swear 't.

Horatio. In faith, my lord, not I.

Marcellus. Nor I, my lord, in faith.

Hamlet. Upon my sword.

Marcellus. We have sworn, my lord, already.

Hamlet. Indeed, upon my sword, indeed.

153 The hilt of a sword, shaped like a cross, was often used for swearing oaths.

Ghost [*cries under the stage*]. Swear.

Hamlet. Ha, ha, boy, sayst thou so? Art thou there, truepenny?
Come on, you hear this fellow in the cellarage.
Consent to swear.

156 truepenny: honest fellow.

Horatio. Propose the oath, my lord.

Hamlet. Never to speak of this that you have seen,
Swear by my sword.

Ghost [*beneath*]. Swear.

Hamlet. *Hic et ubique*? Then we'll shift our ground.
Come hither, gentlemen,

162 *Hic et ubique*: here and everywhere (Latin).

And lay your hands again upon my sword.
Swear by my sword
Never to speak of this that you have heard.

Ghost [*beneath*]. Swear by his sword.

Hamlet. Well said, old mole. Canst work i' th' earth so fast?
A worthy pioner! Once more remove, good friends.

Horatio. O day and night, but this is wondrous strange.

Hamlet. And therefore as a stranger give it welcome.
There are more things in heaven and earth, Horatio,
Than are dreamt of in your philosophy. But come.
Here, as before, never, so help you mercy,
How strange or odd some'er I bear myself
(As I perchance hereafter shall think meet
To put an antic disposition on)
That you, at such times seeing me, never shall,
With arms encumbered thus, or this headshake,
Or by pronouncing of some doubtful phrase,
As "Well, well, we know," or "We could an if we would."
Or "If we list to speak," or "There be an if they might,"
Or such ambiguous giving-out, to note
That you know aught of me—this do swear,
So grace and mercy at your most need help you.

Ghost [*beneath*]. Swear.

Hamlet. Rest, rest, perturbèd spirit.—So, gentlemen,
With all my love I do commend me to you,
And what so poor a man as Hamlet is
May do t' express his love and friending to you,
God willing, shall not lack. Let us go in together,
And still your fingers on your lips, I pray.
The time is out of joint. O cursèd spite
That ever I was born to set it right!
Nay, come, let's go together.

[*They exit.*]

169 pioner: digger, miner.

171 Hamlet tells Horatio to welcome, or accept, the night's events as one would welcome a stranger.

173 your philosophy: the general subject of philosophy (not a particular belief of Horatio's).

174–185 Hamlet reveals that he may have to disguise himself with strange behavior (**antic disposition**); he has them swear not to make any gestures or hints that would give him away.

188–191 Hamlet says that he entrusts himself to them and will do his best to reward them.

193 The . . . joint: Everything is in disorder.

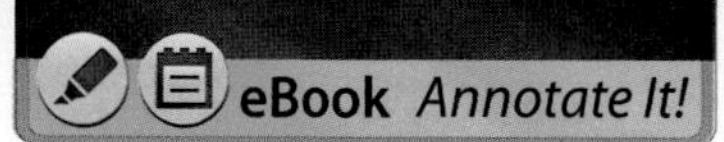

Analyzing the Text

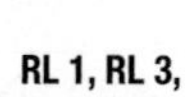

RL 1, RL 3, RL 4, W 4

Cite Text Evidence Support your responses with evidence from the selection.

1. **Analyze** What **mood,** or atmosphere, does Shakespeare establish in Scene 1? Which details help create this mood?
2. **Infer** In Scene 2, Claudius urges Hamlet to stay at court instead of returning to Wittenberg. What might he be concerned about?
3. **Compare** How do Hamlet's comments about Claudius in Scene 2 contrast with the impression Claudius conveys of himself through his speeches? What does this contrast suggest about life at the Danish court?
4. **Draw Conclusions** Reread lines 129–159 of Scene 2. What does this soliloquy suggest about Hamlet's state of mind at this point in the play?
5. **Interpret** Many of Shakespeare's characters use puns in their speech. A **pun** is a play on the multiple meanings of a word or on two words that sound alike but have different meanings. Throughout *Hamlet*, notes in the margin explain many puns that would be unfamiliar to a modern audience. Although puns are often associated with humor, they can also be an effective way to convey serious meaning. For example, in his conversation with Ophelia in Scene 3, Laertes says that Hamlet "himself is subject to his birth" (line 18). Explain how Laertes's statement is enriched by his drawing on two separate meanings of the word *subject*.
6. **Infer** In Scene 5, the Ghost speaks harshly about Gertrude. Why does he insist that Hamlet not take any action against her?
7. **Predict** In lines 175–177 of Scene 5, Hamlet tells Horatio and Marcellus that he might soon have to pretend to act strangely. What does this comment suggest about how he will try to carry out his revenge?
8. **Draw Conclusions** What do lines 193–195 in Scene 5 reveal about Hamlet's attitude toward the responsibility given to him by the Ghost? Why does he feel this way?

PERFORMANCE TASK

Writing Activity: Analysis In Act I, we learn about Hamlet's relationship with his uncle, and we also learn about Ophelia's relationship with her father. Write a brief essay in which you compare the two relationships.

- First, analyze Hamlet's interaction with Claudius in Scene 2, lines 64–128.
- Next, analyze Ophelia's interaction with Polonius in Scene 3, lines 89–137.
- Summarize the key similarities and differences in these relationships.

ACT II

Scene 1 *Polonius's chambers.*

[*Enter old* Polonius *with his man* Reynaldo.]

Polonius. Give him this money and these notes, Reynaldo.

Reynaldo. I will, my lord.

Polonius. You shall do marvelous wisely, good Reynaldo,
Before you visit him, to make inquire
Of his behavior.

Reynaldo. My lord, I did intend it.

Polonius. Marry, well said, very well said. Look you, sir,
Inquire me first what Danskers are in Paris;
And how, and who, what means, and where they keep,
What company, at what expense; and finding
By this encompassment and drift of question
That they do know my son, come you more nearer
Than your particular demands will touch it.
Take you, as 'twere, some distant knowledge of him,
As thus: "I know his father and his friends
And, in part, him." Do you mark this, Reynaldo?

Reynaldo. Ay, very well, my lord.

Polonius. "And, in part, him, but," you may say, "not well.
But if 't be he I mean, he's very wild,
Addicted so and so." And there put on him
What forgeries you please—marry, none so rank
As may dishonor him, take heed of that,
But, sir, such wanton, wild, and usual slips
As are companions noted and most known
To youth and liberty.

Reynaldo. As gaming, my lord.

Polonius. Ay, or drinking, fencing, swearing,
Quarreling, drabbing—you may go so far.

Reynaldo. My lord, that would dishonor him.

Polonius. Faith, no, as you may season it in the charge.
You must not put another scandal on him
That he is open to incontinency;
That's not my meaning. But breathe his faults so quaintly
That they may seem the taints of liberty,

6–12 Polonius tells him to start by asking general questions, because he will find out more through this roundabout approach (**encompassment**) than by asking specific questions about Laertes.

13 Take you: assume.

19–20 put on . . . please: accuse him of whatever faults you wish to make up; **rank:** gross.

22 wanton: reckless.

23–24 As are . . . liberty: that are commonly associated with youth and freedom.

24 gaming: gambling.

26 drabbing: going to prostitutes.

28 you . . . charge: You can soften (**season**) the charge by the way you state it.

30 incontinency: habitual sexual misconduct (as opposed to an occasional lapse).

31–36 Polonius tells him to describe Laertes's faults so subtly that they will seem the faults that come with independence (**taints of liberty**), the sudden urges of an excited mind, a wildness in untamed blood that occurs in most men.

The flash and outbreak of a fiery mind,
A savageness in unreclaimèd blood,
Of general assault.

Reynaldo. But, my good lord—

Polonius. Wherefore should you do this?

Reynaldo. Ay, my lord, I would know that.

Polonius. Marry, sir, here's my drift,
And I believe it is a fetch of wit.
You, laying these slight sullies on my son,
As 'twere a thing a little soiled i' th' working,
Mark you, your party in converse, him you would sound,
Having ever seen in the prenominate crimes
The youth you breathe of guilty, be assured
He closes with you in this consequence:
"Good sir," or so, or "friend," or "gentleman,"
According to the phrase or the addition
Of man and country—

Reynaldo. Very good, my lord.

Polonius. And then, sir, does he this, he does—what was I about to say? By the Mass, I was about to say something. Where did I leave?

Reynaldo. At "closes in the consequence," at "friend, or so, and gentleman."

Polonius. At "closes in the consequence"—ay, marry—
He closes thus: "I know the gentleman.
I saw him yesterday," or "th' other day"
(Or then, or then, with such or such), "and as you say,
There was he gaming, there o'ertook in 's rouse,
There falling out at tennis"; or perchance
"I saw him enter such a house of sale"—
Videlicet, a brothel—or so forth. See you now
Your bait of falsehood take this carp of truth;
And thus do we of wisdom and of reach,
With windlasses and with assays of bias,
By indirections find directions out.
So by my former lecture and advice
Shall you my son. You have me, have you not?

Reynaldo. My lord, I have.

Polonius. God be wi' you. Fare you well.

Reynaldo. Good my lord.

Polonius. Observe his inclination in yourself.

37 Wherefore: why.

40 fetch of wit: clever move.

41–46 Polonius wants Reynaldo to put these small stains (**sullies**) on his son's reputation—similar to the way in which cloth might be dirtied when it is handled—and then ask the person whether he has seen Laertes engaged in the offenses Reynaldo has mentioned (**prenominate crimes**).

46 He closes . . . consequence: he agrees with you in the following way.

48 addition: form of address.

59 o'ertook in 's rouse: overcome by drink.

62 *Videlicet*: namely.

64–66 we of . . . out: we who have wisdom and intelligence (**reach**) find things out indirectly, through roundabout courses (**windlasses**) and indirect tests (**assays of bias**).

71–73 Polonius tells him to observe Laertes's behavior personally and to see that Laertes practices his music.

Reynaldo. I shall, my lord.

Polonius. And let him ply his music.

Reynaldo. Well, my lord.

Polonius. Farewell.

[Reynaldo *exits.*]

[*Enter* Ophelia.]

How now, Ophelia, what's the matter?

Ophelia. O, my lord, my lord, I have been so affrighted!

Polonius. With what, i' th' name of God?

Ophelia. My lord, as I was sewing in my closet,
Lord Hamlet, with his doublet all unbraced,
No hat upon his head, his stockings fouled,
Ungartered, and down-gyvèd to his ankle,
Pale as his shirt, his knees knocking each other,
And with a look so piteous in purport
As if he had been loosèd out of hell
To speak of horrors—he comes before me.

Polonius. Mad for thy love?

Ophelia. My lord, I do not know,
But truly I do fear it.

Polonius. What said he?

Ophelia. He took me by the wrist and held me hard.
Then goes he to the length of all his arm,
And, with his other hand thus o'er his brow,
He falls to such perusal of my face
As he would draw it. Long stayed he so.
At last, a little shaking of mine arm,
And thrice his head thus waving up and down,
He raised a sigh so piteous and profound
As it did seem to shatter all his bulk
And end his being. That done, he lets me go,
And, with his head over his shoulder turned,
He seemed to find his way without his eyes,
For out o' doors he went without their helps
And to the last bended their light on me.

Polonius. Come, go with me. I will go seek the King.
This is the very ecstasy of love,
Whose violent property fordoes itself
And leads the will to desperate undertakings
As oft as any passions under heaven
That does afflict our natures. I am sorry.
What, have you given him any hard words of late?

78 closet: private room.

79 doublet all unbraced: jacket entirely unfastened.

80 fouled: dirty.

81 down-gyvèd to his ankle: fallen down to his ankles (like a prisoner's ankle chains, or gyves).

83 purport: expression.

96 bulk: body.

101 to the last . . . me: kept his eyes upon me the whole time.

103–107 Polonius says that the violent nature (**property**) of this love madness (**ecstasy**) often leads people to do something desperate.

Ophelia. No, my good lord, but as you did command
I did repel his letters and denied
His access to me.

Polonius. That hath made him mad.
I am sorry that with better heed and judgment
I had not coted him. I feared he did but trifle
And meant to wrack thee. But beshrew my jealousy!
By heaven, it is as proper to our age
To cast beyond ourselves in our opinions
As it is common for the younger sort
To lack discretion. Come, go we to the King.
This must be known, which, being kept close, might move
More grief to hide than hate to utter love.
Come.

[*They exit.*]

113 coted: observed.

114 wrack: ruin, seduce; **beshrew my jealousy:** curse my suspicious nature.

115–118 It is as natural for old people to go too far (**cast beyond ourselves**) with their suspicions as it is for younger people to lack good judgment.

119–120 Polonius decides that although it may anger the King, he must be told about this love because keeping it a secret might create even more grief.

Scene 2 *The castle.*

[*Flourish. Enter* King *and* Queen, Rosencrantz *and* Guildenstern *and* Attendants.]

King. Welcome, dear Rosencrantz and Guildenstern.
Moreover that we much did long to see you,
The need we have to use you did provoke
Our hasty sending. Something have you heard
Of Hamlet's transformation, so call it,
Sith nor th' exterior nor the inward man
Resembles that it was. What it should be,
More than his father's death, that thus hath put him
So much from th' understanding of himself
I cannot dream of. I entreat you both
That, being of so young days brought up with him
And sith so neighbored to his youth and havior,
That you vouchsafe your rest here in our court
Some little time, so by your companies
To draw him on to pleasures, and to gather
So much as from occasion you may glean,
Whether aught to us unknown afflicts him thus
That, opened, lies within our remedy.

Queen. Good gentlemen, he hath much talked of you,
And sure I am two men there is not living
To whom he more adheres. If it will please you
To show us so much gentry and goodwill
As to expend your time with us awhile
For the supply and profit of our hope,

6 Sith . . . man: since neither his appearance nor his personality.

10–18 Because Rosencrantz and Guildenstern were childhood friends with Hamlet and are so familiar with his past and his usual manner (**havior**), Claudius asks them to agree to stay (**vouchsafe your rest**) at court awhile to cheer Hamlet up and find out whether he is troubled by something that Claudius is unaware of.

18 opened: revealed.

22 gentry: courtesy.

24 For . . . hope: to aid and fulfill our wishes.

Your visitation shall receive such thanks
As fits a king's remembrance.

Rosencrantz. Both your Majesties
Might, by the sovereign power you have of us,
Put your dread pleasures more into command
Than to entreaty.

Guildenstern. But we both obey,
And here give up ourselves in the full bent
To lay our service freely at your feet,
To be commanded.

29–32 Guildenstern promises that they will devote themselves entirely (**in the full bent**) to the service of the King and Queen.

King. Thanks, Rosencrantz and gentle Guildenstern.

Queen. Thanks, Guildenstern and gentle Rosencrantz.
And I beseech you instantly to visit
My too much changèd son. Go, some of you,
And bring these gentlemen where Hamlet is.

Guildenstern. Heavens make our presence and our
practices
Pleasant and helpful to him!

38 practices: doings (sometimes used to mean "trickery").

Queen. Ay, amen!

[Rosencrantz *and* Guildenstern *exit with some* Attendants.]

[*Enter* Polonius.]

Polonius. Th' ambassadors from Norway, my good lord,
Are joyfully returned.

King. Thou still hast been the father of good news.

42 still: always.

Polonius. Have I, my lord? I assure my good liege
I hold my duty as I hold my soul,
Both to my God and to my gracious king,
And I do think, or else this brain of mine
Hunts not the trail of policy so sure
As it hath used to do, that I have found
The very cause of Hamlet's lunacy.

47–48 Hunts . . . do: does not follow the path of political shrewdness as well as it used to.

King. O, speak of that! That do I long to hear.

Polonius. Give first admittance to th' ambassadors.
My news shall be the fruit to that great feast.

52 fruit: dessert.

King. Thyself do grace to them and bring them in.

[Polonius *exits.*]

He tells me, my dear Gertrude, he hath found
The head and source of all your son's distemper.

Queen. I doubt it is no other but the main—
His father's death and our o'erhasty marriage.

56 the main: the main matter.

King. Well, we shall sift him.

[*Enter* Ambassadors Voltemand *and* Cornelius *with* Polonius.]

Welcome, my good friends.
Say, Voltemand, what from our brother Norway?

Voltemand. Most fair return of greetings and desires.
Upon our first, he sent out to suppress
His nephew's levies, which to him appeared
To be a preparation 'gainst the Polack,
But, better looked into, he truly found
It was against your Highness. Whereat, grieved
That so his sickness, age, and impotence
Was falsely borne in hand, sends out arrests
On Fortinbras, which he, in brief, obeys,
Receives rebuke from Norway, and, in fine,
Makes vow before his uncle never more
To give th' assay of arms against your Majesty.
Whereon old Norway, overcome with joy,
Gives him three-score thousand crowns in annual
fee
And his commission to employ those soldiers,
So levied as before, against the Polack,
With an entreaty, herein further shown,

[*He gives a paper.*]

That it might please you to give quiet pass
Through your dominions for this enterprise,
On such regards of safety and allowance
As therein are set down.

King. It likes us well,
And, at our more considered time, we'll read,
Answer, and think upon this business.
Meantime, we thank you for your well-took labor.
Go to your rest. At night we'll feast together.
Most welcome home!

[Voltemand *and* Cornelius *exit.*]

Polonius. This business is well ended.
My liege, and madam, to expostulate
What majesty should be, what duty is,
Why day is day, night night, and time is time
Were nothing but to waste night, day, and time.
Therefore, since brevity is the soul of wit,
And tediousness the limbs and outward flourishes,
I will be brief. Your noble son is mad.
"Mad" call I it, for, to define true madness,

58 sift him: question Polonius carefully.

59 brother: fellow king.

61 Upon our first: as soon as we brought up the matter.

67 borne in hand: deceived; **arrests:** orders to desist.

69 in fine: finally.

71 give . . . against: challenge militarily.

77–80 give . . . down: allow troops to move through Denmark for this expedition, under the conditions set down for Denmark's security and Fortinbras's permission.

80 likes: pleases.

81 our more considered time: a more suitable time for consideration.

86–89 To inquire into (**expostulate**) the nature of one's duty to the crown would be a waste of time, like trying to figure out the reason for day, night, and time.

90 brevity . . . wit: intelligent speech should be concise.

91 flourishes: decorations.

What is 't but to be nothing else but mad?
But let that go.

Queen. More matter with less art.

Polonius. Madam, I swear I use no art at all.
That he's mad, 'tis true; 'tis true 'tis pity,
And pity 'tis 'tis true—a foolish figure,
But farewell it, for I will use no art.
Mad let us grant him then, and now remains
That we find out the cause of this effect,
Or, rather say, the cause of this defect,
For this effect defective comes by cause.
Thus it remains, and the remainder thus.
Perpend.
I have a daughter (have while she is mine)
Who, in her duty and obedience, mark,
Hath given me this. Now gather and surmise.

[*He reads.*] *To the celestial, and my soul's idol, the most beautified Ophelia—*

That's an ill phrase, a vile phrase; "beautified" is a vile phrase. But you shall hear. Thus: [*He reads.*] *In her excellent white bosom, these, etc.—*

Queen. Came this from Hamlet to her?

Polonius. Good madam, stay awhile. I will be faithful.

[*He reads the letter.*]

Doubt thou the stars are fire,
Doubt that the sun doth move,
Doubt truth to be a liar,
But never doubt I love.

O dear Ophelia, I am ill at these numbers. I have not art to reckon my groans, but that I love thee best, O most best, believe it. Adieu.
Thine evermore, most dear lady, whilst this machine is to him, Hamlet.

This, in obedience, hath my daughter shown me,
And more above, hath his solicitings,
As they fell out by time, by means, and place,
All given to mine ear.

King. But how hath she received his love?

Polonius. What do you think of me?

King. As of a man faithful and honorable.

Polonius. I would fain prove so. But what might you think,

96–99 The Queen asks Polonius to make his point without such a display of rhetoric (**art**). He claims to be speaking plainly about the matter, but then he can't resist making a figure of speech that even he describes as foolish.

105 Perpend: consider.

108 gather and surmise: draw your own conclusions.

114–115 The Queen doubts Hamlet would use such formal and flowery language; Polonius assures her he will read the letter accurately.

116 Doubt: suspect.

120 ill at these numbers: bad at writing in verse.

121 reckon: count, put into metrical verse.

123–124 whilst . . . to him: while I am still in this body (**machine**).

126–128 more above . . . ear: In addition, she has told me all the details of his solicitations as they occurred.

When I had seen this hot love on the wing
(As I perceived it, I must tell you that,
Before my daughter told me), what might you,
Or my dear Majesty your queen here, think,
If I had played the desk or table-book
Or given my heart a winking, mute and dumb,
Or looked upon this love with idle sight?
What might you think? No, I went round to work,
And my young mistress thus I did bespeak:
"Lord Hamlet is a prince, out of thy star.
This must not be." And then I prescripts gave her,
That she should lock herself from his resort,
Admit no messengers, receive no tokens;
Which done, she took the fruits of my advice,
And he, repelled (a short tale to make),
Fell into a sadness, then into a fast,
Thence to a watch, thence into a weakness,
Thence to a lightness, and, by this declension,
Into the madness wherein now he raves
And all we mourn for.

King [*to* Queen]. Do you think 'tis this?

Queen. It may be, very like.

Polonius. Hath there been such a time (I would fain know that)
That I have positively said "'Tis so,"
When it proved otherwise?

King. Not that I know.

Polonius. Take this from this, if this be otherwise.
If circumstances lead me, I will find
Where truth is hid, though it were hid, indeed,
Within the center.

King. How may we try it further?

Polonius. You know sometimes he walks four hours together
Here in the lobby.

Queen. So he does indeed.

Polonius. At such a time I'll loose my daughter to him.
[*To the* King.] Be you and I behind an arras then.
Mark the encounter. If he love her not,
And be not from his reason fall'n thereon,
Let me be no assistant for a state,
But keep a farm and carters.

King. We will try it.

137 played . . . table-book: kept this knowledge hidden within me.

138 given . . . winking: closed the eyes of my heart.

139 with idle sight: saw without really noticing.

142 star: sphere.

143 prescripts: orders.

144 resort: visits.

147–152 Polonius describes the stages of Hamlet's decline: he grew sad, then stopped eating, then suffered from sleeplessness (**a watch**), then turned weak and light-headed, and finally became mad.

157 The actor playing Polonius might point from his head to his shoulder or make a similar gesture while speaking this line.

160 the center: the Earth's center, the most inaccessible place; **try:** test.

163 loose: turn loose (as an animal might be released for mating).

164 arras: a tapestry hung in front of a wall.

[*Enter* Hamlet *reading on a book.*]

Queen. But look where sadly the poor wretch comes reading.

Polonius. Away, I do beseech you both, away.
I'll board him presently. O, give me leave.

171 board him presently: speak to him at once.

[King *and* Queen *exit with* Attendants.]

How does my good Lord Hamlet?

Hamlet. Well, God-a-mercy.

Polonius. Do you know me, my lord?

Hamlet. Excellent well. You are a fishmonger.

175 fishmonger: fish seller.

Polonius. Not I, my lord.

Hamlet. Then I would you were so honest a man.

Polonius. Honest, my lord?

Hamlet. Ay, sir. To be honest, as this world goes, is to be one man picked out of ten thousand.

Polonius. That's very true, my lord.

Hamlet. For if the sun breed maggots in a dead dog, being a good kissing carrion—Have you a daughter?

Polonius. I have, my lord.

Hamlet. Let her not walk i' th' sun. Conception is a blessing, but, as your daughter may conceive, friend, look to 't.

Polonius [*aside*]. How say you by that? Still harping on my daughter. Yet he knew me not at first; he said I was a fishmonger. He is far gone. And truly, in my youth, I suffered much extremity for love, very near this. I'll speak to him again.—What do you read, my lord?

Hamlet. Words, words, words.

Polonius. What is the matter, my lord?

Hamlet. Between who?

Polonius. I mean the matter that you read, my lord.

Hamlet. Slanders, sir; for the satirical rogue says here that old men have gray beards, that their faces are wrinkled, their eyes purging thick amber and plum-tree gum, and that they have a plentiful lack of wit, together with most weak hams; all which, sir, though I most powerfully and potently believe, yet I hold it not honesty to have it thus set down; for yourself, sir, shall grow old as I am, if, like a crab, you could go backward.

Polonius [*aside*]. Though this be madness, yet there is method in 't.—Will you walk out of the air, my lord?

Hamlet. Into my grave?

Polonius. Indeed, that's out of the air. [*Aside.*] How pregnant sometimes his replies are! A happiness that often madness hits on, which reason and sanity could not so prosperously be delivered of. I will leave him and suddenly contrive the means of meeting between him and my daughter.—My lord, I will take my leave of you.

Hamlet. You cannot, sir, take from me anything that I will more willingly part withal—except my life, except my life, except my life.

Polonius. Fare you well, my lord.

Hamlet [*aside*]. These tedious old fools.

[*Enter* Guildenstern *and* Rosencrantz.]

183 a good kissing carrion: good flesh for kissing. (Hamlet seems to be reading at least part of this sentence from his book.)

185 Conception: understanding, being pregnant.

188 harping on: sticking to the subject of.

195 matter: subject matter. (Hamlet plays off another meaning, "the basis of a quarrel.")

201 wit: understanding.

204 honesty: good manners.

208 Polonius asks him to come out of the open air.

211 pregnant: full of meaning; **happiness:** talent for expression.

Polonius. You go to seek the Lord Hamlet. There he is.

Rosencrantz [*to* Polonius]. God save you, sir.

[Polonius *exits.*]

Guildenstern. My honored lord.

Rosencrantz. My most dear lord.

Hamlet. My excellent good friends! How dost thou, Guildenstern? Ah, Rosencrantz! Good lads, how do you both?

Rosencrantz. As the indifferent children of the earth.

229 indifferent: ordinary.

Guildenstern. Happy in that we are not overhappy. On Fortune's cap, we are not the very button.

Hamlet. Nor the soles of her shoe?

Rosencrantz. Neither, my lord.

Hamlet. Then you live about her waist, or in the middle of her favors?

234–238 Hamlet exchanges sexual puns with his childhood friends. References to Fortune's sexual favors and private parts lead up to the traditional saying that the unfaithful Fortune is a prostitute (**strumpet**).

Guildenstern. Faith, her privates we.

Hamlet. In the secret parts of Fortune? O, most true! She is a strumpet. What news?

Rosencrantz. None, my lord, but that the world's grown honest.

Hamlet. Then is doomsday near. But your news is not true. Let me question more in particular. What have you, my good friends, deserved at the hands of Fortune that she sends you to prison hither?

Guildenstern. Prison, my lord?

Hamlet. Denmark's a prison.

Rosencrantz. Then is the world one.

Hamlet. A goodly one, in which there are many confines, wards, and dungeons, Denmark being one o' th' worst.

249 confines: places of confinement; **wards:** cells.

Rosencrantz. We think not so, my lord.

Hamlet. Why, then, 'tis none to you, for there is nothing either good or bad but thinking makes it so. To me, it is a prison.

Rosencrantz. Why, then, your ambition makes it one. 'Tis too narrow for your mind.

Hamlet. O God, I could be bounded in a nutshell and count myself a king of infinite space, were it not that I have bad dreams.

Guildenstern. Which dreams, indeed, are ambition, for the very substance of the ambitious is merely the shadow of a dream.

Hamlet. A dream itself is but a shadow.

Rosencrantz. Truly, and I hold ambition of so airy and light a quality that it is but a shadow's shadow.

Hamlet. Then are our beggars bodies, and our monarchs and outstretched heroes the beggars' shadows. Shall we to th' court? For, by my fay, I cannot reason.

Rosencrantz/Guildenstern. We'll wait upon you.

Hamlet. No such matter. I will not sort you with the rest of my servants, for, to speak to you like an honest man, I am most dreadfully attended. But, in the beaten way of friendship, what make you at Elsinore?

Rosencrantz. To visit you, my lord, no other occasion.

Hamlet. Beggar that I am, I am even poor in thanks; but I thank you, and sure, dear friends, my thanks are too dear a halfpenny. Were you not sent for? Is it your own inclining? Is it a free visitation? Come, come, deal justly with me. Come, come; nay, speak.

Guildenstern. What should we say, my lord?

Hamlet. Anything but to th' purpose. You were sent for, and there is a kind of confession in your looks which your modesties have not craft enough to color. I know the good king and queen have sent for you.

Rosencrantz. To what end, my lord?

Hamlet. That you must teach me. But let me conjure you by the rights of our fellowship, by the consonancy of our youth, by the obligation of our everpreserved love, and by what more dear a better proposer can charge you withal: be even and direct with me whether you were sent for or no.

Rosencrantz [*to* Guildenstern]. What say you?

Hamlet [*aside*]. Nay, then I have an eye of you.—If you love me, hold not off.

Guildenstern. My lord, we were sent for.

260–262 Guildenstern says that the apparently substantial aims of ambition are even less substantial than dreams.

266–267 Hamlet says that according to their logic, only beggars would have real bodies (since they lack ambition), and monarchs and ambitious (**outstretched**) heroes would be the shadows of beggars.

268 fay: faith.

269 wait upon: escort. (Hamlet takes the word to mean "serve" and replies that he would not categorize them with his servants.)

278 too dear a halfpenny: too costly at a halfpenny.

279 free: voluntary.

282 Hamlet sarcastically asks them to give him anything but a straight answer.

285 color: disguise.

288–289 conjure you: ask you earnestly.

289–290 consonancy of our youth: our closeness when we were young.

291–292 by what . . . withal: by whatever you hold more valuable, which someone more skillful than me would use to urge you with.

295 Hamlet reminds them that he is watching.

Hamlet. I will tell you why; so shall my anticipation prevent your discovery, and your secrecy to the King and Queen molt no feather. I have of late, but wherefore I know not, lost all my mirth, forgone all custom of exercises, and, indeed, it goes so heavily with my disposition that this goodly frame, the earth, seems to me a sterile promontory; this most excellent canopy, the air, look you, this brave o'er-hanging firmament, this majestical roof, fretted with golden fire—why, it appeareth nothing to me but a foul and pestilent congregation of vapors. What a piece of work is a man, how noble in reason, how infinite in faculties, in form and moving how express and admirable; in action how like an angel, in apprehension how like a god: the beauty of the world, the paragon of animals—and yet, to me, what is this quintessence of dust? Man delights not me, no, nor women neither, though by your smiling you seem to say so.

Rosencrantz. My lord, there was no such stuff in my thoughts.

Hamlet. Why did you laugh, then, when I said "man delights not me"?

Rosencrantz. To think, my lord, if you delight not in man, what Lenten entertainment the players shall receive from you. We coted them on the way, and hither are they coming to offer you service.

Hamlet. He that plays the king shall be welcome—his Majesty shall have tribute on me. The adventurous knight shall use his foil and target, the lover shall not sigh gratis, the humorous man shall end his part in peace, the clown shall make those laugh whose lungs are tickle o' th' sear, and the lady shall say her mind freely, or the blank verse shall halt for 't. What players are they?

Rosencrantz. Even those you were wont to take such delight in, the tragedians of the city.

Hamlet. How chances it they travel? Their residence, both in reputation and profit, was better both ways.

Rosencrantz. I think their inhibition comes by the means of the late innovation.

Hamlet. Do they hold the same estimation they did when I was in the city? Are they so followed?

Rosencrantz. No, indeed are they not.

298–299 shall my . . . discovery: My saying it first will spare you from revealing your secret.

300 molt no feather: will not be diminished.

304 promontory: a rock jutting out from the sea.

305 brave: splendid.

306 fretted: adorned.

308 congregation: gathering.

309 piece of work: work of art or fine craftsmanship.

311 express: exact, expressive.

312 apprehension: understanding.

314 quintessence of dust: essence, or most refined form, of dust.

322 Lenten entertainment: meager, or spare, reception.

323 coted: passed.

325–332 The king shall receive his praise, the knight shall use his sword and shield, the lover shall not sigh for nothing, the eccentric (**humorous**) character shall play his part in peace, the clown shall make those laugh who do so easily, and the lady shall speak without restraint, or else the blank verse (which has five metrical feet) will limp (**halt**) because of it.

Hamlet. How comes it? Do they grow rusty?

Rosencrantz. Nay, their endeavor keeps in the wonted pace. But there is, sir, an aerie of children, little eyases, that cry out on the top of question and are most tyrannically clapped for 't. These are now the fashion and so berattle the common stages (so they call them) that many wearing rapiers are afraid of goose quills and dare scarce come thither.

Hamlet. What, are they children? Who maintains 'em? How are they escoted? Will they pursue the quality no longer than they can sing? Will they not say afterwards, if they should grow themselves to common players (as it is most like, if their means are no better), their writers do them wrong to make them exclaim against their own succession?

Rosencrantz. Faith, there has been much to-do on both sides, and the nation holds it no sin to tar them to controversy. There was for a while no money bid for argument unless the poet and the player went to cuffs in the question.

Hamlet. Is 't possible?

Guildenstern. O, there has been much throwing about of brains.

Hamlet. Do the boys carry it away?

Rosencrantz. Ay, that they do, my lord—Hercules and his load too.

Hamlet. It is not very strange; for my uncle is King of Denmark, and those that would make mouths at him while my father lived give twenty, forty, fifty, a hundred ducats apiece for his picture in little. 'Sblood, there is something in this more than natural, if philosophy could find it out.

[*A flourish for the* Players.]

Guildenstern. There are the players.

Hamlet. Gentlemen, you are welcome to Elsinore. Your hands, come then. Th' appurtenance of welcome is fashion and ceremony. Let me comply with you in this garb, lest my extent to the players, which, I tell you, must show fairly outwards, should more appear like entertainment than yours. You are welcome. But my uncle-father and aunt-mother are deceived.

337–349 The players had to leave the city due to competition from a company of boy actors—a nest (**aerie**) of young hawks (**little eyases**) who are loudly applauded for their shrill performances. Many fashionable patrons are afraid to attend the public theaters (**common stages**) where adult actors play, fearing satirical attacks from the pens of those who write for the boy actors.

351 escoted: provided for.

351–352 pursue . . . sing: perform only until their voices change.

353 common: adult.

356 succession: future work as actors.

358 tar: provoke.

359–361 no money . . . question: the only profitable plays were satires about this rivalry.

366–367 Ay . . . load: Yes, they've won over the whole theater world.

368–371 Hamlet says that people who made faces (**mouths**) at his uncle while his father was alive now pay up to 100 gold coins for his miniature portrait.

375–381 Hamlet tells Rosencrantz and Guildenstern that since fashion and ceremony should accompany a welcome, he wants to observe these formalities with them so it will not appear that the players get a better reception than they do.

Guildenstern. In what, my dear lord?

Hamlet. I am but mad north-north-west. When the wind is southerly, I know a hawk from a handsaw.

384–385 Hamlet says he is only mad when the wind blows in a certain direction; at other times he can tell one thing from another.

[*Enter* Polonius.]

Polonius. Well be with you, gentlemen.

Hamlet. Hark you, Guildenstern, and you too—at each ear a hearer! That great baby you see there is not yet out of his swaddling clouts.

389 swaddling clouts: cloth used to wrap a newborn baby.

Rosencrantz. Haply he is the second time come to them, for they say an old man is twice a child.

Hamlet. I will prophesy he comes to tell me of the players; mark it.—You say right, sir, a Monday morning, 'twas then indeed.

Polonius. My lord, I have news to tell you.

Hamlet. My lord, I have news to tell you: when Roscius was an actor in Rome—

397 Roscius: a famous Roman actor.

Polonius. The actors are come hither, my lord.

Hamlet. Buzz, buzz.

399 Hamlet dismisses the announcement as old news.

Polonius. Upon my honor—

Hamlet. Then came each actor on his ass.

Polonius. The best actors in the world, either for tragedy, comedy, history, pastoral, pastoral-comical, historical-pastoral, tragical-historical, tragical-comical-historical-pastoral, scene individable, or poem unlimited. Seneca cannot be too heavy, nor Plautus too light. For the law of writ and the liberty, these are the only men.

406 Seneca: a Roman writer of tragedies.

406–407 Plautus: a Roman writer of comedies; **For the . . . liberty:** for plays that follow strict rules of dramatic composition as well as more loosely written plays.

Hamlet. O Jephthah, judge of Israel, what a treasure hadst thou!

Polonius. What a treasure had he, my lord?

Hamlet. Why,

One fair daughter, and no more,
The which he lovèd passing well.

409–426 Jephthah: a biblical figure who sacrifices his beloved daughter after making a thoughtless vow (see Judges 11). Hamlet quotes lines from a ballad based on this story.

Polonius [*aside*]. Still on my daughter.

Hamlet. Am I not i' th' right, old Jephthah?

Polonius. If you call me "Jephthah," my lord: I have a daughter that I love passing well.

Hamlet. Nay, that follows not.

Polonius. What follows then, my lord?

Hamlet. Why,

As by lot, God wot

and then, you know,

It came to pass, as most like it was—

the first row of the pious chanson will show you more, for look where my abridgment comes.

[*Enter the* Players.]

You are welcome, masters; welcome all.—I am glad to see thee well.—Welcome, good friends.—O my old friend! Why, thy face is valanced since I saw thee last. Com'st thou to beard me in Denmark—What, my young lady and mistress! By'r Lady, your ladyship is nearer to heaven than when I saw you last, by the altitude of a chopine. Pray God your voice, like a piece of uncurrent gold, be not cracked within the ring. Masters, you are all welcome. We'll e'en to 't like French falconers, fly at anything we see. We'll have a speech straight. Come, give us a taste of your quality. Come, a passionate speech.

First Player. What speech, my good lord?

Hamlet. I heard thee speak me a speech once, but it was never acted, or, if it was, not above once; for the play, I remember, pleased not the million: 'twas caviary to the general. But it was (as I received it, and others whose judgments in such matters cried in the top of mine) an excellent play, well digested in the scenes, set down with as much modesty as cunning. I remember one said there were no sallets in the lines to make the matter savory, nor no matter in the phrase that might indict the author of affectation, but called it an honest method, as wholesome as sweet and, by very much, more handsome than fine. One speech in 't I chiefly loved. 'Twas Aeneas' tale to Dido, and thereabout of it especially when he speaks of Priam's slaughter. If it live in your memory, begin at this line—let me see, let me see:

The rugged Pyrrhus, like th' Hyrcanian beast—

'tis not so; it begins with Pyrrhus:

The rugged Pyrrhus, he whose sable arms,
Black as his purpose, did the night resemble
When he lay couchèd in th' ominous horse,
Hath now this dread and black complexion smeared
With heraldry more dismal. Head to foot,

425 the first . . . chanson: the first stanza of the religious song.

429 valanced: fringed (with a beard).

431–435 All female roles were played by boys. Hamlet fears that this boy's voice might crack onstage, since he has grown by the height of a thick-soled shoe.

436–437 fly . . . see: take on anything.

437 straight: right away.

444 caviary to the general: like caviar, which is unappreciated by most people.

446 digested: arranged.

447 modesty: restraint.

448 cunning: skill, **sallets:** spicy bits, racey jests.

454–455 Pyrrhus, son of the Greek hero Achilles, killed King Priam to revenge the death of his father during the Trojan War. Aeneas tells the story to Dido, the Queen of Carthage, in Virgil's *Aeneid*.

458 Hyrcanian beast: a tiger.

462 couchèd: concealed; **ominous horse:** wooden horse used by the Greeks to enter Troy.

Now is he total gules, horridly tricked
With blood of fathers, mothers, daughters, sons,
Baked and impasted with the parching streets,
That lend a tyrannous and a damnèd light
To their lord's murder. Roasted in wrath and fire,
And thus o'ersizèd with coagulate gore,
With eyes like carbuncles, the hellish Pyrrhus
Old grandsire Priam seeks.
So, proceed you.

Polonius. 'Fore God, my lord, well spoken, with good accent and good discretion.

First Player. *Anon he finds him*
Striking too short at Greeks. His antique sword,
Rebellious to his arm, lies where it falls,
Repugnant to command. Unequal matched,
Pyrrhus at Priam drives, in rage strikes wide;
But with the whiff and wind of his fell sword
Th' unnervèd father falls. Then senseless Ilium,
Seeming to feel this blow, with flaming top
Stoops to his base, and with a hideous crash
Takes prisoner Pyrrhus' ear. For lo, his sword,
Which was declining on the milky head
Of reverend Priam, seemed i' th' air to stick.
So as a painted tyrant Pyrrhus stood
And, like a neutral to his will and matter,
Did nothing.
But as we often see against some storm
A silence in the heavens, the rack stand still,
The bold winds speechless, and the orb below
As hush as death, anon the dreadful thunder
Doth rend the region; so, after Pyrrhus' pause,
Arousèd vengeance sets him new a-work,
And never did the Cyclops' hammers fall
On Mars's armor, forged for proof eterne,
With less remorse than Pyrrhus' bleeding sword
Now falls on Priam.
Out, out, thou strumpet Fortune! All you gods
In general synod take away her power,
Break all the spokes and fellies from her wheel,
And bowl the round nave down the hill of heaven
As low as to the fiends!

Polonius. This is too long.

Hamlet. It shall to the barber's with your beard.—Prithee say on. He's for a jig or a tale of bawdry, or he sleeps. Say on; come to Hecuba.

465 total gules: all red; **tricked:** adorned.

467 The blood is baked and crusted (**impasted**) from the heat of the burning streets.

470 o'ersizèd: smeared over.

471 carbuncles: fiery red stones.

479 Repugnant to: resisting.

482 unnervèd: strengthless; **senseless Ilium:** the inanimate fortress of Troy.

485 Takes . . . ear: captures Pyrrhus' attention.

488–490 So . . . nothing: Pyrrhus stood still like a tyrant in a painting, suspended between his intentions and taking the actions that would fulfill them.

492 rack: mass of high clouds.

497 Cyclops: one-eyed giants who worked for Vulcan, the Roman god of metalworking.

498 Mars: Roman god of war; **for proof eterne:** to last for eternity.

502 synod: assembly.

503 fellies: section of a wheel's rim.

504 nave: hub of a wheel.

508–509 He's for . . . sleeps: Unless he's hearing a comic song and dance (**jig**) or a bawdy tale, he falls asleep.

509 Hecuba: Priam's wife.

First Player. *But who, ah woe, had seen the moblèd queen—*

Hamlet. "The moblèd queen"?

Polonius. That's good. "Moblèd queen" is good.

First Player. *Run barefoot up and down, threat'ning the flames*
With bisson rheum, a clout upon that head
Where late the diadem stood, and for a robe,
About her lank and all o'erteemèd loins
A blanket, in the alarm of fear caught up—
Who this had seen, with tongue in venom steeped,
'Gainst Fortune's state would treason have pronounced.
But if the gods themselves did see her then
When she saw Pyrrhus make malicious sport
In mincing with his sword her husband's limbs,
The instant burst of clamor that she made
(Unless things mortal move them not at all)
Would have made milch the burning eyes of heaven
And passion in the gods.

Polonius. Look whe'er he has not turned his color and has tears in 's eyes. Prithee, no more.

Hamlet. 'Tis well. I'll have thee speak out the rest of this soon.—Good my lord, will you see the players well bestowed? Do you hear, let them be well used, for they are the abstract and brief chronicles of the time. After your death you were better have a bad epitaph than their ill report while you live.

Polonius. My lord, I will use them according to their desert.

Hamlet. God's bodykins, man, much better! Use every man after his desert and who shall 'scape whipping? Use them after your own honor and dignity. The less they deserve, the more merit is in your bounty. Take them in.

Polonius. Come, sirs.

Hamlet. Follow him, friends. We'll hear a play tomorrow. [*As* Polonius *and* Players *exit,* Hamlet *speaks to the* First Player.] Dost thou hear me, old friend? Can you play "The Murder of Gonzago"?

First Player. Ay, my lord.

Hamlet. We'll ha 't tomorrow night. You could, for a need, study a speech of some dozen or sixteen

510 moblèd: her face was muffled.

514 bisson rheum: blinding tears; **clout:** cloth.

516 o'erteemèd: worn out from childbearing.

519 'Gainst . . . pronounced: would have proclaimed treasonous statements against Fortune's rule.

525 milch: milky, moist with tears.

527 whe'er: whether.

532 abstract: summary.

537 God's bodykins: by God's little body.

548 ha 't: have it.

lines, which I would set down and insert in 't, could you not?

First Player. Ay, my lord.

Hamlet. Very well. Follow that lord—and look you mock him not. [First Player *exits.*] My good friends, I'll leave you till night. You are welcome to Elsinore.

Rosencrantz. Good my lord.

Hamlet. Ay, so, good-bye to you.

[Rosencrantz *and* Guildenstern *exit.*]

Now I am alone.

O, what a rogue and peasant slave am I!
Is it not monstrous that this player here,
But in a fiction, in a dream of passion,
Could force his soul so to his own conceit
That from her working all his visage wanned,
Tears in his eyes, distraction in his aspect,
A broken voice, and his whole function suiting
With forms to his conceit—and all for nothing!
For Hecuba!
What's Hecuba to him, or he to Hecuba,
That he should weep for her? What would he do
Had he the motive and the cue for passion
That I have? He would drown the stage with tears
And cleave the general ear with horrid speech,

561–562 Could . . . wanned: could force his soul into such agreement with his thoughts that his soul made his face turn pale.

564–565 his whole . . . conceit: all of his activity creating outward appearances that express his thoughts.

571 cleave . . . speech: pierce everyone's ears with horrible words.

Make mad the guilty and appall the free,
Confound the ignorant and amaze indeed
The very faculties of eyes and ears. Yet I,
A dull and muddy-mettled rascal, peak
Like John-a-dreams, unpregnant of my cause,
And can say nothing—no, not for a king
Upon whose property and most dear life
A damned defeat was made. Am I a coward?
Who calls me "villain"? breaks my pate across?
Plucks off my beard and blows it in my face?
Tweaks me by the nose? gives me the lie i' th' throat
As deep as to the lungs? Who does me this?
Ha! 'Swounds, I should take it! For it cannot be
But I am pigeon-livered and lack gall
To make oppression bitter, or ere this
I should have fatted all the region kites
With this slave's offal. Bloody, bawdy villain!
Remorseless, treacherous, lecherous, kindless villain!
O vengeance!
Why, what an ass am I! This is most brave,
That I, the son of a dear father murdered,
Prompted to my revenge by heaven and hell,
Must, like a whore, unpack my heart with words
And fall a-cursing like a very drab,
A scullion! Fie upon 't! Foh!
About, my brains!—Hum, I have heard
That guilty creatures sitting at a play
Have, by the very cunning of the scene,
Been struck so to the soul that presently
They have proclaimed their malefactions.
For murder, though it have no tongue, will speak
With most miraculous organ. I'll have these players
Play something like the murder of my father
Before mine uncle. I'll observe his looks;
I'll tent him to the quick. If he do blench,
I know my course. The spirit that I have seen
May be a devil, and the devil hath power
T' assume a pleasing shape; yea, and perhaps,
Out of my weakness and my melancholy,
As he is very potent with such spirits,
Abuses me to damn me. I'll have grounds
More relative than this. The play's the thing
Wherein I'll catch the conscience of the King.

[*He exits.*]

572 appall the free: terrify the innocent.

575 muddy-mettled: weak-spirited; **peak:** mope.

576 John-a-dreams: a dreamy idler; **unpregnant of:** not roused to action by.

579 defeat: destruction.

582–583 gives . . . lungs: calls me a complete liar.

584 'Swounds: by Christ's wounds (an oath).

585 pigeon-livered: meek as a pigeon.

587 kites: birds of prey.

588 offal: entrails.

589 kindless: unnatural.

591 brave: admirable.

595 drab: prostitute.

596 scullion: kitchen servant.

597 About: get to work.

599 cunning of the scene: skill of the performance.

600 presently: immediately.

601 malefactions: crimes.

606 tent . . . quick: probe him in his most vulnerable spot; **blench:** flinch.

612–613 grounds . . . this: a more solid basis for acting than the Ghost's words.

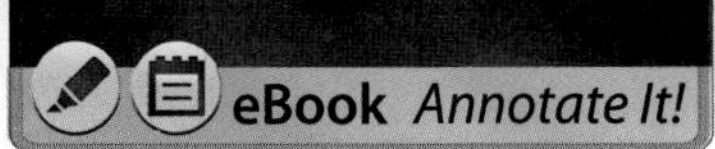

Analyzing the Text

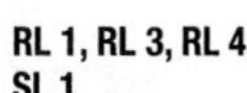
RL 1, RL 3, RL 4, SL 1

Cite Text Evidence Support your responses with evidence from the selection.

1. **Infer** In the opening scene of Act II, how does Polonius want Reynaldo to check on Laertes's conduct? What does this instruction suggest about Polonius's character?
2. **Analyze** In a play, **dramatic irony** occurs when the audience knows something that a character does not know. In lines 88–101 of Scene 1, Ophelia tells Polonius what took place when Hamlet visited her. Explain why this passage is an example of dramatic irony.
3. **Infer** Reread Hamlet's exchange with Polonius in Scene 2, lines 172–219. Polonius says of Hamlet's responses, "Though this be madness, yet there is method in 't." What is the method, or purpose, of Hamlet's behavior in this interaction?
4. **Interpret** In line 246 of Scene 2, Hamlet says to Guildenstern that "Denmark's a prison." Explain that remark in the context of Hamlet's present situation, considering also the role of Rosencrantz and Guildenstern.
5. **Compare** In Scene 2, lines 368–371, Hamlet compares Claudius to a company of boy actors who have chased the adult actors from the city. What does Claudius have in common with the boy actors?
6. **Compare** The play discussed by Hamlet and the players (Scene 2, lines 453–526) tells the story of Pyrrhus seeking revenge on Priam. What are the parallels between this tale and Hamlet's own quest for revenge? What does the conclusion of the tale foreshadow for Hamlet?
7. **Analyze** Summarize Hamlet's comments about the First Player's performance in Scene 2, lines 558–588. What internal conflict is expressed in this soliloquy?
8. **Draw Conclusions** At the end of Act II, Hamlet reveals his plan for testing Claudius's guilt. Why might Shakespeare have chosen to have him use a theatrical performance for this purpose?

PERFORMANCE TASK

Speaking Activity: Discussion Why is Hamlet so cautious?

- Gather evidence from the text about Hamlet's pretending to be mad and about his plan to test Claudius's guilt.
- In a small group, discuss why Hamlet takes these measures. Consider what might happen if instead he tried to immediately take revenge.
- Summarize the group discussion and present your ideas to the class.

ACT III

Scene 1 *The castle.*

[*Enter* King, Queen, Polonius, Ophelia, Rosencrantz, Guildenstern, *and* Lords.]

King. And can you by no drift of conference
Get from him why he puts on this confusion,
Grating so harshly all his days of quiet
With turbulent and dangerous lunacy?

1 drift of conference: steering of conversation.

Rosencrantz. He does confess he feels himself distracted,
But from what cause he will by no means speak.

Guildenstern. Nor do we find him forward to be sounded,
But with a crafty madness keeps aloof
When we would bring him on to some confession
Of his true state.

7 forward to be sounded: interested in being questioned.

Queen. Did he receive you well?

Rosencrantz. Most like a gentleman.

Guildenstern. But with much forcing of his disposition.

12 forcing of his disposition: effort.

Rosencrantz. Niggard of question, but of our demands
Most free in his reply.

13–14 Niggard . . . reply: Reluctant to talk, but willing to answer our questions.

Queen. Did you assay him to any pastime?

15 assay: tempt.

Rosencrantz. Madam, it so fell out that certain players
We o'erraught on the way. Of these we told him,
And there did seem in him a kind of joy
To hear of it. They are here about the court,
And, as I think, they have already order
This night to play before him.

17 o'erraught: overtook.

Polonius. 'Tis most true,
And he beseeched me to entreat your Majesties
To hear and see the matter.

King. With all my heart, and it doth much content me
To hear him so inclined.
Good gentlemen, give him a further edge
And drive his purpose into these delights.

26 give . . . edge: sharpen his interest.

Rosencrantz. We shall, my lord.

[Rosencrantz *and* Guildenstern *and* Lords *exit.*]

King. Sweet Gertrude, leave us too,
For we have closely sent for Hamlet hither,
That he, as 'twere by accident, may here
Affront Ophelia.
Her father and myself (lawful espials)

29 closely: privately.

31 Affront: meet.

32 espials: spies.

Will so bestow ourselves that, seeing unseen,
We may of their encounter frankly judge
And gather by him, as he is behaved,
If't be th' affliction of his love or no
That thus he suffers for.

35 as he is behaved: according to his behavior.

Queen. I shall obey you.
And for your part, Ophelia, I do wish
That your good beauties be the happy cause
Of Hamlet's wildness. So shall I hope your virtues
Will bring him to his wonted way again,
To both your honors.

Ophelia. Madam, I wish it may.

[Queen *exits.*]

Polonius. Ophelia, walk you here.—Gracious, so please you,
We will bestow ourselves. [*To* Ophelia.] Read on this book,
That show of such an exercise may color
Your loneliness.—We are oft to blame in this
('Tis too much proved), that with devotion's visage
And pious action we do sugar o'er
The devil himself.

King [*aside*]. O, 'tis too true!
How smart a lash that speech doth give my conscience.
The harlot's cheek beautied with plast'ring art
Is not more ugly to the thing that helps it
Than is my deed to my most painted word.
O heavy burden!

43 Gracious: Your Grace (addressing the King).

44–49 Polonius tells Ophelia to read a religious book to provide an excuse for being alone. He remarks that many people are guilty of using worship and a devout appearance to cover their sins.

50-55 Claudius compares the heavy makeup that covers up the flaws on a prostitute's cheek to the beautiful words that cover his crime.

Polonius. I hear him coming. Let's withdraw, my lord.

[*They withdraw.*]

[*Enter* Hamlet.]

Hamlet. To be or not to be—that is the question:
Whether 'tis nobler in the mind to suffer
The slings and arrows of outrageous fortune,
Or to take arms against a sea of troubles
And, by opposing, end them. To die, to sleep—
No more—and by a sleep to say we end
The heartache and the thousand natural shocks
That flesh is heir to—'tis a consummation
Devoutly to be wished. To die, to sleep—
To sleep, perchance to dream. Ay, there's the rub,
For in that sleep of death what dreams may come,
When we have shuffled off this mortal coil,
Must give us pause. There's the respect
That makes calamity of so long life.
For who would bear the whips and scorns of time,

57 To be: To exist, to continue living.

59 slings: something thrown or shot.

64 consummation: final ending.

66 rub: obstacle.

68 shuffled . . . coil: cast aside the turmoil of life.

69–70 There's . . . life: That is the consideration that makes us endure misery (**calamity**) for such a long time.

71 time: life in this world.

Th' oppressor's wrong, the proud man's contumely,
The pangs of despised love, the law's delay,
The insolence of office, and the spurns
That patient merit of th' unworthy takes,
When he himself might his quietus make
With a bare bodkin? Who would fardels bear,
To grunt and sweat under a weary life,
But that the dread of something after death,
The undiscovered country from whose bourn
No traveler returns, puzzles the will
And makes us rather bear those ills we have
Than fly to others that we know not of?
Thus conscience does make cowards of us all,
And thus the native hue of resolution
Is sicklied o'er with the pale cast of thought,
And enterprises of great pitch and moment
With this regard their currents turn awry
And lose the name of action.— Soft you now,
The fair Ophelia.— Nymph, in thy orisons
Be all my sins remembered.

Ophelia. Good my lord,
How does your Honor for this many a day?

Hamlet. I humbly thank you, well.

Ophelia. My lord, I have remembrances of yours
That I have longèd long to redeliver.
I pray you now receive them.

Hamlet. No, not I. I never gave you aught.

Ophelia. My honored lord, you know right well you did,
And with them words of so sweet breath composed
As made the things more rich. Their perfume lost,
Take these again, for to the noble mind
Rich gifts wax poor when givers prove unkind.
There, my lord.

Hamlet. Ha, ha, are you honest?

Ophelia. My lord?

Hamlet. Are you fair?

Ophelia. What means your lordship?

Hamlet. That if you be honest and fair, your honesty should admit no discourse to your beauty.

Ophelia. Could beauty, my lord, have better commerce than with honesty?

72 contumely: insults, expressions of contempt.

73 despised: unreturned.

74 office: officials.

74–75 spurns . . . takes: the insults that people of merit receive from the unworthy.

76–77 When . . . bodkin: when he might settle his accounts (**his quietus make**) with merely a dagger (**a bare bodkin**)—that is, end his unhappiness by killing himself.

77 fardels: burdens.

80 bourn: boundary.

81 puzzles: paralyzes.

85 native hue: natural color.

86 cast: shade.

87–89 pitch and moment: height and importance; **with this regard:** for this reason.

89 Soft you: be quiet, enough.

90 orisons: prayers.

104 honest: truthful, chaste.

108 Your honesty . . . beauty: Your chastity should not allow itself to be influenced by your beauty.

110 commerce: dealings.

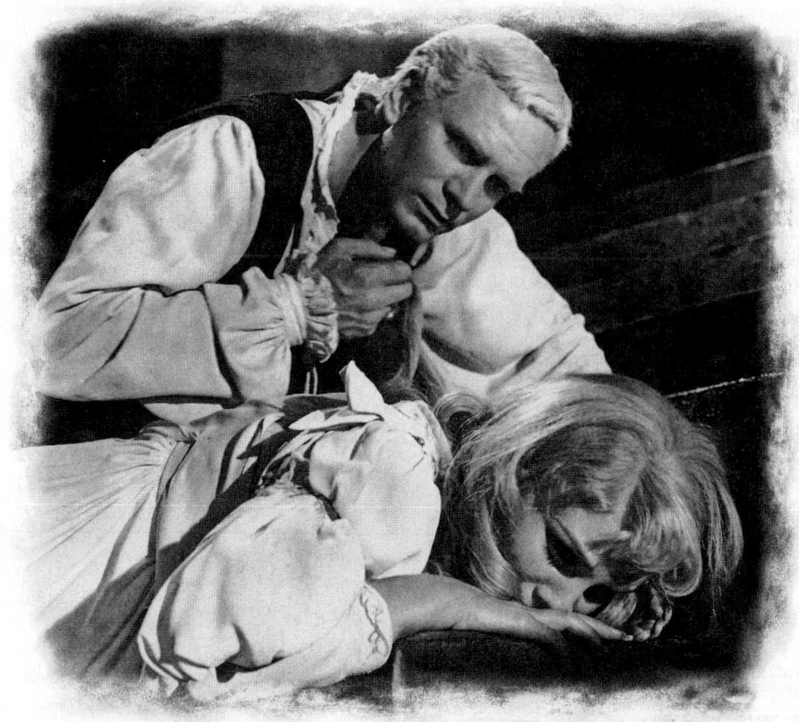

Hamlet. Ay, truly, for the power of beauty will sooner transform honesty from what it is to a bawd than the force of honesty can translate beauty into his likeness. This was sometime a paradox, but now the time gives it proof. I did love you once.

Ophelia. Indeed, my lord, you made me believe so.

Hamlet. You should not have believed me, for virtue cannot so inoculate our old stock but we shall relish of it. I loved you not.

Ophelia. I was the more deceived.

Hamlet. Get thee to a nunnery. Why wouldst thou be a breeder of sinners? I am myself indifferent honest, but yet I could accuse me of such things that it were better my mother had not borne me: I am very proud, revengeful, ambitious, with more offenses at my beck than I have thoughts to put them in, imagination to give them shape, or time to act them in. What should such fellows as I do crawling between earth and heaven? We are arrant knaves all; believe none of us. Go thy ways to a nunnery. Where's your father?

Ophelia. At home, my lord.

114 his: its.

115 This . . . paradox: This once went against the common viewpoint.

116 time: the present age.

118–120 Hamlet's metaphor is of grafting a branch onto a fruit tree: If virtue is grafted onto his sinful nature, the fruit of the grafted tree will still taste of his old nature.

122 nunnery: convent (sometimes used as a slang word for "brothel").

123 indifferent honest: reasonably virtuous.

127 beck: command.

Hamlet. Let the doors be shut upon him that he may play the fool nowhere but in 's own house. Farewell.

Ophelia. O, help him, you sweet heavens!

Hamlet. If thou dost marry, I'll give thee this plague for thy dowry: be thou as chaste as ice, as pure as snow, thou shalt not escape calumny. Get thee to a nunnery, farewell. Or if thou wilt needs marry, marry a fool, for wise men know well enough what monsters you make of them. To a nunnery, go, and quickly too. Farewell.

139 calumny: slander, defamation.

142 monsters: horned cuckolds (men whose wives are unfaithful).

Ophelia. Heavenly powers, restore him!

Hamlet. I have heard of your paintings too, well enough. God hath given you one face, and you make yourselves another. You jig and amble, and you lisp; you nickname God's creatures and make your wantonness your ignorance. Go to, I'll no more on 't. It hath made me mad. I say we will have no more marriage. Those that are married already, all but one, shall live. The rest shall keep as they are. To a nunnery, go.

148 nickname: find new names for.

148–149 make . . . ignorance: use ignorance as an excuse for your waywardness.

[*He exits.*]

Ophelia. O, what a noble mind is here o'erthrown!
The courtier's, soldier's, scholar's, eye, tongue, sword,
Th' expectancy and rose of the fair state,
The glass of fashion and the mold of form,
Th' observed of all observers, quite, quite down!
And I, of ladies most deject and wretched,
That sucked the honey of his musicked vows,
Now see that noble and most sovereign reason,
Like sweet bells jangled, out of time and harsh;
That unmatched form and stature of blown youth
Blasted with ecstasy. O, woe is me
T' have seen what I have seen, see what I see!

155–158 Ophelia starts her description of Hamlet's former self by evoking the princely ideal of statesman, soldier, and scholar. He was the hope and ornament (**expectancy and rose**) of Denmark, a model of behavior and appearance for other people, respected (**observed**) by all who looked upon him.

163–164 blown . . . ecstasy: youth in full bloom withered by madness.

King [*advancing with* Polonius]. Love? His affections do not that way tend;
Nor what he spake, though it lacked form a little,
Was not like madness. There's something in his soul
O'er which his melancholy sits on brood,
And I do doubt the hatch and the disclose
Will be some danger; which for to prevent,
I have in quick determination
Thus set it down: he shall with speed to England
For the demand of our neglected tribute.
Haply the seas, and countries different,

166 affections: feelings.

168–171 Claudius says that Hamlet's melancholy broods on something like a bird sits on an egg; he fears that some danger will hatch from it.

With variable objects, shall expel
This something-settled matter in his heart,
Whereon his brains still beating puts him thus
From fashion of himself. What think you on 't?

177 This . . . heart: this unknown thing that has settled in his heart.

Polonius. It shall do well. But yet do I believe
The origin and commencement of his grief
Sprung from neglected love.— How now, Ophelia?
You need not tell us what Lord Hamlet said;
We heard it all.— My lord, do as you please,
But, if you hold it fit, after the play
Let his queen-mother all alone entreat him
To show his grief. Let her be round with him;
And I'll be placed, so please you, in the ear
Of all their conference. If she find him not,
To England send him, or confine him where
Your wisdom best shall think.

187 be round: speak plainly.

189 find him not: does not learn what is disturbing him.

King. It shall be so.
Madness in great ones must not unwatched go.

[*They exit.*]

Scene 2 *The castle.*

[*Enter* Hamlet *and three of the* Players.]

Hamlet. Speak the speech, I pray you, as I pronounced it to you, trippingly on the tongue; but if you mouth it, as many of our players do, I had as lief the town-crier spoke my lines. Nor do not saw the air too much with your hand, thus, but use all gently; for in the very torrent, tempest, and, as I may say, whirlwind of your passion, you must acquire and beget a temperance that may give it smoothness. O, it offends me to the soul to hear a robustious, periwig-pated fellow tear a passion to tatters, to very rags, to split the ears of the groundlings, who for the most part are capable of nothing but inexplicable dumb shows and noise. I would have such a fellow whipped for o'erdoing Termagant. It out-Herods Herod. Pray you, avoid it.

3 I had as lief: I would just as soon.

9 robustious: boisterous.

9–10 periwig-pated: wig-wearing.

11 groundlings: the spectators who paid the cheapest price for admittance to the theater and stood in an open area in front of the stage.

14–15 Termagant, Herod: noisy, violent figures from early drama.

Player. I warrant your Honor.

Hamlet. Be not too tame neither, but let your own discretion be your tutor. Suit the action to the word, the word to the action, with this special observance, that you o'erstep not the modesty of nature. For anything so o'erdone is from the purpose of playing, whose end, both at the first and now, was and is to hold, as 'twere, the mirror up to nature, to

20 modesty: moderation.

21 is from: strays from.

show virtue her own feature, scorn her own image, and the very age and body of the time his form and pressure. Now this overdone or come tardy off, though it makes the unskillful laugh, cannot but make the judicious grieve, the censure of the which one must in your allowance o'erweigh a whole theater of others. O, there be players that I have seen play and heard others praise (and that highly), not to speak it profanely, that, neither having th' accent of Christians nor the gait of Christian, pagan, nor man, have so strutted and bellowed that I have thought some of nature's journeymen had made men, and not made them well, they imitated humanity so abominably.

24 scorn: something scornful.

25–26 the very... pressure: a true impression of the present.

26 come tardy off: done inadequately.

27 the unskillful: those lacking in judgment.

28–30 the censure... others: You should value the opinion of a single judicious theatergoer over an entire audience that lacks judgment.

Player. I hope we have reformed that indifferently with us, sir.

38 indifferently: fairly well.

Hamlet. O, reform it altogether. And let those that play your clowns speak no more than is set down for them, for there be of them that will themselves laugh, to set on some quantity of barren spectators to laugh too, though in the meantime some necessary question of the play be then to be considered. That's villainous and shows a most pitiful ambition in the fool that uses it. Go make you ready.

42 of them: some among them.

43 barren: dull-witted.

[Players *exit.*]

[*Enter* Polonius, Guildenstern, *and* Rosencrantz.]

How now, my lord, will the King hear this piece of work?

Polonius. And the Queen too, and that presently.

Hamlet. Bid the players make haste. [Polonius *exits.*] Will you two help to hasten them?

Rosencrantz. Ay, my lord.

[*They exit.*]

Hamlet. What ho, Horatio!

[*Enter* Horatio.]

Horatio. Here, sweet lord, at your service.

Hamlet. Horatio, thou art e'en as just a man
As e'er my conversation coped withal.

Horatio. O, my dear lord—

Hamlet. Nay, do not think I flatter,
For what advancement may I hope from thee

56–57 Hamlet says that Horatio is as honorable as any man he has ever dealt with.

That no revenue hast but thy good spirits
To feed and clothe thee? Why should the poor be flattered?
No, let the candied tongue lick absurd pomp
And crook the pregnant hinges of the knee
Where thrift may follow fawning. Dost thou hear?
Since my dear soul was mistress of her choice
And could of men distinguish, her election
Hath sealed thee for herself. For thou hast been
As one in suffering all that suffers nothing,
A man that Fortune's buffets and rewards
Hast ta'en with equal thanks; and blessed are those
Whose blood and judgment are so well commeddled
That they are not a pipe for Fortune's finger
To sound what stop she please. Give me that man
That is not passion's slave, and I will wear him
In my heart's core, ay, in my heart of heart,
As I do thee.—Something too much of this.—
There is a play tonight before the King.
One scene of it comes near the circumstance
Which I have told thee of my father's death.
I prithee, when thou seest that act afoot,
Even with the very comment of thy soul
Observe my uncle. If his occulted guilt
Do not itself unkennel in one speech,
It is a damnèd ghost that we have seen,
And my imaginations are as foul
As Vulcan's stithy. Give him heedful note,
For I mine eyes will rivet to his face,
And, after, we will both our judgments join
In censure of his seeming.

Horatio. Well, my lord.
If he steal aught the whilst this play is playing
And 'scape detecting, I will pay the theft.

[*Sound a flourish.*]

Hamlet. They are coming to the play. I must be idle.
Get you a place.

[*Enter Trumpets and Kettle Drums. Enter* King, Queen, Polonius, Ophelia, Rosencrantz, Guildenstern, *and other* Lords *attendant with the* King's guard *carrying torches.*]

King. How fares our cousin Hamlet?

Hamlet. Excellent, i' faith, of the chameleon's dish. I eat the air, promise-crammed. You cannot feed capons so.

62 candied: flattering.

63 crook...knee: bend the ready joint of the knee (kneel down).

64 thrift: profit.

68 one...nothing: one who experiences everything but is harmed by nothing.

71 blood: passions; **commeddled:** blended.

72 pipe: small wind instrument.

73 stop: a hole in a wind instrument that controls sound.

81 Even...soul: with your most searching observation.

82–86 Hamlet says that if Claudius's hidden (**occulted**) guilt does not reveal (**unkennel**) itself with the speech Hamlet wrote, then the Ghost is in league with the devil and Hamlet's thoughts about Claudius are as foul as the forge of the Roman god of metalworking.

89 censure of his seeming: judgment of how he looks and behaves.

92 be idle: play the fool, be unoccupied.

94–97 Hamlet, taking **fares** to mean "feeds," answers that he eats promises. (Chameleons were said to feed on air.)

King. I have nothing with this answer, Hamlet. These words are not mine.

Hamlet. No, nor mine now. [*To* Polonius.] My lord, you played once i' th' university, you say?

Polonius. That did I, my lord, and was accounted a good actor.

Hamlet. What did you enact?

Polonius. I did enact Julius Caesar. I was killed i' th' Capitol. Brutus killed me.

Hamlet. It was a brute part of him to kill so capital a calf there.—Be the players ready?

108 calf: fool.

Rosencrantz. Ay, my lord. They stay upon your patience.

Queen. Come hither, my dear Hamlet, sit by me.

Hamlet. No, good mother. Here's metal more attractive.

111 metal more attractive: a substance more magnetic.

[Hamlet *takes a place near* Ophelia.]

Polonius [*to the* King]. Oh, ho! Do you mark that?

Hamlet. Lady, shall I lie in your lap?

Ophelia. No, my lord.

Hamlet. I mean, my head upon your lap?

Ophelia. Ay, my lord.

Hamlet. Do you think I meant country matters?

117 country matters: something coarse or indecent, which a rustic from the country might propose.

Ophelia. I think nothing, my lord.

Hamlet. That's a fair thought to lie between maids' legs.

Ophelia. What is, my lord?

Hamlet. Nothing.

Ophelia. You are merry, my lord.

Hamlet. Who, I?

Ophelia. Ay, my lord.

Hamlet. O God, your only jig-maker. What should a man do but be merry? For look you how cheerfully my mother looks, and my father died within 's two hours.

125 Hamlet sarcastically refers to himself as the best jig (comical song and dance) performer.

Ophelia. Nay, 'tis twice two months, my lord.

Hamlet. So long? Nay, then, let the devil wear black, for I'll have a suit of sables. O heavens, die two months ago, and not forgotten yet? Then there's hope a great man's memory may outlive his life half a year. But, by'r Lady, he must build churches, then, or else shall

129–130 Hamlet sarcastically suggests giving up his mourning clothes for luxurious clothing trimmed with furs.

he suffer not thinking on, with the hobby-horse, whose epitaph is "For oh, for oh, the hobby-horse is forgot."

[*The trumpets sound. Dumb show follows.*]

[*Enter a* King *and a* Queen, *very lovingly, the* Queen *embracing him and he her. She kneels and makes show of protestation unto him. He takes her up and declines his head upon her neck. He lies him down upon a bank of flowers. She, seeing him asleep, leaves him. Anon comes in another* man, *takes off his crown, kisses it, pours poison in the sleeper's ears, and leaves him. The* Queen *returns, finds the* King *dead, makes passionate action. The* poisoner *with some three or four come in again, seem to condole with her. The dead body is carried away. The* poisoner *woos the* Queen *with gifts. She seems harsh awhile but in the end accepts his love.*]

[Players *exit.*]

Ophelia. What means this, my lord?

Hamlet. Marry, this is miching mallecho. It means mischief.

Ophelia. Belike this show imports the argument of the play.

[*Enter* Prologue.]

Hamlet. We shall know by this fellow. The players cannot keep counsel; they'll tell all.

Ophelia. Will he tell us what this show meant?

Hamlet. Ay, or any show that you will show him. Be not you ashamed to show, he'll not shame to tell you what it means.

Ophelia. You are naught, you are naught. I'll mark the play.

Prologue.

For us and for our tragedy,
Here stooping to your clemency,
We beg your hearing patiently.

[*He exits.*]

Hamlet. Is this a prologue or the posy of a ring?

Ophelia. 'Tis brief, my lord.

Hamlet. As woman's love.

[*Enter the* Player King *and Queen.*]

Player King. *Full thirty times hath Phoebus' cart gone round*
Neptune's salt wash and Tellus' orbèd ground,

134 not thinking on: being forgotten; **hobby-horse:** a horse-and-rider figure who once performed in morris and may-day dances. Such traditions had been disappearing.

Dumb show: a scene without dialogue.

138 miching mallecho: sneaking misdeed. (The Spanish word **malhecho** means "misdeed.")

139 Belike: perhaps; **argument:** plot.

147 naught: naughty, indecent.

152 posy of a ring: a motto inscribed in a ring.

155–160 The Player King says that they have been united in love and marriage for 30 years. **Phoebus' cart:** the sun god's chariot; **Neptune's salt wash:** the ocean; **Tellus:** Roman goddess of the earth; **Hymen:** god of marriage.

And thirty dozen moons with borrowed sheen
About the world have times twelve thirties been
Since love our hearts and Hymen did our hands
Unite commutual in most sacred bands.

Player Queen. *So many journeys may the sun and moon*
Make us again count o'er ere love be done!
But woe is me! You are so sick of late,
So far from cheer and from your former state,
That I distrust you. Yet, though I distrust,
Discomfort you, my lord, it nothing must.
For women fear too much, even as they love,
And women's fear and love hold quantity,
In neither aught, or in extremity.
Now what my love is, proof hath made you
know, And, as my love is sized, my fear is so:
Where love is great, the littlest doubts are fear;
Where little fears grow great, great love grows there.

Player King. *Faith, I must leave thee, love, and shortly too.*
My operant powers their functions leave to do.
And thou shalt live in this fair world behind,
Honored, beloved; and haply one as kind
For husband shalt thou—

Player Queen. *O, confound the rest!*
Such love must needs be treason in my breast.
In second husband let me be accurst.
None wed the second but who killed the first.

Hamlet. That's wormwood!

Player Queen. *The instances that second marriage move*
Are base respects of thrift, but none of love.
A second time I kill my husband dead
When second husband kisses me in bed.

Player King. *I do believe you think what now you speak,*
But what we do determine oft we break.
Purpose is but the slave to memory,
Of violent birth, but poor validity,
Which now, the fruit unripe, sticks on the tree
But fall unshaken when they mellow be.
Most necessary 'tis that we forget
To pay ourselves what to ourselves is debt.
What to ourselves in passion we propose,
The passion ending, doth the purpose lose.
The violence of either grief or joy
Their own enactures with themselves destroy.
Where joy most revels, grief doth most lament;
Grief joys, joy grieves, on slender accident.

165 distrust you: am worried about you.

168–169 And women's…extremity: Women love and fear in equal measure, loving and fearing either too much or hardly at all.

175 My…do: My vital powers are no longer functioning.

176 behind: after I'm gone.

182 wormwood: a bitter herb.

183–184 The instances…love: People marry a second time for profit, not for love.

189–190 Our intentions are dependent on our memory; they are powerful at first but have little durability (**validity**).

193–194 Most…debt: We inevitably forget promises we have made to ourselves.

197–200 When the violence of extreme grief or joy ceases, so too does the willingness to act upon these emotions. People who feel extreme grief also feel extreme joy, and one passion is likely to follow another without much cause (**on slender accident**).

This world is not for aye, nor 'tis not strange
That even our loves should with our fortunes change;
For 'tis a question left us yet to prove
Whether love lead fortune or else fortune love.
The great man down, you mark his favorite flies;
The poor, advanced, makes friends of enemies.
And hitherto doth love on fortune tend,
For who not needs shall never lack a friend,
And who in want a hollow friend doth try
Directly seasons him his enemy.
But, orderly to end where I begun:
Our wills and fates do so contrary run
That our devices still are overthrown;
Our thoughts are ours, their ends none of our own.
So think thou wilt no second husband wed,
But die thy thoughts when thy first lord is dead.

Player Queen. *Nor earth to me give food, nor heaven light,*
Sport and repose lock from me day and night,
To desperation turn my trust and hope,
An anchor's cheer in prison be my scope.
Each opposite that blanks the face of joy
Meet what I would have well and it destroy.
Both here and hence pursue me lasting strife,
If, once a widow, ever I be wife.

Hamlet. If she should break it now!

201 for aye: forever.

205 The great...flies: When a great man's fortune falls, his closest friend abandons him.

206 advanced: moving up in life.

207 hitherto: to this extent.

210 Directly seasons him: immediately changes him into.

213 devices still: plans always.

218 Sport...night: May the day deny (**lock from**) me its pastimes and night its rest.

220 An anchor's cheer: a religious hermit's fare.

221–222 May each obstacle that turns the face of joy pale meet and destroy everything that I wish to see prosper (**what I would have well**).

Player King. *'Tis deeply sworn. Sweet, leave me here awhile.*
My spirits grow dull, and fain I would beguile
The tedious day with sleep.

[*Sleeps.*]

Player Queen. *Sleep rock thy brain,*
And never come mischance between us twain.

[Player Queen *exits.*]

Hamlet. Madam, how like you this play?

Queen. The lady doth protest too much, methinks.

Hamlet. O, but she'll keep her word.

King. Have you heard the argument? Is there no offense in 't?

Hamlet. No, no, they do but jest, poison in jest. No offense i' th' world.

King. What do you call the play?

Hamlet. "The Mousetrap." Marry, how? Tropically. This play is the image of a murder done in Vienna. Gonzago is the duke's name, his wife Baptista. You shall see anon. 'Tis a knavish piece of work, but what of that? Your Majesty and we that have free souls, it touches us not. Let the galled jade wince; our withers are unwrung.

[*Enter* Lucianus.]

This is one Lucianus, nephew to the king.

Ophelia. You are as good as a chorus, my lord.

Hamlet. I could interpret between you and your love, if I could see the puppets dallying.

Ophelia. You are keen, my lord, you are keen.

Hamlet. It would cost you a groaning to take off mine edge.

Ophelia. Still better and worse.

Hamlet. So you mis-take your husbands.—Begin, murderer. Pox, leave thy damnable faces and begin. Come, the croaking raven doth bellow for revenge.

Lucianus. *Thoughts black, hands apt, drugs fit, and time agreeing,*
Confederate season, else no creature seeing,
Thou mixture rank, of midnight weeds collected,
With Hecate's ban thrice blasted, thrice infected,

231 doth protest too much: overstates her case, makes too many assurances.

233 argument: plot.

238 Tropically: metaphorically.

242 free: guilt-free.

243–244 Let... unwrung: a proverbial expression that means, "Let the guilty flinch; our consciences do not bother us."

246 chorus: a character who explains what will happen in a play.

247–252 An "interpreter" is a narrator in a puppet show. Hamlet says that he could explain what is going on between Ophelia and her lover if he caught them together. When she comments that he is **keen** (sharp, penetrating), he responds with wordplay (using **keen** to mean "sexually aroused") that she finds even more witty but also more offensive.

253 mis-take: take falsely. A reference to the marriage vow to take a husband "for better, for worse."

257 Time is my ally (**Confederate**) and only witness.

259 Hecate's ban: the curse of Hecate, goddess of witchcraft.

Thy natural magic and dire property
On wholesome life usurp immediately.

[*Pours the poison in his ears.*]

Hamlet. He poisons him i' th' garden for his estate. His name's Gonzago. The story is extant and written in very choice Italian. You shall see anon how the murderer gets the love of Gonzago's wife.

[Claudius *rises.*]

Ophelia. The King rises.

Hamlet. What, frighted with false fire?

Queen. How fares my lord?

Polonius. Give o'er the play.

King. Give me some light. Away!

Polonius. Lights, lights, lights!

[*All but* Hamlet *and* Horatio *exit.*]

Hamlet. *Why, let the strucken deer go weep,*
The hart ungallèd play.
For some must watch, while some must sleep:
Thus runs the world away.

Would not this, sir, and a forest of feathers (if the rest of my fortunes turn Turk with me) with two Provincial roses on my razed shoes, get me a fellowship in a cry of players?

Horatio. Half a share.

Hamlet. A whole one, I.
For thou dost know, O Damon dear,
This realm dismantled was
Of Jove himself, and now reigns here
A very very—pajock.

Horatio. You might have rhymed.

Hamlet. O good Horatio, I'll take the ghost's word for a thousand pound. Didst perceive?

Horatio. Very well, my lord.

Hamlet. Upon the talk of the poisoning?

Horatio. I did very well note him.

Hamlet. Ah ha! Come, some music! Come, the recorders!
For if the King like not the comedy,
Why, then, belike he likes it not, perdy.
Come, some music!

261 usurp: steal.

267 false fire: the discharge of a gun loaded without shot.

273 ungallèd: uninjured.

277–279 turn Turk with me: turn against me. Elizabethan theater costumes often included feathers worn on hats and ribbon rosettes on shoes. A fellowship is a share or partnership in a theater company.

282 Damon: in Roman mythology the friend of Pythias.

285 pajock: either "peacock," which had a reputation for lust and cruelty, or "patchock," a savage person. (Presumably the rhyme Horatio hints at is **ass.**)

293 recorders: flute-like wooden wind instruments.

295 perdy: by God (from the French **par dieu**).

[*Enter* Rosencrantz *and* Guildenstern.]

Guildenstern. Good my lord, vouchsafe me a word with you.

Hamlet. Sir, a whole history.

Guildenstern. The King, sir—

Hamlet. Ay, sir, what of him?

Guildenstern. Is in his retirement marvelous distempered.

302 distempered: upset. (Hamlet takes it in the sense of "drunk.")

Hamlet. With drink, sir?

Guildenstern. No, my lord, with choler.

304 choler: anger. (Hamlet takes it in the sense of "biliousness.")

Hamlet. Your wisdom should show itself more richer to signify this to the doctor, for for me to put him to his purgation would perhaps plunge him into more choler.

307 purgation: cleansing of the body of impurities; spiritual cleansing through confession.

Guildenstern. Good my lord, put your discourse into some frame and start not so wildly from my affair.

310 frame: order; **start:** shy away like a nervous or wild horse.

Hamlet. I am tame, sir. Pronounce.

Guildenstern. The Queen your mother, in most great affliction of spirit, hath sent me to you.

Hamlet. You are welcome.

Guildenstern. Nay, good my lord, this courtesy is not of the right breed. If it shall please you to make me a wholesome answer, I will do your mother's commandment. If not, your pardon and my return shall be the end of my business.

318 pardon: permission to leave.

Hamlet. Sir, I cannot.

Rosencrantz. What, my lord?

Hamlet. Make you a wholesome answer. My wit's diseased. But, sir, such answer as I can make, you shall command—or, rather, as you say, my mother. Therefore no more but to the matter. My mother, you say—

Rosencrantz. Then thus she says: your behavior hath struck her into amazement and admiration.

328 admiration: wonder.

Hamlet. O wonderful son that can so 'stonish a mother! But is there no sequel at the heels of this mother's admiration? Impart.

Rosencrantz. She desires to speak with you in her closet ere you go to bed.

332 closet: private room.

Hamlet. We shall obey, were she ten times our mother. Have you any further trade with us?

Rosencrantz. My lord, you once did love me.

Hamlet. And do still, by these pickers and stealers.

337 pickers and stealers: hands (from the Church catechism, "To keep my hands from picking and stealing").

Rosencrantz. Good my lord, what is your cause of distemper? You do surely bar the door upon your own liberty if you deny your griefs to your friend.

Hamlet. Sir, I lack advancement.

Rosencrantz. How can that be, when you have the voice of the King himself for your succession in Denmark?

Hamlet. Ay, sir, but "While the grass grows"—the proverb is something musty.

345–346 The rest of the stale (**musty**) proverb is "the horse starves," suggesting that Hamlet cannot wait so long.

[*Enter the* Players *with recorders.*]

O, the recorders! Let me see one. [*He takes a recorder and turns to* Guildenstern.] To withdraw with you: why do you go about to recover the wind of me, as if you would drive me into a toil?

348–350 withdraw: speak privately. Hamlet uses a hunting metaphor: The hunter moves to the windward side of the prey, causing it to flee toward a net (**toil**).

Guildenstern. O, my lord, if my duty be too bold, my love is too unmannerly.

Hamlet. I do not well understand that. Will you play upon this pipe?

Guildenstern. My lord, I cannot.

Hamlet. I pray you.

Guildenstern. Believe me, I cannot.

Hamlet. I do beseech you.

Guildenstern. I know no touch of it, my lord.

Hamlet. It is as easy as lying. Govern these ventages with your fingers and thumb, give it breath with your mouth, and it will discourse most eloquent music. Look you, these are the stops.

360 ventages: stops, or finger holes, on the recorder.

Guildenstern. But these cannot I command to any utt'rance of harmony. I have not the skill.

Hamlet. Why, look you now, how unworthy a thing you make of me! You would play upon me, you would seem to know my stops, you would pluck out the heart of my mystery, you would sound me from my lowest note to the top of my compass; and there is much music, excellent voice, in this little organ, yet cannot you make it speak. 'Sblood,

369–375 sound me: play upon me like an instrument, investigate me; **compass:** an instrument's range; **organ:** musical instrument; **fret me:** annoy me (also punning on **frets,** the raised bars for fingering a stringed instrument).

do you think I am easier to be played on than a pipe? Call me what instrument you will, though you can fret me, you cannot play upon me.

[*Enter* Polonius.]

God bless you, sir.

Polonius. My lord, the Queen would speak with you, and presently.

Hamlet. Do you see yonder cloud that's almost in shape of a camel?

Polonius. By th' Mass, and 'tis like a camel indeed.

Hamlet. Methinks it is like a weasel.

Polonius. It is backed like a weasel.

Hamlet. Or like a whale.

Polonius. Very like a whale.

Hamlet. Then I will come to my mother by and by.

[*Aside.*] They fool me to the top of my bent.—I will come by and by.

Polonius. I will say so.

Hamlet. "By and by" is easily said. Leave me, friends.

[*All but* Hamlet *exit.*]

'Tis now the very witching time of night,
When churchyards yawn and hell itself breathes out
Contagion to this world. Now could I drink hot blood
And do such bitter business as the day
Would quake to look on. Soft, now to my mother.
O heart, lose not thy nature; let not ever
The soul of Nero enter this firm bosom.
Let me be cruel, not unnatural.
I will speak daggers to her, but use none.
My tongue and soul in this be hypocrites:
How in my words somever she be shent,
To give them seals never, my soul, consent.

[*He exits.*]

387 fool…bent: make me play the fool to the limits of my ability.

388 by and by: before long.

397 Nero: a Roman emperor who put his mother to death.

401–402 Hamlet tells himself that however much she is rebuked (**shent**) in his words, he must not put those words into action (**give them seals**).

Scene 3 *The castle.*

[*Enter* King, Rosencrantz, *and* Guildenstern.]

King. I like him not, nor stands it safe with us
To let his madness range. Therefore prepare you.
I your commission will forthwith dispatch,
And he to England shall along with you.
The terms of our estate may not endure
Hazard so near 's as doth hourly grow
Out of his brows.

Guildenstern. We will ourselves provide.
Most holy and religious fear it is
To keep those many many bodies safe
That live and feed upon your Majesty.

Rosencrantz. The single and peculiar life is bound
With all the strength and armor of the mind
To keep itself from noyance, but much more
That spirit upon whose weal depends and rests
The lives of many. The cess of majesty
Dies not alone, but like a gulf doth draw
What's near it with it; or it is a massy wheel
Fixed on the summit of the highest mount,
To whose huge spokes ten thousand lesser things
Are mortised and adjoined, which, when it falls,
Each small annexment, petty consequence,
Attends the boist'rous ruin. Never alone
Did the king sigh, but with a general groan.

King. Arm you, I pray you, to this speedy voyage,
For we will fetters put about this fear,
Which now goes too free-footed.

Rosencrantz. We will haste us.

[Rosencrantz *and* Guildenstern *exit.*]

[*Enter* Polonius.]

Polonius. My lord, he's going to his mother's closet.
Behind the arras I'll convey myself
To hear the process. I'll warrant she'll tax him home;
And, as you said (and wisely was it said),
'Tis meet that some more audience than a mother,
Since nature makes them partial, should o'erhear
The speech of vantage. Fare you well, my liege.
I'll call upon you ere you go to bed
And tell you what I know.

King. Thanks, dear my lord.

[Polonius *exits.*]

1 him: his behavior.

3 forthwith dispatch: have prepared at once.

5 The terms of our estate: my position as king.

6 near 's: near us.

11 single and peculiar: individual and private.

13 noyance: harm.

14 weal: well-being.

15 cess: cessation, decease.

16 gulf: whirlpool.

17–22 Rosencrantz alludes to Fortune's massive (**massy**) wheel, with the king traditionally shown on the top; when the king falls, everyone connected with him plunges as well.

24 Arm you: prepare yourself.

29 process: proceedings; **tax him home:** strongly rebuke him.

31 meet: fitting.

33 of vantage: in addition.

O, my offense is rank, it smells to heaven;
It hath the primal eldest curse upon 't,
A brother's murder. Pray can I not,
Though inclination be as sharp as will.
My stronger guilt defeats my strong intent,
And, like a man to double business bound,
I stand in pause where I shall first begin
And both neglect. What if this cursèd hand
Were thicker than itself with brother's blood?
Is there not rain enough in the sweet heavens
To wash it white as snow? Whereto serves mercy
But to confront the visage of offense?
And what's in prayer but this twofold force,
To be forestallèd ere we come to fall,
Or pardoned being down? Then I'll look up.
My fault is past. But, O, what form of prayer
Can serve my turn? "Forgive me my foul murder"?
That cannot be, since I am still possessed
Of those effects for which I did the murder:
My crown, mine own ambition, and my queen.
May one be pardoned and retain th' offense?
In the corrupted currents of this world,
Offense's gilded hand may shove by justice,
And oft 'tis seen the wicked prize itself
Buys out the law. But 'tis not so above:
There is no shuffling; there the action lies
In his true nature, and we ourselves compelled,
Even to the teeth and forehead of our faults,
To give in evidence. What then? What rests?
Try what repentance can. What can it not?
Yet what can it, when one cannot repent?
O wretched state! O bosom black as death!
O limèd soul, that, struggling to be free,
Art more engaged! Help, angels! Make assay.
Bow, stubborn knees, and heart with strings of steel
Be soft as sinews of the newborn babe.
All may be well.

[*He kneels.*]

[*Enter* Hamlet.]

Hamlet. Now might I do it pat, now he is a-praying,
And now I'll do 't.

[*He draws his sword.*]

And so he goes to heaven,
And so am I revenged. That would be scanned:
A villain kills my father, and for that,

37 primal eldest curse: the curse of Cain (the son of Adam and Eve who murdered his brother Abel).

46–47 Whereto… offense: What purpose does mercy serve other than to oppose condemnation?

56 th' offense: the benefits of the crime.

57–64 In the corrupt ways (**currents**) of this world, a rich offender can push aside justice, and often the law is bribed with stolen wealth. But that isn't the case in heaven, where there is no evasion (**shuffling**); the true nature of every deed lies exposed, and we must testify against ourselves.

64 rests: remains.

68 limèd: trapped like a bird caught in quicklime (a sticky substance).

69 engaged: entangled; **Make assay:** Make an attempt (addressed to himself).

73 pat: conveniently.

75 would be scanned: needs to be looked at carefully.

I, his sole son, do this same villain send
To heaven.
Why, this is hire and salary, not revenge.
He took my father grossly, full of bread,
With all his crimes broad blown, as flush as May;
And how his audit stands who knows save heaven.
But in our circumstance and course of thought
'Tis heavy with him. And am I then revenged
To take him in the purging of his soul,
When he is fit and seasoned for his passage?
No.
Up sword, and know thou a more horrid hent.

[*He sheathes his sword.*]

When he is drunk asleep, or in his rage,
Or in th' incestuous pleasure of his bed,
At game a-swearing, or about some act
That has no relish of salvation in 't—
Then trip him, that his heels may kick at heaven,
And that his soul may be as damned and black
As hell, whereto it goes. My mother stays.
This physic but prolongs thy sickly days.

[Hamlet *exits.*]

King [*rising*]. My words fly up, my thoughts remain below;
Words without thoughts never to heaven go.

[*He exits.*]

79 hire and salary: something Claudius should pay me to do.

80–84 Hamlet complains that his father was killed without allowing him spiritual preparation (**grossly**). He was immersed in worldly pleasures and his sins were in full bloom. Only heaven knows how his final account stands, but from Hamlet's perspective his father's sins seem a heavy burden.

86 seasoned: prepared.

88 know thou a more horrid hent: wait to be grasped on a more horrible occasion.

95 stays: awaits me.

96 physic: medicine (referring to the postponement of revenge or to Claudius's act of prayer).

Scene 4 *The Queen's private chamber.*

[*Enter* Queen *and* Polonius.]

Polonius. He will come straight. Look you lay home to him.
Tell him his pranks have been too broad to bear with
And that your Grace hath screened and stood between
Much heat and him. I'll silence me even here.
Pray you, be round with him.

Hamlet [*within*]. Mother, mother, mother!

Queen. I'll warrant you. Fear me not. Withdraw,
I hear him coming.

[Polonius *hides behind the arras.*]

[*Enter* Hamlet.]

Hamlet. Now, mother, what's the matter?

Queen. Hamlet, thou hast thy father much offended.

Hamlet. Mother, you have my father much offended.

1 straight: right away; **lay home to:** strongly rebuke.

2 broad: unrestrained.

5 round: blunt.

Queen. Come, come, you answer with an idle tongue.

12 idle: foolish.

Hamlet. Go, go, you question with a wicked tongue.

Queen. Why, how now, Hamlet?

Hamlet. What's the matter now?

Queen. Have you forgot me?

15 forgot me: forgotten who I am; **rood:** cross.

Hamlet. No, by the rood, not so.
You are the Queen, your husband's brother's wife,
And (would it were not so) you are my mother.

Queen. Nay, then I'll set those to you that can speak.

Hamlet. Come, come, and sit you down; you shall not budge.
You go not till I set you up a glass
Where you may see the inmost part of you.

20 glass: mirror.

Queen. What wilt thou do? Thou wilt not murder me?
Help, ho!

Polonius [*behind the arras*]. What ho! Help!

Hamlet. How now, a rat? Dead for a ducat, dead.

25 Dead for a ducat: I'll wager a ducat that I kill him; I'll kill him for a ducat.

[*He kills* Polonius *by thrusting a rapier through the arras.*]

Polonius [*behind the arras*]. O, I am slain!

Queen. O me, what hast thou done?

Hamlet. Nay, I know not. Is it the King?

Queen. O, what a rash and bloody deed is this!

Hamlet. A bloody deed—almost as bad, good mother,
As kill a king and marry with his brother.

Queen. As kill a king?

Hamlet. Ay, lady, it was my word.

[*He pulls* Polonius' *body from behind the arras.*]

Thou wretched, rash, intruding fool, farewell.
I took thee for thy better. Take thy fortune.
Thou find'st to be too busy is some danger.

[*To* Queen.]

Leave wringing of your hands. Peace, sit you down,
And let me wring your heart; for so I shall
If it be made of penetrable stuff,
If damnèd custom have not brazed it so
That it be proof and bulwark against sense.

Queen. What have I done, that thou dar'st wag thy tongue
In noise so rude against me?

Hamlet. Such an act
That blurs the grace and blush of modesty,
Calls virtue hypocrite, takes off the rose
From the fair forehead of an innocent love
And sets a blister there, makes marriage vows
As false as dicers' oaths—O, such a deed
As from the body of contraction plucks
The very soul, and sweet religion makes
A rhapsody of words! Heaven's face does glow
O'er this solidity and compound mass
With heated visage, as against the doom,
Is thought-sick at the act.

Queen. Ay me, what act
That roars so loud and thunders in the index?

Hamlet. Look here upon this picture and on this,
The counterfeit presentment of two brothers.
See what a grace was seated on this brow,
Hyperion's curls, the front of Jove himself,
An eye like Mars' to threaten and command,
A station like the herald Mercury
New-lighted on a heaven-kissing hill,
A combination and a form indeed
Where every god did seem to set his seal
To give the world assurance of a man.

34 too busy: too much of a busybody.

38–39 If…sense: if habitual wickedness (**damnèd custom**) has not so hardened (**brazed**) your heart that it has become armor (**proof**) and fortification against feeling (**sense**).

47 contraction: the marriage contract.

48 sweet religion: marriage vows.

49 rhapsody: senseless jumble.

49–52 Heaven's face looks down shamefully and is sick with sorrow.

53 index: introduction.

55 counterfeit presentment: portraits.

57 Hyperion: the sun god; **front:** brow.

59–60 A station…hill: a stance like that of the winged messenger of the gods.

This was your husband. Look you now what follows.
Here is your husband, like a mildewed ear
Blasting his wholesome brother. Have you eyes?
Could you on this fair mountain leave to feed
And batten on this moor? Ha! Have you eyes?
You cannot call it love, for at your age
The heyday in the blood is tame, it's humble
And waits upon the judgment; and what judgment
Would step from this to this? Sense sure you have,
Else could you not have motion; but sure that sense
Is apoplexed; for madness would not err,
Nor sense to ecstasy was ne'er so thralled,
But it reserved some quantity of choice
To serve in such a difference. What devil was 't
That thus hath cozened you at hoodman-blind?
Eyes without feeling, feeling without sight,
Ears without hands or eyes, smelling sans all,
Or but a sickly part of one true sense
Could not so mope. O shame, where is thy blush?
Rebellious hell,
If thou canst mutine in a matron's bones,
To flaming youth let virtue be as wax
And melt in her own fire. Proclaim no shame
When the compulsive ardor gives the charge,
Since frost itself as actively doth burn,
And reason panders will.

Queen. O Hamlet, speak no more!
Thou turn'st my eyes into my very soul,
And there I see such black and grainèd spots
As will not leave their tinct.

Hamlet. Nay, but to live
In the rank sweat of an enseamèd bed,
Stewed in corruption, honeying and making love
Over the nasty sty!

Queen. O, speak to me no more!
These words like daggers enter in my ears.
No more, sweet Hamlet!

Hamlet. A murderer and a villain,
A slave that is not twentieth part the tithe
Of your precedent lord; a vice of kings,
A cutpurse of the empire and the rule,
That from a shelf the precious diadem stole
And put it in his pocket—

Queen. No more!

Hamlet. A king of shreds and patches—

65–66 Hamlet uses the metaphor of a **mildewed ear** of grain that is blighting (**blasting**) a nearby healthy plant.

68 batten on: grow fat from feeding on; **moor:** barren land.

70 heyday in the blood: sexual excitement.

72–78 Hamlet says that her senses must be paralyzed, because madness would let her choose correctly between Claudius and Hamlet's father. He wonders what devil tricked her in a game.

80 sans all: without the other senses.

82 so mope: be so dazed.

83–89 If hell can stir up rebellion in an older woman's bones, then in young people virtue should be like a candle melting in its own flame.

92 grainèd: ingrained, indelible.

93 leave their tinct: lose their color, fade.

94 enseamèd: greasy, sweaty.

100 tithe: tenth part.

101 vice: buffoon. (The Vice was a clownish villain in medieval morality plays.)

102 cutpurse: thief.

103 diadem: crown.

106 shreds and patches: referring to the patchwork costume of clowns or fools.

[*Enter* Ghost.]
Save me and hover o'er me with your wings,
You heavenly guards!— What would your gracious figure?

Queen. Alas, he's mad.

Hamlet. Do you not come your tardy son to chide,
That, lapsed in time and passion, lets go by
Th' important acting of your dread command?
O, say!

Ghost. Do not forget. This visitation
Is but to whet thy almost blunted purpose.
But look, amazement on thy mother sits.
O, step between her and her fighting soul.
Conceit in weakest bodies strongest works.
Speak to her, Hamlet.

Hamlet. How is it with you, lady?

Queen. Alas, how is 't with you,
That you do bend your eye on vacancy
And with th' incorporal air do hold discourse?
Forth at your eyes your spirits wildly peep,
And, as the sleeping soldiers in th' alarm,
Your bedded hair, like life in excrements,
Start up and stand an end. O gentle son,
Upon the heat and flame of thy distemper
Sprinkle cool patience! Whereon do you look?

Hamlet. On him, on him! Look you how pale he glares.
His form and cause conjoined, preaching to stones,
Would make them capable. [*To the* Ghost.] Do not
look upon me,
Lest with this piteous action you convert
My stern effects. Then what I have to do
Will want true color—tears perchance for blood.

Queen. To whom do you speak this?

Hamlet. Do you see nothing there?

Queen. Nothing at all; yet all that is I see.

Hamlet. Nor did you nothing hear?

Queen. No, nothing but ourselves.

Hamlet. Why, look you there, look how it steals away!
My father, in his habit as he lived!
Look where he goes even now out at the portal!

[Ghost *exits*.]

111 lapsed in time and passion: having let time pass and my passion cool.

116 amazement: bewilderment, shock.

118 Conceit: imagination.

122 incorporal: immaterial.

124–126 Like soldiers awakened by an alarm, your smoothly laid (**bedded**) hair—as if there were life in this outgrowth (**excrements**)—jumps up and stands on end.

130 conjoined: joined together.

131 them capable: the stones responsive.

132–133 convert… effects: alter the stern impression I give.

134 want: lack.

141 in his habit as he lived: in the clothes he wore when alive.

Queen. This is the very coinage of your brain.
This bodiless creation ecstasy
Is very cunning in.

Hamlet. Ecstasy?
My pulse as yours doth temperately keep time
And makes as healthful music. It is not madness
That I have uttered. Bring me to the test,
And I the matter will reword, which madness
Would gambol from. Mother, for love of grace,
Lay not that flattering unction to your soul
That not your trespass but my madness speaks.
It will but skin and film the ulcerous place,
Whiles rank corruption, mining all within,
Infects unseen. Confess yourself to heaven,
Repent what's past, avoid what is to come,
And do not spread the compost on the weeds
To make them ranker. Forgive me this my virtue,
For, in the fatness of these pursy times,
Virtue itself of vice must pardon beg,
Yea, curb and woo for leave to do him good.

Queen. O Hamlet, thou hast cleft my heart in twain!

Hamlet. O, throw away the worser part of it,
And live the purer with the other half!
Good night. But go not to my uncle's bed.
Assume a virtue if you have it not.
That monster, custom, who all sense doth eat,
Of habits devil, is angel yet in this,
That to the use of actions fair and good
He likewise gives a frock or livery
That aptly is put on. Refrain tonight,
And that shall lend a kind of easiness
To the next abstinence, the next more easy;
For use almost can change the stamp of nature
And either . . . the devil or throw him out
With wondrous potency. Once more, good night,
And, when you are desirous to be blest,
I'll blessing beg of you. For this same lord

[*Pointing to* Polonius.]

I do repent; but heaven hath pleased it so
To punish me with this and this with me,
That I must be their scourge and minister.
I will bestow him and will answer well
The death I gave him. So, again, good night.
I must be cruel only to be kind.

144–145 Madness (**ecstasy**) is very skillful at creating this kind of hallucination (**bodiless creation**).

148–155 Hamlet tells his mother to make him repeat his description word for word, a test that madness would skip (**gambol**) away from. He asks her not to use his madness rather than her misdeeds to explain this visitation; such a soothing ointment (**unction**) would merely cover up the sore on her soul, allowing the infection within to grow unseen.

158 this my virtue: my virtuous talk.

159 fatness: grossness; **pursy:** flabby, bloated.

161 curb: bow; **leave:** permission.

167–171 Custom, which consumes our awareness of the evil we habitually do, can also make us grow used to performing good actions.

174 stamp of nature: the traits we are born with.

175 A word seems to be missing in this line.

180 this: Polonius.

181 their scourge and minister: heaven's agent of retribution.

182 answer well: explain.

This bad begins, and worse remains behind.
One word more, good lady.

Queen. What shall I do?

Hamlet. Not this by no means that I bid you do:
Let the bloat king tempt you again to bed,
Pinch wanton on your cheek, call you his mouse,
And let him, for a pair of reechy kisses
Or paddling in your neck with his damned fingers,
Make you to ravel all this matter out
That I essentially am not in madness,
But mad in craft. 'Twere good you let him know,
For who that's but a queen, fair, sober, wise,
Would from a paddock, from a bat, a gib,
Such dear concernings hide? Who would do so?
No, in despite of sense and secrecy,
Unpeg the basket on the house's top,
Let the birds fly, and like the famous ape,
To try conclusions, in the basket creep
And break your own neck down.

Queen. Be thou assured, if words be made of breath
And breath of life, I have no life to breathe
What thou hast said to me.

Hamlet. I must to England, you know that.

Queen. Alack,
I had forgot! 'Tis so concluded on.

Hamlet. There's letters sealed; and my two schoolfellows,
Whom I will trust as I will adders fanged,
They bear the mandate; they must sweep my way
And marshal me to knavery. Let it work,
For 'tis the sport to have the enginer
Hoist with his own petard; and 't shall go hard
But I will delve one yard below their mines
And blow them at the moon. O, 'tis most sweet
When in one line two crafts directly meet.
This man shall set me packing.
I'll lug the guts into the neighbor room.
Mother, good night indeed. This counselor
Is now most still, most secret, and most grave,
Who was in life a foolish prating knave.—
Come, sir, to draw toward an end with you.
Good night, mother.

[*They exit,* Hamlet *tugging in* Polonius.]

185 remains behind: is still to come.

188 bloat: bloated.

189 mouse: a term of endearment.

190 reechy: filthy.

191 paddling in: fingering on.

194 in craft: by clever design or action.

194–202 Although Hamlet has asked his mother not to let Claudius use sexual attentions to unravel the secret that Hamlet is only pretending to be mad, he now sarcastically urges her to go ahead and tell Claudius. He refers to a story about an ape that died trying to imitate the flight of birds it released from a cage, hinting that the Queen will get hurt if she lets out her secret.

208–211 Rosencrantz and Guildenstern have been commanded to escort Hamlet to some treachery.

212–213 to have… petard: to have the maker of military devices blown up (**hoist**) by his own bomb (**petard**).

213–214 and 't… I will: unless I have bad luck I will; **mines:** tunnels.

216 crafts: plots, crafty schemes.

217 Polonius's death will force Hamlet to leave in a hurry.

222 to draw toward an end: to finish up.

Analyzing the Text

RL 1, RL 4, RL 6, SL 1

Cite Text Evidence Support your responses with evidence from the selection.

1. **Interpret** What does Claudius's aside in Scene 1, lines 50–55, reveal about him?
2. **Draw Conclusions** Hamlet's command "Get thee to a nunnery" (Scene 1, line 122) can be interpreted in two ways. Either he wants Ophelia to retreat to a convent, safe from the corruption of the world, or he thinks she is so tainted that she belongs in a brothel. Choose the interpretation that is best supported by his behavior toward her in this scene, and explain your choice. What has caused him to feel this way?
3. **Analyze** Reread lines 58–76 in Scene 2. What does Hamlet admire about Horatio? How does Shakespeare use Horatio to help develop the play's plot?
4. **Analyze** When a character says one thing but means another, it is called **verbal irony.** Find an example of verbal irony in Hamlet's conversation with Claudius and Gertrude in Scene 2, lines 230–236. What message is Hamlet really conveying?
5. **Analyze** An **extended metaphor** is a metaphor in which two things are compared at length and in various ways. Review Hamlet's dialogue in Scene 2, lines 353–375. In what ways does he compare himself to a musical instrument? Is his attitude toward Rosencrantz and Guildenstern consistent with his behavior toward them in Act II, Scene 2, or does this speech signal a change? Explain.
6. **Identify Patterns** How does Hamlet's refusal to kill Claudius while he is praying relate back to what the Ghost said about the circumstances of his own death in Act I, Scene 5?
7. **Draw Conclusions** Hamlet confronts his mother in Scene 4, and she responds with expressions of guilt. Does she seem to realize that Claudius murdered Hamlet's father? Explain why or why not.
8. **Synthesize** Soon after Hamlet decides against killing Claudius while he is praying, he mistakes Polonius for the King and kills him without hesitation. What does this combination of events suggest about revenge?

PERFORMANCE TASK

Speaking Activity: Performance Act out a brief scene or a section of a longer scene.

- In a small group, choose a scene and decide which role will be played by each member.
- Read the scene aloud. Discuss the motivation of each character.
- Decide where performers will enter or exit and where they will stand while reciting the dialogue. Read the stage directions to determine if any sound or lighting effects are needed.
- Perform the scene in front of the class.

ACT IV

Scene 1 *The Castle.*

[*Enter* King *and* Queen, *with* Rosencrantz *and* Guildenstern.]

King. There's matter in these sighs; these profound
heaves
You must translate; 'tis fit we understand them.
Where is your son?

Queen. Bestow this place on us a little while.

[Rosencrantz *and* Guildenstern *exit.*]

Ah, mine own lord, what have I seen tonight!

King. What, Gertrude? How does Hamlet?

Queen. Mad as the sea and wind when both contend
Which is the mightier. In his lawless fit,
Behind the arras hearing something stir,
Whips out his rapier, cries "A rat, a rat,"
And in this brainish apprehension kills
The unseen good old man.

King. O heavy deed!
It had been so with us, had we been there.
His liberty is full of threats to all—
To you yourself, to us, to everyone.
Alas, how shall this bloody deed be answered?
It will be laid to us, whose providence
Should have kept short, restrained, and out of haunt
This mad young man. But so much was our love,
We would not understand what was most fit,
But, like the owner of a foul disease,
To keep it from divulging, let it feed
Even on the pith of life. Where is he gone?

Queen. To draw apart the body he hath killed,
O'er whom his very madness, like some ore
Among a mineral of metals base,
Shows itself pure: he weeps for what is done.

King. O Gertrude, come away!
The sun no sooner shall the mountains touch
But we will ship him hence; and this vile deed
We must with all our majesty and skill
Both countenance and excuse.—Ho, Guildenstern!

[*Enter* Rosencrantz *and* Guildenstern.]

Friends both, go join you with some further aid.
Hamlet in madness hath Polonius slain,

1 matter: significance.

11 brainish apprehension: frenzied belief.

17–19 Claudius worries that the death will be blamed on him (**laid to us**) because he should have had the foresight (**providence**) to keep Hamlet restrained (**short**) and isolated (**out of haunt**).

22 divulging: being revealed.

25–26 O're . . . mineral: vein of gold in a mine.

32 countenance: accept.

33 some further aid: others who can help.

Image Credits: ©John Kobal Foundation/Moviepix/Getty Images

And from his mother's closet hath he dragged him.
Go seek him out, speak fair, and bring the body
Into the chapel. I pray you, haste in this.

[Rosencrantz *and* Guildenstern *exit.*]

Come, Gertrude, we'll call up our wisest friends
And let them know both what we mean to do
And what's untimely done. . . .
Whose whisper o'er the world's diameter,
As level as the cannon to his blank
Transports his poisoned shot, may miss our name
And hit the woundless air. O, come away!
My soul is full of discord and dismay.
[*They exit.*]

40–44 Some words are missing after "untimely done" in line 40. Many editors insert "So haply slander" or a similar phrase. Claudius is hoping that slander, which hits as directly as a cannon fired at point-blank range hits its target, will miss the royal household.

Scene 2 *The Castle.*

[*Enter* Hamlet.]

Hamlet. Safely stowed.

Gentlemen [*within*]. Hamlet! Lord Hamlet!

Hamlet. But soft, what noise? Who calls on Hamlet?
O, here they come.

[*Enter* Rosencrantz, Guildenstern, *and others.*]

Rosencrantz. What have you done, my lord, with the dead body?

Hamlet. Compounded it with dust, whereto 'tis kin.

Rosencrantz. Tell us where 'tis, that we may take it thence
And bear it to the chapel.

Hamlet. Do not believe it.

Rosencrantz. Believe what?

Hamlet. That I can keep your counsel and not mine own. Besides, to be demanded of a sponge, what replication should be made by the son of a king?

Rosencrantz. Take you me for a sponge, my lord?

Hamlet. Ay, sir, that soaks up the King's countenance, his rewards, his authorities. But such officers do the King best service in the end. He keeps them like an ape an apple in the corner of his jaw, first mouthed, to be last swallowed. When he needs

6 compounded: mixed. Hamlet alludes to Genesis 3.19: "dust thou art, and unto dust shalt thou return."

12 demanded of: questioned by.

13 replication: response.

15 countenance: favor.

17–18 like an ape . . . jaw: as an ape keeps food in the corner of its mouth.

what you have gleaned, it is but squeezing you, and, sponge, you shall be dry again.

Rosencrantz. I understand you not, my lord.

Hamlet. I am glad of it. A knavish speech sleeps in a foolish ear.

Rosencrantz. My lord, you must tell us where the body is and go with us to the King.

Hamlet. The body is with the King, but the King is not with the body. The King is a thing—

Guildenstern. A "thing," my lord?

Hamlet. Of nothing. Bring me to him. Hide fox, and all after!

[*They exit.*]

Scene 3 *The castle.*

[*Enter* King *and two or three.*]

King. I have sent to seek him and to find the body.
How dangerous is it that this man goes loose!
Yet must not we put the strong law on him.
He's loved of the distracted multitude,
Who like not in their judgment, but their eyes;
And, where 'tis so, th' offender's scourge is weighed,
But never the offense. To bear all smooth and even,
This sudden sending him away must seem
Deliberate pause. Diseases desperate grown
By desperate appliance are relieved
Or not at all.

[*Enter* Rosencrantz.]

How now, what hath befallen?

Rosencrantz. Where the dead body is bestowed, my lord,
We cannot get from him.

King. But where is he?

Rosencrantz. Without, my lord; guarded, to know your pleasure.

King. Bring him before us.

Rosencrantz. Ho! Bring in the lord.

[*They enter with* Hamlet.]

King. Now, Hamlet, where's Polonius?

Hamlet. At supper.

King. At supper where?

23 sleeps in: is meaningless to.

27–30 Hamlet may be playing off the idea that the king occupies two "bodies": his own mortal body and the office of kingship. Claudius is a king of no account (**of nothing**); the office of kingship does not belong to him.

30 Hide fox . . . after: a cry from a children's game such as hide-and-seek.

4–5 He's loved . . . eyes: He's loved by the confused masses, who choose not by judgment but by appearance.

6 scourge: punishment.

7 To bear . . . even: to manage everything smoothly and evenly.

9 Deliberate pause: carefully thought out.

9–11 Diseases . . . all: Desperate diseases require desperate remedies.

19–21 Hamlet says that a group of crafty (**politic**) worms are dining on him.

Hamlet. Not where he eats, but where he is eaten. A certain convocation of politic worms are e'en at him. Your worm is your only emperor for diet. We fat all creatures else to fat us, and we fat ourselves for maggots. Your fat king and your lean beggar is but variable service—two dishes but to one table. That's the end.

21 Your . . . diet: Worms have the last word when it comes to eating.

24 but variable service: only different courses (of a meal).

King. Alas, alas!

Hamlet. A man may fish with the worm that hath eat of a king and eat of the fish that hath fed of that worm.

King. What dost thou mean by this?

Hamlet. Nothing but to show you how a king may go a progress through the guts of a beggar.

32 progress: royal journey.

King. Where is Polonius?

Hamlet. In heaven. Send thither to see. If your messenger find him not there, seek him i' th' other place yourself. But if, indeed, you find him not within this month, you shall nose him as you go up the stairs into the lobby.

King [*to* Attendants]. Go, seek him there.

Hamlet. He will stay till you come.

[Attendants *exit.*]

King. Hamlet, this deed, for thine especial safety
(Which we do tender, as we dearly grieve
For that which thou hast done) must send thee hence
With fiery quickness. Therefore prepare thyself.
The bark is ready, and the wind at help,
Th' associates tend, and everything is bent
For England.

42 tender: regard, hold dear.

45–47 Claudius says that the sailing vessel (**bark**) is ready, the wind is favorable (**at help**), his fellow travellers wait (**tend**) for him, and everything is ready (**bent**).

Hamlet. For England?

King. Ay, Hamlet.

Hamlet. Good.

King. So is it, if thou knew'st our purposes.

Hamlet. I see a cherub that sees them. But come, for England.
Farewell, dear mother.

52 cherub: angel of knowledge.

King. Thy loving father, Hamlet.

Hamlet. My mother. Father and mother is man and wife,
Man and wife is one flesh, and so, my mother.—
Come, for England.

[*He exits.*]

King. Follow him at foot; tempt him with speed aboard.
Delay it not. I'll have him hence tonight.
Away, for everything is sealed and done
That else leans on th' affair. Pray you, make haste.

[*All but the* King *exit.*]

And England, if my love thou hold'st at aught
(As my great power thereof may give thee sense,
Since yet thy cicatrice looks raw and red
After the Danish sword, and thy free awe
Pays homage to us), thou mayst not coldly set
Our sovereign process, which imports at full,
By letters congruing to that effect,
The present death of Hamlet. Do it, England,
For like the hectic in my blood he rages,
And thou must cure me. Till I know 'tis done,
Howe'er my haps, my joys were ne'er begun.

[*He exits.*]

57 at foot: closely.

60 leans on: is related to.

61–68 Claudius says that if the King of England values his friendship, he will not ignore Claudius's command to have Hamlet killed immediately.

69 hectic: fever.

71 Howe'er my haps: whatever my fortunes.

Scene 4 *Near the coast of Denmark.*

[*Enter* Fortinbras *with his army over the stage.*]

Fortinbras. Go, Captain, from me greet the Danish king.
Tell him that by his license Fortinbras
Craves the conveyance of a promised march
Over his kingdom. You know the rendezvous.
If that his Majesty would aught with us,
We shall express our duty in his eye;
And let him know so.

Captain. I will do 't, my lord.

Fortinbras. Go softly on.

[*All but the* Captain *exit.*]

[*Enter* Hamlet, Rosencrantz, Guildenstern, *and others.*]

Hamlet. Good sir, whose powers are these?

Captain. They are of Norway, sir.

Hamlet. How purposed, sir, I pray you?

Captain. Against some part of Poland.

Hamlet. Who commands them, sir?

Captain. The nephew to old Norway, Fortinbras.

2 license: permission.

3 the conveyance of: escort during.

5–7 Fortinbras says that if the King wishes to see him, he will show his respect in person (**in his eye**).

9 softly: slowly, carefully.

10 powers: forces.

Hamlet. Goes it against the main of Poland, sir,
Or for some frontier?

Captain. Truly to speak, and with no addition,
We go to gain a little patch of ground
That hath in it no profit but the name.
To pay five ducats, five, I would not farm it;
Nor will it yield to Norway or the Pole
A ranker rate, should it be sold in fee.

Hamlet. Why, then, the Polack never will defend it.

Captain. Yes, it is already garrisoned.

Hamlet. Two thousand souls and twenty thousand ducats
Will not debate the question of this straw.
This is th' impostume of much wealth and peace,
That inward breaks and shows no cause without
Why the man dies.—I humbly thank you, sir.

Captain. God be wi' you, sir.

[*He exits.*]

Rosencrantz. Will 't please you go, my lord?

Hamlet. I'll be with you straight. Go a little before.

[*All but* Hamlet *exit.*]

How all occasions do inform against me
And spur my dull revenge. What is a man
If his chief good and market of his time
Be but to sleep and feed? A beast, no more.
Sure He that made us with such large discourse,
Looking before and after, gave us not
That capability and godlike reason
To fust in us unused. Now whether it be
Bestial oblivion or some craven scruple
Of thinking too precisely on th' event
(A thought which, quartered, hath but one part wisdom
And ever three parts coward), I do not know
Why yet I live to say "This thing's to do,"
Sith I have cause, and will, and strength, and means
To do 't. Examples gross as earth exhort me:
Witness this army of such mass and charge,
Led by a delicate and tender prince,
Whose spirit with divine amibition puffed

16 the main: the main part.

18 Truly . . . addition: to speak plainly.

21 To pay . . . it: I would not pay even five ducats a year to rent it.

23 ranker: higher; **in fee:** outright.

27 Will not . . . straw: are not enough to settle this trifling dispute.

28 impostume: puss-filled swelling.

29 without: on the outside.

34 inform against: denounce.

36 market: profit.

38–41 Sure He . . . unused: God would not have given us such a considerable power of reasoning to let it grow moldy from lack of use.

42–43 Bestial . . . event: beast-like forgetfulness or cowardly hesitation from thinking too carefully about the outcome.

48 gross: obvious.

Makes mouths at the invisible event,
Exposing what is mortal and unsure
To all that fortune, death, and danger dare,
Even for an eggshell. Rightly to be great
Is not to stir without great argument,
But greatly to find quarrel in a straw
When honor's at the stake. How stand I, then,
That have a father killed, a mother stained,
Excitements of my reason and my blood,
And let all sleep, while to my shame I see
The imminent death of twenty thousand men
That for a fantasy and trick of fame
Go to their graves like beds, fight for a plot
Whereon the numbers cannot try the cause,
Which is not tomb enough and continent
To hide the slain? O, from this time forth
My thoughts be bloody or be nothing worth!

[*He exits.*]

52 Makes mouths . . . event: makes scornful faces at the unforeseeable outcome.

55–58 True greatness does not lie in refraining from action when there is no great cause but in the willingness to fight whenever honor is at stake.

63 fantasy and trick of fame: illusion of honor.

65–67 Whereon . . . slain: The disputed land does not have enough room for so many men to battle on and is too small a burial ground to hold those who will be killed.

Scene 5 *The castle.*

[*Enter* Horatio, Queen, *and a* Gentleman.]

Queen. I will not speak with her.

Gentleman. She is importunate,
Indeed distract; her mood will needs be pitied.

Queen. What would she have?

Gentleman. She speaks much of her father, says she hears
There's tricks i' th' world, and hems, and beats her heart,
Spurns enviously at straws, speaks things in doubt
That carry but half sense. Her speech is nothing,
Yet the unshaped use of it doth move
The hearers to collection. They aim at it
And botch the words up fit to their own thoughts;
Which, as her winks and nods and gestures yield them,
Indeed would make one think there might be thought,
Though nothing sure, yet much unhappily.

Horatio. 'Twere good she were spoken with, for she may strew
Dangerous conjectures in ill-breeding minds.

Queen. Let her come in.

[Gentleman *exits.*]

[*Aside*] To my sick soul (as sin's true nature is),
Each toy seems prologue to some great amiss.

3 distract: distracted; **mood . . . pitied:** state of mind must be pitied.

6 tricks: deception.

7 Spurns enviously at straws: takes offense at trifles; **in doubt:** without clear meaning.

8–11 Although Ophelia speaks nonsense, her confused manner of speaking moves her listeners to gather some meaning by patching her words together to fit their conjectures.

16 ill-breeding: intent on making trouble.

19 toy: trifle; **amiss:** misfortune.

So full of artless jealousy is guilt,
It spills itself in fearing to be spilt.

[*Enter* Ophelia *distracted.*]

Ophelia. Where is the beauteous Majesty of Denmark?

Queen. How now, Ophelia?

Ophelia [*sings*]. *How should I your true love know*
From another one?
By his cockle hat and staff
And his sandal shoon.

Queen. Alas, sweet lady, what imports this song?

Ophelia. Say you? Nay, pray you, mark.
[*Sings.*] *He is dead and gone, lady,*
He is dead and gone;
At his head a grass-green turf,
At his heels a stone.

Oh, ho!

Queen. Nay, but Ophelia—

Ophelia. Pray you, mark.

[*Sings.*] *White his shroud as the mountain snow—*

[*Enter* King.]

Queen. Alas, look here, my lord.

Ophelia [*sings*]. *Larded all with sweet flowers;*
Which bewept to the ground did not go
With true-love showers.

King. How do you, pretty lady?

Ophelia. Well, God dild you. They say the owl was a baker's daughter. Lord, we know what we are but know not what we may be. God be at your table.

King. Conceit upon her father.

Ophelia. Pray let's have no words of this, but when they ask you what it means, say you this:
[*Sings.*] *Tomorrow is Saint Valentine's day,*
All in the morning betime,
And I a maid at your window,
To be your Valentine.
Then up he rose and donned his clothes
And dupped the chamber door,
Let in the maid, that out a maid
Never departed more.

King. Pretty Ophelia—

20–21 Guilt is so full of clumsy suspicion (**artless jealousy**) that it reveals (**spills**) itself through fear of being revealed.

26 cockle hat: a hat with a scallop shell (worn by pilgrims to show that they had been to an overseas shrine).

27 shoon: shoes.

28 imports: means.

39 Larded: decorated.

41 showers: tears

43 God dild you: God yield, or reward, you.

43–44 Ophelia refers to a legend about a baker's daughter who was turned into an owl because she refused to give Christ bread.

46 Conceit: brooding.

49–67 This song refers to the ancient custom that the first maiden a man sees on St. Valentine's Day will be his sweetheart.

54 dupped: opened.

Ophelia. Indeed, without an oath, I'll make an end on 't:
[*Sings.*] *By Gis and by Saint Charity,*
Alack and fie for shame,
Young men will do 't, if they come to 't;
By Cock, they are to blame.
Quoth she "Before you tumbled me,
You promised me to wed."
He answers:
"So would I 'a done, by yonder sun,
An thou hadst not come to my bed."

King. How long hath she been thus?

Ophelia. I hope all will be well. We must be patient, but I cannot choose but weep to think they would lay him i' th' cold ground. My brother shall know of it. And so I thank you for your good counsel. Come, my coach! Good night, ladies, good night, sweet ladies, good night, good night.

[*She exits.*]

King. Follow her close; give her good watch, I pray you.

[Horatio *exits.*]

O, this is the poison of deep grief. It springs
All from her father's death, and now behold!
O Gertrude, Gertrude,
When sorrows come, they come not single spies,
But in battalions: first, her father slain;
Next, your son gone, and he most violent author
Of his own just remove; the people muddied,
Thick, and unwholesome in their thoughts and whispers
For good Polonius' death, and we have done but greenly
In hugger-mugger to inter him; poor Ophelia
Divided from herself and her fair judgment,
Without the which we are pictures or mere beasts;
Last, and as much containing as all these,
Her brother is in secret come from France,
Feeds on his wonder, keeps himself in clouds,
And wants not buzzers to infect his ear
With pestilent speeches of his father's death,
Wherein necessity, of matter beggared,
Will nothing stick our person to arraign
In ear and ear. O, my dear Gertrude, this,
Like to a murd'ring piece, in many places
Gives me superfluous death.

59 Gis: Jesus.

62 Cock: a substitution for "God" in oaths.

63 tumbled: had sexual intercourse with.

79 spies: soldiers sent ahead as scouts.

82 muddied: confused.

84–85 Claudius says that he has only acted foolishly (**greenly**) by burying Polonius in haste and secrecy.

89–95 Laertes, who has secretly returned from France, is clouded by suspicion and does not lack gossipers who spread rumors of his father's death. And in the absence of facts, the need for some explanation means that Claudius will be accused of the crime.

96 murd'ring piece: a cannon that can kill many men simultaneously with its scattered shot.

97 Gives . . . death: kills me over and over.

[*A noise within.*]

Queen. Alack, what noise is this?

King. Attend!
Where is my Switzers? Let them guard the door.

100 Switzers: Swiss bodyguards.

[*Enter a* Messenger.]

What is the matter?

Messenger. Save yourself, my lord.
The ocean, overpeering of his list,
Eats not the flats with more impiteous haste
Than young Laertes, in a riotous head,
O'erbears your officers. The rabble call him "lord,"
And, as the world were now but to begin,
Antiquity forgot, custom not known,
The ratifiers and props of every word,
They cry "Choose we, Laertes shall be king!"
Caps, hands, and tongues applaud it to the clouds,
"Laertes shall be king! Laertes king!"

102–105 Laertes is overpowering Claudius's officers as quickly as the ocean, rising above its boundary (**list**), floods the level ground.

106–108 as the world . . . word: as if the world had just begun, and ancient tradition and custom, which should confirm and support everything one says, were both forgotten.

110 Caps: caps thrown into the air.

[*A noise within.*]

Queen. How cheerfully on the false trail they cry.
O, this is counter, you false Danish dogs!

113 counter: a hunting term that means "to follow a trail in the wrong direction."

King. The doors are broke.

[*Enter* Laertes *with others.*]

Laertes. Where is this king?—Sirs, stand you all without.

All. No, let's come in!

Laertes. I pray you, give me leave.

All. We will, we will.

Laertes. I thank you. Keep the door. [Followers *exit.*] O, thou vile king,
Give me my father!

Queen. Calmly, good Laertes.

Laertes. That drop of blood that's calm proclaims me bastard,
Cries "cuckold" to my father, brands the harlot
Even here between the chaste unsmirchèd brow
Of my true mother.

121–124 Laertes says that no true son could be calm about his father's murder—that being calm would in effect prove that son to be a bastard.

122 cuckold: a man whose wife is unfaithful.

124 true: faithful.

King. What is the cause, Laertes,
That thy rebellion looks so giant-like?—
Let him go, Gertrude. Do not fear our person.
There's such divinity doth hedge a king
That treason can but peep to what it would,

Acts little of his will.—Tell me, Laertes,
Why thou art thus incensed.—Let him go,
Gertrude.—
Speak, man.

Laertes. Where is my father?

King. Dead.

Queen. But not by him.

King. Let him demand his fill.

Laertes. How came he dead? I'll not be juggled with.
To hell, allegiance! Vows, to the blackest devil!
Conscience and grace, to the profoundest pit!
I dare damnation. To this point I stand,
That both the worlds I give to negligence,
Let come what comes, only I'll be revenged
Most throughly for my father.

King. Who shall stay you?

Laertes. My will, not all the world.
And for my means, I'll husband them so well
They shall go far with little.

King. Good Laertes,
If you desire to know the certainty
Of your dear father, is 't writ in your revenge
That, swoopstake, you will draw both friend and
foe,
Winner and loser?

Laertes. None but his enemies.

King. Will you know them, then?

Laertes. To his good friends thus wide I'll ope my arms
And, like the kind life-rend'ring pelican,
Repast them with my blood.

King. Why, now you speak
Like a good child and a true gentleman.
That I am guiltless of your father's death
And am most sensibly in grief for it,
It shall as level to your judgment 'pear
As day does to your eye.
[*A noise within*] Let her come in.

Laertes. How now, what noise is that?

[*Enter* Ophelia.]

O heat, dry up my brains! Tears seven times salt
Burn out the sense and virtue of mine eye!

126–129 Claudius tells Gertrude not to fear for his personal safety; so much divinity protects (**doth hedge**) a king that treason can only peer (**peep**) from afar at what it would like to do.

135 juggled with: played with, deceived.

144 husband: manage, conserve.

148 swoopstake: a gambling term that means taking all the stakes on the gambling table.

153 pelican: traditionally thought to feed its young with its own blood.

157 sensibly: feelingly.

158 level: plain.

162 virtue: power.

By heaven, thy madness shall be paid with weight
Till our scale turn the beam! O rose of May,
Dear maid, kind sister, sweet Ophelia!
O heavens, is 't possible a young maid's wits
Should be as mortal as an old man's life?
Nature is fine in love, and, where 'tis fine,
It sends some precious instance of itself
After the thing it loves.

Ophelia [*sings*]. *They bore him barefaced on the bier,*
Hey non nonny, nonny, hey nonny,
And in his grave rained many a tear.
Fare you well, my dove.

Laertes. Hadst thou thy wits and didst persuade revenge,
It could not move thus.

Ophelia. You must sing "A-down a-down"—and you "Call him a-down-a."—O, how the wheel becomes it! It is the false steward that stole his master's daughter.

Laertes. This nothing's more than matter.

Ophelia. There's rosemary, that's for remembrance. Pray you, love, remember. And there is pansies, that's for thoughts.

Laertes. A document in madness: thoughts and remembrance fitted.

Ophelia. There's fennel for you, and columbines. There's rue for you, and here's some for me; we may call it herb of grace o' Sundays. You must wear your rue with a difference. There's a daisy. I would give you some violets, but they withered all when my father died. They say he made a good end.
[*Sings.*] *For bonny sweet Robin is all my joy.*

Laertes. Thought and afflictions, passion, hell itself
She turns to favor and to prettiness.

Ophelia [*sings*].
And will he not come again?
And will he not come again?
No, no, he is dead.
Go to thy deathbed.
He never will come again.

His beard was as white as snow,
All flaxen was his poll.
He is gone, he is gone,
And we cast away moan.
God 'a mercy on his soul.

163–164 In his vow to revenge Ophelia's madness, Laertes uses the image of weights being placed on a scale to make it tilt in the opposite direction.

168–169 fine in: refined by; **instance:** token (suggesting that Ophelia has sent her sanity into the grave with her father).

175 persuade: argue rationally for.

176 move thus: have such an effect.

177–178 Ophelia assigns refrains to the others so they can join in the singing.

178 the wheel: perhaps referring to the refrain or a spinning wheel that accompanies the singing.

181 This . . . matter: This nonsense has more meaning than rational speech.

182–192 Rosemary was used to symbolize remembrance at funerals. **Pansies**, a name derived from the French word for thought, **pensée**, was associated with courtship. Ophelia also mentions **fennel** (flattery), **columbines** (adultery or ingratitude), **rue** (repentance, sorrow), the **daisy** (dissembling, false love) and **violets** (faithfulness).

185–186 Laertes finds a lesson (**document**) in Ophelia's linking of thoughts and remembrance.

194 Thought: melancholy; **passion:** suffering.

202 flaxen: pale yellow; **poll:** head.

204 cast away: scatter uselessly.

And of all Christians' souls, I pray God. God be
wi' you.

[*She exits.*]

Laertes. Do you see this, O God?

King. Laertes, I must commune with your grief,
Or you deny me right. Go but apart,
Make choice of whom your wisest friends you will,
And they shall hear and judge 'twixt you and me.
If by direct or by collateral hand
They find us touched, we will our kingdom give,
Our crown, our life, and all that we call ours,
To you in satisfaction; but if not,
Be you content to lend your patience to us,
And we shall jointly labor with your soul
To give it due content.

Laertes. Let this be so.
His means of death, his obscure funeral
(No trophy, sword, nor hatchment o'er his bones,
No noble rite nor formal ostentation)
Cry to be heard, as 'twere from heaven to earth,
That I must call 't in question.

King. So you shall,
And where th' offense is, let the great ax fall.
I pray you, go with me.

[*They exit.*]

213 collateral: indirect.

214 find us touched: find me implicated.

221–222 The traditional burial ceremony (**ostentation**) for a knight included hanging his helmet, sword, and a tablet displaying his coat of arms (**hatchment**) over the tomb.

224 That I . . . question: so that I must demand an explanation.

Scene 6 *The castle.*

[*Enter* Horatio *and others.*]

Horatio. What are they that would speak with me?

Gentleman. Seafaring men, sir. They say they have letters for you.

Horatio. Let them come in. [Gentleman *exits.*] I do not know from what part of the world I should be greeted, if not from Lord Hamlet.

[*Enter* Sailors.]

Sailor. God bless you, sir.

Horatio. Let Him bless thee too.

Sailor. He shall, sir, an 't please Him. There's a letter for you, sir. It came from th' ambassador that was bound for England—if your name be Horatio, as I am let to know it is.

9 an 't: if it.

10 th' ambassador: Hamlet.

[*He hands* Horatio *a letter.*]

Horatio [*reads the letter*]. *Horatio, when thou shalt have overlooked this, give these fellows some means to the King. They have letters for him. Ere we were two days old at sea, a pirate of very warlike appointment gave us chase. Finding ourselves too slow of sail, we put on a compelled valor, and in the grapple I boarded them. On the instant, they got clear of our ship; so I alone became their prisoner. They have dealt with me like thieves of mercy, but they knew what they did: I am to do a good turn for them. Let the King have the letters I have sent, and repair thou to me with as much speed as thou wouldst fly death. I have words to speak in thine ear will make thee dumb; yet are they much too light for the bore of the matter. These good fellows will bring thee where I am. Rosencrantz and Guildenstern hold their course for England; of them I have much to tell thee. Farewell.*
He that thou knowest thine, Hamlet.

Come, I will give you way for these your letters
And do 't the speedier that you may direct me
To him from whom you brought them.

[*They exit.*]

14 overlooked: read; **means:** means of access.

16–17 pirate . . . appointment: pirate ship well equipped for warfare.

21 thieves of mercy: merciful thieves.

22 they knew what they did: their actions were calculated.

24 repair: come.

27 light . . . bore: inadequate for the importance.

32 way: means of access.

Scene 7 *The castle.*

[*Enter* King *and* Laertes.]

King. Now must your conscience my acquittance seal,
And you must put me in your heart for friend,
Sith you have heard, and with a knowing ear,
That he which hath your noble father slain
Pursued my life.

Laertes. It well appears. But tell me
Why you proceeded not against these feats,
So criminal and so capital in nature,
As by your safety, greatness, wisdom, all things else,
You mainly were stirred up.

King. O, for two special reasons,
Which may to you perhaps seem much unsinewed,
But yet to me they're strong. The Queen his mother
Lives almost by his looks, and for myself
(My virtue or my plague, be it either which),

1 my acquittance seal: confirm my innocence.

3 Sith: since.

7 capital: punishable by death.

8 safety: concern for your safety.

9 mainly: greatly.

11 unsinewed: weak.

She is so conjunctive to my life and soul
That, as the star moves not but in his sphere,
I could not but by her. The other motive
Why to a public count I might not go
Is the great love the general gender bear him,
Who, dipping all his faults in their affection,
Work like the spring that turneth wood to stone,
Convert his gyves to graces, so that my arrows,
Too slightly timbered for so loud a wind,
Would have reverted to my bow again,
But not where I have aimed them.

Laertes. And so have I a noble father lost,
A sister driven into desp'rate terms,
Whose worth, if praises may go back again,
Stood challenger on mount of all the age
For her perfections. But my revenge will come.

King. Break not your sleeps for that. You must not think
That we are made of stuff so flat and dull
That we can let our beard be shook with danger
And think it pastime. You shortly shall hear more.
I loved your father, and we love ourself,
And that, I hope, will teach you to imagine—

[*Enter a* Messenger *with letters.*]

How now? What news?

Messenger. Letters, my lord, from Hamlet.
These to your Majesty, this to the Queen.

King. From Hamlet? Who brought them?

Messenger. Sailors, my lord, they say. I saw them not.
They were given me by Claudio. He received them
Of him that brought them.

King. Laertes, you shall hear them.—
Leave us.

[Messenger *exits.*]

[*Reads.*] *High and mighty, you shall know I am set
naked on your kingdom. Tomorrow shall I beg
leave to see your kingly eyes, when I shall (first
asking your pardon) thereunto recount the occasion
of my sudden and more strange return. Hamlet.*
What should this mean? Are all the rest come back?
Or is it some abuse and no such thing?

Laertes. Know you the hand?

15 conjunctive: closely joined.

16 star . . . sphere: In Shakespeare's time, it was believed that each planet moves around the Earth in a hollow sphere.

18 count: account, indictment.

19–25 Claudius says that the common people (**general gender**), through their love for Hamlet, act like a spring with such a high concentration of lime that wood placed in it will become petrified; they change his limitations (**gyves**) into attractive qualities, so that the strong wind of their approval would blow back any arrows that Claudius might shoot at Hamlet.

27 terms: condition.

28–30 Whose worth . . . perfections: If praises can recall Ophelia's former self, her worth placed her at the top of the age.

45 naked: destitute, defenseless.

50 Claudius wonders if this is a deception and no such thing has occurred.

King. 'Tis Hamlet's character. "Naked"—
And in a postscript here, he says "alone."
Can you advise me?

52 character: handwriting.

Laertes. I am lost in it, my lord. But let him come.
It warms the very sickness in my heart
That I shall live and tell him to his teeth
"Thus didst thou."

King. If it be so, Laertes
(As how should it be so? how otherwise?),
Will you be ruled by me?

Laertes. Ay, my lord,
So you will not o'errule me to a peace.

61 So: as long as.

King. To thine own peace. If he be now returned,
As checking at his voyage, and that he means
No more to undertake it, I will work him
To an exploit, now ripe in my device,
Under the which he shall not choose but fall;
And for his death no wind of blame shall breathe,
But even his mother shall uncharge the practice
And call it accident.

63 checking at: turning away from.

65 device: devising.

68 uncharge the practice: not blame the plot.

Laertes. My lord, I will be ruled,
The rather if you could devise it so
That I might be the organ.

72 organ: agent, instrument.

King. It falls right.
You have been talked of since your travel much,

And that in Hamlet's hearing, for a quality
Wherein they say you shine. Your sum of parts
Did not together pluck such envy from him
As did that one, and that, in my regard,
Of the unworthiest siege.

Laertes. What part is that, my lord?

King. A very ribbon in the cap of youth—
Yet needful too, for youth no less becomes
The light and careless livery that it wears
Than settled age his sables and his weeds,
Importing health and graveness. Two months since
Here was a gentleman of Normandy.
I have seen myself, and served against, the French,
And they can well on horseback, but this gallant
Had witchcraft in 't. He grew unto his seat,
And to such wondrous doing brought his horse
As had he been encorpsed and demi-natured
With the brave beast. So far he topped my thought
That I in forgery of shapes and tricks
Come short of what he did.

Laertes. A Norman was 't?

King. A Norman.

Laertes. Upon my life, Lamord.

King. The very same.

Laertes. I know him well. He is the brooch indeed
And gem of all the nation.

King. He made confession of you
And gave you such a masterly report
For art and exercise in your defense,
And for your rapier most especial,
That he cried out 'twould be a sight indeed
If one could match you. The 'scrimers of their nation
He swore had neither motion, guard, nor eye,
If you opposed them. Sir, this report of his
Did Hamlet so envenom with his envy
That he could nothing do but wish and beg
Your sudden coming-o'er, to play with you.
Now out of this—

Laertes. What out of this, my lord?

75–84 The rest of Laertes's qualities combined did not inspire as much envy in Hamlet as this one, which ranks lowest in Claudius's regard. Yet this quality is important even if only a mere decoration (**very ribbon**), because light, carefree clothes (**livery**) are as well-suited to youth as more richly trimmed or sober clothes (**his sables and his weeds**) are to old age, suggesting well-being and dignity.

87 can well: are skillful.

90–91 encorpsed . . . beast: as if he and the horse shared the same body, a double-natured beast (like the mythical centaur, half man and half horse).

91–93 His feats surpassed the ability of Claudius's imagination to reconstruct them.

96 brooch: ornament.

98 made confession of: testified about.

100 art . . . defense: skill and practice in fencing.

103 'scrimers: fencers.

108 play: fence.

King. Laertes, was your father dear to you?
Or are you like the painting of a sorrow,
A face without a heart?

Laertes. Why ask you this?

King. Not that I think you did not love your father,
But that I know love is begun by time
And that I see, in passages of proof,
Time qualifies the spark and fire of it.
There lives within the very flame of love
A kind of wick or snuff that will abate it,
And nothing is at a like goodness still;
For goodness, growing to a pleurisy,
Dies in his own too-much. That we would do
We should do when we would; for this "would" changes
And hath abatements and delays as many
As there are tongues, are hands, are accidents;
And then this "should" is like a spendthrift sigh,
That hurts by easing. But to the quick of th' ulcer:
Hamlet comes back; what would you undertake
To show yourself indeed your father's son
More than in words?

Laertes. To cut his throat i' th' church.

King. No place indeed should murder sanctuarize;
Revenge should have no bounds. But, good Laertes,
Will you do this? Keep close within your chamber.
Hamlet, returned, shall know you are come home.
We'll put on those shall praise your excellence
And set a double varnish on the fame
The Frenchman gave you; bring you, in fine, together
And wager on your heads. He, being remiss,
Most generous, and free from all contriving,
Will not peruse the foils, so that with ease,
Or with a little shuffling, you may choose
A sword unbated, and in a pass of practice
Requite him for your father.

Laertes. I will do 't,
And for that purpose I'll anoint my sword.
I bought an unction of a mountebank
So mortal that, but dip a knife in it,
Where it draws blood no cataplasm so rare,

114 begun by time: created by circumstance.

119 nothing . . . still: Nothing remains at the same level of goodness.

120 pleurisy: excess.

121 his own too-much: its own excess.

121–122 That we . . . would: If one wishes to do something, one should act right away.

123 abatements: lessenings.

125–126 spendthrift sigh . . . easing: an allusion to the idea that sighing brings temporary relief but weakens the heart.

130 should murder sanctuarize: should protect a murderer from punishment.

134 put on those shall: arrange for people to.

136 in fine: finally.

137 remiss: carelessly unsuspicious.

138 generous: noble-minded

141 unbated: not blunted; **pass of practice:** treacherous thrust.

144–149 Laertes bought from a quack doctor an ointment (**unction**) so deadly that no medical dressing (**cataplasm**) can save anyone scratched by it.

Collected from all simples that have virtue
Under the moon, can save the thing from death
That is but scratched withal. I'll touch my point
With this contagion, that, if I gall him slightly,
It may be death.

King. Let's further think of this,
Weigh what convenience both of time and means
May fit us to our shape. If this should fail,
And that our drift look through our bad performance,
'Twere better not assayed. Therefore this project
Should have a back or second that might hold
If this did blast in proof. Soft, let me see.
We'll make a solemn wager on your cunnings—
I ha 't!
When in your motion you are hot and dry
(As make your bouts more violent to that end)
And that he calls for drink, I'll have prepared him
A chalice for the nonce, whereon but sipping,
If he by chance escape your venomed stuck,
Our purpose may hold there.—But stay, what noise?

[*Enter* Queen.]

Queen. One woe doth tread upon another's heel,
So fast they follow. Your sister's drowned, Laertes.

Laertes. Drowned? O, where?

Queen. There is a willow grows askant the brook
That shows his hoar leaves in the glassy stream.
Therewith fantastic garlands did she make
Of crowflowers, nettles, daisies, and long purples,
That liberal shepherds give a grosser name,
But our cold maids do "dead men's fingers" call them.
There on the pendant boughs her coronet weeds
Clamb'ring to hang, an envious sliver broke,
When down her weedy trophies and herself
Fell in the weeping brook. Her clothes spread wide,
And mermaid-like awhile they bore her up,
Which time she chanted snatches of old lauds,
As one incapable of her own distress
Or like a creature native and endued
Unto that element. But long it could not be
Till that her garments, heavy with their drink,
Pulled the poor wretch from her melodious lay
To muddy death.

Laertes. Alas, then she is drowned.

Queen. Drowned, drowned.

150 gall: injure.

153 fit us to our shape: suit our purposes.

153–155 If the plot should fail and our intentions are exposed, it would be better if we never attempted it.

156 back: backup.

157 blast in proof: blow up while tested.

158 cunnings: skills.

159 ha 't: have it.

163 A chalice for the nonce: a cup of wine for the occasion.

164 stuck: thrust.

169 askant: slanting over

170 his hoar: its gray.

171 Therewith . . . make: she used the willow twigs to make elaborate wreaths.

172 long purples: orchids.

173 liberal: free-spoken.

174 cold: chaste.

175 pendant boughs: overhanging branches; **coronet:** made into a wreath or crown.

176 envious sliver: malicious branch.

180 lauds: hymns.

181 incapable: unaware.

182 native and endued: naturally adapted.

Laertes. Too much of water hast thou, poor Ophelia,
And therefore I forbid my tears. But yet
It is our trick; nature her custom holds,
Let shame say what it will. When these are gone,
The woman will be out.—Adieu, my lord.
I have a speech o' fire that fain would blaze,
But that this folly drowns it.

[*He exits.*]

King. Let's follow, Gertrude.
How much I had to do to calm his rage!
Now fear I this will give it start again.
Therefore, let's follow.

[*They exit.*]

189–192 Laertes says that tears are a natural trait (**trick**), which shame cannot prevent. When all his tears are shed, the womanly part of him will be gone.

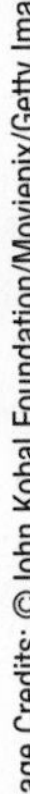
Image Credits: ©John Kobal Foundation/Moviepix/Getty Images

Analyzing the Text

RL 1, RL 3, RL 5, W 10

Cite Text Evidence Support your responses with evidence from the selection.

1. **Cause/Effect** What sequence of events is triggered by the killing of Polonius?
2. **Interpret** What does Claudius's speech at the beginning of Scene 3 (lines 1–11) reveal about the difficult situation he is in?
3. **Draw Conclusions** Reread lines 41–52 in Scene 3. Hamlet has already confided to his mother at the end of Act III that Rosencrantz and Guildenstern have been assigned to lead him into a trap. What does it suggest about his character that he now appears eager to go with them?
4. **Interpret** Reread lines 48–58 in Scene 4. Paraphrase the view of honor that Hamlet praises in the speech. Is this view consistent with his other comments in the scene? Why or why not?
5. **Interpret** Ophelia has fallen into madness following the death of her father. In Scene 5, do her statements and singing suggest she is only disturbed by his death, or is something else troubling her? Explain.
6. **Compare** A **foil** is a character whose traits contrast with those of another character. Very often a minor character is used as a foil to emphasize traits of the main character. Explain how the following characters serve as foils to Hamlet:
   - Fortinbras
   - Laertes
7. **Draw Conclusions** Hamlet sends two letters announcing his return to England, one to Horatio and one to Claudius. Why might Shakespeare have chosen to have him send the letter to Horatio even though it is not needed to advance the plot?
8. **Analyze** In Scene 7, lines 130–142, Claudius describes an elaborate scheme to kill Hamlet. What advantages does this scheme have for both him and Laertes? Based on what has happened so far in the play, what might be a disadvantage of the scheme?

PERFORMANCE TASK

Writing Activity: Journal Entry Write a journal entry by either Rosencrantz or Guildenstern about their mission to take Hamlet to England.

- Describe Hamlet's behavior toward his old friends and the events that led to Claudius's decision to send him away.
- Consider the limited knowledge that Rosencrantz and Guildenstern have about these events. Only include information that your character would be aware of.
- Use an informal, intimate style appropriate for a journal entry.

ACT V

Scene 1 *A churchyard.*

[*Enter* Gravedigger *and* Another.]

Gravedigger. Is she to be buried in Christian burial, when she willfully seeks her own salvation?

Other. I tell thee she is. Therefore make her grave straight. The crowner hath sat on her and finds it Christian burial.

Gravedigger. How can that be, unless she drowned herself in her own defense?

Other. Why, 'tis found so.

Gravedigger. It must be se offendendo; it cannot be else. For here lies the point: if I drown myself wittingly, it argues an act, and an act hath three branches—it is to act, to do, to perform. Argal, she drowned herself wittingly.

Other. Nay, but hear you, goodman delver—

Gravedigger. Give me leave. Here lies the water; good. Here stands the man; good. If the man go to this water and drown himself, it is (will he, nill he) he goes; mark you that. But if the water come to him and drown him, he drowns not himself. Argal, he that is not guilty of his own death shortens not his own life.

Other. But is this law?

Gravedigger. Ay, marry, is 't—crowner's 'quest law.

Other. Will you ha' the truth on 't? If this had not been a gentlewoman, she should have been buried out o' Christian burial.

Gravedigger. Why, there thou sayst. And the more pity that great folk should have count'nance in this world to drown or hang themselves more than their even-Christian. Come, my spade. There is no ancient gentlemen but gard'ners, ditchers, and grave-makers. They hold up Adam's profession.

Other. Was he a gentleman?

Gravedigger. He was the first that ever bore arms.

Other. Why, he had none.

1 Christian burial: Suicides were not allowed Christian funeral rites. The Gravedigger assumes that Ophelia killed herself.

2 salvation: probably a blunder for **damnation**.

4 straight: immediately; **crowner:** coroner; **sat on her:** held an inquest into her death; **finds it:** gave a verdict allowing.

9 se offendendo: a blunder for **se defendendo,** a legal term meaning "in self-defense."

12 Argal: a blunder for Latin **ergo,** "therefore."

13 wittingly: intentionally.

14 goodman: a title used before the name of a profession or craft; **delver:** digger.

17 will he, nill he: willy-nilly, whether he wishes it or not.

23 'quest: inquest.

27 thou sayst: you speak the truth.

28 count'nance: privilege.

30 even-Christian: fellow Christians.

32 hold up: keep up.

34 bore arms: had a coat of arms (the sign of a gentleman).

Gravedigger. What, art a heathen? How dost thou understand the scripture? The scripture says Adam digged. Could he dig without arms? I'll put another question to thee. If thou answerest me not to the purpose, confess thyself—

Other. Go to!

Gravedigger. What is he that builds stronger than either the mason, the shipwright, or the carpenter?

Other. The gallows-maker; for that frame outlives a thousand tenants.

Gravedigger. I like thy wit well, in good faith. The gallows does well. But how does it well? It does well to those that do ill. Now, thou dost ill to say the gallows is built stronger than the church. Argal, the gallows may do well to thee. To 't again, come.

Other. "Who builds stronger than a mason, a shipwright, or a carpenter?"

Gravedigger. Ay, tell me that, and unyoke.

Other. Marry, now I can tell.

Gravedigger. To 't.

Other. Mass, I cannot tell.

[*Enter* Hamlet *and* Horatio *afar off.*]

Gravedigger. Cudgel thy brains no more about it, for your dull ass will not mend his pace with beating. And, when you are asked this question next, say "a grave-maker." The houses he makes lasts till doomsday. Go, get thee in, and fetch me a stoup of liquor.

[*The* Other Man *exits and the* Gravedigger *digs and sings.*]

In youth when I did love, did love,
Methought it was very sweet
To contract—O—the time for—a—my behove,
O, methought there—a—was nothing—a—meet.

Hamlet. Has this fellow no feeling of his business? He sings in grave-making.

Horatio. Custom hath made it in him a property of easiness.

Hamlet. 'Tis e'en so. The hand of little employment hath the daintier sense.

Gravedigger [*sings*].

But age with his stealing steps
Hath clawed me in his clutch,

41 Go to: go on (an expression of impatience).

44 frame: structure

48–50 Now, thou . . . to thee: Since you blasphemously say that the gallows is stronger than the church, you may be headed for the gallows.

53 unyoke: stop work for the day.

56 Mass: by the Mass.

57–58 The Gravedigger tells him to stop beating his brains to figure it out, because a beating won't make a slow donkey pick up its pace.

62–123 The Gravedigger sings a version of a popular Elizabethan song, with some added grunts (**O** and **a**), as he works.

68–69 Custom . . . easiness: Habit has made it easy for him.

71 hath the daintier sense: is more sensitive.

And hath shipped me into the land,
As if I had never been such.

[*He digs up a skull.*]

Hamlet. That skull had a tongue in it and could sing once. How the knave jowls it to the ground as if 'twere Cain's jawbone, that did the first murder! This might be the pate of a politician which this ass now o'erreaches, one that would circumvent God, might it not?

Horatio. It might, my lord.

Hamlet. Or of a courtier, which could say "Good morrow, sweet lord! How dost thou, sweet lord?" This might be my Lord Such-a-one that praised my Lord Such-a-one's horse when he went to beg it, might it not?

Horatio. Ay, my lord.

Hamlet. Why, e'en so. And now my Lady Worm's, chapless and knocked about the mazard with a sexton's spade. Here's fine revolution, an we had the trick to see 't. Did these bones cost no more the breeding but to play at loggets with them? Mine ache to think on 't.

Gravedigger [*sings*].

A pickax and a spade, a spade,
For and a shrouding sheet,
O, a pit of clay for to be made
For such a guest is meet.

[*He digs up more skulls.*]

Hamlet. There's another. Why may not that be the skull of a lawyer? Where be his quiddities now, his quillities, his cases, his tenures, and his tricks? Why does he suffer this mad knave now to knock him about the sconce with a dirty shovel and will not tell him of his action of battery? Hum, this fellow might be in 's time a great buyer of land, with his statutes, his recognizances, his fines, his double vouchers, his recoveries. Is this the fine of his fines and the recovery of his recoveries, to have his fine pate full of fine dirt? Will his vouchers vouch him no more of his purchases, and double ones too, than the length and breadth of a pair of indentures? The very conveyances of his lands will scarcely lie in this box, and must th' inheritor himself have no more, ha?

77 jowls: dashes.

79–81 The skull, which the Gravedigger gets the better of, might have been the head (**pate**) of a schemer who would have tried to get the better of God.

90 chapless: missing the lower jaw; **mazard:** head.

91 revolution: turn of Fortune's wheel; **an:** if.

92 trick: ability.

92–94 Hamlet asks whether the cost of bringing up these people was so low that one may play a game with their bones.

100 quiddities: subtle arguments, quibbles.

101 quillities: subtle distinctions; **tenures:** terms for the holding of property.

103 sconce: head.

104–114 Hamlet lists different legal terms related to the buying and holding of property. **Fines** were documents involved in the transfer of estates; Hamlet also uses the word to refer to the "end result" of the lawyer's legal work and his "elegant" head filled with "small particles" of dirt. He plays similarly off the meanings of other terms.

Horatio. Not a jot more, my lord.

Hamlet. Is not parchment made of sheepskins?

Horatio. Ay, my lord, and of calves' skins too.

Hamlet. They are sheep and calves which seek out assurance in that. I will speak to this fellow.— Whose grave's this, sirrah?

Gravedigger. Mine, sir.

[*Sings.*] *O, a pit of clay for to be made*
For such a guest is meet.

Hamlet. I think it be thine indeed, for thou liest in 't.

Gravedigger. You lie out on 't, sir, and therefore 'tis not yours. For my part, I do not lie in 't, yet it is mine.

Hamlet. Thou dost lie in 't, to be in 't and say it is thine. 'Tis for the dead, not for the quick; therefore thou liest.

Gravedigger. 'Tis a quick lie, sir; 'twill away again from me to you.

Hamlet. What man dost thou dig it for?

Gravedigger. For no man, sir.

Hamlet. What woman then?

Gravedigger. For none, neither.

Hamlet. Who is to be buried in 't?

Gravedigger. One that was a woman, sir, but, rest her soul, she's dead.

Hamlet. How absolute the knave is! We must speak by the card, or equivocation will undo us. By the Lord, Horatio, this three years I have took note of it: the age is grown so picked that the toe of the peasant comes so near the heel of the courtier, he galls his kibe.—How long hast thou been grave maker?

Gravedigger. Of all the days i' th' year, I came to 't that day that our last King Hamlet overcame Fortinbras.

Hamlet. How long is that since?

Gravedigger. Cannot you tell that? Every fool can tell that. It was that very day that young Hamlet was born—he that is mad, and sent into England?

Hamlet. Ay, marry, why was he sent into England?

119 assurance in that: safety in legal documents.

120 sirrah: a term used to address inferiors.

125 out on 't: outside of it.

130 quick: living.

139 absolute: strict, precise.

140 by the card: accurately; **equivocation:** use of words that are vague or have more than one meaning.

142–144 The present age has grown so refined (**picked**) that hardly any distinction remains between a peasant and a courtier; the peasant walks so closely that he chafes (**galls**) the courtier's sore heel (**kibe**).

Gravedigger. Why, because he was mad. He shall recover his wits there. Or if he do not, 'tis no great matter there.

Hamlet. Why?

Gravedigger. 'Twill not be seen in him there. There the men are as mad as he.

Hamlet. How came he mad?

Gravedigger. Very strangely, they say.

Hamlet. How "strangely"?

Gravedigger. Faith, e'en with losing his wits.

Hamlet. Upon what ground?

Gravedigger. Why, here in Denmark. I have been sexton here, man and boy, thirty years.

Hamlet. How long will a man lie i' th' earth ere he rot?

Gravedigger. Faith, if he be not rotten before he die (as we have many pocky corses nowadays that will scarce hold the laying in), he will last you some eight year or nine year. A tanner will last you nine year.

Hamlet. Why he more than another?

Gravedigger. Why, sir, his hide is so tanned with his trade that he will keep out water a great while; and your water is a sore decayer of your whoreson dead body. Here's a skull now hath lien you i' th' earth three-and-twenty years.

Hamlet. Whose was it?

Gravedigger. A whoreson mad fellow's it was. Whose do you think it was?

Hamlet. Nay, I know not.

Gravedigger. A pestilence on him for a mad rogue! He poured a flagon of Rhenish on my head once. This same skull, sir, was, sir, Yorick's skull, the King's jester.

Hamlet. This?

Gravedigger. E'en that.

Hamlet [*taking the skull*]. Let me see. Alas, poor Yorick! I knew him, Horatio—a fellow of infinite jest, of most excellent fancy. He hath bore me on his back a thousand times, and now how abhorred in my imagination it is! My gorge rises at it. Here hung those lips that I have kissed I know not how oft.

163 ground: cause. (The Gravedigger takes it in the sense of "land.")

168 pocky: rotten, infected with syphilis.

169 scarce hold the laying in: barely hold together until they are buried.

174–175 your . . . body: Water is a terrible (**sore**) decayer of vile (**whoreson**) corpses.

175 lien you: lain.

Where be your gibes now? your gambols? your songs? your flashes of merriment that were wont to set the table on a roar? Not one now to mock your own grinning? Quite chapfallen? Now get you to my lady's chamber, and tell her, let her paint an inch thick, to this favor she must come. Make her laugh at that.—Prithee, Horatio, tell me one thing.

Horatio. What's that, my lord?

Hamlet. Dost thou think Alexander looked o' this fashion i' th' earth?

Horatio. E'en so.

Hamlet. And smelt so? Pah!

[*He puts the skull down.*]

Horatio. E'en so, my lord.

Hamlet. To what base uses we may return, Horatio! Why may not imagination trace the noble dust of Alexander till he find it stopping a bunghole?

Horatio. 'Twere to consider too curiously to consider so.

Hamlet. No, faith, not a jot; but to follow him thither, with modesty enough and likelihood to lead it, as thus: Alexander died, Alexander was buried, Alexander returneth to dust; the dust is earth; of earth we make loam; and why of that loam whereto he was converted might they not stop a beer barrel?
Imperious Caesar, dead and turned to clay,
Might stop a hole to keep the wind away.

193 gibes: taunts; **gambols:** pranks.

196 chapfallen: down in the mouth, missing the lower jaw.

197–198 let her . . . come: Even if she covers her face with an inch of makeup, eventually she will have this appearance (**favor**).

201 Alexander: Alexander the Great.

208 bunghole: a hole in a keg or barrel for pouring liquid.

209 curiously: minutely, closely.

211 modesty: moderation.

214 loam: a mixture of clay, sand, and straw used for plastering.

216 Imperious: imperial.

O, that that earth which kept the world in awe
Should patch a wall t' expel the winter's flaw!

[*Enter* King, Queen, Laertes, Lords attendant, *and the corpse of* Ophelia, *with a* Doctor of Divinity.]

But soft, but soft awhile! Here comes the King,
The Queen, the courtiers. Who is this they follow?
And with such maimèd rites? This doth betoken
The corse they follow did with desp'rate hand
Fordo its own life. 'Twas of some estate.
Couch we awhile and mark.

[*They step aside.*]

Laertes. What ceremony else?

Hamlet. That is Laertes, a very noble youth. Mark.

Laertes. What ceremony else?

Doctor. Her obsequies have been as far enlarged
As we have warranty. Her death was doubtful,
And, but that great command o'ersways the order,
She should in ground unsanctified been lodged
Till the last trumpet. For charitable prayers
Shards, flints, and pebbles should be thrown on her.
Yet here she is allowed her virgin crants,
Her maiden strewments, and the bringing home
Of bell and burial.

Laertes. Must there no more be done?

Doctor. No more be done.
We should profane the service of the dead
To sing a requiem and such rest to her
As to peace-parted souls.

Laertes. Lay her i' th' earth,
And from her fair and unpolluted flesh
May violets spring! I tell thee, churlish priest,
A minist'ring angel shall my sister be
When thou liest howling.

Hamlet [*to* Horatio]. What, the fair Ophelia?

Queen. Sweets to the sweet, farewell!
She scatters flowers.
I hoped thou shouldst have been my Hamlet's wife;
I thought thy bride-bed to have decked, sweet maid,
And not have strewed thy grave.

Laertes. O, treble woe
Fall ten times treble on that cursèd head
Whose wicked deed thy most ingenious sense

219 flaw: gust of wind.

222 maimèd: incomplete.

224 Fordo: destroy; **some estate:** high rank.

225 Couch . . . mark: Let us conceal ourselves awhile and observe.

229–233 The priest says he has performed her funeral rites to the extent allowed under church law. The manner of her death was suspicious, and if the King's orders hadn't overruled the procedures, she would have remained buried in unsanctified ground until Judgment Day.

233 For: instead of.

234 Shards: pieces of broken pottery; **should be:** would have been.

235 virgin crants: wreaths placed on the coffin as a sign of virginity.

236 strewments: flowers strewn on a grave.

236–237 bringing . . . burial: being laid to rest in consecrated ground with church bells tolling.

240–241 such rest . . . souls: pray for her to have the same rest as those who died in peace.

245 howling: in hell.

252–253 thy most . . . thee of: deprived you of your excellent mind.

Deprived thee of!—Hold off the earth awhile,
Till I have caught her once more in mine arms.

[*Leaps in the grave.*]

Now pile your dust upon the quick and dead,
Till of this flat a mountain you have made
T' o'ertop old Pelion or the skyish head
Of blue Olympus.

Hamlet [*advancing*]. What is he whose grief
Bears such an emphasis, whose phrase of sorrow
Conjures the wand'ring stars and makes them stand
Like wonder-wounded hearers? This is I,
Hamlet the Dane.

Laertes [*coming out of the grave*].
The devil take thy soul!

Hamlet. Thou pray'st not well.

[*They grapple.*]

I prithee take thy fingers from my throat,
For though I am not splenitive and rash,
Yet have I in me something dangerous,
Which let thy wisdom fear. Hold off thy hand.

King. Pluck them asunder.

Queen. Hamlet! Hamlet!

All. Gentlemen!

Horatio. Good my lord, be quiet.

[Hamlet *and* Laertes *are separated.*]

Hamlet. Why, I will fight with him upon this theme
Until my eyelids will no longer wag!

Queen. O my son, what theme?

Hamlet. I loved Ophelia. Forty thousand brothers
Could not with all their quantity of love
Make up my sum. What wilt thou do for her?

King. O, he is mad, Laertes!

Queen. For love of God, forbear him.

Hamlet. 'Swounds, show me what thou't do.
Woo't weep, woo't fight, woo't fast, woo't tear thyself,
Woo't drink up eisel, eat a crocodile?
I'll do 't. Dost thou come here to whine?
To outface me with leaping in her grave?
Be buried quick with her, and so will I.
And if thou prate of mountains, let them throw

257 Pelion: In Greek mythology, giants placed Mount Pelion on top of Mount Ossa in an attempt to reach the top of Mount Olympus, home of the gods.

260–261 wand'ring stars: planets; **wonder-wounded:** struck with amazement.

265 splenitive: quick-tempered.

279 forbear him: leave him alone.

281 Woo't: wilt thou.

282 eisel: vinegar.

285 quick: alive.

Millions of acres on us, till our ground,
Singeing his pate against the burning zone,
Make Ossa like a wart. Nay, an thou'lt mouth,
I'll rant as well as thou.

Queen. This is mere madness;
And thus awhile the fit will work on him.
Anon, as patient as the female dove
When that her golden couplets are disclosed,
His silence will sit drooping.

Hamlet. Hear you, sir,
What is the reason that you use me thus?
I loved you ever. But it is no matter.
Let Hercules himself do what he may,
The cat will mew, and dog will have his day.

[Hamlet *exits.*]

King. I pray thee, good Horatio, wait upon him.

[Horatio *exits.*]

[*To* Laertes.] Strengthen your patience in our last night's speech.
We'll put the matter to the present push.—
Good Gertrude, set some watch over your son.—
This grave shall have a living monument.
An hour of quiet shortly shall we see;
Till then in patience our proceeding be.

[*They exit.*]

288 Singeing his . . . zone: burning its head in the sphere of the Sun's orbit.

289 Ossa: See note to line 257, **an thou'lt mouth:** if you rant.

290 mere: utter.

292–294 Soon Hamlet will fall as silent as a dove after its twin baby birds (**couplets**) are hatched.

299 wait upon: accompany.

301 to the present push: into immediate action.

Scene 2 *The hall of the castle.*

[*Enter* Hamlet *and* Horatio.]

Hamlet. So much for this, sir. Now shall you see the other.
You do remember all the circumstance?

Horatio. Remember it, my lord!

Hamlet. Sir, in my heart there was a kind of fighting
That would not let me sleep. Methought I lay
Worse than the mutines in the bilboes. Rashly—
And praised be rashness for it: let us know,
Our indiscretion sometime serves us well
When our deep plots do pall; and that should learn us
There's a divinity that shapes our ends,
Rough-hew them how we will—

Horatio. That is most certain.

1 see the other: hear the rest of the story.

6 mutines: mutineers; **bilboes:** shackles, chains.

8 indiscretion: hasty actions.

9 pall: falter; **learn:** teach.

10–11 There's a . . . will: A divine power guides our destinies, despite our clumsy attempts to fashion them ourselves.

Hamlet. Up from my cabin,
My sea-gown scarfed about me, in the dark
Groped I to find out them; had my desire,
Fingered their packet, and in fine withdrew
To mine own room again, making so bold
(My fears forgetting manners) to unfold
Their grand commission; where I found, Horatio,
A royal knavery—an exact command,
Larded with many several sorts of reasons
Importing Denmark's health and England's too,
With—ho!—such bugs and goblins in my life,
That on the supervise, no leisure bated,
No, not to stay the grinding of the ax,
My head should be struck off.

Horatio. Is 't possible?

Hamlet. Here's the commission. Read it at more leisure.
[*Handing him a paper.*]
But wilt thou hear now how I did proceed?

Horatio. I beseech you.

Hamlet. Being thus benetted round with villainies,
Or I could make a prologue to my brains,
They had begun the play. I sat me down,
Devised a new commission, wrote it fair—
I once did hold it, as our statists do,
A baseness to write fair, and labored much
How to forget that learning; but, sir, now
It did me yeoman's service. Wilt thou know
Th' effect of what I wrote?

Horatio. Ay, good my lord.

Hamlet. An earnest conjuration from the King,
As England was his faithful tributary,
As love between them like the palm might flourish,
As peace should still her wheaten garland wear
And stand a comma 'tween their amities,
And many suchlike ases of great charge,
That, on the view and knowing of these contents,
Without debatement further, more or less,
He should those bearers put to sudden death,
Not shriving time allowed.

Horatio. How was this sealed?

Hamlet. Why, even in that was heaven ordinant.
I had my father's signet in my purse,
Which was the model of that Danish seal;

13 scarfed: wrapped.

14 them: Rosencrantz and Guildenstern.

15 Fingered: stole; **in fine:** finally.

20 Larded: embellished.

21 importing: concerning.

22 bugs . . . life: imaginary terrors in my remaining alive.

23 on the supervise: upon reading this; **no leisure bated:** without hesitation.

24 stay: wait for.

30–31 Before Hamlet had time to consider what to do, his brains started working out a plan.

33–36 Like a politician, Hamlet once considered it beneath him to write neatly (as a clerk would), but his handwriting gave him substantial service.

39 tributary: a nation controlled by another.

41 still: always; **wheaten garland:** symbol of peace and prosperity.

42 stand . . . amities: join their friendships.

43 suchlike . . . charge: similar legal phrases of great import beginning with "whereas." (Hamlet is ridiculing official language.)

47 shriving time: time for confession and absolution of sins.

48 ordinant: controlling events.

50 model: likeness.

Folded the writ up in the form of th' other,
Subscribed it, gave 't th' impression, placed it safely,
The changeling never known. Now, the next day
Was our sea-fight; and what to this was sequent
Thou knowest already.

Horatio. So Guildenstern and Rosencrantz go to 't.

Hamlet. Why, man, they did make love to this employment.
They are not near my conscience. Their defeat
Does by their own insinuation grow.
'Tis dangerous when the baser nature comes
Between the pass and fell incensèd points
Of mighty opposites.

Horatio. Why, what a king is this!

Hamlet. Does it not, think thee, stand me now upon—
He that hath killed my king and whored my mother,
Popped in between th' election and my hopes,
Thrown out his angle for my proper life,
And with such cozenage—is 't not perfect conscience
To quit him with this arm? And is 't not to be damned
To let this canker of our nature come
In further evil?

Horatio. It must be shortly known to him from England
What is the issue of the business there.

Hamlet. It will be short. The interim's mine,
And a man's life's no more than to say "one."
But I am very sorry, good Horatio,
That to Laertes I forgot myself,
For by the image of my cause I see
The portraiture of his. I'll court his favors.
But, sure, the bravery of his grief did put me
Into a tow'ring passion.

Horatio. Peace, who comes here?

[*Enter* Osric, *a courtier.*]

Osric. Your lordship is right welcome back to Denmark.

Hamlet. I humbly thank you, sir. [*Aside to* Horatio.]
Dost know this waterfly?

Horatio [*aside to* Hamlet]. No, my good lord.

Hamlet [*aside to* Horatio]. Thy state is the more gracious, for 'tis a vice to know him. He hath much land, and fertile. Let a beast be lord of beasts and his crib shall stand at the king's mess. 'Tis a chough, but, as I say, spacious in the possession of dirt.

52 Subscribed . . . impression: signed and sealed it.

53 changeling: substitution.

54 what to this was sequent: what followed.

58 defeat: destruction.

59 insinuation: worming their way in.

60–62 'Tis . . . opposites: It is dangerous for inferior people to come between the fiercely thrusting sword points of mighty antagonists.

66 The Danish king was elected by a small group of electors.

68 cozenage: deception.

69 quit: pay back.

70–71 come/In: grow into.

74–75 Hamlet says that although he only has a short time in which to act, a man's life is also brief, lasting no longer than it takes to count to one.

78 image: likeness.

80 bravery: showiness.

88–89 Let a . . . mess: If a man owns a lot of livestock, no matter how much he resembles them, he may eat at the king's table.

89 chough: chattering bird.

Osric. Sweet lord, if your lordship were at leisure, I should impart a thing to you from his Majesty.

Hamlet. I will receive it, sir, with all diligence of spirit. Put your bonnet to his right use: 'tis for the head.

Osric. I thank your lordship; it is very hot.

Hamlet. No, believe me, 'tis very cold; the wind is northerly.

Osric. It is indifferent cold, my lord, indeed.

Hamlet. But yet methinks it is very sultry and hot for my complexion.

Osric. Exceedingly, my lord; it is very sultry, as 'twere—I cannot tell how. My lord, his Majesty bade me signify to you that he has laid a great wager on your head. Sir, this is the matter—

Hamlet. I beseech you, remember.

[*He motions to* Osric *to put on his hat.*]

Osric. Nay, good my lord, for my ease, in good faith. Sir, here is newly come to court Laertes—believe me, an absolute gentleman, full of most excellent differences, of very soft society and great showing. Indeed, to speak feelingly of him, he is the card or calendar of gentry, for you shall find in him the continent of what part a gentleman would see.

Hamlet. Sir, his definement suffers no perdition in you, though I know to divide him inventorially would dozy th' arithmetic of memory, and yet but yaw neither, in respect of his quick sail. But, in the verity of extolment, I take him to be a soul of great article, and his infusion of such dearth and rareness as, to make true diction of him, his semblable is his mirror, and who else would trace him, his umbrage, nothing more.

Osric. Your lordship speaks most infallibly of him.

Hamlet. The concernancy, sir? Why do we wrap the gentleman in our more rawer breath?

Osric. Sir?

Horatio [*aside to* Hamlet]. Is 't not possible to understand in another tongue? You will to 't, sir, really.

Hamlet [*to* Osric]. What imports the nomination of this gentleman?

Osric. Of Laertes?

93–106 Men commonly wore their hats indoors but removed them in the presence of superiors. Hamlet mocks not only this show of respect but also Osric's insistence on agreeing with everything Hamlet says.

98 indifferent: somewhat.

100 complexion: temperament.

110–112 Among his compliments, Osric calls Laertes the map or guide (**card or calendar**) of good breeding, one who contains in him (**the continent of**) all the qualities a gentleman would look for.

113–121 Hamlet, mocking Osric's flowery speech, says that nothing has been lost in Osric's definition of Laertes, but the calculations needed to make an inventory of Laertes's excellences would be dizzying, and even then one would fail to capture him. He goes on to say that the only true likeness (**semblable**) of Laertes is his reflection in a mirror, and anyone who wanted to copy him would be nothing more than his shadow (**umbrage**).

123–124 Hamlet asks why they are speaking about Laertes.

128 What imports . . . of: for what purpose are you mentioning.

Horatio [*aside*]. His purse is empty already; all 's golden words are spent.

Hamlet. Of him, sir.

Osric. I know you are not ignorant—

Hamlet. I would you did, sir. Yet, in faith, if you did, it would not much approve me. Well, sir?

Osric. You are not ignorant of what excellence Laertes is—

Hamlet. I dare not confess that, lest I should compare with him in excellence. But to know a man well were to know himself.

Osric. I mean, sir, for his weapon. But in the imputation laid on him by them, in his meed he's unfellowed.

Hamlet. What's his weapon?

Osric. Rapier and dagger.

Hamlet. That's two of his weapons. But, well—

Osric. The King, sir, hath wagered with him six Barbary horses, against the which he has impawned, as I take it, six French rapiers and poniards, with their assigns, as girdle, hangers, and so. Three of the carriages, in faith, are very dear to fancy, very responsive to the hilts, most delicate carriages, and of very liberal conceit.

Hamlet. What call you the "carriages"?

Horatio [*aside to* Hamlet]. I knew you must be edified by the margent ere you had done.

Osric. The carriages, sir, are the hangers.

Hamlet. The phrase would be more germane to the matter if we could carry a cannon by our sides. I would it might be "hangers" till then. But on. Six Barbary horses against six French swords, their assigns, and three liberal-conceited carriages—that's the French bet against the Danish. Why is this all "impawned," as you call it?

Osric. The King, sir, hath laid, sir, that in a dozen passes between yourself and him, he shall not exceed you three hits. He hath laid on twelve for nine, and it would come to immediate trial if your lordship would vouchsafe the answer.

Hamlet. How if I answer no?

131 all 's: all his.

136 approve: commend.

142–143 In the reputation others have given him, his merit (**meed**) is unmatched.

145 Rapier and dagger: a type of fencing with a rapier (sword) held in the right hand and a dagger in the left.

147–153 Against Claudius's wager, Laertes has staked six rapiers and daggers, along with their accessories, such as straps (**hangers**) to hold the swords onto a sword belt (**girdle**), and so forth. Three of the hangers are fancifully designed, well adjusted, finely crafted, and have an elaborate design.

155–156 Horatio jokes that he knew Hamlet would seek explanation in a marginal note.

159 cannon by our sides: an affected term for "hanger," *carriage* normally refers to the wheeled base of a cannon.

165 laid: wagered.

166 passes: bouts, exchanges; **him:** Laertes.

169 vouchsafe the answer: accept the challenge.

Osric. I mean, my lord, the opposition of your person in trial.

Hamlet. Sir, I will walk here in the hall. If it please his Majesty, it is the breathing time of day with me. Let the foils be brought, the gentleman willing, and the King hold his purpose, I will win for him, an I can. If not, I will gain nothing but my shame and the odd hits.

Osric. Shall I deliver you e'en so?

Hamlet. To this effect, sir, after what flourish your nature will.

Osric. I commend my duty to your lordship.

Hamlet. Yours. [Osric *exits.*] He does well to commend it himself. There are no tongues else for 's turn.

Horatio. This lapwing runs away with the shell on his head.

Hamlet. He did comply, sir, with his dug before he sucked it. Thus has he (and many more of the same breed that I know the drossy age dotes on) only got the tune of the time, and, out of an habit of encounter, a kind of yeasty collection, which carries them through and through the most fanned and winnowed opinions; and do but blow them to their trial, the bubbles are out.

[*Enter a* Lord.]

Lord. My lord, his Majesty commended him to you by young Osric, who brings back to him that you attend him in the hall. He sends to know if your pleasure hold to play with Laertes, or that you will take longer time.

Hamlet. I am constant to my purposes. They follow the King's pleasure. If his fitness speaks, mine is ready now or whensoever, provided I be so able as now.

Lord. The King and Queen and all are coming down.

Hamlet. In happy time.

Lord. The Queen desires you to use some gentle entertainment to Laertes before you fall to play.

Hamlet. She well instructs me.

[Lord *exits.*]

Horatio. You will lose, my lord.

174 breathing time of day: usual time for exercise.

175 foils: swords with blunt tips.

182 commend: present to your favor.

185 lapwing: A bird that supposedly left its nest soon after hatching and ran around with its shell on its head—probably a reference to Osric's hat.

187–194 After joking that Osric paid courtesies to his mother's nipple before nursing, Hamlet complains that Osric and his type, popular in this worthless age, have only picked up a fashionable manner of speaking (**the tune of the time**) and a frothy collection of phrases that help them move through refined society (**fanned and winnowed opinions**), but the bubbles burst as soon as they are tested.

201–202 If his . . . whensoever: I am ready at his convenience.

205 In happy time: a polite phrase of welcome.

206 use some gentle entertainment: show some courtesy.

Hamlet. I do not think so. Since he went into France, I have been in continual practice. I shall win at the odds; but thou wouldst not think how ill all's here about my heart. But it is no matter.

Horatio. Nay, good my lord—

Hamlet. It is but foolery, but it is such a kind of gaingiving as would perhaps trouble a woman.

Horatio. If your mind dislike anything, obey it. I will forestall their repair hither and say you are not fit.

Hamlet. Not a whit. We defy augury. There is a special providence in the fall of a sparrow. If it be now, 'tis not to come; if it be not to come, it will be now; if it be not now, yet it will come. The readiness is all. Since no man of aught he leaves knows, what is 't to leave betimes? Let be.

[*A table prepared. Enter Trumpets, Drums, and* Officers *with cushions,* King, Queen, Osric, *and all the state, foils, daggers, flagons of wine, and* Laertes.]

King. Come, Hamlet, come and take this hand from me.

[*He puts* Laertes' *hand into* Hamlet's.]

Hamlet [*to* Laertes]. Give me your pardon, sir. I have done you wrong;
But pardon 't as you are a gentleman. This presence knows,
And you must needs have heard, how I am punished
With a sore distraction. What I have done
That might your nature, honor, and exception
Roughly awake, I here proclaim was madness.
Was 't Hamlet wronged Laertes? Never Hamlet.
If Hamlet from himself be ta'en away.
And when he's not himself does wrong Laertes,
Then Hamlet does it not; Hamlet denies it.
Who does it, then? His madness. If 't be so,
Hamlet is of the faction that is wronged;
His madness is poor Hamlet's enemy.
Sir, in this audience
Let my disclaiming from a purposed evil
Free me so far in your most generous thoughts
That I have shot my arrow o'er the house
And hurt my brother.

Laertes. I am satisfied in nature,
Whose motive in this case should stir me most
To my revenge; but in my terms of honor
I stand aloof and will no reconcilement

215–216 gaingiving: misgiving.

218 repair: coming.

219–224 Hamlet rejects **augury** (attempting to foresee the future by interpreting omens) and declares that since the death of even a sparrow is not left to chance, he is ready to accept any circumstances he encounters; his death will come sooner or later. He concludes that since man knows nothing about the life he leaves behind, what does it matter if he leaves early?

227 presence: royal assembly.

229 sore distraction: severe confusion.

230 exception: disapproval.

237 faction: party.

240 purposed evil: intentional harm.

242 That I have: as if I had.

244–250 Laertes is satisfied in regard to his own feelings (**nature**), but in regard to his honor he will wait until men experienced in such matters have given their authoritative judgment (**voice and precedent**) in favor of reconciliation, which would allow him to keep his reputation undamaged (**name ungored**).

Till by some elder masters of known honor
I have a voice and precedent of peace
To keep my name ungored. But till that time
I do receive your offered love like love
And will not wrong it.

Hamlet. I embrace it freely
And will this brothers' wager frankly play.—
Give us the foils. Come on.

Laertes. Come, one for me.

Hamlet. I'll be your foil, Laertes; in mine ignorance
Your skill shall, like a star i' th' darkest night,
Stick fiery off indeed.

Laertes. You mock me, sir.

Hamlet. No, by this hand.

King. Give them the foils, young Osric. Cousin Hamlet,
You know the wager?

Hamlet. Very well, my lord.
Your Grace has laid the odds o' th' weaker side.

King. I do not fear it; I have seen you both.
But, since he is better, we have therefore odds.

Laertes. This is too heavy. Let me see another.

253 frankly: without any hard feelings.

255 foil: metallic background used to display a jewel (punning on **foils**, referring to the blunted swords).

257 Stick fiery off: stand out brilliantly.

260–261 Hamlet comments that Claudius has bet on (**laid the odds o'**) the weaker fencer. Claudius expresses confidence in Hamlet, but says he has arranged a handicap (**odds**) for Laertes because he has improved.

Hamlet dueling with Laertes (Terence Morgan)

Hamlet. This likes me well. These foils have all a length?

Osric. Ay, my good lord.

265 likes me: pleases me; **have all a length:** are all the same length.

[*Prepare to play.*]

King. Set me the stoups of wine upon that table.—
If Hamlet give the first or second hit
Or quit in answer of the third exchange,
Let all the battlements their ordnance fire.
The King shall drink to Hamlet's better breath,
And in the cup an union shall he throw,
Richer than that which four successive kings
In Denmark's crown have worn. Give me the cups,
And let the kettle to the trumpet speak,
The trumpet to the cannoneer without,
The cannons to the heavens, the heaven to earth,
"Now the King drinks to Hamlet." Come, begin.
And you, the judges, bear a wary eye.

269 quit . . . exchange: gets back at Laertes by scoring the third hit.

272 union: pearl.

275 kettle: kettledrum.

[*Trumpets the while.*]

Hamlet. Come on, sir.

Laertes. Come, my lord.

[*They play.*]

Hamlet. One.

Laertes. No.

Hamlet. Judgment!

Osric. A hit, a very palpable hit.

Laertes. Well, again.

King. Stay, give me drink.—Hamlet, this pearl is thine.
Here's to thy health.

[*He drinks and then drops the pearl in the cup. Drum, trumpets, and shot.*]

Give him the cup.

Hamlet. I'll play this bout first. Set it by awhile.
Come. They play. Another hit. What say you?

Laertes. A touch, a touch. I do confess 't.

King. Our son shall win.

Queen. He's fat and scant of breath.
Here, Hamlet, take my napkin; rub thy brows.
The Queen carouses to thy fortune, Hamlet.

292 fat: sweaty

293 napkin: handkerchief.

[*She lifts the cup.*]

Hamlet. Good madam.

King. Gertrude, do not drink.

Queen. I will, my lord; I pray you pardon me.

[*She drinks.*]

King [*aside*]. It is the poisoned cup. It is too late.

Hamlet. I dare not drink yet, madam—by and by.

Queen. Come, let me wipe thy face.

Laertes [*to* Claudius]. My lord, I'll hit him now.

King. I do not think 't.

Laertes [*aside*]. And yet it is almost against my conscience.

Hamlet. Come, for the third, Laertes. You do but dally.
I pray you pass with your best violence.
I am afeard you make a wanton of me.

304 pass: thrust.

305 make a wanton of me: indulge me as if I were a spoiled child.

Laertes. Say you so? Come on. [*Play.*]

Osric. Nothing neither way.

Laertes. Have at you now!

[Laertes *wounds* Hamlet. *Then in scuffling they change rapiers, and* Hamlet *wounds* Laertes.]

King. Part them. They are incensed.

Hamlet. Nay, come again.

[*The* Queen *falls.*]

Osric. Look to the Queen there, ho!

Horatio. They bleed on both sides.—How is it, my lord?

Osric. How is 't, Laertes?

Laertes. Why as a woodcock to mine own springe, Osric.

[*He falls.*]

I am justly killed with mine own treachery.

314 Laertes says he's been caught like a **woodcock** (a proverbially stupid bird) in his own trap.

Hamlet. How does the Queen?

King. She swoons to see them bleed.

Queen. No, no, the drink, the drink! O, my dear Hamlet!
The drink, the drink! I am poisoned. [*She dies.*]

Hamlet. O villainy! Ho! Let the door be locked.

[Osric *exits.*]

Treachery! Seek it out.

Laertes. It is here, Hamlet. Hamlet, thou art slain.
No med'cine in the world can do thee good.
In thee there is not half an hour's life.
The treacherous instrument is in thy hand,
Unbated and envenomed. The foul practice
Hath turned itself on me. Lo, here I lie,
Never to rise again. Thy mother's poisoned.
I can no more. The King, the King's to blame.

325 unbated: not blunted; **practice:** trick.

Hamlet. The point envenomed too! Then, venom, to
thy work. [*Hurts the* King.]
All Treason, treason!

King. O, yet defend me, friends! I am but hurt.

Hamlet. Here, thou incestuous, murd'rous, damnèd Dane,
Drink off this potion. Is thy union here?

[*Forcing him to drink the poison.*]

Follow my mother.

[King *dies.*]

333 union: a pun on the meanings "pearl" and "marriage." (Claudius is joining his wife in death.)

Laertes. He is justly served.
It is a poison tempered by himself.
Exchange forgiveness with me, noble Hamlet.
Mine and my father's death come not upon thee,
Nor thine on me.

[*Dies.*]

335 tempered: mixed.

Hamlet. Heaven make thee free of it. I follow thee.—
I am dead, Horatio.—Wretched queen, adieu.—
You that look pale and tremble at this chance,
That are but mutes or audience to this act,
Had I but time (as this fell sergeant, Death,
Is strict in his arrest), O, I could tell you—
But let it be.—Horatio, I am dead.
Thou livest; report me and my cause aright
To the unsatisfied.

342 mutes: silent observers (literally, actors without speaking parts).

343 fell sergeant: cruel arresting officer.

Horatio. Never believe it.
I am more an antique Roman than a Dane.
Here's yet some liquor left.

[*He picks up the cup.*]

348 more an antique Roman: a reference to the Roman idea that suicide can be an honorable action following a defeat or the death of a loved one.

Hamlet. As thou'rt a man,
Give me the cup. Let go! By heaven, I'll ha 't.
O God, Horatio, what a wounded name,
Things standing thus unknown, shall I leave behind me!
If thou didst ever hold me in thy heart,
Absent thee from felicity awhile

354 Absent thee from felicity: deny yourself the pleasure of death.

And in this harsh world draw thy breath in pain
To tell my story.

[*A march afar off and shot within.*]

What warlike noise is this?

[*Enter* Osric.]

Osric. Young Fortinbras, with conquest come from Poland,
To th' ambassadors of England gives
This warlike volley.

357–359 Fortinbras, returning triumphant from Poland, has saluted the English ambassadors with a volley of gunfire.

Hamlet. O, I die, Horatio!
The potent poison quite o'ercrows my spirit.
I cannot live to hear the news from England.
But I do prophesy th' election lights
On Fortinbras; he has my dying voice.
So tell him, with th' occurrents, more and less,
Which have solicited—the rest is silence.
O, O, O, O!

[*Dies.*]

360 o'ercrows: triumphs over (like the winner in a cockfight).

362–363 Hamlet predicts that Fortinbras will be elected the new Danish king and gives him his vote (**voice**).

364 occurrents: occurrences.

365 solicited: prompted, brought about. (Hamlet dies before finishing this thought.)

Horatio. Now cracks a noble heart. Good night, sweet prince,
And flights of angels sing thee to thy rest.

[*March within.*]

Why does the drum come hither?

[*Enter* Fortinbras *with the* English Ambassadors *with Drum, Colors, and* Attendants.]

Fortinbras. Where is this sight?

Horatio. What is it you would see?
If aught of woe or wonder, cease your search.

Fortinbras. This quarry cries on havoc. O proud Death,
What feast is toward in thine eternal cell
That thou so many princes at a shot
So bloodily hast struck?

373 This heap of dead bodies (**quarry**) proclaims a massacre (**cries on havoc**).

374 toward: in preparation.

Ambassador. The sight is dismal,
And our affairs from England come too late.
The ears are senseless that should give us hearing
To tell him his commandment is fulfilled,
That Rosencrantz and Guildenstern are dead.
Where should we have our thanks?

381 his: Claudius's.

Horatio. Not from his mouth,
Had it th' ability of life to thank you.
He never gave commandment for their death.
But since, so jump upon this bloody question,

384 so jump upon this bloody question: so soon after this bloody quarrel.

You from the Polack wars, and you from England,
Are here arrived, give order that these bodies
High on a stage be placed to the view,
And let me speak to th' yet unknowing world
How these things came about. So shall you hear
Of carnal, bloody, and unnatural acts,
Of accidental judgments, casual slaughters,
Of deaths put on by cunning and forced cause,
And, in this upshot, purposes mistook
Fall'n on th' inventors' heads. All this can I
Truly deliver.

Fortinbras. Let us haste to hear it
And call the noblest to the audience.
For me, with sorrow I embrace my fortune.
I have some rights of memory in this kingdom,
Which now to claim my vantage doth invite me.

Horatio. Of that I shall have also cause to speak,
And from his mouth whose voice will draw on more.
But let this same be presently performed
Even while men's minds are wild, lest more mischance
On plots and errors happen.

Fortinbras. Let four captains
Bear Hamlet like a soldier to the stage,
For he was likely, had he been put on,
To have proved most royal; and for his passage,
The soldier's music and the rite of war
Speak loudly for him.
Take up the bodies. Such a sight as this
Becomes the field but here shows much amiss.
Go, bid the soldiers shoot.

[*They exit, marching, after the which a peal of ordnance are shot off.*]

387 stage: platform.

390 carnal, bloody, and unnatural acts: Claudius's murder of his brother and marriage to Gertrude.

391 accidental judgments, casual slaughters: punishments that occurred by chance.

392 put on: instigated; **forced:** contrived.

395 deliver: tell the story of.

398–399 Fortinbras says he has some unforgotten claims to Denmark, and this is a favorable time to present them.

401 from his mouth . . . more: the words of Hamlet, whose decision will influence other votes.

402 presently: immediately.

403–404 lest more . . . happen: lest other trouble occur in addition to these plots and accidents.

406 put on: enthroned, and so put to the test.

407 passage: death.

411 field: field of battle.

COLLABORATIVE DISCUSSION With a partner, discuss the reasons why Hamlet continues to capture the interest of critics and readers four centuries after his creation. Cite evidence from the play to support your opinion.

Analyze Language: Soliloquy

RL 4

A **soliloquy** is a long speech performed in a drama by a character alone on the stage. Hamlet delivers seven soliloquies in the first four acts of the play. These soliloquies perform multiple functions: they develop Hamlet's character; they expose his internal conflict; they foreshadow the action to come; they present his perspective on the other characters and events; and they communicate themes. In these speeches, Hamlet speaks the truth as he sees it; no deception is necessary.

Hamlet's language in these speeches is rich and powerful; his words draw the audience into his state of mind and remain memorable long after the play is over. To achieve this lasting impact, Shakespeare uses a variety of techniques.

Language in Hamlet's Soliloquies	
Figures of speech: metaphors, similes, and personification	Act III, Scene 2, 391–393: "'Tis now the very witching time of night, / When churchyards yawn and hell itself breathes out / Contagion to this world." The personification emphasizes Hamlet's heightened awareness of the evil around him.
Allusions	Act I, Scene 2, 139–140: "So excellent a king, that was to this / Hyperion to a satyr. . . . " Hamlet alludes to Hyperion, the sun god, to make the point that his father had integrity—unlike Claudius, whom he compares to a satyr, a mythical half-goat, half-man figure associated with lechery.
Powerful imagery; careful word choices	Act III, Scene 2, 393–395: "Now could I drink hot blood / And do such bitter business as the day / Would quake to look on." The sensory details show the intensity of Hamlet's feelings.

Analyze Drama Elements: Conflict

RL 3

In contrast with many of Shakespeare's tragic heroes, Hamlet's conflicts often result in inaction rather than action. As the play opens, Hamlet is already suffering a profound disillusionment about the nature of women. His subsequent encounter with the Ghost darkens his vision further. Still, he cannot surrender himself to the duty demanded by the Ghost until he has resolved his inner conflict by answering the questions that plague him:

- Is the Ghost an emissary of truth or deception?
- How will the deed affect the fate of his soul?
- How will he live with his conscience if he does or does not kill Claudius?
- How can one reconcile the corruption and nobility within human nature?

By answering these questions, Hamlet achieves the resolution that he needs to act.

Analyzing the Text

RL 1, RL 2, RL 3, RL 4, RL 5, RL 6, W 10, SL 6

Cite Text Evidence Support your responses with evidence from the selection.

1. **Analyze** Review Hamlet's encounter with the Gravedigger and his thoughts about Yorick at the beginning of Act V. Why might Shakespeare have chosen to include this darkly humorous scene here?
2. **Interpret** Why does Hamlet quarrel with Laertes at Ophelia's grave? What does this conflict clarify about his feelings?
3. **Infer** In the story he tells Horatio at the start of Act V, Scene 2, what qualities does Hamlet show that he has not displayed previously?
4. **Analyze** Ideas, customs, behaviors, or institutions are ridiculed in **satire** for the purpose of improving society. Satirists often use irony, wordplay, and exaggeration to poke fun at their targets. Reread Hamlet's exchange of words with Osric in Scene 2, lines 82–184. What customs or behavior is Hamlet ridiculing? Identify examples of techniques used in this satirical passage.
5. **Compare** Reread Hamlet's speech in Scene 2, lines 219–224. How do these thoughts about fate differ from his attitude in earlier speeches?
6. **Infer** As he is dying, Hamlet urges Horatio to stay alive and tell his story. Why is this so important to Hamlet?
7. **Analyze** Choose a soliloquy in the play, such as the famous "To be or not to be" speech in Act III, Scene 1, lines 57–89. Summarize the ideas in the soliloquy, and discuss the literary techniques Shakespeare uses to express them. Provide specific examples.
8. **Draw Conclusions** A **theme** is the central idea that a writer wishes to convey to the audience. Use specific details to explain what message *Hamlet* conveys about each of these subjects:
   - revenge
   - fate
   - the human condition

PERFORMANCE TASK

Speaking Activity: Funeral Speech If you were invited to speak at Hamlet's funeral, what would you say?

- Think about your overall impression of Hamlet's character. What were his admirable qualities, and what were his flaws? What motivated his actions?
- Write a brief speech that you would deliver at Hamlet's funeral. Address the events that led up to his death. Sum up your conclusions about him in a way that fits the occasion.
- Deliver your speech to a small group of classmates.

Language and Style: Paradox

L 5a

A **paradox** is a statement that is seemingly contradictory but actually reveals a truth. Shakespeare uses this literary device frequently in *Hamlet*. By expressing ideas paradoxically, he is able to convey subtle meanings and reinforce the audience's understanding of the duplicitous nature of many of the characters and their actions.

In Act I, Scene 2, Claudius's first speech features examples of paradox and **oxymoron** (a paradox condensed into a brief phrase):

> **Have we (as 'twere with a defeated joy,**
> **With an auspicious and a dropping eye,**
> **With mirth in funeral and with dirge in marriage,**
> **In equal scale weighing delight and dole)**
> **Taken to wife.**

He speaks of "defeated joy," "mirth in funeral," "dirge in marriage," and "weighing delight and dole." These paradoxical expressions tell those assembled that he views his marriage and accession to the throne as a mixed blessing, achieved at the expense of his brother's life. The use of paradox also hints at his own contradictory nature: outwardly virtuous, inwardly scheming and self-centered.

Hamlet also uses paradoxical language in the play. For example, in Act II, Scene 2, lines 309–320, he describes humankind in idealistic terms ("how noble in reason, how infinite in faculties . . . in action how like an angel, in apprehension how like a god") but ends the speech with the dismissive remark, "and yet, to me, what is this quintessence of dust? Man delights not me. . . ." This paradox emphasizes Hamlet's obsession with human corruption.

Note these other instances of paradox in the play:

- **Hamlet:** "it is a custom / More honored in the breach than the observance" (Act I, Scene 4, lines 17–18)
- **Polonius:** "Your bait of falsehood takes this carp of truth; / And thus do we of wisdom and of reach, / With windlasses and with assays of bias, / By indirections find directions out." (Act II, Scene 1, lines 63–66)
- **Hamlet:** "I must be cruel only to be kind." (Act III, Scene 4, line 184)

Practice and Apply Review the context of each example of paradox listed. With a partner, discuss the meaning of each paradox and examine how it deepens the audience's understanding of the character or situation. Then look back at the funeral speech you wrote for the Performance Task that follows Act V. Insert a reference to one of the paradoxes from the play, or create your own paradoxical expression about Hamlet's life.

MEDIA ANALYSIS

Film Versions of Hamlet

Hamlet (1980)

BBC Shakespeare
Directed by Rodney Bennett

AS YOU VIEW Pay attention to the elements that make each film version unique, and generate a list of questions as you watch.

Hamlet (2009)

BBC Shakespeare
Directed by Gregory Doran

COLLABORATIVE DISCUSSION Which version did you prefer? Why? With a partner, discuss the overall effect of each film version and the details that contribute to its impact. Cite specific evidence from the clips to support your ideas.

Analyze Interpretations of Drama

For a director, the chance to make a film of one of Shakespeare's plays is both a great opportunity and a great risk. Although Shakespeare sometimes included descriptions of characters or setting in the dialogue, his texts have few stage directions, and those usually provide only basic information, such as indicating a trumpet flourish. As a result, the director has little guidance but a great deal of freedom to imagine the play's details. Many of Shakespeare's plays have been adapted into more than one film, allowing audiences to experience multiple interpretations of the same play and to evaluate how well each version interprets the source text.

Each director has a personal vision of the film he or she wants to make. This concept is determined by the way the director interprets the play, the film's purpose and intended audience, previous versions of the play, and the particular subject matter of the play. To realize his or her vision, the director must make decisions that include casting, set design, and lighting.

Elements of Film Adaptation
Casting refers to the selection of actors to play the parts. Actors may be chosen based on how their appearance and age fit the image that the director has of the characters. They must also be able to bring out the characters' traits in the way the director envisions. For example, directors casting *Hamlet* would most likely choose actors of different ages for the roles of Hamlet and his mother, since that relationship is an established part of the play. The choice of actors is crucial to the success of the production; the actors determine how the audience responds to the characters and to the film as a whole. Directors may stay true to type or cast against type, perhaps choosing a female Hamlet or an actor whose race or ethnicity differs from what would be expected for a character. In the two clips seen here, the same actor, Patrick Stewart, was chosen to play the role of Claudius.
Set design refers to the scenery, props, furniture, and physical location that create the setting for the film. The set design may be traditional, modern, futuristic, or primitive, or it may spring from the imagination of the director. The setting in which the action of the film takes place Is important to the director's interpretation. It also affects how the audience reacts. Consider the effect of the spacious, modern set of the 2009 film, for example, compared to the set of the 1980 version, which is crowded with furniture and actors. How does each set shape your impression of the Danish court and the interaction among the characters?
Lighting can have a major influence on the mood and perception of character and action. Dim lighting conveys an air of mystery or gloominess and obscures actors' features and actions. Bright lighting cheers up the atmosphere and highlights actors' movements and expressions. In the 2009 film version, the reflective floor creates an interesting play of light and shadow that rivets the audience's attention on Hamlet's gestures and words during his soliloquy.

Analyzing the Text and Media

RL 7, SL 5

Cite Text Evidence Support your responses with evidence from the selections.

1. **Analyze** Describe the setting of the 1980 BBC adaptation. What time and place are indicated by the set and costumes?
2. **Compare** In what ways is the setting of the 2009 adaptation different from the setting of the earlier film? How might audiences respond to each setting?
3. **Interpret** Consider the two actors who play Hamlet. What does each one emphasize about Hamlet's personality and his relationships with the other characters? Explain your response.
4. **Compare** How are Patrick Stewart's performances in the two films similar to and different from each other?
5. **Infer** Reread lines 160-180 in Act I, Scene 2 of the play. What can you infer about Horatio's appearance and personality from Shakespeare's text? How does each director's casting of Horatio either confirm or upend these assumptions?
6. **Analyze** What mood is evoked by the lighting in the 1980 film? Is this mood consistent with the atmosphere in the same scene in Shakespeare's text? Explain.
7. **Critique** In the absence of stage directions, how does each actress playing Gertrude use voice and gesture to mediate matters between Hamlet and Claudius? Where do they use similar choices? Where do their choices differ? Cite specific evidence in to support your response.

PERFORMANCE TASK

Media Activity: Trailer Which film version would you endorse? With a partner, complete these activities.

- Identify your reasons for preferring one film over the other.
- Develop a storyboard for a trailer to be shown in theaters, "plugging" the film you have chosen.
- Match images from the film with each of your reasons. Express your ideas in a way that is specific and engaging.
- Create a video version of your trailer or refine your storyboard for presentation to the class.
- Show your trailer to the class.

Hamlet's Dull Revenge

Literary Criticism by René Girard

AS YOU READ Pay attention to details that reveal how Girard views Hamlet's character. Write down any questions you have as you read.

Hamlet belongs to the **genre** of the revenge tragedy, as hackneyed and yet inescapable in Shakespeare's days as the "thriller" in ours to a television writer. In *Hamlet* Shakespeare turned this necessity for a playwright to go on writing the same old revenge tragedies into an opportunity to debate almost openly for the first time the questions I have tried to define. The weariness with revenge and *katharsis*[1] which can be read, I believe, in the margins of the earlier plays must really exist because, in *Hamlet,* it moves to the center of the stage and becomes fully articulated.

genre (zhän′rə) *n.* a category within an art form, based on style or subject.

Some writers who were not necessarily the most unimaginative found it difficult, we are told, to postpone for the whole duration of the lengthy Elizabethan play an action which had never been in doubt in the first place and which is always the same anyway. Shakespeare can turn this tedious chore into the most brilliant feat of theatrical ***double entendre*** because the tedium of revenge is really what he wants to talk about, and he wants to talk about it in the usual Shakespearean fashion; he will denounce the revenge theater and all its works with the utmost daring without denying his mass audience the *katharsis* it demands, without depriving himself of the dramatic success which is necessary to his own career as a dramatist.

double entendre (dŭb′əl än-tän′drə) *n.* an expression having a double meaning.

If we assume that Shakespeare really had this double goal in mind, we will find that some unexplained details in the play become intelligible and that the function of many obscure scenes becomes obvious.

In order to perform revenge with conviction, you must believe in the justice of your own cause. This is what we noted before, and the revenge seeker will not believe in his own cause unless he believes in

[1] **katharsis:** catharsis, the elimination of tension through the release of repressed emotions.

the guilt of his intended victim. And the guilt of that intended victim **entails** in turn the innocence of that victim's victim. If the victim's victim is already a killer and if the revenge seeker reflects a little too much on the circularity of revenge, his faith in vengeance must collapse.

entail
(ĕn-tāl´) *v.* involve as a consequence.

This is exactly what we have in *Hamlet*. It cannot be without a purpose that Shakespeare suggests the old Hamlet, the murdered king, was a murderer himself. In the various sources of the play there may be indications to that effect, but Shakespeare would have omitted them if he had wanted to strengthen the case for revenge. However nasty Claudius may look, he cannot look nasty enough if he appears in a context of previous revenge; he cannot generate, as a villain, the absolute passion and dedication which is demanded of Hamlet. The problem with Hamlet is that he cannot forget the context. As a result, the crime by Claudius looks to him like one more link in an already long chain, and his own revenge will look like still another link, perfectly identical to all the other links.

In a world where every ghost, dead or alive, can only perform the same action, revenge, or clamor for more of the same from beyond the grave, all voices are interchangeable. You can never know with certainty which ghost is addressing whom. It is one and the same thing for Hamlet to question his own identity and to question the ghost's identity, and his authority.

To seek singularity in revenge is a vain enterprise but to shrink from revenge, in a world which looks upon it as a "sacred duty" is to exclude oneself from society, to become a nonentity once more. There is no way out for Hamlet and he shifts endlessly from one impasse to the other, unable to make up his mind because neither choice makes sense.

If all characters are caught in a cycle of revenge that extends in all directions beyond the limits of its action, *Hamlet* has no beginning and no end. The play collapses. The trouble with the hero is that he does not believe in his play half as much as the critics do. He understands revenge and the theater too well to assume willingly a role chosen for him by others. His sentiments are those, in other words, which we have surmised in Shakespeare himself. What the hero feels in regard to the act of revenge, the creator feels in regard to revenge as theater.

The public wants vicarious victims and the playwright must oblige. Tragedy is revenge. Shakespeare is tired of revenge, and yet he cannot give it up, or he gives up his audience and his identity as a playwright. Shakespeare turns a typical revenge topic, *Hamlet*, into a meditation on his predicament as a playwright. . . .

What Hamlet needs, in order to stir up his vengeful spirit, is a revenge theater more convincing than his own, something less half-hearted than the play Shakespeare is actually writing. Fortunately for the hero and for the spectators who are eagerly awaiting their final bloodbath, Hamlet has many opportunities to watch rousing spectacles during his play and he tries to generate even more, in a conscientious effort to put himself in the right mood for the murder of Claudius. Hamlet must receive from someone else, a mimetic[2] model, the impulse which he does not find in himself. This is what he tried to achieve with his mother, we found, and he did not succeed. He is much more successful with the actor who impersonates for him the role of Hecuba. It becomes obvious, at this point, that the only hope for Hamlet to accomplish what his society—or the spectators—require, is to become as "sincere" a showman as the actor who can shed real tears when he pretends to be the queen of Troy!

Is it not monstrous that this player here,
But in a fiction, in a dream of passion,
Could force his soul so to his own conceit
That from her working all his visage wanned,
Tears in his eyes, distraction in's aspect,
A broken voice, and his whole function suiting
With forms to his conceit? And all for nothing!
For Hecuba!
What's Hecuba to him or he to Hecuba,
That he should weep for her? What would he do
Had he the motive and the cue for passion
That I have?

Another catchy example for Hamlet comes from the army of Fortinbras on its way to Poland. The object of the war is a worthless speck of land. Thousands of people must risk their lives:

Even for an eggshell. Rightly to be great
Is not to stir without great argument,
But greatly to find quarrel in a straw
When Honor's at the stake.

The scene is as ridiculous as it is sinister. It would not impress Hamlet so much if the hero truly believed in the superiority and urgency of his cause. His words constantly betray him, here as in the scene with his mother. As a cue for passion, his revenge motif is no more compelling, really, than the cue of an actor on the stage. He too must *greatly . . . find quarrel in a straw,* he too must stake everything *even for an eggshell.*

The effect of the army scene obviously stems, at least in part, from the large number of people involved, from the almost infinite multiplication of the example which cannot fail to increase its mimetic attraction enormously. Shakespeare is too much a master of mob effects not to remember at this point the cumulative effect of mimetic models. In order to whip up enthusiasm for the war against Claudius,

[2] **mimetic:** relating to imitation.

the same irrational contagion is needed as in the war against Poland. The type of mimetic incitement from which Hamlet "benefits" at this point resembles very much the kind of spectacle which governments never fail to organize for their citizenry when they have decided it is time to go to war: a rousing military parade.

But it is not the actor, ultimately, or the army of Fortinbras; it is Laertes, I believe, who determines Hamlet to act. Laertes provides the most persuasive spectacle not because he provides the "best" example but because his situation parallels that of Hamlet. Being Hamlet's peer, at least up to a point, his passionate stance constitutes the most powerful challenge imaginable. In such circumstances, even the most apathetic man's sense of **emulation** must rise to such a pitch that the sort of disaster that the fulfillment of the revenge demands can finally be achieved.

emulation (ĕm´yə-lā´shən) *n.* competitive imitation.

The simple and unreflective Laertes can shout to Claudius "give me my father" and then leap into his sister's grave in a wild demonstration of grief. Like a well-adjusted gentleman or a consummate actor, he can perform with the utmost sincerity all the actions his social milieu demands, even if they contradict each other. He can mourn the useless death of a human being at one minute and the next he can uselessly kill a dozen more if he is told that his honor is at stake. The death of his father and sister are almost less shocking to him than the lack of pomp and circumstance at their burial. At the rites of Ophelia, Laertes keeps asking the priest for "more ceremony." Laertes is a formalist[3] and he reads the tragedy of which he is a part very much like the formalists of all stripes. He does not question the validity of revenge. He does not question the literary *genre*. He does not question the relationship between revenge and mourning. These are not valid critical questions to him; they never enter his mind, just as it never occurs to most critics that Shakespeare himself could question the validity of revenge.

Hamlet watches Laertes leap into Ophelia's grave and the effect on him is electrifying. The reflective mood of the conversation with Horatio gives way to a wild imitation of the rival's theatrical mourning. At this point, he has obviously decided that he, too, would act according to the demands of society, that he would become another Laertes in other words. He, too, as a result, must leap into the grave of one who has already died, even as he prepares other graves for those still alive:

'Swounds, show me what thou'lt do.
Woo't weep? Woo't fight? Woo't fast? Woo't tear thyself?
Woo't drink up eisel? Eat a crocodile?
I'll do't. Dost thou come here to whine?
To outface me with leaping in her grave?

[3] **formalist:** one who strictly adheres to accepted rules and conventions.

Be buried quick with her, and so will I.

....

I'll rant as well as thou. . . .

Shakespeare can place these incredible lines in the mouth of Hamlet without undermining the dramatic credibility of what follows. Following the lead of Gertrude, the spectators will ascribe the outburst to "madness."

This is mere madness.
And thus awhile the fit will work on him.
Anon, as patient as the female dove
When that her golden couplets are disclosed,
His silence will sit drooping.

A little later Hamlet himself, now calmly determined to kill Claudius, will recall the recent outburst in most significant words:

I am very sorry, good Horatio,
That to Laertes I forgot myself,
For by the image of my cause I see
The portraiture of his. I'll court his favors.
But, sure, the bravery of his grief did put me
Into a towering passion.

Like all victims of mimetic suggestion, Hamlet reverses the true **hierarchy** between the other and himself. He should say: "by the image of *his* cause I see the portraiture of *mine*." This is the correct formula, obviously, for all the spectacles that have influenced Hamlet. The actor's tears and the military display of Fortinbras were already presented as mimetic models. In order to realize that Laertes, too, functions as a model, the last two lines are essential. The cool determination of Hamlet, at this point, is the transmutation[4] of the "towering passion" which he had vainly tried to build up before and which Laertes has finally communicated to him through the "bravery of his grief." This transmutation is unwittingly predicted by Gertrude when she compares Hamlet to the dove who becomes quiet after she has laid her eggs. Gertrude only thinks of Hamlet's previous changes of mood, as sterile as they were sudden, but her metaphor suggests a more tangible accomplishment, the birth of something portentous:

hierarchy (hī´ə-rär´kē) *n.* a ranking of status within a group.

Anon, as patient as the female dove
When that her golden couplets are disclosed,
His silence will sit drooping.

[4] **transmutation:** an alteration or conversion into another form.

COLLABORATIVE DISCUSSION With a partner, discuss whether you agree with Girard's assessment of Hamlet's character. Cite specific textual evidence from the essay to support your ideas.

Analyze Structure: Argument

RI 5

In his critical essay, Girard makes an **argument** about Shakespeare's motivations in writing *Hamlet*. Following a traditional structure for argument, Girard's essay begins with a **claim**, or statement of position on an issue. It includes **reasons** for making the claim. The reasoning is supported by **evidence**—in this case, examples from the text. In a persuasive argument, reasons flow logically from the evidence because the evidence is strong and relevant. When you analyze the structure of an argument and the way it is developed, these kinds of questions can help you assess the validity of the argument:

- What is Girard's claim?
- Does Girard support his claim with reasons? Are the reasons arranged logically, in a way that becomes increasingly convincing and engaging?
- Does Girard cite evidence from the drama to support his reasoning? Is the evidence both relevant and adequate?
- Are there any inconsistencies in Girard's argument?

Determine Central Ideas

RI 2

In his literary criticism "Hamlet's Dull Revenge," Girard develops central ideas related to the character of Hamlet and the Elizabethan theater. **Central ideas** are important points that an author wants to convey about a topic. In an argument, you can think of the claim and the supporting reasons as the central ideas. Readers can determine these central ideas by reading the details in each section of the essay and then inferring the major point—or in the case of argument, the reason—being advanced in that section. The graphic organizer shows how details from lines 71–97 of the essay support a central idea.

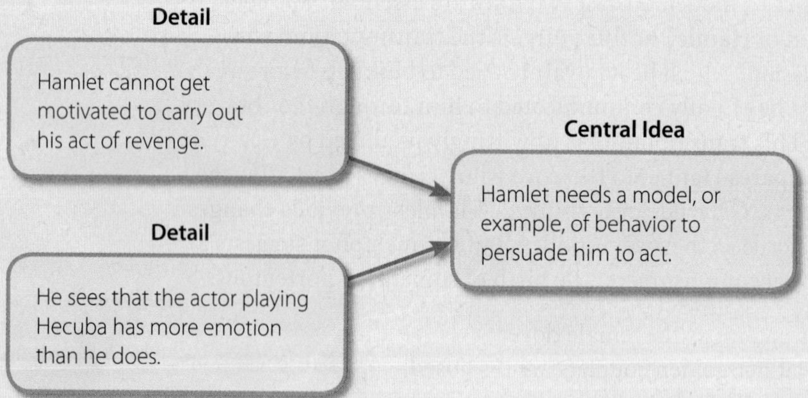

This central idea is one part of the reasoning that supports Girard's claim. Examining how the claim and other central ideas interact and build on one another can help the reader understand Girard's complex and subtle literary analysis.

RI 1, RI 2, RI 4, RI 5, W 1

Analyzing the Text

Cite Text Evidence Support your responses with evidence from the selection.

1. **Summarize** What claim does Girard develop in this essay?
2. **Analyze** What is Girard's explanation for why Hamlet fails to take revenge swiftly? What does he argue is the link between this behavior and revenge theater?
3. **Draw Conclusions** What central idea does Girard begin to develop in lines 25–70?
4. **Analyze** What is Girard's tone toward Shakespeare and his play? Explain how his feelings are revealed through his language as well as his choice of details.
5. **Evaluate** Girard provides three examples of the models that he claims Hamlet needs to work up a taste for vengeance. Identify these examples and discuss how their presentation within the argument strengthens or diminishes Girard's claims.
6. **Critique** According to Girard, what is the relationship between the character of Laertes and revenge theater? Is this interpretation of Laertes' role convincing? Why or why not?
7. **Evaluate** Review the lines spoken by Hamlet that Girard cites. Do these lines effectively support his perspective on Hamlet's state of mind? Explain.
8. **Summarize** Trace the reasoning that Girard uses to support his overall claim, showing the relationships among the central ideas.
9. **Analyze** What is the "something portentous" that Gertrude's birth metaphor refers to in line 195? In Girard's view, how might the phrase be applied to Shakespeare's play as well?

PERFORMANCE TASK

Writing Activity: Argument Does Girard succeed in presenting a valid interpretation of Shakespeare's play *Hamlet*?

- Write a sentence or two summarizing Girard's interpretation.
- Decide whether or not he convincingly supports this reading of the play in his essay.
- Give reasons for your claim and use details from the essay to provide evidence for your opinion.
- Use conventions of standard written English.

Critical Vocabulary

L 6

genre **double entendre** **entail**

emulation **hierarchy**

Practice and Apply Work with a partner and discuss which Critical Vocabulary word is most closely associated with the italicized word in each sentence and why.

1. Which word is most closely associated with *requirement*? Why?
2. Which word goes with *drama* or *novel*? Why?
3. Which word is associated with *rivalry*? Why?
4. Which word goes with *rank*? Why?
5. Which word might be associated with *ambiguity*? Why?

Vocabulary Strategy: Domain-Specific Words and Phrases

To convey his precise meaning, Girard uses **domain-specific words**, terms that are related to the field of literary criticism. The Critical Vocabulary words *genre* and *double entendre* are two examples of this specialized vocabulary. Many times domain-specific words are footnoted. If the words are not explained, following these steps will help you define them.

1. Look closely at the context in which the term is used for familiar phrases or words that give clues to its meaning.
2. Identify word parts—roots, prefixes, or suffixes—as well as the word's part of speech, and use them to help define the term.
3. Consult a print or digital dictionary to determine the exact meaning of the term, referring to a specialized dictionary if necessary.

Practice and Apply Work with a partner to complete these activities.

1. Review this list of words that Girard uses in his essay: *tragedy, katharsis, hero, mimetic, motif, formalist, metaphor.*
2. Use the footnotes, context clues, word parts, and a dictionary to define each word as it applies to literature or literary criticism.
3. Use three of the words to discuss an aspect of the play *Hamlet* with a partner.

Juan Rulfo (1918–1986) *was a Mexican writer. He wrote only one novel and a book of short stories, but they have earned him recognition as one of the finest writers in twentieth-century Latin America. His style, which is characterized by shifting points of view, flashbacks, and a stream-of-consciousness technique, influenced other Latin American authors, including well-known novelist Gabriel García Márquez. Rulfo's childhood and family life were disrupted by political conflict that wracked Mexico in the 1920s; his stories are primarily set in that time period and reflect the hardship and violence that characterized rural Mexicans' struggle to survive.*

Tell Them Not to Kill Me!

Short Story by Juan Rulfo translated by George D. Schade

AS YOU READ Make predictions about the main character in the story. Write down any questions you generate during reading.

"Tell them not to kill me, Justino! Go on and tell them that. For God's sake! Tell them. Tell them please for God's sake."

"I can't. There's a sergeant there who doesn't want to hear anything about you."

"Make him listen to you. Use your wits and tell him that scaring me has been enough. Tell him please for God's sake."

"But it's not just to scare you. It seems they really mean to kill you. And I don't want to go back there."

"Go on once more. Just once, to see what you can do."

"No. I don't feel like going. Because if I do they'll know I'm your son. If I keep bothering them they'll end up knowing who I am and will decide to shoot me too. Better leave things the way they are now."

"Go on, Justino. Tell them to take a little pity on me. Just tell them that."

Justino clenched his teeth and shook his head saying no.

And he kept on shaking his head for some time.

"Tell the sergeant to let you see the colonel. And tell him how old I am—How little I'm worth. What will he get out of killing me?

Nothing. After all he must have a soul. Tell him to do it for the blessed salvation of his soul."

Justino got up from the pile of stones which he was sitting on and walked to the gate of the corral. Then he turned around to say, "All right, I'll go. But if they decide to shoot me too, who'll take care of my wife and kids?"

"Providence will take care of them, Justino. You go there now and see what you can do for me. That's what matters."

They'd brought him in at dawn. The morning was well along now and he was still there, tied to a post, waiting. He couldn't keep still. He'd tried to sleep for a while to calm down, but he couldn't. He wasn't hungry either. All he wanted was to live. Now that he knew they were really going to kill him, all he could feel was his great desire to stay alive, like a recently resuscitated man.

Who would've thought that old business that happened so long ago and that was buried the way he thought it was would turn up? That business when he had to kill Don Lupe. Not for nothing either, as the Alimas tried to make out, but because he had his reasons. He remembered: Don Lupe Terreros, the owner of the Puerta de Piedra—and besides that, his compadre—was the one he, Juvencio Nava, had to kill, because he'd refused to let him pasture his animals, when he was the owner of the Puerta de Piedra and his compadre too.

At first he didn't do anything because he felt compromised. But later, when the drought came, when he saw how his animals were dying off one by one, plagued by hunger, and how his compadre Lupe continued to refuse to let him use his pastures, then was when he began breaking through the fence and driving his herd of skinny animals to the pasture where they could get their fill of grass. And Don Lupe didn't like it and ordered the fence mended, so that he, Juvencio Nava, had to cut open the hole again. So, during the day the hole was stopped up and at night it was opened again, while the stock stayed there right next to the fence, always waiting—his stock that before had lived just smelling the grass without being able to taste it.

And he and Don Lupe argued again and again without coming to any agreement.

Until one day Don Lupe said to him, "Look here, Juvencio, if you let another animal in my pasture, I'll kill it."

And he answered him, "Look here, Don Lupe, it's not my fault that the animals look out for themselves. They're innocent. You'll have to pay for it, if you kill them."

And he killed one of my yearlings.

This happened thirty-five years ago in March, because in April I was already up in the mountains, running away from the summons. The ten cows I gave the judge didn't do me any good, or the lien on my house either, to pay for getting me out of jail. Still later they used up what was left to pay so they wouldn't keep after me, but they kept

"All he could feel was his great desire to stay alive, like a recently resuscitated man."

after me just the same. That's why I came to live with my son on this other piece of land of mine which is called Palo de Venado. And my son grew up and got married to my daughter-in-law Ignacia and has had eight children now. So it happened a long time ago and ought to be forgotten by now. But I guess it's not.

I figured then that with about a hundred pesos everything could be fixed up. The dead Don Lupe left just his wife and two little kids still crawling. And his widow died soon afterward too—they say from grief. They took the kids far off to some relatives. So there was nothing to fear from them.

But the rest of the people took the position that I was still summoned to be tried just to scare me so they could keep on robbing me. Every time someone came to the village they told me, "There are some strangers in town, Juvencio."

And I would take off to the mountains, hiding among the madrone thickets and passing the days with nothing to eat but herbs. Sometimes I had to go out at midnight, as though the dogs were after me. It's been that way my whole life. Not just a year or two. My whole life.

And now they'd come for him when he no longer expected anyone, confident that people had forgotten all about it, believing that he'd spend at least his last days peacefully. "At least," he thought, "I'll have some peace in my old age. They'll leave me alone."

He'd clung to this hope with all his heart. That's why it was hard for him to imagine that he'd die like this, suddenly, at this time of life, after having fought so much to ward off death, after having spent his best years running from one place to another because of the alarms, now when his body had become all dried up and leathery from the bad days when he had to be in hiding from everybody.

Hadn't he even let his wife go off and leave him? The day when he learned his wife had left him, the idea of going out in search of her didn't even cross his mind. He let her go without trying to find out at all who she went with or where, so he wouldn't have to go down to the village. He let her go as he'd let everything else go, without putting up a fight. All he had left to take care of was his life, and he'd do that, if nothing else. He couldn't let them kill him. He couldn't. Much less now.

But that's why they brought him from there, from Palo de Venado. They didn't need to tie him so he'd follow them. He walked alone, tied by his fear. They realized he couldn't run with his old body, with those skinny legs of his like dry bark, cramped up with the fear of dying. Because that's where he was headed. For death. They told him so.

That's when he knew. He began to feel that stinging in his stomach that always came on suddenly when he saw death nearby, making his eyes big with fear and his mouth swell up with those mouthfuls of sour water he had to swallow unwillingly. And that thing that made his feet heavy while his head felt soft and his heart pounded with all its force against his ribs. No, he couldn't get used to the idea that they were going to kill him.

There must be some hope. Somewhere there must still be some hope left. Maybe they'd made a mistake. Perhaps they were looking for another Juvencio Nava and not him.

He walked along in silence between those men, with his arms fallen at his sides. The early-morning hour was dark, starless. The wind blew slowly, whipping the dry earth back and forth, which was filled with that odor like urine that dusty roads have.

His eyes, that had become squinty with the years, were looking down at the ground, here under his feet, in spite of the darkness. There in the earth was his whole life. Sixty years of living on it, of holding it tight in his hands, of tasting it like one tastes the flavor of meat. For a

long time he'd been crumbling it with his eyes, savoring each piece as if it were the last one, almost knowing it would be the last.

Then, as if wanting to say something, he looked at the men who were marching along next to him. He was going to tell them to let him loose, to let him go; "I haven't hurt anybody, boys," he was going to say to them, but he kept silent. "A little further on I'll tell them," he thought. And he just looked at them. He could even imagine they were his friends, but he didn't want to. They weren't. He didn't know who they were. He watched them moving at his side and bending down from time to time to see where the road continued.

He'd seen them for the first time at nightfall, that dusky hour when everything seems scorched. They'd crossed the furrows trodding on the tender corn. And he'd gone down on account of that—to tell them that the corn was beginning to grow there. But that didn't stop them.

He'd seen them in time. He'd always had the luck to see everything in time. He could've hidden, gone up in the mountains for a few hours until they left and then come down again. Already it was time for the rains to have come, but the rains didn't come and the corn was beginning to wither. Soon it'd be all dried up.

So it hadn't even been worthwhile, his coming down and placing himself among those men like in a hole, never to get out again.

And now he continued beside them, holding back how he wanted to tell them to let him go. He didn't see their faces, he only saw their bodies, which swung toward him and then away from him. So when he started talking he didn't know if they'd heard him. He said, "I've never hurt anybody." That's what he said. But nothing changed. Not one of the bodies seemed to pay attention. The faces didn't turn to look at him. They kept right on, as if they were walking in their sleep.

Then he thought that there was nothing else he could say, that he would have to look for hope somewhere else. He let his arms fall again to his sides and went by the first houses of the village, among those four men, darkened by the black color of the night.

"Colonel, here is the man."

They'd stopped in front of the narrow doorway. He stood with his hat in his hand, respectfully, waiting to see someone come out. But only the voice came out, "Which man?"

"From Palo de Venado, colonel. The one you ordered us to bring in."

"Ask him if he ever lived in Alima," came the voice from inside again.

"Hey, you. Ever lived in Alima?" the sergeant facing him repeated the question.

"Yes. Tell the colonel that's where I'm from. And that I lived there till not long ago."

"Ask him if he knew Guadalupe Terreros."

“He began to feel that stinging in his stomach that always came on suddenly when he saw death nearby.”

“He says did you know Guadalupe Terreros?”

“Don Lupe? Yes. Tell him that I knew him. He’s dead.”

Then the voice inside changed tone: “I know he died,” it said. And the voice continued talking, as if it was conversing with someone there on the other side of the reed wall.

“Guadalupe Terreros was my father. When I grew up and looked for him they told me he was dead. It’s hard to grow up knowing that the thing we have to hang on to to take roots from is dead. That’s what happened to us.

“Later on I learned that he was killed by being hacked first with a machete and then an ox goad[1] stuck in his belly. They told me he lasted more than two days and that when they found him, lying in an arroyo,[2] he was still in agony and begging that his family be taken care of.

“As time goes by you seem to forget this. You try to forget it. What you can’t forget is finding out that the one who did it is still alive, feeding his rotten soul with the illusion of eternal life. I couldn’t forgive that man, even though I don’t know him; but the fact that I know where he is makes me want to finish him off. I can’t forgive his still living. He should never have been born.”

From here, from outside, all he said was clearly heard. Then he ordered, “Take him and tie him up awhile, so he’ll suffer, and then shoot him!”

“Look at me, colonel!” he begged. “I’m not worth anything now. It won’t be long before I die all by myself, crippled by old age. Don’t kill me!”

“Take him away!” repeated the voice from inside.

---

[1] **ox goad:** a long stick with a pointed end used to control or guide oxen.

[2] **arroyo** (ə-roi´ō): a dry or frequently waterless streambed often found in arid regions.

"I've already paid, colonel. I've paid many times over. They took everything away from me. They punished me in many ways. I've spent about forty years hiding like a leper, always with the fear they'd kill me at any moment. I don't deserve to die like this, colonel. Let the Lord pardon me, at least. Don't kill me! Tell them not to kill me!"

There he was, as if they'd beaten him, waving his hat against the ground. Shouting.

Immediately the voice from inside said, "Tie him up and give him something to drink until he gets drunk so the shots won't hurt him."

Finally, now, he'd been quieted. There he was, slumped down at the foot of the post. His son Justino had come and his son Justino had gone and had returned and now was coming again.

He slung him on top of the burro. He cinched him up tight against the saddle so he wouldn't fall off on the road. He put his head in a sack so it wouldn't give such a bad impression. And then he made the burro giddap, and away they went in a hurry to reach Palo de Venado in time to arrange the wake for the dead man.

"Your daughter-in-law and grandchildren will miss you," he was saying to him. "They'll look at your face and won't believe it's you. They'll think the coyote has been eating on you when they see your face full of holes from all those bullets they shot at you."

COLLABORATIVE DISCUSSION With a partner, discuss the predictions you made as you read the story. Were you surprised by the revelations about Juvencio's past or by the way he died? Cite specific textual evidence to support your ideas.

Analyze Structure

RL 5

Authors make deliberate choices about how to structure a story to convey their meaning and to achieve a particular aesthetic, or artistic, impact. Rulfo uses a variety of narrative techniques that affect how readers understand both the plot and the characters of his story.

- **Shifting point of view:** The story begins with a third-person narrator, moves to first person, and then shifts back to third person. To analyze the purpose and effect of these changes, readers should consider what each narrator says, how each perspective relates to the other and to the story as a whole, and how the shifting point of view might affect the reader's response to the story.
- **Flashback:** Flashbacks are accounts of conversations or events that occurred before the beginning of the story. Rulfo's flashbacks help readers understand the main character and important plot points. They also build suspense as they delay the story's climax.
- **Conclusion:** Rulfo's decision to conclude his story abruptly is deliberate. Think about what purpose such a sudden ending might serve.

Analyze Point of View: Irony

RL 6

The point of view from which a story is narrated influences readers' understanding of events and characters. In Rulfo's short story, he shifts between first- and third-person narrators, which enables readers to understand Juvencio's feelings about his present situation, as well as the events that led him there.

Initially, Juvencio is a sympathetic character—a frightened old man talking to his son. As the story develops and readers learn more details, their perceptions of Juvencio change. A contrast develops between expectations and reality. This **irony** can be analyzed by comparing Juvencio's words, and what they suggest about his motives and actions, to the story that emerges as more details unfold. The following passage from the story is a good example.

> **I figured then that with about a hundred pesos everything could be fixed up. The dead Don Lupe left just his wife and two little kids still crawling. And his widow died soon afterward too—they say from grief. They took the kids far off to some relatives.**

Here, Juvencio presents the wife and children of the murdered Don Lupe as threats that have been neutralized, not as victims deserving compassion. This callous attitude is surprising based on Juvencio's words and actions earlier in the story. It is ironic that the initially sympathetic character of Juvencio actually turns out to be selfish and cold-hearted. As you analyze the story, think about what actually happens versus what you expected to happen.

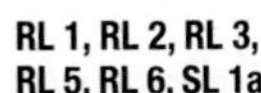

Analyzing the Text

Cite Text Evidence Support your responses with evidence from the selection.

1. **Analyze** What impression of the main character and his situation is created by the opening dialogue in which he begs his son to mediate? Explain.
2. **Draw Conclusions** In the story, Juvencio states that "he had to kill Don Lupe." What does this line reveal about how he views his deed? What do his further thoughts in lines 41–101 make clear to readers?
3. **Analyze** How does the author structure the story to reveal the details about Juvencio's life? Does the author use a straightforward chronological order? Explain.
4. **Interpret** Why is the sentence "So there was nothing to fear from them" (lines 73–74) ironic? What does it foreshadow?
5. **Evaluate** Identify where the point of view shifts from third person to first person in the story. Why does the author use the first person to have Juvencio narrate this part of the story? Does the change significantly affect the tone of the narrative?
6. **Analyze** Review the details that are revealed about Juvencio's crime prior to line 158. How does each new fact affect readers' perception of his integrity and his character? Explain what makes these revelations ironic.
7. **Cite Evidence** What is ironic about Juvencio's capture and his fierce desire to live? Cite details from the story that illustrate the irony.
8. **Draw Conclusions** Structurally, the dialogue between Juvencio and the Colonel balances the initial conversation between Juvencio and his son. What other purposes does it serve?
9. **Draw Conclusions** Why does the author choose to end the story without describing Juvencio's actual death? Cite details from the story to support your answer.

PERFORMANCE TASK

Speaking Activity: Discussion What is the central theme of this story, and how does the author's use of irony help develop this theme? Jot down details that support your ideas.

- In a small group, discuss the theme you have identified and cite several examples of how the author's use of irony supports this theme.
- As a group, examine the support and decide on the central theme.
- Create a group chart that summarizes your conclusions. Present it to the class.

Language and Style: Vary Syntax for Effect

L 3a

Syntax refers to the way in which words are arranged in a sentence. To keep readers interested and to draw attention to particular ideas, writers vary their syntax. For example, they might use inverted word order, alternate long sentences with short ones, or even include sentence fragments.

Read this passage from the story.

And I would take off to the mountains, hiding among the madrone thickets and passing the days with nothing to eat but herbs. Sometimes I had to go out at midnight, as though the dogs were after me. It's been that way my whole life. Not just a year or two. My whole life.

The author could have chosen not to vary the syntax:

And I would take off to the mountains, hiding among the madrone thickets and passing the days with nothing to eat but herbs. Sometimes I had to go out at midnight, as though the dogs were after me. It's been that way my whole life, not just for a year or two but for my whole life.

The two sentence fragments at the end of the original passage grab readers' attention. They are abrupt and unexpected. The meaning stands out because the syntax is different from the syntax of the previous sentences. In the second version, the two fragments are incorporated into a longer sentence. Visually, they don't catch the readers' attention, nor do they stand out when the sentence is read. The forcefulness of the two ideas is lost.

In formal writing, these methods can be used to vary syntax.

Method to Vary Syntax	Original	Revised
Revise a sentence to begin with a phrase or subordinate clause.	Don Lupe's son gave the old man something to drink out of pity.	Out of pity for the old man, Don Lupe's son gave him something to drink.
Invert the word order.	The old man shuffled along behind the soldiers.	Behind the soldiers shuffled the old man.
Combine two short sentences to clarify the relationship between ideas.	Juvencio becomes less sympathetic as the narrative unfolds. Still, his motive for killing Don Lupe remains vexingly strong.	Although Juvencio becomes less sympathetic as the narrative unfolds, his motive for killing Don Lupe remains vexingly strong.

Practice and Apply Rewrite this paragraph, varying the syntax for effect. Share your rewritten version with a partner and discuss your changes.

One puzzling aspect of the story is Rulfo's use of the word *compadre*. In Spanish, it means both "buddy" and "godfather." It's difficult to tell from the context of the story which meaning applies. If it means "buddy," it could make Juvencio's anger toward Don Lupe more justified. If it means "godfather," it could make Juvencio's murder more abhorrent.

Alex Kotlowitz *wrote one of the most important books of the twentieth century, according to the New York Public Library. That book, entitled* There Are No Children Here, *tells the story of two brothers trying to survive in a public housing project in Chicago. Much of his writing, in both books and articles, focuses on topics related to race and poverty. In addition to being a senior lecturer at Northwestern University, he contributes regularly to the* New York Times Magazine *and other publications. His most recent book is* Never a City So Real, *a portrait of Chicago.*

Blocking the Transmission of Violence

Feature Article by Alex Kotlowitz

AS YOU READ Pay attention to details that help you understand the connection between infectious diseases and violence.

Last summer, Martin Torres was working as a cook in Austin, Tex., when, on the morning of Aug. 23, he received a call from a relative. His 17-year-old nephew, Emilio, had been murdered. According to the police, Emilio was walking down a street on Chicago's South Side when someone shot him in the chest, possibly the culmination of an ongoing dispute. Like many killings, Emilio's received just a few sentences in the local newspapers. Torres, who was especially close to his nephew, got on the first Greyhound bus to Chicago. He was grieving and plotting **retribution**. "I thought, Man, I'm going to take care of business," he told me recently. "That's how I live. I was going hunting. This is my own blood, my nephew."

retribution (rĕt′rə-byo͞o′shən) *n.* appropriate punishment or revenge.

Torres, who is 38, grew up in a dicey section of Chicago, and even by the standards of his neighborhood he was a rough character. His nickname was Packman, because he was known to always pack a gun. He was first shot when he was 12, in the legs with buckshot by members of a rival gang. He was shot five more times, including once through the jaw, another time in his right shoulder and the last time—seven years ago—in his right thigh, with a .38-caliber bullet that is still lodged there. On his chest, he has tattooed a tombstone with the name "Buff" at its center, a tribute to a friend who was killed on his 18th birthday. Torres was the head of a small Hispanic gang, and though he is no longer active, he still wears two silver studs in his left ear, a sign of his **affiliation.**

affiliation (ə-fĭl´ē-ā´shən) *n.* association with.

When he arrived in Chicago, he began to ask around, and within a day believed he had figured out who killed his nephew. He also began drinking a lot. . . . He borrowed two guns, a .38 and a .380, from guys he knew. He would, he thought, wait until after the funeral to track down his nephew's assailants.

Zale Hoddenbach looks like an ex-military man. He wears his hair cropped and has a trimmed goatee that highlights his angular jaw. He often wears T-shirts that fit tightly around his muscled arms, though he also carries a slight paunch. When he was younger, Hoddenbach, who is also 38, belonged to a gang that was under the same umbrella as Torres's, and so when the two men first met 17 years ago at Pontiac Correctional Center, an Illinois maximum-security prison, they became friendly. Hoddenbach was serving time for armed violence; Torres for possession of a stolen car and a gun (he was, he says, on his way to make a hit). "Zale was always in segregation, in the hole for fights," Torres told me. "He was aggressive." In one scuffle, Hoddenbach lost the sight in his right eye after an inmate pierced it with a shank.[1] Torres and Hoddenbach were at Pontiac together for about a year but quickly lost touch after they were both released.

Shortly after Torres arrived in Chicago last summer, Hoddenbach received a phone call from Torres's brother, the father of the young man who was murdered. He was worried that Torres was preparing to seek revenge and hoped that Hoddenbach would speak with him. When Hoddenbach called, Torres was thrilled. He immediately thought that his old prison buddy was going to join him in his search for the killer. But instead Hoddenbach tried to talk him down, telling him retribution wasn't what his brother wanted. "I didn't understand what the hell he was talking about," Torres told me when I talked to him six months later. "This didn't seem like the person I knew." The next day Hoddenbach appeared at the wake, which was held at New Life Community Church, housed in a low-slung former factory. He spent the day by Torres's side, sitting with him, talking to him, urging him to respect his brother's wishes. When Torres went to the parking lot for a smoke, his hands shaking from agitation, Hoddenbach would follow. "Because of our relationship, I thought there was a chance," Hoddenbach told me. "We were both cut from the same cloth." Hoddenbach knew from experience that the longer he could delay Torres from heading out, the more chance he'd have of keeping him from shooting someone. So he let him vent for a few hours. Then Hoddenbach started laying into him with every argument he could

[1] **shank:** a crude, homemade knife.

Zale Hoddenbach, a CeaseFire interrupter

think of: *Look around, do you see any old guys here? I never seen so many young kids at a funeral. Look at these kids, what does the future hold for them? Where do we fit in? Who are you to step on your brother's wishes?*

The stubborn core of violence in American cities is troubling and perplexing. Even as homicide rates have declined across the country—in some places, like New York, by a remarkable amount—gunplay continues to plague economically struggling minority communities. For 25 years, murder has been the leading cause of death among African-American men between the ages of 15 and 34, according to the Centers for Disease Control and Prevention. . . .

The traditional response has been more focused policing and longer prison sentences, but law enforcement does little to disrupt a street code that allows, if not encourages, the settling of squabbles with deadly force. Zale Hoddenbach, who works for an organization called CeaseFire, is part of an unusual effort to apply the principles of public health to the brutality of the streets. CeaseFire tries to deal with these quarrels on the front end. Hoddenbach's job is to suss out[2] smoldering disputes and to intervene before matters get out of hand. His job title

[2] **suss out:** to discover or figure out.

is violence interrupter, a term that while not artful seems bluntly self-explanatory. Newspaper accounts usually refer to the organization as a gang-intervention program, and Hoddenbach and most of his colleagues are indeed former gang leaders. But CeaseFire doesn't necessarily aim to get people out of gangs—nor interrupt the drug trade. It's almost blindly focused on one thing: preventing shootings.

CeaseFire's founder, Gary Slutkin, is an epidemiologist and a physician who for 10 years battled infectious diseases in Africa. He says that violence directly mimics infections like tuberculosis and AIDS, and so, he suggests, the treatment ought to mimic the regimen applied to these diseases: go after the most infected, and stop the infection at its source. "For violence, we're trying to interrupt the next event, the next transmission, the next violent activity," Slutkin told me recently. "And the violent activity predicts the next violent activity like H.I.V. predicts the next H.I.V. and TB predicts the next TB." Slutkin wants to shift how we think about violence from a moral issue (good and bad people) to a public health one (healthful and unhealthful behavior).

Every Wednesday afternoon, in a Spartan room on the 10th floor of the University of Illinois at Chicago's public-health building, 15 to 25 men—and two women—all violence interrupters, sit around tables arranged in a circle and **ruminate** on the rage percolating in the city. Most are in their 40s and 50s, though some, like Hoddenbach, are a bit younger. All of them are black or Hispanic and in one manner or another have themselves been privy to, if not participants in, the brutality of the streets.

ruminate (ro͞o′mə-nāt′) *v.* to consider or think about carefully; contemplate.

On a Wednesday near the end of March, Slutkin made a rare appearance; he ordinarily leaves the day-to-day operations to a staff member. Fit at 57, Slutkin has a somewhat disheveled appearance—tie askew, hair uncombed, seemingly forgetful. Some see his presentation as a calculated effort to disarm. "Slutkin does his thing in his Slutkinesque way," notes Carl Bell, a psychiatrist who has long worked with children exposed to neighborhood violence and who admires CeaseFire's work. "He seems kind of disorganized, but he's not." Hoddenbach told me: "You can't make too much of that guy. In the beginning, he gives you that look like he doesn't know what you're talking about."

Slutkin had come to talk with the group about a recent high-profile incident outside Crane Tech High School on the city's West Side. An 18-year-old boy was shot and died on the school's steps, while nearby another boy was savagely beaten with a golf club. Since the beginning of the school year, 18 Chicago public-school students had been killed. (Another six would be murdered in the coming weeks.) The interrupters told Slutkin that there was a large police presence at the school, at least temporarily muffling any hostilities there, and that the police were even escorting some kids to and from

> For violence, we're trying to interrupt the next event, the next transmission, the next violent activity.

school. They then told him what was happening off the radar in their neighborhoods. There was the continuing discord at another high school involving a group of girls ("They'd argue with a stop sign," one of the interrupters noted); a 14-year-old boy with a gang tattoo on his forehead was shot by an older gang member just out of prison; a 15-year-old was shot in the stomach by a rival gang member as he came out of his house; and a former CeaseFire colleague was struggling to keep himself from losing control after his own sons were beaten. There was also a high-school basketball player shot four times; a 12-year-old boy shot at a party; gang members arming themselves to counter an egging of their freshly painted cars; and a high-ranking gang member who was on life support after being shot, and whose sister was overheard talking on her cellphone in the hospital, urging someone to "get those straps together. Get loaded."

These incidents all occurred over the previous seven days. In each of them, the interrupters had stepped in to try to keep one act of **enmity** from spiraling into another. Some had more success than others. Janell Sails prodded the guys with the egged cars to go to a car wash and then persuaded them it wasn't worth risking their lives over a stupid prank. At Crane Tech High School, three of the interrupters fanned out, trying to convince the five gangs involved in the conflict to lie low, but they conceded that they were unable to reach some of the main players. Many of the interrupters seem bewildered by what they see as a wilder group of youngsters now running the streets and by a gang structure that is no longer top-down but is instead made up of many small groups—which they refer to as cliques—whose members are answerable to a handful of peers. . . .

enmity (ĕn′mĭ-tē) *n.* hatred or hostility towards an enemy.

It became clear as they delivered their reports that many of the interrupters were worn down. One of them, Calvin Buchanan, whose street name is Monster and who just recently joined CeaseFire, showed the others six stitches over his left eye; someone had cracked a beer bottle on his head while he was mediating an argument between two men. The other interrupters applauded when Buchanan told them that, though tempted, he restrained himself from getting even.

When Slutkin finally spoke, he first praised the interrupters for their work. "Everybody's overreacting, and you're trying to cool them down," he told them. He then asked if any of them had been experiencing jitteriness or fear. He spent the next half-hour teaching stress-reduction exercises. If they could calm themselves, he seemed to be saying, they could also calm others. I recalled what one of the interrupters told me a few weeks earlier: "We helped create the madness, and now we're trying to debug it."

In the public-health field, there have long been two schools of thought on derailing violence. One focuses on environmental factors, specifically trying to limit gun purchases and making guns safer. The other tries to influence behavior by introducing school-based curricula like antidrug and safe-sex campaigns.

Slutkin is going after it in a third way—as if he were trying to contain an infectious disease. The fact that there's no vaccine or medical cure for violence doesn't dissuade him. He points out that in the early days of AIDS, there was no treatment either. In the short run, he's just trying to halt the spread of violence. In the long run, though, he says he hopes to alter behavior and what's considered socially acceptable.

Slutkin's perspective grew out of his own experience as an infectious-disease doctor. In 1981, six years out of the University of Chicago Pritzker School of Medicine, Slutkin was asked to lead the TB program in San Francisco. With an influx of new refugees from Cambodia, Laos and Vietnam, the number of cases in the city had nearly doubled. Slutkin chose to concentrate on those who had the most active TB; on average, they were infecting 6 to 10 others a year. Slutkin hired Southeast Asian outreach workers who could not only locate the infected individuals but who could also stick with them for nine months, making sure they took the necessary medication. These outreach workers knew the communities and spoke the languages, and they were able to persuade family members of infected people to be tested. Slutkin also went after the toughest cases—26 people with drug-resistant TB. The chance of curing those people was slim, but Slutkin reckoned that if they went untreated, the disease would continue to spread. "Gary wasn't constrained by the textbook," says Eric Goosby, who worked in the clinic and is now the chief executive of the Pangaea Global AIDS Foundation. Within two years, the number of TB cases, at least among these new immigrants, declined sharply.

Slutkin then spent 10 years in Africa, first in refugee camps in Somalia and then working, in Uganda and other countries, for the World Health Organization to curtail the spread of AIDS. . . . After leaving Africa, Slutkin returned to Chicago, where he was raised and where he could attend to his aging parents. . . . It was 1995, and there had been a series of horrific murders involving children in the city. He was convinced that longer sentences and more police officers had made little difference. "Punishment doesn't drive behavior," he told me. "Copying and modeling and the social expectations of your peers is what drives your behavior."

Borrowing some ideas (and the name) from a successful Boston program, Slutkin initially established an approach that exists in one form or another in many cities: outreach workers tried to get youth and young adults into school or to help them find jobs. These outreach workers were also doing dispute mediation. . . . One of Slutkin's colleagues, Tio Hardiman, brought up an uncomfortable truth: the program wasn't reaching the most **bellicose**, those most likely to pull a trigger. So in 2004, Hardiman suggested that, in addition to outreach workers, they also hire men and women who had been deep into street life, and he began recruiting people even while they were still in prison. Hardiman told me he was looking for those "right there on the edge." (The interrupters are paid roughly $15 an hour, and those working full time receive benefits from the University of Illinois at Chicago, where CeaseFire is housed.) The new recruits, with strong connections to the toughest communities, would focus solely on sniffing out clashes that had the potential to escalate. They would intervene in potential acts of retribution—as well as try to defuse seemingly minor spats that might erupt into something bigger, like disputes over women or insulting remarks.

bellicose (bĕl′ĭ-kōs′) *adj.* aggressively inclined to fight.

As CeaseFire evolved, Slutkin says he started to realize how much it was drawing on his experiences fighting TB and AIDS. "Early intervention in TB is actually treatment of the most infectious people," Slutkin told me recently. "They're the ones who are infecting others. So treatment of the most infectious spreaders is the most effective strategy known and now accepted in the world." And, he continued, you want to go after them with individuals who themselves were once either infectious spreaders or at high risk for the illness. In the case of violence, you use those who were once hard-core, once the most belligerent, once the most uncontrollable, once the angriest. They are the most convincing messengers. It's why, for instance, Slutkin and his colleagues asked sex workers in Uganda and other nations to spread the word to other sex workers about safer sexual behavior. Then, Slutkin said, you train them, as you would paraprofessionals[3]. . . .

The first step to containing the spread of an infectious disease is minimizing transmission. The parallel in Slutkin's Chicago work is thwarting retaliations, which is precisely what Hoddenbach was trying to do in the aftermath of Emilio Torres's murder. But Slutkin is also looking for the equivalent of a cure. The way public-health doctors think of curing disease when there are no drug treatments is by changing behavior. Smoking is the most obvious example. Cigarettes are still around. And there's no easy remedy for lung cancer

[3] **paraprofessionals:** specialized workers who assist physicians, attorneys, or other professionals.

or emphysema. So the best way to deal with the diseases associated with smoking is to get people to stop smoking. In Uganda, Slutkin and his colleagues tried to change behavior by encouraging people to have fewer sexual partners and to use condoms. CeaseFire has a visible public-communications campaign, which includes billboards and bumper stickers (which read, “Stop. Killing. People.”). It also holds rallies—or what it calls “responses”—at the sites of killings. But much research suggests that peer or social pressure is the most effective way to change behavior. “It was a real turning point for me,” Slutkin said, “when I was working on the AIDS epidemic and saw research findings that showed that the principal determinant of whether someone uses a condom or not is whether they think their friends use them.” Daniel Webster, a professor of public health at Johns Hopkins University who has looked closely at CeaseFire, told me, “The guys out there doing the interruption have some prestige and reputation, and I think the hope is that they start to change a culture so that you can retain your status, retain your manliness and be able to walk away from events where all expectations were that you were supposed to respond with lethal force.”

As a result, the interrupters operate in a netherworld between upholding the law and upholding the logic of the streets. They're not meant to be a substitute for the police, and indeed, sometimes the interrupters negotiate disputes involving illicit goings-on. They often walk a fine line between mediating and seeming to condone criminal activity. At one Wednesday meeting this past December, the interrupters argued over whether they could dissuade stickup artists from shooting their victims; persuading them to stop robbing people didn't come up in the discussion. . . .

Relying on hardened types—the ones who, as Webster of Johns Hopkins says, have some prestige on the streets—is risky. They have prestige for a reason. Hoddenbach, who once beat someone so badly he punctured his lungs, is reluctant to talk about his past. “I don't want to be seen as a monster,” he told me. . . . Hoddenbach always worked. He did maintenance on train equipment and towed airplanes at a private airport. But he was also active in a Hispanic street gang and was known for his **unmitigated** aggression. He served a total of eight years in the state penitentiary, the last stay for charges that included aggravated battery. He was released in 2002.

unmitigated
(ŭn-mĭt´ĭ-gā´tĭd) *adj.* complete and undiminishing.

In January, I was with Slutkin in Baltimore, where he spoke about CeaseFire to a small gathering of local civic leaders at a private home. During the two-hour meeting, Slutkin never mentioned that the interrupters were ex-felons. When I later asked him about that omission, he conceded that talking about their personal histories “is a dilemma. I haven't solved it.” I spent many hours with Hoddenbach and the others, trying to understand how they chose to make the transition from gangster to peacemaker, how they put thuggery

Gary Slutkin, founder of CeaseFire

behind them. It is, of course, their street savvy and reputations that make them effective for CeaseFire. (One supporter of the program admiringly called it "a terrifying strategy" because of the inherent risks.) Some CeaseFire workers have, indeed, reverted to their old ways. One outreach worker was fired after he was arrested for possession of an AK-47 and a handgun. Another outreach worker and an interrupter were let go after they were arrested for dealing drugs. Word-of-mouth allegations often circulate, and privately, some in the police department worry about CeaseFire's workers returning to their old habits.

Not all the interrupters I talked to could articulate how they had made the transition. Some, like Hoddenbach, find religion—in his case, Christianity. He also has four children he feels responsible for, and has found ways to decompress, like going for long runs. (His brother Mark speculated that "maybe he just wants to give back what he took out.") I once asked Hoddenbach if he has ever apologized to anyone he hurt. We were with one of his old friends from the street, who started guffawing, as if I had asked Hoddenbach if he ever wore dresses. "I done it twice," Hoddenbach told us—quickly silencing his friend and saving me from further embarrassment. (One apology was to the brother of the man whose lungs he'd punctured; the other was to a rival gang member he shot.) . . .

Recently I went out to lunch with Hoddenbach and Torres. It had been four months since Torres buried his nephew. Torres, who looked worn and agitated (he would get up periodically to smoke a cigarette outside), seemed paradoxically both grateful to and annoyed at Hoddenbach. In the end, Hoddenbach had persuaded him not to avenge his nephew's murder. Torres had returned the guns and quickly left town. This was his first visit back to Chicago. "I felt like a punk," he told me, before transferring to the present tense. "I feel shameful." He said he had sought revenge for people who weren't related to him—"people who weren't even no blood to me." But he held back in the case of his nephew. "I still struggle with it," he said. On the ride over to the restaurant, Torres had been playing a CD of his nephew's favorite rap songs. It got him hyped up, and he blurted out to Hoddenbach, "I feel like doing something." Hoddenbach chided him and shut off the music. "Stop being an idiot," he told Torres.

"Something made me do what Zale asked me to do," Torres said later, looking more puzzled than comforted. "Which is respect my brother's wishes."

When Slutkin heard of Hoddenbach's intervention, he told me: "The interrupters have to deal with how to get someone to save face. In other words, how do you not do a shooting if someone has insulted you, if all of your friends are expecting you to do that? . . . In fact, what our interrupters do is put social pressure in the other direction."

He continued: "This is cognitive dissonance.[4] Before Zale walked up to him, this guy was holding only one thought. So you want to put another thought in his head. It turns out talking about family is what really makes a difference." Slutkin didn't take this notion to the interrupters; he learned it from them. . . .

Baltimore, Newark and Kansas City, Mo., have each replicated components of the CeaseFire model and have received training from the Chicago staff. In Baltimore, the program, which is run by the city, combines the work of interrupters and outreach workers and has been concentrated in one East Baltimore neighborhood. (The program recently expanded to a second community.) Early research out of the Johns Hopkins Bloomberg School of Public Health shows that in the East Baltimore neighborhood there were on average two shootings a month just before the program started. During the first four months that interrupters worked the streets, there had not been a single incident.

"My eyes rolled immediately when I heard what the model was," says Webster of Johns Hopkins, who is studying the Baltimore project. Webster knew the forces the interrupters were up against and considered it wishful thinking that they could effectively mediate disputes. "But when I looked closer at the data," Webster continues,

[4] **cognitive dissonance:** having contradictory or conflicting ideas or attitudes.

> "The interrupters have to deal with how to get someone to save face."

"and got to know more about who these people were and what they were doing, I became far less skeptical and more hopeful. We're going to learn from it. And it will evolve." George Kelling, a Rutgers professor of criminal justice who is helping to establish an effort in Newark to reduce homicide, helped develop the "broken window" theory of fighting crime: addressing small issues quickly. He says a public-health model will be fully effective only if coupled with other efforts, including more creative policing and efforts to get gang members back to school or to work. But he sees promise in the CeaseFire model. "I had to overcome resistance," Kelling told me, referring to the introduction of a similar program in Newark. "But I think Slutkin's on to something."

Most of the police officials I spoke with, in both Chicago and Baltimore, were grateful for the interrupters. James B. Jackson, now the first deputy superintendent in Chicago, was once the commander of the 11th district, which has one of the highest rates of violent crime in the city. Jackson told me that after his officers investigated an incident, he would ask the police to pull back so the interrupters could mediate. He understood that if the interrupters were associated with the police, it would jeopardize their standing among gang members. "If you look at how segments of the population view the police department, it makes some of our efforts problematic," Baltimore's police commissioner, Frederick H. Bealefeld III, told me. "It takes someone who knows these guys to go in and say, 'Hey, lay off.' We can't do that."

Like many new programs that taste some success, CeaseFire has ambitions that threaten to outgrow its capacity. Slutkin has put much of his effort on taking the project to other cities (there's interest from Los Angeles, Oakland and Wilmington, Delaware, among others), and he has consulted with the State Department about assisting in Iraq and in Kenya. (CeaseFire training material has been made available to the provincial reconstruction teams in Iraq.) Meanwhile, their Chicago project is underfinanced, and the interrupters seem stressed from the amount of work they've taken on. . . .

Slutkin says that it makes sense to purify the water supply if—and only if—you acknowledge and treat the epidemic at hand. In other words, antipoverty measures will work only if you treat violence. It would seem intuitive that violence is a result of economic deprivation, but the relationship between the two is not static. People who have little expectation for the future live recklessly. On the other side of the coin, a community in which arguments are settled by gunshots is unlikely to experience economic growth and opportunity. In his book "The Bottom Billion," Paul Collier argues that one of the characteristics of many developing countries that suffer from entrenched poverty is what he calls the conflict trap, the inability to escape a cycle of violence, usually in the guise of civil wars. Could the same be true in our inner cities, where the **ubiquity** of guns and gunplay pushes businesses and residents out and leaves behind those who can't leave, the most impoverished?

ubiquity (yo͞o-bĭk´wĭ-tē) *n.* constant presence or prevalence.

In this, Slutkin sees a direct parallel to the early history of seemingly incurable infectious diseases. "Chinatown, San Francisco in the 1880s," Slutkin says. "Three ghosts: malaria, smallpox and leprosy. No one wanted to go there. Everybody blamed the people. Dirty. Bad habits. Something about their race. Not only is everybody afraid to go there, but the people there themselves are afraid at all times because people are dying a lot and nobody really knows what to do about it. And people come up with all kinds of other ideas that are not scientifically grounded—like putting people away, closing the place down, pushing the people out of town. Sound familiar?"

COLLABORATIVE DISCUSSION How did an infectious disease doctor get involved in stopping violence? With a partner, discuss how Dr. Slutkin's career in Africa connects to what he is doing now in Chicago. Cite specific textual evidence from the article to support your ideas.

Analyze Ideas and Events

RI 3

The feature article "Blocking the Transmission of Violence" includes a great deal of information. To enable readers to understand how all the ideas interact and fit together, Alex Kotlowitz chooses a problem-solution organization. The graphic organizer shows how readers can use this organization to help them analyze the development of the author's major points:

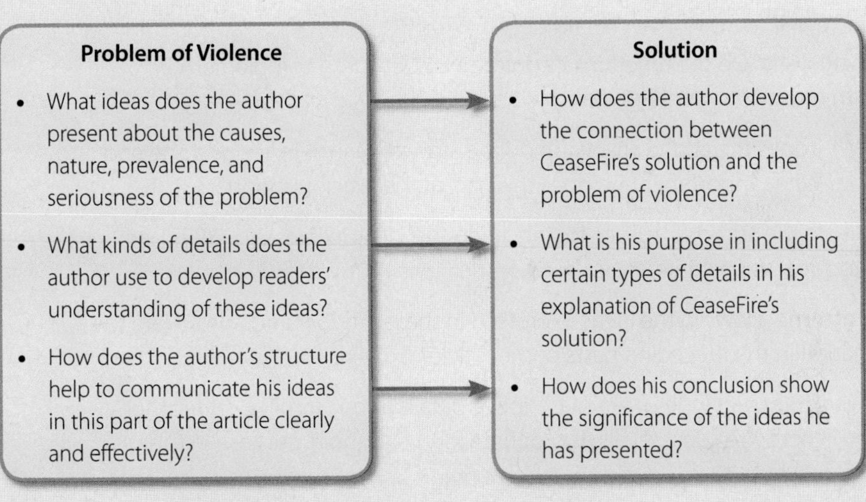

Support Inferences: Draw Conclusions

RI 1

Kotlowitz expects readers to draw their own conclusions from the ideas and details he shares in "Blocking the Transmission of Violence." When readers **draw conclusions**, they use textual evidence as well as their own prior knowledge and experience to make a judgment or statement of belief. Conclusions are often universal in that they can apply to a situation or issue beyond what is in the text.

From the information in this article, readers can draw several conclusions about the problem of violence and possible solutions, using these strategies:

- Examine both the ideas and supporting details that the author includes in his discussion of the problem and solution.
- Use this information to make inferences, or logical assumptions, about specific facets of violence or about CeaseFire.
- Combine the information and your inferences to arrive at a new understanding that applies to the subject beyond the context of this article.

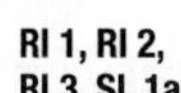

Analyzing the Text

RI 1, RI 2, RI 3, SL 1a

Cite Text Evidence Support your responses with evidence from the selection.

1. **Cause/Effect** What motive triggers Martin Torres's desire to commit an act of violence? Why did the author place this account at the beginning of the article?
2. **Draw Conclusions** What does the list of incidents discussed at the CeaseFire meeting illustrate about the prevalence and nature of violence? What effect is this list likely to have on readers?
3. **Draw Conclusions** Do the functions performed by CeaseFire complement or conflict with those of law enforcement?
4. **Analyze** Why does the author follow up on the story of Martin Torres near the end of his article? What important ideas does this part of the article support?
5. **Infer** What are the author's reasons for including the ideas in lines 391–399? Cite evidence to support your inference.
6. **Identify Patterns** How do the ideas expressed in the last two paragraphs relate to the information in the preceding parts of the article? Explain.
7. **Critique** The author includes many descriptive details about Torres, Hoddenbach, Slutkin, and others. Are such details appropriate for the author's purpose in this article? Why or why not?

PERFORMANCE TASK

Speaking Activity: Discussion In a small group, discuss your conclusions about whether CeaseFire is the type of organization that could work in many different communities confronting the problem of violence.

- Jot down the ideas from the article that you think offer the most valuable insight into the problems of violence and the potential solutions.
- Apply the insights from the article to communities beyond Chicago—your own community or a community whose violent conflicts are frequently in the headlines.
- Bring your notes to a group conversation. Present your conclusions and listen to others' conclusions. As a group, discuss the pros and cons of CeaseFire and write a statement that summarizes the group's ideas.

Critical Vocabulary

retribution **affiliation** **ruminate** **enmity**

bellicose **unmitigated** **ubiquity**

Practice and Apply Complete the sentence in a way that shows your understanding of the Critical Vocabulary word.

1. The *bellicose* expression on his face alerted those around him that . . .
2. The *ubiquity* of thieves in the neighborhood meant . . .
3. It is important to stop displays of *enmity* early on because . . .
4. The ex-convict was proud of his *affiliation* with CeaseFire because . . .
5. They met to *ruminate* on possible solutions before they made a decision because . . .
6. His *unmitigated* rage was frightening because . . .
7. The impulse to seek *retribution* should be restrained because . . .

Vocabulary Strategy: Latin Roots

The Critical Vocabulary words *affiliation* and *bellicose* are both derived from Latin roots. Knowing the meaning of their roots can help readers to define many related words, such as those shown in the chart.

Root/Meaning	Related Words
bellum: war	**bellicose**, belligerence, rebel, rebellious, antebellum
filius: son	**affiliation**, affiliate, filial

Practice and Apply Work with a partner to complete the steps.

1. Define each of the related words in the chart. Use your knowledge of the meaning of their roots. Check your definition in the dictionary to confirm.
2. For each word, write a sentence that includes context clues to help convey the word's meaning.
3. Read your sentences to another pair. Discuss your use of each word.

L 2

Language and Style: Direct and Indirect Quotations

In his article, Alex Kotlowitz includes both direct and indirect quotations. **Direct quotations** are a speaker's exact words. They are set off by quotation marks and usually by a comma. **Indirect quotations** are the writer's restatement of a speaker's words. They are often introduced by *that* and are not punctuated with quotation marks, showing that the exact words are not recorded. Writers will often use indirect quotations when it is the idea they want to convey rather than the expression of the idea.

Kotlowitz includes a direct quotation from Torres in the first paragraph of his article:

> **"I thought, Man, I'm going to take care of business," he told me recently. "That's how I live. I was going hunting. This is my own blood, my nephew."**

The author could have chosen to present most of Torres's comments as an indirect quotation:

> **Torres said to me that he was going to get revenge for his nephew's death. He explained that it was how he lived; he was "going hunting."**

Notice the difference between the two versions. In the first, Torres's own words show his raw emotion. Readers can more clearly hear his voice as he uses the expression "Man" and talks about his "own blood." The second version conveys the idea without the emotion or sense of the speaker's personality.

Kotlowitz uses direct quotations for effect, when restating the speaker's words would dilute their impact. He uses indirect quotations when he wants to integrate the information more smoothly into his own writing and use it to support a point that he is making.

The chart shows different ways to punctuate direct quotations:

Punctuation of Direct Quotations	
with tag at beginning	The writer said, "I saw that in certain groups violence is a way to live up to social expectations."
with tag interrupting the quotation	"He taught us that violence is not a solution," the teen said, "but the way to start another problem."
with tag after the quotation	"We need to mediate in the hopes that we can reach a peaceful settlement," said the interrupter.
to introduce a long quotation	The interrupter told me the philosophy behind CeaseFire: "We want to prevent shootings . . ."

Practice and Apply Return to the article. Copy several of the direct quotations that the author includes. Rewrite them as indirect quotations. Analyze the way the change affects the impact of that part of the article.

Wisława Szymborska (1923–2012) *was born in Poland and remained there throughout her life. She lived modestly, supporting herself with a full-time job at a literary magazine. Though her body of work includes only about 400 poems, it was remarkable enough to be recognized with a Nobel Prize in 1996. In her Nobel lecture, she compared poets to scientists because, just as scientists need to question what they know through rigorous experimentation, poets need to question what they know through writing. Though her poetry is sometimes seen as political, she considered her work to be more prosaic, dealing with ordinary people and life.*

Hatred

Poem by Wisława Szymborska

AS YOU READ Pay attention to the details that characterize hatred. Write down any questions you generate during reading.

See how efficient it still is,
how it keeps itself in shape—
our century's hatred.
How easily it vaults the tallest obstacles.
How rapidly it pounces, tracks us down.

It's not like other feelings.
At once both older and younger.
It gives birth itself to the reasons
that give it life.
When it sleeps, it's never eternal rest.
And sleeplessness won't sap its strength; it feeds it.

One religion or another—
whatever gets it ready, in position.
One fatherland or another—
whatever helps it get a running start.
Justice also works well at the outset
until hate gets its own momentum going.

Hatred. Hatred.
Its face twisted in a grimace
of erotic ecstasy.

Oh these other feelings,
listless weaklings.
Since when does brotherhood
draw crowds?
Has compassion
ever finished first?
Does doubt ever really rouse the rabble?
Only hatred has just what it takes.

Gifted, diligent, hard-working.
Need we mention all the songs it has composed?
All the pages it has added to our history books?
All the human carpets it has spread
over countless city squares and football fields?

Let's face it:
it knows how to make beauty.
The splendid fire-glow in midnight skies.
Magnificent bursting bombs in rosy dawns.
You can't deny the inspiring pathos of ruins
and a certain bawdy humor to be found
in the sturdy column jutting from their midst.

Hatred is a master of contrast—
between explosions and dead quiet,
red blood and white snow.
Above all, it never tires
of its leitmotif—the impeccable executioner
towering over its soiled victim.
It's always ready for new challenges.
If it has to wait awhile, it will.
They say it's blind. Blind?
It has a sniper's keen sight
and gazes unflinchingly at the future
as only it can.

COLLABORATIVE DISCUSSION What impression of hatred does the poet create? With a partner, discuss the details that create a vivid image of hatred. Cite specific textual details from the poem to support your ideas.

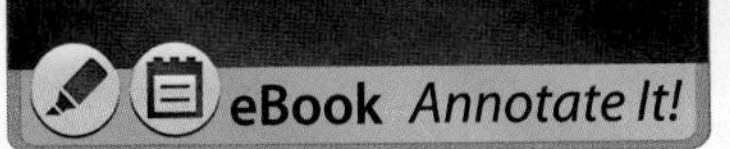

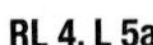

Determine Figurative Meanings: Personification

Personification is a figure of speech in which human qualities are given to objects, animals, ideas, or emotions. By imagining the non-human subject as human, the writer can express insights and abstractions in a concrete way that readers in turn can visualize and connect to their own realm of experience.

To convey her insights into the nature of hatred, Szymborska personifies the powerful emotion. She develops her message by commenting on hatred's actions, habits, accomplishments, and other attributes as if it were human. By the end of the poem, a detailed picture of hatred has been drawn; readers can almost see it standing before them: "Gifted, diligent, hard-working."

RL 1, RL 4, RL 6, W 3d, L 5a

Analyzing the Text

Cite Text Evidence Support your responses with evidence from the selection.

1. **Analyze** What image of hatred is created by the personification in lines 1–5 and 12–20? What words contribute to this image?
2. **Synthesize** Explain the ideas about hatred conveyed through the apparent contradictions, or paradoxes, in lines 6–11.
3. **Compare** How does the poet use personification in lines 21–28 to contrast hatred with compassion, brotherhood, and doubt?
4. **Analyze** How would you describe the poem's tone? Cite evidence to support your response.
5. **Draw Conclusions** The poet locates phrases that seem to portray hatred positively—such as "it knows how to make beauty" (line 35)—near details that show how hatred triggers destruction. What message about hatred is the poet conveying through this juxtaposition?

PERFORMANCE TASK

Writing Activity: Comparison Why is personification an effective literary device?

- Choose three stanzas of "Hatred." Rewrite them, conveying the ideas without the use of personification.
- In a small group, read your rewritten version. Together, discuss how the absence of personification alters the poem's meaning and impact.
- Present your group's conclusions to the class.

Language and Style: Repetition and Parallelism

L 3

In poetry, the techniques of repetition and parallelism affect both sound and sense. They draw attention to key words or phrases, and they can contribute to the rhythm and tone of a poem.

Notice how the poet uses **repetition**, the repeating of key words and phrases, in "Hatred":

Need we mention all the songs it has composed?
All the pages it has added to our history books?
All the human carpets it has spread . . .

The repetition of "all" directs readers' attention to the thought contained in each line. The meaning of the word itself emphasizes hatred's far-reaching impact.

Parallelism, using similar grammatical constructions to express ideas that are related or equal in importance, appears in these lines from "Hatred":

Hatred is a master of contrast—
between explosions and dead quiet,
red blood and white snow.

The repeated grammatical construction of two nouns and modifiers joined by the conjunction *and* draws attention to the contrasts; in doing so, the poet shows how hatred multiplies its violent effects. She could have written the lines in this way:

Hatred is a master of contrast—
between explosions and dead quiet,
with red blood on white snow.

The change in structure makes the last line less dramatic and shifts the rhythm, deemphasizing the last image.

Parallelism and repetition can be used together to add drama and tension to lines.

How easily it vaults the tallest obstacles.
How rapidly it pounces, tracks us down.

The repetition of *how* along with the same grammatical construction at the beginning of each line adds almost a physical punch to the lines, emphasizing the athleticism of hatred.

Practice and Apply Write a brief poem in the style of Szymborska, personifying an emotion such as happiness or nervousness. Include examples of both repetition and parallelism in your poem. Exchange your work with a partner and share feedback on each other's use of personification, repetition, and parallelism.

Write an Analytical Essay

W 2a–f Write informative/explanatory texts.
W 4 Produce clear and coherent writing.
W 5 Develop and strengthen writing.
W 9a–b Draw evidence from literary or informational texts.

The title character in *Hamlet* feels trapped in a cycle of violence that he cannot break. Consider *Hamlet* and the other texts in the collection. How does violence affect people's ability to control their future? For example, does violence limit people's choices or prevent them from changing their circumstances? Write an analytical essay on the effects of violence as presented in the collection.

An effective analytical essay

- expresses a thesis statement about the effect of violence on the future as it is portrayed in *Hamlet* and one other selection
- engages the reader with an observation, quotation, or detail
- organizes central ideas in a logically structured body that develops the thesis statement
- includes relevant textual evidence to illustrate central ideas
- uses transitions and text structures to create a cohesion between sections of the text and among ideas
- has a concluding section that follows logically from the body

Mentor Text See how this example from "Blocking the Transmission of Violence" uses transitions that indicate the sequence of events to create cohesion.

> "Slutkin then spent 10 years in Africa, first in refugee camps in Somalia and then working, in Uganda and other countries, for the World Health Organization to curtail the spread of AIDS. . . . After leaving Africa, Slutkin returned to Chicago, where he was raised and where he could attend to his aging parents. . . ."

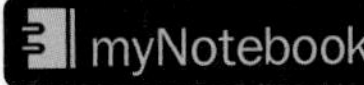

Use the annotation tools in your eBook to find evidence to support your analysis. Save each piece of evidence to your notebook.

PLAN

Analyze the Texts Review *Hamlet* and one other text in this collection. Pay attention to the effects of violence in each text.

- Make notes about specific acts of violence mentioned in the texts.
- Consider how violence affects the characters' or people's ability to control their future.
- Compare and contrast Shakespeare's portrayal of violence in *Hamlet* with that of one other writer. Note similarities and differences in the two writers' views about violence's effect on one's future.
- List details, examples, and quotations that support your conclusions.

ACADEMIC VOCABULARY

As you develop your ideas about violence, be sure to use these words.

drama
integrity
mediate
restrain
trigger

Get Organized Organize your details and evidence in an outline.

- Write your thesis statement about the way violence affects people's future in the texts. For example, you might say that the texts suggest that people can avoid getting caught in a cycle of violent acts when they receive help from others.
- Search for an interesting quotation or detail from one of the texts to engage readers in your introduction.
- Decide what organizational pattern you will use for your essay. For example, you might present your central ideas about violence point by point, referring to the texts as you develop each point. Or, you could present your ideas about one text and then the other.
- Use your organizational pattern to arrange into a logical order the textual evidence you have gathered in support of your central ideas.
- Write down some ideas for your conclusion that reflect your own perspective on how violence affects people's future.

Interactive Lessons

To help you plan your essay, complete the following lesson:

- Writing Informative Texts: Organizing Ideas

PRODUCE

Draft Your Essay Write a draft of your essay, following your outline.

- Write a clear thesis statement so that readers will understand your view on the topic. Include an attention-grabbing detail or quotation.
- Present your details, quotations, and examples from the selections in logically ordered paragraphs. Each paragraph should have a central idea with evidence to support it.
- Use transitions and text structures to link sections of the text and to clarify the relationships among your ideas.
- Write a satisfying conclusion that summarizes your analysis.

As you draft your analytical essay, remember that this kind of writing requires formal language and a respectful tone.

myWriteSmart

Write your rough draft in *my*WriteSmart. Focus on getting your ideas down, rather than on perfecting your choice of language.

Interactive Lessons

To help you draft your essay, complete the following lesson:

- Writing Informative Texts: Elaboration

Language and Style: Text Structures

Note the clear organization of text in the following passage from "Blocking the Transmission of Violence."

> "Some had more success than others. Janell Sails prodded the guys with the egged cars to go to a car wash and then persuaded them it wasn't worth risking their lives over a stupid prank. At Crane Tech High School, three of the interrupters fanned out, trying to convince the five gangs involved in the conflict to lie low, but they conceded that they were unable to reach some of the main players."

The writer makes a statement about the interrupters' attempts to stop violence from spreading and then provides specific examples to support it. Look for places where you can use text structures to clarify your ideas and make your essay more clear and cohesive.

REVISE

Have your partner or a group of peers review your draft in *my*WriteSmart. Ask your reviewers to note any evidence that does not support the thesis statement.

Improve Your Draft Have your partner or a group of peers review your draft. Use the following chart to revise your draft.

Questions	Tips	Revision Techniques
Does the essay include a clear thesis statement?	**Highlight** the thesis statement.	**Add** or **clarify** your thesis statement.
Are central ideas organized in a clear and logical way?	**Note** any instances where ideas may not be in a clear, logical order.	**Reorder** ideas so that they are presented in a clear and logical way.
Does relevant text evidence support your central ideas?	**Underline** details, quotations, and examples that support your central ideas.	**Elaborate** with text evidence that supports your central ideas. **Delete** evidence that is not relevant.
Do transitions and text organization create cohesion within the essay?	**Underline** transitions that link ideas and sections within the text. **Note** where text organization clarifies ideas.	**Add** transitions to link ideas and sections. **Reword** sections so that text is organized more clearly.
Does the conclusion summarize your analysis?	**Highlight** the summary of your analysis.	**Add** one or more sentences to summarize your analysis and explain your perspective.

Interactive Lessons

To help you revise your essay, complete the following lesson:

- Writing as a Process: Revising and Editing

PRESENT

Publish Online If your school has a website where you can post your writing, work with your classmates to publish your collection of essays online. First, review your own essay and look for places to add links to online sources that readers may find helpful, such as a video clip from a theatrical production or film version of *Hamlet*. Then, as a group, create a front page that introduces the collection and invites readers to explore the individual essays. You might also consider setting up a blog to allow readers to comment on the essays.

PERFORMANCE TASK A RUBRIC
ANALYTICAL ESSAY

	Ideas and Evidence	Organization	Language
4	• An eloquent introduction includes the titles and authors of the selections; the thesis statement presents a unique perspective on the topic as it relates to the texts. • Specific, relevant details support the central ideas. • A satisfying concluding section summarizes the analysis.	• Central ideas and supporting evidence are organized effectively and logically throughout the essay. • Varied transitions successfully show the relationships between ideas.	• The analysis has an appropriately formal style and a knowledgeable, objective tone. • Language is precise and captures the writer's thoughts with originality. • Sentence beginnings, lengths, and structures vary and have a rhythmic flow. • Spelling, capitalization, and punctuation are correct. If handwritten, the essay is legible. • Grammar and usage are correct.
3	• The introduction identifies the titles and authors of the selections but could be more engaging; the thesis statement adequately sets up the analysis. • One or two central ideas need more support. • The concluding section summarizes most of the analysis.	• The organization of central ideas and supporting evidence is confusing in a few places. • A few more transitions are needed to clarify the relationships between ideas.	• The style becomes informal in a few places, and the tone does not always communicate confidence. • Most language is precise. • Sentence beginnings, lengths, and structures vary somewhat. • Several spelling, capitalization, and punctuation mistakes occur. If handwritten, the essay is mostly legible. • Some grammatical and usage errors are repeated in the essay.
2	• The introduction identifies the titles and the authors of the selections; the thesis statement only hints at the main idea of the analysis. • Details support some central ideas but are often too general. • The concluding section gives an incomplete summary of the analysis and merely restates the thesis statement.	• Most central ideas are organized logically, but many supporting details are out of place. • More transitions are needed throughout the essay to connect ideas.	• The style is informal in many places, and the tone reflects a superficial understanding of the selections. • Language is repetitive or vague at times. • Sentence structures barely vary, and some fragments or run-on sentences are present. • Spelling, capitalization, and punctuation are often incorrect but do not make reading the essay difficult. If handwritten, the essay may be partially illegible. • Grammar and usage are incorrect in many places, but the writer's ideas are still clear.
1	• The appropriate elements of an introduction are missing. • Details and evidence are irrelevant or missing. • The analysis lacks a concluding section.	• A logical organization is not used; ideas are presented randomly. • Transitions are not used, making the essay difficult to understand.	• The style and tone are inappropriate. • Language is inaccurate, repetitive, and vague. • Repetitive sentence structure, fragments, and run-on sentences make the writing monotonous and difficult to follow. • Spelling, capitalization, and punctuation are incorrect throughout. If handwritten, the essay may be partially or mostly illegible. • Many grammatical and usage errors change the meaning of the writer's ideas.

PERFORMANCE TASK B

Interactive Lessons
To help you complete this task, use
- *Writing Arguments*
- *Writing as a Process*

Write an Argument

In the anchor text "Blocking the Transmission of Violence," you learned about the violence interrupters' mission to act as mediators and prevent acts of revenge. Do you think revenge is always misguided, or is it justified in some cases? Write an argument stating your position.

W 1a–e Write arguments.
W 4 Produce clear and coherent writing.
W 5 Develop and strengthen writing.
W 9a–b Draw evidence from literary or informational texts.

An effective argument

- states a clear claim on whether revenge is always misguided or whether it is sometimes justified
- develops the claim with valid reasons and relevant evidence from texts from the collection
- addresses opposing claims with well-supported counterclaims
- establishes clear, logical relationships among claims, counterclaims, reasons, and evidence through the use of transitions
- uses specific rhetorical devices to support claims and assertions
- has a satisfying conclusion that effectively summarizes the claim
- maintains a formal tone through the use of standard English

PLAN

Analyze the Texts Reread "Blocking the Transmission of Violence" and take notes about how revenge is viewed by the CeaseFire organization as well as victims of violence like Torres. Do they believe that revenge is always misguided, or do they think that it is justified in some cases? What reasons do they give? Pay attention to specific details, and gather evidence from the text. Then choose one other text from this collection and take notes on the ideas it conveys about revenge. Save evidence in *my*Notebook, in a folder titled *Collection 4 Performance Task B.*

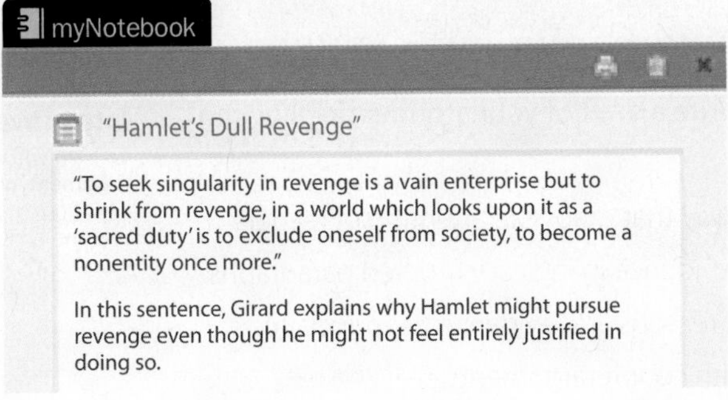

ACADEMIC VOCABULARY

As you develop your argument about revenge, be sure to use these words.

drama
integrity
mediate
restrain
trigger

Make a Claim Based on the ideas conveyed in the texts, write a claim that clearly and concisely states your position on revenge. Remember that you will have to provide sufficient evidence from the texts to convince your audience of your position.

Interactive Lessons

To help you plan your argument, complete the following lessons in Writing Arguments:

- What is a Claim?
- Support: Reasons and Evidence

Build Your Argument Create a graphic organizer that clearly outlines the reasons and evidence that support your claim.

- Begin with your claim stating your position on revenge.
- Outline several reasons that support your claim. Provide textual evidence including details, examples, and quotations to support each reason.
- Make a concluding statement that summarizes your argument.

Develop Counterclaims In an argument you will need to anticipate opposing claims, or objections from opponents, and develop counterclaims to refute them.

- Share your graphic organizer to present your claim, reasons, and evidence with a partner. Allow your partner to respond with opposing claims.
- Take notes about the opposing claims and how to refute them. Ask your partner for feedback on how to improve your argument.

Use Rhetorical Devices Consider including these rhetorical devices to support any claims and assertions in your argument:

- **Logical appeals** are attempts to gain support based on facts and reason.
- **Appeals to emotion** or **ethics** are designed to elicit a strong response, but may not necessarily be based on facts.
- **Anecdotes** are personal stories about your own life.
- **Case studies** use the example of a person, group, or event to illustrate a point.
- **Analogies** are comparisons of two things that are similar in some way.

PRODUCE

Draft Your Argument Write a draft of your argument, following your outline:

Interactive Lessons

To help you draft your argument, use:

- Writing as a Process: Planning and Drafting

- Introduce your claim in a way that grabs the attention of readers.
- Present your reasons and evidence in logically ordered paragraphs.
- Use transitions to connect reasons and evidence to your claim.
- Refute opposing claims with counterarguments.
- Incorporate rhetorical devices to strengthen your claim.
- Use formal language and a respectful tone.
- Write a conclusion that summarizes your position.

Language and Style: Use Rhetorical Devices

Rhetorical devices can strengthen your argument. Read the following passage from "Blocking the Transmission of Violence."

> "In the end, Hoddenbach had persuaded him not to avenge his nephew's murder. Torres had returned the guns and quickly left town."

Note how Kotlowitz uses Torres's experience as a case study of someone who realized that getting revenge through drastic measures is not justified. Using this case study strengthens his point about how acts of revenge can be misguided.

REVISE

myWriteSmart

Have your partner or a group of peers review your draft in *my*WriteSmart. Ask your reviewers to note any reasons that do not support the claim or that lack sufficient evidence.

Improve Your Draft

Have a partner or group of peers use the chart to review your draft.

Questions	Tips	Revision Techniques
Does the introduction include a claim that states a position on the issue?	**Underline** the claim of the argument.	**Add** a claim that clearly states a position on the issue.
Is the claim supported by valid reasons and supporting evidence?	**Highlight** the reasons and evidence that support the claim.	**Add** reasons and evidence if the claim is not supported.
Are opposing claims addressed with well-supported counterclaims?	**Underline** any opposing claims. **Highlight** counterclaims that address the opposing claims.	**Elaborate** by adding opposing claims and counterclaims to refute them, as needed.
Do transitions establish links between claims, reasons, and evidence?	**Underline** transitions to connect reasons and evidence to the claim.	**Clarify** the relationship between the claim and its reasons and evidence by adding transitions.
Are rhetorical devices included to support your claim?	**Highlight** any rhetorical devices.	**Add** appropriate rhetorical devices to support claims.
Does the conclusion effectively summarize the claim?	**Underline** the statement that summarizes the claim.	**Add** a sentence that summarizes the claim.

Interactive Lessons

To help you revise your argument, complete the following lesson:

- Writing as a Process: Revising and Editing

PRESENT

Exchange Essays

When your final draft is completed, exchange essays with a new partner. Read your partner's essay and provide feedback. Be sure to point out aspects of the essay that are particularly strong, as well as areas that could be improved.

PERFORMANCE TASK B RUBRIC

ARGUMENT

	Ideas and Evidence	Organization	Language
4	• The introduction is memorable and persuasive; the claim clearly states a position on a substantive topic. • Valid reasons and relevant evidence from the texts convincingly support the writer's claim. • Counterclaims are anticipated and effectively addressed with counterarguments. • Claims and assertions are supported by a variety of specific rhetorical devices. • The concluding section effectively summarizes the claim.	• The reasons and textual evidence are organized consistently and logically throughout the argument. • Varied transitions logically connect reasons and textual evidence to the writer's claim.	• The writing reflects a formal style and an objective, or controlled, tone. • Sentence beginnings, lengths, and structures vary and have a rhythmic flow. • Spelling, capitalization, and punctuation are correct. If handwritten, the argument is legible. • Grammar and usage are correct.
3	• The introduction could do more to capture the reader's attention; the claim states a position on an issue. • Most reasons and evidence from the texts support the writer's claim, but they could be more convincing. • Counterclaims are anticipated, but the counterarguments need to be developed more. • Rhetorical devices are included, but some do not directly support the claim. • The concluding section restates the claim.	• The organization of reasons and textual evidence is confusing in a few places. • A few more transitions are needed to connect reasons and textual evidence to the writer's claim.	• The style is informal in a few places, and the tone is defensive at times. • Sentence beginnings, lengths, and structures vary somewhat. • Several spelling and capitalization mistakes occur, and punctuation is inconsistent. If handwritten, the argument is mostly legible. • Some grammatical and usage errors are repeated in the argument.
2	• The introduction is ordinary; the claim identifies an issue, but the writer's position is not clearly stated. • The reasons and evidence from the texts are not always logical or relevant. • Counterclaims are anticipated but not addressed logically. • The relationship between rhetorical devices and the claim is not clear. • The concluding section includes an incomplete summary of the claim.	• The organization of reasons and textual evidence is logical in some places, but it often doesn't follow a pattern. • Many more transitions are needed to connect reasons and textual evidence to the writer's position.	• The style becomes informal in many places, and the tone is often dismissive of other viewpoints. • Sentence structures barely vary, and some fragments or run-on sentences are present. • Spelling, capitalization, and punctuation are often incorrect but do not make reading the argument difficult. If handwritten, the argument may be partially illegible. • Grammar and usage are incorrect in many places, but the writer's ideas are still clear.
1	• The introduction is missing. • Significant supporting reasons and evidence from the texts are missing. • Counterclaims are neither anticipated nor addressed. • Rhetorical devices are not included. • The concluding section is missing.	• An organizational strategy is not used; reasons and textual evidence are presented randomly. • Transitions are not used, making the argument difficult to understand.	• The style is inappropriate, and the tone is disrespectful. • Repetitive sentence structure, fragments, and run-on sentences make the writing monotonous and hard to follow. • Spelling and capitalization are often incorrect, and punctuation is missing. If handwritten, the argument may be partially or mostly illegible. • Many grammatical and usage errors change the meaning of the writer's ideas.

Taking Risks

“It is only by risking our persons from one hour to another that we live at all.”

—William James

Taking Risks

From mythical heroes to contemporary scientists, the individuals shown in this collection face the choice of taking a big risk.

COLLECTION

PERFORMANCE TASK Preview

At the end of this collection, you will have the opportunity to complete a task:

- Present an argument on the importance of taking risks in life, citing examples from texts in the collection.

ACADEMIC VOCABULARY

Study the words and their definitions in the chart below. You will use these words as you discuss and write about the texts in this collection.

Word	Definition	Related Forms
assurance (ə-shŏor′əns) *n.*	a guarantee or pledge	assure, assured
collapse (kə-lăps′) *v.*	to break down or fall apart suddenly and cease to function	collapsed, collapsible
conceive (kən-sēv′) *v.*	to understand or form in the mind; to devise	conceivable, conceivably
devote (dĭ-vōt′) *v.*	to give one's entire energy or attention to something or someone	devoted, devotee, devotion
vision (vĭzh′ən) *n.*	ability to see; insight	visionary

HISTORY VIDEO

Beowulf

Epic Poem by The Beowulf Poet translated by Burton Raffel

Background *The epic poem* Beowulf *grew from a rich oral tradition. In large wooden halls similar to the one described in the poem, poet-singers entertained groups of Anglo-Saxon warriors with tales celebrating great heroes. Sometime between the seventh and ninth centuries, a poet unified the accounts of the hero Beowulf, composing the Anglo-Saxon epic that survives today.*

The Angles and the Saxons, as well as other Germanic tribes, came to England from northern Europe starting in the mid-fifth century. Their culture became the basis for English culture, and their languages fused into Old English, the Anglo-Saxon language. They struggled to survive the challenges of nature and frequent wars against new invaders. Anglo-Saxons lived communally for protection; devoted to their lord, they reserved their greatest loyalty for him and their kin. They believed in wyrd, *or fate, rather than in an afterlife, but they hoped that acquiring fame and treasure through acts of valor would give them a kind of immortality. For this reason, poets were highly valued: their poems passed down the history of the Anglo-Saxons, taught their values, and ensured that great warriors would be remembered even after their society collapsed.*

By the time the epic Beowulf *was written down by a monk in the beginning of the eleventh century, the Anglo-Saxons had converted to Christianity. Thus, in the final version of the poem, Christian references are mingled with the original pagan beliefs. The poem is translated here from Old English; the characteristics of oral poetry remain, however, helping readers to hear the splendor of the epic.*

AS YOU READ Pay attention to how the poet sustains suspense during each of Beowulf's battles. Write down any questions you generate during reading.

GRENDEL

Hrothgar (hrôth´gär´), *king of the Danes, has built a wonderful mead hall called Herot* (hĕr´ət), *where his subjects congregate and make merry. As this selection opens, a fierce and powerful monster named Grendel prepares to invade the mead hall.*

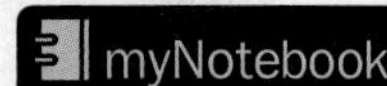

As you read, mark up the text. Save your work to ***my*Notebook**.

- Highlight details
- Add notes and questions
- Add new words to ***my*WordList**

A powerful monster, living down
In the darkness, growled in pain, impatient
As day after day the music rang
Loud in that hall, the harp's rejoicing
Call and the poet's clear songs, sung
Of the ancient beginnings of us all, recalling
The Almighty making the earth, shaping
These beautiful plains marked off by oceans,
Then proudly setting the sun and moon
To glow across the land and light it;
The corners of the earth were made lovely with trees
And leaves, made quick with life, with each
Of the nations who now move on its face. And then
As now warriors sang of their pleasure:
So Hrothgar's men lived happy in his hall
Till the monster stirred, that demon, that fiend,
Grendel, who haunted the moors, the wild
Marshes, and made his home in a hell
Not hell but earth. He was spawned in that slime,
Conceived by a pair of those monsters born
Of Cain, murderous creatures banished
By God, punished forever for the crime
Of Abel's death. The Almighty drove
Those demons out, and their exile was bitter,
Shut away from men; they split
Into a thousand forms of evil—spirits
And fiends, goblins, monsters, giants,
A brood forever opposing the Lord's
Will, and again and again defeated.

17 moors (mŏŏrz): broad, open regions with patches of bog.

19 spawned: given birth to.

21 Cain: the eldest son of Adam and Eve. According to the Bible (Genesis 4), he murdered his younger brother, Abel.

Then, when darkness had dropped, Grendel
Went up to Herot, wondering what the warriors
Would do in that hall when their drinking was done.
He found them sprawled in sleep, suspecting
Nothing, their dreams undisturbed. The monster's
Thoughts were as quick as his greed or his claws:
He slipped through the door and there in the silence
Snatched up thirty men, smashed them
Unknowing in their beds and ran out with their bodies,

The blood dripping behind him, back
To his lair, delighted with his night's slaughter.
At daybreak, with the sun's first light, they saw
How well he had worked, and in that gray morning
Broke their long feast with tears and laments
For the dead. Hrothgar, their lord, sat joyless
In Herot, a mighty prince mourning
The fate of his lost friends and companions,
Knowing by its tracks that some demon had torn
His followers apart. He wept, fearing
The beginning might not be the end. And that night
Grendel came again, so set
On murder that no crime could ever be enough,
No savage assault quench his lust
For evil. Then each warrior tried
To escape him, searched for rest in different
Beds, as far from Herot as they could find,
Seeing how Grendel hunted when they slept.
Distance was safety; the only survivors
Were those who fled him. Hate had triumphed.
So Grendel ruled, fought with the righteous,
One against many, and won; so Herot
Stood empty, and stayed deserted for years,
Twelve winters of grief for Hrothgar, king
Of the Danes, sorrow heaped at his door
By hell-forged hands. His misery leaped
The seas, was told and sung in all
Men's ears: how Grendel's hatred began,
How the monster relished his savage war
On the Danes, keeping the bloody feud
Alive, seeking no peace, offering
No truce, accepting no settlement, no price
In gold or land, and paying the living
For one crime only with another. No one
Waited for reparation from his plundering claws:
That shadow of death hunted in the darkness,
Stalked Hrothgar's warriors, old
And young, lying in waiting, hidden
In mist, invisibly following them from the edge
Of the marsh, always there, unseen.
So mankind's enemy continued his crimes,
Killing as often as he could, coming
Alone, bloodthirsty and horrible. Though he lived
In Herot, when the night hid him, he never
Dared to touch king Hrothgar's glorious
Throne, protected by God—God,
Whose love Grendel could not know. But Hrothgar's

73 reparation: something done to make amends for loss or suffering. In Germanic society, someone who killed another person was generally expected to make a payment to the victim's family as a way of restoring peace.

84 The reference to God shows the influence of Christianity on the Beowulf Poet.

Heart was bent. The best and most noble
Of his council debated remedies, sat
In secret sessions, talking of terror
And wondering what the bravest of warriors could do.
And sometimes they sacrificed to the old stone gods,
Made heathen vows, hoping for Hell's
Support, the Devil's guidance in driving
Their **affliction** off. That was their way,
And the heathen's only hope, Hell
Always in their hearts, knowing neither God
Nor His passing as He walks through our world, the Lord
Of Heaven and earth; their ears could not hear
His praise nor know His glory. Let them
Beware, those who are thrust into danger,
Clutched at by trouble, yet can carry no solace
In their hearts, cannot hope to be better! Hail
To those who will rise to God, drop off
Their dead bodies and seek our Father's peace!

91 heathen (hē´thən): pagan; non-Christian. Though the Beowulf Poet was a Christian, he recognized that the characters in the poem lived before the Germanic tribes were converted to Christianity, when they still worshiped "the old stone gods."

affliction (ə-flĭk´shən) *n.* something that causes suffering or pain.

BEOWULF

So the living sorrow of Healfdane's son
Simmered, bitter and fresh, and no wisdom
Or strength could break it: that agony hung
On king and people alike, harsh
And unending, violent and cruel, and evil.
In his far-off home Beowulf, Higlac's
Follower and the strongest of the Geats—greater
And stronger than anyone anywhere in this world—
Heard how Grendel filled nights with horror
And quickly commanded a boat fitted out,
Proclaiming that he'd go to that famous king,
Would sail across the sea to Hrothgar,
Now when help was needed. None
Of the wise ones regretted his going, much
As he was loved by the Geats: the omens were good,
And they urged the adventure on. So Beowulf
Chose the mightiest men he could find,
The bravest and best of the Geats, fourteen
In all, and led them down to their boat;
He knew the sea, would point the prow
Straight to that distant Danish shore. . . .

104 Healfdane's son: Hrothgar.

109–110 Higlac's follower: a warrior loyal to Higlac (hĭg´lăk´), king of the Geats (and Beowulf's uncle).

Beowulf and his men sail over the sea to the land of the Danes to offer help to Hrothgar. They are escorted by a Danish guard to Herot, where Wulfgar, one of Hrothgar's soldiers, tells the king of their arrival. Hrothgar is ready to welcome the young prince and his men.

Then Wulfgar went to the door and addressed
The waiting seafarers with soldier's words:
"My lord, the great king of the Danes, commands me
To tell you that he knows of your noble birth
And that having come to him from over the open
Sea you have come bravely and are welcome.
Now go to him as you are, in your armor and helmets,
But leave your battle-shields here, and your spears,
Let them lie waiting for the promises your words
May make."
Beowulf arose, with his men
Around him, ordering a few to remain
With their weapons, leading the others quickly
Along under Herot's steep roof into Hrothgar's
Presence. Standing on that prince's own hearth,
Helmeted, the silvery metal of his mail shirt
Gleaming with a smith's high art, he greeted
The Danes' great lord:
"Hail, Hrothgar!
Higlac is my cousin and my king; the days
Of my youth have been filled with glory. Now Grendel's
Name has echoed in our land: sailors
Have brought us stories of Herot, the best
Of all mead-halls, deserted and useless when the moon
Hangs in skies the sun had lit,
Light and life fleeing together.
My people have said, the wisest, most knowing
And best of them, that my duty was to go to the Danes'
Great king. They have seen my strength for themselves,
Have watched me rise from the darkness of war,

139 mail shirt: flexible body armor made of metal links or overlapping metal scales.

140 smith's high art: the skilled craft of a blacksmith (a person who fashions objects from iron).

142 cousin: here, a general term for a relative. Beowulf is actually Higlac's nephew.

Dripping with my enemies' blood. I drove
Five great giants into chains, chased
All of that race from the earth. I swam
In the blackness of night, hunting monsters
Out of the ocean, and killing them one
By one; death was my errand and the fate
They had earned. Now Grendel and I are called
Together, and I've come. Grant me, then,
Lord and protector of this noble place,
A single request! I have come so far,
Oh shelterer of warriors and your people's loved friend,
That this one favor you should not refuse me—
That I, alone and with the help of my men,
May **purge** all evil from this hall. I have heard,
Too, that the monster's scorn of men
Is so great that he needs no weapons and fears none.
Nor will I. My lord Higlac
Might think less of me if I let my sword
Go where my feet were afraid to, if I hid
Behind some broad linden shield: my hands
Alone shall fight for me, struggle for life
Against the monster. God must decide
Who will be given to death's cold grip.
Grendel's plan, I think, will be
What it has been before, to invade this hall
And gorge his belly with our bodies. If he can,
If he can. And I think, if my time will have come,
There'll be nothing to mourn over, no corpse to prepare
For its grave: Grendel will carry our bloody
Flesh to the moors, crunch on our bones
And smear torn scraps of our skin on the walls
Of his den. No, I expect no Danes
Will fret about sewing our shrouds, if he wins.
And if death does take me, send the hammered
Mail of my armor to Higlac, return
The inheritance I had from Hrethel, and he
From Wayland. Fate will unwind as it must!"

Hrothgar replied, protector of the Danes:
"Beowulf, you've come to us in friendship, and because
Of the reception your father found at our court.
Edgetho had begun a bitter feud,
Killing Hathlaf, a Wulfing warrior:
Your father's countrymen were afraid of war,
If he returned to his home, and they turned him away.
Then he traveled across the curving waves
To the land of the Danes. I was new to the throne,

purge (pûrj) *v.* to eliminate or wash away.

172 linden shield: a shield made from the wood of a linden tree.

172–174 Beowulf insists on fighting Grendel without weapons.

185 shrouds: cloths in which dead bodies are wrapped.

188 Hrethel (hrĕth´əl): a former king of the Geats—Higlac's father and Beowulf's grandfather.

189 Wayland: a famous blacksmith and magician.

193 Edgetho (ĕj´thō): Beowulf's father

194 Wulfing: a member of another Germanic tribe.

Then, a young man ruling this wide
Kingdom and its golden city: Hergar,
My older brother, a far better man
Than I, had died and dying made me,
Second among Healfdane's sons, first
In this nation. I bought the end of Edgetho's
Quarrel, sent ancient treasures through the ocean's
Furrows to the Wulfings; your father swore
He'd keep that peace. My tongue grows heavy,
And my heart, when I try to tell you what Grendel
Has brought us, the damage he's done, here
In this hall. You see for yourself how much smaller
Our ranks have become, and can guess what we've lost
To his terror. Surely the Lord Almighty
Could stop his madness, smother his lust!
How many times have my men, glowing
With courage drawn from too many cups
Of ale, sworn to stay after dark
And stem that horror with a sweep of their swords.
And then, in the morning, this mead-hall glittering
With new light would be drenched with blood, the benches
Stained red, the floors, all wet from that fiend's
Savage assault—and my soldiers would be fewer
Still, death taking more and more.
But to table, Beowulf, a banquet in your honor:
Let us toast your victories, and talk of the future."
    Then Hrothgar's men gave places to the Geats,
Yielded benches to the brave visitors
And led them to the feast. The keeper of the mead
Came carrying out the carved flasks,
And poured that bright sweetness. A poet
Sang, from time to time, in a clear
Pure voice. Danes and visiting Geats
Celebrated as one, drank and rejoiced....

THE BATTLE WITH GRENDEL

After the banquet, Hrothgar and his followers leave Herot, and Beowulf and his warriors remain to spend the night. Beowulf reiterates his intent to fight Grendel without a sword and, while his followers sleep, lies waiting, eager for Grendel to appear.

    Out from the marsh, from the foot of misty
Hills and bogs, bearing God's hatred,
Grendel came, hoping to kill
Anyone he could trap on this trip to high Herot.
He moved quickly through the cloudy night,

Up from his swampland, sliding silently
Toward that gold-shining hall. He had visited Hrothgar's
Home before, knew the way—
But never, before nor after that night,
Found Herot defended so firmly, his reception
So harsh. He journeyed, forever joyless,
Straight to the door, then snapped it open,
Tore its iron fasteners with a touch
And rushed angrily over the threshold.
He strode quickly across the inlaid
Floor, snarling and fierce: his eyes
Gleamed in the darkness, burned with a gruesome
Light. Then he stopped, seeing the hall
Crowded with sleeping warriors, stuffed
With rows of young soldiers resting together.
And his heart laughed, he relished the sight,
Intended to tear the life from those bodies
By morning; the monster's mind was hot
With the thought of food and the feasting his belly
Would soon know. But fate, that night, intended
Grendel to gnaw the broken bones
Of his last human supper. Human
Eyes were watching his evil steps,
Waiting to see his swift hard claws.
Grendel snatched at the first Geat
He came to, ripped him apart, cut
His body to bits with powerful jaws,
Drank the blood from his veins and bolted
Him down, hands and feet; death
And Grendel's great teeth came together,
Snapping life shut. Then he stepped to another
Still body, clutched at Beowulf with his claws,
Grasped at a strong-hearted wakeful sleeper
—And was instantly seized himself, claws
Bent back as Beowulf leaned up on one arm.
    That shepherd of evil, guardian of crime,
Knew at once that nowhere on earth
Had he met a man whose hands were harder;
His mind was flooded with fear—but nothing
Could take his talons and himself from that tight
Hard grip. Grendel's one thought was to run
From Beowulf, flee back to his marsh and hide there:
This was a different Herot than the hall he had emptied.
But Higlac's follower remembered his final
Boast and, standing erect, stopped
The monster's flight, fastened those claws
In his fists till they cracked, clutched Grendel

246 threshold: the strip of wood or stone at the bottom of a doorway.

Closer. The **infamous** killer fought
For his freedom, wanting no flesh but retreat,
Desiring nothing but escape; his claws
Had been caught, he was trapped. That trip to Herot
Was a miserable journey for the writhing monster!
The high hall rang, its roof boards swayed,
And Danes shook with terror. Down
The aisles the battle swept, angry
And wild. Herot trembled, wonderfully
Built to withstand the blows, the struggling
Great bodies beating at its beautiful walls;
Shaped and fastened with iron, inside
And out, artfully worked, the building
Stood firm. Its benches rattled, fell
To the floor, gold-covered boards grating
As Grendel and Beowulf battled across them.
Hrothgar's wise men had fashioned Herot
To stand forever; only fire,
They had planned, could shatter what such skill had put
Together, swallow in hot flames such splendor
Of ivory and iron and wood. Suddenly
The sounds changed, the Danes started
In new terror, cowering in their beds as the terrible
Screams of the Almighty's enemy sang
In the darkness, the horrible shrieks of pain
And defeat, the tears torn out of Grendel's
Taut throat, hell's captive caught in the arms
Of him who of all the men on earth
Was the strongest.

That mighty protector of men
Meant to hold the monster till its life
Leaped out, knowing the fiend was no use
To anyone in Denmark. All of Beowulf 's
Band had jumped from their beds, ancestral
Swords raised and ready, determined
To protect their prince if they could. Their courage
Was great but all wasted: they could hack at Grendel
From every side, trying to open
A path for his evil soul, but their points
Could not hurt him, the sharpest and hardest iron
Could not scratch at his skin, for that sin-stained demon
Had bewitched all men's weapons, laid spells
That blunted every mortal man's blade.
And yet his time had come, his days
Were over, his death near; down
To hell he would go, swept groaning and helpless

infamous
(ĭn′fə-məs) *adj.* having a bad reputation.

taut
(tôt) *adj.* tense or tightly flexed.

To the waiting hands of still worse fiends.
Now he discovered—once the afflictor
Of men, tormentor of their days—what it meant
To feud with Almighty God: Grendel
Saw that his strength was deserting him, his claws
Bound fast, Higlac's brave follower tearing at
His hands. The monster's hatred rose higher,
But his power had gone. He twisted in pain,
And the bleeding sinews deep in his shoulder
Snapped, muscle and bone split
And broke. The battle was over, Beowulf
Had been granted new glory: Grendel escaped,
But wounded as he was could flee to his den,
His miserable hole at the bottom of the marsh,
Only to die, to wait for the end
Of all his days. And after that bloody
Combat the Danes laughed with delight.
He who had come to them from across the sea,
Bold and strong-minded, had driven affliction
Off, purged Herot clean. He was happy,
Now, with that night's fierce work; the Danes
Had been served as he'd boasted he'd serve them; Beowulf,
A prince of the Geats, had killed Grendel,
Ended the grief, the sorrow, the suffering
Forced on Hrothgar's helpless people
By a bloodthirsty fiend. No Dane doubted
The victory, for the proof, hanging high
From the rafters where Beowulf had hung it, was the monster's
Arm, claw and shoulder and all.

339 sinews (sĭn´yo͞oz): the tendons that connect muscles to bones.

And then, in the morning, crowds surrounded
Herot, warriors coming to that hall
From faraway lands, princes and leaders
Of men hurrying to behold the monster's
Great staggering tracks. They gaped with no sense
Of sorrow, felt no regret for his suffering,
Went tracing his bloody footprints, his beaten
And lonely flight, to the edge of the lake
Where he'd dragged his corpselike way, doomed
And already weary of his vanishing life.
The water was bloody, steaming and boiling
In horrible pounding waves, heat
Sucked from his magic veins; but the swirling
Surf had covered his death, hidden
Deep in murky darkness his miserable
End, as hell opened to receive him.

Then old and young rejoiced, turned back
From that happy **pilgrimage**, mounted their hard-hooved
Horses, high-spirited stallions, and rode them
Slowly toward Herot again, retelling
Beowulf 's bravery as they jogged along.
And over and over they swore that nowhere
On earth or under the spreading sky
Or between the seas, neither south nor north,
Was there a warrior worthier to rule over men.
(But no one meant Beowulf 's praise to belittle
Hrothgar, their kind and gracious king!)
And sometimes, when the path ran straight and clear,
They would let their horses race, red
And brown and pale yellow backs streaming
Down the road. And sometimes a proud old soldier
Who had heard songs of the ancient heroes
And could sing them all through, story after story,
Would weave a net of words for Beowulf 's
Victory, tying the knot of his verses
Smoothly, swiftly, into place with a poet's
Quick skill, singing his new song aloud
While he shaped it, and the old songs as well. . . .

pilgrimage (pĭl´grə-mĭj) *n.* a journey to a historical or religious site.

GRENDEL'S MOTHER

Although one monster has died, another still lives. From her lair in a cold and murky lake, where she has been brooding over her loss, Grendel's mother emerges, bent on revenge.

So she reached Herot,
Where the Danes slept as though already dead;
Her visit ended their good fortune, reversed
The bright vane of their luck. No female, no matter

400 vane: a device that turns to show the direction the wind is blowing—here associated metaphorically with luck, which is as changeable as the wind.

How fierce, could have come with a man's strength,
Fought with the power and courage men fight with,
Smashing their shining swords, their bloody,
Hammer-forged blades onto boar-headed helmets,
Slashing and stabbing with the sharpest of points.
The soldiers raised their shields and drew
Those gleaming swords, swung them above
The piled-up benches, leaving their mail shirts
And their helmets where they'd lain when the terror took hold of
them.
To save her life she moved still faster,
Took a single victim and fled from the hall,
Running to the moors, discovered, but her supper
Assured, sheltered in her dripping claws.
She'd taken Hrothgar's closest friend,
The man he most loved of all men on earth;
She'd killed a glorious soldier, cut
A noble life short. No Geat could have stopped her:
Beowulf and his band had been given better
Beds; sleep had come to them in a different
Hall. Then all Herot burst into shouts:
She had carried off Grendel's claw. Sorrow
Had returned to Denmark. They'd traded deaths,
Danes and monsters, and no one had won,
Both had lost! …

404 boar-headed helmets: Germanic warriors often wore helmets bearing the images of wild pigs or other fierce creatures in the hope that the images would increase their ferocity and protect them against their enemies.

Devastated by the loss of his friend, Hrothgar sends for Beowulf and recounts what Grendel's mother has done. Then Hrothgar describes the dark lake where Grendel's mother has dwelt with her son.

They live in secret places, windy
Cliffs, wolf-dens where water pours
From the rocks, then runs underground, where mist
Steams like black clouds, and the groves of trees
Growing out over their lake are all covered
With frozen spray, and wind down snakelike
Roots that reach as far as the water
And help keep it dark. At night that lake
Burns like a torch. No one knows its bottom,
No wisdom reaches such depths. A deer,
Hunted through the woods by packs of hounds,
A stag with great horns, though driven through the forest
From faraway places, prefers to die
On those shores, refuses to save its life
In that water. It isn't far, nor is it
A pleasant spot! When the wind stirs
And storms, waves splash toward the sky,

As dark as the air, as black as the rain
That the heavens weep. Our only help,
Again, lies with you. Grendel's mother
Is hidden in her terrible home, in a place
You've not seen. Seek it, if you dare! Save us,
Once more, and again twisted gold,
Heaped-up ancient treasure, will reward you
For the battle you win!". . .

447–449 Germanic warriors placed great importance on amassing treasure as a way of acquiring fame and temporarily defeating fate.

THE BATTLE WITH GRENDEL'S MOTHER

Beowulf accepts Hrothgar's challenge, and the king and his men accompany the hero to the dreadful lair of Grendel's mother. Fearlessly, Beowulf prepares to battle the terrible creature.

He leaped into the lake, would not wait for anyone's
Answer; the heaving water covered him
Over. For hours he sank through the waves;
At last he saw the mud of the bottom.
And all at once the greedy she-wolf
Who'd ruled those waters for half a hundred
Years discovered him, saw that a creature
From above had come to explore the bottom
Of her wet world. She welcomed him in her claws,
Clutched at him savagely but could not harm him,
Tried to work her fingers through the tight
Ring-woven mail on his breast, but tore
And scratched in vain. Then she carried him, armor
And sword and all, to her home; he struggled
To free his weapon, and failed. The fight
Brought other monsters swimming to see
Her catch, a host of sea beasts who beat at
His mail shirt, stabbing with tusks and teeth
As they followed along. Then he realized, suddenly,
That she'd brought him into someone's battle-hall,
And there the water's heat could not hurt him,
Nor anything in the lake attack him through
The building's high-arching roof. A brilliant
Light burned all around him, the lake
Itself like a fiery flame.
Then he saw
The mighty water witch, and swung his sword,
His ring-marked blade, straight at her head;
The iron sang its fierce song,
Sang Beowulf's strength. But her guest

476 His ring-marked blade: For the battle with Grendel's mother, Beowulf has been given an heirloom sword with an intricately etched blade.

Discovered that no sword could slice her evil
Skin, that Hrunting could not hurt her, was useless
Now when he needed it. They wrestled, she ripped
And tore and clawed at him, bit holes in his helmet,
And that too failed him; for the first time in years
Of being worn to war it would earn no glory;
It was the last time anyone would wear it. But Beowulf
Longed only for fame, leaped back
Into battle. He tossed his sword aside,
Angry; the steel-edged blade lay where
He'd dropped it. If weapons were useless he'd use
His hands, the strength in his fingers. So fame
Comes to the men who mean to win it
And care about nothing else! He raised
His arms and seized her by the shoulder; anger
Doubled his strength, he threw her to the floor.
She fell, Grendel's fierce mother, and the Geats'
Proud prince was ready to leap on her. But she rose
At once and repaid him with her clutching claws,
Wildly tearing at him. He was weary, that best
And strongest of soldiers; his feet stumbled
And in an instant she had him down, held helpless.
Squatting with her weight on his stomach, she drew
A dagger, brown with dried blood, and prepared
To avenge her only son. But he was stretched
On his back, and her stabbing blade was blunted
By the woven mail shirt he wore on his chest.
The hammered links held; the point
Could not touch him. He'd have traveled to the bottom of the earth,
Edgetho's son, and died there, if that shining
Woven metal had not helped—and Holy
God, who sent him victory, gave judgment
For truth and right, Ruler of the Heavens,
Once Beowulf was back on his feet and fighting.

Then he saw, hanging on the wall, a heavy
Sword, hammered by giants, strong
And blessed with their magic, the best of all weapons
But so massive that no ordinary man could lift
Its carved and decorated length. He drew it
From its scabbard, broke the chain on its hilt,
And then, savage, now, angry
And desperate, lifted it high over his head
And struck with all the strength he had left,
Caught her in the neck and cut it through,
Broke bones and all. Her body fell
To the floor, lifeless, the sword was wet

480 Hrunting (hrŭn′tĭng): the name of Beowulf's sword. (Germanic warriors' swords were possessions of such value that they were often given names.)

With her blood, and Beowulf rejoiced at the sight.
The brilliant light shone, suddenly,
As though burning in that hall, and as bright as Heaven's
Own candle, lit in the sky. He looked
At her home, then following along the wall
Went walking, his hands tight on the sword,
His heart still angry. He was hunting another
Dead monster, and took his weapon with him
For final revenge against Grendel's vicious
Attacks, his nighttime raids, over
And over, coming to Herot when Hrothgar's
Men slept, killing them in their beds,
Eating some on the spot, fifteen
Or more, and running to his **loathsome** moor
With another such sickening meal waiting
In his pouch. But Beowulf repaid him for those visits,
Found him lying dead in his corner,
Armless, exactly as that fierce fighter
Had sent him out from Herot, then struck off
His head with a single swift blow. The body
Jerked for the last time, then lay still.
The wise old warriors who surrounded Hrothgar,
Like him staring into the monsters' lake,
Saw the waves surging and blood
Spurting through. They spoke about Beowulf,
All the graybeards, whispered together
And said that hope was gone, that the hero
Had lost fame and his life at once, and would never
Return to the living, come back as triumphant
As he had left; almost all agreed that Grendel's
Mighty mother, the she-wolf, had killed him.
The sun slid over past noon, went further
Down. The Danes gave up, left
The lake and went home, Hrothgar with them.
The Geats stayed, sat sadly, watching,
Imagining they saw their lord but not believing
They would ever see him again.
—Then the sword
Melted, blood-soaked, dripping down
Like water, disappearing like ice when the world's
Eternal Lord loosens invisible
Fetters and unwinds icicles and frost
As only He can, He who rules
Time and seasons, He who is truly
God. The monsters' hall was full of
Rich treasures, but all that Beowulf took
Was Grendel's head and the hilt of the giants'

loathsome (lōth′səm) *adj.* hateful or repulsive.

550 graybeards: old men.

Jeweled sword; the rest of that ring-marked
Blade had dissolved in Grendel's steaming
Blood, boiling even after his death.
And then the battle's only survivor
Swam up and away from those silent corpses;
The water was calm and clean, the whole
Huge lake peaceful once the demons who'd lived in it
Were dead.
Then that noble protector of all seamen
Swam to land, rejoicing in the heavy
Burdens he was bringing with him. He
And all his glorious band of Geats
Thanked God that their leader had come back unharmed;
They left the lake together. The Geats
Carried Beowulf 's helmet, and his mail shirt.
Behind them the water slowly thickened
As the monsters' blood came seeping up.
They walked quickly, happily, across
Roads all of them remembered, left
The lake and the cliffs alongside it, brave men
Staggering under the weight of Grendel's skull,
Too heavy for fewer than four of them to handle—
Two on each side of the spear jammed through it—
Yet proud of their ugly load and determined
That the Danes, seated in Herot, should see it.
Soon, fourteen Geats arrived
At the hall, bold and warlike, and with Beowulf,
Their lord and leader, they walked on the mead-hall
Green. Then the Geats' brave prince entered
Herot, covered with glory for the daring
Battles he had fought; he sought Hrothgar
To salute him and show Grendel's head.
He carried that terrible trophy by the hair,
Brought it straight to where the Danes sat,
Drinking, the queen among them. It was a weird
And wonderful sight, and the warriors stared. . . .

578 that noble protector of all seamen: Beowulf, who will be buried in a tower that will serve as a navigational aid to sailors.

604 queen: Welthow, wife of Hrothgar.

COLLABORATIVE DISCUSSION How does the poet keep readers on the edge of their seats? With a partner, discuss the ways in which the poet builds suspense. Cite specific textual evidence from the poem to support your ideas.

RL 3

Analyze Story Elements: Characteristics of an Epic

An **epic** is a long narrative poem that celebrates a hero's deeds. Traditional epics, such as *Beowulf*, began as oral poems and were retold by poets over many generations before they were finally written down. Epic poems share certain conventions and characteristics:

- The hero is a person of noble birth or high position who performs great deeds of strength and courage.
- The hero battles supernatural creatures and may undergo dangerous journeys in order to fulfill a quest.
- The hero's character traits reflect the ideals of the culture.
- The story conveys universal themes—themes found in the literature of all time periods and cultures—such as the importance of honor and the conflict between good and evil.
- The style features formal diction (word choice and syntax) and a serious tone (expression of the writer's attitude toward a subject).
- The dialogue often includes long speeches by major characters.

RL 4

Analyze Language: Old English Poetry

Anglo-Saxon poets used techniques that made their verse easier to chant. This chart describes important techniques found in *Beowulf*:

Technique	Example
Alliteration is the repetition of consonant sounds at the beginning of words. This device helps unify the lines.	The **h**igh **h**all **r**ang, its **r**oof boards swayed,
The poem's strong **rhythm** is created by four stresses, or beats, in each line.	Grendel came, hoping to kill
A **caesura** is a pause that divides the line, with each part having two stresses. Usually, at least one stressed syllable in the first part alliterates with a stressed syllable in the second part.	Out from the marsh, // from the foot of misty Hills and bogs, // bearing God's hatred,
Kennings are metaphorical compound words or phrases substituted for simple nouns.	The kennings "Higlac's follower" and "protector of men" are used in place of the name "Beowulf."

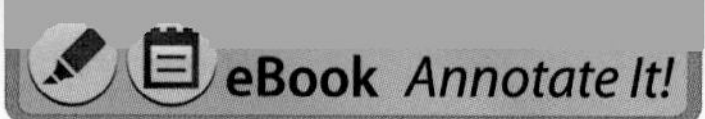

Analyzing the Text

RL 1, RL 2, RL 3, RL 4, W 2

Cite Text Evidence Support your responses with evidence from the selection.

1. **Draw Conclusions** Reread lines 15–29 and 81–85, which show the influence of Christianity on the epic. What is the purpose of referring to Hrothgar and Grendel in terms of their relationship to God?
2. **Analyze** How does Beowulf's speech in lines 141–175 contribute to his characterization?
3. **Analyze** Reread the following passages. How does the poet's use of alliteration influence the mood or tone of each passage?
    - "A powerful monster, living . . . growled in pain" (lines 1–2)
    - "My tongue grows heavy . . . In this hall." (lines 207–210)
    - "Herot trembled . . . across them." (lines 293–300)
4. **Analyze** Explain what is revealed in the following passages about Anglo-Saxon values and beliefs.
    - "And I think, if my time will have come . . . as it must!" (lines 179–189)
    - "I bought the end of Edgetho's . . . keep that peace." (lines 204–207)
    - "And over and over they swore . . . gracious king!)" (lines 381–386)
    - "Seek it, if you dare! . . . battle you win!'" (lines 446–449)
5. **Draw Conclusions** Identify details about setting in lines 450–474. Why might the poet have chosen to provide such a detailed description of the setting of Beowulf's battle with Grendel's mother? How does this description influence the reader's impression of the battle?
6. **Analyze** What universal themes are conveyed by the descriptions of battles between Beowulf and Grendel and between Beowulf and Grendel's mother?
7. **Analyze** Identify kennings associated with Grendel and Grendel's mother. How do these phrases convey the poet's attitude toward the characters?

PERFORMANCE TASK

Writing Activity: Comparison How do heroes reveal the traits prized most highly by a culture?

- Identify Beowulf's qualities and what they reveal about the Anglo-Saxon culture.
- Choose a fictional hero from contemporary American culture. Explain what this character's traits reveal about values of modern society.
- Compare the values of Anglo-Saxons and modern Americans in a well-organized essay.

Critical Vocabulary

affliction **purge** **infamous**

taut **pilgrimage** **loathsome**

Practice and Apply Explain whether the words in each pair are synonyms, antonyms, or unrelated.

1. pilgrimage/restoration
2. loathsome/appealing
3. taut/slack
4. affliction/burden
5. infamous/honorable
6. purge/expel

Vocabulary Strategy: Homophones

When listening to poetry read aloud, the audience has to be able to recognize **homophones.** These are words that have the same pronunciation but different spellings and meanings. Listeners can use context clues to figure out which word is intended. For example, the Vocabulary word *taut* is a homophone found in line 311: "the tears torn out of Grendel's/Taut throat." Although *taut* is pronounced in exactly the same way as the past tense of *teach*, the position of the word in the sentence indicates that it is an adjective, not a verb, and other context clues help to define the word as "stretched tight."

Practice and Apply Complete each of these sentences with the correct choice from the homophones in parentheses. Define the word you choose.

1. The sun (shown, shone) brightly, lighting up the (guilt, gilt) on the walls of Hrothgar's hall.
2. Beowulf tells Hrothgar how he swam the (straight, strait) killing monsters in the blackness of the night.
3. When the weeping was over, the hall was silent with the (wait, weight) of the Danes' (mourning, morning).
4. The (pain, pane) from his injury was too much for Grendel to (bare, bear).
5. Each (birth, berth) in the hall held a vigilant Geat, alert to Grendel's approach.
6. The arrival of Grendel's mother turned the (vein, vane, vain) of the Danes' luck back in the other direction.
7. The (foul/fowl) mist over the lake hinted at the danger that (weighted, waited) beneath.
8. A talented (bard, barred) sang about Beowulf's miraculous (feet, feat) of courage.

Language and Style: Mood

L3

Mood is the feeling or atmosphere that a writer creates for the reader. Poets may use imagery, figurative language, and word choices to create this atmosphere.

In lines 425–449, the Beowulf poet describes the lake in which Grendel's mother lives. Read this passage from the poem:

They live in secret places, windy
Cliffs, wolf-dens where water pours
From the rocks, then runs underground, where mist
Steams like black clouds, and the groves of trees
Growing out over their lake are all covered
With frozen spray, and wind down snakelike
Roots that reach as far as the water
And help to keep it dark. At night that lake
Burns like a torch. . . .
. . . When the wind stirs
And storms, waves splash toward the sky,
As dark as the air, as black as the rain
That the heavens weep. . . .

Notice these literary devices used by the poet:

- imagery ("windy cliffs," "water pours from the rocks," "frozen spray")
- similes ("mist steams like black clouds," "snakelike roots," "that lake burns like a torch," "waves . . . as dark as the air, as black as the rain")
- personification ("the rain that the heavens weep")
- words with sinister connotations ("secret," "black," "dark")

These devices create an ominous, foreboding mood. This mood helps to develop the impression of Grendel's mother as the epitome of evil and darkness. The mood adds to the suspense as readers wonder whether Beowulf will make it back out of such a horrifying place alive. It also foreshadows the magnitude of the conflict that is about to occur.

Practice and Apply Complete these activities independently.

1. Choose a passage from the poem that conveys a distinct mood—for example, lines 15–40, 233–268, or 474–505. Identify the mood of the passage you've chosen and the words and phrases that help to create this mood.
2. Using the words and phrases you identified, write an original passage that creates a similar mood.
3. Read your passage aloud to a partner. Have your partner identify the mood and evaluate your success in conveying it.

HISTORY VIDEO

Background *The* Challenger *shuttle explosion marked the nation's first tragedy during a flight to space. The disaster, which occurred on January 28, 1986, killed the entire crew just moments after takeoff, including Christa McAuliffe, a high-school teacher who had been selected to pioneer NASA's Teacher in Space program. On the morning of the launch, students in schools across the country gathered to watch the event on live television. That evening, President Ronald Reagan addressed the nation.*

Explosion of the Space Shuttle *Challenger*:

Address to the Nation

Speech by Ronald Reagan

AS YOU READ Pay attention to Reagan's comments about the *Challenger* crew. Write down questions you generate during reading.

Ladies and gentlemen, I'd planned to speak to you tonight to report on the state of the Union, but the events of earlier today have led me to change those plans. Today is a day for mourning and remembering.

Nancy and I are pained to the core by the tragedy of the shuttle *Challenger*. We know we share this pain with all of the people of our country. This is truly a national loss.

Nineteen years ago, almost to the day, we lost three astronauts in a terrible accident on the ground.[1] But we've never lost an astronaut in flight; we've never had a tragedy like this. And perhaps we've forgotten the courage it took for the crew of the shuttle; but they, the Challenger Seven, were aware of the dangers, but overcame them and did their jobs brilliantly. We mourn seven heroes: Michael Smith, Dick Scobee, Judith Resnik, Ronald McNair, Ellison Onizuka, Gregory Jarvis, and Christa McAuliffe. We mourn their loss as a nation together.

For the families of the seven, we cannot bear, as you do, the full impact of this tragedy. But we feel the loss, and we're thinking

[1] **Nineteen years . . . ground:** In 1967, the crew of Apollo 1 died when a fire broke out while it was on the launch pad.

about you so very much. Your loved ones were daring and brave, and they had that special grace, that special spirit that says, "Give me a challenge and I'll meet it with joy." They had a hunger to explore the universe and discover its truths. They wished to serve, and they did. They served all of us.

We've grown used to wonders in this century. It's hard to dazzle us. But for 25 years the United States space program has been doing just that. We've grown used to the idea of space, and perhaps we forget that we've only just begun. We're still pioneers. They, the members of the *Challenger* crew, were pioneers.

And I want to say something to the schoolchildren of America who were watching the live coverage of the shuttle's takeoff. I know it is hard to understand, but sometimes painful things like this happen. It's all part of the process of exploration and discovery. It's all part of taking a chance and expanding man's horizons. The future doesn't belong to the fainthearted; it belongs to the brave. The *Challenger* crew was pulling us into the future, and we'll continue to follow them.

I've always had great faith in and respect for our space program, and what happened today does nothing to diminish it. We don't hide our space program. We don't keep secrets and cover things up. We do it all up front and in public. That's the way freedom is, and we wouldn't change it for a minute.

We'll continue our quest in space. There will be more shuttle flights and more shuttle crews and, yes, more volunteers, more civilians, more teachers in space. Nothing ends here; our hopes and our journeys continue.

I want to add that I wish I could talk to every man and woman who works for NASA or who worked on this mission and tell them: "Your dedication and professionalism have moved and impressed us for decades. And we know of your anguish. We share it."

There's a coincidence today. On this day 390 years ago, the great explorer Sir Francis Drake died aboard ship off the coast of Panama. In his lifetime the great frontiers were the oceans, and an historian later said, "He lived by the sea, died on it, and was buried in it." Well, today we can say of the *Challenger* crew: Their dedication was, like Drake's, complete.

The crew of the space shuttle *Challenger* honored us by the manner in which they lived their lives. We will never forget them, nor the last time we saw them, this morning, as they prepared for their journey and waved goodbye and "slipped the surly bonds of earth" to "touch the face of God."[2]

---

[2] **"slipped . . . God":** references to the first and last lines of "High Flight," a poem by John G. Magee, Jr.

COLLABORATIVE DISCUSSION With a partner, discuss whether you think Reagan responded effectively to the tragic deaths of the crew members.

Delineate and Evaluate an Argument

RI 8

President Reagan's response to the tragedy of the *Challenger* explosion includes an argument about the space program. Think about these questions to delineate and evaluate his argument.

- **Claim:** Is Reagan's claim, or position, about the space program credible and supported by logical reasoning and evidence?
- **Reasoning:** Upon what premises—statements affirming or denying something—is President Reagan's argument based? Does he make any logical errors in presenting his conclusions? For example, does he make any generalizations that are too broad?
- **Evidence:** Are the facts, examples, and other details included in the speech valid, authoritative, relevant, and sufficient? Is President Reagan able to support his vision of the future with evidence?

The answers to these questions will help you outline President Reagan's argument and look critically at the flow of ideas. Examining the relationships between ideas will help you evaluate the strength of his argument.

Determine Author's Purpose

RI 6

The author of a speech writes for one or more **purposes**, which may include to inform, to persuade, to express opinions, or to influence an audience's emotions. The reader often has to infer the author's purpose. As you identify and analyze the purposes of Reagan's speech, consider how he uses these persuasive techniques to help achieve them and add power to his message.

Persuasive Techniques	Examples
Emotional appeals sway an audience by focusing on strong feelings.	President Reagan identifies with Americans' grief by using phrases such as "painful things like this happen" and "we know of your anguish."
Appeals to loyalty rely on people's affiliation with a particular group.	President Reagan's use of the pronouns *us* and *we* appeals to Americans' sense of patriotism.
Appeals by association connect a cause with another widely accepted idea.	President Reagan compares the space program to the exploration of other frontiers.

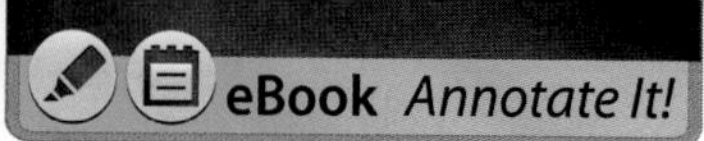

Analyzing the Text

RI 6, RI 8, SL 1c, SL 2, SL 3

Cite Text Evidence Support your responses with evidence from the selection.

1. **Identify** What is Reagan's claim about the future of the space program?
2. **Identify** What premise about the space program does Reagan express in lines 22–26? How does this premise relate to his claim?
3. **Analyze** What specific groups of people does Reagan directly address in his speech? How do the assurances he makes to them impact his message?
4. **Interpret** What values does President Reagan suggest all Americans share in his appeals to their sense of patriotism?
5. **Analyze** According to Reagan, how are the *Challenger* astronauts similar to Sir Francis Drake? Is this a valid comparison? Explain why or why not.
6. **Analyze** Identify two purposes of Reagan's speech. How do the style and content of the speech contribute to his purposes?
7. **Evaluate** Is Reagan's statement that tragedies like the *Challenger* explosion are "all part of the process of exploration and discovery" valid? What types of evidence does Reagan provide to support this idea? What types of evidence does he not address?
8. **Critique** John G. Magee, Jr., died a few months after writing the poem "High Flight," which expresses his feelings about being a World War II pilot. Is Reagan's quote from the poem an effective way to end his speech? Explain your response.

PERFORMANCE TASK

Speaking Activity: Discussion President Reagan postponed his State of the Union address to deliver his speech on the *Challenger* explosion on television. Watch a video of the speech and then evaluate it in a small group discussion.

1. As you watch the speech, note how Reagan's tone of voice, facial expressions, and eye contact help support his message.
2. Discuss the power and effectiveness of Reagan's speech. Pose and respond to questions that probe Reagan's use of reasoning and evidence. Assess the premises on which his claim is based, his links among ideas, word choice, points of emphasis, and tone.
3. Take notes during the discussion and then write a brief summary of the group's conclusions.

Anthony Doerr *has won many awards for his short stories, including four O. Henry prizes and Britain's Sunday Times EFG Short Story Award for "The Deep." In an interview with the journal* Fugue, *he explained that it is vital not to become used to life's wonder but to keep trying to see what is special about the world. He also described his desire to shake up structure and language so that readers are struck anew by some element in life or nature. He currently lives in Boise, Idaho, and writes for the* Boston Globe *and the* New York Times *when not at work on his fiction.*

The Deep

Short Story by Anthony Doerr

AS YOU READ Pay attention to details the author adds to develop Tom's character throughout the story. Write down any questions you generate during reading.

TOM IS BORN in 1914 in Detroit, a quarter mile from International Salt. His father is offstage, unaccounted for. His mother operates a six-room, underinsulated boardinghouse populated with locked doors, behind which drowse the grim possessions of **itinerant** salt workers: coats the color of mice, tattered mucking boots, aquatints[1] of undressed women, their breasts faded orange. Every six months a miner is fired or drafted or dies and is replaced by another, so that very early in his life Tom comes to see how the world continually drains itself of young men, leaving behind only objects—empty tobacco pouches, bladeless jack-knives, salt-caked trousers—mute, incapable of memory.

itinerant (ī-tĭn´ər-ənt) *adj.* migrant, or travelling from site to site.

Tom is four when he starts fainting. He'll be rounding a corner, breathing hard, and the lights will go out. Mother will carry him indoors, set him on the armchair, and send someone for the doctor.

[1] **aquatints:** prints that resemble watercolor paintings.

Atrial septal defect. Hole in the heart. The doctor says blood sloshes from the left side to the right side. His heart will have to do three times the work. Life span of sixteen. Eighteen if he's lucky. Best if he doesn't get excited.

Mother trains her voice into a whisper. *Here you go, there you are, sweet little Tomcat.* She smothers the windows with curtains. She moves Tom's cot into an upstairs closet—no bright lights, no loud noises. Mornings she serves him a glass of buttermilk, then points him to the brooms or steel wool. *Go slow,* she'll say. He scrubs the coal stove, sweeps the marble stoop. Every so often he peers up from his work and watches the face of the oldest boarder, Mr. Weems, as he troops downstairs, a fifty-year-old man hooded against the cold, off to descend in an elevator a thousand feet underground. Tom imagines his descent, **sporadic** and dim lights passing and receding, cables rattling, a half dozen other miners squeezed into the cage beside him, each thinking his own thoughts, sinking down into that city beneath the city, where mules stand waiting and oil lamps burn in the walls and glittering rooms of salt recede into vast arcades beyond the farthest reaches of the light.

sporadic
(spə-răd´ĭk) *adj.* occasional; occurring at random intervals.

Sixteen, thinks Tom. *Eighteen if I'm lucky.*

School is a three-room shed aswarm with the offspring of salt workers, coal workers, ironworkers. Irish kids, Polish kids, Armenian kids. *Don't run, don't fight,* whispers Mother. *No games.* For Tom the schoolyard seems a thousand acres of sizzling pandemonium. His first day, he lasts an hour. Mother finds him beneath a tablecloth with his fist in his mouth. *Shhh,* she says, and crawls under there with him and wraps her arms around his like ropes.

He seesaws in and out of the early grades. By the time he's ten, he's in remedial everything. *I'm trying,* he mumbles, but letters spin off pages and hang themselves in the branches outside. *Dunce,* the other boys declare, and to Tom that seems about right.

Tom sweeps, scrubs, scours the stoop with pumice one square inch at a time. *Slow as molasses in January,* says Mr. Weems, but he winks at Tom when he says it.

Every day, all day, the salt finds its way in. It encrusts washbasins, settles on the rims of baseboards. It spills out of the boarders, too: from ears, boots, handkerchiefs. Furrows of glitter gather in the bedsheets; a daily lesson in insidiousness.

Start at the center, then scrub out to the edges. Linens on Thursdays. Toilets on Fridays.

He's twelve when Ms. Fredericks asks the children to give reports. Ruby Hornaday goes sixth. Ruby has flames for hair, Christmas for a birthday, and a drunk for a daddy. She's one of two girls to make it to fourth grade.

She reads from notes in controlled terror. *If you think the lake is big you should see the sea. It's three-quarters of Earth. And that's just the surface.* Someone throws a pencil. The creases in Ruby's forehead deepen. *Land animals live on ground or in trees rats and worms and gulls and such. But sea animals they live everywhere they live in the waves and they live in mid water and they live in canyons six and a half miles down.*

She passes around a thick, red book. Inside are blocks of text and full-color photographic plates that make Tom's heart boom in his ears. A blizzard of green fish. A kingdom of purple corals. Five orange starfish cemented to a rock.

Ruby says, *Detroit used to have palm trees and corals and seashells. Detroit used to be a sea three miles deep.*

Ms. Fredericks says, *Ruby, where did you get that book?* but by then Tom is hardly breathing. See-through flowers with poison tentacles and fields of clams and pink monsters with kingdoms of whirling needles on their backs. He tries to say, *Are these real?* but quicksilver bubbles rise from his mouth and float up to the ceiling. When he goes over, the desk goes over with him.

The doctor says it's best if Tom stays out of school. *Keep indoors,* the doctor says. *If you get excited, think of something blue.* Mother lets him come downstairs for meals and chores only. Otherwise he's to stay in his closet. *We have to be more careful, Tomcat,* she whispers, and sets her palm on his forehead.

Tom spends long hours on the floor beside his cot, assembling and reassembling the same jigsaw puzzle: a Swiss village. Five hundred pieces, nine of them missing. Sometimes Mr. Weems sits and reads to Tom from adventure novels. They're blasting a new vein down in the mines and little cascades of plaster sift from the ceiling. In the lulls between Mr. Weems's words, Tom can feel explosions **reverberate** up through a thousand feet of rock and shake the fragile pump in his chest.

reverberate
(rĭ-vûr′bə-rāt′) *v.* to vibrate or resonate.

He misses school. He misses the sky. He misses everything. When Mr. Weems is in the mine and Mother is downstairs, Tom often slips to the end of the hall and lifts aside the curtains and presses his forehead to the glass. Children run the snowy lanes and lights glow in the foundry windows and train cars trundle beneath elevated conduits. First-shift miners emerge from the mouth of the hauling elevator in groups of six and bring out cigarette cases from their overalls and strike matches and spill like little salt-dusted insects out into the night, while the darker figures of the second-shift miners stamp their feet in the cold, waiting outside the cages for their turn in the pit.

In dreams he sees waving sea fans and milling schools of grouper and underwater shafts of light. He sees Ruby Hornaday push open the door of his closet. She's wearing a copper diving helmet; she leans over his cot and puts the window of her helmet an inch from his face.

He wakes with a shock and heat pooled in his groin. He thinks, *Blue, blue, blue.*

One drizzly Saturday when Tom is thirteen, the bell rings. He's scrubbing behind the stove, Mother is changing linens upstairs, and Mr. Weems is in the armchair reading the newspaper. When Tom opens the door, Ruby Hornaday is standing on the stoop in the rain.

Hello. Tom blinks a dozen times. Raindrops set a thousand intersecting circles upon the puddles in the road. Ruby holds up a jar: six black tadpoles squirm in an inch of water.

Seemed like you were interested in water creatures.

Tom tries to answer, but the whole sky is rushing through the open door into his mouth.

You're not going to faint again, are you?

Mr. Weems stumps into the foyer. *Jesus, boy, she's damp as a church, you got to invite a lady in.*

Ruby stands on the tiles and drips. Mr. Weems grins. Tom mumbles, *My heart.*

Ruby holds up the jar. *Keep 'em if you want. They'll be frogs before long.* Drops shine in her eyelashes. Rain glues her shirt to her clavicles. *Well, that's something,* says Mr. Weems. He nudges Tom in the back. *Ain't it, Tom?*

Tom is opening his mouth. He's saying, *Maybe I could*—when Mother comes down the stairs in her big, black shoes. *Trouble,* hisses Mr. Weems. Heat crashes over Tom like a wave.

Mother dumps the tadpoles in a ditch. Her face says she's composing herself but her eyes say she's going to wipe all this away.

Image Credits: ©Eric Anthony Johnson/Photolibrary/Getty Images

Mr. Weems leans over the dominoes and whispers, *Mother's as hard as a cobblestone, but we'll crack her, Tom, you wait.*

Tom whispers, *Ruby Hornaday,* into the space above his cot. *Ruby Hornaday. Ruby Hornaday.* A strange and uncontainable joy inflates dangerously in his chest.

Mr. Weems has long conversations with Mother in the kitchen. Tom overhears scraps: *Boy needs to move his legs. Boy should get some air.*

Mother's voice is a whip. *He's sick.*

He's alive! What're you saving him for? How much time he got left?

Mother consents to let Tom retrieve coal from the depot and tinned goods from the commissary. Tuesdays he'll be allowed to walk to the butcher's in Dearborn. *Careful, Tomcat, don't hurry.*

Tom moves through the colony that first Tuesday with something close to rapture in his veins. Down the long gravel lanes, past pit cottages and surface mountains of blue and white salt, the warehouses like dark cathedrals, the hauling machines like demonic armatures.[2] All around him the monumental industry of Detroit pounds and clangs. The boy tells himself he is a treasure hunter, a hero from one of Mr. Weems's adventure stories, a knight on important errands, a spy behind enemy lines. He keeps his hands in his pockets and his head down and his gait slow, but his soul charges ahead, sparking through the gloom.

In May of that year, 1929, fourteen-year-old Tom is walking along the lane thinking spring happens beneath the snow, beyond the walls—spring happens in the dark while you dream—when Ruby Hornaday steps out of the weeds. She has a shriveled rubber hose coiled over her shoulder and a swim mask in one hand and a tire pump in the other. *Need your help.* Tom's pulse soars.

I got to go to the butcher's.

Your choice. Ruby turns to go. But really there's no choice at all.

She leads him west, away from the mine, through mounds of rusting machines. They hop a fence, cross a field gone to seed, and walk a quarter mile through pitch pines to a marsh where cattle egrets stand in the cattails like white flowers.

In my mouth, she says, and starts picking up rocks. *Out my nose. You pump, Tom. You understand?* In the green water two feet down Tom can make out the dim shapes of fish gliding through weedy enclaves.

Ruby pitches the far end of the hose into the water. With waxed cord she binds the other end to the pump. Then she fills her pockets with rocks. She wades out, looks back, says, *You pump*, and puts the hose into her mouth. The swim mask goes over her eyes; her face goes into the water.

[2] **armatures:** metal frames upon which sculptures are formed.

The marsh closes over Ruby's back, and the hose trends away from the bank. Tom begins to pump. The sky slides along over-head. Loops of garden hose float under the light out there, shifting now and then. Occasional bubbles rise, moving gradually farther out.

One minute, two minutes. Tom pumps. His heart does its fragile work. He should not be here. He should not be here while this skinny, spellbinding girl drowns herself in a marsh. If that's what she's doing. One of Mr. Weems's similes comes back to him from some dingy corner of memory: *You're trembling like a needle to the pole.*

After four or five minutes underwater, Ruby comes up. A neon mat of algae clings to her hair, and her bare feet are great boots of mud. She pushes through the cattails. Strings of saliva hang off her chin. Her lips are blue. Tom feels dizzy. The sky turns to liquid.

Incredible, pants Ruby. *Absolutely incredible.* She holds up her wet, rock-filled trousers with both hands, and looks at Tom through the wavy lens of her swim mask. His blood storms through its lightless tunnels.

He has to trot to make the butcher's by noon. It is the first time Tom can remember permitting himself to run, and his legs feel like glass and his breath like quicksand. At the end of the lane, a hundred yards from home, he stops and pants with the basket of meat in his arms and spits a pat of blood into the dandelions. Sweat soaks his shirt. Dragonflies dart and hover. Swallows inscribe letters across the sky. The lane seems to ripple and fold and straighten itself out again.

Just a hundred yards more. He forces his heart to settle. *Everything*, Tom thinks, *follows a path worn by those who have gone before: egrets, clouds, tadpoles. Everything.*

The following Tuesday Ruby meets him at the end of the lane. And the Tuesday after that. They hop the fence, cross the field; she leads him places he's never dreamed existed. Places where the structures of the saltworks become white mirages on the horizon. Places where sunlight washes through groves of maples and makes the ground quiver with leaf-shadow. They peer into a foundry where shirtless men in masks pour molten iron from one vat into another; they climb a tailings pile where a lone sapling grows like a single hand thrust up from the underworld. Tom knows he's risking everything, but how can he stop? How can he say no? To say no to Ruby Hornaday would be to say no to the world.

Some Tuesdays Ruby brings along her red book, with its images of corals and jellies and underwater men breathing from hoses. She tells him that when she grows up she'll go to parties where hostesses row guests offshore and everyone puts on special helmets and goes for strolls along the sea bottom. She tells him she'll be a diver who sinks herself a half mile into the sea in a steel ball with one window. In the basement of the ocean she'll find a world of lights: schools of fish glittering green, whole galaxies wheeling through the black.

In the ocean, says Ruby, *the rocks are alive and half the plants are animals.*

They hold hands; they chew Indian gum. She stuffs his mind full of kelp forests and seascapes and dolphins. *When I grow up*, thinks Tom. *When I grow up . . .*

Four more times Ruby walks around beneath the surface of a River Rouge marsh while Tom stands on the bank working the pump. Four more times he watches her rise back out like a fever. *Amphibian.* She laughs. *It means two lives.*

Then Tom runs to the butcher's and runs home, and his heart races, and spots spread like inkblots in front of his eyes. *Blue, blue blue.* But how does he know the blue he sees is the right color? Sometimes in the afternoons, when he stands up from his chores, his vision slides away in violet streaks and is a long while returning. Other colors spiral through his mind's eye, too: the glowing white of the salt tunnels, the red of Ruby's book, the orange of her hair—he imagines her all grown up, standing on the bow of a ship, and feels a core of lemon yellow light flaring brighter and brighter within him. It spills from the slats between his ribs, from between his teeth, from the pupils of his eyes. He thinks: *It is so much! So much!*

So now you're fifteen. And the doctor says sixteen?

Eighteen if I'm lucky.

Ruby turns her book over and over in her hands. *What's it like? To know you won't get all the years you should?*

I don't feel so shortchanged when I'm with you, he says, but his voice breaks at *short-* and the sentence falls apart.

They kiss only that one time. It is clumsy. He shuts his eyes and leans in, but something shifts and Ruby is not where he expects her to be. Their teeth clash. When he opens his eyes, she is looking off to her left, smiling slightly, smelling of mud, and the thousand tiny blonde hairs on her upper lip catch the light.

The second-to-last time Tom and Ruby are together, on the last Tuesday of October, 1929, everything is strange. The hose leaks, Ruby is upset, a curtain has fallen somehow between them.

Go back, Ruby says. *It's probably noon already. You'll be late.* But she sounds as if she's talking to him through a tunnel. Freckles flow and bloom across her face. The light goes out of the marsh.

On the long path through the pitch pines it begins to rain. Tom makes it to the butcher's and back home with the basket and the ground veal, yet when he opens the door to Mother's parlor the curtains seem to blow inward. The chairs seem to leave their places and come scraping toward him.

The daylight thins to a pair of beams, waving back and forth. Mr. Weems passes in front of his eyes, but Tom hears no footsteps, no voices: only an internal rushing and the wet metronome of his exhalations. Suddenly he's staring through a thick, foggy window into a world of immense pressure. Mother's face disappears and reappears. Her lips say, *Haven't I given enough? Lord God, haven't I tried?* Then she's gone.

In something deeper than a dream Tom walks the salt roads a thousand feet beneath the house. At first it's all darkness, but after what might be a minute or a day or a year, he sees little flashes of green light out there in distant galleries, hundreds of feet away. Each flash initiates a chain reaction of further flashes beyond it, so that if he turns in a slow circle he can perceive great flowing signals of light in all directions, tunnels of green arcing out into the blackness—each flash glowing for only a moment before fading, but in that moment repeating everything that came before, everything that will come next. Like days, like hours, like heartbeats.

He wakes to a deflated world. The newspapers are full of suicides; the price of gas has tripled. The miners whisper that the saltworks is in trouble. The Ford plant is shedding men; the foundry shuts down.

Quart milk bottles sell for a dollar apiece. There's no butter, hardly any meat. Most nights Mother serves only cabbage and soda bread. Salt.

No more trips to the butcher or the depot or the commissary. No more outside. He waits for Ruby to come to the door.

By November, Mother's boarders are vanishing. Mr. Beeson goes first, then Mr. Fackler. Still, Ruby doesn't come. Her face doesn't appear among the faces Tom watches from the upstairs window. Each morning he clambers out of his closet and carries his traitorous heart down to the kitchen like an egg. Images of Ruby climb the undersides of his eyelids, and he rubs them away.

No addresses, mumbles Mr. Weems. *The world is swallowing people like candy, boy. No one is leaving addresses.*

Mr. Hanson goes next, then Mr. Heathcock. By April the saltworks is operating only two days a week, and Mr. Weems, Mother, and Tom are alone at supper.

Sixteen. Eighteen if he's lucky. Tom moves his few things into one of the empty boarders' rooms on the first floor, and Mother doesn't say a word. He thinks of Ruby Hornaday: her pale blue eyes, her loose flames of hair. *Is she out there in the city, somewhere, right now? Or is she three thousand miles away?* Then he puts his questions aside.

Mother catches a fever in 1931. It eats her from the inside. She still puts on her high-waisted dresses, ties on her apron. She still cooks every meal and presses Mr. Weems's suit every Sunday. But within a month she has become somebody else, an empty demon in Mother's clothes—perfectly upright at the table, eyes smoldering, nothing on her plate.

> **“The world is swallowing people like candy, boy. No one is leaving addresses.”**

She has a way of putting her hand on Tom's forehead while he works. Tom will be hauling coal or mending a pipe or sweeping the parlor, the sun glowing behind the curtains, and Mother will appear from nowhere and put her icy palm over his eyebrows, and he'll close his eyes and feel his heart tear just a little more.

Amphibian. It means two lives.

Mr. Weems is let go. He puts on his suit, packs up his dominoes, and leaves an address downtown.

I thought no one was leaving addresses.

You're true as a map, Tom. True as the magnet to the iron. And tears spill from the old miner's eyes.

One blue, icy morning not long after that, for the first time in Tom's memory, Mother is not at the stove when he enters the kitchen. He finds her upstairs sitting on her bed, fully dressed in her coat and shoes and with her rosary clutched to her chest. The room is spotless, the house wadded with silence.

Now remember, payments are due on the fifteenth. Her voice is ash. *The flashing on the roof needs replacing. There's ninety-one dollars in the dresser.*

Mother, Tom says.

Shhh, Tomcat, she hisses. *Don't get yourself worked up.*

Tom manages two more payments. Then the saltworks closes and the bank comes for the house. He walks in a daze through blowing sleet to the end of the lane and turns right and staggers over the dry weeds awhile till he finds the old path and walks beneath the creaking pitch pines to Ruby's marsh. Ice has interlocked in the shallows, but the water in the center is dark as molten pewter.

He stands there a long time. Into the gathering darkness he says, *I'm still here, but where are you?* His blood sloshes to and fro, and snow gathers in his eyelashes, and three ducks come spiraling out of the night and land silently on the water.

The next morning he walks past the padlocked gate of International Salt with fourteen dollars in his pocket. He rides the trackless trolley downtown for a nickel and gets off on Washington

Boulevard. Between the buildings the sun comes up the color of steel, and Tom raises his face to it but feels no warmth at all. He passes catatonic drunks squatting on upturned crates, motionless as statues, and storefront after storefront of empty windows. In a diner a goitrous[3] waitress brings him a cup of coffee with little shining disks of fat floating on top.

The streets are filled with faces, dull and wan, lean and hungry; none belongs to Ruby. He drinks a second cup of coffee and eats a plate of eggs and toast, and then another. A woman emerges from a doorway and flings a pan out onto the sidewalk, and the wash water flashes in the light a moment before falling. In an alley a mule lies on its side, asleep or dead. Eventually the waitress says, *You moving in?* and Tom goes out. He walks slowly toward the address he's copied and recopied onto a sheet of Mother's writing paper. Frozen furrows of plowed snow are shored up against the buildings, and the little golden windows high above seem miles away.

It's a boardinghouse. Mr. Weems is at a lopsided table playing dominoes by himself. He looks up, says, *Holy ghosts sure as gravity,* and spills his tea.

By a miracle Mr. Weems has a grandniece who manages the owl shift in the maternity ward at City General. Maternity is on the fourth floor. In the elevator Tom cannot tell if he is ascending or descending. The niece looks him up and down and checks his eyes and chest for fever and hires him on the spot. *World goes to Hades, but babies still get born,* she says, and issues him white coveralls.

Rainy nights are the busiest. Full moons and holidays are tied for second. God forbid a rainy holiday with a full moon. Ten hours a night, six nights a week, Tom roves the halls with carts of laundry, taking soiled blankets down to the cellar, bringing clean blankets up. He brings up meals, brings down trays.

Doctors walk the rows of beds injecting expectant mothers with morphine and something called scopolamine that makes them forget. Sometimes there are screams. Sometimes Tom's heart pounds for no reason he can identify. In the delivery rooms there's always new blood on the tiles to replace the old blood Tom has just mopped away.

The halls are bright at every hour, but out the windows the darkness presses very close, and in the leanest hours of those nights Tom gets a sensation like the hospital is deep underwater, the floor rocking gently, the lights of neighboring buildings like glimmering schools of fish, the pressure of the sea all around.

He turns eighteen, nineteen. All the listless figures he sees: children humped around the hospital entrance, their eyes vacant with hunger;

[3] **goitrous** (goiˊtrəs): having a swelled area, usually in the neck and caused by an enlarged thyroid gland.

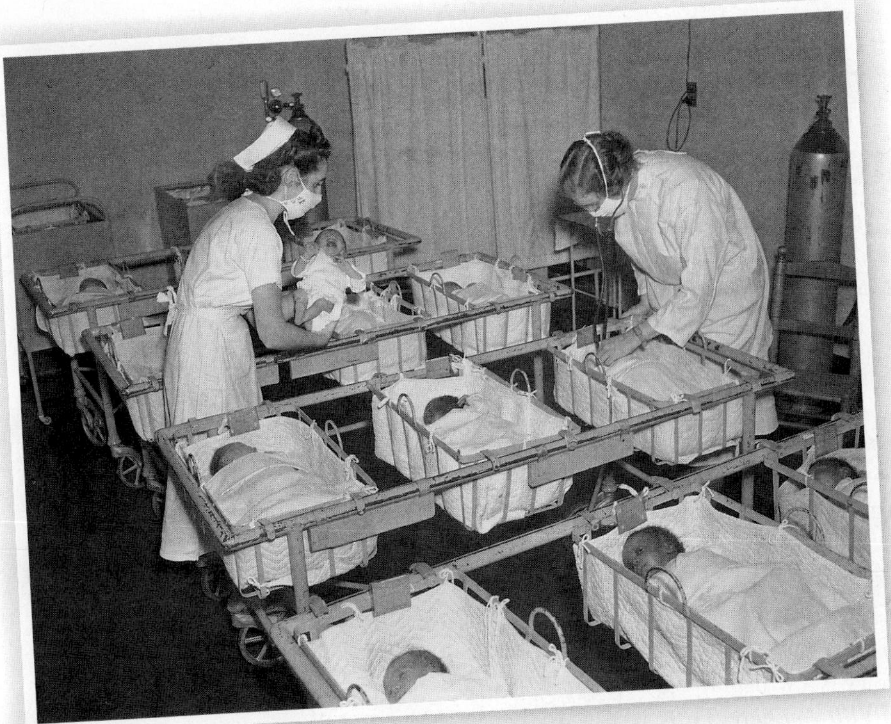

farmers pouring into the parks; families sleeping without cover—people for whom nothing left on earth could be surprising. There are so many of them, as if somewhere out in the countryside great factories pump out thousands of new men every minute, as if the ones shuffling down the sidewalks are but fractions of the immense multitudes behind them.

And yet is there not goodness, too? Are people not helping one another in these ruined places? Tom splits his wages with Mr. Weems. He brings home discarded newspapers and wrestles his way through the words on the funny pages. He turns twenty, and Mr. Weems bakes a mushy pound cake full of eggshells and sets twenty matches in it, and Tom blows them all out.

He faints at work: once in the elevator, twice in the big, pulsing laundry room in the basement. Mostly he's able to hide it. But one night he faints in the hall outside the waiting room, and a nurse named Fran hauls him into a closet. *Can't let them see you like that*, she says, and he washes back into himself.

Fran's face is brown, lived-in. She sits him on a chair in the corner and wipes his forehead. The air is warm, steamy; it smells like soap. For a moment he feels like throwing his arms around her neck and telling her everything.

The closet is more than a closet. On one wall is a two-basin sink; heat lamps are bolted to the undersides of the cabinets. Set in the opposite wall are two little doors.

> **Is there not goodness, too? Are people not helping one another in these ruined places?**

Tom returns to the chair in the corner of this room whenever he starts to feel dizzy. Three, four, occasionally ten times a night, he watches a nurse carry an utterly newborn baby through the little door on the left and deposit it on the counter in front of Fran.

She plucks off little knit caps and unwraps blankets. Their bodies are scarlet or imperial purple; they have tiny, bright red fingers, no eyebrows, no kneecaps, no expression except a constant, bewildered wince. Her voice is a whisper: *Why here you are, there you go, okay now, baby, just lift you here.* Their wrists are the circumference of Tom's pinkie.

Fran takes a new washcloth from a stack, dips it in warm water, and wipes every inch of the creature—ears, scrotum, armpits, eyelids—washing away bits of placenta,[4] dried blood, all the milky fluids that accompanied it into this world. Meanwhile the child stares up at her with blank, memorizing eyes, peering into the newness of all things. Knowing what? Only light and dark, only mother, only fluid.

Fran dries the baby and splays her fingers beneath its head and tugs its hat back on. She whispers, *Here you are, see what a good girl you are, down you go,* and with one free hand lays out two new, crisp blankets, and binds the baby—wrap, wrap, turn—and sets her in a rolling bassinet for Tom to wheel into the nursery, where she'll wait with the others beneath the lights like loaves of bread.

In a magazine Tom finds a color photograph of a three-hundred-year-old skeleton of a bowhead whale, stranded on a coastal plain in some place called Finland and covered with moss. He tears it out, studies it in the lamplight. *See,* he murmurs to Mr. Weems, *how the flowers closest to it are brightest? See how the closest leaves are the darkest green?*

Tom is twenty-one and fainting three times a week when he sees, among the drugged, dazed mothers in their rows of beds, the

[4] **placenta:** an organ connecting the mother and unborn fetus that provides nutrients and removes waste.

unmistakable face of Ruby Hornaday. Flaming orange hair, freckles sprayed across her cheeks, hands folded in her lap, and a thin gold wedding ring on her finger. The material of the ward ripples. Tom leans on the handle of his cart to keep from falling.

Blue, he thinks. *Blue, blue, blue.*

He retreats to the chair in the corner of the washing room and tries to suppress his heart. *Any minute*, he thinks, *her baby could come through the door.*

Two hours later, he pushes his cart into the postdelivery room, and Ruby is gone. Tom's shift ends; he rides the elevator down. Outside, and icy January rain settles lightly on the city. The street-lights glow yellow. The early morning avenues are empty except for the occasional automobile, passing with a damp sigh. Tom steadies a hand against the bricks and closes his eyes.

A police officer helps him home. Tom lies on his stomach in his rented bed all that day and recopies the letter until little suns burst behind his eyes. *Deer Ruby, I saw you in the hospital and I saw your baby to. His eyes are viry prety. Fran sez later they will probly get blue. Mother is gone and I am lonely as the arctic see.*

That night at the hospital Fran finds the address. Tom includes the photo of the whale skeleton from the magazine and sticks on an extra stamp for luck. He thinks: *See how the flowers closest to it are brightest. See how the closest leaves are the darkest green.*

He sleeps, pays his rent, walks the thirty-one blocks to work, and checks the mail each day. And each day winter pales and spring strengthens and Tom loses a little bit of hope.

One morning over breakfast, Mr. Weems looks to him with concern and says, *You ain't even here, Tom. You got one foot across the river. You got to pull back to our side.*

But three weeks later, it comes. *Dear Tom, I liked hearing from you. It hasn't been ten years but it feels like a thousand. I'm married, you probably guessed that. The baby is Arthur. Maybe his eyes will turn blue. They just might.*

A bald president is on the stamp. The paper smells like paper, nothing more. Tom runs a finger beneath every word, sounding it out. Making sure he hasn't missed anything.

I know your married and I dont want anything but happyness for you but maybe I can see you one time? We could meet at the acquareyem. If you dont rite back thats okay I no why.

Two more weeks. *Dear Tom, I don't want anything but happiness for you, too. How about next Tuesday? I'll bring the baby, okay?*

The next Tuesday, the first one in May, Tom leaves the hospital after his shift. His vision wavers at the edges, and he hears Mother's voice: *Be careful, Tomcat. It's not worth the risk.* He walks slowly to the end of the block and catches the first trolley to Belle Isle, where he steps off into a golden dawn.

There are few cars about, all parked, one a Ford with a huge present wrapped in yellow ribbon on the backseat. An old man with a crumpled face rakes the gravel paths. The sunlight hits the dew and sets the lawns aflame.

The face of the aquarium is Gothic and wrapped in vines. Tom finds a bench outside and waits for his pulse to steady. The reticulated[5] glass roofs of the flower conservatory reflect a passing cloud. Eventually a man in overalls opens the gate, and Tom buys two tickets, then thinks about the baby and buys a third. He returns to the bench with the three tickets in his trembling fingers.

By eleven the sky is filled with a platinum haze and the island is busy. Men on bicycles crackle along the paths. A girl flies a yellow kite.

Tom?

Ruby Hornaday materializes before him—shoulders erect, hair newly short, pushing a chrome-and-canvas baby buggy. He stands quickly, and the park bleeds away and then restores itself.

Sorry I'm late, she says.

She's dignified, slim. Two quick strokes for eyebrows, the same narrow nose. No makeup. No jewelry. Those pale blue eyes and that hair.

She cocks her head slightly. *Look at you. All grown up.*

I have tickets, he says.

How's Mr. Weems?

Oh, he's made of salt, he'll live forever.

They start down the path between the rows of benches and the shining trees. Occasionally she takes his arm to steady him, though her touch only disorients him more.

I thought maybe you were far away, he says. *I thought maybe you went to sea.*

Ruby doesn't say anything. She parks the buggy and lifts the baby to her chest—he's wrapped in a blue afghan—and then they're through the turnstile.

The aquarium is dim and damp and lined on both sides with glass-fronted tanks. Ferns hang from the ceiling, and little boys lean across the brass railings and press their noses to the glass. *I think he likes it*, Ruby says. *Don't you, baby?* The boy's eyes are wide open. Fish swim slow ellipses through the water.

They see **translucent** squid with corkscrew tails, sparkling pink octopi like floating lanterns, cowfish in blue and violet and gold. **Iridescent** green tiles gleam on the domed ceiling and throw wavering patterns of light across the floor.

In a circular pool at the very center of the building, dark shapes race back and forth in coordination. *Jacks*, Ruby murmurs. *Aren't they?*

translucent (trăns-lo͞oʹsənt) *adj.* semitransparent.

iridescent (ĭr′ĭ-dĕsʹənt) *adj.* having colors that change when seen from different angles.

[5] **reticulated:** having lines with a net-like pattern.

Tom blinks.

You're pale, she says.

Tom shakes his head.

She helps him back out into the daylight, beneath the sky and the trees. The baby lies in the buggy sucking his lips, and Ruby guides Tom to a bench.

Cars and trucks and even a limousine pass slowly along the white bridge, high over the river. The city glitters in the distance.

Thank you, says Tom.

For what?

For this.

How old are you now, Tom?

Twenty-one. Same as you. A breeze stirs the trees, and the leaves vibrate with light. Everything is radiant.

World goes to Hades, but babies still get born, whispers Tom.

Ruby peers into the buggy and adjusts something, and for a moment the back of her neck shows between her hair and collar. The sight of those two knobs of vertebrae, sheathed in her delicate skin, fills Tom with a longing that cracks the lawns open. For a moment it seems Ruby is being slowly dragged away from him, as if he were a swimmer caught in a rip, and with every stroke the back of her neck recedes farther into the distance. Then she sits back, and the park heels over, and he can feel the bench become solid beneath him once more.

I used to think, Tom says, *that I had to be careful with how much I lived. As if life was a pocketful of coins. You only got so much and you didn't want to spend it all in one place.*

Ruby looks at him. Her eyelashes whisk up and down.

But now I know life is the one thing in the world that never runs out. I might run out of mine, and you might run out of yours, but the world will never run out of life. And we're all very lucky to be part of something like that.

She holds his gaze. *Some deserve more luck than they've gotten.*

Tom shakes his head. He closes his eyes. *I've been lucky, too. I've been absolutely lucky.*

The baby begins to fuss, a whine building to a cry, and Ruby says, *Hungry.*

A trapdoor opens in the gravel between Tom's feet, black as a keyhole, and he glances down.

You'll be okay?

I'll be okay.

Good-bye, Tom. She touches his forearm once, and then she goes, pushing the buggy through the crowds. He watches her disappear in pieces, first her legs, then her hips, then her shoulders, and finally the back of her bright head.

And then Tom sits, hands in his lap, alive for one more day.

COLLABORATIVE DISCUSSION How would you describe Tom? With a partner, discuss how his relationships and life experiences help you understand the kind of person he is. Cite specific textual evidence from the story to support your ideas.

Determine Themes

RL 2

The **theme** of a short story is a message or central idea it conveys about life or human nature, particularly through the development of plot and character. It is not necessarily the subject of the story, though it does often revolve around a particular conflict in the plot. Themes are generally implied rather than directly stated. In a complex story such as "The Deep," there may be more than one theme, and the themes may interact and build on one another as the story develops.

By analyzing story elements, readers can get clues about theme in "The Deep." Ask yourself these questions:

- Does the story's title suggest a theme?
- What is the central conflict in the story? Is it resolved?
- What is revealed about Tom through his reaction to the conflict?
- Does Tom change over the course of the story? If so, what message does the change convey to readers?
- How do the actions of the other characters in the story, and their interactions with Tom, hint at a theme?

Analyze Story Elements: Setting

RL 3

Authors make critical choices about the **setting** of their stories, deciding not only when and where the action will take place but also how important a role the setting will play. In "The Deep," the setting has a significant effect on the mood, the characters, and the conflict. It also contributes to the development of themes. The setting of "The Deep" involves the physical place and a specific time period, as well as the economic conditions that resulted from the historical era known as the Great Depression.

This chart shows how the setting of a story can affect readers' perceptions of characters as the story develops.

Setting		Effect
Detroit, near the salt mines: • underinsulated boardinghouse • "the salt finds its way in" • the salt "encrusts washbasins . . . spills out of the boarders" • the miners "spill like little salt-dusted insects out into the night"	▶	The boardinghouse's location near the salt mines and the pervasiveness of this gritty salt create a gray, grim mood. The characters, and the lives they live, are drab and comfortless. Salt is a preservative, though food preserved with salt lacks the vitality of fresh food. This idea mirror's the dull routine of Tom's life, designed to keep him alive without really living.

eBook *Annotate It!*

Analyzing the Text

RL 1, RL 2, RL 3, RL 4, SL 1a

Cite Text Evidence Support your responses with evidence from the selection.

1. **Compare** How does the way Tom is treated by Mr. Weems differ from the way he is treated by his mother? What motivates their attitudes toward his health?
2. **Cite Evidence** Identify examples of metaphors and similes that the author uses to describe Tom's interactions with Ruby. How does this figurative language help reveal Tom's thoughts and feelings about her?
3. **Interpret** Reread lines 251–256. What does the author convey with the statement, "The light goes out of the marsh"?
4. **Cause/Effect** The story is set during the Great Depression. In what ways does this historical event affect Tom's life? How does the author use these changes to develop his character?
5. **Analyze** A **symbol** is a person, place, or thing that stands for something beyond itself. What do the following places and things symbolize for Tom?
   - the marsh
   - the hospital
   - the whale skeleton
6. **Synthesize** Identify two themes in the story. Explain how these themes interact and build on each other.
7. **Evaluate** Throughout the story, Tom struggles with the fear that he will die young. How does Tom resolve this conflict at the end of the story? Do you find this resolution effective? Explain.

PERFORMANCE TASK

Speaking Activity: Discussion What is the significance of the story's title?

- Review the story, jotting down ideas about what you see as the significance of the title as well as specific references to water or "the deep."
- Meet in a small group and share ideas about the meaning of the title, including how it relates to a possible theme. Does it have more than one meaning in the story?
- Summarize the important ideas from your discussion, and present them to the class.

Critical Vocabulary

L 5b

itinerant **sporadic** **reverberate**

translucent **iridescent**

Practice and Apply Explain which of the two situations best fits each Critical Vocabulary word's meaning.

itinerant	(a) a door-to-door salesperson	(b) a store owner
sporadic	(a) a bell that tolls every hour	(b) a bell that rings when there is a fire
reverberate	(a) shouting in a canyon	(b) shouting down the street
translucent	(a) a window with frosted glass	(b) a window with closed shutters
iridescent	(a) an oil slick on a road	(b) a muddy puddle on a sidewalk

Vocabulary Strategy: Analyze Nuances in Word Meanings

Writers choose words carefully, deciding which ones to use based on shades of difference, or **nuances,** in their meaning. For example, the Critical Vocabulary word *translucent* and the word *transparent* have a similar **denotation,** or literal meaning, but there are subtle differences between them that affect the mood of the story. As used in "The Deep," *translucent* means something that transmits light but that can't be completely seen through. *Transparent* refers to something that transmits light and that can be seen through. Read this sentence from the story: "They see translucent squid with corkscrew tails. . . ." The word *transparent* would not be accurate, nor would it evoke the same image that the word *translucent* does.

Practice and Apply Complete these activities with a partner.

1. The words in each pair are similar in meaning but not exactly identical. Look up the definition of each word in a dictionary, or use the meaning in the text to define the Critical Vocabulary word in each pair.
   - itinerant/migrant
   - iridescent/colorful
   - sporadic/periodic
   - fragile/feeble
2. Explain the nuance in meaning between the words in each pair.
3. Choose one of the pairs and write a sentence for each word that illustrates its exact meaning. Share your sentences with the class.

Language and Style: Tone

L 3

In a work of fiction, the author creates a narrative **tone**. That is, the author chooses words and arranges them in a way that conveys the narrator's attitude toward the characters and events.

In "The Deep," the author intersperses lush, flowing descriptions with ideas expressed in a terse, or abrupt, syntax. These two passages from the text illustrate the differing styles:

> **Tom moves through the colony that first Tuesday with something close to rapture in his veins. Down the long gravel lanes, past pit cottages and surface mountains of blue and white salt, the warehouses like dark cathedrals, the hauling machines like demonic armatures.**
>
> **Quart milk bottles sell for a dollar apiece. There's no butter, hardly any meat. Most nights Mother serves only cabbage and soda bread. Salt.**

The first passage describes Tom's internal world, the world experienced through his newly awakened senses. The narrator's tone, created by powerful words, figurative language, and the melodious rhythm of the prose, might be described as reverential or sensitive. The second passage describes the physical world that Tom inhabits, with all of its limitations. The abrupt, disjointed sentences and humdrum vocabulary suggest the harshness of this existence. The narrator's tone here is matter-of-fact and unsentimental.

Practice and Apply A writer may show any number of attitudes toward a subject, such as formal, casual, serious, lighthearted, sarcastic, or mournful. Complete these activities to show your understanding of tone.

1. Choose an actual incident from your life as the basis for a brief narrative.
2. Before writing, think about the tone you want to convey. After writing, replace and rearrange words to better reflect your desired tone.
3. Read your narrative to a partner and discuss whether or not you effectively communicated your tone.

Michael Specter *has written for the* Washington Post *and the* New York Times; *currently he is a staff writer for the* New Yorker. *He often covers topics related to science, technology, and public health. Specter has received awards for articles on the AIDS epidemic in Africa and for his war reporting. His 2009 book* Denialism *reflects his growing concern over opposition to science by various groups and individuals, which he believes could have disastrous consequences for the planet.*

The Mosquito Solution

Science Article by Michael Specter

AS YOU READ Pay attention to the clues that tell you how the author feels about "the mosquito solution." Write down any questions you generate during reading.

Can genetic modification eliminate a deadly tropical disease?

Few people, unless they travel with an electron microscope,[1] would ever notice the egg of an *Aedes aegypti* mosquito. But the insects follow us nearly everywhere we go. *Aedes* can breed in a teaspoon of water, and their eggs have been found in tin cans, beer bottles, barrels, jugs, flower vases, cups, tanks, tubs, storm drains, cisterns, cesspools, catch basins, and fishponds. They mate in the dew of spider lilies, ape plants, guava trees, palm fronds, in the holes of rocks formed from lava, and in coral reefs. More than any other place, perhaps, *Aedes aegypti* thrive in the moist, hidden gullies of used automobile tires.

[1] **electron microscope:** an instrument that uses beams of electrons rather than light to magnify tiny objects.

As adults, the mosquitoes are eerily beautiful: jet black, with white spots on the thorax[2] and white rings on their legs. Yet *Aedes* are among the deadliest creatures on earth. Before a vaccine was discovered in the nineteen-thirties, the mosquito transmitted the yellow-fever virus to millions of people, with devastating efficiency. During the Spanish-American War, U.S. troops suffered more casualties from yellow fever than from enemy fire. The mosquito also carries dengue, one of the most rapidly spreading viral diseases in the world. According to the World Health Organization, dengue infects at least fifty million people a year. For the fortunate, a case of dengue resembles a mild form of influenza. But more than half a million people become seriously ill from the disease. Many develop dengue shock syndrome or a hemorrhagic fever that leaves them vomiting and, often, bleeding from the nose, mouth, or skin. The pain can be so excruciating that the virus has a commonly invoked nickname: break-bone fever.

There is no vaccine or cure for dengue, or even a useful treatment. The only way to fight the disease has been to poison the insects that carry it. That means bathing yards, roads, and public parks in a fog of insecticide. Now there is another approach, promising but experimental: a British biotechnology company called Oxitec has developed a method to modify the genetic structure of the male *Aedes* mosquito, essentially transforming it into a mutant capable of destroying its own species. A few weeks ago, I found myself standing in a dank, **fetid** laboratory at Moscamed, an insect-research facility in the Brazilian city of Juazeiro, which has one of the highest dengue rates in the world. A plastic container about the size of an espresso cup sat on a bench in front of me, and it was filled with what looked like black tapioca: a granular, glutinous[3] mass containing a million eggs from Oxitec's engineered mosquito. Together, the eggs weighed ten grams, about the same as a couple of nickels.

fetid
(fĕt´ĭd) *adj.* having an unpleasant odor; bad-smelling.

Oxitec, which is short for Oxford Insect Technologies, has essentially transformed Moscamed into an **entomological** assembly line. In one tightly controlled, intensely humid space, mosquitoes are hatched, nurtured, fed a combination of goat's blood and fish food, then bred. Afterward, lab technicians destroy the females they have created and release the males to pursue their only real purpose in life: to find females in the wild and mate with them. Eggs fertilized by those genetically modified males will hatch normally, but soon after, and well before the new mosquitoes can fly, the fatal genes will prevail, killing them all. The goal is both simple and audacious: to overwhelm the native population of *Aedes aegypti* and wipe them out, along with the diseases they carry.

entomological
(ĕn´tə-mə-lŏj´ĭ-kəl) *adj.* related to the study of insects.

The engineered mosquitoes, known officially as OX513A, lead a brief but privileged life. The entire process, from creation to

[2] **thorax:** the part of a body between the head and abdomen.

[3] **glutinous:** thick and sticky, like glue.

destruction, takes less than two weeks. The eggs, oval spheres no longer than a millimetre, are milky white when laid. Within a couple of hours they harden, forming a protective cuticle and turning shiny and black. Looking around the lab, I saw long white sheets lining the shelves; each sheet was covered in tens of thousands of pin-sized dots and resembled some sort of computer code. The eggs can survive that way for a year; after four days, however, they are plunged into jam jars filled with water at twenty-seven degrees Celsius—a temperature that enables the eggs to hatch in less than an hour.

"These mosquitoes are relatively easy to breed and cost almost nothing to transport," Andrew McKemey, Oxitec's chief field officer, said as he led me around the lab. McKemey, a lanky man who was dressed in a green madras shirt and khaki cargo pants, spends much of his time in Brazil, teaching local scientists how to manufacture the company's prize product. The lab churns out about four million mutant eggs a week, and will soon increase production to ten million. "That's a start," McKemey said. "In theory, we can build hundreds of millions of mosquitoes in this place."

The field trial, which began a year ago, is a collaboration between Moscamed, Oxitec, and the University of São Paulo. Preliminary results have been impressive: the group recently collected a sample of eggs in two neighborhoods where the engineered mosquitoes had been released, and found that eighty-five per cent of them were genetically modified. With a large enough number of those eggs, the *Aedes* population would fall, and so would the incidence of dengue. "This is not a **panacea**," Giovanini Coelho, who coordinates the Brazilian Ministry of Health's National Program for Control of Dengue, told me. "I am not saying this alone will solve the problem or that there are no risks. There are always risks—that's why we start with small studies in geographically isolated neighborhoods. But people are dying here, and this mosquito is resistant to many insecticides. We really do need something better than what we have."

panacea (păn′ə-sē′ə) *n.* a cure or solution for all problems.

In Juazeiro, where few families remain unaffected by dengue, the Moscamed team and its mosquitoes are treated with reverence. The researchers drive around in white vans that have pictures of mosquitoes and the word *transgenico*[4] painted on the side. They try to visit every house in areas where they release mosquitoes, to explain that OX513A "are friendly bugs that protect you against dengue" and that, because the scientists are targeting *Aedes aegypti* where they live, under sofas and in back yards, the engineered mosquitoes can kill their brethren without harming any other plant or animal.

It's an elegant approach to a health crisis that threatens much of the world, but it will take more than biological success to make it work. That's because OX513A is not like other mosquitoes. In fact, it's like nothing else on earth—a winged creature, made by man, then released

[4] ***transgenico*** (trăns-jĕn′ĭ-kô): a Spanish term meaning "genetically modified."

into the wild. Despite the experiment's scientific promise, many people regard the tiny insect as a harbinger of a world where animals are built by nameless scientists, nurtured in beakers, then set loose—with consequences, no matter how noble the intention, that are impossible to anticipate or control. "This mosquito is Dr. Frankenstein's monster, plain and simple," Helen Wallace, the executive director of the British environmental organization GeneWatch, said. "To open a box and let these man-made creatures fly free is a risk with dangers we haven't even begun to contemplate."

There are more than three thousand species of mosquito, but the vast majority take no interest in us; they feed mostly on rotting fruit and other sources of sugar. Only a few hundred species, including *Aedes aegypti*, need blood to survive. (The males never bite, but without a blood meal the females would be unable to nourish their eggs.) Mosquito mating habits can be brutal. "In the most successful encounters, the pair may become so tightly locked together that the male has some difficulty escaping in the end," the late Harvard entomologist Andrew Spielman wrote in his 2001 book, "Mosquito: The Story of Man's Deadliest Foe." "An unfortunate few males manage to get away only by leaving their sex organs behind." Yet Spielman also noted that the briefest exchanges can be highly productive: "A single minute or so of passion allows her to produce all the fertile eggs she will ever lay."

There has never been a more effective killing machine. Researchers estimate that mosquitoes have been responsible for half the deaths in human history. Malaria accounts for much of the mortality, but mosquitoes also transmit scores of other potentially fatal infections, including yellow fever, dengue fever, chikungunya, lymphatic filariasis, Rift Valley fever, West Nile fever, and several types of encephalitis. Despite our technical sophistication, mosquitoes pose a greater risk to a larger number of people today than ever before. Like most other pathogens, the viruses and parasites borne by mosquitoes evolve rapidly to resist pesticides and drugs. Many insecticides once used against *Aedes aegypti* are now considered worthless.

Aedes aegypti is an invasive species in the Americas. It most likely arrived on slave boats from Africa in the seventeenth century, along with the yellow fever it carried. The mosquitoes bred easily in the casks that provided drinking water on sailing ships. During the eighteenth century, a severe yellow-fever epidemic swept through New England and Philadelphia, as well as other American port cities; it took another century to discover that mosquitoes were the bearers of the disease.

Traditional mosquito control all but eradicated *Aedes aegypti* (and the diseases it carries) from the United States fifty years ago. But globalization has been good to mosquitoes, particularly species like *Aedes aegypti*, which travel easily and can lie dormant in containers for months. In recent years, the mosquito and dengue have returned to Texas, Hawaii, and Florida. The disease has also been transmitted for the first time in France and Croatia. "We have dragged mosquitoes around the world in billions of used tires," Paul Reiter told me. Reiter, a professor of medical entomology at the Pasteur Institute, in Paris, is one of the world's experts on the natural history of mosquito-borne diseases. Before moving to France, he spent more than two decades in the Dengue Branch of the Centers for Disease Control, devoting a surprising amount of his time to studying tires. He found that they are ideal incubators for mosquitoes: tires absorb heat, trap rainwater, and nurture bacteria in the puddles they create. The exponential growth of dengue fever—the number of cases reported to the World Health Organization has increased thirtyfold since 1965—can, at least in part, be attributed to the enormous increase in tire exports.

Aedes aegypti don't fly far or live long; a major traveller would move a few hundred yards and, on average, survive as an adult for ten days. But it is a particularly wily insect. Most mosquitoes are noisy enough to wake a sleeping man and slow enough that one bite is all they'll get before escaping or being crushed with an angry swat. *Aedes aegypti* feed during the day and strike in silence; they mostly stay low to the ground, preferring to bite people in the ankles or legs. The mosquito is highly sensitive to motion—as you move, it will, too, often stabbing its victim several times during each feeding, depositing pathogens with every bite and, in turn, increasing its chances of picking up dengue from infected people to pass along to others. (Unlike most mosquitoes, which can lay hundreds of eggs in a single raft the size of a grain of rice, *Aedes aegypti* usually deposits its eggs in multiple locations, thereby raising the odds that some will survive.)

Dengue has always been considered a tropical illness. But its mode of transport, the mosquito, rarely lives more than a hundred yards from the vector's principal source of sustenance—us—and as our demographics have changed so have those of the mosquito. *Aedes aegypti* has adapted to the city with great dexterity. Even the most effective modern larvicides often miss the mosquito's well-hidden urban breeding grounds. "Dengue is a terrible disease, just terrible," Reiter said. "Its danger is impossible to exaggerate. And none of the methods used right now for dengue control are working. None."

It is not easy for an egg to become an OX513A. Most were originally modified in Oxitec's laboratories, in the English countryside not far from Oxford, where scientists, working with glass needles so small they can be seen only under a powerful microscope, insert two genes into eggs no bigger than a grain of salt. One gene carries instructions to manufacture far too much of a protein required to maintain healthy new cells; the results are lethal. Scientists keep the gene at bay, and the mosquitoes alive, by placing the antibiotic tetracycline in the insects' food. The drug latches on to the protein and acts as a switch that can turn it on or off. As long as tetracycline is present, the mosquitoes live and reproduce normally and can be bred for generations. Once they are released from the lab, however, the antidote is gone; the lethal gene goes unchecked. Within days the males, along with any eggs they help to create, will perish. In fact, Oxitec has already modified all the *Aedes aegypti* eggs the world may ever need.

The other gene is a fluorescent marker—the molecular version of a branding iron—that helps distinguish normal mosquitoes from modified ones. The naked eye sees nothing, but under the microscope the larvae give off a rich red glow, like a soft neon sign. Most of the altered eggs will die. Others will fail to incorporate the new genes into their DNA; these are useless, because the process succeeds only when the genes work their way into the critical germ cells the eggs need to reproduce. The task is difficult and tedious: the technicians can go through thousands of eggs to hit on just one that will pass the new genes to the next generation of mosquitoes. But once a sufficient number of eggs have been correctly modified they can, after many generations, produce millions of mutant mosquitoes.

OX513A are raised in the relative splendor of the laboratory. After they hatch, they are moved from petri dishes to plastic tanks the size of a home aquarium. Males are fed sugar; females, first lured by the smell of human sweat, feed on goat's blood obtained weekly from a nearby abattoir. "Thank God for that place," McKemey said with a laugh. "You can't make mosquitoes without blood." He stood in the close quarters of the rearing room as all around him eggs were morphing into larvae, hatching in the type of long trays bakers use to store loaves of bread. Across the room, in transparent, water-filled pails covered with cheesecloth, thousands of larvae, known to biologists as wrigglers, were frantically trying to work themselves out of their cases and emerge as pupae, the final stage before becoming an adult.

Adolescent mosquitoes have enormous heads and prominent eyes; under the microscope they look like sea horses or miniature versions of E.T.[5] While the mosquitoes are still sheathed in their cases, their transparent wings are pinned behind their bodies. By this point, the mosquito has begun breathing through its syphon, a curling, segmented tube that pokes above the surface of the water like a snorkel. When the moment is right, the pupae inhale, expand their abdomens, burst their cases, and emerge head first as adults. "It's thrilling to see," McKemey said, as we watched the young mosquitoes take their first tentative flights. "I never tire of it."

The Oxitec mosquito grew out of a pest-control method called sterile insect technique, or SIT, which has been used for decades. Billions of insects, all sterilized by intense bursts of radiation, have been reared in laboratories like Moscamed and released to mate in the wild. In 1982, SIT, which prevents the organism from reproducing,

---

[5] **E.T.:** Extraterrestrial, referring to the central character in the movie of that name.

A mosquito larva shown through an electron microscope

successfully eradicated the screw-worm—a parasite that attacks the flesh of warm-blooded animals—from North America. But radiation is difficult to use properly on insects as small as mosquitoes. Administer too little and they remain virile; zap them too powerfully and the insects are left so weak that they are unfit to compete for mates.

In the early nineties, Oxitec's chief scientist, Luke Alphey, was investigating the developmental genetics of *Drosophila*, the common fruit fly. One day, Alphey, now a visiting professor of zoology at Oxford, bumped into a colleague who was talking about sterile insect technique. Alphey, who knew little about the field, began to think about how to supplant radiation with the practices of modern molecular biology. Alphey is reserved, with a mop of brown hair and pensive eyes; one can practically see his brain in motion as he works out a scientific problem. His goal was not exactly to sterilize the males but to alter their genes so that any **progeny** would die. If he could do that without using radiation, he reasoned, the insects should be fit to compete sexually for wild females.

progeny (prŏj′ə-nē) *n.* offspring or descendants.

Alphey faced several scientific hurdles. He would have to engineer only males. (Female mosquitoes bite, so genetically modified females could, in theory, pass novel proteins to humans, with unknown consequences.) "I was trying to think of ways around the radiation issue," he said. "I wondered, What if the engineered lethal system could be sex-specific? It turns out that, with *Aedes aegypti*, females are considerably larger than the males. That was a lucky break, because it means you can easily separate them on the basis of their size."

Once released, the males would have to live long enough to impregnate females, and they would need to be healthy enough to compete with wild males for the right to do so. "You want the insect to breed successfully in the lab but to be dependent on an antidote that will no longer be available in nature," Alphey said. "It was difficult to know how to do that." But chance again intervened: he happened to attend a seminar at which researchers described using tetracycline as a switch to turn off a gene. "The molecule prevents the deadly gene from working," Alphey said. "It was a perfect solution."

In 2002, Oxitec was spun off as a company apart from the university. Alphey began to speak at tropical-disease meetings and in dengue-infested countries; he also gathered support from private investors and public-health philanthropies, including the Gates Foundation and the Wellcome Trust. In 2010, the company ran a series of field trials in the Cayman Islands, releasing 3.3 million genetically altered mosquitoes on sixteen hectares[6] of land. OX513A became the first engineered mosquito set free on the planet.

The number of wild *Aedes aegypti* mosquitoes in the area fell by eighty per cent in two months. It was only a test of feasibility; no one knew how it might affect the local ecology or whether it would actually reduce the incidence of dengue. Environmental activists feared that the release of engineered insects could set off a cascade of events that nobody would be able to control.

"They don't know how it will function in the real environment," Silvia Ribeiro, the director in Latin America for an environmental organization called the ETC Group, said. "And once they release it they can't take it back." In 2010, Oxitec began a smaller trial in Malaysia. But the Brazilian experiment has been the biggest test so far, and it has laid the groundwork for Oxitec's battle over entry into the world's most significant market: the United States.

In 2009, Key West, Florida, suffered its first dengue outbreak in seventy-three years. There were fewer than thirty confirmed cases—a trifling number compared with the millions who are infected each year in South America, Africa, and Asia. There are just twenty thousand full-time residents in Key West, but, with more than two million visitors each year, the town is highly dependent on tourists. I was there during spring break, which is not the best time to visit unless you have a particular interest in keggers, tequila, or Eagles cover bands.

"They feed this town," a woman who runs a cigar stand told me as we watched scores of sunburned students work their way down Truman Street and head toward Jimmy Buffett's bar, Margaritaville,

---

[6] **hectares:** metric units of area measurement, with one hectare equivalent to 10,000 square meters.

"Environmental activists feared that the release of engineered insects could set off a cascade of events."

ground zero for the aggressively laid-back Key West life style. "Sometimes it's a little gross out there," she said. "But take the tourists away and we are just a bunch of taco stands, bars, and beach bums."

Even a small dengue outbreak in Key West would send a troubling message. After 2009, the Florida Keys Mosquito Control District added ten inspectors to join the battle against *Aedes aegypti*. In 2010, there were twice as many cases. "Clearly, we have the potential for serious dengue outbreaks," Michael S. Doyle told me. Doyle, an entomologist, is the district's executive director. He moved to Key West in 2011, after spending five years at the Centers for Disease Control. "Part of our problem is the image of dengue," he said. "A couple of hundred cases here could be devastating to the tourist economy.

"Think about it," he continued. "Somebody in Milwaukee is cruising through Web sites and asks his wife, 'Where should we go on vacation, honey, Key West or some place in the Caribbean?' And the wife says, 'Hey, didn't I hear something about dengue in Key West?'" We were sitting in a café not far from Ernest Hemingway's house, the city's most heavily visited tourist site. Like many public buildings, the café has open windows and no screens; mosquitoes danced in the air beside us. "We live with open doors and windows," Doyle said. "And they live with us. We are an ideal host."

Doyle is a soft-spoken man with rimless eyeglasses and a neatly trimmed mustache. He pointed out that, when it comes to contracting dengue, the way people live is as important as where they live: from 1980 to 1999, Texas reported sixty-four cases of dengue along the Rio Grande, whereas there were more than sixty thousand cases in the Mexican states just across the river. "The population of *Aedes aegypti* was actually larger in Texas," he said. But Texans have screens on their windows (and keep the windows closed), drive air-conditioned cars, and spend little time outdoors.

Doyle wanted to lower the risk of a dengue outbreak in Key West, but the district was already spending more than a million dollars a year on insecticide, and he was loath to dump more chemicals in people's yards. Then a colleague attended a meeting of the American Society for Tropical Medicine and Hygiene and told him about OX513A. "I remember thinking that if this actually worked we would win in every possible way," he said. "Other approaches are more costly and more environmentally challenging. The data looked solid, and certainly we need to think differently about mosquito control than we have in the past."

In March, Doyle invited Luke Alphey, Oxitec's founder, and Hadyn Parry, its chief executive, to explain their approach at a town meeting. It would be the first in a series of hearings intended to explore the possibility of testing the mosquitoes in one relatively isolated Key West neighborhood. "I don't really know what to expect," Alphey told me early on the day of the meeting. "But I hope the people of Key West understand that they have been lucky. Because they are living in a sea of dengue."

Opponents mobilized within hours of receiving notice of the meeting. Boldly colored flyers, stating that the mosquito-control board was "planning on releasing and testing genetically modified (man-made) mosquitoes on you, your family and the environment," were pasted onto half the city's walls.

Before the meeting, I ran into Chris O'Brien, an artfully dishevelled woman with shoulder-length hair and searching blue eyes. She was dressed in the peaches and pinks one associates with southern Florida. She was also wearing combat boots. O'Brien is a "conch," a term that describes people who are born, raised, and spend their lives in Key West. Her children and grandchildren are conchs, too.

"People live with mosquitoes here," she said. "We always have. We have had no dengue for two years and maybe, at most, we will have a few cases. It's not a huge deal. Certainly not big enough to bring in an unnatural insect about which we know so little. You are in much more danger of being hit by a car."

It is impossible to predict the likelihood of a dengue outbreak based on the number of past infections. All it takes is the presence of the mosquito and the virus. Key West has plenty of the former; the rest is a matter of aggressive pest control—and chance. Once infectious mosquitoes start biting humans, an epidemic can erupt within weeks, as the virus moves from vector to host and back again. O'Brien, like many of her fellow-protesters, had been briefed by the Friends of the Earth about the concept of introducing man-made creatures into the local environment. "How do we know the females won't breed and bite people?" she asked. "They would have enzymes in their bodies that don't exist in real life. What would happen if they bit us? Getting rid of dengue would be wonderful, of course, but what would happen if we did succeed and these mosquitoes simply vanished from the earth? Isn't there a food chain to worry about?"

Those are reasonable concerns. But ecologists are quick to note that *Aedes aegypti* have been in America for only two hundred years or so; that's not enough time for a species to make an evolutionary impact. Many biologists argue that if *Aedes aegypti*, or, indeed, all mosquitoes, were to disappear, the world wouldn't miss them, and other insects would quickly fill their ecological niche—if they have one. "More than most other living things, the mosquito is a self-serving creature," Andrew Spielman has written. "She doesn't aerate the soil, like ants and worms. She is not an important pollinator of plants, like the bee. She does not even serve as an essential food item for some other animal. She has no 'purpose' other than to perpetuate her species. That the mosquito plagues human beings is really, to her, incidental. She is simply surviving and reproducing."

Not everyone agrees with Spielman's assessment. "Genetic modification leads to both intended and unintended effects," Ricarda Steinbrecher, of EcoNexus, a not-for-profit, public-interest research organization based in England, says. In a lengthy letter to government regulators in Malaysia, she stressed that there could be **ancillary** impacts "if the mosquitoes are eliminated altogether." For instance, what would happen to those fish, frogs, other insects, and arthropods that feed on larval or adult mosquitoes? "What if their interactions with other organisms in the environment change?" she wrote. "There is also the question of what will fill the gap or occupy the niche should the target mosquitoes have been eliminated. Will other pests increase in number? Will targeted diseases be able to switch vectors? Will these vectors be easier or more difficult to control?"

ancillary (ăn′sə-lĕr′ē) *adj.* additional and related.

It would be irresponsible to deploy transgenic insects widely without adequate answers to those questions, but most have been addressed in environmental-impact statements and by independent research. If the results were put to the vote of biologists, the overwhelming response would be: the potential benefits far outweigh the risks. There are no birds, fish, or other insects that depend solely on *Aedes aegypti*. It doesn't pollinate flowers or regulate the growth of plants. It is not what entomologists call a "keystone" species in the United States.

"It is frankly difficult to see a downside," Daniel Strickman, the national program leader in veterinary and medical entomology at the Agricultural Research Service, told me. "My job is to try and prevent human disease by modifying behavior and killing mosquitoes. So I come at it from that perspective. I am biased against mosquitoes. And *Aedes aegypti* cause immense damage. Raging epidemics of dengue would affect our economy badly. Go back to the days of yellow fever in this country and it had real demographic consequences. Whole towns died. Life expectancies in certain areas were reduced." Strickman added, "I look at this new approach and there is nothing greener. It's targeted at one species. If the sole question is what will happen if we kill off this single species of mosquito, it doesn't seem like a close call."

Mark Q. Benedict agrees. Benedict, an entomologist at the University of Perugia, has researched genetically modified insects for years and written about them extensively. "There are unanswered questions and there always will be," he said. "But there are also unanswered questions about the effect of insecticides on children, and we use them every day to try and kill the very same mosquitoes. It's important to remember: we're already trying to wipe this species out, and for good reason. The risk involved in eliminating them is very, very small. The risk in letting them multiply is enormous."

Environmentalists have expressed concern about what might happen if some of the modified females survived and, while biting people, injected them with an engineered protein. Oxitec separates males from females, but, with so many mosquitoes, a few genetically modified females inevitably slip by—Oxitec puts the number at about one in three thousand. "This is a nightmare scenario, and we don't have any published data that answers this question," Eric Hoffman, a food-and-technology policy campaigner for Friends of the Earth, told me. Hoffman has assiduously followed the Oxitec experiments. Reiter says that none of the protein introduced into transgenic mosquitoes enters its salivary glands—which means it couldn't spread to the humans it bites. In addition, he has recognized nothing in the genetic structure of the modified mosquitoes that could cause humans harm. But he and others are eager to see papers published, by groups unconnected to Oxitec, that confirm those conclusions.

The biggest question raised by the creation of OX513A is who will regulate it and how. In Brazil, a single government body—the National Technical Commission on Biosafety—oversees the approval of all genetically modified organisms. In the United States, however, the regulatory structure is far more complex. It's not clear whether engineered mosquitoes will be regarded as animals, under the jurisdiction of the Department of Agriculture, or as drugs, governed by the Food and Drug Administration.

> "We're already trying to wipe this species out, and for good reason."

"I would be so eager to have a clear regulatory situation in the United States," Alphey told me, his frustration at the process barely held in check. "We do not want to move forward unless one is properly in place." To the consternation of many, Oxitec recently applied to the F.D.A. for approval of its mosquito. "We are concerned that Oxitec has been less than forthcoming in their statements to the public," Hoffman told me. "They are saying that these mosquitoes are sterile, but they are not sterile, since they impregnate females. They are genetically modified, and the public needs to know that." Oxitec does call its mosquitoes sterile, but has not denied that they are genetically modified; almost all their literature says as much. "There is no layman's term for 'passes on an autocidal gene that kills offspring,'" Alphey said. "'Sterile' is the closest common term. OX513A is sterile in very much the same sense as radiation-sterilized insects are sterile." Hoffman stops short of calling Alphey's message deceptive, but he certainly doesn't agree. "This country just doesn't have the law or regulations necessary to move this project forward right now," he said.

In Key West, the Oxitec scientists, along with Doyle and his team from the mosquito-control district, faced a packed room at the Harvey Government Center. It was a warm, sunny day, and many in the crowd had left work early to be there. Doyle explained how a small experiment might proceed; Oxitec made its case; then the floor was opened to the public. The meeting quickly became emotional and, at times, rancorous. Oxitec—a small company that had emerged from a zoology department—was portrayed as an international conglomerate willing to "play God" and endanger an American paradise. The insects were referred to as "robo-Franken mosquitoes." More than a dozen people rose to speak; none defended the project or noted that, if successful, it would reduce a health threat and ease the county's heavy reliance on insecticides. Overwhelmingly, the people with whom I spoke said they assumed that this decision had already been made; the meeting was taken up with accusations of lies and secrecy. But nothing had been decided. Every question asked, at the meeting or later, in writing, was forwarded to state regulators for their consideration.

"It breaks my heart to think that you guys have the nerve to come here and do this to our community," one woman said. "Anything genetically modified should not be touched. I have a feeling that"—she pointed to Doyle and his colleagues on the dais— "your minds are made up. I know it. I can just sense it. I feel the vibe." She concluded to thunderous applause. Another speaker, Rick Worth, was even more direct. "I, for one, don't care about your scientific crap," he said. "I don't care about money you spend. You are not going to cram something down my throat that I don't want. I am no guinea pig."

One afternoon before leaving Brazil, I found myself inching along the rutted dirt roads of a neighborhood called Itaberaba, with Aldo Malavasi, the highly animated director of Moscamed. Itaberaba is only a few miles from the center of Juazeiro, and, as we drove, loudspeakers on the front of the car announced our arrival. "We are here to talk about the transgenic mosquito project," the speakers said. "We are here to explain this program to you and answer your questions." Malavasi, a large and charismatic man, said, "There is only one way to get people on your side: talk to them. This is a new technology. It is scary. But it also carries tremendous possibilities. People are not stupid. You just have to tell them all of that. Lay it out so they can decide." Moscamed has spoken to nearly everyone living in the affected areas. When a team leaves a house, they etch the outlines of a mosquito on the doorframe, so that colleagues will know which houses still need to be visited.

Bahia is one of Brazil's most important fruit-growing regions. We passed warehouses full of guavas, mangoes, limes, pineapples, and papayas. The scent of rotted fruit filled the humid air. People live in small, brightly painted cottages in these towns, and it seemed that at least one member of every family had had dengue. It isn't as hard to explain to them the value of a modified mosquito as it is of, say, modified corn. "You tell people you are messing with soybeans or corn and they get suspicious," Malavasi said. "This is different. They have suffered."

When it comes to genetic engineering, acceptance clearly depends on the product. Opponents often invoke a one-sided interpretation of the "precautionary principle," which argues against introducing activities into the environment that, in theory, could cause harm to human health. The sentiment is difficult to dispute, but so is the fact that dengue fever strikes tens of millions of people every year, that the threat is growing, and that there is no treatment or cure. The worry about theoretical risks tends to overwhelm any discussion of possible benefits. Many people, particularly in the rich Western world, object to modified food, but such complaints are almost never aired against the same scientific process when it is used to make insulin or heart medicine. "Sometimes I despair of these issues," Paul Reiter, who has advised Oxitec, told me. "The objections so rarely have anything to do with the science or the safety of the research. It is an opposition driven by fear. I understand that, but this technology has been used in a different form for years." He was referring to sterile insect technique. "The Oxitec approach is safer and more environmentally **benign**," Reiter said. "If the phrase 'genetically modified' was not attached, I don't think people would even mind."

benign (bĭ-nīn´) *adj.* harmless.

Malavasi shrugged when I brought up the opposition. "I know this sounds like science fiction," he said. "And I am not naïve. But to get rid of the virus, we have to get rid of the mosquitoes. And, at least in this small experiment, it's working." He noted that the name of the program, the Projeto *Aedes* Transgenico—the Transgenic *Aedes* Project—was not accidental. "We put the word 'transgenic' right in the name of the program for everyone to see," he said. "We hide nothing."

We had stopped at a random spot on an unmarked road. The heat was oppressive as we emerged from the car; a small stream burbled by the roadside. "We are in mosquito heaven," Malavasi said. As he spoke, a team from Moscamed began unloading several casserole-size Tupperware containers from the back of their van. The containers had white plastic lids, and one by one they were flipped open, releasing thousands of male mosquitoes. Each time a top was removed, scores of the tiny insects would alight, briefly, on the researchers' bodies—not to bite but to orient themselves. It was the first time they had experienced freedom. For a moment, they seemed reluctant to fly away. Then, almost as a unit, they would lift off and, after hovering for a few seconds in the moist afternoon air, form a kind of flying carpet, and set off to fulfill their destiny.

COLLABORATIVE DISCUSSION Does the author believe that OX513A should be used to combat dengue? What does he think about its opponents? With a partner, discuss the details in the article that help you understand the author's perspective on his subject.

Summarize the Text

RI 2

When readers **summarize**, they identify the central ideas and most important details in a text and retell them in their own words. Summarizing a long, fact-filled article such as "The Mosquito Solution" enables readers to remember key points and better understand how they relate to one another.

"The Mosquito Solution" discusses numerous facts about the *Aedes aegypti* mosquito and Oxitec's approach to neutralizing the threat it poses to humans. The article also describes the strenuous opposition that researchers have encountered as they try to persuade communities to test their genetically modified pest. Ideas about these topics are developed over the course of the article.

To make sure that you understand all the important ideas in the article, summarize each major section or passage in one or two sentences. For example, these sentences summarize lines 182–209: "OX513A mosquitoes are genetically altered by the insertion of two genes. One gene leads to the destruction of the mosquito and its eggs after it has mated; the other tells scientists whether the egg has been modified." Notice that in this summary, only the essential details have been included, and the summary shows how they are related.

Support Inferences: Draw Conclusions

RI 1

In his article, Specter provides extensive information on a complex and controversial issue. Readers can use evidence from the text and their own knowledge to make **inferences**, or logical assumptions, about things that are not directly stated in the text. For example, readers might infer from statements and actions by some people opposed to the release of OX513A that they made up their minds before listening to any scientific arguments.

Inferences can be the basis for **conclusions**, or more general statements about a text. The following chart shows a conclusion that is based on evidence in lines 173–181 and on an inference about this evidence.

Evidence	Inference	Conclusion
Aedes aegypti have adapted to city habitats. Pesticides cannot eradicate them in urban areas. They are carriers of dengue.	Populated areas could be at high risk of a dengue epidemic.	If traditional methods cannot offer assurance that such a dangerous pest can be controlled, then alternative approaches should be tried.

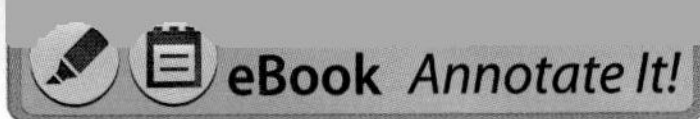

Analyzing the Text

RI 1, RI 2, RI 3, W 1

Cite Text Evidence Support your responses with evidence from the selection.

1. **Summarize** Write a brief summary of the information that explains why the *Aedes aegypti* mosquito poses such a danger to humans.
2. **Interpret** Why does the author call OX513A "an elegant approach" to the health crisis?
3. **Summarize** Reread lines 243–279, and summarize how the OX513A mosquito was developed. Why might the author have chosen to include such a detailed explanation of this process?
4. **Compare** How do the reactions of the Juazeiro residents to the use of OX513A mosquitoes compare with the reactions of the Key West residents? What might account for the differences in the reactions of the two populations?
5. **Evaluate** Why do groups such as Friends of the Earth and EcoNexus devote time to voicing their concerns about OX513A? Does this article provide sufficient evidence to support or refute their concerns? Explain.
6. **Draw Conclusions** Has Oxitec done enough to reassure the residents of Key West that it would be safe to release OX513A into their community? Identify the evidence and inferences you used to draw this conclusion.
7. **Draw Conclusions** How does the regulation of genetically modified organisms in Brazil differ from the regulation of them in the United States? Which system do you consider preferable? Explain the basis for this conclusion.

PERFORMANCE TASK

Writing Activity: Argument Is OX513A a safe solution to the problem of the *Aedes aegypti* mosquito? Write a brief argument expressing your conclusion and present it to the class.

- State your claim.
- Develop reasons and draw evidence from the text in support of them.
- Anticipate and refute a counterclaim—for example, address the use of pesticides.
- Present your conclusion.

Make sure to organize your support logically, and include statistics and examples as necessary.

Critical Vocabulary

L6

fetid	**entomological**	**panacea**
progeny	**ancillary**	**benign**

Practice and Apply Use a complete sentence to answer each question and demonstrate that you understand the meaning of each Critical Vocabulary word.

1. Why are the *fetid* conditions within tires an *entomological* paradise?
2. In what way are the *progeny* of OX513A rendered *benign* in terms of their threat to humans?
3. What *ancillary* issues prevent OX513A from being called a *panacea* for the problem of mosquitoes?

Vocabulary Strategy: Scientific Terms

In order to convey his information accurately, the author of "The Mosquito Solution" relies on **scientific terms** related to his topic, such as the Critical Vocabulary words *entomological* and *progeny*. These words have specialized meanings in the context of his article; to replace them with more familiar terms would decrease the precision of his writing. Readers can define scientific terms by following a series of steps:

- Read footnotes or other explanations within the text.
- Use the context of the article, as well as the passage and sentence, to determine meaning.
- Identify familiar word parts, such as roots or affixes, and use their meanings to help define the word.
- Consult a print or digital college-level dictionary. Refer to a specialized dictionary as needed.

Practice and Apply With a partner, complete these activities.

1. Locate these terms in the text: *hemorrhagic fever* (line 22), *insecticide* (line 28), *biotechnology* (line 29), *mutant* (line 31), *pathogens* (line 130), *parasites* (line 130), *larvae* (line 201), *pupae* (line 221), *syphon* (line 226).
2. Use context clues, word parts, or a college-level dictionary to define each term.

Present an Argument

Why do the characters and people in the texts in this collection take the risks they do? What do they learn from their risk-taking experiences? Synthesize your ideas by preparing and presenting an argument about the importance of taking risks in life.

W 9a–b Draw evidence from literary or informational texts.

SL 4 Present information, findings, and supporting evidence.

An effective argument

- introduces a precise and logical claim about taking risks
- has a logical sequence for claims and counterclaims, including transitions
- provides evidence from *Beowulf* and one other text that illustrates the claim
- has a satisfying conclusion that supports the argument presented

PLAN

Gather Evidence Review and analyze the texts in this collection.

- Reread *Beowulf*, identifying and taking notes on the risks Beowulf takes. Consider the poet's vision regarding why Beowulf took certain risks and what he learned from them.
- Choose one other text from the collection, also identifying and analyzing the risks that the characters or people in that text take.
- Note details, examples, and quotations that support your ideas about risk taking.

Once you have reviewed the texts, write a precise claim that summarizes your thoughts about the importance of taking risks in life. This will be the thesis statement of your speech, which you will need to support with sufficient textual evidence.

Use the annotation tools in your eBook to find evidence that supports your ideas about taking risks. Save each piece of evidence to your notebook.

Get Organized Create an outline to organize your claim, details, and evidence. This will make writing your speech easier.

- Write your claim at the top of your outline. Consider how you will engage your audience at the beginning of your speech.
- List the central ideas that support your claim.
- For each central idea, cite evidence that supports it.
- Consider possible counterclaims listeners might make. Prepare counterarguments with evidence to refute the counterclaims.

ACADEMIC VOCABULARY

As you share your ideas, be sure to incorporate these words.

assurance
collapse
conceive
devote
vision

PRODUCE

Write Your Speech Draft a logically organized speech, following your outline. Consider your purpose and audience. Remember to include

- an introduction that immediately grabs the interest of your audience
- a logically ordered body, including varied transitions between the main sections of your speech
- details, quotations, and examples from the texts to support your claim and to refute counterclaims
- rhetorical devices that will support your argument, such as analogy, appealing to logic, and appealing to emotion
- language and structures appropriate for a speech
- a variety of grammatical structures that will create cohesion and keep your audience engaged
- a conclusion that leaves your audience with a lasting impression

Write your rough draft in *my*WriteSmart. Focus on getting your ideas down, rather than perfecting your choice of language.

Interactive Lessons

To help you draft your argument, complete the following lessons from *Giving a Presentation*:

- The Content of Your Presentation
- Style in Presentation

Language and Style: Rhetorical Devices

Rhetorical devices can enhance your argument. Read this passage from "The Mosquito Solution."

> "'This mosquito is Dr. Frankenstein's monster, plain and simple,' Helen Wallace, the executive director of the British environmental organization GeneWatch, said."

Wallace uses an analogy comparing the mosquito to Dr. Frankenstein's monster. This analogy appeals to people's emotions by relating something unknown (genetically modified mosquitos) to something readers can relate to (the horrific monster created by Dr. Frankenstein). Other rhetorical devices, such as appealing to logic by using reasons or appealing to people's ethical beliefs, can also help support an argument. Add one or more of these devices to your argument.

REVISE

Practice Your Speech You will need to make your speech come alive with appropriate expression, volume, and gestures. Mark places in your draft where you might want to emphasize a word, insert a pause, or use gestures to convey meaning or emotion. Then practice your speech with a partner. Remember to speak loudly enough, to vary your pitch and tone, and to maintain eye contact.

Have your partner or a group of peers review your draft in *my*WriteSmart. Ask your reviewers to note any evidence that does not support the claim.

Interactive Lessons

To help you practice your speech, complete this lesson:

- Giving a Presentation: Delivering Your Presentation

Have your partner use the questions in the chart to review your speech.

Questions	Tips	Revision Techniques
Does the introduction grab the audience's attention and present a precise claim?	**Highlight** sentences that get the audience interested. **Underline** the claim.	**Add** an interesting opening sentence. **Add** a claim that states your position. **Rework** the existing claim to make it more precise.
Do at least two valid reasons support the claim? Is each reason supported by relevant and sufficient evidence?	**Underline** each reason. **Highlight** each piece of supporting evidence.	**Add** reasons or **rework** existing ones to make them more valid. **Add** relevant evidence to ensure that your support is sufficient.
Do rhetorical devices support the claims?	**Highlight** sentences that contain analogy, appeals to reason, and appeals to emotion or ethical beliefs.	**Add** rhetorical devices to support claims.
Are potential counterclaims refuted with counterarguments?	**Underline** potential counterclaims. **Highlight** counterarguments that address those objections.	**Add** counterclaims and counterarguments to fairly address potential concerns the audience might have.
Are claims ordered logically? Do varied transitions link the parts of the argument?	**Number** the claims and rank them by their strength. **Highlight** the words that link major sections of the argument.	**Reorder** claims so that they will have the greatest impact on the audience. **Add** links between sections to create clarity and cohesion.
Does the concluding section restate and support the argument?	**Underline** the restatement of the argument.	**Add** a restatement of the argument.

Evaluate and Revise After you and your partner have presented your speeches, give each other feedback. Use the rubric on the next page to evaluate your partner's speech as well as your own. Then revise your draft based on your partner's feedback and your own observations.

PRESENT

Deliver Your Speech Present your speech to the whole class. The audience should listen, take notes, and be prepared to respond.

- Speak clearly at an appropriate volume and pace.
- At the end of your speech, invite questions or comments.
- Find out which aspects were strong and which could be improved.
- Thank your audience for their time and attention.

PERFORMANCE TASK RUBRIC
ARGUMENT

	Ideas and Evidence	Organization	Language
4	• The introduction is intriguing and informative; the thesis statement precisely identifies a claim. • The claim is strongly developed with relevant facts, concrete details, interesting quotations, and examples from the texts. • Varied rhetorical devices support assertions throughout the speech. • The concluding section supports the ideas presented.	• The organization of claims, counterclaims, and counterarguments is effective and logical throughout the speech. • Varied transitions are well crafted and successfully link major sections of the speech.	• The speech reflects a formal style and an objective, knowledgeable tone. • Language is vivid and precise. • Sentence beginnings, lengths, and structures vary and have a rhythmic flow. • Grammar and usage are correct.
3	• The introduction could do more to attract the audience's curiosity; the thesis statement identifies a claim. • One or two key points could use additional support in the form of relevant facts, concrete details, quotations, and examples from the texts. • Some rhetorical devices support assertions. • The concluding section mostly supports the ideas presented.	• The organization is confusing in a few places. • A few more transitions are needed to link major sections of the speech.	• The style is inconsistent in a few places, and the tone is subjective at times. • Vague language is used in a few places. • Sentence beginnings, lengths, and structures vary somewhat. • Some grammatical and usage errors are repeated in the speech.
2	• The introduction provides some information about a claim but does not include a thesis statement. • Most key points need additional support in the form of relevant facts, concrete details, quotations, and examples from the texts. • More rhetorical devices are needed to support assertions. • The concluding section is confusing and does not follow from the ideas presented.	• The organization is confusing in some places and often doesn't follow a pattern. • More transitions are needed throughout.	• The style is too informal; the tone conveys subjectivity and a lack of understanding of the topic. • Vague, general language is used in many places. • Sentence structures barely vary, and some fragments or run-on sentences are present. • Grammar and usage are incorrect in many places, but the speaker's ideas are still clear.
1	• The appropriate elements of an introduction are missing. • Facts, details, quotations, and examples from the texts are missing. • Rhetorical devices are not used to support assertions. • The speech lacks an identifiable concluding section.	• A logical organization is not used; information is presented randomly. • Transitions are not used, making the speech difficult to follow.	• The style and tone are inappropriate for the speech. • Language is too vague or general to convey the information. • Repetitive sentence structure, fragments, and run-on sentences make the speech monotonous and difficult to follow. • Many grammatical and usage errors change the meaning of the speaker's ideas.

Finding Ourselves in Nature

"How often I've wanted to escape to a wilderness where a human hand has not been in everything."

—Linda Hogan

COLLECTION 6

Finding Ourselves in Nature

This collection reveals personal insights gained through encounters with the natural world.

COLLECTION

PERFORMANCE TASK Preview

At the end of this collection, you will have the opportunity to complete a task:

- Write a personal narrative in which you describe and reflect on a memorable encounter with nature. Compare your experience with those portrayed in "Living Like Weasels" and another selection in the collection.

ACADEMIC VOCABULARY

Study the words and their definitions in the chart below. You will use these words as you discuss and write about the texts in this collection.

Word	Definition	Related Forms
encounter (ĕn-koun´tər) *n.*	an unplanned or unexpected meeting	counter, encounter (v.)
intensity (ĭn-tĕn´sĭ-tē) *n.*	high degree of concentration, power, or force	intense, intensify, Intensive
restore (rĭ-stôr´) *v.*	to bring back to original condition; to renew; to revive	restoration, restorative
theme (thēm) *n.*	an idea that is implied or that recurs in a work; a message conveyed in a literary work	thematic
visualize (vĭzh´o͞o-ə-līz´) *v.*	to form a mental image of something or someone	envision, revision, vision, visual

Annie Dillard (b. 1945) *was born and raised in Pittsburgh. Her parents encouraged her to explore intellectual and creative interests and to reject conformity. Dillard has written in many different genres; her books range widely in subject matter, though she is best known for writing about nature.* Pilgrim at Tinker Creek, *her 1974 nonfiction narrative about the fields, creeks, and woods near Roanoke, Virginia, won the Pulitzer Prize and has been compared to Thoreau's* Walden.

Living Like Weasels

Essay by Annie Dillard

AS YOU READ Pay attention to the details that help you understand Dillard's attitude toward nature. Write down any questions you generate during reading.

myNotebook

As you read, mark up the text. Save your work to ***my*Notebook**.

- Highlight details
- Add notes and questions
- Add new words to ***my*WordList**

A WEASEL IS WILD. Who knows what he thinks? He sleeps in his underground den, his tail draped over his nose. Sometimes he lives in his den for two days without leaving. Outside, he stalks rabbits, mice, muskrats, and birds, killing more bodies than he can eat warm, and often dragging the carcasses home. Obedient to instinct, he bites his prey at the neck, either splitting the jugular vein at the throat or crunching the brain at the base of the skull, and he does not let go. One naturalist refused to kill a weasel who was socketed into his hand deeply as a rattlesnake. The man could in no way pry the tiny weasel off, and he had to walk half a mile to water, the weasel dangling from his palm, and soak him off like a stubborn label.

And once, says Ernest Thompson Seton[1]—once, a man shot an eagle out of the sky. He examined the eagle and found the dry skull of a weasel fixed by the jaws to his throat. The **supposition** is that the eagle had pounced on the weasel and the weasel swiveled and bit as

supposition (sŭp′ə-zĭsh′ən) *n.* something thought to be the case; an assumed truth or hypothesis.

[1] **Ernest Thompson Seton:** (1860–1946) author, artist, and naturalist known for his portrayals of wildlife.

instinct taught him, tooth to neck, and nearly won. I would like to have seen that eagle from the air a few weeks or months before he was shot: was the whole weasel still attached to his feathered throat, a fur pendant? Or did the eagle eat what he could reach, gutting the living weasel with his **talons** before his breast, bending his beak, cleaning the beautiful airborne bones?

talon
(tăl´ən) *n.* the claw of a predator bird.

I have been reading about weasels because I saw one last week. I startled a weasel who startled me, and we exchanged a long glance.

Twenty minutes from my house, through the woods by the quarry and across the highway, is Hollins Pond, a remarkable piece of shallowness, where I like to go at sunset and sit on a tree trunk. Hollins Pond is also called Murray's Pond; it covers two acres of bottomland near Tinker Creek with six inches of water and six thousand lily pads. In winter, brown-and-white steers stand in the middle of it, merely dampening their hooves; from the distant shore they look like miracle itself, complete with miracle's nonchalance. Now, in summer, the steers are gone. The water lilies have blossomed and spread to a green horizontal plane that is terra firma to plodding blackbirds, and tremulous ceiling to black leeches, crayfish, and carp.

This is, mind you, suburbia. It is a five-minute walk in three directions to rows of houses, though none is visible here. There's a 55 mph highway at one end of the pond, and a nesting pair of wood ducks at the other. Under every bush is a muskrat hole or a beer can. The far end is an alternating series of fields and woods, fields and woods, threaded everywhere with motorcycle tracks—in whose bare clay wild turtles lay eggs.

So. I had crossed the highway, stepped over two low barbed-wire fences, and traced the motorcycle path in all gratitude through the wild rose and poison ivy of the pond's shoreline up into high grassy fields. Then I cut down through the woods to the mossy fallen tree where I sit. This tree is excellent. It makes a dry, upholstered bench at the upper, marshy end of the pond, a plush jetty raised from the thorny shore between a shallow blue body of water and a deep blue body of sky.

The sun had just set. I was relaxed on the tree trunk, ensconced in the lap of lichen, watching the lily pads at my feet tremble and part dreamily over the thrusting path of a carp. A yellow bird appeared to my right and flew behind me. It caught my eye; I swiveled around—and the next instant, **inexplicably,** I was looking down at a weasel, who was looking up at me.

inexplicably
(ĭn-ĕk´splĭ-kə-blē) *adv.* in a way that is hard or impossible to explain.

Weasel! I'd never seen one wild before. He was ten inches long, thin as a curve, a muscled ribbon, brown as fruitwood, soft-furred, alert. His face was fierce, small and pointed as a lizard's; he would have made a good arrowhead. There was just a dot of chin, maybe two brown hairs' worth, and then the pure white fur began that spread down his underside. He had two black eyes I didn't see, any more than you see a window.

The weasel was stunned into stillness as he was emerging from beneath an enormous shaggy wild rose bush four feet away. I was stunned into stillness twisted backward on the tree trunk. Our eyes locked, and someone threw away the key.

Our look was as if two lovers, or deadly enemies, met unexpectedly on an overgrown path when each had been thinking of something else: a clearing blow to the gut. It was also a bright blow to the brain, or a sudden beating of brains, with all the charge and intimate grate of rubbed balloons. It emptied our lungs. It felled the forest, moved the fields, and drained the pond; the world dismantled and tumbled into that black hole of eyes. If you and I looked at each other that way, our skulls would split and drop to our shoulders. But we don't. We keep our skulls. So.

He disappeared. This was only last week, and already I don't remember what shattered the enchantment. I think I blinked, I think I retrieved my brain from the weasel's brain, and tried to memorize what I was seeing, and the weasel felt the yank of separation, the careening splashdown into real life and the urgent current of instinct. He vanished under the wild rose. I waited motionless, my mind suddenly full of data and my spirit with pleadings, but he didn't return.

Please do not tell me about "approach-avoidance conflicts."[2] I tell you I've been in that weasel's brain for sixty seconds, and he was in mine. Brains are private places, muttering through unique and secret tapes—but the weasel and I both plugged into another tape simultaneously, for a sweet and shocking time. Can I help it if it was a blank?

What goes on in his brain the rest of the time? What does a weasel think about? He won't say. His journal is tracks in clay, a spray of feathers, mouse blood and bone: uncollected, unconnected, loose-leaf, and blown.

I would like to learn, or remember, how to live. I come to Hollins Pond not so much to learn how to live as, frankly, to forget about it. That is, I don't think I can learn from a wild animal how to live in particular—shall I suck warm blood, hold my tail high, walk with my footprints precisely over the prints of my hands?—but I might learn something of mindlessness, something of the purity of living in the physical senses and the dignity of living without bias or motive. The weasel lives in necessity and we live in choice, hating necessity and dying at the last **ignobly** in its talons. I would like to live as I should, as the weasel lives as he should. And I suspect that for me the way is like

ignobly
(ĭg-nō´blē) *adv.*
dishonorably.

[2] **approach-avoidance conflicts:** a state of psychological conflict or indecision that occurs when an individual is faced with a situation that has both positive and negative characteristics.

the weasel's: open to time and death painlessly, noticing everything, remembering nothing, choosing the given with a fierce and pointed will.

I missed my chance. I should have gone for the throat. I should have lunged for that streak of white under the weasel's chin and held on, held on through mud and into the wild rose, held on for a dearer life. We could live under the wild rose wild as weasels, mute and uncomprehending. I could very calmly go wild. I could live two days in the den, curled, leaning on mouse fur, sniffing bird bones, blinking, licking, breathing musk, my hair tangled in the roots of grasses. Down is a good place to go, where the mind is single. Down is out, out of your ever-loving mind and back to your careless senses. I remember muteness as a prolonged and giddy fast, where every moment is a feast of utterance received. Time and events are merely poured, unremarked, and ingested directly, like blood pulsed into my gut through a jugular vein. Could two live that way? Could two live under the wild rose, and explore by the pond, so that the smooth mind of each is as everywhere present to the other, and as received and as unchallenged, as falling snow?

We could, you know. We can live any way we want. People take vows of poverty, chastity, and obedience—even of silence—by choice. The thing is to stalk your calling in a certain skilled and supple way, to locate the most tender and live spot and plug into that pulse. This is yielding, not fighting. A weasel doesn't "attack" anything; a weasel lives as he's meant to, yielding at every moment to the perfect freedom of single necessity.

I think it would be well, and proper, and obedient, and pure, to grasp your one necessity and not let it go, to dangle from it limp wherever it takes you. Then even death, where you're going no matter how you live, cannot you part. Seize it and let it seize you up aloft even, till your eyes burn out and drop; let your musky flesh fall off in shreds, and let your very bones unhinge and scatter, loosened over fields, over fields and woods, lightly, thoughtless, from any height at all, from as high as eagles.

COLLABORATIVE DISCUSSION Why does Dillard go to Hollins Pond? With a partner, discuss the role that nature plays in the author's life. Cite specific evidence from the essay to support your ideas.

Analyze Style

RI 6

Annie Dillard's style—her unique and beautiful way of communicating ideas—makes readers feel as if they are experiencing the events that she writes about and the emotions that she is feeling. To analyze how she achieves this immediacy, note the elements of her style described in the chart:

Stylistic Elements
Word Choice Dillard carefully chooses words with connotations, or shades of meaning, to evoke a particular emotional response in the reader. For example, she describes herself as being "ensconced in the lap of lichen." The word *ensconced* suggests a cozy security; this suggestion is reinforced by her choice of the word *lap*.
Alliteration Particularly in significant passages, Dillard repeats consonant sounds at the beginning of words to add emphasis and draw attention to ideas.
Syntax Dillard often writes long sentences to clarify connections between ideas and create a smooth, flowing rhythm in her prose. Periodically she disrupts this rhythm with short sentences that convey a sense of surprise or wonder.
Tone Through her choice of words and phrases, Dillard achieves a conversational tone that establishes an intimacy with her readers. For example, she opens her essay by saying "A weasel is wild. Who knows what he thinks?" These simple sentences give the impression that she is speaking directly to her audience.

Determine Figurative Meanings

RI 4, L 5a

Another important element of Dillard's style is **figurative language**, language that communicates ideas beyond the literal meanings of the words. She uses both **metaphors** (which compare two things directly) and **similes** (which compare things using the word *like* or *as*) to suggest ideas that create an impression in readers' minds. Consider this sentence from her essay:

> **The water lilies have blossomed and spread to a green horizontal plane that is terra firma to plodding blackbirds, and tremulous ceiling to black leeches, crayfish, and carp.**

In this passage, Dillard compares the water lilies in the pond to "terra firma"—solid ground—for blackbirds and to a flimsy, trembling ceiling to those creatures that live below it. Her metaphors help readers visualize the mass of water lilies that carpet the surface of the pond, as well as the teeming life both below and above the water.

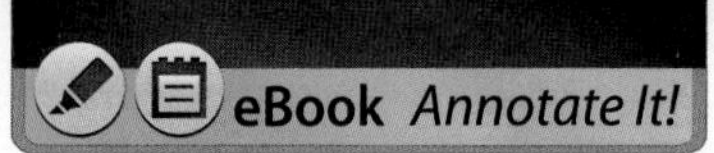

Analyzing the Text

RI 1, RI 2, RI 3, RI 4, RI 6, W 3a, W 3e, L 5a

Cite Text Evidence Support your responses with evidence from the selection.

1. **Infer** What idea about the weasel is communicated in the first two paragraphs of the essay? Identify words and phrases that develop this idea.
2. **Analyze** In lines 24–49, Dillard juxtaposes images of nature with evidence of human habitation. Explain how these lines relate to her overall purpose.
3. **Analyze** What does Dillard compare the weasel to in lines 56–62? What impression of the weasel is evoked by this figurative language?
4. **Cite Evidence** How does Dillard convey the intensity of her encounter with the weasel in lines 63–75? Consider how these stylistic elements contribute to the effectiveness of this passage:
   - word choice
   - tone
   - use of alliteration
   - syntax
5. **Analyze** What contrast between humans and the weasel does Dillard make in lines 94–106? How does she feel about these differences? Explain.
6. **Draw Conclusions** Identify the similes and metaphors in lines 107–122. Think about what Dillard is describing in this paragraph. What function does this figurative language fulfill?
7. **Interpret** What does Dillard mean in lines 127–128 when she writes, "A weasel doesn't 'attack' anything; a weasel lives as he's meant to"?
8. **Connect** Explain how Dillard unifies her essay by connecting the ideas in the first two paragraphs to those in her last two paragraphs. What central idea do these paragraphs develop?

PERFORMANCE TASK

Writing Activity: Essay In her essay, Dillard's observation of the weasel leads her to reflect on her own life. Write your own personal essay, following these steps.

- Write about a memorable event in your life.
- Explain how this event led to an insight about your own life or about the human condition.
- Organize your ideas into a unified essay.

Critical Vocabulary

supposition **talon** **inexplicably** **ignobly**

Practice and Apply Create a semantic map for each Critical Vocabulary word. Follow the example given here, which is for a word that appears in line 31 of the essay. Use a dictionary or thesaurus as needed.

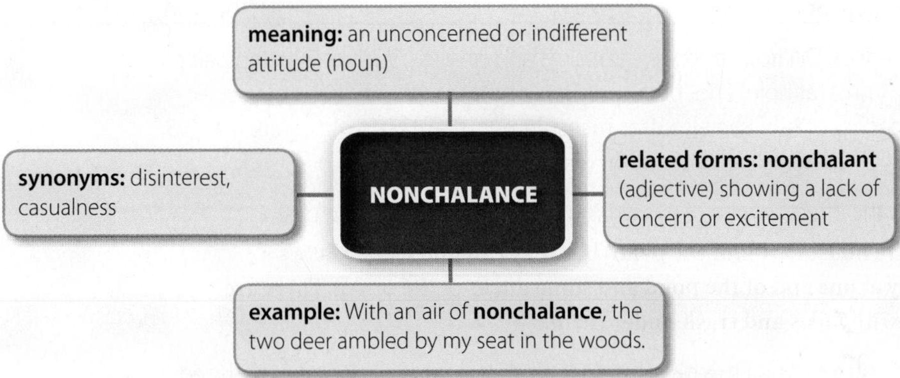

Vocabulary Strategy: Domain-Specific Words

As she writes about nature, Dillard uses **domain-specific words**—vocabulary associated with a specific field of study. Such words allow her to be more precise and concise in her writing. Domain-specific words also help broaden readers' knowledge of nature. The Critical Vocabulary word *talons* in line 20 is an example of a domain-specific word.

Another domain-specific word, *carcasses*, occurs in line 5. To determine the meaning of this word, readers can follow these steps:

- Read the sentence in which the word *carcasses* appears and the adjacent sentences. Identify possible context clues, such as "killing" and "bodies."
- Identify the root of the word to see if you recognize it. Then look for any prefix or suffix that might indicate the word's part of speech, number, or tense. The suffix –*es* indicates that *carcasses* is a plural noun.
- Use a dictionary to confirm meaning. *Carcass* is defined as "a dead body, especially one killed for food."

Practice and Apply Work in a small group to complete these activities.

1. Identify additional domain-specific words that appear in the essay.
2. Write a definition for each word using context clues or a dictionary.
3. Share your words and definitions with the class. Together, write sample sentences for each domain-specific word.

Language and Style: Use Precise Details

L 3

One characteristic of Dillard's style is her use of **precise details**. These details make it less likely that readers will overlook or misinterpret her meaning. Read the following passage from her essay:

> **It is a five-minute walk in three directions to rows of houses, though none is visible here. There's a 55 mph highway at one end of the pond, and a nesting pair of wood ducks at the other. Under every bush is a muskrat hole or a beer can.**

In these sentences, Dillard uses concrete words and phrases, such as "nesting pair of wood ducks," "muskrat hole," and "beer can." These phrases create vivid and specific pictures in readers' minds. She also uses measurements—"five-minute walk" and "55 mph highway"—to make her description more specific.

Contrast the effectiveness of her writing with this version of the passage:

> **There are houses around the pond, but they can't be seen. There's a highway at one end of the pond and some ducks at the other. There are bushes with holes and trash under them.**

Notice how vague and dull this description is. Concrete words have been replaced with imprecise adjectives and nouns, such as "some" and "trash." Not only are these words open to interpretation, the sharp contrast between nature and civilization set up in the first passage is lost.

The chart shows some ways to make writing more precise.

Method	Example
Use appositives or prepositional phrases to provide additional description or clarity to explanations.	"Was the whole weasel still attached to his feathered throat, a fur pendant?" "It covers two acres of bottomland near Tinker Creek with six inches of water and six thousand lily pads."
Include specific adjectives, adverbs, nouns, and verbs.	"In winter, brown-and-white steers stand in the middle of it, merely dampening their hooves." "He was ten inches long, thin as a curve, a muscled ribbon, brown as fruitwood, soft-furred, alert."

Practice and Apply Revise your personal essay from the Performance Task, following these guidelines.

1. Replace vague adjectives, adverbs, nouns, or verbs with concrete and specific words. Original: I fell a long distance. Revision: I plummeted 15 feet.
2. Add prepositional phrases or appositives that more precisely define, explain, or describe. Revision: From the cliff's edge, I plummeted 15 feet, splashing into a sparkling glacial lake.

COMPARE TEXTS

Background *In the early twentieth century, American poetry was heavily influenced by the literary movement known as modernism. Poets such as Ezra Pound, T. S. Eliot, and William Carlos Williams experimented with literary form, rarely using regular meter or rhyme schemes. They also avoided moral commentary, preferring to let images speak for themselves, which often made their poems difficult to interpret. Yet some famous poets of the period, including Robert Frost and Elinor Wylie, continued to use traditional forms and expressed their ideas more directly.*

Wild Peaches | Spring and All

Poem by Elinor Wylie | Poem by William Carlos Williams

Elinor Wylie (1885–1928) *led a life marked by scandal and personal tragedy, yet her poetry is restrained and traditional in form. She published her first volume anonymously in 1912. Her second volume,* Nets to Catch the Wind, *published in 1921, is considered by many critics to contain her best poems, including the widely anthologized "Velvet Shoes" and the poem in this lesson, "Wild Peaches." Her work was well received by critics and readers during her lifetime; she went on to write three more volumes of poetry as well as four novels. After Wylie's death, her poetry fell out of fashion, but since the 1980s it has experienced a revival of interest.*

William Carlos Williams (1883–1963) *lived an outwardly conventional life as a full-time medical doctor in the city of his birth, Rutherford, New Jersey, yet his poetry was highly innovative. Inspired by his friendship with Ezra Pound, Williams developed a poetic style that was direct, vigorous, and unfettered by previous poetic conventions of form. His volume* Spring and All *contains not only this selection but some of his most famous poems, including the important "The Red Wheelbarrow." Modestly acclaimed in his lifetime, Williams is now recognized for significantly influencing several new schools of poetry, including the Beat movement.*

AS YOU READ Notice how each poet uses imagery to help readers visualize nature. Write down any questions you generate during reading.

Wild Peaches
by Elinor Wylie

1

When the world turns completely upside down
You say we'll emigrate to the Eastern Shore[1]
Aboard a river-boat from Baltimore;
We'll live among wild peach trees, miles from town,
You'll wear a coonskin cap, and I a gown
Homespun, dyed butternut's dark gold colour.
Lost, like your lotus-eating ancestor,[2]
We'll swim in milk and honey till we drown.

The winter will be short, the summer long,
The autumn amber-hued, sunny and hot,
Tasting of cider and of scuppernong;[3]
All seasons sweet, but autumn best of all.
The squirrels in their silver fur will fall
Like falling leaves, like fruit, before your shot.

2

The autumn frosts will lie upon the grass
Like bloom[4] on grapes of purple-brown and gold.
The misted early mornings will be cold;
The little puddles will be roofed with glass.
The sun, which burns from copper into brass,
Melts these at noon, and makes the boys unfold
Their knitted mufflers; full as they can hold,
Fat pockets dribble chestnuts as they pass.

Peaches grow wild, and pigs can live in clover;
A barrel of salted herrings lasts a year;
The spring begins before the winter's over.
By February you may find the skins
Of garter snakes and water moccasins[5]
Dwindled and harsh, dead-white and cloudy-clear.

---

[1] **Eastern Shore:** land on the east side of the Chesapeake Bay, part of the Delmarva Peninsula.

[2] **lotus-eating ancestor:** an allusion to the *Odyssey,* in which Odysseus encounters a lotus-eating society whose diet makes people forget their cares and become lazy.

[3] **scuppernong:** a type of grape native to the southeastern United States.

[4] **bloom:** a white, powdery coating that can form on the surface of fruits.

[5] **water moccasins:** thick-bodied, venomous snakes, also called cottonmouths.

3

When April pours the colours of a shell
Upon the hills, when every little creek
Is shot with silver from the Chesapeake
In shoals new-minted by the ocean swell,
When strawberries go begging, and the sleek
Blue plums lie open to the blackbird's beak,
We shall live well—we shall live very well.

The months between the cherries and the peaches
Are brimming cornucopias which spill
Fruits red and purple, sombre-bloomed and black;
Then, down rich fields and frosty river beaches
We'll trample bright persimmons, while you kill
Bronze partridge, speckled quail, and canvasback.[6]

4

Down to the Puritan marrow of my bones
There's something in this richness that I hate.
I love the look, austere, immaculate,
Of landscapes drawn in pearly monotones.
There's something in my very blood that owns
Bare hills, cold silver on a sky of slate,
A thread of water, churned to milky spate[7]
Streaming through slanted pastures fenced with stones.

I love those skies, thin blue or snowy gray,
Those fields sparse-planted, rendering meagre sheaves;
That spring, briefer than apple-blossom's breath,
Summer, so much too beautiful to stay,
Swift autumn, like a bonfire of leaves,
And sleepy winter, like the sleep of death.

[6] **canvasback:** a type of diving duck.

[7] **spate:** rising or flowing water.

Spring and All

by William Carlos Williams

By the road to the contagious hospital[8]
under the surge of the blue
mottled clouds driven from the
northeast—a cold wind. Beyond, the
waste of broad, muddy fields
brown with dried weeds, standing and fallen

patches of standing water
the scattering of tall trees

All along the road the reddish
purplish, forked, upstanding, twiggy
stuff of bushes and small trees
with dead, brown leaves under them
leafless vines—

Lifeless in appearance, sluggish
dazed spring approaches—

They enter the new world naked,
cold, uncertain of all
save that they enter. All about them
the cold, familiar wind—

Now the grass, tomorrow
the stiff curl of wildcarrot leaf

One by one objects are defined—
It quickens: clarity, outline of leaf

But now the stark dignity of
entrance—Still, the profound change
has come upon them: rooted, they
grip down and begin to awaken

[8] **contagious hospital:** a medical facility for people with infectious diseases.

COLLABORATIVE DISCUSSION What adjectives would you apply to each poet's descriptive style? With a partner, compare your impressions of the landscape created by the imagery in each poem. Cite specific evidence from the poems to support your ideas.

COMPARE TEXTS

Demonstrate Knowledge of Foundational Works

RL 9

For many centuries, poets who wrote about landscapes often followed the conventions of **pastoral** literature, which presents idealized scenes of nature populated with innocent shepherds and nymphs. Pastoral poems have a regular meter and rhyme, and they feature highly artificial language. The popularity of this genre faded in the 18th century, but echoes of it live on even today. Some modern poets have played off the tradition by alluding to pastoral themes, such as the carefree existence of country folk and the contrast between rural and urban life. Others have responded by rejecting any idealization of nature.

Both Wylie and Williams describe scenes of nature in their poems. To compare their depictions of landscape, examine the following elements:

- the types of images that appear in each poem, and the way in which these images are presented to allow the reader to visualize the landscape
- how each poet's word choices contribute to the speaker's tone
- the theme conveyed by each poem

Analyze Structure

RL 5

Though both poems share a focus on nature, Wylie and Williams chose very different ways of presenting their ideas. "Wild Peaches" has a **traditional form**, with a regular pattern of rhyme and meter and mostly regular grouping of lines. "Spring and All" is an example of **organic form** because its free verse does not follow any fixed rules.

"Wild Peaches"	"Spring and All"
Wylie predominantly uses **iambic pentameter,** a pattern of alternating unstressed and stressed syllables in ten-syllable lines. Parts 1, 2, and 4 are **sonnets,** fourteen-line poems that have a regular pattern of end rhyme. Wylie end-stops many of her lines, using semicolons, commas, or periods.	Williams's free verse does not have a regular meter or pattern of end rhyme. He uses **enjambment,** the continuation of a phrase or clause over a line break. Williams uses dashes at the end of several of his lines. The two periods in the poem occur within lines, not at the end of lines.

Consider how the authors' choices affect the meaning and aesthetic impact of their poems.

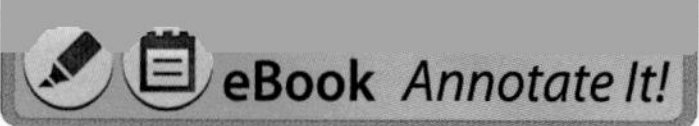

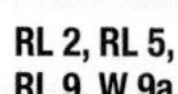

Analyzing the Text

Cite Text Evidence Support your responses with evidence from the selections.

1. **Cite Evidence** Identify details that Wylie uses to idealize the Eastern shore landscape in parts 1–3 of the poem. What expectation do these details create for readers?
2. **Analyze** What conflict does Wylie introduce with the lines "Down to the Puritan marrow of my bones / There's something in this richness that I hate"? How do the lines in the stanza develop this conflict?
3. **Draw Conclusions** What do the words "briefer," "too beautiful to stay," and "sleep of death" in the last stanza of Wylie's poem suggest about nature's bounty and a life of plenty and ease? Do these ideas support or overturn the conventions of pastoral poetry? Explain.
4. **Evaluate** How does Wylie use the structure of "Wild Peaches" to help develop the poem's ideas? Would an organic form have been as effective? Why or why not?
5. **Analyze** Although William Carlos Williams rejected traditional verse forms, he still believed that it was important to use poetic devices to distinguish verse from prose. What poetic devices does he use in "Spring and All"? How do these devices draw attention to significant images in the poem?
6. **Draw Conclusions** What theme does "Spring and All" convey about nature? Discuss how this theme relates to the conventions of pastoral poetry.
7. **Compare** Compare the tones of "Wild Peaches" and "Spring and All." How does the tone of each poem reflect the role of the speaker?
8. **Evaluate** Both poems end with a shift in thought or a reversal of expectations. Discuss the shift or reversal in each poem, and explain whether you think it provides an effective conclusion.

PERFORMANCE TASK

Writing Activity: Opinion Which poem speaks to you on a more personal level? Why?

- Choose your favorite of the two poems. Identify reasons that you prefer it, including ideas related to content, style, and form. Incorporate details from the poem to support your reasons.
- Consider why the other poem does not appeal to you in the same way. Identify specific reasons.
- Organize your ideas logically and present them in a brief written analysis.

Background *Dan Horgan grew up on a farm in California. He loved the outdoors and created his first garden at age nine, planting tulips and rimming the edge with rocks. When he came home from serving in the Vietnam War, Horgan needed to restore his inner balance. He did so by designing landscapes that incorporated both rocks and plants. Then, in the 1990s, he was galvanized by the work of artist Andy Goldsworthy to focus on creating art just with rocks. His art pieces are built and left in the environments that inspired them, keeping Horgan close to the nature that he loves.*

MEDIA ANALYSIS

Being Here: The Art of Dan Horgan

Documentary directed by Russ Spencer

AS YOU VIEW Pay attention to the methods the filmmaker uses to reveal Horgan's personality and attitude toward his art.

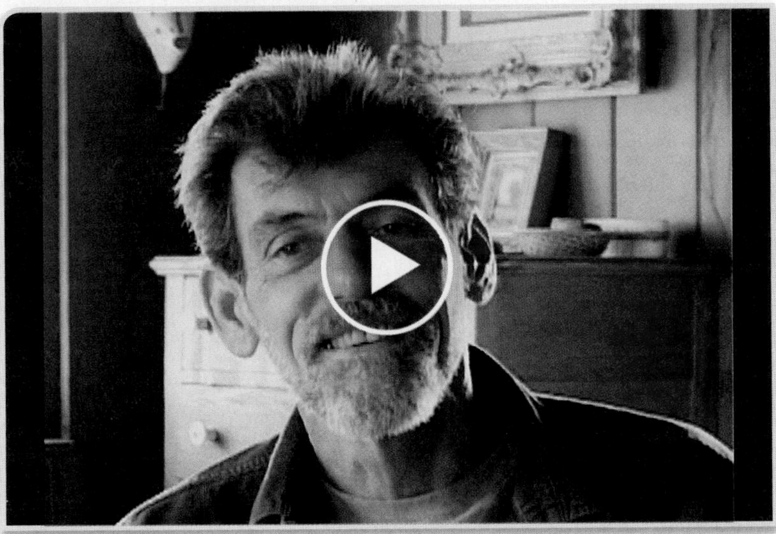

Image Credits: ©Bison Films

COLLABORATIVE DISCUSSION What is your impression of Horgan? With a partner, discuss how the filmmaker uses his craft to convey important aspects of the artist's character.

Integrate and Evaluate Information

RI 7

A documentary is a nonfiction film that provides information about a social, political, or historical subject. In this film about artist Dan Horgan, the filmmaker provides footage of Horgan and his works as well as an audio track with background music and the artist's commentary on his process. To evaluate how these different media build the audience's understanding of the subject, consider what these features contribute to the film:

Visual	Sound
• the movement of the camera • the variety of camera angles used • the synchronization of the commentary with the images • the appearance of the artist at the beginning and at the close of this segment	• the sound of the artist's own voice talking about the creative process • the content of the artist's commentary • the choice of background music

Analyzing the Media

RI 7, SL 5

Cite Text Evidence Support your responses with evidence from the selection.

1. **Analyze** What camera techniques are used to film Horgan's art, such as the *Navajo Sentinel?* Explain how these techniques influence the audience's perception of the art.
2. **Cite Evidence** How do Horgan's insights about his creative process help viewers understand the choice of materials, location, form, and themes of his work? Cite specific comments that relate to these ideas in your response.
3. **Evaluate** Explain how the different media used by the filmmaker all work together to help achieve the purpose of this documentary.

PERFORMANCE TASK

Media Activity: Art Analysis Complete these activities independently.

- Review the clip, identifying two or three of Horgan's works that provoke a reaction in you.
- Create speaking notes that explain what you see, feel, and think about the form, materials, location, and meaning of each work. Draw from what you have learned about Horgan's art in the video.
- Present your critique to the class, pausing the film at each work of art that you have chosen.
- Invite classmates to share their ideas about the work as well.

Linda Hogan *has received many awards for her writing. Much of her work focuses on environmental themes, often from a Native American perspective. She especially wants to help people understand the importance of ecologically sound, indigenous environmental practices. Hogan says she had no idea that writing would become her profession. In her private journals, she found herself focusing on nature and realized that she could convey her ideas to a wider audience by making them public. She is currently the Writer in Residence for the Chickasaw Nation.*

Dwellings

Essay by Linda Hogan

AS YOU READ Consider what you learn about the author from the details in this essay. Write down any questions you generate during reading.

Not far from where I live is a hill that was cut into by the moving water of a creek. Eroded this way, all that's left of it is a broken wall of earth that contains old roots and pebbles woven together and exposed. Seen from a distance, it is only a rise of raw earth. But up close it is something wonderful, a small cliff dwelling that looks almost as intricate and well made as those the Anasazi[1] left behind when they vanished mysteriously centuries ago. This hill is a place that could be the starry skies of night turned inward into the thousand round holes where solitary bees have lived and died. It is a hill of tunneling rooms. At the mouths of some of the excavations, half-circles of clay beetle out like awnings shading a doorway. It is earth that was turned to clay in the mouths of the bees and spit out as they mined deeper into their dwelling places.

This place where the bees reside is at an angle safe from rain. It faces the southern sun. It is a warm and intelligent architecture

[1] **Anasazi** (ä′nə-sä′zē): an ancient Native American culture of the American Southwest.

of memory, learned by whatever memory lives in the blood. Many of the holes still contain the gold husks of dead bees, their faces dry and gone, their flat eyes gazing out from death's land toward the other uninhabited half of the hill that is across the creek from these catacombs.

The first time I found the residence of the bees, it was dusty summer. The sun was hot, and land was the dry color of rust. Now and then a car rumbled along the dirt road and dust rose up behind it before settling back down on older dust. In the silence, the bees made a soft droning hum. They were alive then, and working the hill, going out and returning with pollen, in and out through the holes, back and forth between daylight and the cooler, darker regions of inner earth. They were flying an invisible map through air, a map charted by landmarks, the slant of light, and a circling story they told one another about the direction of food held inside the center of yellow flowers.

Sitting in the hot sun, watching the small bees fly in and out around the hill, hearing the summer birds, the light breeze, I felt right in the world. I belonged there. I thought of my own dwelling places, those real and those imagined. Once I lived in a town called Manitou, which means "Great Spirit," and where hot mineral springwater gurgled beneath the streets and rose up into open wells. I felt safe there. With the underground movement of water and heat a constant reminder of other life, of what lives beneath us, it seemed to be the center of the world.

A few years after that, I wanted silence. My daydreams were full of places I longed to be, shelters and solitudes. I wanted a room apart from others, a hidden cabin to rest in. I wanted to be in a redwood forest with trees so tall the owls called out in the daytime. I daydreamed of living in a vapor cave a few hours away from here. Underground, warm, and moist, I thought it would be the perfect world for staying out of cold winter, for escaping the noise of living.

And how often I've wanted to escape to a wilderness where a human hand has not been in everything. But those were only dreams of peace, of comfort, of a nest inside stone or woods, a sanctuary where a dream or life wouldn't be invaded.

Years ago, in the next canyon west of here, there was a man who followed one of those dreams and moved into a cave that could only be reached by climbing down a rope. For years he lived there in comfort, like a troglodite.[2] The inner weather was stable, never too hot, too cold, too wet, or too dry. But then he felt lonely. His utopia needed a woman. He went to town until he found a wife. For a while after the marriage, his wife climbed down the rope along with him, but before long she didn't want the mice scurrying about in the cave, or the untidy bats that wanted to hang from stones of the ceiling. So they built a door.

[2] **troglodite:** a mythical or prehistoric cave dweller.

Because of the closed entryway, the temperature changed. They had to put in heat. Then the inner moisture of earth warped the door, so they had to have air-conditioning, and after that the earth wanted to go about life in its own way and it didn't give in to the people.

In other days and places, people paid more attention to the strong-headed will of earth. Once homes were built of wood that had been felled from a single region in a forest. That way, it was thought, the house would hold together more harmoniously, and the family of walls would not fall or lend themselves to the unhappiness or arguments of the inhabitants.

An Italian immigrant to Chicago, Aldo Piacenzi, built birdhouses that were dwellings of harmony and peace. They were the incredible spired shapes of cathedrals in Italy. They housed not only the birds, but also his memories, his own past. He painted them the watery blue of his Mediterranean, the wild rose of flowers in a summer field. Inside them was straw and the droppings of lives that layed eggs, fledglings who grew there. What places to inhabit, the bright and sunny birdhouses in dreary alleyways of the city.

One beautiful afternoon, cool and moist, with the kind of yellow light that falls on earth in these arid regions, I waited for barn swallows to return from their daily work of food gathering. Inside the tunnel where they live, hundreds of swallows had mixed their saliva with mud and clay, much like the solitary bees, and formed nests that were perfect as a potter's bowl. At five in the evening, they returned all at once, a dark, flying shadow. Despite their enormous numbers and the crowding together of nests, they didn't pause for even a moment before entering the nests, nor did they crowd one another. Instantly they vanished into the nests. The tunnel went silent. It held no outward signs of life.

But I knew they were there, filled with the fire of living. And what a marriage of elements was in those nests. Not only mud's earth and water, the fire of sun and dry air, but even the elements contained one another. The bodies of prophets and crazy men were broken down in that soil.

I've noticed often how when a house is abandoned, it begins to sag. Without a tenant, it has no need to go on. If it were a person, we'd say it is depressed or lonely. The roof settles in, the paint cracks, the walls and floorboards warp and slope downward in their own natural ways, telling us that life must stay in everything as the world whirls and tilts and moves through boundless space.

One summer day, cleaning up after long-eared owls where I work at a rehabilitation facility for birds of prey, I was raking the gravel floor of a flight cage. Down on the ground, something looked like it was moving. I bent over to look into the pile of bones and pellets I'd just raked together. There, close to the ground, were two fetal mice. They were new to the planet, pink and hairless. They were so tenderly young. Their faces had swollen blue-veined eyes. They were nestled in a mound of feathers, soft as velvet, each one curled up smaller than an infant's ear, listening to the first sounds of earth. But the ants were biting them. They turned in agony, unable to pull away, not yet having the arms or legs to move, but feeling, twisting away from, the pain of the bites. I was horrified to see them bitten out of life that way. I dipped them in water, as if to take away the sting, and let the ants fall in the bucket. Then I held the tiny mice in the palm of my hand. Some of the ants were drowning in the water. I was trading one life for another, exchanging the lives of ants for those of mice, but I hated their suffering, and hated even more that they had not yet grown to a life, and already they inhabited the miserable world of pain. Death and life feed each other. I know that.

Inside these rooms where birds are healed, there are other lives besides those of mice. There are fine gray globes the wasps have woven together, the white cocoons of spiders in a corner, the downward tunneling anthills. All these dwellings are inside one small walled space, but I think most about the mice. Sometimes the downy nests fall out of the walls where their mothers have placed them out of the way of their enemies. When one of the nests falls, they are so well made and soft, woven mostly from the chest feathers of birds. Sometimes the leg of a small quail holds the nest together like a slender cornerstone with dry, bent claws. The mice have adapted to life in the presence of their enemies, adapted to living in the thin wall between beak and beak, claw and claw. They move their nests often, as if a new rafter or wall will protect them from the inevitable fate of all our returns home to the deeper, wider nest of earth that houses us all.

One August at Zia Pueblo[3] during the corn dance I noticed tourists picking up shards of all the old pottery that had been made and broken there. The residents of Zia know not to take the bowls and pots left behind by the older ones. They know that the fragments of those earlier lives need to be smoothed back to earth, but younger nations, travelers from continents across the world who have come to inhabit this land, have little of their own to grow on. The pieces of earth that were formed into bowls, even on their way home to dust, provide the new people a lifeline to an unknown land, help them remember that they live in the old nest of earth.

It was in early February, during the mating season of the great horned owls. It was dusk, and I hiked up the back of a mountain to where I'd heard the owls a year before. I wanted to hear them again, the voices so tender, so deep, like a memory of comfort. I was halfway up the trail when I found a soft, round nest. It had fallen from one of the

---

[3] **Zia Pueblo:** a small community in central New Mexico.

bare-branched trees. It was a delicate nest, woven together of feathers, sage, and strands of wild grass. Holding it in my hand in the rosy twilight, I noticed that a blue thread was entwined with the other gatherings there. I pulled at the thread a little, and then I recognized it. It was a thread from one of my skirts. It was blue cotton. It was the unmistakable color and shape of a pattern I knew. I liked it, that a thread of my life was in an abandoned nest, one that had held eggs and new life. I took the nest home. At home, I held it to the light and looked more closely. There, to my surprise, nestled into the gray-green sage, was a gnarl of black hair. It was also unmistakable. It was my daughter's hair, cleaned from a brush and picked up out in the sun beneath the maple tree, or the pit cherry where birds eat from the overladen, fertile branches until only the seeds remain on the trees.

I didn't know what kind of nest it was, or who had lived there. It didn't matter. I thought of the remnants of our lives carried up the hill that way and turned into shelter. That night, resting inside the walls of our home, the world outside weighed so heavily against the thin wood of the house. The sloped roof was the only thing between us and the universe. Everything outside of our wooden boundaries seemed so large. Filled with night's citizens, it all came alive. The world opened in the thickets of the dark. The wild grapes would soon ripen on the vines. The burrowing ones were emerging. Horned owls sat in treetops. Mice scurried here and there. Skunks, fox, the slow and holy porcupine, all were passing by this way. The young of the solitary bees were feeding on pollen in the dark. The whole world was a nest on its humble tilt, in the maze of the universe, holding us.

COLLABORATIVE DISCUSSION With a partner, discuss how the ideas and thoughts included in this essay create a portrait of the author. Cite specific evidence from the text to support your ideas.

Support Inferences

RI 1

Inferences are logical assumptions that readers make by combining evidence from the text with their own prior knowledge and experience. Inferences are important in reading because authors may not be explicit about the connections they want you to make. In this reflective essay, the author develops ideas from personal observations of the natural world and human interactions with nature. Hogan states some of her ideas explicitly; others must be inferred by readers from the details in the text.

Consider this passage, in which the author describes the experience of a man who created a dwelling in nature:

> **For years he lived there in comfort, like a troglodite. The inner weather was stable, never too hot, too cold, too wet, or too dry. . . . but before long she [his wife] didn't want the mice scurrying about in the cave, or the untidy bats that wanted to hang from stones of the ceiling. So they built a door. Because of the closed entryway, the temperature changed. They had to put in heat. Then the inner moisture of earth warped the door, so they had to have air-conditioning, and after that the earth wanted to go about life in its own way and it didn't give in to the people.**

These details show that when the man accepted what nature provided, conditions were perfect. When he added his own "improvements," he upset the balance of nature and suffered the consequences; he had to compensate for more and more deficiencies. From this account, readers can infer the author's message—that humans would be happier if they could find a way to live in greater harmony with nature.

Comprehend Literary Nonfiction: Cultural Context

RI 10

The **cultural context** of a work refers to the traditions, beliefs, and values that influenced its creation. As a Native American, Hogan's perspective is shaped by the key beliefs and values of her culture. These include an acute awareness of the connection between all living things; the realization that humans are restored when they live in harmony with their environment; a deep respect for other species of animal and plant life; and the belief that humans have a responsibility to care for nature.

To analyze the impact of the author's cultural context on "Dwellings," readers can look for the way those values are revealed in these aspects of the essay:

- the choice of topic
- the author's description of elements of nature
- the author's direct statements of theme
- the author's actions
- the kinds of details the author notices
- the author's reflections on what she observes

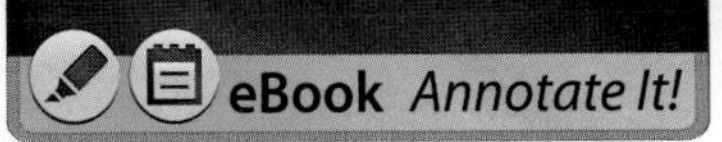

RI 1, RI 2, RI 3, RI 4, RI 6, RI 10, W 2

Analyzing the Text

Cite Text Evidence Support your responses with evidence from the selection.

1. **Infer** Note the details that Hogan uses in lines 14–39 to describe the community of bees. What is the tone of this description? What might the bees represent for the author to make her have this attitude?
2. **Analyze** Explain why the author felt "safe" in Manitou. How might her perceptions of this place reflect her Native American beliefs?
3. **Compare** What characteristics do the dwellings in lines 64–77 have in common? Are these characteristics viewed positively or negatively by the author?
4. **Analyze** In lines 82–83, the author says that swallows form "nests that were perfect as a potter's bowl." Explain the literal meaning of this simile as well as what it implies.
5. **Cite Evidence** Cite evidence that reveals the author's belief in the interconnectedness of all things.
6. **Analyze** What does the author's work at the wildlife facility reveal about the relationship between her values and her life?
7. **Synthesize** Based on the author's descriptions of various dwellings she has encountered, what would be her idea of an ideal dwelling?
8. **Draw Conclusions** In the last sentence of the essay, the author states, "The whole world was a nest on its humble tilt, in the maze of the universe, holding us." What does this statement suggest about her overall purpose in writing this essay?

PERFORMANCE TASK

Writing Activity: Comparison Do Annie Dillard and Linda Hogan share the same view of nature?

- Review Hogan's essay and Dillard's "Living Like Weasels" (also in this collection). Identify each author's perspective and the details that reveal that view of nature.
- Include direct quotations as well as original analysis of each author's work. Organize your ideas logically and in a way that shows the comparison clearly.
- Be sure to follow the conventions of standard written English.

Language and Style: Appositives and Appositive Phrases

Writers may provide additional information about a noun or pronoun in a sentence by using **appositives** and **appositive phrases**. An appositive is a noun or pronoun that identifies or renames another noun or pronoun. An appositive phrase includes an appositive and its modifiers.

Read this sentence from the essay:

An Italian immigrant to Chicago, Aldo Piacenzi, built birdhouses that were dwellings of harmony and peace.

The author could have expressed the same ideas this way:

Aldo Piacenzi was an Italian immigrant to Chicago. He built birdhouses that were dwellings of harmony and peace.

In the original text, the appositive ("Aldo Piacenzi") clarifies who the Italian immigrant is. Though the second version is correct, the original sentence flows more naturally and is more concise.

The chart shows the two types of appositives and appositive phrases.

Appositive/Appositive Phrase	Example
Essential: Provides information that is necessary to identify the preceding noun or pronoun. It is not set off by commas, and the meaning of the sentence would be altered by deleting it.	Hogan's book *Mean Spirits* was nominated for a Pulitzer Prize. (The title *Mean Spirits* is an appositive for the word *book*. Without it, readers would not know which of Hogan's books was nominated.)
Nonessential: Adds extra information to a noun or pronoun that is already clearly identified. It is set off by commas. If it were deleted, the meaning of the sentence would still be clear.	Hogan, an active public speaker, has given talks on environmental issues. (The appositive phrase *an active public speaker* adds more information but is not required for the sentence to make sense.)

Practice and Apply Add an appositive or an appositive phrase to the italicized noun or pronoun in each of these sentences. Share your sentences with a partner. Discuss how the appositive or appositive phrase affects the meaning of each sentence.

1. The *hummingbird* prefers the nectar from red flowers.
2. The *car* raised a cloud of dust as it sped along the dirt road.
3. She worked to rehabilitate *eagles*.
4. Her *home* was built on the edge of a redwood forest.
5. The enthusiastic hiker she met was a *botanist*.

Rick Bass (b. 1958) *grew up in Texas, where he became interested in nature at an early age. He studied geology at Utah State University and worked as a petroleum geologist for several years. During his lunch hours he started writing short stories. Since then, he has written and edited over 25 books, both fiction and nonfiction, and has received many literary awards. His passion for nature is reflected in his environmental activism as well as his writing. He moved to Montana in 1987 and is involved in efforts to protect areas such as the Glacier National Park.*

The Hermit's Story

Short Story by Rick Bass

AS YOU READ Think about whether Ann's story is credible or not. Write down any questions you generate during reading.

An ice storm, following seven days of snow; the vast fields and drifts of snow turning to sheets of glazed ice that shine and shimmer blue in the moonlight, as if the color is being **fabricated** not by the bending and absorption of light but by some chemical reaction within the glossy ice; as if the source of all blueness lies somewhere up here in the north—the core of it beneath one of those frozen fields; as if blue is a thing that emerges, in some parts of the world, from the soil itself, after the sun goes down.

fabricate (făb´rĭ-kāt´) *v.* to construct or make.

Blue creeping up fissures and cracks from depths of several hundred feet; blue working its way up through the gleaming ribs of Ann's buried dogs; blue trailing like smoke from the dogs' empty eye sockets and nostrils—blue rising like smoke from chimneys until it reaches the surface and spreads laterally and becomes entombed, or trapped—but still alive, and smoky—within those moonstruck fields of ice.

Blue like a scent trapped in the ice, waiting for some soft release, some thawing, so that it can continue spreading.

It's Thanksgiving. Susan and I are over at Ann and Roger's house for dinner. The storm has knocked out all the power down in town —it's a clear, cold, starry night, and if you were to climb one of the mountains on snowshoes and look forty miles south toward where town lies, instead of seeing the usual small scatterings of light—like fallen stars, stars sunken to the bottom of a lake, but still glowing—you would see nothing but darkness—a bowl of silence and darkness in balance for once with the mountains up here, rather than opposing or complementing our darkness, our peace.

As it is, we do not climb up on snowshoes to look down at the dark town—the power lines dragged down by the clutches of ice—but can tell instead just by the way there is no faint glow over the mountains to the south that the power is out: that this Thanksgiving, life for those in town is the same as it always is for us in the mountains, and it is a good feeling, a familial one, coming on the holiday as it does—though doubtless too the townspeople are feeling less snug and cozy about it than we are.

We've got our lanterns and candles burning. A fire's going in the stove, as it will all winter long and into the spring. Ann's dogs are asleep in their straw nests, breathing in that same blue light that is being exhaled from the skeletons of their ancestors just beneath and all around them. There is the faint, good smell of cold-storage meat—slabs and slabs of it—coming from down in the basement, and we have just finished off an entire chocolate pie and three bottles of wine. Roger, who does not know how to read, is examining the empty bottles, trying to read some of the words on the labels. He recognizes the words *the* and *in* and *USA*. It may be that he will never learn to read—that he will be unable to — but we are in no rush, and—unlike his power lifting—he has all of his life in which to accomplish this. I for one believe that he will learn it.

Ann has a story for us. It's about one of the few clients she's ever had, a fellow named Gray Owl, up in Canada, who owned half a dozen speckled German shorthaired pointers and who hired Ann to train them all at once. It was twenty years ago, she says—her last good job.

She worked the dogs all summer and into the autumn, and finally had them ready for field trials. She took them back up to Gray Owl—way up in Saskatchewan—driving all day and night in her old truck, which was old even then, with dogs piled up on top of each other, sleeping and snoring: dogs on her lap, dogs on the seat, dogs on the floorboard. How strange it is to think that most of us can count on one hand the number of people we know who are doing what they most want to do for a living. They invariably have about them a kind of wildness and calmness both, possessing somewhat the grace of animals that are fitted intricately and polished into this world. An academic such as myself might refer to it as a kind of biological confidence. Certainly I think another word for it could be *peace*.

Ann was taking the dogs up there to show Gray Owl how to work them: how to take advantage of their newly found talents. She could be a sculptor or some other kind of artist, in that she speaks of her work as if the dogs are rough blocks of stone whose internal form exists already and is waiting only to be chiseled free and then released by her, beautiful, into the world.

Basically, in six months the dogs had been transformed from gangling, bouncing puppies into six raging geniuses, and she needed to show their owner how to control them, or rather, how to work with them. Which characteristics to nurture, which ones to discourage. With all dogs, Ann said, there was a tendency, upon their leaving her **tutelage**—unlike a work of art set in stone or paint—for a kind of chitinous[1] encrustation to set in, a sort of oxidation, upon the dogs leaving her hands and being returned to someone less knowledgeable and passionate, less committed than she. It was as if there were a tendency in the world for the dogs' greatness to disappear back into the stone.

tutelage (to͞ot′l-ĭj) *n.* instructional authority.

So she went up there to give both the dogs and Gray Owl a check-out session. She drove with the heater on and the window down; the cold Canadian air was invigorating, cleaner, farther north. She could smell the scent of the fir and spruce, and the damp alder and cottonwood leaves beneath the many feet of snow. We laughed at her when she said it, but she told us that up in Canada she could taste the fish in the streams as she drove alongside creeks and rivers.

She listened to the only radio station she could pick up as she drove, but it was a good one. She got to Gray Owl's around midnight. He had a little guest cabin but had not heated it for her, uncertain as to the day of her arrival, so she and the six dogs slept together on a cold mattress beneath mounds of elk hides: their last night together. She had brought a box of quail with which to work the dogs, and she built a small fire in the stove and set the box of quail next to it.

The quail muttered and cheeped all night and the stove popped and hissed and Ann and the dogs slept for twelve hours straight, as if submerged in another time, or as if everyone else in the world were submerged in time—encased in stone—and as if she and the dogs were pioneers, or survivors of some kind: upright and exploring the present, alive in the world, free of that strange chitin.

She spent a week up there, showing Gray Owl how his dogs worked. She said he scarcely recognized them afield, and that it took a few days just for him to get over his amazement. They worked the dogs both individually and, as Gray Owl came to understand and appreciate what Ann had crafted, in groups. They traveled across snowy hills on snowshoes, the sky the color of snow, so that often it was like moving through a dream, and except for the rasp of the snowshoes beneath

[1] **chitinous** (kīt′n-əs): like a hard, biological substance found in the shells or exoskeletons of certain creatures.

them, and the pull of gravity, they might have believed they had ascended into some sky-place where all the world was snow.

They worked into the wind—north—whenever they could. Ann would carry birds in a pouch over her shoulder—much as a woman might carry a purse—and from time to time would fling a startled bird out into that dreary, icy snowscape—and the quail would fly off with great haste, a dark feathered buzz bomb disappearing quickly into the teeth of cold, and then Gray Owl and Ann and the dog, or dogs, would go find it, following it by scent only, as always.

Snot icicles would be hanging from the dogs' nostrils. They would always find the bird. The dog, or dogs, would point it, at which point Gray Owl or Ann would step forward and flush it—the beleaguered bird would leap into the sky again—and then once more they would push on after it, pursuing that bird toward the horizon as if driving it with a whip. Whenever the bird wheeled and flew downwind, they'd quarter away from it, then get a mile or so downwind from it and push it back north.

When the quail finally became too exhausted to fly, Ann would pick it up from beneath the dogs' noses as they held point staunchly, put the tired bird in her game bag and replace it with a fresh one, and off they'd go again. They carried their lunch in Gray Owl's day pack, as well as emergency supplies—a tent and some dry clothes—in case they should become lost, and around noon each day (they could rarely see the sun, only an eternal ice-white haze, so that they relied instead only on their rhythms within) they would stop and make a pot of tea on the sputtering little gas stove. Sometimes one or two of the quail would die from exposure, and they would cook that on the stove and eat it out there in the tundra, tossing the feathers up into the wind as if to launch one more flight and feeding the head, guts, and feet to the dogs.

Perhaps seen from above their tracks would have seemed aimless and wandering rather than with the purpose, the focus that was burning hot in both their and the dogs' hearts—perhaps someone viewing the tracks could have discerned the pattern, or perhaps not—but it did not matter, for their tracks—the patterns, direction, and tracing of them—were obscured by the drifting snow, sometimes within minutes after they were laid down.

Toward the end of the week, Ann said, they were finally running all six dogs at once, like a herd of silent wild horses through all that snow, and as she would be going home the next day, there was no need to conserve any of the birds she had brought, and she was turning them loose several at a time: birds flying in all directions; the dogs, as ever, tracking them to the ends of the earth.

It was almost a whiteout that last day, and it was hard to keep track of all the dogs. Ann was sweating from the exertion as well as the tension of trying to keep an eye on, and evaluate, each dog—the sweat was freezing on her in places, so that it was as if she were developing

"They might have **believed** they had ascended into some **sky-place** where all the world was **snow**."

an ice skin. She jokingly told Gray Owl that next time she was going to try to find a client who lived in Arizona, or even South America. Gray Owl smiled and then told her that they were lost, but no matter, the storm would clear in a day or two.

They knew it was getting near dusk—there was a faint dulling to the sheer whiteness, a kind of increasing heaviness in the air, a new density to the faint light around them—and the dogs slipped in and out of sight, working just at the edges of their vision.

The temperature was dropping as the north wind increased—"No question about which way south is; we'll turn around and walk south for three hours, and if we don't find a road, we'll make camp," Gray Owl said—and now the dogs were coming back with frozen quail held gingerly in their mouths, for once the birds were dead, they were allowed to retrieve them, though the dogs must have been puzzled that there had been no shots. Ann said she fired a few rounds of the cap pistol into the air to make the dogs think she had hit those birds. Surely they believed she was a goddess.

They turned and headed south—Ann with a bag of frozen birds over her shoulder, and the dogs, knowing that the hunt was over now, all around them, once again like a team of horses in harness, though wild and prancy.

After an hour of increasing discomfort—Ann's and Gray Owl's hands and feet numb, and ice beginning to form on the dogs' paws, so that the dogs were having to high-step—they came in day's last light to the edge of a wide clearing: a terrain that was remarkable and soothing for its lack of hills. It was a frozen lake, which meant—said Gray Owl—they had drifted west (or perhaps east) by as much as ten miles.

Ann said that Gray Owl looked tired and old and guilty, as would any host who had caused his guest some unasked-for inconvenience. They knelt down and began massaging the dogs' paws and then lit the little stove and held each dog's foot, one at a time, over the tiny blue flame to help it thaw out.

Gray Owl walked out to the edge of the lake ice and kicked at it with his foot, hoping to find fresh water beneath for the dogs; if they ate too much snow, especially after working so hard, they'd get violent diarrhea and might then become too weak to continue home the next day, or the next, or whenever the storm quit.

Ann said she could barely see Gray Owl's outline through the swirling snow, even though he was less than twenty yards away. He kicked once at the sheet of ice, the vast plate of it, with his heel, then disappeared below the ice.

Ann wanted to believe that she had blinked and lost sight of him, or that a gust of snow had swept past and hidden him, but it had been too fast, too total: she knew that the lake had swallowed him. She was sorry for Gray Owl, she said, and worried for his dogs—afraid they would try to follow his scent down into the icy lake, and be lost as well—but what she was most upset about, she said—to be perfectly honest—was that Gray Owl had been wearing the little day pack with the tent and emergency rations. She had it in her mind to try to save Gray Owl, and to try to keep the dogs from going through the ice, but if he drowned, she was going to have to figure out how to try to get that day pack off of the drowned man and set up the wet tent in the blizzard on the snowy prairie and then crawl inside and survive. She would have to go into the water naked, so that when she came back out—if she came back out—she would have dry clothes to put on.

The dogs came galloping up, seeming as large as deer or elk in that dim landscape, against which there was nothing else to give them perspective, and Ann whoaed them right at the lake's edge, where they stopped immediately, as if they had suddenly been cast with a sheet of ice.

Ann knew they would stay there forever, or until she released them, and it troubled her to think that if she drowned, they too would die—that they would stand there motionless, as she had commanded them, for as long as they could, until at some point—days later, perhaps—they would lie down, trembling with exhaustion—they might lick at some snow, for moisture—but that then the snows would cover them, and still they would remain there, chins resting on their front paws, staring straight ahead and unseeing into the storm, wondering where the scent of her had gone.

Ann eased out onto the ice. She followed the tracks until she came to the jagged hole in the ice through which Gray Owl had plunged. She was almost half again lighter than he, but she could feel the ice crackling beneath her own feet. It sounded different too, in a way she could not place—it did not have the squeaky, percussive resonance of the lake-ice back home—and she wondered if Canadian ice froze differently or just sounded different.

She got down on all fours and crept closer to the hole. It was right at dusk. She peered down into the hole and dimly saw Gray Owl standing down there, waving his arms at her. He did not appear to be swimming. Slowly, she took one glove off and eased her bare hand down into the hole. She could find no water, and **tentatively**, she reached deeper.

tentatively (tĕn′tə-tĭv-lē) *adv.* with uncertainty; cautiously.

Gray Owl's hand found hers and he pulled her down in. Ice broke as she fell, but he caught her in his arms. She could smell the wood smoke in his jacket from the alder he burned in his cabin. There was no water at all, and it was warm beneath the ice.

"This happens a lot more than people realize," he said. "It's not really a phenomenon; it's just what happens. A cold snap comes in October, freezes a skin of ice over the lake—it's got to be a shallow one, almost a marsh. Then a snowfall comes, insulating the ice. The lake drains in fall and winter—percolates down through the soil"—he stamped the spongy ground beneath them—"but the ice up top remains. And nobody ever knows any differently. People look out at the surface and think, *Aha, a frozen lake.*" Gray Owl laughed.

"Did you know it would be like this?" Ann asked.

"No," he said. "I was looking for water. I just got lucky."

Ann walked back to shore beneath the ice to fetch her stove and to release the dogs from their whoa command. The dry lake was only about eight feet deep, but it grew shallow quickly closer to shore, so that Ann had to crouch to keep from bumping her head on the overhead ice, and then crawl; and then there was only space to wriggle, and to emerge she had to break the ice above her by bumping and then battering it with her head and elbows, like the struggles of some embryonic hatchling; and when she stood up, waist-deep amid sparkling shards of ice—it was nighttime now—the dogs barked ferociously at her, but remained where she had ordered them to stay, and she was surprised at how far off course she was when she climbed out; she had traveled only twenty feet, but already the dogs were twice that far away from her. She knew humans had a poorly evolved, almost nonexistent sense of direction, but this error—over such a short distance—shocked her. It was as if there were in us a thing—an impulse, a catalyst—that denies our ever going straight to another thing. Like dogs working left and right into the wind, she thought, before converging on the scent.

Except that the dogs would not get lost, while she could easily imagine herself and Gray Owl getting lost beneath the lake, walking in circles forever, unable to find even the simplest of things: the shore.

She gathered the stove and dogs. She was tempted to try to go back in the way she had come out—it seemed so easy—but considered the consequences of getting lost in the other direction, and instead followed her original tracks out to where Gray Owl had first dropped through the ice. It was true night now, and the blizzard was still blowing hard, plastering snow and ice around her face like a mask. The dogs did not want to go down into the hole, so she lowered them to Gray Owl and then climbed gratefully back down into the warmth herself.

The air was a thing of its own—recognizable as air, and breathable, as such, but with a taste and odor, an essence, unlike any other air they'd ever breathed. It had a different density to it, so that smaller, shallower breaths were required; there was very much the feeling that if they breathed in too much of the strange, dense air, they would drown.

They wanted to explore the lake, and were thirsty, but it felt like a victory simply to be warm—or rather, not cold—and they were so exhausted that instead they made pallets out of the dead marsh grass that rustled around their ankles, and they slept curled up on the tiniest of hammocks, to keep from getting damp in the pockets and puddles of dampness that still lingered here and there.

All eight of them slept as if in a nest, heads and arms draped across other ribs and hips, and it was, said Ann, the best and deepest sleep she'd ever had—the sleep of hounds, the sleep of childhood—and how long they slept, she never knew, for she wasn't sure, later, how much of their subsequent time they spent wandering beneath the lake, and then up on the prairie, homeward again—but when they awoke, it was still night, or night once more, and clearing, with bright stars visible through the porthole, their point of embarkation; and even from beneath the ice, in certain places where, for whatever reasons—temperature, oxygen content, wind scour—the ice was clear rather than glazed, they could see the spangling of stars, though more dimly; and strangely, rather than seeming to distance them from the stars, this phenomenon seemed to pull them closer, as if they were up in the stars, traveling the Milky Way, or as if the stars were embedded in the ice.

It was very cold outside—up above—and there was a steady stream, a current like a river, of the night's colder, heavier air plunging down through their porthole, as if trying to fill the empty lake with that frozen air—but there was also the hot muck of the earth's massive respirations breathing out warmth and being trapped and protected beneath that ice, so that there were warm currents doing battle with the lone cold current.

The result was that it was breezy down there, and the dogs' noses twitched in their sleep as the images brought by these scents painted themselves across their sleeping brains in the language we call dreams but which, for the dogs, and perhaps for us, was reality: the scent of an owl *real*, not a dream; the scent of bear, cattail, willow, loon, *real*, even though they were sleeping, and even though those things were not visible, only over the next horizon.

The ice was contracting, groaning and cracking and squeaking up tighter, shrinking beneath the great cold—a concussive, grinding sound, as if giants were walking across the ice above—and it was this sound that had awakened them. They snuggled in warmer among the rattly dried yellowing grasses and listened to the tremendous clashings, as if they were safe beneath the sea and were watching waves of starlight sweeping across their hiding place; or as if they were in some place, some position, where they could watch mountains being born.

After a while the moon came up and washed out the stars. The light was blue and silver and seemed, Ann said, to be like a living thing. It filled the sheet of ice just above their heads with a shimmering cobalt light, which again rippled as if the ice were moving, rather than the earth itself, with the moon tracking it—and like deer drawn by gravity getting up in the night to feed for an hour or so before settling back in, Gray Owl and Ann and the dogs rose from their nests of straw and began to travel.

"You didn't—you know—*engage?*" Susan asks: a little mischievously, and a little proprietary, perhaps.

Ann shakes her head. "It was too cold," she says. I sneak a glance at Roger but cannot read his expression. Is he in love with her? Does she own his heart?

"But you would have, if it hadn't been so cold, right?" Susan asks, and Ann shrugs.

"He was an old man—in his fifties—and the dogs were around. But yeah, there was something about it that made me think of . . . those things," she says, careful and precise as ever.

"I would have done it anyway," Susan says. "Even if it was cold, and even if he was a hundred."

"We walked a long way," Ann says, eager to change the subject. "The air was damp down there, and whenever we'd get chilled, we'd stop and make a little fire out of a bundle of dry cattails." There were little pockets and puddles of swamp gas pooled here and there, she said, and sometimes a spark from the cattails would ignite one of those, and all around these little pockets of gas would light up like when you toss gas on a fire—these little explosions of brilliance, like flashbulbs, marsh pockets igniting like falling dominoes, or like children playing hopscotch—until a large-enough flash-pocket was reached—sometimes thirty or forty yards away from them, by this point—that the puff of flame would blow a chimney-hole through the ice, venting the other pockets, and the fires would crackle out, the scent of grass smoke sweet in their lungs, and they could feel gusts of warmth from the little flickering fires, and currents of the colder, heavier air sliding down through the new vent-holes and pooling around their ankles. The moonlight would strafe down through those rents in the ice, and shards of moon-ice would be glittering and spinning like diamond-motes in those newly vented columns of moonlight; and they pushed on, still lost, but so alive.

The mini-explosions were fun, but they frightened the dogs, and so Ann and Gray Owl lit twisted bundles of cattails and used them for torches to light their way, rather than building warming fires, though occasionally they would still pass through a pocket of methane and a stray ember would fall from their torches, and the whole chain of fire and light would begin again, culminating once more with a vent-hole being blown open and shards of glittering ice tumbling down into their lair . . .

What would it have looked like, seen from above—the orange blurrings of their wandering trail beneath the ice; and what would the sheet of lake-ice itself have looked like that night—throbbing with the ice-bound, **subterranean** blue and orange light of moon and fire? But again, there was no one to view the spectacle: only the travelers themselves, and they had no perspective, no vantage or loft from which to view or judge themselves. They were simply pushing on from one fire to the next, carrying their tiny torches. The beauty in front of them was enough.

subterranean (sŭb′tə-rā′nē-ən) *adj.* underground.

They knew they were getting near a shore—the southern shore, they hoped, as they followed the glazed moon's lure above—when the dogs began to encounter shore birds that had somehow found

"They pushed on, still lost, but so alive."

their way beneath the ice through small fissures and rifts and were taking refuge in the cattails. Small winter birds—juncos, nuthatches, chickadees—skittered away from the smoky approach of their torches; only a few late-migrating (or winter-trapped) snipe held tight and steadfast, and the dogs began to race ahead of Gray Owl and Ann, working these familiar scents—blue and silver ghost-shadows of dog-muscle weaving ahead through slants of moonlight.

The dogs emitted the odor of adrenaline when they worked, Ann said—a scent like damp fresh-cut green hay—and with nowhere to vent, the odor was dense and thick around them, so that Ann wondered if it too might be flammable, like the methane—if in the dogs' passions they might literally immolate themselves.

They followed the dogs closely with their torches. The ceiling was low—about eight feet, as if in a regular room—so that the tips of their torches' flames seared the ice above them, leaving a drip behind them and transforming the milky, almost opaque cobalt and orange ice behind them, wherever they passed, into wandering ribbons of clear ice, translucent to the sky—a script of flame, or buried flame, ice-bound flame—and they hurried to keep up with the dogs.

Now the dogs had the snipe surrounded, as Ann told it, and one by one the dogs went on point, each dog freezing as it pointed to the birds' hiding places, and it was the strangest scene yet, Ann said, seeming surely underwater; and Gray Owl moved in to flush the birds, which launched themselves with vigor against the roof of the ice above, fluttering like bats; but the snipe were too small, not powerful enough to break through those frozen four inches of water (though they could fly four thousand miles to South America each year and then back to Canada six months later—is freedom a lateral component, or a vertical one?), and as Gray Owl kicked at the clumps of frost-bent cattails where the snipe were hiding and they burst into flight, only to hit their heads on the ice above them, they came tumbling back down, raining limp and unconscious back to their soft grassy nests.

The dogs began retrieving them, carrying them gingerly, delicately—not preferring the taste of snipe, which ate only earth-worms—and Ann and Gray Owl gathered the tiny birds from the dogs, placed them in their pockets, and continued on to the shore, chasing that moon, the ceiling lowering to six feet, then four, then to a crawlspace, and after they had bashed their way out (with elbows, fists, and forearms) and stepped back out into the frigid air, they tucked the still-unconscious snipe into little crooks in branches, up against the trunks of trees and off the ground, out of harm's way, and passed on, south—as if late in their own migration—while the snipe rested, warm and terrified and heart-fluttering, but saved, for now, against the trunks of those trees.

Long after Ann and Gray Owl and the pack of dogs had passed through, the birds would awaken, their bright dark eyes luminous in the moonlight, and the first sight they would see would be the frozen marsh before them, with its chain of still-steaming vent-holes stretching back across all the way to the other shore. Perhaps these were birds that had been unable to migrate owing to injuries, or some genetic absence. Perhaps they had tried to migrate in the past but had found either their winter habitat destroyed or the path down there so fragmented and fraught with danger that it made more sense—to these few birds—to ignore the tuggings of the stars and seasons and instead to try to carve out new lives, new ways of being, even in such a stark and severe landscape: or rather, in a stark and severe period—knowing that lushness and bounty were still retained within that landscape. That it was only a phase; that better days would come. That in fact (the snipe knowing these things with their blood, ten-million-years-in-the-world), the austere times were the very thing, the very imbalance, that would summon the resurrection of that frozen richness within the soil—if indeed that richness, that magic, that hope, did still exist beneath the ice and snow. Spring would come like its own green fire, if only the injured ones could hold on.

And what would the snipe think or remember, upon reawakening and finding themselves still in that desolate position, desolate place and time, but still alive, and with hope?

Would it seem to them that a thing like grace had passed through, as they slept—that a slender winding river of it had passed through and rewarded them for their faith and endurance?

Believing, stubbornly, that that green land beneath them would blossom once more. Maybe not soon; but again.

If the snipe survived, they would be among the first to see it. Perhaps they believed that the pack of dogs, and Gray Owl's and Ann's advancing torches, had only been one of winter's dreams. Even with the proof—the scribings—of grace's passage before them—the vent-holes still steaming—perhaps they believed it was only one of winter's dreams.

It would be curious to tally how many times any or all of us reject, or fail to observe, moments of grace. Another way in which I think Susan and I differ from most of the anarchists and militia members up here is that we believe there is still green fire in the hearts of our citizens, beneath this long snowy winter—beneath the chitin of the **insipid**. That there is still something beneath the surface: that our souls and spirits are still of more worth, more value, than the glassine, latticed ice-structures visible only now at the surface of things. We still believe there's something down there beneath us, as a country. Not that we're better than other countries, by any means, but that we're luckier. That ribbons of grace are still passing through and around us—even now, and for whatever reasons, certainly unbeknownst to us, and certainly undeserved, unearned.

insipid
(ĭn-sĭp´ĭd) *adj.* dull; lacking color or zest.

Gray Owl, Ann, and the dogs headed south for half a day until they reached the snow-scoured road on which they'd parked. The road looked different, Ann said, buried beneath snowdrifts, and they didn't know whether to turn east or west. The dogs chose west, and so Gray Owl and Ann followed them. Two hours later they were back at their truck, and that night they were back at Gray Owl's cabin; by the next night Ann was home again. She says that even now she still sometimes has dreams about being beneath the ice—about living beneath the ice—and that it seems to her as if she was down there for much longer than a day and a night; that instead she might have been gone for years.

It was twenty years ago, when it happened. Gray Owl has since died, and all those dogs are dead now too. She is the only one who still carries—in the flesh, at any rate—the memory of that passage.

Ann would never discuss such a thing, but I suspect that it, that one day and night, helped give her a model for what things were like for her dogs when they were hunting and when they went on point: how the world must have appeared to them when they were in that trance, that blue zone, where the odors of things wrote their images across the dogs' hot brainpans. A zone where sight, and the appearance of things—*surfaces*—disappeared, and where instead their essence—the heat molecules of scent—was revealed, illuminated, circumscribed, possessed.

I suspect that she holds that knowledge—the memory of that one day and night—especially since she is now the sole possessor—as tightly, and securely, as one might clench some bright small gem in one's fist: not a gem given to one by some favored or beloved individual but, even more valuable, some gem found while out on a walk—perhaps by happenstance, or perhaps by some unavoidable rhythm of fate—and hence containing great magic, great strength.

Such is the nature of the kinds of people living, scattered here and there, in this valley.

COLLABORATIVE DISCUSSION Do you believe that the events in Ann's story could happen? With a partner, discuss the details in the text that support your view of whether the occurrence is or is not real. Cite specific evidence from the story to support your ideas.

Determine Theme

RL 2, RL 10

The **theme** of a story is an underlying message about life or human experience that the author wants to share with readers. This message is implied by the author as the story unfolds. A story may have more than one theme. In "The Hermit's Story," the characters' interaction with nature is key to understanding and appreciating the story's theme. For instance, think about how nature is presented as mysterious and unpredictable. Look for repeating patterns and symbols. See if you identify with any of the characters or with a particular event that is recounted in the story.

Asking and answering questions such as these will help you draw accurate conclusions about this story's theme or themes:

- What is the setting of the story Ann tells, and how does it create conflict for the characters?
- How do the characters' actions, as well as the setting itself, resolve the conflict?
- How does narrator feel about the events in the story? What words and phrases convey his attitude?
- How does the outer story influence the way readers understand Ann's story?
- Is it significant that the events Ann recounts occurred two decades earlier?

Analyze Structure: Frame Story

RL 5

A **frame story** is a narrative structure in which one or more stories are told within a story. Typically, the opening and closing of the story constitute the frame, and another story is told within that frame. Chaucer's *The Canterbury Tales* and the Arabic classic *One Thousand and One Nights* are well-known frame stories. This literary device can help make a story more believable by grounding a fantastical narrative in an ordinary experience—in the case of "The Hermit's Story," a dinner party. Authors might also choose this structure because the ideas in the frame can contribute to readers' understanding of the inner story; because it creates new meaning for the work as a whole; or simply because it enhances the story's aesthetic impact.

The frame story in "The Hermit's Story" introduces a setting and characters and provides a context for the inner story. To analyze the significance of the frame story structure, readers should note these elements:

Point of View The first-person narrator of the frame story *retells* Ann's story instead of having Ann tell it directly. Think about why the author chooses to do this.
Parallels in Setting The settings of the two stories are similar. In what way might these parallels contribute to the theme of the overall story?
Interruptions of Inner Story by Frame Story Characters At one point, the guests break into Ann's story to have a conversation; later in Ann's story, the narrator comments on what she has said. Think about the purpose of these interruptions.

Analyzing the Text

RL 1, RL 2, RL 3, RL 4, RL 5, SL 1a

Cite Text Evidence Support your responses with evidence from the selection.

1. **Connect** Which details in the frame are similar to details in Ann's description of her story's setting? What do these details suggest about nature?
2. **Interpret** The narrator uses the word *grace* in line 60 and lines 434–461. What idea does he suggest through the use of this word?
3. **Cite Evidence** Which sensory details does Bass include to highlight the unusual nature of Ann's experience under the ice?
4. **Infer** What is Ann's perspective on her experience? Which words and phrases indicate this attitude?
5. **Analyze** What theme is conveyed by Ann's conflict with nature and by the resolution of this conflict?
6. **Interpret** Reread lines 495–512. What lasting effect does Ann's experience under the ice have on her? Why does the narrator find it to be significant?
7. **Evaluate** Does narrating Ann's story within the frame of a dinner party make it more believable? Identify specific details from the text to support your response.
8. **Critique** Why might the author have chosen to call his story "The Hermit's Story"? Is this an effective and appropriate title? Explain why or why not?

PERFORMANCE TASK

Speaking Activity: Discussion Some critics have suggested that Bass views nature as mystical—having a spiritual significance. Do you agree?

- Identify and jot down details that describe nature in the story. Use them to draw your own conclusion about Bass's view.
- In a small group, share your conclusion and support for it. Reach a consensus, or analyze reasons for conflicting views.
- Summarize important ideas generated by the discussion.
- Present your summary of the discussion to the class.

Critical Vocabulary

L 4c, L 5b

fabricate **tutelage** **tentatively**

subterranean **insipid**

Practice and Apply Complete each sentence in a way that shows comprehension of the Critical Vocabulary word.

1. The story she told was far from *insipid* because . . .
2. The guests wondered if she *fabricated* the events because . . .
3. The animals were safe in their *subterranean* world because . . .
4. They stepped out onto the ice *tentatively* because . . .
5. Her *tutelage* of the dogs was necessary because . . .

Vocabulary Strategy: Consult a Thesaurus

A **thesaurus,** or a dictionary of synonyms (words that share a similar meaning), can be used to expand your vocabulary and make better word choices in your own writing. A print thesaurus might be organized alphabetically or by subject with an alphabetical index; an online thesaurus allows the user to search for synonyms of a word.

When choosing a synonym, it is important to remember that not all word choices will precisely match the intended meaning of the original word. There are usually subtle distinctions, or nuances, that make some words more suitable alternatives. For example, *eminent* and *notorious* are both valid synonyms of the word *famous*, but *eminent* has a positive connotation and *notorious* a negative one. It is important to choose synonyms that create the right impact when you write.

Practice and Apply With a partner, use a thesaurus to replace each Critical Vocabulary word with a synonym that best fits the word's meaning as it is used in the sentence. Consult a dictionary to confirm your choices.

1. He required extra *tutelage* in order to be the kicker for the team.
2. The child approached the dogs *tentatively*.
3. The two *fabricated* a plan that would get them home safely.
4. She would be a good speaker if her insights were less *insipid*.
5. The group shunned publicity, preferring to stay *subterranean*.

Present a Personal Narrative

This collection explores people's interactions with nature. Review the anchor text, "Living Like Weasels," and the other selections. Think about how the texts convey ideas and insights about the natural world. Write and present a personal narrative in which you describe and reflect on your own experience in nature.

W 3a–e Write narratives.
W 4 Produce clear and coherent writing.
W 5 Develop and strengthen writing.
W 9a–b Draw evidence from literary or informational texts.
SL 4 Present information, findings, and supporting evidence

An effective narrative presentation

- explores a significant personal experience the speaker had with the natural world
- establishes a first-person point of view
- uses sensory language to vividly describe people, places, and events
- narrates a logical sequence of events with the use of transitions
- uses narrative techniques, including dialogue, pacing, and description, to re-create the writer's experience
- engages the audience through volume, eye contact, and gestures
- concludes by reflecting on the experience and connecting it to a broader theme

Mentor Text See how this example from "Living Like Weasels" uses sensory language to vividly describe a weasel.

> "He was ten inches long, thin as a curve, a muscled ribbon, brown as fruitwood, soft-furred, alert. His face was fierce, small and pointed as a lizard's; he would have made a good arrowhead."

PLAN

Use the annotation tools in your eBook to find interesting ideas and details about nature. Save each example to your notebook.

Find Inspiration Reread "Living Like Weasels" and one other narrative text in the collection. Take notes about any new perspectives or understanding about the natural world that you gain from the texts. Jot down any ideas or insights inspired by the selections that you want to communicate in your personal narrative. How do these ideas or insights relate to your own experiences with nature?

Brainstorm Write down some ideas for your own narrative. What experience(s) with the natural world have you had that resulted in a new understanding of nature? Think about a hike, a camping trip, a walk in the park, a day at the beach, or a picnic. Then, create a semantic map to generate ideas for your narrative. Include details about themes, people, setting, and events.

Get Organized Organize your notes, using an outline or a graphic organizer. Decide on the structure of your narrative. Look back at the texts you read to help you. Ask yourself these questions about each one:

- How does the story begin? What techniques are used to engage the audience?
- How does the writer develop the narrative? What is the sequence of events? How are the main ideas organized?
- How does the writer use setting, people or characters, conflict, and events to reveal a theme about the natural world?
- How does the narrative end? Is there a final reflection on nature?

Flesh out your narrative with descriptive details. Visualize the places and people in your narrative, and write down details about them. Be sure to include qualities and characteristics that make them unique. Reveal the insight you gained from your experience.

ACADEMIC VOCABULARY

As you draft your personal narrative, be sure to use these words.

encounter
intensity
restore
theme
visualize

Interactive Lessons

To help you structure your narrative, complete the following lesson in Writing Narratives:
• Narrative Structure

PRODUCE

my WriteSmart

Write your rough draft in *my*WriteSmart. Focus on getting your ideas down rather than on perfecting your choice of language.

Draft Your Narrative Write a draft of your narrative, following your notes, outline, and/or graphic organizers.

- Begin by introducing your audience to the setting, people, and experience that will be central to the narrative.
- Describe a chronological sequence of events.
- Write from the first-person point of view, and allow your own unique voice to shine through.
- Use sensory language and descriptive details to make the setting, people, and events realistic for your audience.
- Provide a powerful conclusion. A personal narrative should reflect on the events and connect the experience to a broad theme.

REVISE

Have your partner or a group of peers review your draft in *my*WriteSmart. Ask your reviewers to note where you might add descriptive details or sensory language.

Practice Your Presentation When you deliver your narrative, you will need to make it come alive through your use of volume, eye contact, and gestures. Mark places in the text where you might emphasize a word, use gestures, or make eye contact to convey meaning. Practice your speech to make sure you can pronounce every word correctly.

Review Your Draft Have a partner or group of peers review your draft. Use the following chart to revise your draft.

Questions	Tips	Revision Techniques
Does the beginning of the narrative introduce the setting and people?	**Underline** details that reveal the setting. **Highlight** the names of the important people in the narrative.	**Add** information about the setting and people, if needed.
Does the narrative relate a clear, logical sequence of events?	**Number** the sequence of events as they appear in the narrative.	**Reorder** events in chronological order, if needed.
Is the point of view consistent throughout?	**Note** any instances where the point of view changes.	**Change** any pronouns to make the point of view consistent.
Does the narrative use sensory language to describe people, places, and events?	**Highlight** details that appeal to the senses.	**Elaborate** with sensory details about people, places, and events.
Are narrative techniques such as dialogue, pacing, and description included?	**Note** at least one example of each narrative technique in your story.	**Elaborate** by adding more narrative techniques as needed.
Does the conclusion reflect on the experience and connect it to a broader theme?	**Underline** sentences that reflect on the experience. **Highlight** sentences that connect the experience to a broader theme.	**Add** sentences that reflect on the experience or connect the experience to a broader theme, if needed.

Interactive Lessons

To help you edit your presentation, complete the following lesson in *Giving a Presentation:*

- The Content of Your Presentation: Narrative

Language and Style: Add Details

Read the following passage from Rick Bass's "The Hermit's Story."

> "She worked the dogs all summer and into the autumn, and finally had them ready for field trials. She took them back up to Gray Owl—way up in Saskatchewan—driving all day and night in her old truck, which was old even then. . . ."

Note how Bass includes phrases that provide detail on the time ("all summer and into the autumn"), place ("back up to Gray Owl"), and manner ("driving all day and night in her old truck"). Look for places where you can expand sentences by adding details that convey information about actions and effectively re-create your experience.

PRESENT

Deliver Your Narrative When your final draft is completed, read your narrative to a small group. Use your voice and gestures to present a lively reading of the narrative. Be prepared to answer questions or respond to comments from your group members.

PERFORMANCE TASK RUBRIC

PERSONAL NARRATIVE

	Ideas and Evidence	Organization	Language
4	• The introduction creates a vivid impression, clearly establishes the setting, and identifies the experience. • Descriptive details, realistic dialogue, and reflection dramatically re-create the experience. • The conclusion powerfully summarizes the importance of the experience and connects it to a broader theme.	• The organization is effective; ideas are arranged logically and events are organized chronologically. • The pace is effective. • Well-chosen transitions clearly connect ideas and show the sequence of events.	• A consistent, first-person point of view creates a unique voice. • Sensory language is used creatively to describe people, places, and events in vivid ways. • Sentence beginnings, lengths, and structures vary and have a rhythmic flow. • Spelling, capitalization, and punctuation are correct. If handwritten, the narrative is legible. • Grammar and usage are correct.
3	• The introduction identifies the experience but could do more to present the setting and engage readers. • More descriptive details, dialogue, and reflection are needed to re-create the experience. • The conclusion summarizes most of the writer's ideas and feelings about the experience.	• The organization of ideas is generally logical; the sequence of events is confusing in a few places. • At times, the pace is too slow or too fast. • A few more transitions are needed to explain the sequence of events.	• The point of view shifts from the first person in a few places. • More sensory language is needed to describe people, places, and events. • Sentence beginnings, lengths, and structures vary somewhat. • Several spelling, capitalization, and punctuation mistakes occur. If handwritten, the narrative is mostly legible. • Some grammatical and usage errors are repeated in the narrative.
2	• The introduction is mundane; it mentions an experience and hints at the setting. • A few descriptive details create lively scenes, but most details are commonplace; dialogue and reflection are lacking. • The conclusion lacks any reflection on the importance of the experience.	• The organization of ideas often doesn't follow a pattern; the sequence of events is sometimes confusing. • The pace is somewhat choppy and distracting to the reader. • More transitions are needed throughout to clarify the sequence of events.	• The narrative frequently shifts from the first-person point of view. • The narrative lacks sensory language in many key parts. • Sentence structures barely vary, and some fragments or run-on sentences are present. • Spelling, capitalization, and punctuation are often incorrect but do not cause confusion. If handwritten, the narrative may be partially illegible. • Grammar and usage are incorrect in many places.
1	• The introduction does not focus on an experience or establish a setting. • Details, dialogue, and reflection are irrelevant or missing. • The narrative lacks a conclusion.	• The narrative is not organized; information and details are presented randomly. • The pace is ineffective. • Transitions are not used, making the narrative difficult to understand.	• The narrative lacks a consistent point of view. • Sensory language is not used. • Repetitive sentence structure, fragments, and run-on sentences make the writing hard to follow. • Spelling, capitalization, and punctuation are mostly incorrect. If handwritten, the narrative may be partially or mostly illegible. • Many grammatical and usage errors change the meaning of the writer's ideas.

Writing Arguments

Many of the Performance Tasks in this book ask you to craft an argument in which you support your ideas with text evidence. Any argument you write should include the following sections and characteristics.

Introduction

Clearly state your **claim**—the point your argument makes. As needed, provide context or background information to help readers understand your position, possibly citing expert opinions to establish the knowledge base for your claim. Note the most common opposing views as a way to distinguish and clarify your ideas. From the very beginning, make it clear for readers why your claim is strong; consider providing an overview of your reasons or a quotation that emphasizes your view in your introduction.

EXAMPLES

Vague claim: Social media is good for learning.	**Precise, knowledgeable claim:** According to a leading digital news source, teachers across the nation find that social media helps students make gains in education.
Opposing views presented without reference to writer's claim: Teachers complain that students can't pay attention anymore.	**Writer's claim distinguished from opposing view:** While one recent study said teachers blame social media for students' diminishing attention spans, the study also showed that today's connected students are more self-sufficient learners.
Confusing relationship of ideas: A Portland, Oregon, teacher piloted a social media site in her own classroom. Grades will increase and absenteeism will decrease school-wide.	**Logical relationship of ideas:** If the recent experience of a program piloted in Portland, Oregon, is any indication, social media sites around each school subject area will cause grades and attendance to improve within a year.

Development of Claims

The body of your argument must provide logical reasons for your claim and thoroughly support those reasons with relevant evidence. A **reason** tells why your claim is valid; **evidence** provides specific examples that illustrate a reason. In developing your claim, you should also refute **counterclaims,** or opposing views, with reasons and evidence. To demonstrate that you have thoroughly considered your view, provide a well-rounded look at both the strengths and limitations of your claim and opposing claims. Consider how much your audience may already know about your topic to avoid boring or confusing them. Consider, too, your audience's values; by failing to recognize their biases, you may miss the mark entirely.

EXAMPLES

Claim lacking reasons: Teachers should use social media.	**Claim developed by reasons:** Social media is a big part of most students' lives, and it's not going away; it makes sense to use social media to advance educational goals.
Omission of limitations: If educators ignore social media, they are totally disconnected from students' reality.	**Fair discussion of limitations:** Of course, other digital tools, like search engines and educational websites, also engage students and play a significant role in their education.
Inattention to audience's knowledge: Most adults probably don't understand that social media is where young people get together online.	**Awareness of audience's knowledge:** If you're one of the nearly 50% of adults in the U.S. that use social media, you already understand its potential for enhancing communication.

continued

Ignorance of audience's bias: Teachers don't understand that sitting in a classroom is boring; we can't wait to check our phones!	**Recognition of audience's bias:** If teachers feel they must compete with social media for students' attention, it makes sense to engage them through that media.

Links Among Ideas

Even the strongest reasons and evidence will fail to sway readers if it is unclear how the reasons relate to the central claim of an argument. Use transitional words and phrases, and also clauses and even entire sentences, as bridges between ideas you have already discussed and ideas you are introducing. By demonstrating control over your language and syntax through the skilled use of transitional expressions, you'll enhance your credibility as a writer. Virginia Tufte's ***Artful Sentences*** is a well-known guide to syntax.

EXAMPLES

Transitional word linking reason to claim: Even students who are uncomfortable speaking up in class will interact with teachers and other students through a virtual community; **therefore,** social media allows more students to become engaged in the learning process.
Transitional phrase linking reason and evidence: Social media can help students feel better about themselves. **According to one study,** about half the students who labeled themselves as "shy" said that social media helped them feel more confident and outgoing.
Transitional clause linking claim and counterclaim: With social media's omnipresence in the world outside of school, it makes no sense for classrooms to be utterly disconnected. **But valid concerns create obstacles to the widespread use of social media in schools:** educators worry about the safety and privacy issues surrounding its use.

Appropriate Style and Tone

An effective argument is most often written in a direct and formal style. The style and tone you choose in an argument should not be an afterthought—the way you express your argument can either drive home your ideas or detract from them. Even as you argue in favor of your viewpoint, take care to remain objective in tone; avoid using loaded language when discussing opposing claims.

EXAMPLES

Informal style, inattention to conventions: Social media in schools makes sense—just get it done!	**Formal style:** Because in-school social media offers so many educational as well as emotional benefits, it is logical for our school to create or adopt a social media site.
Biased tone: Nervous Nellies need to Google *social media safe for schools* and stop wringing their hands.	**Objective tone:** While its detractors have valid safety and privacy concerns, social media specifically designed for school settings already exists and is easy to adopt.

Conclusion

Your conclusion may range from a sentence to a full paragraph, but it must wrap up your argument in a satisfying way; a conclusion that sounds tacked-on helps your argument no more than providing no conclusion at all. A strong conclusion is a logical extension of the argument you have presented. It carries forth your ideas through an inference, question, quotation, or challenge.

EXAMPLES

Inference: The migration to social media in the classroom will require a leap by administrators and teachers.
Quotation: To paraphrase Marshall MacLuhan, the (social) medium is the message.
Question: Students have gotten the message; have educators?
Challenge: If so, they need to do more than nod to social media through Twitter feeds; they need to adopt and implement fully functional, school-wide social media tools.

Writing Informative Texts

Most of the Performance Tasks in this book ask you to write informational or explanatory texts in which you present a topic and examine it thoughtfully, through a well-organized analysis of relevant content. Any informative or explanatory text that you create should include the following parts and features.

Introduction

Develop a strong **thesis statement.** That is, clearly state your **topic** and the **organizational framework** through which you will develop a unified composition, in which each new idea logically flows from and extends the one before it. For example, you might state that your text will compare ideas, examine causes and effects, or analyze a single text or a group of texts.

EXAMPLE

Topic: Shakespeare's *Hamlet*
Sample Thesis Statements
Compare-contrast analysis: Hamlet and his foil Laertes represent two different views of revenge—Laertes being unequivocal about the need to repay bloodshed with bloodshed, and Hamlet perseverating about the futility of vengeance.
Cause-effect analysis: Hamlet's hesitancy to undertake revenge inadvertently causes the deaths of many characters in the play.
Evaluation: Hamlet's "To be or not to be" soliloquy is often interpreted as a contemplation of suicide; however, this interpretation is not borne out by the hero's actions throughout the play.

Clarifying the organizational framework up front will help you organize the body of your essay, suggesting **headings** you can use to guide your readers or graphics that might illustrate the text. Most important, it can help you identify any ideas that you may need to clarify. For example, if you are analyzing the cause and effect of the deaths in *Hamlet,* you may use the following framework:

Initial cause: Hamlet hesitates to heed the will of his father's ghost.

▼

He pretends madness while investigating his uncle's guilt.

▼

Polonius spies on Hamlet due to his strange behavior.

▼

Hamlet accidentally kills Polonius.

▼

Ophelia, distraught at her father's murder by her beloved, kills herself, etc.

Development of the Topic

In the body of your text, flesh out the organizational framework you established in your introduction with strong supporting paragraphs. Include only the most significant evidence relevant to your topic. If you are using outside sources, don't rely on a single source, and make sure the sources you do use are reputable and current. The table shows the types of support you might use to develop different types of topics. It also shows how transitions link text sections, create cohesion, and clarify the relationships among ideas.

Types of Support in Explanatory/ Informative Texts (in italics)	Uses of Transitions in Explanatory/ Informative Texts
Fact: *While Hamlet could not have known that his elaborate ruse to "catch the conscience of the king" would ultimately result in a pile of dead bodies, it certainly seemed unnecessary.* After all, *there were three other witnesses to the ghost.*	The entire transitional sentence introduces a fact supporting Hamlet's excessive hesitancy.
Concrete details: Hamlet doesn't truly understand the inevitability of death until he holds it in his hands, contemplating *the skull of Yorick,* the jester to whom he was close as a child.	A transitional clause explains the significance of a concrete detail in a literary evaluation.
Textual evidence: Unlike Hamlet, who barely seems to know where to direct his angst, Laertes' rage after Ophelia's death is immediate and visceral: *"O, treble woe / Fall ten times treble on that cursèd head / Whose wicked deed thy most ingenious sense / Deprived of thee!"*	The phrase *Unlike Hamlet* signals the use of a quotation from Act V, Scene 1, to support comparison between Hamlet and Laertes.

You can't always include all of the information you'd like to in a short essay, but you can plan to point readers directly to useful **multimedia links** either in the body of or at the end of your essay.

Style and Tone

Use formal English to establish your credibility as a source of information. To project authority, use the language of the domain, or field, that you are writing about. However, be sure to define unfamiliar terms and avoid jargon. Provide extended definitions when your audience is likely to have limited knowledge of the topic. Using quotations from reputable sources can also give your text authority; be sure to credit the source of quoted material. In general, keep the tone neutral, avoiding slangy or biased expressions. However, don't shy away from figurative language: Well-placed metaphors, similes, and analogies can convey a complex idea more succinctly than a paragraph of strictly objective language.

Informal, biased language: Who knows why we do what we do, but still, it's no accident that Hamlet was so spineless.	**Formal style, neutral tone, with figurative language to express complex ideas:** Assigning causation to the actions of literary characters may seem as pointless as playing a game of "What if?" with history. Shakespeare made the characters do what they do to forward the plot. However, ample evidence suggests that Shakespeare intended to highlight the consequences of Hamlet's equivocating nature.

Conclusion

Wrap up your essay with a concluding statement or section that sums up or extends the information in your essay.

EXAMPLES

Articulate implications: Though Shakespeare makes all of the play's character's pay dearly for Hamlet's hesitation, he was not condemning his lack of certitude. Instead, he was making a broader statement about turmoil we all face when confronted with a moral dilemma.
Emphasize significance: If "To be, or not to be" is not a question about suicide but about fear of death, Hamlet's change of heart in Act V makes much more sense. He never contemplated taking his own life to avoid dealing with unpleasant reality; his struggle was always with whether he should risk his life in the first place.

Writing Narratives

When you compose a fictional tale or a factual account of something that happened to you, you are writing in the narrative mode. That means telling a story with a beginning, a climax, and a conclusion. Though there are important differences between fictional and nonfiction narratives, you use similar processes to develop them.

Identify a Significant Problem or Situation, or Make an Observation

For a nonfiction narrative, dig into your memory bank for a significant problem you dealt with or an important observation you've made about life. For fiction, try to invent a problem or situation that can unfold in interesting ways.

EXAMPLES

Observation (nonfiction)	Grandparents are often the best people to turn to when you're feeling isolated or ashamed.
Situation (fiction)	Marissa's parents didn't understand what she meant by "gap year." They thought she wanted to work in retail rather than go to college.

Establish a Point of View

Decide who will tell your story. If you are writing a reflective essay about an important experience or person in your own life, you will be the narrator of the events you relate. If you are writing a work of fiction, you can choose to create a first-person narrator or tell the story from the third-person point of view. In that case, the narrator can focus on one character or reveal the thoughts and feelings of all the characters. The examples below show the differences between a first- and third-person narrator.

First-person narrator (nonfiction)	When I smashed the rear end of my mother's car in the library parking lot, she just shook her head in utter disbelief; then she extended her hand, silently demanding the key back. I would never drive that car again, her look told me.
Third-person narrator (fiction)	She felt her stomach tighten as her parents stared at her blankly. She realized this would be a difficult conversation.

Gather Details

To make real or imaginary experiences come alive, you will need to use techniques such as description and dialogue. The questions in the left column in the chart can help you imagine or recall details that will flesh out your narrative. You don't have to respond in full sentences, but try to capture the sights, sounds, and feelings that bring your narrative to life.

Who, What, When, Where?	Narrative Techniques
People: Who are the people or characters involved in the experience? What did they look like? What did they do or say?	**Description:** My mother's lips pursed, eyes burning; my grandfather's wrinkled fingers holding the newspaper as he sits in his chair. **Dialogue:** "Did I ever tell you about the time your mother totaled my sedan?" Grampa asked.
Experience: What led up to or caused the event? What is the main event in the experience? What happened as a result of the event?	**Description:** I didn't have to go to the library to do homework; I was hoping to see a girl I had a crush on. She wasn't even there. The only thing that got crushed was my mother's bumper. Why are the parking spaces so small? For ruining the bumper on her new car, it seemed I had lost driving privileges indefinitely.

continued

Who, What, When, Where?	Narrative Techniques
Places: When and where did the events take place? What were the sights, sounds, and smells of this place?	**Description:** It happened during my junior year. I had just gotten my license, and I was just getting used to the independence it brought me. Other than the surprisingly strong jarring my body felt when I hit the other car, and the loud crunch, I also remember the smell of beef stew that was simmering in the house when I got home.

Sequence Events

Before you begin writing, list the key events of the experience or story in chronological, or time, order. Place a star next to the point of highest tension—for example, the point at which a key decision determines the outcome of events. In fiction, this point is called the climax, but a gripping nonfiction narrative will also have a climactic event.

To build suspense—the uncertainly a reader feels about what will happen next—you'll want to think about the pacing or rhythm of your narrative. Consider disrupting the chronological order of events by beginning at the end and then starting over. Or interrupt the forward progression or flow of events with a flashback, which takes the reader to an earlier point in the narrative. Another way to build suspense is with multiple plot lines.

Use Vivid Language

As you revise, make an effort to use vivid language. Use precise words and phrases to describe feelings and action. Use telling details to show, rather than directly state, what a character is like. Use sensory language that lets readers see, feel, hear, smell, and taste what you or your characters experienced. Overall, select language that conveys a consistent tone throughout your narrative.

First Draft	Revision
I heard a crash and felt a thump.	The unpleasant sound of metal hitting metal—hard—hit my ears as my head snapped back against the headrest. [sensory details]
My mother glared at me, and my grandfather just sat there.	While my mother stood in mute judgment, my peripheral vision caught my grandfather's head peeking around the newspaper, which was quivering in his hands. Was he suppressing laughter? [telling details]
I was angry and embarrassed.	As I lay on my bed, replaying the accident in my mind, I castigated myself for being so careless and for having lost my driving privileges in the dubious pursuit of a girl who probably didn't even know my name. [precise words and phrases]

Conclusion

At the conclusion of the narrative, you or your narrator will reflect on the meaning of the events. The conclusion should follow logically from the climactic moment of the narrative. The narrator of a personal narrative usually reflects on the significance of the experience—the lessons learned or the legacy left. A fictional narrative will end with the resolution of the conflict described over the course of the story.

EXAMPLE

> The next day, Grampa took me out to drive—in *his* car.
>
> "I like what it says on that rearview mirror," Grampa said.
>
> "'Objects in the mirror are closer than they appear'?"
>
> "Old age is like looking into the rearview mirror. It gives you a broader perspective. When your mom totaled my car, I was just as angry with her as she is with you. But now I can see that I was more scared than angry. And what you need isn't to have the keys taken away—well, not for long, anyway—but to practice driving. So buckle up. And check your mirrors."

Conducting Research

W 2a–f, W 7, W 8

The Performance Tasks in this book will require you to complete research projects related to the texts you've read in the collections. Whether the topic is stated in a Performance Task or is one you generate, the following information will guide you through your research project.

Focus Your Research and Formulate a Question

Some topics for a research project can be effectively covered in three pages; others require an entire book for a thorough treatment. Begin by developing a topic that is neither too narrow nor too broad for the time frame of the assignment. Also check your school and local libraries and databases to help you determine how to choose your topic. If there's too little information, you'll need to broaden your focus; if there's too much, you'll need to limit it.

With a topic in hand, formulate a research question; it will keep you on track as you conduct your research. A good research question cannot be answered in a single word and should be open-ended. It should require investigation. You can also develop related research questions to explore your topic in more depth.

EXAMPLES

Possible topics about George Orwell	• How Orwell's writings reflect the concerns of the day—too broad • How Big Brother is like Stalin—too narrow • What ideas or events inspired Orwell to write *1984*?
Research question	• How was Orwell's own world like the world he presents in *1984*?
Related questions	• What threats to personal freedom existed in Britain after World War II? • What was occurring in the Soviet Union at that time? • Why do people compare Big Brother to Stalin?

Locate and Evaluate Sources

To find answers to your research question, you'll need to investigate primary and secondary sources, whether in print or digital formats. **Primary sources** contain original, firsthand information, such as diaries, autobiographies, interviews, speeches, and eyewitness accounts. **Secondary sources** provide other people's versions of primary sources in encyclopedias, newspaper and magazine articles, biographies, and documentaries.

Your search for sources begins at the library and on the World Wide Web. Use **advanced search features** to help you find things quickly. Add a minus sign (-) before a word that should not appear in your results. Use an asterisk (*) in place of unknown words. List the name of and location of each possible source, adding comments about its potential usefulness. Assessing, or evaluating, your sources in an important step in the research process. Your goal is to use sources that are credible, or reliable and trustworthy, and that are appropriate to your task, purpose, and audience.

Criteria for Assessing Sources	
Relevance: It covers the target aspect of my topic and helps me achieve my purpose for writing.	• How will the source be useful in answering my research question?
Accuracy: It includes information that can be verified by more than one authoritative source.	• Is the information up-to-date? Are the facts accurate? How can I verify them? • What qualifies the author to write about this topic? Is he or she an authority?

continued

Criteria for Assessing Sources	
Objectivity: It presents multiple viewpoints on the topic.	• What, if any, biases can I detect? Does the writer favor one view of the topic?
Coverage: It covers the topic at a level appropriate for my grade level and audience.	• Is the treatment of the material too juvenile for my audience? Is it too advanced?

Incorporating and Citing Source Material

When you draft your research project, you'll need to include material from your sources. This material can be **direct quotations, summaries,** or **paraphrases** of the original source material. Two well-known **style manuals** provide information on how to cite a range of print and digital sources: the ***MLA Handbook for Writers of Research Papers*** (published by the Modern Language Association) and Kate L. Turabian's ***A Manual for Writers of Research Papers, Theses, and Dissertations*** (published by The University of Chicago Press). Both style manuals provide a wealth of information about conducting, formatting, drafting, and presenting your research, including guidelines for citing sources within the text (called parenthetical citations) and preparing the list of Works Cited, as well as correct use of the mechanics of writing. Your teacher will indicate which style manual you should use. The following examples use the format in the ***MLA Handbook.***

EXAMPLES

Direct quotation [The writer is citing an analysis by literary critic Isaac Deutcher.]	Orwell was satirizing the English and not the Soviets when he created a party that didn't try to "indoctrinate the working class" (35).
Summary [The writer is summarizing a passage from a study of the Cold War.]	Many Europeans (especially the French) respected the Communists not only for helping to win World War II but also for resisting the Nazis (24–25).
Paraphrase [The writer is para-phrasing, or stating in his own words, the same passage summarized above. Since paraphrases include more details from the original passage, they are longer than the summaries.]	Many people respected the Soviet Union's Red Army, which had fought mightily against the Nazis and had been largely responsible for their defeat. . . . French people linked the Communists with their own brave resistance fighters in France (24–25).

As you write, it's important not to rely too heavily on any one source but to synthesize information from a variety of sources. Furthermore, any material from sources must be completely documented, or you will commit **plagiarism,** the unauthorized use of someone else's words or ideas. Plagiarism is not honest. As you take notes for your research project, be sure to keep complete information about your sources so that you can cite them correctly in the body of your paper. This applies to all sources, whether print or digital. Having complete information will also enable you to prepare the list of Works Cited. The list of Works Cited, which concludes your research project, provides author, title, and publication information for both print and digital sources. The following section shows the ***MLA Handbook's*** citation formats for a variety of sources.

MLA Citation Guidelines

You may be able to find free websites that help you create citations for research papers. While these sites may save time, you should always check your citations carefully before you turn in your paper. The MLA (Modern Language Association) has developed guidelines for documenting research. You can follow these examples to create the Works Cited list for your research paper.

Books

One author

Orwell, George. *1984 and Related Readings*. 1949. Evanston: McDougal, 1998. Print.

Two authors or editors

Isaacs, Jeremy, and Taylor Downing. *Cold War: An Illustrated History, 1945–1991*. Boston: Little, 1998. Print.

Three authors or editors

Randolph, Carolyn, Catherine Coleman, and Thomas Mullens. *The Soviet Union During the Stalin Years*. Dallas: Strom, 2008. Print.

Four or more authors or editors

List only the first author followed by the abbreviation* et al.*, which means "and others."

Reed, Nahid, et al. *Orwell the Satirist*. Milwaukee: Steuben, 2008. Print.

Parts of Books

An introduction, a preface, a foreword, or an afterword written by someone other than the author or authors of a work

Symons, Julian. Introduction. *Nineteen Eighty-Four*. By George Orwell. New York: Knopf, 1992. ix–xiii. Print.

A poem, a short story, an essay, or a chapter in a collection of works

Pritchett, V.S. "1984." *Twentieth Century Interpretations of 1984*. Ed. Samuel Hynes. Englewood Cliffs: Prentice, 1971. 20–23. Print.

A poem, a short story, an essay, or a chapter in an anthology of works by several authors

Orwell, George. "Shooting an Elephant." *The Great English and American Essays*. Ed. Edmund Fuller. New York: Avon, 1964. Print.

A novel or play in a collection

Orwell, George. *Animal Farm*. The Penguin Complete Novels of George Orwell. Harmondsworth, Eng.: Penguin, 1983. Print.

Magazines, Newspapers, and Encyclopedias

An article in a newspaper

Vincent, Anne-Marie. "In the Land of Big Brother: Six Decades Later." *Fairview Press* 7 July 2008: B12. Print.

An article in a newspaper accessed from a database

Schorer, Mark. "An Indignant and Prophetic Novel." *New York Times* 12 June 1949: BR1. *ProQuest Historical Newspapers*. Web. 9 Apr. 2010.

An article in a magazine or journal

Mayers, Oswald J. "The Road to 1984: George Orwell, the life that shaped the vision." *Library Journal* 15 Nov. 1986: 68. Print.

An article in an encyclopedia

Fisher, Christopher T. "Cold War." *Encyclopedia of Espionage, Intelligence, and Security*.

Eds. K. Lee Lerner and Brenda Wilmoth Lerner. 3 vols. Detroit: Gale, 2004.

Miscellaneous Nonprint Sources

An interview

Delibes, Taisha. Personal interview. 19 Mar. 2011.

A video recording or film

Nineteen Eighty-Four. Dir. Michael Radford. Perf. John Hurt, Richard Burton, Suzanna Hamilton, and Cyril Cusack. 1984. MGM, 2003. DVD.

A sound recording

Fears, J. Rufus. "George Orwell, *1984*." *Books That Have Made History: Books That Can Change Your Life*. Part 2 of 3. Chantilly, VA: Teaching Company, 2005. CD.

Electronic Publications

A document from an Internet site

Author or compiler	Title or description of document	Title of Internet site
Bixby, Ilana.	"George Orwell's London."	*George Orwell: Lone Crusader.*

Site sponsor	Date of Internet site	Medium of Publication	Date of access
Orwell Institute.	Jan. 2008.	Web.	9 Apr. 2010.

An Online Book or E-Book

Bloom, Harold. *George Orwell's Nineteen Eighty-Four*. New York: Chelsea, 1996. *Netlibrary*.

A CD-ROM

"Stalin, Joseph." *Britannica Student Encyclopedia*. 2004 ed. Chicago: Encyclopædia Britannica, 2004. CD-ROM.

Participating in Collaborative Discussions

SL 1a-d

Often, class activities, including the Performance Tasks in this book, will require you to work collaboratively with classmates. Whether your group will analyze a work of literature or try to solve a community problem, use the following guidelines to ensure a productive discussion.

Prepare for the Discussion

A productive discussion is one in which all the participants bring useful information and ideas to share. If your group will discuss a short story the class read, first re-read and annotate a copy of the story. Your annotations will help you quickly locate evidence to support your points. Participants in a discussion about an important issue should first research the issue and bring notes or information sources that will help guide the group. If you disagree with a point made by another group member, your case will be stronger if you back it up with specific evidence from your sources.

EXAMPLES

Disagreeing without evidence: Our school should not have done away with vocational training. Not everyone wants to go to college.

Providing evidence for disagreement: Not everyone wants to go to college, and I have proof: I'm one of them. I want to be an electrician, and four-year colleges don't prepare electricians.

Set Ground Rules

Your group's rules will depend on what you are expected to accomplish. A discussion of a poem's theme will be unlikely to produce a consensus; however, a discussion aimed at developing a solution to a problem should result in one strong proposal arrived at with the participation of all group members. Answer the following questions to set ground rules that fit your group's purpose:

- What will this group produce? A range of ideas, a single decision, a plan of action, or something else?
- How much time is available? How much of that time should be allotted to each part of our discussion (presenting ideas, summarizing or voting on final ideas, creating a product such as a written analysis or speech)?
- What roles need to be assigned within the group? Do we need a leader, a note-taker, a timekeeper, or other specific roles?
- What is the best way to synthesize our group's ideas? Should we take a vote, list group members as "for" or "against" in a chart, or use some other method to reach consensus or sum up the results of the discussion?

Move the Discussion Forward

Everyone in the group should be actively involved in synthesizing ideas. To make sure this happens, ask questions that draw out ideas, especially from less-talkative members. If an idea or statement is confusing, try to paraphrase it, or ask the speaker to explain more about it. If you disagree with a statement, say so politely and explain in detail why you disagree.

SAMPLE DISCUSSION

Effective Behavior	How It Works
Support others' contributions. Tyra states that she believes the ultimate goal of a high school education is to enable students to go to college. She mentions how important it has been in her family that she will be the first to go to college, and the same is true of several of her friends' families. Virgil listens attentively to Tyra. He has just come from a meeting with the school's guidance counselor. He is interested in options for developing a fulfilling career by learning a trade.	Tyra shares her opinion, supporting it with evidence. Virgil disagrees with Tyra but still listens carefully. He avoids making faces or rolling his eyes while Tyra presents her views.
State your own views thoughtfully. When Tyra finishes speaking, Virgil restates her points to make sure he understands her perspective. He comments, "I understand Tyra's position because in my family it is also important to succeed. But college training doesn't prepare everyone for his or her idea of a successful career. People who want to learn a trade, like plumbing or auto mechanics, won't get the training they need in a traditional four-year college. How can high school help prepare students with these ambitions?"	Virgil verifies that he understands Tyra's point. Then, he offers another viewpoint, supporting it with an example. As Virgil did, Tyra listens carefully and respectfully as he explains his perspective.

Respond to Ideas

In a diverse group, everyone may have a different perspective on the topic of discussion, and that's a good thing. Consider what everyone has to say, and don't resist changing your view if other group members provide convincing evidence for theirs. If, instead, you feel more strongly than ever about your view, don't hesitate to say so and provide relevant reasons. Before wrapping up the discussion, try to synthesize the claims made on both sides. That means pulling sometimes contradictory ideas together to arrive at a new understanding.

SAMPLE DISCUSSION

Effective Behavior	How It Works
Synthesize various viewpoints to arrive at a new, alternative understanding. Andreas speaks next. First he summarizes Tyra's and Virgil's opposing views, and then he offers an alternative. "It may look like there is a contradiction here. Either high school spends its limited budget to prepare students for a four-year college, or it re-introduces vocational training at the expense of some parts of the college prep program. What if high school maintains its college-track emphasis but also develops an apprenticeship program with local employers who can teach vocational skills?"	By combining both arguments, Andreas creates an alternative view of the issue. This expands the discussion by allowing different viewpoints to coexist.
Justify your views or consider new ones. Tyra considers what Andreas has said. She prepares to offer more evidence that preparing everyone for a college track is the most reasonable route and extends her argument to respond to Virgil's point as well. Perhaps community colleges can open vocational classes to students who haven't earned their high school degrees yet. She decides to mention this when her turn comes up again. Andreas's point makes Virgil think, too. He makes a note to ask the group, "I think Andreas makes a good point. What other ways could the school provide early access to vocational training?" His question will also expand the discussion.	Tyra and Virgil consider Andreas's point. Andreas's alternative offers an opportunity to delve into the original question and expand their own arguments. Through the contributions of each participant, the discussion has led to a true collaboration about the topic.

Debating an Issue

SL 1a-d, SL 3, SL 4

The selection and collection Performance Tasks in this text will direct you to engage in debates about issues relating to the selections you are reading. Use the guidelines that follow to have a productive and balanced argument about both sides of an issue.

The Structure of a Formal Debate

If you've ever tried to settle a disagreement with a friend or sibling, you've used persuasive techniques to engage in a debate—a discussion in which individuals or teams argue opposing sides of an issue. In a **formal debate,** two teams, each with three members, present their arguments on a given proposition or policy statement. One team argues for the proposition or statement, and the other team argues against it. Each debater must consider the proposition closely and must research both sides of it. To argue convincingly either for or against a proposition, a debater must be familiar with both sides of the issue.

Plan the Debate

The purpose of a debate is to allow participants and audience members to consider both sides of an issue. Use these planning suggestions to hold a balanced and productive debate:

- **Identify Debate Teams** Form groups of six members based on the issue that the Performance Tasks involves. Three members of the team will argue for the affirmative side of the issue—that is, they support the issue. The other three members will argue for the negative side of the issue—that is, they will not support the issue.
- **Appoint a Moderator** The moderator plays a neutral role in the debate, promoting a civil discussion and keeping everyone on task. The moderator begins by introducing the topic of the debate and then recognizes speakers, alternating between affirmative and negative.
- **Assign Debate Roles** One team member introduces the team's claim with supporting reasons and evidence. Another team member exchanges questions with a member of the opposing team to clarify and challenge reasoning. The last member presents a strong closing argument.

Prepare Briefs and Rebuttals

A **brief** is an outline of the debate, accounting for the evidence and arguments of both sides of the **proposition** (topic). Debaters also prepare a **rebuttal,** a follow-up speech to support their arguments and counter the opposition's. Propositions are usually one of four types:

- **Proposition of fact**—Debaters determine whether a statement is true or false. An example is "Social media is changing society for the better."
- **Proposition of value**—Debators determine the value of a person, place, or thing. An example is "Every individual has a moral obligation to help people in need."
- **Proposition of problem**—Debators determine whether a problem exists and whether it requires action.
- **Proposition of policy**—Debators determine the action that will be taken. An example is "The federal government should invest more money to develop alternative energy sources."

Use the following steps to prepare a brief:

- **Gather Information** Consult a variety of primary and secondary sources to gather the most reliable, up- to-date information about the proposition.
- **Identify Key Ideas** Sort out the important points, and arrange them in order of importance.
- **List Arguments For and Against Each Key Idea** Look for strong arguments that support your side of the proposition, and also note those that support your opponents' side.
- **Support Your Arguments** Find facts, quotations, expert opinions, and examples that support your arguments and counter your opponents' arguments.
- **Write the Brief** Begin your brief with a statement of the proposition. Then list the

arguments and evidence that support both sides of the proposition.

The rebuttal is the opportunity to rebuild your case. Use the following steps to build a strong rebuttal:

- Listen to your opponents respectfully. Note the points you wish to overturn.
- Defend what the opposition has challenged.
- Cite weaknesses in their arguments, such as points they overlooked.
- Present counterarguments and supporting evidence.
- Offer your summary arguments. Restate and solidify your stance.

Hold the Debate

A well-run debate can be a vehicle for expressing your opinions in an assertive but respectful manner. Participating in a debate challenges you to synthesize comments made on both sides of an issue, pose probing questions, clarify ideas, and appreciate divergent perspectives.

FORMAL DEBATE FORMAT

Speaker	Role	Time
Affirmative Speaker 1	Present the claim and supporting evidence for the affirmative ("pro") side of the argument.	5 minutes
Negative Speaker 1	Ask probing questions that will prompt the other team to address flaws in the argument.	3 minutes
Affirmative Speaker 2	Respond to the questions posed by the opposing team and counter any concerns.	3 minutes
Negative Speaker 2	Present the claim and supporting evidence for the negative ("con") side of the argument.	5 minutes
Affirmative Speaker 3	Summarize the claim and evidence for the affirmative side and explain why your reasoning is more valid.	3 minutes
Negative Speaker 3	Summarize the claim and evidence for the negative side and explain why your reasoning is more valid.	3 minutes

Evaluate the Debate

Use the following guidelines to evaluate a team in a debate:

- What was the proposition, or premise, being debated? Was each team's stance with respect to the topic— whether affirmative or negative—clear?
- How effectively did the team present reasons and evidence, including evidence from the texts, to support the proposition? Were the links among ideas clear?
- Did the team avoid fallacious, or flawed, reasoning? Did the team avoid disguising exaggerated or distorted evidence with persuasive rhetoric? In general, was the team's word choice appropriate?
- How effectively did the team rebut, or respond to, arguments made by the opposing team?
- Did the speakers maintain eye contact and speak at an appropriate rate and volume?
- Did the speakers observe proper debate etiquette—that is, did they follow the moderator's instructions, stay within their allotted time limits, and treat their opponents respectfully? Did they use verbal techniques of emphasis and tone to highlight their argument rather than to ridicule their opponent?

Reading Arguments

RI 5, RI 6

An argument expresses a position on an issue or problem and supports it with reasons and evidence. Being able to analyze and evaluate arguments will help you distinguish between claims you should accept and those you should not.

Analyzing an Argument

A sound argument should appeal strictly to reason. However, arguments are often used in texts that also contain other types of persuasive devices. An argument includes the following:

- A **claim** is the writer's position on an issue or problem.
- **Support** is any material that serves to prove a claim. In an argument, support usually consists of reasons and evidence.
- **Reasons** are declarations made to justify an action, decision, or belief—for example, "You should sleep on a good mattress in order to avoid spinal problems."
- **Evidence** consists of the specific references, quotations, facts, examples, and opinions that support a claim. Evidence may also consist of statistics, reports of personal experience, or the views of experts.
- A **counterargument** is an argument made to oppose another argument. A good argument anticipates the opposition's objections and provides counterarguments to disprove or answer them.

Claim	Winston Churchill's contribution to victory in World War II was significant.
Reason	Churchill's strong leadership and persuasive rhetoric raised the morale of British citizens and soldiers.
Evidence	British citizens and soldiers never let London fall to the Germans, and British soldiers played a key role in the defeat of Germany.
Counter-argument	His ideas seemed impractical and he was unpopular with much of England, but he succeeded in leading Britain to victory.

Practice and Apply

Use a chart like the one shown to identify the claim, reasons, evidence, and counterargument in the following article.

Should Soft Drinks Be Banned from Schools?

A new substance has joined the list of those banned on school grounds: soft drinks. As the number of obese teenagers rises, there is a growing movement to limit the products of empty calories that are available in school vending machines. Los Angeles has banned the sale of soft drinks on the district's high school and elementary campuses. Other districts are debating whether to implement similar policies. Activists who favor the soda ban say schools must make a choice between student health and vending machine revenues.

Advocates of banning sodas point out that a typical can of soda has at least 10 teaspoons of sugar. Its 140 calories contain no vitamins, minerals, fiber, or other nutritional value. Poor eating habits contribute to teenage obesity. Dr. Jonathan E. Fielding, director of public health for Los Angeles County, describes obesity as a fast-growing, chronic disease that is "entirely preventable."

However, not everyone agrees that carbonated soft drinks are a hazard to students' health. A Georgetown University study found no link between obesity and the soda consumption of 12- to 16-year-olds. Surgeon General David Satcher, while concerned about unhealthy eating habits, considers lack of physical activity another important cause of excess weight.

Some schools are responding to the problem by expanding instead of restricting students' choices. A pilot program that offered Metro Detroit students a choice of pop or flavored milk was so successful that the district installed 80 more milk machines. . . . Other schools offer students a selection of juice-based drinks. Stakes on both sides of the question are high: student health versus

continued

the $750 million that students put into school vending machines each year. The evidence currently available does not prove that the availability of soda pop in school vending machines causes obesity. Until that evidence is provided, I believe banning pop is an extreme solution. Instead, schools should keep both students and the budget healthy by offering both soft drinks and healthier alternatives.

Recognizing Persuasive Techniques

Persuasive texts typically rely on more than just the logical appeal of an argument to be convincing. They also rely on ethical and emotional appeals, as well as other **persuasive techniques**—devices that can sway you to adopt a position or take an action.

The chart shown here explains several of these techniques. Learn to recognize them, and you will be less likely to be influenced by them.

Persuasive Technique	Example
Appeals by Association	
Bandwagon appeal Suggests that a person should believe or do something because "everyone else" does	Don't be the last person on earth to use High Speed TurboWhip for your Internet needs.
Testimonial Relies on endorsements from well-known people or satisfied customers	Seven top chefs from Sonoma County recommend Fivar Cutlery— why not feature it at your next dinner party?
Snob appeal Taps into people's desire to be special or part of an elite group	Diamondshire Hotels provide luxurious accommo-dations in a premier setting.
Transfer Connnects a product, candidate, or cause with a positive emotion or idea	Volunteer with Elderly Help and go home happy—you've touched the life of someone special.
Appeal to loyalty Relies on people's affiliation with a particular group	Buy a bumper sticker from the Skooner Seahawks today and show your true team spirit!
Emotional Appeals	
Appeals to pity, fear, or vanity Use strong feelings, rather than facts, to persuade	Help! Bear Habitat needs refurbishing. Without your dona-tion, polar bears at Cityside Zoo will die!
Word Choice	
Glittering generality Makes a generalization that includes a word or phrase with positive connotations, such as *freedom* or *action-packed,* to promote a product or idea.	Elect E. Willmington and preserve dignity and honor.

Practice and Apply

Identify the persuasive techniques used in the model.

Our city high schools are failing, and they need your help. Half of this city's freshmen drop out before their senior prom. Inner-city students need quality education and well-trained teachers. Your signature on our petition can make it happen and will show your loyalty to our city. Our petition demands re-evaluation of the city's fiscal priorities and a promise that more funds will be allocated for teachers next year. Sign our petition and you'll be in good company. Respected elected officials such as Alderman Donna Jones and County Clerk Tony Fitzharmon support this effort 100 percent. By signing, you will be on the frontline of a most important battle—the battle for the minds of our youth.

Analyzing Logic and Reasoning

When you evaluate the credibility of an argument, look closely at the writer's logic and reasoning. To do this, it is helpful to identify the type of reasoning the writer is using.

The Inductive Mode of Reasoning

When a writer leads from specific evidence to a general principle or generalization, that writer is using **inductive reasoning** to make **inferences,** or logical assumptions, and draw conclusions from them. Here is an example of inductive reasoning.

The Inductive Mode of Reasoning
Specific Facts **Fact 1** *Oliver Twist* is about the hard life of a young orphan boy. **Fact 2** *Great Expectations* is about a poor young man who is given money to become a gentleman. **Fact 3** *David Copperfield* is about a young man's growth into adulthood.
Generalization One of Charles Dickens's main themes is that of a young person maturing into adulthood, often under challenging circumstances.

Strategies for Determining the Soundness of Inductive Arguments

Ask yourself the following questions to evaluate an inductive argument:

- **Is the evidence valid and does it provide sufficient support for the conclusion?** Inaccurate facts lead to inaccurate conclusions. Make sure all facts are accurate.
- **Does the conclusion follow logically from the evidence?** Make sure the writer has used sound reasons—those that can be proved—as a basis for the conclusion and has avoided logical fallacies, such as circular reasoning.
- **Is the evidence drawn from a large enough sample?** Even though there are only three facts listed above, the sample is large enough to support the claim. By qualifying the generalization with words such as *sometimes*, *some*, or *many*, the writer indicates that the generalization is limited to a specific group.

The Deductive Mode of Reasoning

When a writer arrives at a conclusion by applying a general principle to a specific situation, the writer is using **deductive reasoning** to make inferences and draw conclusions. Here's an example.

Practices that harm others should be outlawed.	General principle or premise
Secondhand smoke has been proven to harm others.	Specific situation
Cigarette smoking in public should be outlawed.	Specific conclusion

Strategies for Determining the Soundness of Deductive Arguments

Ask yourself the following questions to evaluate a deductive argument:

- **Is the general principle stated, or is it implied?** Note that writers often use deductive reasoning in an argument without stating the general principle. They assume readers will understand the principle. You need to identify the writer's implicit assumptions.
- **Is the general principle sound?** Don't assume the general principle is sound. Ask yourself whether it is really true based on the evidence.
- **Is the conclusion valid?** To be valid, a conclusion in a deductive argument must follow logically from the general principle and the specific situation.

The following chart shows two conclusions drawn from the same general principle.

General Principle: All members of the soccer fan club wore red yesterday to support their team.	
Accurate Deduction	**Inaccurate Deduction**
Aida is a member of the soccer fan club; therefore, Aida wore red yesterday.	Clyde wore red yesterday; therefore Clyde is a member of the soccer fan club.

The inference that Clyde must be a member of the soccer fan club because he wore red leads to an inaccurate conclusion; Clyde may have chosen red for another reason.

Practice and Apply

Identify the mode of reasoning used in this passage. Determine whether the argument is sound and valid.

Some literary critics believe that numerous works attributed to William Shakespeare may actually have been written by other authors of the time. Edward de Vere was the 17th earl of Oxford and a contemporary of William Shakespeare's. He was a nobleman in Queen Elizabeth I's court, highly educated and very well traveled. Although de Vere was a writer in his early years, no literary manuscripts exist from later in his life. He seemed to have mysteriously stopped writing. Sir Francis Bacon, also a contemporary of Shakespeare's, wrote prolifically throughout his life. Experts note that his correspondences, memoirs,

continued

and notebooks express "coincidences" and parallels with the life of the Bard.

Another writer close to Shakespeare was poet and dramatist Christopher Marlowe. He was allegedly stabbed to death in a bar fight in 1593, but many believe his death was faked and that he lived a long and secret life as a spy for the queen.

All of these three men had the occasion and the talent to have written a number of plays using the nom de plume of William Shakespeare. Therefore, Shakespeare was not the sole author of the works that bear his name.

Identifying Faulty Reasoning

Sometimes an argument at first appears to make sense, but as you take a closer look at the reasoning, you can see it isn't valid, because it is based on a fallacy. A **fallacy** is an error in logic based on inaccurate inferences or invalid assumptions. Learn to recognize these common fallacies.

Type of Fallacy	Definition	Example
Circular reasoning	Supporting a statement by simply repeating it in different words	That restaurant is popular because more people **go there than to any other restaurant in town.**
Either/or fallacy	A statement that suggests that there are only two choices available in a situation that really offers more than two options	**Either** you come pick me up, **or** I will be stranded here forever.
Oversimplification	An explanation of a complex situation or problem as if it were much simpler than it is	If you make the manager laugh during the interview, **you will get the job.**
Overgeneralization	A generalization that is too broad. You can often recognize overgeneralizations by the use of words such as *all, everyone, every time, anything, no one,* and *none.*	**No one ever** wants to wear a bicycle helmet.

continued

Stereotyping	A dangerous type of overgeneralization. Stereotypes are broad statements about people on the basis of their gender, ethnicity, race, or political, social, professional, or religious group.	**People from big cities** are unfriendly.
Attacking the person or name-calling	An attempt to discredit an idea by attacking the person or group associated with it. Candidates often engage in name-calling during political campaigns.	The mayor's new program was developed by a **fool.**
Evading the issue	Refuting an objection with arguments and evidence that do not address its central point	Yes, I broke the window, **but then I mowed the lawn—doesn't the lawn look nice?**
Non sequitur	A conclusion that does not follow logically from the "proof" offered to support it. A non sequitur is sometimes used to win an argument by diverting the reader's attention to proof that can't be challenged.	I'm against building the new stadium, **because I've lived in this town my whole life.**
False cause	The mistake of assuming that because one event occurred after another event, the first event caused the second one to occur	My brother sang in the shower this morning, **so when he auditioned for the spring musical this afternoon, he got the lead role.**
False analogy	A comparison that doesn't hold up because of a critical difference between the two subjects	If you are unable to understand T. S. Eliot, **you probably won't understand modernism.**
Hasty generalization	A conclusion drawn from too little evidence or from evidence that is biased	My job interview did not go well. **I'll never get a job.**

Practice and Apply

Look for examples of faulty reasoning in the following argument. Identify each one, and explain why you identified it as such.

Let's address the proposed expansion of our airport. Opponents claim that the land west of the airport is wetlands and that we can't build on wetlands. Those people are dreamy-eyed do-gooders. Of course you can build on wetlands. Like my father said before me—hard work pays off, and you get what you want. We are now competing internationally, so we need to expand in order to be competitive globally. If we expand runways, it will solve all our city's problems.

Evaluating Persuasive Texts

Learning how to evaluate the credibility of persuasive texts by identifing bias will help you become more selective when doing research and also help you improve your own reasoning and arguing skills. **Bias** is an inclination for or against a particular opinion or viewpoint. A writer may reveal a strongly positive or negative opinion on an issue by presenting only one way of looking at it or by heavily weighting the evidence on one side of the argument. Additionally, the presence of either of the following is often a sign of bias:

Loaded language consists of words with strongly positive or negative connotations that are intended to influence a reader's attitude.

EXAMPLE

A vote for our candidate is a vote to secure your financial future, to ensure safe streets for your children, and to guarantee prosperity for people of all ages. (*Secure future, safe for children*, and *guarantee prosperity* are phrases of loaded language with positive connotations.)

Propaganda is any form of communication that is so distorted that it conveys false or misleading information. Many logical fallacies, such as name-calling, the either/or fallacy, and false causes, are often used in propaganda. The following example shows an oversimplification. The writer uses one fact to support a particular point of view but does not reveal another fact that does not support that viewpoint.

EXAMPLE

Since that new restaurant opened on our block, it is impossible to find a parking place on the street. (The writer does not include the fact that two new apartment buildings recently opened, adding to the demand for street parking.)

Strategies for Evaluating Evidence

It is important to have a set of standards by which you can evaluate persuasive texts. Use the questions below to help you critically assess facts and opinions that are presented as evidence.

- **Are the facts presented verifiable?** Facts can be proved by eyewitness accounts, authoritative sources such as encyclopedias and almanacs, experts, or research.
- **Are the claims presented credible?** Any opinions offered should be supported by facts, research, eyewitness accounts, or the opinions of experts on the topic.
- **Is the evidence thorough?** Thorough evidence leaves no reasonable questions unanswered. If a choice is offered, background for making the choice should be provided. If taking a side is called for, all sides of the issue should be presented.
- **Is the evidence biased?** Be alert to evidence that contains loaded language and other signs of bias.
- **Is the evidence authoritative?** The people, groups, or organizations that provided the evidence should have credentials that verify their credibility.
- **Is it important that the evidence be current?** Where timeliness is crucial, as in the areas of medicine and technology, the evidence should reflect the latest developments in the areas.

Practice and Apply

Read the argument below. Identify the facts, opinions, and elements of bias.

It is time to end the logging industry's destruction of the world's oldest and largest rain forests. Despite protests from environmentalists and conservationists, nature-hating, big-money interests still pay millions to have pristine forests mowed down, just to make roads! This is so their toxic, diesel-pumping logging trucks can haul cut-up pieces of the world's most precious woodlands to the mills. The worst part is that taxpayers fund the whole process—to the tune of $60 million a year. I don't know about you, but I'm going to make sure my hard-earned money isn't contributing to the destruction of the planet.

Strategies for Evaluating an Argument

Make sure that all or most of the following statements are true:

- The argument presents a claim or thesis.
- In a deductive argument, the claim is connected to its support by a **general principle,** or assumption, that most readers would readily agree with. Valid general principle: ***It is the job of a corporation to provide adequate health benefits to full-time employees.*** Invalid general principle: ***It is the job of a corporation to ensure its employees are healthy and physically fit.***
- The reasons make sense.
- The reasons are presented in a logical and effective order.
- The claim and all reasons are adequately supported by sound, credible evidence.
- The evidence is adequate, accurate, and appropriate.
- The logic is sound. There are no instances of faulty reasoning.
- The argument adequately anticipates and addresses reader concerns and counterclaims with counterarguments.

Practice and Apply

Use the preceding criteria to evaluate the strength of the following editorial.

This city should submit a bid to host the summer Olympics. The building and development to plan such an event would take years, but it would also create jobs, lower unemployment, and boost the city's economy. We must face facts: either we submit a bid to host the games, or our city will never grow.

Families citywide would be ecstatic to think that talented, famous people from all over the world would be invited to their lovely communities. There's no doubt families would open up their homes to guests from overseas, because they want our city to be considered the friendliest in the United States.

Some people claim that being a host city is not as important as building new schools, so surplus money should go toward education. These antagonists have simply been too lazy to do proper research. Two other U.S. cities that have hosted the games profited immensely, which means our city could put millions of dollars toward education after the games. You wouldn't want to deprive your child of the chance to see Olympic athletes in action, would you?

We can't afford not to make the bid—and we can't afford not to win it! If the mayor decides not to put in a bid for our city, he'll be just like every other politician, always making wrong choices. So, write a letter to your alderman today, encouraging a vote for the summer games. Our city will be better for it.

L 1, L 2, L 2a, L 3a, L 4a, L 4b

Grammar

Writing that has a lot of mistakes can confuse or even annoy a reader. A business letter with a punctuation error might lead to a miscommunication and delay a reply. A sentence fragment might lower your grade on an essay. Paying attention to grammar, punctuation, and capitalization rules can make your writing clearer and easier to read.

Quick Reference: Parts of Speech

Part of Speech	Function	Examples
Noun	names a person, a place, a thing, an idea, a quality, or an action	
common	serves as a general name, or a name common to an entire group	king, monster, ship, ocean
proper	names a specific, one-of-a-kind person, place, or thing	Chaucer, London, Thames River
singular	refers to a single person, place, thing, or idea	woman, river, leaf, flame
plural	refers to more than one person, place, thing, or idea	women, rivers, leaves, flames
concrete	names something that can be perceived by the senses	rose, church, bell, sky
abstract	names something that cannot be perceived by the senses	contentment, honor, faith, trust
compound	expresses a single idea through a combination of two or more words	sunshine, middle class, mother-in-law
collective	refers to a group of people or things	crop, crew, family
possessive	shows who or what owns something	Burns's, mice's, nature's, fields'
Pronoun	takes the place of a noun or another pronoun	
personal	refers to the person making a statement, the person(s) being addressed, or the person(s) or thing(s) the statement is about	I, me, my, mine, we, us, our, ours, you, your, yours, she, he, it, her, him, hers, his, its, they, them, their, theirs
reflexive	follows a verb or preposition and refers to a preceding noun or pronoun	myself, yourself, herself, himself, itself, ourselves, yourselves, themselves
intensive	emphasizes a noun or another pronoun	(same as reflexives)

continued

Part of Speech	Function	Examples
demonstrative	points to one or more specific persons or things	this, that, these, those
interrogative	signals a question	who, whom, whose, which, what
indefinite	refers to one or more persons or things not specifically mentioned	both, all, most, many, anyone, everybody, several, none, some
relative	introduces an adjective clause by relating it to a word in the clause	who, whom, whose, which, that
Verb	expresses an action, a condition, or a state of being	
action	tells what the subject does or did, physically or mentally	run, reaches, listened, consider, decides, dreamed
linking	connects the subject to something that identifies or describes it	am, is, are, was, were, sound, taste, appear, feel, become, remain, seem
auxiliary	precedes the main verb in a verb phrase	be, have, do, can, could, will, would, may, might
transitive	directs the action toward someone or something; always has an object	The wind **snapped** the young tree in half.
intransitive	does not direct the action toward someone or something; does not have an object	The young tree **snapped.**
Adjective	modifies a noun or pronoun	**frightened** man, **two** epics, **enough** time
Adverb	modifies a verb, an adjective, or another adverb	walked **out, really** funny, **far** away
Preposition	relates one word to another word	at, by, for, from, in, of, on, to, with
Conjunction	joins words or word groups	
coordinating	joins words or word groups used the same way	and, but, or, for, so, yet, nor
correlative	used as a pair to join words or word groups used the same way	both . . . and, either . . . or, neither . . . nor
subordinating	introduces a clause that cannot stand by itself as a complete sentence	although, after, as, before, because, when, if, unless
Interjection	expresses emotion	whew, yikes, uh-oh

Quick Reference: The Sentence and Its Parts

The diagrams that follow will give you a brief review of the essentials of a sentence and some of its parts.

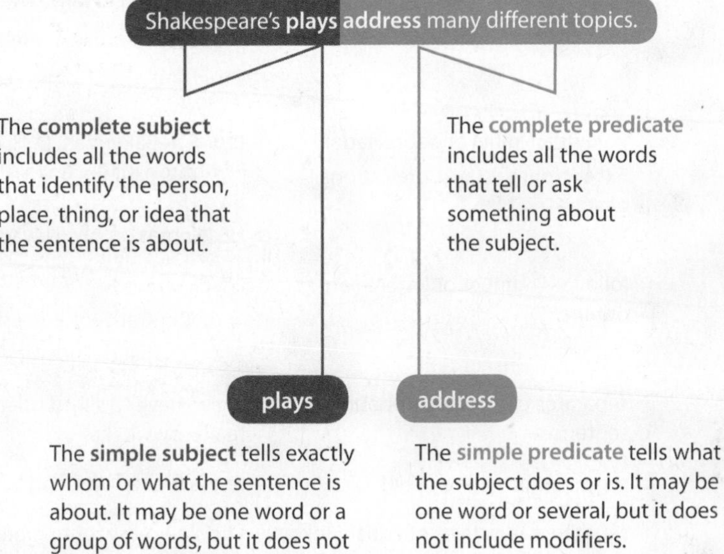

Every word in a sentence is part of a complete subject or a complete predicate.

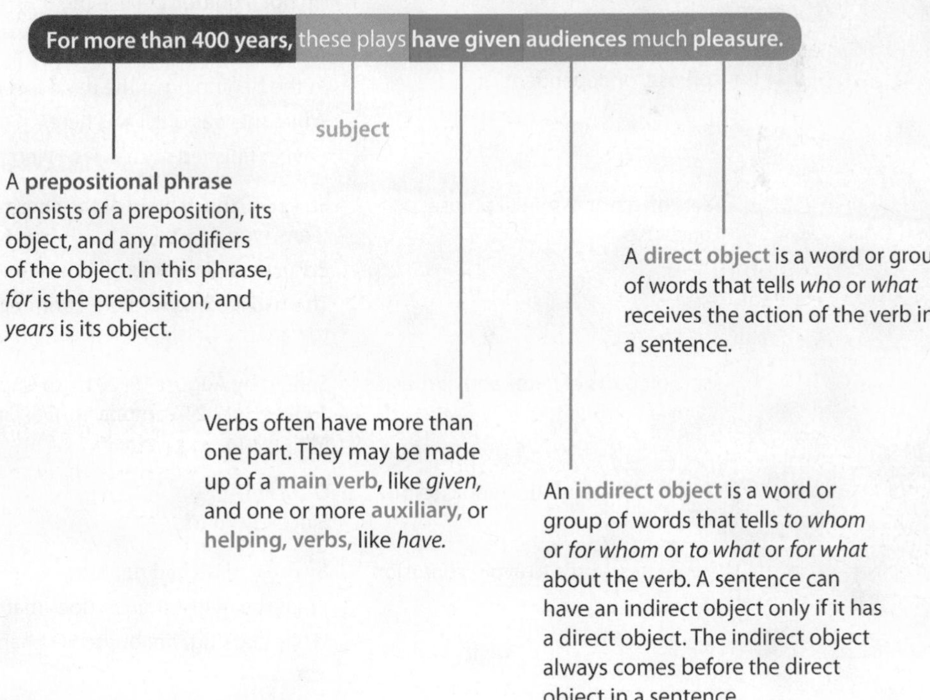

Quick Reference: Punctuation

Mark	Function	Examples
End Marks period, question mark, exclamation point	end a sentence	The games begin today. Who is your favorite contestant? What a play Jamie made!
period	follows an initial or abbreviation **Exception:** postal abbreviations of states	Prof. Ted Bakerman, D. H. Lawrence, Houghton Mifflin Co., P.M., A.D., oz., ft., Blvd., St. NE (Nebraska), NV (Nevada)
period	follows a number or letter in an outline	I. Volcanoes A. Central-vent 1. Shield
Comma	separates parts of a compound sentence	I have never disliked poetry, but now I really love it.
	separates items in a series	She is brave, loyal, and kind.
	separates adjectives of equal rank that modify the same noun	The slow, easy route is best.
	sets off a term of address	O wind, if winter comes . . . Come to the front, children.
	sets off a parenthetical expression	Hard workers, as you know, don't quit. I'm not a quitter, believe me.
	sets off an introductory word, phrase, or dependent clause	Yes, I forgot my key. At the beginning of the day, I feel fresh. While she was out, I was here. Having finished my chores, I went out.
	sets off a nonessential phrase or clause	Ed Pawn, the captain of the chess team, won. Ed Pawn, who is the captain, won. The two leading runners, sprinting toward the finish line, finished in a tie.
	sets off parts of dates and addresses	Send it by August 18, 2010, to Cherry Jubilee, Inc., 21 Vernona St., Oakland, Minnesota.
	follows the salutation and closing of a letter	Dear Jim, Sincerely yours,
	separates words to avoid confusion	By noon, time had run out. What the minister does, does matter. While cooking, Jim burned his hand.

Part of Speech	Function	Examples
Semicolon	separates items in a series if one or more items contain commas	We invited my sister, Jan; her friend, Don; my uncle Jack; and Mary Dodd.
	separates parts of a compound sentence that are not joined by a coordinating conjunction	The small books are on the top shelves; the large books are below. I dusted the books; however, I didn't wipe the shelves.
	separates parts of a compound sentence when the parts contain commas	After I ran out of money, I called my parents; but only my sister was home, unfortunately.
Colon	introduces a list	Those we wrote were the following: Dana, John, and Will.
	introduces a long quotation	Mary Wollstonecraft wrote: "It appears to me necessary to dwell on these obvious truths, because females have been insulted. . . ."
	follows the salutation of a business letter	Dear Ms. Williams: Dear Senator Wiley:
	separates certain numbers	1:28 P.M., Genesis 2:5
Dash	indicates an abrupt break in thought	I was thinking of my mother—who is arriving tomorrow—just as you walked in.
Parentheses	enclose less-important material	Throughout her life (though some might think otherwise), she worked hard. The temperature on this July day (would you believe it?) is 65 degrees!
Hyphen	joins parts of a compound adjective before a noun	She lives in a first-floor apartment.
	joins parts of a compound with *all-*, *ex-*, *self-*, or *-elect*	The president-elect is a well-respected woman.
	joins parts of a compound number (to ninety-nine)	Today, I turn twenty-one.
	joins parts of a fraction	My cup is one-third full.
	joins a prefix to a word beginning with a capital letter	The post-Victorian era was marked by great technological advancements.
	indicates that a word is divided at the end of a line	Yeats knew Lady Gregory, an influen-tial Irish gentlewoman.

continued

Part of Speech	Function	Examples
Apostrophe	used with *s* to form the possessive of a noun or an indefinite pronoun	my friend's book, my friends' books, anyone's guess, somebody else's problem
	replaces one or more omitted letters in a contraction or numbers in a date	don't (omitted *o*), he'd (omitted *woul*), the class of '99 (omitted *19*)
	used with *s* to form the plural of a letter	I had two A's on my report card.
Quotation Marks	set off a speaker's exact words	Sara said, "I'm finally ready." "I'm ready," Sara said, "finally." Did Sara say, "I'm ready"? Sara said, "I'm ready!"
	set off the title of a story, an article, a short poem, an essay, a song, or a chapter	So far, we've read Swift's essay "A Modest Proposal," Eliot's poem "Preludes," and Joyce's short story "Araby."
Ellipses	replace material omitted from a quotation	"Candide listened attentively . . . for he thought Miss Cunegund excessively handsome. . . ."
Italics	indicate the title of a book, a play, a magazine, a long poem, an opera, a film, or a TV series, or the names of ships, trains, and spacecraft	***The Canterbury Tales, The Tragedy of Macbeth, Rolling Stone, Beowulf, Aida, Shakespeare in Love, The Office, Titanic***

Quick Reference: Capitalization

Category	Examples
People and Titles	
Names and initials of people	Samuel Johnson, E. M. Forster
Titles used before or in place of names	Professor Holmes, Senator Long
Deities and members of religious groups	Jesus, Allah, Buddha, Zeus, Baptists, Roman Catholics
Names of ethnic and national groups	Hispanics, Jews, African Americans
Geographical Names	
Cities, states, countries, continents	New York, Maine, Haiti, Africa
Regions, bodies of water, mountains	the South, Lake Erie, Mount Katahdin
Geographic features, parks	Continental Divide, Everglades, Yellowstone
Streets and roads, planets	55 East Ninety-fifth Street, Maple Lane, Venus, Jupiter
Organizations, Events, Etc.	
Companies, organizations, teams	General Motors, Lions Club, Utah Jazz
Buildings, bridges, monuments	the Alamo, Golden Gate Bridge, Lincoln Memorial
Documents, awards	the Constitution, World Cup
Special named events	Super Bowl, World Series
Government bodies, historical periods and events	the Supreme Court, U.S. Senate, Harlem Renaissance, World War II
Days and months, holidays	Friday, May, Easter, Memorial Day
Specific cars, boats, trains, planes	Mustang, *Titanic, California Zephyr*
Proper Adjectives	
Adjectives formed from proper nouns	American League teams, French cooking, Dickensian period, Arctic waters
First Words and the Pronoun *I*	
First word in a sentence or quotation	This is it. He said, "Let's go."
First word of sentence in parentheses that is not within another sentence	The spelling rules are covered in another section. (Consult that section for more information.)
First words in the salutation and closing of a letter	Dear Madam, Very truly yours,
First word in each line of most poetry Personal pronoun *I*	Then am I A happy fly If I live Or if I die.
First word, last word, and all important words in a title	"A Vindication of the Rights of Woman," *Waiting for Godot*

1 Nouns

A **noun** is a word used to name a person, a place, a thing, an idea, a quality, or an action. Nouns can be classified in several ways.

1.1 COMMON NOUNS

Common nouns are general names, common to entire groups.

EXAMPLES: *mountain, country, lake*

1.2 PROPER NOUNS

Proper nouns name specific, one-of-a-kind things.

Common	Proper
mountain, country, lake	Mt. Everest, Italy, Lake Michigan

1.3 SINGULAR AND PLURAL NOUNS

A noun may take a singular or a plural form, depending on whether it names a single person, place, thing, or idea or more than one. Make sure you use appropriate spellings when forming plurals.

Singular	Plural
church, lily, wife	churches, lilies, wives

1.4 COMPOUND AND COLLECTIVE NOUNS

Compound nouns are formed from two or more words but express a single idea. They are written as single words, as separate words, or with hyphens. Use a dictionary to check the correct spelling of a compound noun.

EXAMPLES: *sunshine, middle class, mother-in-law*

Collective nouns are singular nouns that refer to groups of people or things.

EXAMPLES: *army, flock, class, species*

1.5 POSSESSIVE NOUNS

A **possessive noun** shows who or what owns something.

EXAMPLES: *Conrad's, jury's, children's*

2 Pronouns

A **pronoun** is a word that is used in place of a noun or another pronoun. The word or word group to which the pronoun refers is called its **antecedent.**

2.1 PERSONAL PRONOUNS

Personal pronouns change their form to express person, number, gender, and case. The forms of these pronouns are shown in the following chart.

	Nominative	Objective	Possessive
Singular			
First Person	I	me	my, mine
Second Person	you	you	your, yours
Third Person	she, he, it	her, him, it	her, hers, his, its
Plural			
First Person	we	us	our, ours
Second Person	you	you	your, yours
Third Person	they	them	their, theirs

2.2 AGREEMENT WITH ANTECEDENT

Pronouns should agree with their antecedents in number, gender, and person.

If an antecedent is singular, use a singular pronoun.

EXAMPLE: ***Gulliver*** *reaches Lilliput after his ship breaks apart.*

If an antecedent is plural, use a plural pronoun.

EXAMPLES: *The* ***Lilliputians*** *shoot their arrows into Gulliver. Gulliver cuts the* ***arrows*** *into pieces as they fly through the air.*

The gender of a pronoun must be the same as the gender of its antecedent.

EXAMPLES: *The **king** enjoys spending his time with Gulliver. The **queen** places Gulliver in her hand.*

The person of the pronoun must be the same as the person of its antecedent. As the chart in Section 2.1 shows, a pronoun can be in first-, second-, or third-person form.

EXAMPLE: ***They** invite Gulliver into their home.*

Practice and Apply

Rewrite each sentence so that the underlined pronoun agrees with its antecedent.

1. The readers of *Gulliver's Travels* love the book as an adventure story, but you like the humor too.
2. In the book, Gulliver travels to strange lands that she never could have imagined.
3. You would be surprised, too, to find their arms and legs suddenly tied down.
4. At first, the Lilliputians fear for its lives.

2.3 PRONOUN CASE

Personal pronouns change form to show how they function in sentences. Different functions are shown by different cases. The three cases are **nominative, objective,** and **possessive.** For examples of these pronouns, see the chart in Section 2.1.

A **nominative pronoun** is used as a subject or a predicate nominative in a sentence.

An **objective pronoun** is used as a direct object, an indirect object, or the object of a preposition.

SUBJECT OBJECT OBJECT OF PREPOSITION

He explained it to me.

A **possessive pronoun** shows ownership. The pronouns *mine, yours, hers, his, its, ours,* and *theirs* can be used in place of nouns.

EXAMPLE: *These letters are yours.*

The pronouns *my, your, her, his, its, our,* and *their* are used before nouns.

EXAMPLE: *These are your letters.*

WATCH OUT! Many spelling errors can be avoided if you watch out for *its* and *their.* Don't confuse the possessive pronoun *its* with the contraction *it's,* meaning "it is" or "it has." The homonyms *they're* (a contraction of *they are*) and *there* ("in that place") are often mistakenly used for *their.*

TIP To decide which pronoun to use in a comparison, such as "He tells better tales than (I or me)," fill in the missing word(s): *He tells better tales than I **tell.***

Practice and Apply

Replace the underlined words in each sentence with an appropriate pronoun, and identify the pronoun as a nominative, objective, or possessive pronoun.

1. Percy Bysshe Shelley was a romantic poet.
2. Percy Bysshe Shelley's friend Lord Byron was also a well-known poet.
3. The writer Mary Wollstonecraft Shelley was Shelley's wife.
4. Mary's novel *Frankenstein* has entertained readers for nearly 200 years.
5. Many film versions of *Frankenstein* exist.

2.4 REFLEXIVE AND INTENSIVE PRONOUNS

These pronouns are formed by adding *-self* or *-selves* to certain personal pronouns. Their forms are the same, and they differ only in how they are used.

A **reflexive pronoun** follows a verb or a preposition and reflects back on an earlier noun or pronoun.

EXAMPLES: *He threw himself forward.*
Danielle mailed herself the package.

Intensive pronouns intensify or emphasize the nouns or pronouns to which they refer.

EXAMPLES: *The queen herself would have been amused.*
I saw it myself.

WATCH OUT! Avoid using *hisself* or *theirselves.* Standard English does not include these forms.

NONSTANDARD: *He had painted hisself into a corner.*

STANDARD: *He had painted himself into a corner.*

2.5 DEMONSTRATIVE PRONOUNS

Demonstrative pronouns point out things and persons near and far.

	Singular	Plural
Near	this	these
Far	that	those

2.6 INDEFINITE PRONOUNS

Indefinite pronouns do not refer to specific persons or things and usually have no antecedents. The chart shows some commonly used indefinite pronouns.

Singular	Plural	Singular or Plural	
another	both	all	none
anybody	few	any	some
no one	many	more	most
neither	several		

TIP Indefinite pronouns that end in *one, body,* or *thing* are always singular.

INCORRECT: *Anyone who wants their research report can pick it up later today.*

CORRECT: *Anyone who wants his or her research report can pick it up later today.*

If the indefinite pronoun might refer to either a male or a female, *his or her* may be used to refer to it, or the sentence may be rewritten.

EXAMPLES: *Everybody wants his or her report back. All the students want their reports back.*

2.7 INTERROGATIVE PRONOUNS

An **interrogative pronoun** is used to ask a question. The interrogative pronouns are *who, whom, whose, which,* and *what.*

EXAMPLES: *Who is going to the store? What time are we leaving?*

TIP *Who* is used as a subject; *whom*, as an object. To find out which pronoun you need to use in a question, change the question to a statement.

QUESTION: *(Who/Whom) did you meet there?*

STATEMENT: *You met (?) there.*

Since the verb has a subject (*you*), the needed word must be the object form, *whom.*

EXAMPLE: *Whom did you meet there?*

WATCH OUT! A special problem arises when you use an interrupter, such as *do you think,* within a question.

EXAMPLE: *(Who/Whom) do you believe is the more influential musician?*

If you eliminate the interrupter, it is clear that the word you need is *who.*

2.8 RELATIVE PRONOUNS

Relative pronouns relate, or connect, dependent (or subordinate) clauses to the words they modify in sentences. The relative pronouns are *that, what, whatever, which, whichever, who, whoever, whom, whomever,* and *whose.*

Sometimes short sentences with related ideas can be combined by using a relative pronoun.

SHORT SENTENCE: *William Blake was underappreciated by his contemporaries.*

RELATED SENTENCE: *William Blake was both an artist and a poet.*

COMBINED SENTENCE: *William Blake, who was both an artist and a poet, was underappreciated by his contemporaries.*

Practice and Apply

Choose the appropriate interrogative or relative pronoun from the words in parentheses.

1. William Blake wrote *Songs of Innocence,* (who, which) was a collection of poems.
2. (Who, Whom) or what was the inspiration for these poems?
3. Blake based the poems on street ballads and rhymes (that, what) children sang.
4. Blake was a visionary (whom, who) was ahead of his time.

2.9 PRONOUN REFERENCE PROBLEMS

The referent of a pronoun should always be clear.

An **indefinite reference** occurs when the pronoun *it, you,* or *they* does not clearly refer to a specific antecedent.

UNCLEAR: *When making bread, they must not overknead the dough.*

CLEAR: *When making bread, a baker must not overknead the dough.*

A **general reference** occurs when the pronoun *it, this, that, which,* or *such* is used to refer to a general idea rather than a specific antecedent.

UNCLEAR: *Jamie practices piano every day. This has made her an accomplished musician.*

CLEAR: *Jamie practices piano every day. Practicing has made her an accomplished musician.*

Ambiguous means "having more than one possible meaning." An **ambiguous reference** occurs when a pronoun could refer to two or more antecedents.

UNCLEAR: *Sarah talked to Beth while she folded laundry.*

CLEAR: *While Sarah folded laundry, she talked to Beth.*

Practice and Apply

Rewrite the following sentences to correct indefinite, ambiguous, and general pronoun references.

1. In "The Wife of Bath's Tale," it tells about a knight who is sent on a quest to find out what women most desire.
2. The knight is given the choice of either accepting the quest or being put to death. This makes him sorrowful.
3. An old woman provides the knight with the correct answer. This saves his life.
4. The queen agrees to the old woman's request that she marry the knight as a reward.

3 Verbs

A **verb** is a word that expresses an action, a condition, or a state of being.

3.1 ACTION VERBS

Action verbs express mental or physical activity.

EXAMPLES: *I walked to the store.*

3.2 LINKING VERBS

Linking verbs join subjects with words or phrases that rename or describe them.

EXAMPLES: *You are my friend.*

3.3 PRINCIPAL PARTS

Action and linking verbs typically have four principal parts, which are used to form verb tenses. The principal parts are the **present,** the **present participle,** the **past,** and the **past participle.**

Action verbs and some linking verbs also fall into two categories: regular and irregular. A **regular verb** is a verb that forms its past and past participle by adding *-ed* or *-d* to the present form.

Present	Present Participle	Past	Past Participle
shift	(is) shifting	shifted	(has) shifted
hope	(is) hoping	hoped	(has) hoped
stop	(is) stopping	stopped	(has) stopped
marry	(is) marrying	married	(has) married

An **irregular verb** is a verb that forms its past and past participle in some other way than by adding *-ed* or *-d* to the present form.

Present	Present Participle	Past	Past Participle
bring	(is) bringing	brought	(has) brought
swim	(is) swimming	swam	(has) swum
steal	(is) stealing	stole	(has) stolen
grow	(is) growing	grew	(has) grown

3.4 VERB TENSE

The **tense** of a verb indicates the time of the action or state of being. An action or state of being can occur in the present, the past, or the future. There are six tenses, each expressing a different range of time.

The **present tense** expresses an action or state that is happening at the present time, occurs regularly, or is constant or generally true. Use the present part.

NOW: *That ballad sounds great.*

REGULAR: *I read every day.*

GENERAL: *The sun rises in the east.*

The **past tense** expresses an action that began and ended in the past. Use the past part.

EXAMPLE: *The storyteller finished his tale.*

The **future tense** expresses an action or state that will occur. Use *shall* or *will* with the present part.

EXAMPLE: *They will attend the next festival.*

The **present perfect tense** expresses an action or state that (1) was completed at an indefinite time in the past or (2) began in the past and continues into the present. Use *have* or *has* with the past participle.

EXAMPLE: *Poetry has inspired readers throughout the ages.*

The **past perfect tense** expresses an action in the past that came before another action in the past. Use *had* with the past participle.

EXAMPLE: *The messenger had traveled for days before he delivered his knight's response.*

The **future perfect tense** expresses an action in the future that will be completed before another action in the future. Use *shall have* or *will have* with the past participle.

EXAMPLE: *They will have finished the novel before seeing the movie version of the tale.*

TIP The past-tense form of an irregular verb is not paired with an auxiliary verb, but the past-perfect-tense form of an irregular verb is always paired with an auxiliary verb.

INCORRECT: *I have went to that restaurant before.*

INCORRECT: *I gone to that restaurant before.*

CORRECT: *I have gone to that restaurant before.*

3.5 PROGRESSIVE FORMS

The progressive forms of the six tenses show ongoing actions. Use forms of *be* with the present participles of verbs.

PRESENT PROGRESSIVE: *She is rehearsing her lines.*

PAST PROGRESSIVE: *She was rehearsing her lines.*

FUTURE PROGRESSIVE: *She will be rehearsing her lines.*

PRESENT PERFECT PROGRESSIVE: *She has been rehearsing her lines.*

PAST PERFECT PROGRESSIVE: *She had been rehearsing her lines.*

FUTURE PERFECT PROGRESSIVE: *She will have been rehearsing her lines.*

WATCH OUT! Do not shift from tense to tense needlessly. Watch out for these special cases:

- In most compound sentences and in sentences with compound predicates, keep the tenses the same.

  INCORRECT: *We work hard, and they paid us well.*

  CORRECT: *We work hard, and they pay us well.*

- If one past action happened before another, indicate this with a shift in tense.

  INCORRECT: *They wished they started earlier.*

  CORRECT: *They wished they had started earlier.*

Practice and Apply

Identify the tense of the verb(s) in each of the following sentences. If you find an unnecessary tense shift, correct it.

1. The tales of King Arthur and his knights were popular in the Middle Ages, and they continue to be popular today.
2. Gawain, Arthur's nephew, bravely accepts the Green Knight's challenge and will agree to the pact proposed by the Green Knight.
3. After Gawain cuts off the Green Knight's head, the Green Knight remained alive.
4. Gawain meets the Green Knight again, just as the Green Knight had instructed him to do the year before.
5. This time Gawain receives the blow of the Green Knight's ax, but he did not die.

3.6 ACTIVE AND PASSIVE VOICE

The voice of a verb tells whether its subject performs or receives the action expressed by the verb. When the subject performs the action, the verb is in the **active voice.** When the subject is the receiver of the action, the verb is in the **passive voice.**

Compare these two sentences:

ACTIVE: *Gawain and the Green Knight make a pact with each other.*

PASSIVE: *A pact is made between Gawain and the Green Knight.*

To form the passive voice, use a form of **be** with the past participle of the verb.

WATCH OUT! Use the passive voice sparingly. It can make writing awkward and less direct.

AWKWARD: *A meeting between the two knights is arranged.*

BETTER: *The two knights arrange a meeting.*

There are occasions when you will choose to use the passive voice because

- You want to emphasize the receiver: *The king was shot.*
- The doer is unknown: *My books were stolen.*
- The doer is unimportant: *French is spoken here.*

Practice and Apply

For the four items below, identify the boldfaced verb phrase as active or passive.

1. King Arthur **was confronted** by the Green Knight.
2. The Green Knight **had been searching** for someone brave enough to meet his challenge.
3. Gawain **did** not **want** King Arthur to subject himself to the challenge.
4. The Green Knight **was struck** by the ax.

4 Modifiers

Modifiers are words or groups of words that change or limit the meanings of other words. Adjectives and adverbs are common modifiers.

4.1 ADJECTIVES

Adjectives modify nouns and pronouns by telling which one, what kind, how many, or how much.

WHICH ONE: *this, that, these, those*

EXAMPLE: *That girl used to live in my neighborhood.*

WHAT KIND: *large, unique, anxious, moldy*

EXAMPLE: *I bought a unique lamp at the yard sale.*

HOW MANY: *ten, many, several, every, each*

EXAMPLE: *I wake up at the same time every day.*

HOW MUCH: *more, less, little, barely*

EXAMPLE: *We bought more food than we could possibly eat.*

4.2 PREDICATE ADJECTIVES

Most adjectives come before the nouns they modify, as in the previous examples. A **predicate adjective,** however, follows a linking verb and describes the subject.

EXAMPLE: *My friends are very intelligent.*

Be especially careful to use adjectives (not adverbs) after such linking verbs as *look, feel, grow, taste,* and *smell.*

EXAMPLE: *The weather grows cold.*

4.3 ADVERBS

Adverbs modify verbs, adjectives, and other adverbs by telling where, when, how, or to what extent.

WHERE: *The children played outside.*

WHEN: *The author spoke yesterday.*

HOW: *We walked slowly behind the leader.*

TO WHAT EXTENT: *He worked very hard.*

Adverbs may occur in many places in sentences, both before and after the words they modify.

EXAMPLES: *Suddenly the wind shifted.*
The wind suddenly shifted.
The wind shifted suddenly.

4.4 ADJECTIVE OR ADVERB?

Many adverbs are formed by adding *-ly* to adjectives.

EXAMPLES: *sweet, sweetly; gentle, gently*

However, *-ly* added to a noun will usually yield an adjective.

EXAMPLES: *friend, friendly; woman, womanly*

4.5 COMPARISON OF MODIFIERS

Modifiers can be used to compare two or more things. The form of a modifier shows the degree of comparison. Both adjectives and adverbs have three forms: the **positive,** the **comparative,** and the **superlative.**

The **positive form** is used to describe individual things, groups, or actions.

EXAMPLES: *Jonathan Swift was a great satirist.*
He had a savage wit.

The **comparative form** is used to compare two things, groups, or actions.

EXAMPLES: *I think Jonathan Swift was a greater satirist than Voltaire.*
Swift had a more savage wit.

The **superlative form** is used to compare more than two things, groups, or actions.

EXAMPLES: *I think Jonathan Swift was the greatest satirist who ever lived.*
Swift had the most savage wit of any writer.

4.6 REGULAR COMPARISONS

Most one-syllable and some two-syllable adjectives and adverbs have comparatives and superlatives formed by adding *-er* and *-est.* All three-syllable and most two syllable modifiers have comparatives and superlatives formed with *more* and *most.*

Modifier	Comparative	Superlative
tall	taller	tallest
kind	kinder	kindest
droopy	droopier	droopiest
expensive	more expensive	most expensive
wasteful	more wasteful	most wasteful

WATCH OUT! Note that spelling changes must sometimes be made to form the comparatives and superlatives of modifiers.

EXAMPLES: *friendly, friendlier* (Change *y* to *i*, and add the ending.)
sad, sadder (Double the final consonant, and add the ending.)

4.7 IRREGULAR COMPARISONS

Some commonly used modifiers have irregular comparative and superlative forms. They are listed in the following chart.

Modifier	Comparative	Superlative
good	better	best
bad	worse	worst
far	farther *or* further	farthest *or* futhest
little	less *or* lesser	least
many	more	most
well	better	best
much	more	most

4.8 PROBLEMS WITH MODIFIERS

Study the tips that follow to avoid common mistakes:

Farther* and *Further Use *farther* for distances; use *further* for everything else.

Double Comparisons Make a comparison by using *-er/-est* or by using *more/most.* Using *-er* with *more* or using *-est* with *most* is incorrect.

INCORRECT: *I like her more better than she likes me.*

CORRECT: *I like her better than she likes me.*

Illogical Comparisons An illogical or confusing comparison results when two unrelated things are compared or when something is compared with itself. The word *other* or the word *else* should be used in a comparison of an individual member to the rest of a group.

ILLOGICAL: *I think the orchid is more beautiful than any flower.* (implies that the orchid isn't a flower)

LOGICAL: *I think the orchid is more beautiful than any other flower.* (identifies that the orchid is a flower)

Bad* vs. *Badly *Bad,* as an adjective, is used before a noun or after a linking verb. *Badly,* always an adverb, never modifies a noun. Be sure to use the right form after a linking verb.

INCORRECT: *Ed felt badly after his team lost.*

CORRECT: *Ed felt bad after his team lost.*

Good* vs. *Well *Good,* as an adjective, is used before a noun or after a linking verb. *Well* is often an adverb meaning "expertly" or "properly." *Well* can also be used as an adjective after a linking verb when it means "in good health."

INCORRECT: *Helen writes very good.*

CORRECT: *Helen writes very well.*

CORRECT: *Yesterday I felt bad; today I feel well.*

Double Negatives If you add a negative word to a sentence that is already negative, the result will be an error known as a double negative. When using *not* or *-n't* with a verb, use *any-* words, such as *anybody* or *anything,* rather than *no-* words, such as *nobody* or *nothing,* later in the sentence.

INCORRECT: *I don't have no money.*

CORRECT: *I don't have any money.*

Using *hardly, barely,* or *scarcely* after a negative word is also incorrect.

INCORRECT: *They couldn't barely see two feet ahead.*

CORRECT: *They could barely see two feet ahead.*

Misplaced Modifiers Sometimes a modifier is placed so far away from the word it modifies that the intended meaning of the sentence is unclear. Prepositional phrases and participial phrases are often misplaced. Place modifiers as close as possible to the words they modify.

MISPLACED: *The ranger explained how to find ducks in her office.* (The ducks were not in the ranger's office.)

CLEARER: *In her office, the ranger explained how to find ducks.*

Dangling Modifiers Sometimes a modifier doesn't appear to modify any word in a sentence. Most dangling modifiers are participial phrases or infinitive phrases.

DANGLING: *Coming home with groceries, our parrot said, "Hello!"*

CLEARER: *Coming home with groceries, we heard our parrot say, "Hello!"*

Practice and Apply

Choose the correct word or words from each pair in parentheses.

1. Sir Launcelot was King Arthur's (most favorite, favoritest) knight.
2. Launcelot, however, (wasn't, was) hardly loyal to Arthur.
3. He made the (most gravest, gravest) mistake when he fell in love with Gwynevere, the king's wife.
4. King Arthur felt (bad, badly) about their friendship coming to an end, but what could he do?
5. Launcelot tried to make peace with the king, but Sir Gawain, the king's nephew, didn't want (nothing, anything) to do with Launcelot.
6. Gawain challenged Launcelot to a battle, and Gawain initially fought very (good, well).

continued

7. After three hours of battle, however, Launcelot became the (stronger, more strong) of the two men.
8. Though Gawain was injured in the battle, he wouldn't let (anything, nothing) stop him from fighting Launcelot again.
9. Launcelot felt (badly, bad) about having to fight Gawain once more, but he knew he had to do it.
10. Once again, Launcelot spared Gawain's life, proving himself to be the (nobler, noblest) of all knights.

5 Prepositions, Conjunctions, and Interjections

5.1 PREPOSITIONS

A preposition is a word used to show the relationship between a noun or a pronoun and another word in the sentence.

Commonly Used Prepositions			
above	down	near	through
at	for	of	to
before	from	on	up
below	in	out	with
by	into	over	without

A preposition is always followed by a word or group of words that serves as its object. The preposition, its object, and modifiers of the object are called the **prepositional phrase.** In each example below, the prepositional phrase is highlighted, and the object of the preposition is in boldface type.

EXAMPLES: *The future of the entire* ***kingdom*** *is uncertain.*
We searched through the deepest ***woods.***

Prepositional phrases may be used as adjectives or as adverbs. The phrase in the first example is used as an adjective modifying the noun *future.* In the second example, the phrase is used as an adverb modifying the verb *searched.*

WATCH OUT! Prepositional phrases must be as close as possible to the word they modify.

MISPLACED: *We have clothes for leisurewear of many colors.*

CLEARER: *We have clothes of many colors for leisurewear.*

5.2 CONJUNCTIONS

A conjunction is a word used to connect words, phrases, or sentences. There are three kinds of conjunctions: **coordinating conjunctions, correlative conjunctions,** and **subordinating conjunctions.**

Coordinating conjunctions connect words or word groups that have the same function in a sentence. Such conjunctions include *and, but, or, for, so, yet,* and *nor.*

Coordinating conjunctions can join nouns, pronouns, verbs, adjectives, adverbs, prepositional phrases, and clauses in a sentence.

These examples show coordinating conjunctions joining words of the same function:

EXAMPLES: *I have many friends but few enemies.* (two noun objects)
We ran out the door and into the street. (two prepositional phrases)
They are pleasant yet seem aloof. (two predicates)
We have to go now, or we will be late. (two clauses)

Correlative conjunctions are similar to coordinating conjunctions. However, correlative conjunctions are always used in pairs.

Correlative Conjunctions		
both . . . and	neither . . . nor	whether . . . or
either . . . or	not only . . . but also	

Subordinating conjunctions introduce subordinate clauses—clauses that cannot stand by themselves as complete sentences. The subordinating conjunction shows how the subordinate clause relates to the rest of the sentence. The relationships include time, manner, place, cause, comparison, condition, and purpose.

Subordinating Conjunctions	
Time	after, as, as long as, as soon as, before, since, until, when, whenever, while
Manner	as, as if
Place	where, wherever
Cause	because, since
Comparison	as, as much as, than
Condition	although, as long as, even if, even though, if, provided that, though, unless, while
Purpose	in order that, so that, that

In the example below, the boldface word is the conjunction, and the highlighted words form a subordinate clause:

EXAMPLE: ***Though** Grendel is a loathsome beast, Beowulf does not fear him.*

Beowulf does not fear him is an independent clause because it can stand alone as a complete sentence. *Though Grendel is a loathsome beast* cannot stand alone as a complete sentence; it is a subordinate clause.

Conjunctive adverbs are used to connect clauses that can stand by themselves as sentences. Conjunctive adverbs include *also, besides, finally, however, moreover, nevertheless, otherwise,* and *then.*

EXAMPLE: *She loved the fall; however, she also enjoyed winter.*

5.3 INTERJECTIONS

Interjections are words used to show strong emotion, such as *wow* and *cool.* Often followed by an exclamation point, they have no grammatical relationship to any other part of a sentence.

EXAMPLE: *Beowulf seizes Grendel, grasping the monster in his fists. Unbelievable!*

6 The Sentence and Its Parts

A **sentence** is a group of words used to express a complete thought. A complete sentence has a subject and a predicate.

6.1 KINDS OF SENTENCES

There are four basic types of sentences.

Types	Definition	Example
Declarative	states a fact, a wish, an intent, or a feeling	I just finished reading *Macbeth.*
Interrogative	asks a question	Have you ever read it?
Imperative	gives a command or direction	You must read it sometime.
Exclamatory	expresses strong feeling or excitement	It's so compelling!

6.2 COMPOUND SUBJECTS AND PREDICATES

A compound subject consists of two or more subjects that share the same verb. They are typically joined by the coordinating conjunction *and* or *or.*

EXAMPLE: *The knight and his horse rode into the forest.*

A compound predicate consists of two or more predicates that share the same subject. They too are typically joined by a coordinating conjunction, usually *and, but,* or *or.*

EXAMPLE: *Sir Gawain beheaded the Green Knight but did not kill him.*

6.3 COMPLEMENTS

A **complement** is a word or group of words that completes the meaning of the sentence. Some sentences contain only a subject and a verb. Most sentences, however, require additional words placed after the verb to complete the meaning of the sentence. There are three kinds of complements: direct objects, indirect objects, and subject complements.

Direct objects are words or word groups that receive the action of action verbs. A direct object answers the question *what* or *whom.*

EXAMPLES: *The students asked many questions.* (Asked what?)
The teacher quickly answered the students. (Answered whom?)

Indirect objects tell to whom or what or for whom or what the actions of verbs are performed. Indirect objects come before direct objects. In the examples that follow, the indirect objects are highlighted.

EXAMPLES: *My sister usually gave her friends good advice.* (Gave to whom?)
Her brother sent the store a heavy package. (Sent to what?)

Subject complements come after linking verbs and identify or describe the subjects. A subject complement that names or identifies a subject is called a **predicate nominative.** Predicate nominatives include **predicate nouns** and **predicate pronouns.**

EXAMPLES: *My friends are very hard workers.*
The best writer in the class is she.

A subject complement that describes a subject is called a **predicate adjective.**

EXAMPLE: *The pianist appeared very energetic.*

7 Phrases

A **phrase** is a group of related words that does not contain a subject and a predicate but functions in a sentence as a single part of speech.

7.1 PREPOSITIONAL PHRASES

A **prepositional phrase** is a phrase that consists of a preposition, its object, and any modifiers of the object. Prepositional phrases that modify nouns or pronouns are called **adjective phrases.** Prepositional phrases that modify verbs, adjectives, or adverbs are **adverb phrases.**

ADJECTIVE PHRASE: *The central character of the story is a villain.*

ADVERB PHRASE: *He reveals his nature in the first scene.*

7.2 APPOSITIVES AND APPOSITIVE PHRASES

An **appositive** is a noun or pronoun that identifies or renames another noun or pronoun. An **appositive phrase** includes an appositive and modifiers of it.

An appositive can be either **essential** or **nonessential.** An **essential appositive** provides information that is needed to identify what is referred to by the preceding noun or pronoun.

EXAMPLE: *The poet Percy Bysshe Shelley frequently used nature as the subject of his poems.*

A **nonessential appositive** adds extra information about a noun or pronoun whose meaning is already clear. Nonessential appositives and appositive phrases are set off with commas.

EXAMPLE: *The skylark, a bird noted for its melodious song, is the subject of one of Shelley's poems.*

8 Verbals and Verbal Phrases

A **verbal** is a verb form that is used as a noun, an adjective, or an adverb. A **verbal phrase** consists of a verbal along with its modifiers and complements. There are three kinds of verbals: **infinitives, participles,** and **gerunds.**

8.1 INFINITIVES AND INFINITIVE PHRASES

An **infinitive** is a verb form that usually begins with to and functions as a noun, an adjective, or an adverb. An **infinitive phrase** consists of an infinitive plus its modifiers and complements. The examples that follow show several uses of infinitive phrases.

NOUN: *To travel the world is my long-term plan.* (subject)
I'm trying to find a solution. (direct object)
Her greatest wish was to return to her native country. (predicate nominative)

ADJECTIVE: *We supported his goal to become a pilot.* (adjective modifying *goal*)

ADVERB: *To prepare for the marathon, Julie maintained a strict exercise regimen.* (adverb modifying *maintained*)

Because infinitives usually begin with *to,* it is usually easy to recognize them. However, sometimes *to* may be omitted.

EXAMPLE: *Should you dare [to] speak these forbidden words, a curse will fall upon you.*

8.2 PARTICIPLES AND PARTICIPIAL PHRASES

A **participle** is a verb form that functions as an adjective. Like adjectives, participles modify nouns and pronouns. Most participles are present-participle forms, ending in *-ing,* or past-participle forms ending in *-ed* or *-en.* In the examples that follow, the participles are highlighted:

MODIFYING A NOUN: *The crying baby needed a nap.*

MODIFYING A PRONOUN: *Scared, she decided not to walk home alone.*

Participial phrases are participles with all their modifiers and complements.

MODIFYING A NOUN: *The light streaming in through the window woke up the boy.*

MODIFYING A PRONOUN: *Walking across the field, she thought she saw a fox.*

8.3 DANGLING AND MISPLACED PARTICIPLES

A participle or participial phrase should be placed as close as possible to the word that it modifies. Otherwise the meaning of the sentence may not be clear.

MISPLACED: *The boys were looking for squirrels searching the trees.*

CLEARER: *The boys searching the trees were looking for squirrels.*

A participle or participial phrase that does not clearly modify anything in a sentence is called a **dangling participle.** A dangling participle causes confusion because it appears to modify a word that it cannot sensibly modify. Correct a dangling participle by providing a word for the participle to modify.

DANGLING: *Running like the wind, my hat fell off.* (The hat wasn't running.)

CLEARER: *Running like the wind, I lost my hat.*

8.4 GERUNDS AND GERUND PHRASES

A **gerund** is a verb form ending in *-ing* that functions as a noun. Gerunds may perform any function nouns perform.

SUBJECT: *Running is my favorite pastime.*

DIRECT OBJECT: *I truly love running.*

INDIRECT OBJECT: *You should give running a try.*

SUBJECT COMPLEMENT: *My deepest passion is running.*

OBJECT OF PREPOSITION: *Her love of running keeps her strong.*

Gerund phrases are gerunds with all their modifiers and complements.

SUBJECT: *Wishing on a star never got me far.*

OBJECT OF PREPOSITION: *I will finish before leaving the office.*

APPOSITIVE: *Her avocation, flying airplanes, finally led to full-time employment.*

Practice and Apply

Identify the underlined phrases as appositive phrases, infinitive phrases, participial phrases, or gerund phrases.

1. In D. H. Lawrence's story "The Rocking-Horse Winner," the protagonist becomes obsessed with betting on horses.
2. The protagonist, a young boy, starts to win a lot of money from the races.
3. Feeling unbeatable, the boy continues to bet more and more money.
4. He wants to win as much as possible but makes himself sick in the process.
5. After the boy dies of his illness, the mother discovers that having a lot of money isn't so important after all.

9 Clauses

A **clause** is a group of words that contains a subject and a verb. There are two kinds of clauses: independent clauses and subordinate clauses.

9.1 INDEPENDENT AND SUBORDINATE CLAUSES

An **independent clause** can stand alone as a sentence, as the word **independent** suggests.

INDEPENDENT CLAUSE: *T. S. Eliot wrote a poem called "The Naming of Cats."*

A sentence may contain more than one independent clause.

EXAMPLE: *T. S. Eliot wrote a poem called "The Naming of Cats," and he also wrote a poem called "The Hollow Men."*

In the preceding example, the coordinating conjunction *and* joins two independent clauses.

A **subordinate clause** cannot stand alone as a sentence. It is subordinate to, or dependent on, an independent clause.

EXAMPLE: *Although Eliot was born in America, he later moved to England.*

The highlighted clause cannot stand by itself; it must be joined with an independent clause to form a complete sentence.

9.2 ADJECTIVE CLAUSES

An **adjective clause** is a subordinate clause used as an adjective. It usually follows the noun or pronoun it modifies. Adjective clauses are typically introduced by the relative pronoun *who, whom, whose, which,* or *that.*

EXAMPLES: *"The Naming of Cats" is the poem that I like best.*
The poem, which is very humorous, discusses the difficulty of naming cats.
I think the people who enjoy the poem most are cat lovers.

An adjective clause can be either essential or nonessential. An **essential adjective clause** provides information that is necessary to identify the preceding noun or pronoun.

EXAMPLE: *Eliot was a poet who wrote about many different topics.*

A **nonessential adjective clause** adds additional information about a noun or pronoun whose meaning is already clear. Nonessential clauses are set off with commas.

EXAMPLE: *Eliot, who was always fond of Lewis Carroll, decided to try his hand at humor.*

TIP The relative pronouns **whom, which,** and **that** may sometimes be omitted when they are objects in adjective clauses.

EXAMPLE: *The names [that] I like best are Augustus and Demeter.*

9.3 ADVERB CLAUSES

An **adverb clause** is a subordinate clause that is used to modify a verb, an adjective, or an adverb. It is introduced by a subordinating conjunction.
Adverb clauses typically occur at the beginning or end of sentences.

MODIFYING A VERB: *When we need you, we will call.*

MODIFYING AN ADVERB: *I'll stay here where there is shelter from the rain.*

MODIFYING AN ADJECTIVE: *Roman felt as good as he had ever felt.*

9.4 NOUN CLAUSES

A **noun clause** is a subordinate clause that is used as a noun. A noun clause may be used as a subject, a direct object, an indirect object, a predicate nominative, or the object of a preposition. Noun clauses are introduced either by pronouns, such as *that, what, who, whoever, which,* and *whose*, or by subordinating conjunctions, such as *how, when, where, why,* and *whether.*

TIP Because the same words may introduce adjective and noun clauses, you need to consider how a clause functions within its sentence. To determine if a clause is a noun clause, try substituting *something* or *someone* for the clause. If you can do it, it is probably a noun clause.

EXAMPLES: *I asked her when I should leave.* ("I asked her something." The clause is a noun clause, direct object of the verb *asked.*)
Whoever decides to go can get a ride with me. ("Someone can get a ride with me." The clause is a noun clause, functioning as the subject of the sentence.)

10 The Structure of Sentences

When classified by their structure, there are four kinds of sentences: simple, compound, complex, and compound-complex.

10.1 SIMPLE SENTENCES

A **simple sentence** is a sentence that has one independent clause and no subordinate clauses. Various parts of simple sentences may be compound, and simple sentences may contain grammatical structures such as appositive and verbal phrases.

EXAMPLES: *William Blake, a rare talent, wrote poetry and created art.* (an appositive phrase and a compound predicate)
Inspired by both the human and the divine, Blake wanted to share his unique vision with the world. (a participial phrase and an infinitive phrase)

10.2 COMPOUND SENTENCES

A **compound sentence** consists of two or more independent clauses. The clauses in compound sentences are joined with commas and coordinating conjunctions *(and, but, or, nor, yet, for, so)* or with semicolons. Like simple sentences, compound sentences do not contain any subordinate clauses.

EXAMPLES: *I like to exercise, but it can be difficult to find the time. I went to the store first; then I went to the bank.*

WATCH OUT! Do not confuse compound sentences with simple sentences that have compound parts.

EXAMPLE: *He vacuumed the floor and shook out the rugs.* (Here *and* joins parts of a compound predicate, not a compound sentence.)

10.3 COMPLEX SENTENCES

A **complex sentence** consists of one independent clause and one or more subordinate clauses. Each subordinate clause can be used as a noun or as a modifier. If it is used as a modifier, a subordinate clause usually modifies a word in the independent clause, and the independent clause can stand alone. However, when a subordinate clause is a noun clause, it is a part of the independent clause; the two cannot be separated.

MODIFIER: *As soon as I am finished with this, I will move on to the next project.*

NOUN CLAUSE: *We're going to the park with whoever else wants to come along.* (The noun clause is the object of the preposition *with* and cannot be separated from the rest of the sentence.)

10.4 COMPOUND-COMPLEX SENTENCES

A **compound-complex sentence** contains two or more independent clauses and one or more subordinate clauses. Compound-complex sentences are, simply, both compound and complex. If you start with a compound sentence, all you need to do to form a compound-complex sentence is add a subordinate clause.

COMPOUND: *We're going to the baseball game, and then we're going to get some ice cream.*

COMPOUND-COMPLEX: *We're going to the baseball game that begins at six o'clock, and then we're going to get some ice cream.*

10.5 PARALLEL STRUCTURE

When you write sentences, make sure that coordinate parts are equivalent, or **parallel,** in structure.

NOT PARALLEL: *I am going to hike and swimming.* (*To hike* is an infinitive; *swimming* is a gerund.)

PARALLEL: *I am going hiking and swimming.* (*Hiking* and *swimming* are both gerunds.)

NOT PARALLEL: *I like steak and to eat potatoes.* (*Steak* is a noun; *to eat potatoes* is a phrase.)

PARALLEL: *I like steak and potatoes.* (*Steak* and *potatoes* are both nouns.)

11 Writing Complete Sentences

Remember that, a sentence is a group of words that expresses a complete thought. In formal writing, try to avoid both sentence fragments and run-on sentences.

11.1 CORRECTING FRAGMENTS

A **sentence fragment** is a group of words that is only part of a sentence. It does not express a complete thought and may be confusing to a reader or listener. A sentence fragment may be lacking a subject, a predicate, or both.

FRAGMENT: *Went for a boat ride.* (no subject)

CORRECTED: *We went for a boat ride.*

FRAGMENT: *People of all ages.* (no predicate)

CORRECTED: *People of all ages tried to water ski.*

FRAGMENT: *After the boat ride.* (neither subject nor predicate)

CORRECTED: *We dried off by the fire after the boat ride.*

In your writing, fragments may be a result of haste or incorrect punctuation. Sometimes fixing a fragment will be a matter of attaching it to a preceding or following sentence.

FRAGMENT: *We saw the two girls. Waiting for the bus to arrive.*

CORRECTED: *We saw the two girls waiting for the bus to arrive.*

11.2 CORRECTING RUN-ON SENTENCES

A **run-on sentence** is made up of two or more sentences written as though they were one. Some run-ons have no punctuation within them. Others may have only commas where conjunctions or stronger punctuation marks are necessary. Use your judgment in correcting run-on sentences, as you have choices. You can make a run-on two sentences if the thoughts are not closely connected. If the thoughts are closely related, you can keep the run-on as one sentence by adding a semicolon or a conjunction.

RUN-ON: *We found a place for the picnic by a small pond it was three miles from the village.*

MAKE TWO SENTENCES: *We found a place for the picnic by a small pond. It was three miles from the village.*

RUN-ON: *We found a place for the picnic by a small pond it was perfect.*

USE A SEMICOLON: *We found a place for the picnic by a small pond; it was perfect.*

ADD A CONJUNCTION: *We found a place for the picnic by a small pond, and it was perfect.*

WATCH OUT! When you form compound sentences, make sure you use appropriate punctuation: a comma before a coordinating conjunction, a semicolon when there is no coordinating conjunction. A very common mistake is to use a comma alone instead of a comma and a conjunction. This error is called a **comma splice.**

INCORRECT: *He finished the apprenticeship, he left the village.*

CORRECT: *He finished the apprenticeship, and he left the village.*

Practice and Apply

Rewrite the following paragraph, correcting all fragments and run-ons.

The Book of Margery Kempe details the tremendous difficulties that Kempe experiences. After the birth of her first child. She sees demons and fears for her own life, her keepers restrain her so that she cannot do harm to herself. She says that one day she is visited by Jesus. And that, afterwards, she becomes calm and rational again. After this transformative experience, Kempe goes on to become a preacher. And a religious visionary.

12 Subject-Verb Agreement

The subject and verb in a clause must agree in number. Agreement means that if the subject is singular, the verb is also singular, and if the subject is plural, the verb is also plural.

12.1 BASIC AGREEMENT

Fortunately, agreement between subjects and verbs in English is simple. Most verbs show the difference between singular and plural only in the third person of the present tense. In the present tense, the third-person singular form ends in *-s.*

Present-Tense Verb Forms	
Singular	**Plural**
I eat	we eat
you eat	you eat
she, he, it eats	they eat

12.2 AGREEMENT WITH *BE*

The verb *be* presents special problems in agreement, because this verb does not follow the usual verb patterns.

Forms of *Be*			
Present Tense		**Past Tense**	
Singular	**Plural**	**Singular**	**Plural**
I am	we are	I was	we were
you are	you are	you were	you were
she, he, it is	they are	she, he, it was	they were

12.3 WORDS BETWEEN SUBJECT AND VERB

A verb agrees only with its subject. When words come between a subject and a verb, ignore them when considering proper agreement. Identify the subject and make sure the verb agrees with it.

EXAMPLES: *Several items in the storage unit need to be thrown out.*
Many of the puppies in the litter are smaller than others.

12.4 AGREEMENT WITH COMPOUND SUBJECTS

Use plural verbs with most compound subjects joined by the word *and.*

EXAMPLE: *My mother and her sisters call each other every Sunday.*

To confirm that you need a plural verb, you could substitute the plural pronoun *they* for *my mother and her sisters.*

If a compound subject is thought of as a unit, use a singular verb. Test this by substituting the singular pronoun *it.*

EXAMPLE: *Liver and onions [it] is Robert's least favorite dish.*

Use a singular verb with a compound subject that is preceded by *each, every,* or *many a.*

EXAMPLE: *Every man, woman, and child is being ordered off the ship.*

When the parts of a compound subject are joined by *or, nor,* or the correlative conjunctions *either . . . or* or *neither . . . nor,* make the verb agree with the noun or pronoun nearest the verb.

EXAMPLES: *Cheddar or Swiss is my favorite cheese.*
Either my brother or my sisters are coming to pick me up.
Neither I nor my two friends were here at the time of the accident.

12.5 PERSONAL PRONOUNS AS SUBJECTS

When using a personal pronoun as a subject, make sure to match it with the correct form of the verb *be.* (See the chart in Section 12.2.) Note especially that the pronoun *you* takes the forms *are* and *were,* regardless of whether it is singular or plural.

WATCH OUT! *You is* and *you was* are nonstandard forms and should be avoided in writing and speaking. *We was* and *they was* are also forms to be avoided.

INCORRECT: *You is facing the wrong direction.*

CORRECT: *You are facing the wrong direction.*

INCORRECT: *We was telling ghost stories.*

CORRECT: *We were telling ghost stories.*

12.6 INDEFINITE PRONOUNS AS SUBJECTS

Some indefinite pronouns are always singular; some are always plural.

Singular Indefinite Pronouns		
another	everybody	no one
anybody	everyone	nothing

continued

anyone	everything	one
anything	much	somebody
each	neither	someone
either	nobody	something

EXAMPLES: *Each of the writers was given an award.*
Somebody in the room upstairs is sleeping.

Plural Indefinite Pronouns			
both	few	many	several

EXAMPLES: *Many of the books in our library are not in circulation.*
Few have been returned recently.

Still other indefinite pronouns may be either singular or plural.

Singular or Plural Indefinite Pronouns		
all	more	none
any	most	some

The number of the indefinite pronoun *any* or *none* often depends on the intended meaning.

EXAMPLES: *Any of these topics has potential for a good article.* (any one topic)
Any of these topics have potential for good articles. (all of the many topics)

The indefinite pronouns *all, some, more, most,* and *none* are singular when they refer to quantities or parts of things. They are plural when they refer to numbers of individual things. Context will usually give a clue.

EXAMPLES: *All of the flour is gone.* (referring to a quantity)
All of the flowers are gone. (referring to individual items)

12.7 INVERTED SENTENCES

Problems in agreement often occur in inverted sentences beginning with *here* or *there;* in questions beginning with *how, when, why, where,* or *what;* and in inverted sentences beginning with phrases. Identify the subject—wherever it is—before deciding on the verb.

EXAMPLES: *There clearly are far too many cooks in this kitchen.*
What is the correct ingredient for this stew?
Far from the embroiled cooks stands the master chef.

Practice and Apply

Locate the subject of each clause in the sentences below. Then choose the correct verb.

1. The work *A History of the English Church and People* (contain, contains) important historical information.
2. Few books (is, are) as valuable for researching early British history.
3. Many stories in the book (discuss, discusses) the spread of Christianity in England.
4. During the fifth century, both the pagan faith and the Christian faith (were, was) present in Britain.
5. Each of King Edwin's counselors (was, were) in agreement that the king should convert to Christianity.
6. Neither the counselors nor the king (were, was) convinced that he should continue to follow the pagan faith.
7. In the end, none of the pagan temples and altars (was, were) left standing.

12.8 SENTENCES WITH PREDICATE NOMINATIVES

When a predicate nominative serves as a complement in a sentence, use a verb that agrees with the subject, not the complement.

EXAMPLES: *The poems of John Keats are one component of this book.* (The subject is the plural noun *poems,* not *component,* and it takes the plural verb *are.*)
One component of this book is the poems of John Keats. (The subject is the singular noun *component,* and it takes the singular verb *is.*)

12.9 *DON'T* AND *DOESN'T* AS AUXILIARY VERBS

The auxiliary verb *doesn't* is used with singular subjects and with the personal pronouns *she, he,* and *it.* The auxiliary verb *don't* is used with plural subjects and with the personal pronouns *I, we, you,* and *they.*

SINGULAR: *He doesn't have time to wait any longer.*
Doesn't Emily know where to meet us?

PLURAL: *We don't think we can make it to the party.*
The campers don't have enough wood to build a fire.

12.10 COLLECTIVE NOUNS AS SUBJECTS

Collective nouns are singular nouns that name groups of persons or things. *Family,* for example, is the collective name of a group of individuals. A collective noun takes a singular verb when the group acts as a single unit. It takes a plural verb when the members of the group act separately.

EXAMPLES: *Her family is moving to another state.* (The family as a whole is moving.)
Her family are carrying furniture out to the truck. (The individual members are carrying furniture.)

12.11 RELATIVE PRONOUNS AS SUBJECTS

When the relative pronoun *who, which,* or *that* is used as a subject in an adjective clause, the verb in the clause must agree in number with the antecedent of the pronoun.

SINGULAR: *The scent that wafts through the air is jasmine.*

The antecedent of the relative pronoun *that* is the singular *scent;* therefore, *that* is singular and must take the singular verb *wafts.*

PLURAL: *The muffins, which are an old family recipe, get eaten quickly.*

The antecedent of the relative pronoun *which* is the plural *muffins.* Therefore, *which* is plural, and it takes the plural verb *are.*

L 1a, L 1b, L 2b, L 4, L 4a–c, L 5, L 6

Vocabulary and Spelling

The key to becoming an independent reader is to develop a toolkit of vocabulary strategies. By learning and practicing the strategies, you'll know what to do when you encounter unfamiliar words while reading. You'll also know how to refine the words you use for different situations—personal, school, and work.

Being a good speller is important when communicating your ideas in writing. Learning basic spelling rules and checking your spelling in a dictionary will help you spell words that you may not use frequently.

1 Using Context Clues

The context of a word is made up of the punctuation marks, words, sentences, and paragraphs that surround the word. A word's context can give you important clues about its meaning.

1.1 GENERAL CONTEXT

Sometimes you need to infer the meaning of an unfamiliar word by reading all the information in a passage.

Since he has received perfect scores on all of the tests, I'd say his forte is definitely history.

You can tell from the context that *forte* means "strength."

1.2 SPECIFIC CONTEXT CLUES

Sometimes writers help you understand the meanings of words by providing specific clues such as those shown in the chart.

Specific Context Clues		
Type of Clue	**Key Words/ Phrases**	**Example**
Definition or restatement of the meaning of the word	or, which is, that is, in other words, also known as, also called	During the last week of the *dog days*—**that hot period of summer from July to early September**—our town was hit by a hurricane.
Example following an unfamiliar word	such as, like, as if, for example, especially, including	The hurricane wreaked *havoc,* including **downed power lines, toppled trees, and flooded roads.**
Comparison with a more familiar word or concept	as, like, also, similar to, in the same way, likewise	The detective we hired was as *tenacious* **as a bulldog.**
Contrast with a familiar word or experience	unlike, but, however, although, on the other hand, on the contrary	The reporter was usually **focused,** but today he was *preoccupied.*
Synonym	An unfamiliar word is followed by a familiar word with a similar meaning	A reporter *impassively* relayed what happened in an equally **unemotional** account.

1.3 IDIOMS, SLANG, AND FIGURATIVE LANGUAGE

Use context clues to figure out the meanings of idioms, figurative language, and slang.

An **idiom** is an expression whose overall meaning is different from the meaning of the individual words.

With only seconds left before the bell, Alison made it to class by the skin of her teeth. (*By the skin of her teeth* means "just in time.")

Figurative language is language that communicates meaning beyond the literal meaning of the words.

His heart was on the verge of love. (*Verge* means "the point beyond which something is likely to occur.")

Slang is informal language composed of made-up words and ordinary words that are used to mean something different from their meanings in formal English.

We both thought the movie was really cool because of all the special effects. (*Cool* means "excellent.")

2 Analyzing Word Structure

Many words can be broken into smaller parts, such as base words, roots, prefixes, and suffixes.

2.1 BASE WORDS

A **base word** is a word part that by itself is also a word. Other words or word parts can be added to base words to form new words.

2.2 ROOTS

A **root** is a word part that contains the core meaning of the word. Many English words contain roots that come from older languages such as Greek, Latin, Old English (Anglo-Saxon), and Norse. Knowing the meaning of a word's root can help you determine the word's meaning.

Root	Meaning	Example
log (Greek)	word; study	epilogue, ecology
card (Greek)	heart	cardiogram
stat (Greek)	standing	static
meter (Greek)	measure	thermometer
hydra / hydro (Greek)	water	hydraulics
cosm / cosmo (Greek)	world	cosmic
ped (Latin)	foot	pedestrian
pel / pul (Latin)	drive; thrust	repel, repulse
equ / equi (Latin)	equal	equitable

2.3 PREFIXES

A **prefix** is a word part attached to the beginning of a word. Most prefixes come from Greek, Latin, or Old English.

Prefix	Meaning	Example
di- / dia- (Greek)	through	dissect
micro- (Greek)	small	microphone
a- (Anglo-Saxon)	in, on; away	asleep
quad- (Latin)	four	quadrangle
pro- (Latin)	forward	progress

2.4 SUFFIXES

A **suffix** is a word part that appears at the end of a root or base word to form a new word. Some suffixes do not change word meaning. These suffixes are

- added to nouns to change the number of persons or objects
- added to verbs to change the tense

- added to modifiers to change the degree of comparison

Suffix	Meaning	Example
-s, -es	to change the number of a noun	trunk + s = trunks
-d, -ed, -ing	to change verb tense	sprinkle + d = sprinkled
-er, -est	to change the degree of comparison in modifiers	cold + er = colder icy + est = iciest

Other suffixes can be added to a root or base to change the word's meaning. These suffixes can also determine a word's part of speech.

Suffix	Meaning	Example
-ence	state or condition of	independence
-ous	full of	furious
-ate	to make	activate
-ly, -ily	manner	quickly

Strategies for Understanding Unfamiliar Words

- Look for any prefixes or suffixes. Remove them to isolate the base word or the root.
- See if you recognize any elements—prefix, suffix, root, or base—of the word. You may be able to guess its meaning by analyzing one or two elements.
- Use the context in the sentence and the word parts to make a logical guess about the word's meaning.
- Consult a dictionary to see whether you are correct.

Practice and Apply

Make inferences about the meanings of the following words from the fields of science and math. Consider what you have learned in this section about Greek, Latin, and Old English (Anglo-Saxon) word parts.

cardiology	hydrometer
perimeter	pathology
diameter	microcosm
diagram	hydrostatic
cosmology	electrocardiogram
quadruped	propulsion

3 Understanding Word Origins

3.1 ETYMOLOGIES

Etymologies show the origin and historical development of a word. When you study a word's history and origin, you can find out when, where, and how the word came to be. Histories of language and dictionaries are valuable tools for exploring how forms and meanings of words have changed through time:

boy•cott (boiˊkŏtˊ) *tr.v.* **boy·cott•ed, boy·cott·ing, boy·cotts** To abstain from or act together in abstaining from using, buying, dealing with, or participating in as an expression of protest or disfavor or as a means of coercion: *boycott a business; boycott merchants; boycott buses; boycott an election. n.* The act or an instance of boycotting. [After Charles C. *Boycott* (1832–1897), English land agent in Ireland.]

quo•rum (kwôrˊəm) *n.* **1.** The minimal number of officers and members of a committee or organization, usually a majority, who must be present for valid transaction of business. **2.** A select group. **3.** The minimal density of bacterial cells that results in altered gene expression in a population of bacteria. [Middle English, quorum of justices of the peace, from Latin *quōrum*, of whom (from the wording of a commission naming certain persons as members of a body), genitive pl. of *quī*, who; see **kʷo-** in Indo-European roots.]

Practice and Apply

Trace the etymology of the words below, often used in the fields of history and political science.

appropriate	filibuster	referendum
carpetbagger	immigrate	secession
caucus	impeach	tariff
communism	pacifism	veto
constitution	ratify	

3.2 WORD FAMILIES

Words that have the same root make up a word family and have related meanings. The chart shows a common Greek and a common Latin root. Notice how the meanings of the example words are related to the meanings of their roots.

Latin Root	*gen:* "race, kind"
English Words	**generalize** to reduce to a general form, class, law **generation** a stage in the life cycle **regenerate** to form or create anew **engender** to bring into existence **generic** relating to a group or class
Greek Root	*log:* "speech, word, reason"
English Words	**apology** an expression of regret **epilogue** a short poem or speech **monologue** a long speech made by one person **syllogism** reasoning from the general to the specific **logic** a system of reasoning

3.3 WORDS FROM CLASSICAL MYTHOLOGY

The English language includes many words from classical mythology. You can use your knowledge of these myths to understand the origins and meanings of these words. For example, *herculean task* refers to the strongman Hercules. Thus, you can guess that *herculean task* means "a job that is large or difficult." The chart shows a few common words from mythology.

Greek	Roman	Norse
panic	cereal	Wednesday
atlas	mercurial	gun
adonis	Saturday	berserk
mentor	January	valkyrie

Practice and Apply

Look up the etymology of each word in the chart, and locate the myth associated with it. Use the information from the myth to explain the origin and meaning of each word.

3.4 FOREIGN WORDS

The English language includes words from diverse languages, such as French, Dutch, Spanish, Italian, and Chinese. Many words stayed the way they were in their original language. Histories of the language trace how similar words become integrated into English.

French	Dutch	Spanish	Italian
entrée	maelstrom	rodeo	pasta
nouveau riche	trek	salsa	opera
potpourri	cookie	bronco	vendetta
tête-à-tête	snoop	tornado	grotto

4 Understanding the English Language

The English language has a documented history of 1,400 years, but its earliest beginnings stretch back to the speakers of Proto-Indo-European who ranged from India to Europe. Proto-Indo-European gave rise to many languages, including English, Swedish, Hindi, Greek, Russian, Polish, Italian, French, Spanish, and German—now collectively referred to as Indo-European. Here's a brief overview of the development of English:

- **Proto-English:** Besides the Romans who spoke Latin, the early inhabitants of Britain were Britons and Celts. The Angles, Saxons, and Jutes—Germanic peoples—arrived around 449 A.D. Proto English incorporated Latin words as well as those drawn from the languages of the Britons, Celts, and the Germanic peoples.
- **Old English:** From about the mid-fifth century to the twelfth century, Old English, the language of the Anglo-Saxons, was the spoken language in Britain. Latin remained the language of writing and of the church, schools, and international relations. Old English would be unintelligible to the speaker of Modern English, given the differences in its grammar, spellings, and pronunciations. The most well-known work in Old English is the epic poem *Beowulf.*
- **Middle English:** After the Norman Conquest in 1066, the nobility spoke Anglo-Norman. Middle English, derived from Anglo-Norman, thrived from the late eleventh century to the late fifteenth century. It also underwent significant changes in grammar and vocabulary. The most famous writer of this period is Geoffrey Chaucer, whose *The Canterbury Tales* remains a staple of the English literature curriculum.
- **Early Modern English:** During the fifteenth century, the so-called "Great Vowel Shift" occurred—a major change in the pronunciation of English. Conventions of spelling were also being established during this time. With the spread of a London-based dialect and the standardization that results from printing, Early Modern English is recognizable to the speaker of Modern English. For example, William Shakespeare, the great English dramatist, wrote during the late phase of Early Modern English, The first edition of the *King James Bible* also was published during this time. Early Modern English lasted until about the seventeenth century.
- **Modern English:** Modern English emerged in the late seventeenth century and continues to the present day. Its development was spurred by Samuel Johnson's *Dictionary of the English Language*, published in 1755, which standardized spelling and usage. The significant characteristic of contemporary Modern English is its extensive vocabulary, which partly arises from technological and scientific developments, as well as from the worldwide variety of its speakers. As various communication devices are increasingly adopted, technology-specific language and vocabulary—such as that used in texting—further influence English. Thus, the development of English continues in the present day.

5 Synonyms and Antonyms

5.1 SYNONYMS

A **synonym** is a word with a meaning similar to that of another word. You can find synonyms in a thesaurus or a dictionary. In a dictionary, synonyms are often given as part of the definition of a word. The following word pairs are synonyms:

dry/arid enthralled/fascinated
gaunt/thin

5.2 ANTONYMS

An **antonym** is a word with a meaning opposite that of another word. The following word pairs are antonyms:

friend/enemy   absurd/logical
courteous/rude   languid/energetic

6 Denotation and Connotation

6.1 DENOTATION

A word's dictionary meaning is called its **denotation.** For example, the denotation of the word *rascal* is "an unethical, dishonest person."

6.2 CONNOTATION

The images or feelings you connect to a word add a finer shade of meaning, called **connotation.** The connotation of a word goes beyond the word's basic dictionary definition. Writers use connotations of words to communicate positive or negative feelings.

Positive	Neutral	Negative
save	store	hoard
fragrance	smell	stench
display	show	flaunt

Make sure you understand the denotation and connotation of a word when you read it or use it in your writing.

7 Analogies

An **analogy** is a comparison between two things that are similar in some way but are otherwise dissimilar. Analogies are sometimes used in writing when unfamiliar subjects or ideas are explained in terms of familiar ones. Analogies often appear on tests as well, usually in a format like this:

TERRIER : DOG :: A) rat : fish
B) kitten : cat
C) trout : fish
D) fish : trout
E) poodle : collie

Follow these steps to determine the correct answer:

- Read the part in capital letters as "*terrier* is to *dog* as . . ."
- Read the answer choices as "*rat* is to *fish*," "*kitten* is to *cat*," and so on.
- Ask yourself how the words *terrier* and *dog* are related. (A terrier is a type of dog.)
- Ask yourself which of the choices shows the same relationship. (A kitten is a kind of cat, but not in the same way that a terrier is a kind of dog. A kitten is a baby cat. A trout, however, is a type of fish in the sense that a terrier is a type of dog. Therefore, the answer is C.)

8 Homonyms and Homophones

8.1 HOMONYMS

Homonyms are words that have the same spelling and sound but have different origins and meanings.

I don't want to bore you with a story about how I had to bore through the living room wall.

Bore can mean "cause a person to lose interest," but an identically spelled word means " drill a hole."

My dog likes to bark while it scratches the bark on the tree in the backyard.

Bark can refer to what a dog does to make a sound, but an identically spelled word means "the outer covering of a tree." Each word has a different meaning and its own dictionary entry.

Sometimes only one of the meanings of two homonyms may be familiar to you. Use context clues to help you figure out the meaning of an unfamiliar word.

8.2 HOMOPHONES

Homophones are words that sound alike but have different meanings and spellings. The following homophones are frequently misused:

it's/its	they're/their/there
to/too/two	stationary/stationery

Many misused homophones are pronouns and contractions. Whenever you are unsure whether to write *your* or *you're* and *who's* or *whose,* ask yourself if you mean *you are* or *who is/has.* If you do, write the contraction. For other homophones, such as *scent* and *sent,* use the meaning of the word to help you decide which one to use.

9 Words with Multiple Meanings

Some words have acquired additional meanings over time that are based on the original meaning.

EXAMPLES: *I was in a hurry, so I jammed my clothes into the suitcase.*
Unfortunately, I jammed my finger in the process.

These two uses of **jam** have different meanings, but they have the same origin. You will find all the meanings of *jam* listed in the dictionary.

10 Specialized Vocabulary

Specialized vocabulary includes technical vocabulary, domain-specific language, and jargon. Each term refers to the use of language specific to a particular field of study or work. Of these three terms, *jargon* has the strongest connotation, suggesting a kind of language that is difficult to understand or unintelligible to anyone not involved in that field of study or work.

Science, mathematics, history, and literature all have domain-specific vocabularies. For example, science includes words such as *photosynthesis* and *biome* which indicate specific scientific processes or concepts. In literature, words such as *foreshadowing, motif,* and *irony* enable you and others to use a common vocabulary to discuss and interpret literary works.

To figure out specialized terms, you can use context clues and reference sources, such as dictionaries on specific subjects, atlases, or manuals. Many of the resources you use in school include reference aids for that particular subject area. For example, this textbook includes a "Glossary of Literary and Informational Terms," as well as a "Glossary of Academic Vocabulary."

11 Preferred and Contested Usage

English is a constantly evolving language, and standard usage is affected by time and place. For example, Americans often use different words and phrases than the British. Within the United States itself, people speak and write differently than they did 200 years ago. English usage even varies depending on whether the setting is formal or informal. Some nonstandard usages are contested but may become accepted and standard over time. Consult references like *The American Heritage Dictionary of the English Language, Fifth Edition* and its website to determine whether a usage is acceptable. See the chart for some common usage problems and preferred and contested usages.

The English language continues to change, and technology plays a part in that. The increasing use of texting as a means of communications has created a contested language all its own. Terms like *IMO* (*in my opinion*) and *LOL* (*laughing out loud*) have become a commonly used part of the vocabulary.

ain't	*Ain't* is nonstandard. Avoid *ain't* in formal speaking and in all writing other than dialogue.
all right	*All right* means "satisfactory," "unhurt," "safe," "correct," or, as a reply to a question or a preface to a remark, "yes." Although some dictionaries include *alright* as an optional spelling, it is contested and has not become standard usage.
can, may	*Can* expresses ability; *may* expresses possibility.
hopefully	Used as an adverb, as in the following sentence, the term is uncontested. EXAMPLE: We waited hopefully for the announcement of the election results last night. Some contest the use of *hopefully* as a disjunct, that is, as an adverb that expresses the speaker's comments on the content of a statement. EXAMPLE: Hopefully the candidate I like wins. Merriam–Webster's online dictionary says the second use is "entirely standard."
like, as if, as though	In formal situations, avoid using *like* for the conjunction *as if* or *as though* to introduce a subordinate clause. INFORMAL: I feel like I have the flu. FORMAL: I feel as if I have the flu.
literally, figuratively	*Literally* means "in a strict sense." It is sometimes used in non-literal situations for emphasis, when *figuratively* is the more appropriate term. This type of use is contested. UNCONTESTED: I literally baked five-dozen cupcakes. CONTESTED: He literally went nuts. Usage experts for *The American Heritage Dictionary* suggest that the term is acceptable when used as an intensive adverb.
off, off of	Do not use *off* or *off of* for *from.* NONSTANDARD: I got some good advice off that mechanic. STANDARD: I got some good advice from that mechanic.
some, somewhat	In formal situations, avoid using *some* to mean "to some extent." Use *somewhat.* INFORMAL: Tensions between the nations began to ease some. FORMAL: Tensions between the nations began to ease somewhat.
who, whom	*Who* is used as a subject or a predicate nominative. *Whom* is used as a direct object, an indirect object or an object of a preposition. However, in spoken English, most people use *who* instead of *whom* in all cases.

12 Using Reference Sources

12.1 DICTIONARIES

A **general dictionary** will tell you not only a word's definitions but also its pronunciation, its parts of speech, and its history and origin. A **specialized dictionary** focuses on terms related to a particular field of study or work. Use a dictionary to check the spelling of any word you are unsure of in your English class and other subjects as well.

12.2 THESAURI

A **thesaurus** (plural, thesauri) is a dictionary of synonyms. A thesaurus can be helpful when you find yourself using the same modifiers over and over again.

12.3 SYNONYM FINDERS

A **synonym finder** is often included in word-processing software. It enables you to highlight a word and be shown a display of its synonyms.

12.4 GLOSSARIES

A **glossary** is a list of specialized terms and their definitions. It is often found in the back of textbooks and sometimes includes pronunciations. In fact, this textbook has three glossaries: the **Glossary of Literary and Informational Terms, the Glossary of Academic Vocabulary,** and the **Glossary of Vocabulary.** Use these glossaries to help you understand how terms are used in this textbook.

13 Spelling Rules

Consult and employ the following English spelling rules as you write, achieving increasing accuracy.

13.1 WORDS ENDING IN A SILENT *E*

Before adding a suffix beginning with a vowel or ***y*** to a word ending in a silent ***e,*** drop the ***e*** (with some exceptions).

amaze + -ing = amazing

love + -able = lovable

create + -ed = created

nerve + -ous = nervous

Exceptions: *change + -able = changeable; courage + -ous = courageous.*

When adding a suffix beginning with a consonant to a word ending in a silent ***e,*** keep the ***e*** (with some exceptions).

late + -ly = lately

spite + -ful = spiteful

noise + -less = noiseless

state + -ment = statement

Exceptions: *truly, argument, ninth, wholly, awful,* and others.

When a suffix beginning with ***a*** or ***o*** is added to a word with a final silent ***e,*** the final ***e*** is usually retained if it is preceded by a soft ***c*** or a soft ***g.***

bridge + -able = bridgeable

peace + -able = peaceable

outrage + -ous = outrageous

advantage + -ous = advantageous

When a suffix beginning with a vowel is added to words ending in ***ee*** or ***oe,*** the final silent ***e*** is retained.

agree + -ing = agreeing

free + -ing = freeing

hoe + -ing = hoeing

see + -ing = seeing

13.2 WORDS ENDING IN *Y*

Before adding most suffixes to a word that ends in ***y*** preceded by a consonant, change the ***y*** to ***i.***

easy + -est = easiest

crazy + -est = craziest

silly + -ness = silliness

marry + -age = marriage

Exceptions: *dryness, shyness,* and *slyness.*

However, when you add ***-ing,*** the ***y*** does not change.

empty + -ed = emptied but

empty + -ing = emptying

When adding a suffix to a word that ends in ***y*** preceded by a vowel, the ***y*** usually does not change.

play + -er = player

employ + -ed = employed

coy + -ness = coyness

pay + -able = payable

13.3 WORDS ENDING IN A CONSONANT

In one-syllable words that end in one consonant preceded by one short vowel, double the final consonant before adding a suffix beginning with a vowel, such as ***-ed*** or ***-ing.***

dip + -ed = dipped **set + -ing = setting**

slim + -est = slimmest **fit + -er = fitter**

The rule does not apply to words of one syllable that end in a consonant preceded by two vowels.

feel + -ing = feeling **peel + -ed = peeled**

reap + -ed = reaped **loot + -ed = looted**

In words of more than one syllable, double the final consonant when (1) the word ends with one consonant preceded by one vowel and (2) the word is accented on the last syllable.

be•gin´ per•mit´ re•fer´

In the following examples, note that in the new words formed with suffixes, the accent remains on the same syllable:

be•gin´ + -ing = be•gin´ ning = beginning

per•mit´ + -ed = per•mit´ ted = permitted

Exceptions: In some words with more than one syllable, though the accent remains on the same syllable when a suffix is added, the final consonant is nevertheless not doubled, as in the following examples:

tra´vel + -er = tra´vel•er = traveler

mar´ket + -er = mar´ket•er = marketer

In the following examples, the accent does not remain on the same syllable; thus, the final consonant is not doubled:

re•fer´ + -ence = ref´er•ence = reference

con•fer´ + -ence = con´fer•ence = conference

13.4 PREFIXES AND SUFFIXES

When adding a prefix to a word, do not change the spelling of the base word. When a prefix creates a double letter, keep both letters.

dis- + approve = disapprove

re- + build = rebuild

ir- + regular = irregular

mis- + spell = misspell

anti- + trust = antitrust

il- + logical = illogical

When adding ***-ly*** to a word ending in ***l,*** keep both ***l***'s, and when adding ***-ness*** to a word ending in ***n,*** keep both ***n***'s.

careful + -ly = carefully

sudden + -ness = suddenness

final + -ly = finally

thin + -ness = thinness

13.5 FORMING PLURAL NOUNS

To form the plural of most nouns, just add ***-s.***

prizes dreams circles stations

For most singular nouns ending in ***o,*** add ***-s.***

solos halos studios photos pianos

For a few nouns ending in ***o,*** add ***-es.***

heroes tomatoes potatoes echoes

When the singular noun ends in ***s, sh, ch, x,*** or ***z,*** add ***-es.***

waitresses brushes ditches

axes buzzes

When a singular noun ends in ***y*** with a consonant before it, change the ***y*** to ***i*** and add ***-es.***

army—armies	**candy—candies**
baby—babies	**diary—diaries**
ferry—ferries	**conspiracy—conspiracies**

When a vowel (***a, e, i, o, u***) comes before the ***y***, just add ***-s.***

boy—boys	**way—ways**
array—arrays	**alloy—alloys**
weekday—weekdays	**jockey—jockeys**

For most nouns ending in ***f*** or ***fe,*** change the ***f*** to ***v*** and add ***-es*** or ***-s.***

life—lives	**calf—calves**
knife—knives	**thief—thieves**
shelf—shelves	**loaf—loaves**

For some nouns ending in ***f,*** add ***-s*** to make the plural.

roofs chiefs reefs beliefs

Some nouns have the same form for both singular and plural.

deer sheep moose salmon trout

For some nouns, the plural is formed in a special way.

man—men	**goose—geese**
ox—oxen	**woman—women**
mouse—mice	**child—children**

For a compound noun written as one word, form the plural by changing the last word in the compound to its plural form.

stepchild—stepchildren firefly—fireflies

If a compound noun is written as a hyphenated word or as two separate words, change the most important word to the plural form.

brother-in-law—brothers-in-law

life jacket—life jackets

13.6 FORMING POSSESSIVES

If a noun is singular, add ***'s.***

mother—my mother's car

Ross—Ross's desk

Exception: The *s* after the apostrophe is dropped after *Jesus', Moses',* and certain names in classical mythology (*Hermes'*). These possessive forms can be pronounced easily.

If a noun is plural and ends with ***s,*** just add an apostrophe.

parents—my parents' car

the Santinis—the Santinis' house

If a noun is plural but does not end in ***s,*** add ***'s.***

people—the people's choice

women—the women's coats

13.7 SPECIAL SPELLING PROBLEMS

Only one English word ends in ***-sede:*** *supersede.* Three words end in ***-ceed:*** *exceed, proceed,* and *succeed.* All other verbs ending in the sound "seed" (except for the verb *seed*) are spelled with ***-cede.***

concede precede recede secede

In words with ***ie*** or ***ei,*** when the sound is long ***e*** (as in *she*), the word is spelled ***ie*** except after ***c*** (with some exceptions).

***i* before e**	**thief**	**relieve**	**field**
piece	**grieve**	**pier**	
except after c	**conceit**	**perceive**	**ceiling**
receive	**receipt**		

Exceptions: *either, neither, weird, leisure, seize.*

14 Commonly Confused Words

Words	Definition	Example
accept/except	The verb ***accept*** means "to receive or believe"; ***except*** is usually a preposition meaning "excluding."	**Except** for some of the more extraordinary events, I can **accept** that the *Odyssey* recounts a real journey.
advice/advise	***Advise*** is a verb; ***advice*** is a noun naming that which an ***adviser*** gives.	I **advise** you to take that job. Whom should I ask for **advice?**
affect/effect	As a verb, ***affect*** means "to influence." ***Effect*** as a verb means "to cause." If you want a noun, you will almost always want ***effect.***	Did Circe's wine **affect** Odysseus's mind? It did **effect** a change in Odysseus's men. In fact, it had an **effect** on everyone else who drank it.
all ready/ already	***All ready*** is an adjective meaning "fully ready." ***Already*** is an adverb meaning "before or by this time."	He was **all ready** to go at noon. I have **already** seen that movie.
allusion/ illusion	An ***allusion*** is an indirect reference to something. An ***illusion*** is a false picture or idea.	There are many **allusions** to the works of Homer in English literature. The world's apparent flatness is an **illusion.**
among/ between	***Between*** is used when you are speaking of only two things. ***Among*** is used for three or more.	**Between** *Hamlet* and *King Lear,* I prefer the latter. Emily Dickinson is **among** my favorite poets.
bring/take	***Bring*** is used to denote motion toward a speaker or place. ***Take*** is used to denote motion away from such a person or place.	**Bring** the books over here, and I will **take** them to the library.
fewer/less	***Fewer*** refers to the number of separate, countable units. ***Less*** refers to bulk quantity.	We have **less** literature and **fewer** selections in this year's curriculum.
leave/let	***Leave*** means "to allow something to remain behind." ***Let*** means "to permit."	The librarian will **leave** some books on display but will not **let** us borrow any.
lie/lay	***Lie*** means "to rest or recline." It does not take an object. ***Lay*** always takes an object.	Rover loves to **lie** in the sun. We always **lay** some bones next to him.
loose/lose	***Loose*** (lo͞os) means "free, not restrained"; ***lose*** (lo͞oz) means "to misplace or fail to find."	Who turned the horses **loose?** I hope we won't **lose** any of them.
precede/ proceed	***Precede*** means "to go or come before." Use ***proceed*** for other meanings.	Emily Dickinson's poetry **precedes** that of Alice Walker. You may **proceed** to the next section of the test.

continued

Words	Definition	Example
than/then	Use ***than*** in making comparisons; use ***then*** on all other occasions.	Who can say whether Amy Lowell is a better poet **than** Denise Levertov? I will read Lowell first, and **then** I will read Levertov.
their/there/ they're	***Their*** means "belonging to them." ***There*** means "in that place." ***They're*** is the contraction for "they are."	**There** is a movie playing at 9 P.M. **They're** going to see it with me. Sakara and Jessica drove away in **their** car after the movie.
two/too/to	***Two*** is the number. ***Too*** is an adverb meaning "also" or "very." Use ***to*** before a verb or as a preposition.	Meg had **to** go **to** town, **too.** We had **too** much reading **to** do. **Two** chapters is **too** many.

Glossary of Literary and Informational Terms

Act An act is a major unit of action in a play, similar to a chapter in a book. Depending on their lengths, plays can have as many as five acts.

See also Drama; Scene.

Allegory An allegory is a work with two levels of meaning, a literal one and a symbolic one. In such a work, most of the characters, objects, settings, and events represent abstract qualities. Personification is often used in traditional allegories. As in a fable or parable, the purpose of an allegory may be to convey truths about life, to teach religious or moral lessons, or to criticize social institutions.

Alliteration Alliteration is the repetition of consonant sounds at the beginnings of words. Poets use alliteration to impart a musical quality to their poems, to create mood, to reinforce meaning, to emphasize particular words, and to unify lines or stanzas.

Allusion An allusion is an indirect reference to a person, place, event, or literary work with which the author believes the reader will be familiar.

Almanac *See* Reference Works.

Ambiguity Ambiguity is a technique in which a word, phrase, or event has more than one meaning or can be interpreted in more than one way. Some writers deliberately create this effect to give richness and depth of meaning.

Analogy An analogy is a point-by-point comparison between two things for the purpose of clarifying the less familiar of the two subjects.

Anapest *See* Meter.

Anecdote An anecdote is a brief story that focuses on a single episode or event in a person's life and that is used to illustrate a particular point.

Anglo-Saxon Poetry Anglo-Saxon poetry, which was written between the 7th and 12th centuries, is characterized by a strong rhythm, or cadence, that makes it easily chanted or sung. It was originally recited by **scops,** poet-singers who traveled from place to place. Lines of Anglo-Saxon poetry are unified through alliteration and through use of the same number of accented syllables in each line. Typically, a line is divided by a **caesura,** or pause, into two parts, with each part having two accented syllables. Usually, one or both of the accented syllables in the first part share a similar sound with an accented syllable in the second part.

Another characteristic of Anglo-Saxon poetry is the use of **kennings,** metaphorical compound words or phrases substituted for simple nouns. Kennings from *Beowulf* include "shepherd of evil" for Grendel, and "folk-king" for Beowulf.

Antagonist An antagonist is usually the principal character in opposition to the **protagonist,** or hero of a narrative or drama. The antagonist can also be a force of nature.

See also Character; Protagonist.

Antithesis Antithesis is a figure of speech in which sharply contrasting words, phrases, clauses, or sentences are juxtaposed to emphasize a point. In a true antithesis, both the ideas and the grammatical structures are balanced.

Aphorism An aphorism is a brief statement that expresses a general observation about life in a witty, pointed way incorporating **subtlety,** or careful distinctions. Unlike proverbs, which may stem from oral folk tradition, aphorisms originate with specific authors.

Apostrophe Apostrophe is a figure of speech in which an object, an abstract quality, or an absent or imaginary person is addressed directly, as if present and able to understand. Writers use apostrophe to express powerful emotions.

Appeals by Association Appeals by association imply that one will gain acceptance or prestige by taking the writer's position.

Appeal to Authority An appeal to authority calls upon experts or others who warrant respect.

Appeal to Reason *See* Logical Appeal.

Archetype An archetype is a pattern in literature that is found in a variety of works from different cultures throughout the ages. An archetype can be a plot, a character, an image, or a setting. For example, the association of death and rebirth with winter and spring is an archetype common to many cultures.

Argument An argument is speech or writing that expresses a position on an issue or problem and supports it with reasons and evidence. An argument often takes into account other points of view, anticipating and answering objections that opponents of the position might raise.

See also Claim; Counterargument; Evidence; General Principle.

Aside In drama, an aside is a short speech directed to the audience, or another character, that is not heard by the other characters on stage.

See also Soliloquy.

Assonance Assonance is the repetition of a vowel sound in two or more stressed syllables that do not end with the same consonant. Poets use assonance to emphasize certain words, to impart a musical quality, to create a mood, or to unify a passage. An example of assonance is the repetition of the long *e* sound in the following sentence. Note that the repeated sounds are not always spelled the same.

> What I fear is that I will seem invisible,
> and all my tears will go unnoticed.

See also Alliteration; Consonance; Rhyme.

Assumption An assumption is an opinion or belief that is taken for granted. It can be about a specific situation, a person, or the world in general. Assumptions are often unstated.

See also General Principle.

Atmosphere *See* Mood.

Audience Audience is the person or persons who are intended to read or hear a piece of writing. The intended audience of a work determines its form, its style, its tone, and the details included.

Author's Message An author's message is the main idea or theme of a particular work.

See also Main Idea; Theme.

Author's Perspective An author's perspective is a unique combination of ideas, values, feelings, and beliefs that influences the way the writer looks at a topic. Tone, or attitude, often reveals an author's perspective.

See also Author's Purpose; Tone.

Author's Position An author's position is his or her opinion on an issue or topic.

See also Claim.

Author's Purpose A writer usually writes for one or more of these purposes: to inform, to entertain, to express himself or herself, or to persuade readers to believe or do something. For example, the purpose of a news report is to inform; the purpose of an editorial is to persuade the readers or audience to do or believe something.

Autobiographical Essay *See* Essay.

Autobiography An autobiography is a writer's account of his or her own life. Autobiographies often convey profound insights as writers recount past events from the perspective of greater understanding and distance. A formal autobiography involves a sustained, lengthy narrative of a person's history, but other autobiographical narratives may be less formal and briefer. Under the general category of autobiography fall such writings as diaries, journals, memoirs, and letters. Both formal and informal autobiographies provide revealing insights into the writer's character, attitudes, and motivations, as well as some understanding of the society in which the writer lived.

See also Diary; Memoir.

Ballad A ballad is a narrative poem that was originally intended to be sung. Traditional folk ballads, written by unknown authors and handed down orally, usually depict ordinary people in the midst of tragic events and adventures of love and bravery. They tend to begin abruptly, focus on a single incident, use dialogue and repetition, and suggest more than they actually state. They often contain supernatural elements.

Typically, a ballad consists of four-line stanzas, or quatrains, with the second and fourth lines of each stanza rhyming. Each stanza has a strong rhythmic pattern, usually with four stressed syllables in the first and third lines and three stressed syllables in the second and fourth lines. The rhyme scheme is usually ***abcb*** or ***aabb.***

A **literary ballad** is a ballad with a single author. Modeled on the early English and Scottish folk ballads, literary ballads became popular during the romantic period.

See also Narrative Poem; Rhyme; Rhythm.

Bias Bias is an inclination toward a particular judgment on a topic or issue. A writer often reveals a strongly positive or strongly negative opinion by presenting only one way of looking at an issue or by heavily weighting the evidence. Words with intensely positive or negative connotations are often a signal of a writer's bias.

Bibliography A bibliography is a list of books and other materials related to the topic of a text. Bibliographies can be good sources of works for further study on a subject.

See also Works Consulted.

Biography A biography is a type of nonfiction in which a writer gives a factual account of someone else's life. Written in the third person, a biography may cover a person's entire life or focus on only an important part of it. Modern biography includes a popular form called **fictionalized biography,** in which writers use their imaginations to re-create past conversations and to elaborate on some incidents.

Blank Verse Blank verse is unrhymed poetry written in **iambic pentameter.** Because iambic pentameter resembles the natural rhythm of spoken English, it has been considered the most suitable meter for dramatic verse in English. Shakespeare's plays are written largely in blank verse. Blank verse has also been used frequently for long poems.

See also Iambic Pentameter; Meter; Rhythm.

Business Correspondence Business correspondence includes all written business communications, such as business letters, e-mails, and memos. Business correspondence is to the point, clear, courteous, and professional.

Caesura A caesura is a pause or a break in a line of poetry. Poets use a caesura to emphasize the word or phrase that precedes it or to vary the rhythmical effects.

See also Anglo-Saxon Poetry.

Cast of Characters The cast of characters is a list of all the characters in a play, usually in the order of appearance. This list is found at the beginning of a script.

Cause and Effect A **cause** is an event or action that directly results in another event or action. An **effect** is the direct or logical outcome of an event or action. Basic **cause-and- effect relationships** include a single cause with a single effect, one cause with multiple effects, multiple causes with a single effect, and a chain of causes and effects. The concept of cause and effect also provides a way of organizing a piece of writing. It helps a writer show the relationships between events or ideas.

Character Characters are the people, and sometimes animals or other beings, who take part in the action of a story or novel. Events center on the lives of one or more characters, referred to as **main characters.** The other characters, called **minor characters,** interact with the main characters and help move the story along.

Characters may also be classified as either static or dynamic. **Static characters** tend not to change much over the course of the story. They do not experience life-altering moments and seem to act the same, even though their situations may change. In contrast, **dynamic characters** evolve as individuals, learning from their experiences and growing emotionally.

See also Antagonist; Characterization; Foil; Motivation; Protagonist.

Characterization Characterization refers to the techniques that writers use to develop characters. There are four basic methods of characterization:

- A writer may use physical description.
- A character's nature may be revealed through his or her own speech, thoughts, feelings, or actions.

- The speech, thoughts, feelings, and actions of other characters can be used to develop a character.
- The narrator can make direct comments about the character's nature.

See also Character; Narrator.

Chorus In the theater of ancient Greece, the chorus was a group of actors who commented on the action of the play. Between scenes, the chorus sang and danced to musical accompaniment, giving insights into the message of the play. The chorus is often considered a kind of ideal spectator, representing the response of ordinary citizens to the tragic events that unfold. Certain dramatists have continued to employ this classical convention as a way of representing the views of the society being depicted.

See also Drama.

Chronological Order Chronological order is the arrangement of events in their order of occurrence. This type of organization is used both in fictional narratives and in historical writing, biography, and autobiography.

Claim In an argument, a claim is the writer's position on an issue or problem. Although an argument focuses on supporting one claim, a writer may make more than one claim in a work.

Clarify Clarifying is a reading strategy that helps a reader to understand or make clear what he or she is reading. Readers usually clarify by rereading, reading aloud, or discussing.

Classification Classification is a pattern of organization in which objects, ideas, or information is presented in groups, or classes, based on common characteristics.

Cliché A cliché is an overused expression. "Better late than never" and "hard as nails" are common examples. Good writers generally avoid clichés unless they are using them in dialogue to indicate something about characters' personalities.

Climax In a plot structure, the climax, or turning point, is the moment when the reader's interest and emotional intensity reach a peak. The climax usually occurs toward the end of a story and often results in a change in the characters or a solution to the conflict.

See also Plot; Resolution.

Comedy A comedy is a dramatic work that is light and often humorous in tone, usually ending happily with a peaceful resolution of the main conflict. A comedy differs from a **farce** by having a more believable plot, more realistic characters, and less boisterous behavior.

See also Drama; Farce.

Comic Relief Comic relief consists of humorous scenes, incidents, or speeches that are included in a serious drama to provide a reduction in emotional intensity. Because it breaks the tension, comic relief allows an audience to prepare emotionally for events to come.

Compare and Contrast To compare and contrast is to identify similarities and differences in two or more subjects. Compare-and-contrast organization can be used to structure a piece of writing, serving as a framework for examining the similarities and differences in two or more subjects.

Complication A complication is an additional factor or problem introduced into the rising action of a story to make the conflict more difficult. In some cases, a plot complication presents a character with a moral dilemma or quandry that seems to make it harder or nearly impossible for a character to get what he or she wants.

Conceit *See* Extended Metaphor.

Conclusion A conclusion is a statement of belief based on evidence, experience, and reasoning. A **valid conclusion** is a conclusion that logically follows from the facts or statements upon which it is based. A **deductive conclusion** is one that follows from a particular generalization or premise. An **inductive conclusion** is a broad conclusion or generalization that is reached by arguing from specific facts and examples.

Conflict A conflict is a struggle between opposing forces that is the basis of a story's plot. An **external conflict** pits a character against nature, society, or another character. An **internal**

conflict is a conflict between opposing forces within a character.

See also Antagonist; Plot.

Connect Connecting is a reader's process of relating the content of a text to his or her own knowledge and experience.

Connotation Connotation is the emotional response evoked by a word, in contrast to its **denotation,** which is its literal meaning. *Kitten,* for example, is defined as "a young cat." However, the word also suggests, or connotes, images of softness, warmth, and playfulness.

Consonance Consonance is the repetition of consonant sounds within and at the ends of words, as in the following example:

> He ate most of the fruit in the kitchen yesterday.

See also Alliteration; Assonance.

Consumer Documents Consumer documents are printed materials that accompany products and services. They are intended for the buyers or users of the products or services and usually provide information about use, care, operation, or assembly. Some common consumer documents are applications, contracts, warranties, manuals, instructions, package inserts, labels, brochures, and schedules.

Context Clues When you encounter an unfamiliar word, you can often use context clues as aids for understanding. Context clues are the words and phrases surrounding the word that provide hints about the word's meaning.

Contradiction *See* Paradox

Controlling Idea *See* Thesis Statement.

Controlling Image *See* Extended Metaphor; Imagery.

Counterargument A counterargument is an argument made to oppose another argument. A good argument anticipates opposing viewpoints and provides counterarguments to refute (disprove) or answer them.

Counterclaim *See* Counterargument.

Couplet A couplet is a rhymed pair of lines. A simple couplet may be written in any rhythmic pattern.

A **heroic couplet** consists of two rhyming lines written in iambic pentameter. The term *heroic* comes from the fact that English poems having heroic themes and elevated style have often been written in iambic pentameter.

Creation Myth *See* Myth.

Credibility *Credibility* refers to the believability or trustworthiness of a source and the information it contains.

Critical Essay *See* Essay.

Critical Review A critical review is an evaluation or critique by a reviewer or critic. Different types of reviews include film reviews, book reviews, music reviews, and artshow reviews.

Dactyl *See* Meter.

Database A database is a collection of information that can be quickly and easily accessed and searched and from which information can be easily retrieved. It is frequently presented in an electronic format.

Debate A debate is an organized exchange of opinions on an issue. In academic settings, *debate* usually refers to a formal contest in which two opposing teams defend and attack a proposition.

See also Argument.

Deductive Reasoning Deductive reasoning is a way of thinking that begins with a generalization, presents a specific situation, and then advances with facts and evidence to a logical conclusion. The following passage has a deductive argument imbedded in it: "All students in the drama class must attend the play on Thursday. Since Ava is in the class, she had better show up." This deductive argument can be broken down as follows: generalization— all students in the drama class must attend the play on Thursday; specific situation—Ava is a student in the drama class; conclusion—Ava must attend the play.

Denotation *See* Connotation.

Dénouement *See* Plot.

Description Description is writing that helps a reader to picture scenes, events, and characters. It helps the reader understand exactly what someone or something is like. To create description, writers often use sensory images—words and phrases that enable the reader to see, hear, smell, taste, or feel the subject described—and figurative language. Effective description also relies on precise nouns, verbs, adjectives, and adverbs, as well as carefully selected details.

See also Diction; Figurative Language; Imagery.

Dialect Dialect is a particular variety of language spoken in one place by a distinct group of people. A dialect reflects the colloquialisms, grammatical constructions, distinctive vocabulary, and pronunciations that are typical of a region. At times writers use dialect to establish or emphasize settings, as well as to develop characters.

Dialogue Dialogue is conversation between two or more characters in either fiction or nonfiction. In drama, the story is told almost exclusively through dialogue, which moves the plot forward and reveals characters' motives.

See also Drama.

Diary A diary is a writer's personal day-to-day account of his or her experiences and impressions. Most diaries are private and not intended to be shared. Some, however, have been published because they are well written and provide useful perspectives on historical events or on the everyday life of particular eras.

Diction A writer's or speaker's choice of words is called diction. Diction includes both vocabulary (individual words) and syntax (the order or arrangement of words). Diction can be formal or informal, technical or common, abstract or concrete. In the following complex sentence, the diction is formal.

See also Connotation; Style.

Dictionary *See* Reference Works.

Drama Drama is literature in which plot and character are developed through dialogue and action; in other words, drama is literature in play form. It is performed on stage and radio and in films and television. Most plays are divided into acts, with each act having an emotional peak, or climax, of its own. The acts sometimes are divided into scenes; each scene is limited to a single time and place. Most contemporary plays have two or three acts, although some have only one act.

See also Act; Dialogue; Scene; Stage Directions.

Dramatic Irony *See* Irony.

Dramatic Monologue A dramatic monologue is a lyric poem in which a speaker addresses a silent or absent listener in a moment of high intensity or deep emotion, as if engaged in private conversation. The speaker proceeds without interruption or argument, and the effect on the reader is that of hearing just one side of a conversation. This technique allows the poet to focus on the feelings, personality, and motivations of the speaker.

See also Lyric Poetry; Soliloquy.

Draw Conclusions To draw a conclusion is to make a judgment or arrive at a belief based on evidence, experience, and reasoning.

Dynamic Character *See* Character.

Editorial An editorial is an opinion piece that usually appears on the editorial page of a newspaper or as part of a news broadcast. The editorial section of a newspaper presents opinions rather than objective news reports.

See also Op-Ed Piece.

Either/Or Fallacy An either/or fallacy is a statement that suggests that there are only two possible ways to view a situation or only two options to choose from. In other words, it is a statement that falsely frames a dilemma, giving the impression that no options exist but the two presented — for example, "Either we stop the construction of a new airport, or the surrounding suburbs will become ghost towns."

Elegy An elegy is an extended meditative poem in which the speaker reflects upon death—often in tribute to a person who has died recently—or on an equally serious subject. Most elegies are written in formal, dignified language and are serious in tone.

Elizabethan (Shakespearean) Sonnet *See* Sonnet.

Emotional Appeals Emotional appeals are messages that evoke strong feelings—such as fear, pity, or vanity—in order to persuade instead of using facts and evidence to make a point. An **appeal to fear** is a message that taps into people's fear of losing their safety or security. An **appeal to pity** is a message that taps into people's sympathy and compassion for others to build support for an idea, a cause, or a proposed action. An **appeal to vanity** is a message that attempts to persuade by tapping into people's desire to feel good about themselves.

Encyclopedia *See* Reference Works.

End Rhyme *See* Rhyme.

English (Shakespearean) Sonnet *See* Sonnet.

Epic Hero An epic hero is a larger-than-life figure who often embodies the ideals of a nation or race. Epic heroes take part in dangerous adventures and accomplish great deeds. Many undertake long, difficult journeys and display great courage and superhuman strength.

Epic Poem An epic is a long narrative poem on a serious subject presented in an elevated or formal style. An epic traces the adventures of a hero whose actions consist of courageous, even superhuman, deeds, which often represent the ideals and values of a nation or race. Epics typically address universal issues, such as good and evil, life and death, and sin and redemption. *Beowulf* is an enduring epic of the Anglo-Saxon period.

Epic Simile *See* Simile.

Epitaph An epitaph is an inscription on a tomb or monument to honor the memory of a deceased person. The term *epitaph* is also used to describe any verse commemorating someone who has died. Although a few humorous epitaphs have been composed, most are serious in tone.

Epithet An epithet is a brief phrase that points out traits associated with a particular person or thing.

Essay An essay is a brief work of nonfiction that offers an opinion on a subject. The purpose of an essay may be to express ideas and feelings, to analyze, to inform, to entertain, or to persuade. In a **persuasive essay,** a writer attempts to convince readers to adopt a particular opinion or to perform a certain action. Most persuasive essays present a series of facts, reasons, or examples in support of an opinion or proposal.

Essays can be formal or informal. A **formal essay** examines a topic in a thorough, serious, and highly organized manner. An **informal essay** presents an opinion on a subject, but not in a completely serious or formal tone. Characteristics of this type of essay include humor, a personal or confidential approach, a loose and sometimes rambling style, and often a surprising or unconventional topic. Mary Wollstonecraft's ***A Vindication of the Rights of Woman*** is a formal essay, meant to analyze and persuade.

A **personal essay** is a type of informal essay. Personal essays allow writers to express their viewpoints on subjects by reflecting on events or incidents in their own lives.

Ethical Appeals Ethical appeals establish a writer's credibility and trustworthiness with an audience. When a writer links a claim to a widely accepted value, for example, the writer not only gains moral support for that claim but also establishes a connection with readers.

Evaluate To evaluate is to examine something carefully and judge its value or worth. Evaluating is an important skill for gaining insight into what you read. A reader can evaluate the actions of a particular character, for example, or can form an opinion about the value of an entire work.

Evidence Evidence is the specific pieces of information that support a claim. Evidence can take the form of facts, quotations, examples, statistics, or personal experiences.

Exaggeration *See* Hyperbole.

Exemplum An exemplum is a short anecdote or story that helps illustrate a particular moral point. Developed in the Middle Ages, this form was widely used by Geoffrey Chaucer in *The Canterbury Tales.*

Exposition *See* Plot.

Expository Essay *See* Essay.

Extended Metaphor Like any metaphor, an extended metaphor is a comparison between two essentially unlike things that nevertheless have something in common. It does not contain the word *like* or *as.* In an extended metaphor, two things are compared at length and in various ways—perhaps throughout a stanza, a paragraph, or even an entire work.

Like an extended metaphor, a **conceit** parallels two essentially dissimilar things on several points. A conceit, though, is a more elaborate, formal, and ingenious comparison than the ordinary extended metaphor. Sometimes a conceit forms the framework of entire poem.

See also Figurative Language; Metaphor; Simile.

External Conflict *See* Conflict.

Fact versus Opinion A **fact** is a statement that can be proved or verified. An **opinion**, on the other hand, is a statement that cannot be proved because it expresses a person's beliefs, feelings, or thoughts.

See also Inference; Generalization.

Fallacy A fallacy is an error in reasoning. Typically, a fallacy is based on an incorrect inference or a misuse of evidence. Some common logical fallacies are **circular reasoning, either/or fallacy, oversimplification, overgeneralization,** and **stereotyping.**

See also Either/Or Fallacy; Logical Appeal; Overgeneralization

Falling Action *See* Plot.

Farce A farce is a type of exaggerated comedy that features an absurd plot, ridiculous situations, and humorous dialogue. The main purpose of a farce is to keep an audience laughing. The characters are usually **stereotypes,** or simplified examples of different traits or qualities. Comic devices typically used in farces include mistaken identity, deception, wordplay—such as puns and double meanings—and exaggeration.

See also Comedy; Stereotype.

Faulty Reasoning *See* Fallacy.

Feature Article A feature article is a main article in a newspaper or a cover story in a magazine. A feature article is focused more on entertaining than on informing. Features are lighter or more general than hard news and tend to be about human interest or lifestyles.

Fiction Fiction refers to works of prose that contain imaginary elements. Although fiction, like nonfiction, may be based on actual events and real people, it differs from nonfiction in that it is shaped primarily by the writer's imagination. The two major types of fiction are novels and short stories. The four basic elements of a work of fiction are **character, setting, plot,** and **theme.**

See also Novel; Short Story.

Figurative Language Figurative language is language that communicates ideas beyond the literal meaning of words. Figurative language can make descriptions and unfamiliar or difficult ideas easier to understand. Special types of figurative language, called **figures of speech,** include **simile, metaphor, personification, hyperbole,** and **apostrophe.**

Figures of Speech *See* Figurative Language.

First-Person Point of View *See* Point of View.

Flashback A flashback is a scene that interrupts the action of a narrative to describe events that took place at an earlier time. It provides background helpful in understanding a character's present situation.

Foil A foil is a character whose traits contrast with those of another character. A writer might use a minor character as a foil to emphasize the positive traits of the main character.

See also Character.

Folk Ballad *See* Ballad.

Folk Tale A folk tale is a short, simple story that is handed down, usually by word of mouth, from generation to generation. Folk tales include legends, fairy tales, myths, and fables. Folk tales often teach family obligations or societal values.

See also Legend; Myth.

Foot *See* Meter.

Foreshadowing Foreshadowing is a writer's use of hints or clues to indicate events that will occur later in a story. Foreshadowing creates suspense and at the same time prepares the reader for what is to come.

Form At its simplest, form refers to the physical arrangement of words in a poem—the length and placement of the lines, the grouping of lines into stanzas, and any graphical element that enhances the poem's meaning. The term can also refer to other kinds of patterning in poetry—anything from rhythm and other sound patterns to the design of a traditional poetic type, such as a sonnet or dramatic monologue.

See also Genre; Stanza.

Frame Story A frame story exists when a story is told within a narrative setting or frame—hence creating a story within a story.

> **Examples:** The collection of tales in Chaucer's *The Canterbury Tales,* including "The Wife of Bath's Tale," are set within a frame story. The frame is introduced in "The Prologue," in which 30 characters on a pilgrimage to Canterbury agree to tell stories to pass the time.

Free Verse Free verse is poetry that does not have regular patterns of rhyme and meter. The lines in free verse often flow more naturally than do rhymed, metrical lines and thus achieve a rhythm more like that of everyday human speech.

See also Meter; Rhyme.

Functional Documents *See* Consumer Documents; Workplace Documents.

Generalization A generalization is a broad statement about a class or category of people, ideas, or things, based on a study of only some of its members.

See also Overgeneralization.

General Principle In an argument, a general principle is an assumption that links the support to the claim. If one does not accept the general principle as a truth, then the support is inadequate because it is beside the point.

Genre Genre refers to the distinct types into which literary works can be grouped. The four main literary genres are fiction, poetry, nonfiction, and drama.

Gothic Literature Gothic literature is characterized by grotesque characters, bizarre situations, and violent events.

Government Publications Government publications are documents produced by government organizations. Pamphlets, brochures, and reports are just some of the many forms these publications may take. Government publications can be good resources for a wide variety of topics.

Graphic Aid A graphic aid is a visual tool that is printed, handwritten, or drawn. Text features such as charts, diagrams, graphs, photographs, and maps can all be graphic aids. Sometimes captions are included with a graphic aid to convey information.

Graphic Organizer A graphic organizer is a visual illustration of a verbal statement that helps a reader understand a text. Charts, tables, webs, and diagrams can all be graphic organizers. Graphic organizers and graphic aids can look the same. However, graphic organizers and graphic aids do differ in how they are used. Graphic aids are the visual representations that people encounter when they read informational texts. Graphic organizers are visuals that people construct to help them understand texts or organize information.

Graphics *See* Form.

Haiku Haiku is a form of Japanese poetry in which 17 syllables are arranged in three lines of 5, 7, and 5 syllables. The rules of haiku are strict. In addition to the syllabic count, the poet must create a clear picture that will evoke a strong emotional response in the reader. Nature is a particularly important source of inspiration for Japanese haiku poets, and details from nature are often the subjects of their poems.

Hero A hero, or **protagonist,** is a central character in a work of fiction, drama, or epic poetry. A traditional hero possesses good qualities that enable him or her to triumph over an antagonist who is bad or evil in some way.

The term ***tragic hero,*** first used by the Greek philosopher Aristotle, refers to a central character in a drama who is dignified or noble. According to Aristotle, a tragic hero possesses a defect, or tragic flaw, that brings about or contributes to his or her downfall. This flaw may be poor judgment, pride, weakness, or an excess of an admirable quality. The tragic hero, Aristotle noted, recognizes his or her flaw and its consequences, but only after it is too late to change the course of events. The characters Macbeth and Hamlet in Shakespeare's tragedies are tragic heroes.

A **cultural hero** is a hero who represents the values of his or her culture. Such a hero ranks somewhere between ordinary human beings and the gods. The role of a cultural hero is to provide a noble image that will inspire and guide the actions of mortals. Beowulf is a cultural hero.

In more recent literature, heroes do not necessarily command the attention and admiration of an entire culture. They tend to be individuals whose actions and decisions reflect personal courage. The conflicts they face are not on an epic scale but instead involve moral dilemmas presented in the course of living. Such heroes are often in a struggle with established authority because their actions challenge accepted beliefs.

See also Epic; Protagonist; Tragedy.

Heroic Couplet *See* Couplet.

Historical Context The historical context of a literary work refers to the social conditions that inspired or influenced its creation. To understand and appreciate some works, the reader must relate them to events in history.

Historical Documents Historical documents are writings that have played a significant role in human events or are themselves records of such events. The Declaration of Independence, for example, is a historical document.

Historical Writing Historical writing is the systematic telling, often in narrative form, of the past of a nation or group of people. Historical writing generally has the following characteristics: (1) it is concerned with real events; (2) it uses chronological order; and (3) it is usually an objective retelling of facts rather than a personal interpretation.

See also Primary Sources; Secondary Sources.

How-To Book A how-to book is a book that is written to explain how to do something—usually an activity, a sport, or a household project.

Humor In literature there are three basic types of humor, all of which may involve exaggeration or irony. **Humor of situation** is derived from the plot of a work. It usually involves exaggerated events or situational irony, which occurs when something happens that is different from what was expected. **Humor of character** is often based on exaggerated personalities or on characters who fail to recognize their own flaws, a form of dramatic irony. **Humor of language** may include sarcasm, exaggeration, puns, or verbal irony, which occurs when what is said is not what is meant.

See also Comedy; Farce; Irony.

Hyperbole Hyperbole is a figure of speech in which the truth is exaggerated for emphasis or for humorous effect.

See also Figurative Language; Understatement.

Iamb *See* Meter.

Iambic Pentameter Iambic pentameter is a metrical pattern of five feet, or units, each of which is made up of two syllables, the first unstressed and the second stressed. Iambic pentameter is the most common meter used in English poetry; it is the meter used in blank verse and in the sonnet.

See also Blank Verse; Meter; Sonnet.

Idiom An idiom is a common figure of speech whose meaning is different from the literal meaning of its words. For example, the phrase "raining cats and dogs" does not literally mean that cats and dogs are falling from the sky; the expression means "raining heavily."

Imagery The term *imagery* refers to words and phrases that create vivid sensory experiences for the reader. The majority of images are visual, but imagery may also appeal to the senses of smell, hearing, taste, and touch. In addition, images may re-create sensations of heat (thermal), movement (kinetic), or bodily tension (kinesthetic). Effective writers of both prose and poetry frequently use imagery that appeals to more than one sense simultaneously.

When an image describes one sensation in terms of another, the technique is called **synesthesia.**

A poet may use a **controlling image** to convey thoughts or feelings. A controlling image is a single image or comparison that extends throughout a literary work and shapes its meaning. A controlling image is sometimes an **extended metaphor.**

See also Description; Kinesthetic Imagery.

Implied Main Idea *See* Main Idea.

Index The index of a book is an alphabetized list of important topics and details covered in the book and the page numbers on which they can be found. An index can be used to quickly find specific information about a topic.

Inductive Reasoning Inductive reasoning is the process of logical reasoning from observations, examples, and facts to a general conclusion or principle.

Inference An inference is a logical assumption that is based on observed facts and one's own knowledge and experience.

Informal Essay *See* Essay.

Informational Text Informational text is a category of writing that includes exposition, argument, and functional documents. These texts normally provide factual, historical, or technical information. However, the term also covers texts that make logical or emotional arguments in defense of a position. Examples include biographies, journalism, essays, narrative histories, instruction manuals, and speeches.

Interior Monologue *See* Monologue; Stream of Consciousness.

Internal Conflict *See* Conflict.

Internal Rhyme *See* Rhyme.

Internet The Internet is a global, interconnected system of computer networks that allows for communication through e-mail, listservers, and the World Wide Web.

Interview An interview is a conversation conducted by a writer or reporter in which facts or statements are elicited from another person, recorded, and then broadcast or published.

Irony Irony is a contrast between expectation and reality. This incongruity often has the effect of surprising the reader or viewer. The techniques of irony include hyperbole, understatement, and sarcasm. Irony is often subtle and easily overlooked or misinterpreted.

There are three main types of irony. **Situational irony** occurs when a character or the reader expects one thing to happen but something else actually happens. **Verbal irony** occurs when a writer or character says one thing but means another. An example of verbal irony is the title of Jonathan Swift's essay "A Modest Proposal." The reader soon discovers that the narrator's proposal is outrageous rather than modest and unassuming. **Dramatic irony** occurs when the reader or viewer knows something that a character does not know.

Italian (Petrarchan) Sonnet *See* Sonnet.

Journal A journal is a periodical publication issued by a legal, medical, or other professional organization. Alternatively, the term may be used to refer to a diary or daily record.

See also Diary.

Kenning *See* Anglo-Saxon Poetry.

Kinesthetic Imagery Kinesthetic imagery re-creates the tension felt through muscles, tendons, or joints in the body.

See also Imagery.

Legend A legend is a story passed down orally from generation to generation and popularly believed to have a historical basis. While some legends may be based on real people or situations, most of the events are either greatly exaggerated or fictitious. Like myths, legends may incorporate supernatural elements and magical deeds. But legends differ from myths in that they claim to be stories about real human beings and are often set in a particular time and place.

Letters *Letters* refers to the written correspondence exchanged between acquaintances, friends, or family members. Most letters are private and not designed for publication. However, some are published and read by a wider audience because they are written by well-known public figures or provide important information about the period in which they were written.

Limited Point of View *See* Point of View.

Line The line is the core unit of a poem. In poetry, line length is an essential element of the poem's meaning and rhythm. There are a variety of terms to describe the way a line of poetry ends or is connected to the next line. Line breaks, where a line of poetry ends, may coincide with grammatical units. However, a line break may also occur in the middle of a grammatical or syntactical unit, creating a pause or emphasis. Poets use a variety of line breaks to play with meaning, thereby creating a wide range of effects.

Literary Ballad *See* Ballad.

Literary Criticism Literary criticism refers to writing that focuses on a literary work or a genre, describing some aspect of it, such as its origin, its characteristics, or its effects.

Literary Nonfiction Literary nonfiction is informational text that is recognized as being of artistic value or that is about literature. Autobiographies, biographies, essays, and eloquent speeches typically fall into this category.

Loaded Language Loaded language consists of words with strongly positive or negative connotations intended to influence a reader's or listener's attitude.

Logical Appeal A logical appeal relies on logic and facts, appealing to people's reasoning or intellect rather than to their values or emotions. Flawed logical appeals—that is, errors in reasoning—are considered logical fallacies.

See also Fallacy.

Logical Argument A logical argument is an argument in which the logical relationship between the support and the claim is sound.

Lyric A lyric is a short poem in which a single speaker expresses personal thoughts and feelings. Most poems other than dramatic and narrative poems are lyrics. In ancient Greece, lyrics were meant to be sung—the word ***lyric*** comes from the word ***lyre,*** the name of a musical instrument that was used to accompany songs. Modern lyrics are not usually intended for singing, but they are characterized by strong, melodic rhythms. Lyrics can be in a variety of forms and cover many subjects, from love and death to everyday experiences. They are marked by imagination and create for the reader a strong, unified impression.

See also Poetry.

Main Character *See* Character.

Main Idea A main idea is the central, controlling, or most important, idea about a topic that a writer or speaker conveys. It can be the central idea of an entire work or of just a paragraph. Often, the main idea of a paragraph is expressed in a topic sentence. However, a main idea may just be implied, or suggested, by details. A main idea and supporting details can serve as a basic pattern of organization in a piece of writing, with the central idea about a topic being supported by details.

Major Character *See* Character.

Make Inferences *See* Inference.

Maxim A maxim is a brief and memorable statement of general truth, one that often imparts guidance or advice.

Memoir A memoir is a form of autobiographical writing in which a person recalls significant events and people in his or her life. Most memoirs share the following characteristics: (1) they usually are structured as narratives told by the writers themselves, using the first-person point of view; (2) although some names may be changed to protect privacy, memoirs are true accounts of actual events; (3) although basically personal, memoirs may deal with newsworthy events having a significance beyond the confines of the writer's life; (4) unlike strictly historical accounts, memoirs often include the writers' feelings and opinions about historical events, giving the reader insight into the impact of history on people's lives.

See also Autobiography.

Metaphor A metaphor is a figure of speech that compares two things that have something in common. Unlike similes, metaphors do not use the words *like* or *as* but make comparisons directly.

See also Extended Metaphor; Figurative Language; Simile.

Meter Meter is the repetition of a regular rhythmic unit in a line of poetry. Each unit, known as a **foot,** has one stressed syllable (indicated by a ´) and either one or two unstressed syllables (indicated by a ˘). The four basic types of metrical feet are the **iamb,** an unstressed syllable followed by a stressed syllable; the **trochee,** a stressed syllable followed by an unstressed syllable; the **anapest,** two unstressed syllables followed by a stressed syllable; and the **dactyl,** a stressed syllable followed by two unstressed syllables.

Two words are typically used to describe the meter of a line. The first word identifies the type of metrical foot— iambic, trochaic, anapestic, or dactylic—and the second word indicates the number of feet in a line: **monometer** (one foot); **dimeter** (two feet); **trimeter** (three feet); **tetrameter** (four feet); **pentameter** (five feet); **hexameter** (six feet); and so forth.

See also Free Verse; Iambic Pentameter; Rhythm; Scansion.

Minor Character *See* Character.

Mise en Scène *Mise en scène* is a term from the French that refers to the various physical aspects of a dramatic presentation, such as lighting, costumes, scenery, makeup, and props.

Modernism Modernism was a movement roughly spanning the time period between the two world wars, 1914–1945. Modernist writers departed from 19th century traditions, such as **realism**, preferring more flexible, experimental approaches emphasizing subjectivity and fragmentation, such as **stream-of-consciousness** and **free verse.** Modernist works often focus on the theme of the alienation of the individual.

Monitor Monitoring is the strategy of checking your comprehension as you are reading and modifying the strategies you are using to suit your needs. Monitoring may include some or all of the following strategies: **questioning, clarifying, visualizing, predicting, connecting,** and **rereading.**

Monologue In a drama, the speech of a character who is alone on stage, voicing his or her thoughts, is known as a monologue. In a short story or a poem, the direct presentation of a character's unspoken thoughts is called an **interior monologue.** An interior monologue may jump back and forth between past and present, displaying thoughts, memories, and impressions just as they might occur in a person's mind.

See also Stream of Consciousness; Dramatic Monologue.

Mood Mood is the feeling or atmosphere that a writer creates for the reader. The writer's use of connotation, imagery, figurative language, sound and rhythm, and descriptive details all contribute to the mood.

See also Connotation; Description; Diction; Figurative Language; Imagery; Style; Tone.

Motif A motif is a recurring word, phrase, image, object, idea, or action in a work of literature. Motifs function as unifying devices and often relate directly to one or more major themes.

Motivation Motivation is the stated or implied reason behind a character's behavior. The grounds for a character's actions may not be obvious, but they should be comprehensible and consistent, in keeping with the character as developed by the writer.

See also Character.

Myth A myth is a traditional story, passed down through generations, that explains why the world is the way it is. Myths are essentially religious because they present supernatural events and beings and articulate the values and beliefs of a cultural group.

Narrative A narrative is any type of writing that is primarily concerned with relating an event or a series of events. A narrative can be imaginary, as is a short story or novel, or factual, as is a newspaper account or a work of history. The word ***narration*** can be used interchangeably with ***narrative,*** which comes from the Latin word meaning "tell."

See also Fiction; Nonfiction; Novel; Plot; Short Story.

Narrative Poem A narrative poem is a poem that tells a story using elements of character, setting, and plot to develop a theme. Epics, such as ***Beowulf*** and the ***Iliad,*** are narrative poems, as are ballads.

See also Ballad.

Narrator The narrator of a story is the character or voice that relates the story's events to the reader.

Naturalism An extreme form of realism, naturalism in fiction involves the depiction of life objectively and precisely, without idealizing. However, the naturalist creates characters who are victims of environmental forces and internal drives beyond their comprehension and control. Naturalistic fiction conveys the belief that universal forces result in an indifference to human suffering.

See also Realism.

Neoclassicism *Neoclassicism* refers to the attitudes toward life and art that dominated English literature during the Restoration and the 18th century. Neoclassicists respected order, reason, and rules and viewed humans as limited and imperfect. To them, the intellect was more important than emotions, and society was more important than the individual. Imitating classical literature, neoclassical writers developed a style that was characterized by strict form, logic, symmetry, grace, good taste, restraint, clarity, and conciseness. Their works were meant not only to delight readers but also to instruct them in moral virtues and correct social behavior. Among the literary forms that flourished during the neoclassical period were the essay, the literary letter, and the epigram. The heroic couplet was the dominant verse form, and satire and parody prevailed in both prose and poetry.

See also Romanticism.

News Article A news article is a piece of writing that reports on a recent event. In newspapers, news articles are usually written in a concise manner to report the latest news, presenting the most important facts first and then more detailed information. In magazines, news articles are usually more elaborate than those in newspapers because they are written to provide both information and analysis. Also, news articles in magazines do not necessarily present the most important facts first.

Nonfiction Nonfiction, or informational text, is writing about real people, places, and events. Unlike fiction, nonfiction is largely concerned with factual information, although the writer shapes the information according to his or her purpose and viewpoint. Biography, autobiography, and newspaper articles are examples of nonfiction.

See also Autobiography; Biography; Diary; Essay; Letters; Memoir.

Novel A novel is an extended work of fiction. Like the short story, a novel is essentially the product of a writer's imagination. The most obvious difference between a novel and a short story is length. Because the novel is considerably longer, a novelist can develop a wider range of characters and a more complex plot.

Octave *See* Sonnet.

Ode An ode is a complex lyric poem that develops a serious and dignified theme. Odes appeal to both the imagination and the intellect, and many commemorate events or praise people or elements of nature.

Off Rhyme *See* Rhyme.

Omniscient Point of View *See* Point of View.

Onomatopoeia Onomatopoeia is the use of words whose sounds echo their meanings, such as ***buzz, whisper, gargle,*** and ***murmur.*** Onomatopoeia as a literary technique goes beyond the use of simple echoic words, however. Skilled writers, especially poets, choose words whose sounds in combination suggest meaning.

Op-Ed Piece An op-ed piece is an opinion piece that usually appears opposite ("op") the editorial page of a newspaper. Unlike editorials, op-ed pieces are written and submitted by named writers.

Oral Literature Oral literature is literature that is passed from one generation to another by performance or word of mouth. Folk tales, fables, myths, chants, and legends are part of the oral tradition of cultures throughout the world.

See also Folk Tale; Legend; Myth.

Organization *See* Pattern of Organization.

Overgeneralization An overgeneralization is a generalization that is too broad. You can often recognize overgeneralizations by the appearance of words and phrases such as ***all, everyone, every time, any, anything, no one,*** and ***none.*** Consider, for example, this statement: "None of the sanitation workers in our city really care about keeping the environment clean." In all probability, there are many exceptions. The writer can't possibly know the feelings of every sanitation worker in the city.

Overstatement *See* Understatement.

Overview An overview is a short summary of a story, a speech, or an essay. It orients the reader by providing a preview of the text to come.

Oxymoron *See* Paradox.

Parable A parable is a brief story that is meant to teach a lesson or illustrate a moral truth. A parable is more than a simple story, however. Each detail of the parable corresponds to some aspect of the problem or moral dilemma to which it is directed.

Paradox A paradox is a statement that seems to contradict, or oppose, itself but, in fact, reveals some element of truth. Paradox is found frequently in the poetry of the 16th and 17th centuries. A special kind of concise paradox is the **oxymoron**, which brings together two contradictory terms. Examples are "cruel kindness" and "brave fear."

Parallel Plot A parallel plot is a particular type of plot in which two stories of equal importance are told simultaneously. The story moves back and forth between the two plots.

Parallelism Parallelism is the use of similar grammatical constructions to express ideas that are related or equal in importance. The parallel elements may be words, phrases, sentences, or paragraphs.

See also Repetition.

Paraphrase Paraphrasing is the restating of information in one's own words.

See also Summarize.

Parody Parody is writing that imitates either the style or the subject matter of a literary work for the purpose of criticism, humorous effect, or flattering tribute.

Pattern of Organization A pattern of organization is a particular arrangement of ideas and information. Such a pattern may be used to organize an entire composition or a single paragraph within a longer work. The following are the most common patterns of organization: **cause-and-effect, chronological order, compare-and-contrast, classification, deductive, inductive, order of importance, problemsolution, sequential,** and **spatial.**

See also Cause and Effect; Chronological Order; Classification; Compare and Contrast; Problem-Solution Order; Sequential Order.

Periodical A periodical is a publication that is issued at regular intervals of more than one day. For example, a periodical may be a weekly, monthly, or quarterly journal or magazine. Newspapers and other daily publications generally are not classified as periodicals.

Persona *See* Speaker.

Personal Essay *See* Essay.

Personification Personification is a figure of speech in which human qualities are attributed to an object, animal, or idea. Writers use personification to communicate feelings and images in a concise, concrete way.

See also Figurative Language; Metaphor; Simile.

Persuasion Persuasion is the art of swaying others' feelings, beliefs, or actions. Persuasion normally appeals to both the intellect and the emotions of readers. **Persuasive techniques** are the methods used to influence others to adopt certain opinions or beliefs or to act in certain ways. Types of persuasive techniques include emotional appeals, ethical appeals, logical appeals, and loaded language. When used properly, persuasive techniques can add depth to writing that's meant to persuade. Persuasive techniques can, however, be misused to cloud factual information, disguise poor reasoning, or unfairly exploit people's emotions in order to shape their opinions.

See also Appeals by Association; Appeal to Authority; Emotional Appeals; Ethical Appeals; Loaded Language; Logical Appeal.

Persuasive Writing Persuasive writing is intended to convince a reader to adopt a particular opinion or to perform a certain action. Effective persuasion usually appeals to both the reason and the emotions of an audience.

Petrarchan Sonnet *See* Sonnet.

Plot The plot is the sequence of actions and events in a literary work. Generally, plots are built around a **conflict**—a problem or struggle between two or more opposing forces. Plots usually progress through stages: exposition, rising action, climax, and falling action.

The **exposition** provides important background information and introduces the setting, characters, and conflict. During the **rising action,** the conflict becomes more intense, and suspense builds as the main characters struggle to resolve their problem. The **climax** is the turning point in the plot when the outcome of the conflict becomes clear, usually resulting in a change in the characters or a solution to the conflict. After the climax, the **falling action** shows the effects of the climax. As the falling action begins, the suspense is over but the results of the decision or action that caused the climax are not yet fully worked out. The **resolution,** or **dénouement,** which often blends with the falling action, reveals the final outcome of events and ties up loose ends.

See also Climax; Complication; Conflict.

Poetry Poetry is language arranged in lines. Like other forms of literature, poetry attempts to re-create emotions and experiences. Poetry, however, is usually more condensed and suggestive than prose.

Poems often are divided into stanzas, or paragraph-like groups of lines. The stanzas in a poem may contain the same number of lines or may vary in length. Some poems have definite patterns of meter and rhyme. Others rely more on the sounds of words and less on fixed rhythms and rhyme schemes. The use of figurative language is also common in poetry.

The form and content of a poem combine to convey meaning. The way that a poem is arranged on the page, the impact of the images, the sounds of the words and phrases, and all the other details that make up a poem work together to help the reader grasp its central idea.

See also Form; Free Verse; Meter; Rhyme; Rhythm; Stanza..

Point of View Point of view refers to the narrative perspective from which events in a story or novel are narrated.

In the **first-person point of view,** the narrator is a character in the work who tells everything in his or her own words and uses the pronouns *I, me,* and *my.* In the **third-person point of view,** events are related by a voice outside the action, not by one of the characters. A third-person narrator uses pronouns like *he, she,* and *they.* In the **third-person omniscient point of view,** the narrator is an all-knowing, objective observer who stands outside the action and reports what different characters are thinking. In the **third-person limited point of view,** the narrator stands outside the action and focuses on one character's thoughts, observations, and feelings.

See also Narrator.

Predict Predicting is a reading strategy that involves using text clues to make a reasonable guess about what will happen next in a story.

Primary Sources Primary sources are accounts of events written by people who were directly involved in or witness to the events. Primary sources include materials such as diaries, letters, wills, and public documents. They also can include historical narratives in which the writer sets out to describe the specific experience of participating in or observing an event.

See also Secondary Sources; Sources.

Prior Knowledge Prior knowledge is the knowledge a reader already possesses about a topic. This information might come from personal experiences, expert accounts, books, films, or other sources.

Problem-Solution Order Problem-solution order is a pattern of organization in which a problem is stated and analyzed and then one or more solutions are proposed and examined. Writers use words and phrases such as ***propose, conclude, reason for, problem, answer,*** and ***solution*** to connect ideas and details when writing about problems and solutions.

Prologue A prologue is an introductory scene in a drama.

Prop Prop, an abbreviation of ***property,*** refers to a physical object that is used in a stage production.

Propaganda Propaganda is a form of communication that may use distorted, false, or misleading information. It usually refers to manipulative political discourse.

Prose Generally, ***prose*** refers to all forms of written or spoken expression that are not in verse. The term, therefore, may be used to describe very different forms of writing—short stories as well as essays, for example.

Protagonist The protagonist is the main character in a work of literature, who is involved in the central conflict of the story. Usually, the protagonist changes after the central conflict reaches a climax. He or she may be a hero and is usually the one with whom the audience tends to identify.

See also Antagonist; Character; Tragic Hero.

Psychological Fiction An offshoot of **realism,** psychological fiction focuses on the conflicts and motivations of its characters. In such literature, plot events are often less important than the inner workings of each character's mind. A technique closely associated with psychological fiction is **stream of consciousness,** which presents the random flow of a character's thoughts. Though psychological fiction is often viewed as a 20th-century invention found in the writing of Virginia Woolf, James Joyce, and others, earlier writers—such as George Eliot, Elizabeth Gaskell, and Thomas Hardy—can be said to employ this technique in varying degrees.

See also Realism.

Public Documents Public documents are documents that were written for the public to provide information that is of public interest or concern. They include government documents, speeches, signs, and rules and regulations.

See also Government Publications.

Purpose *See* Author's Purpose.

Quatrain A quatrain is a four-line stanza.

See also Poetry; Stanza.

Realism As a general term, ***realism*** refers to any effort to offer an accurate and detailed portrayal of actual life. Thus, critics talk about Shakespeare's realistic portrayals of his characters and praise the medieval poet Chaucer for his realistic descriptions of people from different social classes.

More specifically, realism refers to a literary method developed in the 19th century. The realists based their writing on careful observations of ordinary life, often focusing on the middle or lower classes. They attempted to present life objectively and honestly, without the sentimentality or idealism that had colored earlier literature. Typically, realists developed their settings in great detail in an effort to re-create a specific time and place for the reader. Elements of realism can be found in the novels of Jane Austen and Charles Dickens, but it is not fully developed until the fiction of George Eliot.

See also Naturalism.

Recurring Theme *See* Theme.

Reference Works General reference works are sources that contain facts and background information on a wide range of subjects. More specific reference works contain in-depth information on a single subject. Most reference works are good sources of reliable information because they have been reviewed by experts. The following are some common reference works: **encyclopedias, dictionaries, thesauruses, almanacs, atlases, chronologies, biographical dictionaries,** and **directories.**

Reflective Essay *See* Essay.

Refrain In poetry, a refrain is part of a stanza, consisting of one or more lines that are repeated regularly, sometimes with changes, often at the ends of succeeding stanzas.

Repetition Repetition is a technique in which a sound, word, phrase, or line is repeated for emphasis or unity. Repetition often helps to reinforce meaning and create an appealing rhythm. The term includes specific devices associated with both prose and poetry, such as **alliteration** and **parallelism.**

See also Alliteration; Parallelism; Sound Devices.

Resolution *See* Plot.

Review *See* Critical Review.

Rhetorical Devices *See* Analogy; Repetition; Rhetorical Questions

Rhetorical Questions Rhetorical questions are those that do not require a reply. Writers use them to suggest that their arguments make the answer obvious or self-evident.

Rhyme Words rhyme when the sounds of their accented vowels and all succeeding sounds are identical, as in ***amuse*** and ***confuse.*** For true rhyme, the consonants that precede the vowels must be different. Rhyme that occurs at the end of lines of poetry is called **end rhyme.** End rhymes that are not exact but approximate are called **off rhyme,** or **slant rhyme.** Rhyme that occurs within a single line is called **internal rhyme.**

Rhyme Scheme A rhyme scheme is the pattern of end rhyme in a poem. A rhyme scheme is charted by assigning a letter of the alphabet, beginning with ***a,*** to each line. Lines that rhyme are given the same letter.

See also Ballad; Couplet; Quatrain; Rhyme; Sonnet.

Rhythm Rhythm is a pattern of stressed and unstressed syllables in a line of poetry. Poets use rhythm to bring out the musical quality of language, to emphasize ideas, to create mood, to unify a work, and to heighten emotional response. Devices such as alliteration, rhyme, assonance, consonance, and parallelism often contribute to creating rhythm.

See also Anglo-Saxon Poetry; Ballad; Meter; Spenserian Stanza.

Rising Action *See* Plot.

Romance The romance has been a popular narrative form since the Middle Ages. Generally, the term refers to any imaginative adventure concerned with noble heroes, gallant love, a chivalric code of honor, daring deeds, and supernatural events. Romances usually have faraway settings, depict events unlike those of ordinary life, and idealize their heroes as well as the eras in which the heroes live. Medieval romances often are lighthearted in tone, consist of a number of episodes, and involve one or more characters in a quest.

Romanticism *Romanticism* refers to a literary movement that flourished in Britain and Europe throughout much of the 19th century. Romantic writers looked to nature for their inspiration, idealized the distant past, and celebrated the individual. In reaction against neoclassicism, their treatment of subjects was emotional rather than rational, imaginative rather than analytical. The romantic period in English literature is generally viewed as beginning with the publication of ***Lyrical Ballads,*** poems by William Wordsworth and Samuel Taylor Coleridge.

See also Neoclassicism.

Sarcasm Sarcasm, a type of **verbal irony,** refers to a critical remark expressed in a mocking fashion. In some cases, a statement is sarcastic because its literal meaning is the opposite of its actual meaning.

See also Irony.

Satire Satire is a literary technique in which ideas, customs, behaviors, or institutions are ridiculed for the purpose of improving society. Satire may be gently witty, mildly abrasive, or bitterly critical, and it often uses exaggeration to force readers to see something in a more critical light. Often, a satirist distances himself or herself from a subject by creating a fictional speaker—usually a calm and often naïve observer—who can address the topic without revealing the true emotions of the writer. Whether the object of a satiric work is an individual person or a group of people, the force of the satire will almost always cast light on foibles and failings that are universal to human experience.

There are two main types of satire, named for the Roman satirists Horace and Juvenal; they differ chiefly in tone. **Horatian satire** is playfully amusing and seeks to correct vice or foolishness with gentle laughter and sympathetic understanding. **Juvenalian satire** provokes a darker kind of laughter. It is biting and criticizes corruption or incompetence with scorn and outrage. Jonathan Swift's "A Modest Proposal" is an example of Juvenalian satire.

See also Irony.

Scanning Scanning is the process of searching through writing for a particular fact or piece of information. When you scan, your eyes sweep across a page, looking for key words that may lead you to the information you want.

Scansion The process of determining meter is known as scansion. When you scan a line of poetry, you mark its stressed (´) and unstressed syllables (˘) in order to identify the rhythm.

See also Meter.

Scene In drama, a scene is a subdivision of an act. Each scene usually establishes a different time or place.

See also Act; Drama.

Scenery Scenery is a painted backdrop or other structures used to create the setting for a play.

Screenplay A screenplay is a play written for film.

Script The text of a play, film, or broadcast is called a script.

Secondary Sources Accounts written by people who were not directly involved in or witnesses to an event are called secondary sources. A history textbook is an example of a secondary source.

See also Primary Sources; Sources.

Sensory Details Sensory details are words and phrases that appeal to the reader's senses of sight, hearing, touch, taste, and smell. For example, the sensory detail "a fine film of rain" appeals to the senses of sight and touch. Sensory details stimulate the reader to create images in his or her mind.

See also Imagery.

Sequential Order A pattern of organization that shows the order in which events or actions occur is called sequential order. Writers typically use this pattern of organization to explain steps or stages in a process.

Sestet *See* Sonnet.

Setting The setting of a literary work refers to the time and place in which the action occurs. A story can be set in an imaginary place, such as an enchanted castle, or a real place, such as London or Hampton Court. The time can be the past, the present, or the future. In addition to time and place, setting can include the larger historical and cultural contexts that form the background for a narrative. Setting is one of the main elements in fiction and often plays an important role in what happens and why.

Setting a Purpose The process of establishing specific reasons for reading a text is called setting a purpose.

Shakespearean (English) Sonnet
See Sonnet.

Short Story A short story is a work of fiction that centers on a single idea and can be read in one sitting. Generally, a short story has one main conflict that involves the characters, keeps the story moving, and stimulates readers' interest.

See also Fiction.

Sidebar A sidebar is additional information set in a box alongside or within a news or feature article. Popular magazines often make use of sidebar information.

Signal Words Signal words are words and phrases that indicate what is to come in a text. Readers can use signal words to discover a text's pattern of organization and to analyze the relationships among the ideas in the text.

Simile A simile is a figure of speech that compares two things that have something in common, using a word such as ***like*** or ***as.*** Both poets and prose writers use similes to intensify emotional response, stimulate vibrant images, provide imaginative delight, and concentrate the expression of ideas.

An **epic simile** is a long comparison that often continues for a number of lines. It does not always contain the word ***like*** or ***as.***

See also Figurative Language; Metaphor.

Situational Irony *See* Irony.

Slant Rhyme *See* Rhyme.

Soliloquy A soliloquy is a speech in a dramatic work in which a character speaks his or her thoughts aloud. Usually the character is on the stage alone, not speaking to other characters and perhaps not even consciously addressing the audience. (If there are other characters on stage, they are ignored temporarily.) The purpose of a soliloquy is to reveal a character's inner thoughts, feelings, and plans to the audience. Soliloquies are characteristic of Elizabethan drama.

Sonnet A sonnet is a lyric poem of 14 lines, commonly written in **iambic pentameter.** For centuries the sonnet has been a popular form because it is long enough to permit development of a complex idea, yet short and structured enough to challenge any poet's skills. Sonnets written in English usually follow one of two forms.

The **Petrarchan,** or **Italian, sonnet,** introduced into English by Sir Thomas Wyatt, is named after Petrarch, the 14th century Italian poet. This type of sonnet consists of two parts, called the **octave** (the first eight lines) and the **sestet** (the last six lines). The usual rhyme scheme for the octave is ***abbaabba.*** The rhyme scheme for the sestet may be ***cdecde, cdccdc,*** or a similar variation. The octave generally presents a problem or raises a question, and the sestet resolves or comments on the problem.

The **Shakespearean,** or **English, sonnet** is sometimes called the **Elizabethan sonnet.** It consists of three quatrains, or four-line units, and a final couplet. The typical rhyme scheme is ***abab cdcd efef gg.*** In the English sonnet, the rhymed couplet at the end of the sonnet provides a final commentary on the subject developed in the three quatrains. Shakespeare's sonnets are the finest examples of this type of sonnet.

A variation of the Shakespearean sonnet is the **Spenserian sonnet,** which has the same structure but uses the interlocking rhyme scheme ***abab bcbc cdcd ee.***

Some poets have written a series of related sonnets that have the same subject. These are called **sonnet sequences,** or **sonnet cycles**. Toward the end of the 16th century, writing sonnet sequences became fashionable, with a common subject being love for a beautiful but unattainable woman.

See also Iambic Pentameter; Lyric; Meter; Quatrain.

Sound Devices *See* Alliteration; Assonance; Consonance; Meter; Onomatopoeia; Repetition; Rhyme; Rhyme Scheme; Rhythm.

Sources A source is anything that supplies information. **Primary sources** are materials written or created by people who were present at events, either as participants or as observers. Letters, diaries, autobiographies, speeches, and photographs are primary sources. **Secondary sources** are records of events that were created sometime after the events occurred; the writers were not directly involved or were not present when the events took place. Encyclopedias, textbooks, biographies, most newspaper and magazine articles, and books and articles that interpret or review research are secondary sources.

Spatial Order Spatial order is a pattern of organization that highlights the physical positions or relationships of details or objects. This pattern of organization is typically found in descriptive writing. Writers use words and phrases such as ***on the left, to the right, here, over there, above, below, beyond, nearby,*** and ***in the distance*** to indicate the arrangement of details.

Speaker The speaker of a poem, like the narrator of a story, is the voice that talks to the reader. In some poems, the speaker can be identified with the poet. In other poems, the poet invents a fictional character, or a persona, to play the role of the speaker. *Persona* is a Latin word meaning "actor's mask."

Speech A speech is a talk or public address. The purpose of a speech may be to entertain, to explain, to persuade, to inspire, or any combination of these aims.

Stage Directions *See* Drama.

Stanza A stanza is a group of lines that form a unit in a poem. A stanza is usually characterized by a common pattern of meter, rhyme, and number of lines. During the 20th century, poets experimented more freely with stanza form than did earlier poets, sometimes writing poems without any stanza breaks.

Static Character *See* Character.

Stereotype A stereotype is an oversimplified image of a person, group, or institution. Sweeping generalizations about "all English people" or "every used-car dealer" are stereotypes. Simplified or stock characters in literature are often called stereotypes. Such characters do not usually demonstrate the complexities of real people.

Stereotyping Stereotyping is a dangerous type of overgeneralization. Stereotypes are broad statements made about people on the basis of their gender, ethnicity, race, or political, social, professional, or religious group.

Stream of Consciousness Stream of consciousness is a technique that was developed by modernist writers to present the flow of a character's seemingly unconnected thoughts, responses, and sensations. A character's stream of consciousness is often expressed as an interior monologue, which may reveal the inner experience of the character on many levels of consciousness.

See also Characterization; Modernism; Point of View; Psychological Fiction; Style.

Structure The structure of a literary work is the way in which it is put together—the arrangement of its parts. In poetry, structure refers to the arrangement of words and lines to produce a desired effect. A common structural unit in poetry is the stanza, of which there are numerous types. In prose, structure is the arrangement of larger units or parts of a selection. Paragraphs, for example, are a basic unit in prose, as are chapters in novels and acts in plays. The structure of a poem, short story, novel, play, or nonfiction selection usually emphasizes certain important aspects of content.

See also Form; Stanza.

Style Style is the distinctive way in which a work of literature is written. Style refers not so much to what is said but how it is said. Word choice, sentence length, tone, imagery, and use of dialogue all contribute to a writer's style. A group of writers might exemplify common stylistic characteristics, as, for example, in the case of the 17th-century metaphysical poets, who employed complex meanings and unconventional rhythms and figurative language to achieve dramatic effect.

Subtlety *See* Aphorism.

Summarize To summarize is to briefly retell, or encapsulate, the main ideas of a piece of writing in one's own words.

See also Paraphrase.

Supernatural Tale A supernatural tale is a story that goes beyond the bounds of reality, usually by involving supernatural elements—beings, powers, or events that are unexplainable by known forces or laws of nature.

In many supernatural tales, **foreshadowing**—hints or clues that point to later events—is used to encourage readers to anticipate the unthinkable. Sometimes readers are left wondering whether a supernatural event has really taken place or is the product of a character's imagination. In an effective supernatural tale, the writer manipulates readers' feelings of curiosity and fear to produce a mounting sense of excitement.

Support Support is any material that serves to prove a claim. In an argument, support typically consists of reasons and evidence. In persuasive texts and speeches, however, support may include appeals to the needs and values of the audience.

See also General Principle.

Supporting Detail *See* Main Idea.

Surprise Ending A surprise ending is an unexpected plot twist at the end of a story.

See also Irony.

Suspense Suspense is the excitement or tension that readers feel as they become involved in a story and eagerly await the outcome.

See also Plot.

Symbol A symbol is a person, place, or object that has a concrete meaning in itself and also stands for something beyond itself, such as an idea or feeling.

Synesthesia *See* Imagery.

Synthesize To synthesize information is to take individual pieces of information and combine them with other pieces of information and with prior knowledge or experience to gain a better understanding of a subject or to create a new product or idea.

Text Features Text features are design elements that indicate the organizational structure of a text and help make the key ideas and the supporting information understandable. Text features include headers, boldface type, italic type, bulleted or numbered lists, sidebars, captions, and graphic aids such as charts, tables, timelines, illustrations, and photographs.

Theme A theme is an underlying message that a writer wants the reader to understand. It is a perception about life or human nature that the writer shares with the reader. In most cases, themes are not stated directly but must be inferred. In addition, there may be more than one theme in a work of literature.

Recurring themes are themes found in a variety of works. For example, authors from varying backgrounds might convey similar themes having to do with the importance of family values. **Universal themes** are themes that are found throughout the literature of all time periods.

Thesaurus *See* Reference Works.

Thesis Statement In an argument, a thesis statement, or controlling idea, is an expression of the claim that the writer or speaker is trying to support. In an essay, a thesis statement is an expression, in one or two sentences, of the main idea or purpose of the piece of writing.

Third-Person Point of View *See* Point of View.

Title The title of a literary work introduces readers to the piece and usually reveals something about its subject or theme. Although works are occasionally untitled or, in the case of some poems, merely identified by their first line, most literary works have been deliberately and carefully named. Some titles are straightforward, stating exactly what the reader can expect to discover in the work. Others hint at the subject and force the reader to search for interpretations.

Tone Tone is a writer's attitude toward his or her subject. A writer can communicate tone through diction, choice of details, and direct statements of his or her position. Unlike mood, which refers to the emotional response of the reader to a work, tone reflects the feelings of the writer. To identify the tone of a work of literature, you might find it helpful to read the work aloud, as if giving a dramatic reading before an audience. The emotions that you convey in an oral reading should give you hints as to the tone of the work.

> **Examples:** The tone of Jonathan Swift's "A Modest Proposal" is searingly ironic. In "The Prologue" from *The Canterbury Tales,* Chaucer's jovial tone accounts for much of the work's humor.

See also Connotation; Diction; Mood; Style.

Topic Sentence The topic sentence of a paragraph states the paragraph's main idea. All other sentences in the paragraph provide supporting details.

Tragedy A tragedy is a dramatic work that presents the downfall of a dignified character who is involved in historically, morally, or socially significant events. The main character, or **tragic hero,** has a **tragic flaw,** a quality that leads to his or her destruction. The events in a tragic plot are set in motion by a decision that is often an error in judgment caused by the tragic flaw. Succeeding events are linked in a cause-and-effect relationship and lead inevitably to a disastrous conclusion, usually death. Shakespeare's plays ***Macbeth, Hamlet, Othello,*** and ***King Lear*** are famous examples of tragedies.

Tragic Flaw *See* Hero; Tragedy.

Tragic Hero *See* Hero; Tragedy.

Traits *See* Character.

Transcript A transcript is a written record of words originally spoken aloud.

Trochee *See* Meter.

Turning Point *See* Climax.

Understatement Understatement is a technique of creating emphasis by saying less than is actually or literally true. It is the opposite of **overstatement,** a form of **hyperbole,** or exaggeration. One of the primary devices of **irony,** understatement can be used to develop a humorous effect, to create satire, or to achieve a restrained tone.

See also Hyperbole; Irony.

Universal Theme *See* Theme.

Verbal Irony *See* Irony.

Verisimilitude Verisimilitude refers to the appearance of truth and actuality.

Visualize Visualizing is the process of forming a mental picture based on written or spoken information.

Voice The term **voice** refers to a writer's unique use of language that allows a reader to "hear" a human personality in his or her writing. The elements of style that determine a writer's voice include sentence structure, diction, and tone. For example, some writers are noted for their reliance on short, simple sentences, while others make use of long, complicated ones. Certain writers use concrete words, such as *lake* or *cold,* which name things that you can see, hear, feel, taste, or smell. Others prefer abstract terms such as *memory,* which name things that cannot be perceived with the senses. A writer's tone also leaves its imprint on his or her personal voice. The term *voice* can be applied to the narrator of a selection, as well as to the writer.

See also Diction; Tone.

Website A website is a collection of "pages" on the World Wide Web that is usually devoted to one specific subject. Pages are linked together and are accessed by clicking hyperlinks or menus, which send the user from page to page within the site. Websites are created by companies, organizations, educational institutions, branches of the government, the military, and individuals.

Word Choice *See* Diction.

Wordplay Wordplay is the intentional use of more than one meaning of a word to express ambiguities, multiple interpretations, and irony.

Workplace Documents Workplace documents are materials that are produced or used within a work setting, usually to aid in the functioning of the workplace. They include job applications, office memos, training manuals, job descriptions, and sales reports. Workplace documents often include text features, such as captions, graphics, and headers, that make key ideas and supporting information understandable.

Works Cited A list of works cited lists names of all the works a writer has referred to in his or her text. This list often includes not only books and articles but also nonprint sources.

Works Consulted A list of works consulted names all the works a writer consulted in order to create his or her text. It is not limited just to those works cited in the text.

See also Bibliography.

Using the Glossaries

The following glossaries list the Academic Vocabulary and Critical Vocabulary words found in this book in alphabetical order. Use these glossaries just as you would a dictionary—to determine the meanings, parts of speech, pronunciation, and syllabication of words. (Some technical, foreign, and more obscure words in this book are not listed here but are defined for you in the footnotes that accompany many of the selections.)

Many words in the English language have more than one meaning. These glossaries give the meanings that apply to the words as they are used in this book. Words closely related in form and meaning are listed together in one entry (for instance, ***consumption*** and ***consume***), and the definition is given for the first form.

The following abbreviations are used to identify parts of speech of words:

adj. adjective ***adv.*** adverb ***n.*** noun ***v.*** verb

Each word's pronunciation is given in parentheses. A guide to the pronunciation symbols appears in the Pronunciation Key below. The stress marks in the Pronunciation Key are used to indicate the force given to each syllable in a word. They can also help you determine where words are divided into syllables.

For more information about the words in the glossaries or for information about words not listed in them, consult a dictionary.

Pronunciation Key

Symbol	Examples
ă	**pat**
ā	**pay**
ä	**father**
âr	**care**
b	**bib**
ch	**church**
d	**deed, milled**
ĕ	**pet**
ē	**bee**
f	**fife, phase, rough**
g	**gag**
h	**hat**
hw	**which**
ĭ	**pit**
ī	**pie, by**
îr	**pier**
j	**judge**
k	**kick, cat, pique**
l	**lid, needle*** (nēd´l)
m	**mum**
n	**no, sudden*** (sud´n)
ng	**thing**
ŏ	**pot**
ō	**toe**
ô	**caught, paw**
oi	**noise**
ŏŏ	**took**
ōō	**boot**
ŏŏr	lure
ôr	**core**
ou	**out**
p	**pop**
r	**roar**
s	**sauce**
sh	**ship, dish**
t	**tight, stopped**
th	**thin**
th	**this**
ŭ	**cut**
ûr	**urge, term, firm, word, heard**
v	**valve**
w	**with**
y	**yes**
z	**zebra, xylem**
zh	**vision, pleasure, garage**
ə	**about, item, edible, gallop, circus**
ər	**butter**

Sounds in Foreign Words

Symbol	Examples
KH	*German* **ich, ach;** *Scottish* **loch**
N (bôn)	*French*, **bon fin**
œ	*French* **feu, oeuf;** *German* **schön**
ü	*French* **tu;** *German* **über**

* In English the consonants *l* and *n* often constitute complete syllables by themselves.

Stress Marks

The relevant emphasis with which the syllables of a word or phrase are spoken, called stress, is indicated in three different ways. The strongest, or primary, stress is marked with a bold mark (**´**). An intermediate, or secondary, level of stress is marked with a similar but lighter mark (´). The weakest stress is unmarked. Words of one syllable show no stress mark.

Glossary of Academic Vocabulary

accumulate (ə-kyoom´yə-lāt´) *v.* to gather or pile up.

appreciation (ə-prē´shē-ā´shən) *n.* recognition of the quality, significance, or value of someone or something.

assurance (ə-shŏŏr´əns) *n.* a guarantee or pledge.

bias (bī´əs) *n.* predisposition toward; preference for one thing over another.

collapse (kə-lăps´) *v.* to break down or fall apart suddenly and cease to function.

complementary (kŏm´plə-mĕn´tə-rē) *adj.* completing; forming a whole.

conceive (kən-sēv´) *v.* to understand or form in the mind; to devise.

conform (kən-fôrm´) *v.* to be similar to or match something or someone; to act or be in accord or agreement.

controversy (kŏn´trə-vûr´sē) *n.* public disagreement, argument.

convince (kən-vĭns´) *n.* persuade or lead to agreement by means of argument.

devote (dĭ-vōt´) *v.* to give one´s entire energy or attention to something or someone.

drama (drä´mə) *n.* a prose or verse composition that is intended to be acted out.

encounter (ĕn-koun´tər) *n.* an unplanned or unexpected meeting.

ethics (ĕth´ĭks) *n.* rules of conduct or set of principles.

exploit (ĭk-sploit´) *v.* to take advantage of; to use for selfish or unethical purposes.

inclinations (ĭn´klə-nā´shənz) *n.* leanings toward; propensities for.

integrity (ĭn-tĕg´rĭ-tē) *n.* quality of being ethically or morally upright.

intensity (ĭn-tĕn´sĭ-tē) *n.* high degree of concentration, power, or force.

mediate (mē´dē-āt´) *v.* to settle differences between two individuals or groups.

persistence (pər-sĭs´təns) *n.* the act or quality of holding firmly to a purpose or task in spite of obstacles.

predominance (prĭ-dŏm´ə-nəns) *n.* superiority in control, force, or influence.

radical (răd´ĭ-kəl) *adj.* extreme; desirous of change in established institutions or practices.

reinforce (rē´ĭn-fôrs´) *v.* to strengthen; to give more force to.

restore (rĭ-stôr´) *v.* to bring back to original condition; to renew; to revive.

restrain (rĭ-strān´) *v.* to hold back or control.

tension (tĕn´shən) *n.* mental strain or excitement.

theme (thēm) *n.* an idea that is implied or that recurs in a work; a message conveyed in a literary work.

trigger (trĭg´ər) *v.* to set off a chain of events.

vision (vĭzh´ən) *n.* ability to see; insight.

visualize (vĭzh´ōō-ə-līz´) *v.* to form a mental image of something or someone.

Glossary of Critical Vocabulary

abrogate (ăb´rə-gāt´) *v.* to revoke or nullify.

acrid (ăk´rĭd) *adj.* strongly unpleasant in smell or taste.

adamant (ăd´ə-mənt) *adj.* inflexible and insistent; unchanging.

admonition (ăd´mə-nĭsh´ən) *n.* critical advice.

affiliation (ə-fĭl´ē-ā´shən) *n.* association with.

affliction (ə-flĭk´shən) *n.* something that causes suffering or pain.

ancillary (ăn´sə-lĕr´ē) *adj.* additional and related.

anomaly (ə-nŏm´ə-lē) *n.* peculiarity; an unusual example.

apparition (ăp´ə-rĭsh´ən) *n.* an unexpected, unexplained vision; a ghostly image of a person.

bellicose (bĕl´ĭ-kōs´) *adj.* aggressively inclined to fight.

benign (bĭ-nīn´) *adj.* harmless.

bequeath (bĭ-kwēth´) *v.* to pass on to heirs.

calamity (kə-lăm´ĭ-tē) *n.* a disaster or catastrophe.

cognitive (kŏg´nĭ-tĭv) *adj.* related to knowledge or understanding.

cohort (kō´hôrt´) *n.* a companion or associate.

collateral (kə-lăt´ər-əl) *adj.* additional; accompanying.

congenial (kən-jēn´yəl) *adj.* agreeable; sympathetic.

counterintuitive (koun´tər-ĭn-to͞o´ĭ-tĭv) *adj.* contrary to what one expects.

degenerate (dĭ-jĕn´ə-rāt´) *v.* to decline in quality.

desultory (dĕs´əl-tôr´ē) *adj.* lacking a fixed plan.

discredit (dĭs-krĕd´ĭt) *v.* to damage the reputation of.

dissimulation (dĭ-sĭm´yə-lā´shən) *n.* deceit or pretense.

double entendre (dŭb´əl än-tän´drə) *n.* an expression having a double meaning.

emulation (ĕm´yə-lā´shən) *n.* competitive imitation.

engender (ĕn-jĕn´dər) *v.* to bring into existence.

enmity (ĕn´mĭ-tē) *n.* hatred or hostility towards an enemy.

entail (ĕn-tāl´) *v.* involve as a consequence.

entomological (ĕn´tə-mə-lŏj´ĭ-kəl) *adj.* related to the study of insects.

eviscerate (ĭ-vĭs´ə-rāt´) *v.* to remove the necessary or important parts of.

extortionist (ĭk-stôr´shən-ĭst) *n.* one who obtains something by force or threat.

extricate (ĕk´strĭ-kāt´) *v.* to free from difficulty.

fabricate (făb´rĭ-kāt´) *v.* to construct or make.

facile (făs´əl) *adj.* easy to make or understand.

fetid (fĕt´ĭd) *adj.* having an unpleasant odor; bad-smelling.

genre (zhän´rə) *n.* a category within an art form, based on style or subject.

hierarchy (hī´ə-rär´kē) *n.* a ranking of status within a group.

hypocrite (hĭp´ə-krĭt´) *n.* one who professes good qualities but does not demonstrate or possess them.

ignobly (ĭg-nō´blē) *adv.* dishonorably.

implicit (ĭm-plĭs´ĭt) *adj.* understood but not directly stated.

indigenous (ĭn-dĭj´ə-nəs) *adj.* native to a land.

inducement (ĭn-do͞os´mənt) *n.* an incentive or stimulus.

inexplicably (ĭn-ĕk´splĭ-kə-blē) *adv.* in a way that is hard or impossible to explain.

infamous (ĭn´fə-məs) *adj.* having a bad reputation.

innate (ĭ-nāt´) *adj.* possessed at birth.

insipid (ĭn-sĭp´ĭd) *adj.* dull; lacking color or zest.

insurgency (ĭn-sûr´jən-sē) *n.* rebellion or revolt.

inviolate (ĭn-vī´ə-lĭt) *adj.* secure against change or violation.

iridescent (ĭr´ĭ-dĕs´ənt) *adj.* having colors that change when seen from different angles.

itinerant (ī-tĭn´ər-ənt) *adj.* migrant, or travelling from site to site.

loathsome (lōth´səm) *adj.* hateful or repulsive.

malleable (măl´ē-ə-bəl) *adj.* able to be shaped or molded.

marginal (mär´jə-nəl) *adj.* just meeting a very low standard of success.

motley (mŏt´lē) *adj.* unusually varied or mixed.

naïveté (nī´ēv-tā´) *n.* lack of knowledge or experience.

panacea (păn´ə-sē´ə) *n.* a cure or solution for all problems.

paraphernalia (păr´ə-fər-nāl´yə) *n.* necessary equipment or utensils.

pilgrimage (pĭl´grə-mĭj) *n.* a journey to a historical or religious site.

preamble (prē´ăm´bəl) *n.* an introductory statement.

prodigious (prə-dĭj´əs) *adj.* remarkably great; huge.

progeny (prŏj´ə-nē) *n.* offspring or descendants.

pugnacious (pŭg-nā´shəs) *adj.* belligerent, inclined to quarrel.

purge (pûrj) *v.* to eliminate or wash away.

rampant (răm´pənt) *adj.* growing wildly without restraint or limit.

rebuke (rĭ-byo͞ok´) *v.* to reprimand or scold.

recalcitrant (rĭ-kăl´sĭ-trənt) *adj.* uncooperative and resistant of authority.

reparations (rĕp´ə-rā´shəns) *n.* compensation or payment from a nation for damage or injury during a war.

resolution (rĕz´ə-lo͞o´shən) *n.* determination.

retribution (rĕt´rə-byo͞o´shən) *n.* appropriate punishment or revenge.

reverberate (rĭ-vûr´bə-rāt´) *v.* to vibrate or resonate.

rudiment (ro͞o´də-mənt) *n.* basic principle or aspect.

ruminate (ro͞o´mə-nāt´) *v.* to consider or think about carefully; contemplate.

savvy (săv´ē) *adj.* shrewd, confidently clever.

scalloped (skŏl´əpt) *adj.* having a wavy edge, border, or design.

scrupulous (skro͞o´pyə-ləs) *adj.* honorable; moral.

signify (sĭg´nə-fī´) *v.* to have meaning or importance.

solace (sŏl´ĭs) *v.* give comfort or relief to.

sovereignty (sŏv´ər-ĭn-tē) *n.* independent rule or authority.

sporadic (spə-răd´ĭk) *adj.* occasional; occurring at random intervals.

stoic (stō´ĭk) *adj.* enduring difficulty without expressing emotion or complaint.

subterranean (sŭb´tə-rā´nē-ən) *adj.* underground.

supposition (sŭp´ə-zĭsh´ən) *n.* something thought to be the case; an assumed truth or hypothesis.

susceptibility (sə-sĕp´tə-bĭl´ĭ-tē) *n.* vulnerability or the likeliness to be affected.

talon (tăl´ən) *n.* the claw of a predator bird.

taut (tôt) *adj.* tense or tightly flexed.

tentatively (tĕn´tə-tĭv-lē) *adv.* with uncertainty; cautiously.

translucent (trăns-lo͞o´sənt) *adj.* semitransparent.

tutelage (to͞ot´l-ĭj) *n.* instructional authority.

tyranny (tĭr´ə-nē) *n.* oppressive rule by an absolute power.

ubiquity (yo͞o-bĭk´wĭ-tē) *n.* constant presence or prevalence.

unmitigated (ŭn-mĭt´ĭ-gā´tĭd) *adj.* complete and undiminishing.

vindication (vĭn´dĭ-kā´shən) *n.* justification.

virtue (vûr´cho͞o) *n.* purity or virginity.

Index of Skills

D

Q

R

S

T

Index of Titles and Authors

Acknowledgments

Excerpt from *The American Heritage Dictionary of the English Language, Fifth Edition.* Text copyright © 2011 by Houghton Mifflin Harcourt. Adapted and reprinted by permission of Houghton Mifflin Harcourt Publishing Company.

Excerpt from *Beowulf* translated by Burton Raffel. Text copyright © 1963 by Burton Raffel. Text copyright renewed © 1991 by Burton Raffel. Reprinted by permission of Dutton Signet, a division of Penguin Group (USA), Inc. and Russell & Volkening on behalf of the author.

Excerpts from "Blocking the Transmissions of Violence" by Alex Kotlowitz from *The New York Times Magazine,* May 4, 2008. Text copyright © 2008. Reprinted by permission of PARS International on behalf of the New York Times. All rights reserved.

Excerpts from *The Canterbury Tales* by Geoffrey Chaucer, translated by Nevill Coghill. Text copyright © 1951, 1958, 1960, 1975, 1977 by Nevill Coghill. Reprinted by permission of Penguin Group UK and Curtis Brown Group, Ltd., London on behalf of the Estate of Nevill Coghill.

"The Clan of One-Breasted Women" from *Refuge: An Unnatural History of Family and Place* by Terry Tempest Williams. Text copyright © 1991 by Terry Tempest Williams. Originally published in *Northern Lights,* Vol. 6, No. 1. Reprinted by permission of Vintage Books, a division of Random House, Inc. and Brandt & Hochman Literary Agents, Inc. on behalf of the author. Any third party use of this material, outside of this publication, is prohibited. Interested parties must apply directly to Random House, Inc. for permission. All rights reserved.

"The Deep" from *Memory Wall* by Anthony Doerr. Text copyright © 2010 by Anthony Doerr. Originally appeared in *Zoetrope.* Reprinted by permission of International Creative Management, Inc. on behalf of the author.

"Dwellings" from *Dwellings: A Spiritual History of the Living World* by Linda Hogan. Text copyright © 1995 by Linda Hogan. Reprinted by permission of W. W. Norton & Company, Inc. and Beth Vesel Literary Agency on behalf of the author.

Excerpt from "Hamlet's Dull Revenge" by René Girard from *Stanford Literature Review 1,* Fall 1984. Text copyright © 1984 by René Girard. Reprinted by permission of René Girard.

"Hatred" from *View with a Grain of Sand* by Wisława Szymborska, translated by Stanislaw Barariczak and Clare Cavanagh. Text copyright © 1993 by Wisława Szymborska. Reprinted by permission of Houghton Mifflin Harcourt Publishing Company.

"The Hermit's Story" by Rick Bass. Text copyright © 1998 by Rick Bass. First appeared in *The Paris Review.* Reprinted by permission of Rick Bass.

"Imagine the Angels of Bread" from *Imagine the Angels of Bread* by Martín Espada. Text copyright © 1996 by Martín Espada. Reprinted by permission of W. W. Norton & Company, Inc.

"In Scattered Protest, Saudi Women Take the Wheel" by Neil MacFarquhar and Dina Salah Amer from *The New York Times,* June 17, 2011. Text copyright © 2011 by the New York Times. Reprinted by permission of PARS International on behalf of the New York Times. All rights reserved.

Excerpt from "Interview of Martín Espada" by Bill Moyers at martinespada.net. Text copyright © 2007 by Martín Espada. Reprinted by permission of Martín Espada.

"Living Like Weasels" from *Teaching a Stone to Talk* by Annie Dillard. Text copyright © 1982 by Annie Dillard. Reprinted by permission of HarperCollins Publishers and Russell & Volkening on behalf of the author.

"Mallam Sile" from *The Prophet of Zongo Street* by Mohammed Naseehu Ali. Text copyright © 2005 by Mohammed Naseehu Ali. Reprinted by permission of HarperCollins Publishers.

"Marita's Bargain" from *Outliers* by Malcolm Gladwell. Text copyright © 2008 by Malcolm Gladwell. Reprinted by permission of Little, Brown and Company. All rights reserved.

"The Men We Carry in Our Minds" from *The Paradise of Bombs* by Scott Russell Sanders. First published in *Mildweed Chronicle.* Text copyright © 1984 by Scott Russell Sanders. Reprinted by permission of Scott Russell Sanders.

"The Mosquito Solution" by Michael Specter from *The New Yorker,* July 9 and 16, 2012. Text copyright © 2012 by Michael Specter. Reprinted by permission of Michael Specter.

"My Father's Sadness" from *Monsoon History* by Shirley Geok-Lin Lim. Text copyright © 1994 by Shirley Geok-Lin Lim. Reprinted by permission of Shirley Geok-Lin Lim.

Excerpt from on-stage conversation with Robert Finch, Utah Museum of Natural History, October 1987. Text copyright © 1987 by Terry Tempest Williams. Reprinted by permission of Terry Tempest Williams.

"The Secret to Raising Smart Kids" from *Scientific American,* November 28, 2007. Text copyright © 2007 by Scientific American. Reprinted by permission of Scientific American.

Excerpt from "Speech on the Vietnam War, New York City, April 4, 1967" by Martin Luther King, Jr. Text copyright © 1967 by Martin Luther King, Jr. Text copyright renewed © 1991 by Coretta Scott King. Reprinted by permission of Writers House LLC on behalf of the Heirs of the Estate of Martin Luther King, Jr.

"Spring and All" from *The Collected Poems: Volume I, 1909-1939* by William Carlos Williams. Text copyright © 1938 by New Directions Publishing Corp. Reprinted by permission of New Directions Publishing Corp. and Carcanet Press Ltd.

"Tell Them Not to Kill Me!" from *The Burning Plain and Other Stories* by Juan Rulfo, translated by George D. Schade. Text copyright © 1967 by Fondo de Cultura Económica, Mexico. Translation copyright © 1967 by George D. Schade. Text copyright renewed © 1996 by George D. Schade. Reprinted by permission of the University of Texas Press and Agencia Literaria Carmen Balcells S.A. on behalf of the author.

Excerpts from *Third World America* by Alison Wright. Text copyright © 2009 by Alison Wright. Adapted and reprinted by permission of Alison Wright.

"A Walk to the Jetty" from *Annie John* by Jamaica Kincaid. Text copyright © 1983, 1984, 1985 by Jamaica Kincaid. Reprinted by permission of Farrar, Straus and Giroux, LLC.